Life-writing in the History of Archaeology
Critical perspectives

Edited by Clare Lewis and
Gabriel Moshenska

First published in 2023 by
UCL Press
University College London
Gower Street
London WC1E 6BT

Available to download free: www.uclpress.co.uk

Collection © Editors, 2023
Text © Contributors, 2023
Images © Contributors and copyright holders named in captions, 2023

The authors have asserted their rights under the Copyright, Designs and Patents Act 1988 to be identified as the authors of this work.

A CIP catalogue record for this book is available from The British Library.

Any third-party material in this book is not covered by the book's Creative Commons licence. Details of the copyright ownership and permitted use of third-party material is given in the image (or extract) credit lines. If you would like to reuse any third-party material not covered by the book's Creative Commons licence, you will need to obtain permission directly from the copyright owner.

This book is published under a Creative Commons Attribution-Non-Commercial 4.0 International licence (CC BY-NC 4.0), https://creativecommons.org/licenses/by-nc/4.0/. This licence allows you to share and adapt the work for non-commercial use providing attribution is made to the author and publisher (but not in any way that suggests that they endorse you or your use of the work) and any changes are indicated. Attribution should include the following information:

Lewis, C. and Moshenska, G. (eds). 2023. *Life-writing in the History of Archaeology: Critical perspectives*. London: UCL Press. https://doi.org/10.14324/111.9781800084506

Further details about Creative Commons licences are available at https://creativecommons.org/licenses/

ISBN: 978-1-80008-452-0 (Hbk.)
ISBN: 978-1-80008-451-3 (Pbk.)
ISBN: 978-1-80008-450-6 (PDF)
ISBN: 978-1-80008-453-7 (epub)
DOI: https://doi.org/10.14324/111.9781800084506

Life-writing in the History of Archaeology

Contents

List of figures and tables   vii
List of contributors   xi
Acknowledgements   xvii

Introduction   1
Gabriel Moshenska and Clare Lewis

Part I: Critical perspectives   23

1. Biography in science studies and the historiography of archaeology: Some methodological guidelines   25
Marc-Antoine Kaeser

2. A plea for 'higher criticism' in disciplinary history: Life-writing sources in the history of German-speaking Egyptology   45
Thomas L. Gertzen

3. Toward a prosopography of archaeology from the margins   73
Thea De Armond

4. Crafting an institution, reshaping a discipline: Intellectual biography, the archive and philanthropic culture   91
Jeffrey Abt

5. An epistolary corpus: Beyond the margins of 'official' archives, T. E. Peet's First World War correspondence   119
Clare Lewis

6. Archaeology, social networks and lives: 'Dig writing' and the history of archaeology   153
Bart Wagemakers

Part II: Sources and networks 181

7 The accidental linguist: Herbert Thompson's contribution
   to Egyptian language studies traced through his archive 183
   Catherine Ansorge

8 Margerie Venables Taylor (1881–1963): An unsung
   heroine of Roman Britain? 213
   Martha Lovell Stewart

9 Father Alfred-Louis Delattre (1850–1932) versus Paul Gauckler
   (1866–1911): The struggle to control archaeology at
   Carthage at the turn of the twentieth century 233
   Joann Freed

10 Hugh Falconer: Botanist, palaeontologist, controversialist 265
   Tim Murray

11 Personal and professional connections in early
   nineteenth-century Egyptology: The letters of Conrad
   Leemans to Thomas Pettigrew 281
   Gabriel Moshenska

12 Life-writing Vere Gordon Childe from secret
   surveillance files 299
   Katie Meheux

Part III: Reflections on practice 329

13 Alternative narratives in the history of archaeology:
   Exploring diaries as a form of reflexivity 331
   Oscar Moro Abadía

14 Archaeologists, curators, collectors and donors:
   Reflecting on the past through archaeological lives 353
   David W. J. Gill

15 The ghosts of Ann Mary Severn Newton: Grief,
   an imagined life and (auto)biography 379
   Debbie Challis

Index 405

List of figures and tables

Figures

1.1	Édouard Desor (1811–1882) posing at the photographer's studio with his dog Rino.	31
1.2	The base camp of Louis Agassiz and his companions' expeditions on the middle moraine of the Aar Glacier (ca. 1840).	32
1.3	La Tène antiquities from Friedrich Schwab's collection: one of the displays produced for the Paris World Exhibition in 1867. The public presentation of the collection, as well as the diffusion of these phototypical prints, have greatly contributed to the notoriety of La Tène (Neuchâtel, Switzerland) and its subsequent election as the eponymous site of the Second European Iron Age.	35
1.4	Édouard Desor's diary, July 10th–11th 1850, during the geological survey on the shores of Lake Mackinaw (Michigan, USA) — a difficult scientific terrain, where Édouard Desor had to retreat after his conflict with Louis Agassiz at Harvard University, which closed the doors of the American academic world to him.	38
1.5	Antoine Poidebard (1878–1955), French pioneer of aerial detection in archaeology.	40
2.1	Georg Steindorff.	51
2.2	Steindorff's 'J'accuse'-letter, (a) page 1/2 and (b) 2/2.	52
2.3	Rudolf Anthes.	57
2.4	Anthes' "list of German Egyptologists", (a) page 1/3, (b) page 2/3, (c) page 3/3.	58
2.5	Hans Gustav Güterbock.	60
4.1	'Orientalist', from the Bristol, Pennsylvania, *Courier*, 14 September 1932.	93

4.2	Poster, ca. January–February 1896.	94
4.3	Nubian expedition photographer Friedrich Koch, with unidentified Egyptian assistant, Great Hypostyle Hall, Temple of Ramses II, Abu Simbel, late January–early February 1906, P. 2403.	97
4.4	Breasted's 'Rough Sketch: Design for Proposed Floating Laboratory on the Nile', prepared ca. April 1907 and revised ca. April 1914.	101
4.5	'Diagram Visualizing the Rise of Civilization in the Orient and Its Transition Thence to Europe', from Breasted's 'Origins of Civilization', *Scientific Monthly* 10, no. 3 (March 1920): 267.	106
4.6	Oriental Institute building from the northwest, designed by Oscar Harold Murray and completed in 1931, ca. 1931, P. 18730/N. 10872.	109
5.1	Portrait of Patricia (daughter of T. E. Peet) aged two years; no location stated [1916]. Peet MS5.5.	127
5.2	Peet's first drawing to his daughter, Peet MSS 4.2.11. T. E. Peet letter to Patricia (undated).	130
5.3	Too and Tee, Peet's Turin Papyrus notes, Gardiner's handwritten hieroglyph m and G17, Gardiner's Sign List. Peet MSS 4.2.3 Letter from T. E. Peet to Patricia (undated); Gardiner Correspondence AHG/42.230.55 Letter from T. E. Peet to A. H. Gardiner (26th November 1928); Griffith MSS 21 Letter from Gardiner to Griffith 22nd May 1896; A. H. Gardiner, Egyptian Grammar (Oxford: Griffith Institute, 1957) G17, p.469.	131
5.4	Buzbug and Gardiner's sign list L2 compared. Peet MSS 4.2.7. Letter from T. E. Peet to Patricia (8th August 1918); A. H. Gardiner, Egyptian Grammar (Oxford: Griffith Institute, 1957) L2, p.477.	135
5.5	EES Income by type 1919–1939 (£).	140
6.1	Three dimensions and sources for dig writing.	157
6.2	Kathleen Kenyon (standing in the centre) supervising local labourers at Tell es-Sultan. Photo by expedition photographer Peter Dorrell.	159
6.3	Bill Power (right) and Muhammed exposing a Neolithic skeleton in Square E.	162
6.4	Drawing made by Henk Franken of the construction to lift the rush mat.	162

6.5	View from the excavation camp. Women from the refugee camp and the United Nations Relief and Works Administration truck near Elisha's Fountain. Tell es-Sultan in the background.	165
6.6	Kathleen Kenyon (left) and her team visit Roland de Vaux at his site Tell el-Far'ah (North).	168
6.7	Sometimes there was time for relaxation. Team member Awni Dajani – later Director of the Department of Antiquities – invited the team to his property at Ain Duke for a picnic in 1952. Kenyon in the middle right, Dajani on the lower left.	173
7.1	Page from a notebook containing notes from various sources including the Cairo Museum and Saqqara and a photograph of a hand-drawn plan of the Monastery of Apa Jeremias at Saqqara.	193
7.2	Lawrence Alma-Tadema (1836–1912) '94 degrees in the shade', a young Herbert Thompson painted in 1876 in a cornfield in Godstone, Surrey. Oil on canvas, 35.3 x 21.6 cm.	194
7.3	Notebook containing sketches and hieroglyphic texts from a museum visit to the Musée de Boulogne in 1909.	196
7.4	Notes and letters to Thompson from colleagues both local and abroad.	197
7.5	Notes for Thompson's publication on 'The archive of Siut' and on Tomb IV at Siut.	200
8.1	Portrait of Miss M.V. Taylor at 80, illustrating an article published in *The Times*, 31 July 1961: 'The Happy Scholar'.	214
10.1	Dr Hugh Falconer, 1844, Salted paper print from a paper negative. 37.3 × 26.7 cm (14 11/16 × 10 1/2 in.), 88.XM.57.40.	267
12.1	Vere Gordon Childe with a teddy bear given to him by students from Brno University, now in the Czech Republic.	302
12.2	The Marx Memorial Library, 7a Clerkenwell Green, London. The library, founded in 1933, was kept under observation by MI5 because of its close association with the CPGB.	304
12.3	Childe at Oxford, wearing graduation robes and probably dating to 1916/1917.	309
12.4	Archaeologists and Activists. Gordon Childe (centre) and Roly Wason (right) with Finnish archaeologist Carl Axel Nordman (left in hat), on a field trip during Nordman's visit to Scotland in 1932. Finnish Heritage Agency.	314

12.5	A letter to Childe from Zonoff, Second Secretary of the Soviet Embassy in London, 21 February 1944. Evidence of his growing engagement, both intellectual and political, with Marxism and the Soviet Union.	315
14.1	The funerary monument of the Disney family in the churchyard of St Mary the Virgin, Fryerning in Essex. It contains the remains of Dr John Disney, founder of the chair of archaeology at Cambridge.	355
14.2	The Egyptianising grave of Sir Gardner Wilkinson in the churchyard of St Dingat's at Llandingad near Llandovery in Carmarthenshire, Wales.	358
14.3	The grave of Humfry Payne in the cemetery at Mycenae. A paperback copy of *The Traveller's Journey is Done*, the biography by his widow, Dilys Powell, had been placed by the gravestone by a passing group of mourners who had written messages inside the cover (2004).	362
15.1	The two large drawings by Mary Severn Newton of the colossal sculpture of Artemisia and Mausolos are reproduced as plates in Charles Newton Travels and Discoveries. Vol. II (1865); (a), Plate 8, (b) Plate 10.	380
15.2	The Mary Newton family tree.	383
15.3	Princess Beatrice of Battenberg by Richard James Lane, after Ann Mary Newton (née Severn), lithograph, 1858.	387
15.4	Mary Severn Newton, Amazons and Greeks - Frieze of the Mausoleum of Halicarnassos, Travels and Discoveries. Vol. II (1865), Plate 14.	392
15.5	Mary Severn Newton, Self-portrait (1863).	392
15.6	Mary Severn Newton, Fragment of Frieze of the Mausoleum Bas-relief Amazon in the Museum of the Seraglio, Travels and Discoveries. Vol. II (1865), Plate I.	395
15.7	Photograph of the gravestone for Mary Severn Newton and Charles Newton in Kensal Green Cemetery.	399

Table

5.1	Table 5.1 T. E. Peet's Career.	123

List of contributors

'About the author' sections in books and journals are a unique form of micro-life-writing, and it would be remiss of us not to draw your attention to it here. Typically less than 200 words long and written in the third person, they tend to include a variety of information, including professional affiliations present and past, research interests, notable publications and honours, such as election to learned societies. Sometimes they refer to works in progress or intended, or less formal affiliations and affinities. Taken as a corpus, scholars' mini-bios can be used to trace career trajectories, scholarly fashions and unfulfilled ambitions. Together with studies of collaboration and co-publishing, they can contribute to tracing scholarly networks and invisible colleges, and to mark changes in practices of academic self-fashioning.

Jeffrey Abt is Professor Emeritus in the James Pearson Duffy Department of Art and Art History, Wayne State University, Detroit, Michigan. He earned BFA and MFA degrees at Drake University and pursued curatorial and administrative work at the Wichita Art Museum, the Special Collections Research Center of the University of Chicago and the University's Smart Museum of Art before coming to Wayne State. He's an artist and writer, his artwork is in museum and corporate collections throughout America, and he has exhibited in solo and group exhibitions in America and abroad. Abt's books include *American Egyptologist: The life of James Henry Breasted and the creation of his Oriental Institute* (University of Chicago Press, 2012) and *Valuing Detroit's Art Museum: A history of fiscal abandonment and rescue* (Palgrave Macmillan, 2017) and *Too Jewish or Not Jewish Enough: Ritual objects and avant-garde art at the Jewish Museum of New York* (Berghahn, 2023).

Catherine Ansorge studied Archaeology and Anthropology at Girton College. She was Librarian of the Oriental Studies Faculty in Cambridge (now Faculty of Asian and Middle Eastern Studies), then Head of the Near and Middle Eastern Department in Cambridge University Library.

She researches the history and provenance of manuscripts and archives as observed through the academic tradition of Middle Eastern studies at Cambridge, dating from the early seventeenth century to present times. She has published on the lives and exploits of the manuscript collectors and travellers whose personal papers, libraries and acquisitions, often from abroad, now form the core of Cambridge resources.

Debbie Challis is Events Producer at the Portico Library Manchester. She has published widely on the history of archaeology in the context of modern political history and ideology, including *The Archaeology of Race: The eugenic ideas of Francis Galton and Flinders Petrie* (2013). More recently she has written on reproductive justice and maternal loss, including in the catalogue for the British Library's exhibition *Unfinished Business. The fight for women's rights* (2020) and her memoir/history on these issues is forthcoming.

Thea De Armond is a historian and field archaeologist. She teaches at New Mexico State University. Her research interests include historiography, 'infrapolitics' and everyday resistance, and histories of archaeology, particularly in central and eastern Europe.

Joann Freed is Professor Emerita of Archaeology and Classical Studies at Wilfrid Laurier University and Adjunct Professor in the Department of History, Classics, and Religious Studies at the University of Alberta. Her book, *Bringing Carthage Home: The excavations of Nathan Davis, 1856–1859* (Oxbow Books) published in 2011. She has studied Father Alfred-Louis Delattre (1850–1932) and his early excavations at Carthage since 1990, first working with amphoras excavated by Delattre at the National Museum of Carthage, then in a bibliography of his publications (*CEDAC Carthage* 2001). She is writing a life of Delattre, largely based on papers in the Archives of the White Fathers in Rome.

Thomas L. Gertzen studied Egyptology, Assyriology and Greco-Roman archaeology at universities in Münster, Berlin (FU), and Oxford. In 2013 he was awarded a PhD in history by the Department of History of Science at Humboldt University, Berlin, with his dissertation on the Berlin School of Egyptology. Thereafter he participated in various research projects on the history of Ancient Near Eastern Studies and Egyptology at, among others, the University of British Columbia (Canada), Near Eastern Department on the History of German Egyptology during the Third Reic, and at Leipzig University on the Steindorff-Project about the history of German Egyptology in the twentieth century. He also took part in research within the framework of the Moses Mendelssohn

Center for European-Jewish Studies, Potsdam. Currently he is collaborating with the Egyptological Seminar of Göttingen University in a wide-scale project evaluating the academic and ideological impact of the writings of the German Orientalist Paul de Lagarde. Gertzen has published the results of this research, including a concise biography of Hermann Grapow, and an introduction to the disciplinary history of Egyptology. He is the research coordinator for the DFG-KFG "Rethinking Oriental Despotism" at Freie Universität, Berlin.

David W. J. Gill is honorary professor in the Centre for Heritage at the University of Kent, and Academic Associate in the Centre for Archaeology and Heritage at the University of East Anglia (UEA). He is a former Rome Scholar at the British School at Rome and Sir James Knott Fellow at Newcastle University. He curated the Greek and Roman collections at the Fitzwilliam Museum, University of Cambridge, before moving to Swansea University where he was Reader in Mediterranean Archaeology. He was awarded his chair in archaeological heritage through UEA, and was director of the Heritage Futures research unit at the University of Suffolk. He received the Outstanding Public Service Award from the Archaeological Institute of America (AIA) for his research on cultural property.

Marc-Antoine Kaeser is the director of the Laténium, the main archaeology museum in Switzerland, and a professor at the University of Neuchâtel. Trained both as a historian of science and as a prehistorian, he has published widely on the history of archaeology and natural sciences, and on the epistemology prehistoric research. His current interests include wetland prehistory and Celtic archaeology, the history of collections, the politics of archaeology as well as the relevance of public outreach in heritage valorisation.

Clare Lewis is a lecturer (teaching) in the Arts and Sciences department of UCL and is lead personal tutor on the Societies Pathway of the undergraduate degree. Alongside this she is completing her PhD in Egyptian Archaeology and History of Science at the UCL Institute of Archaeology. This research takes the inaugural lecture as a prism for analysis of the formation of Egyptology in universities in England from W.M. Flinders Petrie at University College London (1892) to the present day.

Katie Meheux works for UCL Library, Culture, Collections, and Open Science as the librarian for the Institute of Archaeology. An archaeologist by training, her research focuses on the history of archaeology, with an interest in the twentieth-century development of the profession within contemporary political, social, and cultural contexts, both national and international. Her publications focus particularly on the political life and career of Vere Gordon Childe. Katie is a Fellow of the Society of Antiquaries and a member of HARN (Histories of Archaeology Research Network).

Oscar Moro Abadía is a Professor at Memorial University of Newfoundland. He specialises in history and epistemology of archaeology. Together with Manuel R. González Morales (Universidad de Cantabria), he has recently co-edited a special issue of the *Journal of Archaeological Method and Theory* devoted to current developments in the study of Pleistocene and Holocene images (September 2020). Moreover, with Martin Porr, he has co-edited the volume *Ontologies of Rock Art: Images, relational approaches and Indigenous knowledge* (Routledge, 2021).

Gabriel Moshenska is associate professor in public archaeology at UCL Institute of Archaeology. His research focuses on nineteenth- and twentieth-century British archaeology including the history of learned societies and congresses, public spectacles, and public protests. He is currently working on a biography of the surgeon and antiquarian Thomas Pettigrew.

Tim Murray is Emeritus Professor at La Trobe and Honorary Professorial Fellow at the University of Melbourne. He has published over 30 books, including *Exploring the Archaeology of Immigration and the Modern City in Nineteenth century Australia* with Penny Crook; *The Commonwealth Block, Melbourne: A historical archaeology*; a volume of essays on the history of archaeology: *From Antiquarian to Archaeologist: The history and philosophy of archaeology*; a single volume history of archaeology: *Milestones in Archaeology*; and many book chapters and journal articles. His research interests span the history and philosophy of archaeology, global historical archaeology and the archaeology of Australia. He is also actively involved in e-humanities research into managing large archaeological databases. He is a Fellow of the Society of Antiquaries of London and of the Australian Academy of the Humanities.

Martha Lovell Stewart is a postgraduate research student at Durham University. Her PhD project in the history of archaeology explores Roman frontier studies and the work of British scholar Eric Birley (1906–1995). She read Classics and Ancient History at Christ Church, Oxford, and is particularly interested in the disciplinary legacy of epigraphy and papyrology.

Bart Wagemakers is a lecturer in Ancient and Religious History at the Institute Archimedes at the University of Applied Sciences Utrecht. He is the coordinator of the Non-Professional Archaeological Photographs project (www.npaph.com), which aims to record and preserve the unofficial documentation created by participants and visitors of archaeological expeditions, making this material accessible to the public via a series of digital archives and publications. This project, and a long-term interest in the history of archaeology, led Wagemakers to initiate the Jericho off the Record project, focusing on the oral and visual history of the Second British Expedition to Tell es-Sultan, from 1952–1958.

Acknowledgements

The editors would like to thank the contributors to this volume for their patience during its protracted production, as well as for the opportunity to showcase their research and writing here. We would also like to extend our gratitude to Panos Kratimenos for his assistance with copyediting the text. Our thanks also to the staff of UCL Press for their support in bringing this book to life.

Our gratitude to UCL Institute of Archaeology for a generous grant to support the indexing of this volume.

We would also like to thank Pamela Jane Smith for her encouragement and support of early-career scholars in the history of archaeology, and in archaeological life-writing in particular.

Introduction
Critical approaches to life-writing in the history of archaeology
Gabriel Moshenska and Clare Lewis

Introduction

Life-writing is a literal translation of 'biography', but in practice it represents a far broader category of texts and related forms. This diversity has given rise to a fast-growing body of scholarship around life-writing, ranging across disciplines, from memory studies and linguistics to the history and philosophy of science. Life-writing has played a vital role in the emergence and development of archaeology, from the memoirs of early–modern antiquarian travellers to the rise of 'object biography' approaches in the late twentieth century. There is even a distinctively archaeological form of life-writing – the field notebook – with its own curious history partly shared across other field sciences.[1] Practitioners of archaeological life-writing have observed that the reconstruction of an archaeological life from scraps of text, ephemera and memories can resemble the interpretation of an ancient site from its scattered fragments.

The lives of archaeologists are intimately entangled with their work, both in practice and in the popular imagination. This public fascination, in turn, has encouraged the publication of archaeological travelogues, diaries, memoirs and 'lives of the great explorers'-type compendia. Some of these like Amelia Edwards' 1877 *A Thousand Miles up the Nile* sold in very high quantities, while newspapers often sponsored archaeological expeditions in return for exclusive reports from the trench's edge.[2] In the twentieth century, the popular understanding of archaeology was shaped by best-sellers such as C. W. Ceram's *Götter, Gräber und Gelehrte*, Mary Chubb's *Nefertiti Lived Here* and Mortimer Wheeler's *Still Digging*.[3]

The history of archaeology has a long and inglorious tradition of life-writing in the form of poorly researched hagiography: what we might call the 'Great Men of Archaeology' genre. This is a widely recognised issue in the nineteenth and twentieth-century historiographies of science, technology, medicine and other disciplines.[4] Writings of this kind tend to reinforce a narrow vision of archaeology as an individualistic, destructive, acquisitive, colonialist, male-dominated endeavour. The popular success of these sorts of writings explains, in part, the widespread and enduring scepticism towards the intellectual values of life-writing by historians throughout much of the twentieth century.[5] We would not, of course, dismiss the considerable impact of popular life-writing on the development and popularisation of archaeology.

The justifiable suspicion towards life-writing by historians, and by historians of science in particular, began to shift in the later twentieth century in light of developments in interdisciplinary science studies as well as the growth of feminist and postcolonial scholarship.[6] The revival of life-writing in the history of science can now be seen in retrospect as an important step towards what has been called a 'biographical turn' in the humanities more generally.[7] It is these new approaches, and the new-found openness to the rich variety of life-writing sources, methods and outputs that provide the context for this book.

In discussions of the biographical turn, there is general recognition that life-writing was marginal to academic history for most of the twentieth century and was generally viewed as atheoretical and lacking in rigour. This was in part a backlash to the widespread success of biography in popular history writing – a disdain that has lately transformed at least in some cases into an appreciation for the public engagement value of the field.[8] The 'turn' itself has been described as a growing acceptance of the academic values of life-writing, beginning in the early 1980s and continuing into the twenty-first century. While the origins of this process lie within historiography, the biographical turn has moved beyond history to influence other fields, first in the humanities and subsequently more widely: 'the biographical turn has initiated a methodological and theoretical turn'.[9] So far, the impacts of this turn in the history of archaeology have been overwhelmingly positive.

What is this book for? It is at once a scholarly resource, an exploration and an argument. First, of course, we offer the requisite disclaimers. There can be no claim in a book of this type and length to any sort of comprehensive coverage of the field of life-writing in the history of archaeology. The lacunae are many, obvious and largely unavoidable, and we look forward with genuine interest to the novel and radical works that will hopefully emerge at least in part in reaction to the arguments presented here.

Our primary aim is to begin to trace the outlines of critical approaches to life-writing in the history of archaeology as an important and emerging field, and one that draws upon a broad and distinctive set of sources and methods. In the process, we believe that we are offering a snapshot of the state of the art of this field at an important stage in its own history – while pointing firmly to the disclaimers above. As part of this exploration we are particularly interested in shining a light on the interdisciplinary contexts of life-writing in the history of archaeology as part of intellectual history, of science studies and of other cognate disciplines. This is reflected in the individual chapters, and in particular through their engagement with theoretical and critical methodological discourses.

One of the most important developments in the history of archaeology has been its growing separation from the field of archaeology itself, where it often gave the impression of being a respectable activity for antiquarian-minded professors in their retirement years. Marc-Antoine Kaeser, one of the pioneers of the field, offered a redefinition of 'internalism' in the history of science to refer to studies carried out by practitioners of disciplines, rather than 'externalist' studies by historians, sociologists or philosophers.[10] This is by way of introduction to our wider point: that life-writing in the history of archaeology has a considerable instrumental value for advancing archaeological knowledge, developing frameworks of archaeological research practice and contributing to archaeological training and pedagogy. Building on this, there are also clear values in archaeological life-writing as a medium for public engagement, collaborative and participatory work, and a variety of forms of learning and communication within and beyond the discipline.[11]

In summary then, this book is intended to promote a more critically conscious approach to life-writing in the history of archaeology that strengthens the field and its related areas of activity, and drives and reinforces positive developments in historical and historiographical discourses. As Kaeser has argued:

> writing history at the micro scale of a single scientist makes it possible to encompass all the social, political, intellectual, cultural and religious factors which interact in the construction of archaeological knowledge, to grasp the changing relations shared by these factors, and also to underscore the dynamics which sustain such relations.[12]

So much for our positive aims in assembling this volume. What, in turn, is this book against? As we celebrate the wide diversity of forms of life-writing in the history of archaeology, we are naturally opposed to narrow, prescriptive approaches to the field, particularly those grounded in elitist attitudes and prejudices. There is no good reason to assert a hierarchy of life-writing with scholarly monographs at its peak. That said, we are working at least in part in reaction to the long-standing tradition of poorly researched, overly simplistic, and hagiographic forms of life-writing in archaeology, particularly those that focus on single elite individuals (we would include self-serving autobiography in this category). Thomas Söderqvist has drawn attention to the longstanding use of 'hagiographical' as a derogatory term in discussions of life-writing in the history of science.[13] One of the useful outcomes of the increasingly critical approach to the subject of life-writing might be a move towards more constructive frameworks of critique and evaluation.

We hope to encourage and amplify life-writing that counteracts the manifold erasures in these forms of writing: the erasure of women, working class and minority archaeologists, of hired labourers, technicians and others, and their contributions, achievements and lives. This is a fast-growing area of scholarship, and hopefully will continue to grow and thrive.[14] We are also conscious of how many forms of life-writing, including obituaries and the creation of personal archives, have been used to erase infidelities, diverse sexualities, abrasive and exuberant personalities, ill health, racism and extremist ideologies, professional misconduct, and other human factors.[15] These exercises in editing and erasure are themselves part of the history of the history of archaeology, and they form an important part of the corpus of our subject.[16]

What do we mean by 'critical approaches' to life-writing? This is perhaps best delineated as an aim for the volume as a whole, rather than for every single contribution. Critical approaches to life-writing are those attempts or methods that problematise the underlying assumptions of the practice, and place their efforts in conscious tension with previous practices. They include exercises in life-writing that foreground methodology, social theory, ethics, and other explanatory and practice-focused intellectual frameworks.

One useful point of reference for outlining critical approaches in this field comes from historian of anthropology George Stocking's autobiographical writings. Stocking makes numerous references to 'anxiety' in his approach to his work, describing it as 'an historiographical category' and reflecting on its interplay with authority, significance, method, identity and other related categories.[17] He identifies 'just the right amount of anxiety' as a key ingredient in conducting interesting and successful research, and in bringing it to successful conclusions. For Stocking, anxiety is a monitoring tool in intellectual work: one that warns when research is becoming too personal, assists in maintaining appropriate scholarly 'distance', identifies threats and hazards, and repels boredom. At the same time, anxiety – like critique more generally – can become paralysing and restricting in practice. We would argue, with Stocking and others, that an appropriate degree of intellectual anxiety encourages methodological rigour and ethical caution in both the broad direction of life-writing research and in its finer details as well.[18]

As the subject of a fashionable and fast-growing field of study, life-writing has inspired numerous books, a dedicated journal and research centres at several universities.[19] The term 'life-writing' itself is usually traced back to Virginia Woolf's autobiographical essay *A Sketch of the Past*, a reflection on memory and narrative written while she was engaged in her biography of the artist Roger Fry.[20] From this starting point, life-writing has for some time served as a challenge to the traditional limits of biography and autobiography, and has come to encompass a dizzying variety of forms and sources. These include, in no particular order or priority: diaries, wills, tweets, photographs, eulogies, secret police files, films, medical records and the 'about the author' sections of academic publications. Smith and Watson's seminal *Reading Autobiography* includes an appendix that lists distinct forms including 'jockography', a specific form of sports memoir; 'ecobiography' that weaves together narratives of person and place; and 'prosopography', the collective study of the lives of members of a group or community.[21] Life-writing studies engages with concepts of language, narrative, identity and the self. An emerging discipline in its own right, it has a tangled intellectual ancestry touching upon literature, history, anthropology and many other fields.

How should we conceptualise life-writing? Smith and Watson regard it as a set of practices, creating forms of writing that take individual lives as their focus or frame. Life-writing studies, in turn, is a part of the humanities and social sciences, with all the intellectual infrastructure that this implies. In turn, scholars of the so-called biographical turn have tended to approach life-writing as a research methodology, part of a growing arsenal of techniques that have radicalised and revitalised the humanities from the 1980s onwards, and have since spread more widely across the scholarly map. In this model, life-writing is frequently compared to – and often overlaps with – approaches such as microhistory, and certainly there are overlaps and synergies with this and other cognate fields.[22]

Accounts of archaeological life-writing

How have historians of archaeology viewed life-writing? It is worth examining the diverse viewpoints and perspectives, and in particular to consider the prevalence of instrumental argumentation – that is, the perceived need to justify such work. The invaluable *Who Was Who in Egyptology* was conceived by Warren Dawson in the 1930s, first published in 1951 and subsequently updated by others through several editions. *Who Was Who* is a rare archaeological example of the biographical encyclopaedia, grounded in the nineteenth century 'national biography' model, and more common in histories of science and medicine.[23] In his preface to the first edition, Dawson argues that, due to the relative youth of the discipline, Egyptology's 'history is very much bound up with the lives of its personnel'.[24] He sets out some of his aims for the volume, including the need to highlight the contributions of lesser-known scholars, and the value of brief accounts with detailed references to point researchers in the direction of more detailed archives. However, Dawson's primary stated aim is to assist scholars, curators and librarians in tracing the histories of museum objects, particularly those 'received in the days when registers were not so carefully kept as they are now'.[25]

Half a century later, Colin Wallace made an eloquent argument for a similar biographical dictionary of Romano-British archaeologists, aimed not only at providing context for their research, as Dawson argued above, but as a foundation for further, richer histories of the discipline.[26] Wallace draws on the arguments made by Evert Baudou for a 'problem oriented' approach to archaeological biography, arguing that this more-applied perspective to life-writing constitutes a historiographical middle-ground between general disciplinary overviews and narrative biographies.[27]

Published some 50 years after Dawson's *Who Was Who*, Tim Murray's two-volume *Encyclopedia of Archaeology: The Great Archaeologists* is a very different type of work: a collection of commissioned essays, some by distinguished authors who were themselves featured as subjects in the collection.[28] Murray's epilogue is a meditation on archaeological biography and its broader intellectual contexts at a time when the history of archaeology was beginning to grow as a field of scholarship, in part through the support of institutions such as the Society of American Archaeologists and the journals *Antiquity* and *Current Anthropology*:

> It has been my goal to argue for both radical and conservative roles for biography writing in archaeology and to stress its very great value in helping us to understand the social and cultural elements of archaeological knowledge.[29]

Murray discusses the variety of approaches taken by the authors of the 58 biographical essays in his encyclopaedia. This includes relatively straightforward studies of the acknowledged pioneers and 'Greats' of the field, and others – he highlights Leo Klejn's studies of Kossinna and Schliemann – aimed in part at demythologising controversial figures. However, he also draws attention to a set of essays where the authors' connections to their subjects make the writing semi-autobiographical. Murray notes that there is a value in such intellectual genealogies, particularly in cases where the scholar in question is still influential and shaping the discipline. This chain of connection approach and the very idea of intellectual ancestors (often, in academia, through networks of PhD supervision) would appear to reinforce the power of elite individuals and institutions. However, Murray argues that it has further values, including emphasising the social as well as the scholarly dimension of disciplinary histories, and allowing space for alternative histories of institutions and communities.[30]

First published in 1992, a few years before Murray's essay, but in a very different scholarly context, Douglas Givens' ruminations on archaeological biography place it within the diverse constellation of approaches to writing disciplinary histories.[31] He considers and (rightly, in our view) rejects R. G. Collingwood's dismissal of life-writing as ahistorical or antihistorical. Instead, like Murray, Givens draws on Jacob Gruber's studies in the history of anthropology to advocate for archaeological life-writing as intellectual history, an exercise in contextualisation. While Murray noted the interconnectedness of biography and autobiography in some of this work, Givens – following Gruber – points out the temporal limitations of such writing.[32] Much of the professionalisation of archaeology and its growth within universities took place within living memory (Givens is writing 30 years before us), and while the living pose challenges to scholarship, Givens argues that biography is of relatively lesser value in the histories of younger disciplines.

Maintaining this more cautious approach, Givens takes a prescriptive approach to archaeological biography. Drawing on his experience as biographer of A. V. Kidder, he outlines a systematic approach: first set out an intellectual and professional life-narrative based on a timeline; next add nodes of personal and institutional affiliation or connection; finally turn one's attention to the subject's scholarly and public outputs and activities.[33] However, he is also alert to the values of archaeological biography as an engaging medium that presents historical knowledge at an individual scale within a narrative of personal life and conflicts that are more likely to hold a reader's attention.

Recent developments

The two decades since Murray's encyclopaedia was published have seen a notable growth in research and publication in the history of archaeology, and with it a set of theoretical advancements that have thrust the field closer to its cognate disciplines in the social and historical studies of science, and intellectual history more broadly.

One of the earliest and most enduring of these changes has been the rapid growth in studies of women's lives and careers in archaeology. This has included encyclopaedic efforts such as the *Breaking Ground* project at Brown University; the *Trowelblazers* project with a wider remit to trace pioneering women in archaeology, palaeontology and geology; and systematic efforts (often against resistance) to expand and enhance the coverage of women in archaeology on Wikipedia.[34] There is also a growing number of substantial, monograph-length studies of individual women including Lydia Carr's study of Tessa Wheeler, Kathleen Sheppard's life of Margaret Murray and David Gill's biography of Winifred Lamb.[35] Some of these efforts to highlight often hitherto-neglected women are allied to other radical strands in the history of archaeology aimed at highlighting the 'hidden hands' of paid archaeological labourers, local and indigenous collaborators, and others. Within and beyond this work we can see a trend in highlighting archaeological work away from the field such as teaching, fundraising, and the distribution of finds.[36] The work of Pamela Jane Smith, Amara Thornton and others has examined the significance of social networks in the development of archaeology, bringing to light webs of social relations, intellectual labour and influence, economic power and other strands where women's contributions to archaeology have often been hidden or devalued.[37]

One of the vital drivers of research innovation is funding, and the most notable funded project in the history of archaeology boom has been the *Archives of European Archaeology (AREA)* project, based around a network of partner institutions across Europe (see Kaeser's chapter in this volume).[38] A number of conferences and workshops were held under the auspices of this project, leading to publications such as *Archives, Ancestors, Practices* which included numerous examples of, and historiographical reflections, on archaeological life-writing.[39] Dedicated book series are another indication of sub-disciplinary maturity: *Oxford Studies in the History of Archaeology* is a prestigious series albeit one which has notably not (to date) published any archaeological life-writing (although Oxford University Press itself has); while Archaeopress publishes the fast-growing *Archaeological Lives* series dedicated to 'autobiographies, biographies, diaries, correspondence, collected essays, and monographs'.[40]

It is perhaps a reflection of the rapid growth in the history of archaeology that some archaeologists' lives seem entangled in life-writing. The Gordon Childe industry has seen numerous biographies including monographs by Barbara McNairn, Bruce Trigger, Sally Green and most recently Terry Irving; as well as several edited collections and innumerable articles, including a heap of essays and an unpublished monograph by his former student Peter Gathercole.[41] Katie Meheux's chapter in this volume highlights new sources and provides new insights into his life and politics: further evidence that Childe remains a rich and relevant part of disciplinary history. The plethora of Childe studies also illuminates some of the ways that a set of biographers can choose to focus on different traits of the same individual, drawing on different sources, and resulting in markedly diverse pictures of their subject.[42] Michael Shortland and Richard Yeo argue that the myth of 'personal coherence' has shaped biography by allowing room for many biographers to write about the same person, so that each may find a different coherent or unified story to tell. This myth has, at the same time, stunted biography in that, by artificially imposing coherence, it may not present the actual life of the subject, but a romanticised, fictionalised account.[43]

Another life entangled in the history of archaeology is that of Leo Klejn, subject of a remarkable biography by Stephen Leach.[44] Outside of his native Soviet Union, Klejn's thought was often encountered by Western archaeologists in the form of published interviews and letters, the latter in part an attempt to subvert political restrictions. In the history of archaeology, as in Murray's biographical encyclopaedia, Klejn is both historian and subject. His remarkable life and work have been written about extensively, most notably in Leach's book, but he has also contributed significantly to the history of Russian and Soviet archaeology, including a monograph in the Oxford series mentioned above, and to the study of the lives of some of its leading figures, such as Nikolai Marr and Boris Rybakov.[45]

Amongst the most significant recent works on life-writing in the history of archaeology are those of Marc-Antoine Kaeser, author of a biography of the German-Swiss scientist and prehistorian Édouard Desor.[46] Kaeser has written on the practice of archaeological life-writing, the use of primary sources, and – consistently – on the links between life-writing and microhistory, from the perspective of the historiography of science.[47] In his study of the use of personal archives in life-writing, Kaeser notes both the restrictions of the discipline – the life of a real person – as well as the opportunities for forging connections and links across often disparate fields and disciplines:

> the uniqueness of a biography ... lies precisely in the possibility to easily bundle a great variety of topics without the risk of anachronism. While focusing on a single individual, the biographer can take note of, document and analyze connections amongst topics or events that may initially appear to be completely independent.[48]

This is also, arguably, a part of what makes the researching, writing and of course the reading of life-writing so rewarding and enjoyable.

In surveying the development of archaeological life-writing, it is particularly interesting and instructive to consider two books published exactly 30 years apart. Jacquetta Hawkes' *Mortimer Wheeler: Adventurer in Archaeology* appeared in 1982, and Lydia Carr's *Tessa Verney Wheeler: Women and Archaeology Before World War Two* in 2012.[49] As the three decades dividing them would suggest, the two books are as different in tone and approach as their married subjects. Hawkes opens with an announcement that 'Mortimer Wheeler will rise from these pages as a Hero figure', and while she later qualifies this statement to reassure us that 'I do not announce an idolatrous biography', the personal friendship between author and subject shapes the feel of the book and limits its scope.[50] In contrast, Carr regrets that Verney Wheeler has 'vanished into the footnotes of archaeology's history', and sets out to correct it: 'In this work, she is rediscovered and reconsidered.'[51]

Inevitably, in studying a husband and wife, Hawkes and Carr draw upon many of the same published, archival and family sources, although Hawkes had the advantage of a great many more living informants as well as her own personal friendship with her subject, while Carr in turn has the advantage of access to Hawkes' own research materials. Hawkes' description of her research and her acknowledgements of support highlight the interconnectedness of different forms of life-writing: she thanks Stuart Piggott for access to his (then unpublished) obituary of Wheeler for the Royal Society, and Max Mallowan for the text of his Memorial Address.[52] Passage of time is important in life-writing. Carr points out that Hawkes' work is sometimes vague about Wheeler's infidelities, in part – perhaps – because some of those involved were still living at the time of publication.[53]

Hawkes is an exceptional writer, and *Adventurer in Archaeology* is a classic of archaeological life-writing, albeit a flawed one. Carr's work, embedded in twenty-first century academic scholarship, is comparatively far more concerned with the historiography of archaeology and with the practice of archaeological life-writing, which she terms 'archaeobiography'.[54] This word was first used rather differently by Bonnie Clark to describe archaeologically informed life-writing, typically in historical archaeology.[55] In the case of Verney Wheeler, Carr is clear that she sets out to conduct a theoretically informed – but not theory-laden – piece of research, including in its relationship to feminist scholarship: 'This biography is not a gender study; it is the study of a woman.' Following Clark, she also considers the quasi-archaeological nature of life history research:

> Archaeobiography ... has yet to find a firm definition. For this author's purposes, it must be seen as the methodical, careful extraction of usable data from the waterfall of papers and ephemera that make up a subject's life. Pamela Jane Smith, among others, has commented on the peculiar symmetry existing between this form of understanding a scholar and the techniques used to comprehend an archaeological site.[56]

Following in the typological tradition of Smith and Watson, we offer up Carr's vision of archaeobiography as a distinctive disciplinary approach to writing the lives of archaeologists that plays on the metaphorically archaeological nature of researching a life, and acknowledges the blurring of archaeological and personal archives as both sources for, and forms of, archaeological life-writing.

Snapshots of a growing field: the chapters of this book

The chapters collected in this volume represent a range of perspectives, approaches and theoretical framings of archaeological life-writing. Together they offer an overview of some of the main strands within the biographical turn in the history of archaeology. In the opening section devoted to critical reflections on the discipline, Kaeser surveys the recent theoretical and methodological developments in the field, based to a considerable extent, as he points out, on the growing body of archive-based research by early career academics. He situates these developments – including the rise of 'microhistories' and tensions between studies of individuals and collectives – within their wider contexts in the history and sociology of science. The model of life-writing as microhistorical practice is one that recurs in several of the chapters in this volume. De Armond's consideration of microhistorical approaches to archaeological life-writing builds on Kaeser's definitions to consider the marginal, more truly 'micro' lives that constitute fragments of the history of archaeology, drawing on the example of the archaeologist Gisela Weyde. De Armond's call for a prosopography from the margins considers some potential theoretical and methodological approaches to writing lives that do not fit within more common approaches, and are often erased even in fine-grained historical studies: a counterbalance to what she describes as 'prosopographies of the privileged'.

Several of the chapters in this volume focus on lives in Egyptian archaeology and Egyptology, reflecting in part a resurgence of interest in the history and historiography of these sub-disciplines. Like Abt, Meheux and others in this volume, Lewis's study of Egyptologist T. E. Peet's wartime letters uses a specific and hitherto ignored or neglected set of primary sources, and uses them to shed new light on an otherwise well-known figure in the discipline. In Lewis' work these sources are personal letters from Peet, who was serving in the First World War, to his daughter Patricia, then aged just three. Lewis compares these letters to two other documentary strands in Peet's archives, noting the complex interplay of public and private lives, agency and self-representation. Gertzen's chapter grapples with the challenges of writing histories of Egyptology, a field that he argues developed along markedly distinctive lines in German-speaking contexts. In surveying key works in this field to date, Gertzen observes the different forms and influences of history writers' moral judgements, most notably in studies of scholars active during the Third Reich.

One of the strengths of this volume is its illumination of the variety of angles and perspectives on the history of archaeology that pertain, in often very different ways, to practices of life-writing. Abt's study of philanthropy and the economic histories of the discipline is one such study, highlighting the particular value of appeals for funding as documents that demonstrate archaeologists' abilities to write for, and appeal to, non-specialist audiences. Abt focuses on the relationship between archaeologist James Henry Breasted and philanthropist John D. Rockefeller, showing how the need to shape research to the interests of funders could profoundly shape the direction of research project, institutions and individual careers. To the plethora of specific forms of life-writing outlined by Smith and Watson, and discussed earlier, Wagemakers' chapter adds another: 'dig writing' – that is, histories of specific archaeological excavations told in biographical form and using the same types of sources as life-writing. To illustrate this, he collected a wide range of sources relating to Kenyon's Jericho excavations including images, letters, film and a dig diary. The account that emerges from these and other sources illustrates the full richness of the 'dig' experience: worries about funding, difficult labour relations, cross-cultural misunderstandings, ill-health, local politics, social relationships and romances, and fallings-out. Wagemakers presents dig writing as a distinct form of history writing, but like life-writing it shares features with related fields, such as microhistory and prosopography.

Following the more theoretically focused chapters in the first parts of this book, the chapters in the central section illuminate and embody a variety of different sources, aims and approaches to archaeological life-writing. Ansorge's account of the pleasingly comprehensive Herbert Thompson archive blends description of the holdings – including a physical description of the material itself – with an account of his life and works. In outlining Thompson's career in Egyptian language studies, Ansorge makes a case for the value of studying an individual scholar primarily through his or her own, singular archive: the wider contexts are present and acknowledged, but viewed from the 'interior' of one personal and professional life. The accounts of the movements of archives, personal libraries, ancient texts and artefacts further illustrate the networked nature of life-writing studies, with Cambridge University Library emerging as a notable nexus in the trajectories of so many of these materials. The uses, limitations and absence or survival of personal letters as a source for life-writing is one of the recurring themes in this volume. Moshenska's chapter focuses on the correspondence between two scholars of ancient Egypt in the early nineteenth century: the British surgeon Thomas Pettigrew and the Dutch curator Conrad Leemans. The letters that Leemans sent over several years combine personal warmth and professional minutiae, and also shed light on the operation of intellectual networks: Leemans asks Pettigrew's assistance for several of his acquaintances passing through London, including the young archaeologist Karl Lepsius.

As we have discussed elsewhere in this chapter, much of the most valuable recent work in archaeological life-writing has focused on the hitherto marginalised. Stewart's study of the scholar of Roman Britain Margerie Venables Taylor includes several of the mechanisms by which women's contributions to the development of archaeology have been neglected, including under-representation in academic posts and overshadowing by prominent men – in this case Francis Haverfield. In examining the entanglement of Haverfield and Taylor's work and careers, Stewart highlights the gap left by Taylor's deliberate disposal of her personal papers. She examines Taylor's obituary of Haverfield – a significant piece of life-writing – to argue that Taylor's subsequent labours at the Roman Society and its journal can be understood as the posthumous continuation of her longstanding collaborative work with Haverfield, in part alongside his other protégé R.G. Collingwood.

Historical disputes are often intellectually stimulating topics for study, and Freed's examination of Alfred-Louis Delattre and Paul Gauckler's work in Tunisian archaeology provides detailed context for the two men as well as for their conflict: a French conflict, as she describes it, on Tunisian soil. This dispute developed over several years and encompassed the most powerful dimensions of French society including church, state and the École Normale. Freed demonstrates the longstanding impacts of this dispute in the contemporary reception of both men's work, and argues for the importance of histories and life-histories in the practice of archaeology. Past controversies also shape Murray's study of Hugh Falconer. This chapter and Falconer's remarkable achievements are a reminder of the startling breadth of interests and achievements that characterised the intellectual lives of Victorian polymaths, ranging across medicine, botany and palaeontology as well as archaeology. It is also a reminder of the deep roots in Empire that enabled and shaped many of these interests. Murray outlines the intellectual disputes that coloured Falconer's legacy even in the immediate aftermath of his death and shed light on a life's work that has hitherto appeared in fragments, mostly as it relates to other, more prominent scholars of his era.

In his critical engagements with the methods of life-writing, Kaeser highlights the challenges of the archive, such as the illusory 'reality effect' of primary sources, and discusses the difficulties that biographers can face in engaging with earlier, less critical studies of their subjects. Few archaeologists have been so extensively studied since their death as Vere Gordon Childe, but Meheux's chapter provides a novel perspective, drawing on the files accumulated by the UK Security Service over decades of surveillance and monitoring. Meheux offers a subtle reinterpretation of Childe's relationship with communism and with left-wing culture more broadly. While taking an appropriately cautious approach to the files, she offers a subtle interpretation of Childe's ideologies and activism, often focused around pacifism, in the nuanced and changing contexts of left-wing political activism from the First World War to the Cold War.

The final section of this book focuses on more personal reflections on the practice of archaeological life-writing. Moro Abadía's chapter is built around fragments of diary that he wrote during a study trip in Paris, while researching archaeologist André Leroi-Gourhan. He describes his engagement with literature and documents, as well as meetings with colleagues, as he traces *inter alia* the influences of Anette Laming-Emperaire's work on Leroi-Gourhan's thought. The diary and its analysis is an exercise in reflexivity, as well as an intriguing insight into the working practices of a historian of archaeology. Gill's chapter reflects on his own prolific writings on lives in Classical archaeology, emerging from provenance and collections history research in a museum context, and later in writing on the development of the discipline. He describes his contributions to a range of life-writing project including several studies of Winifred Lamb, ranging over several years and the discovery of new sets of sources, as well as work on the revision and expansion of the *Oxford Dictionary of National Biography*.

At the close of the book, Challis' study of artist Ann Mary Severn Newton describes a brief, brilliant life caught between the demands of family, finances and professional practice in archaeological illustration. She reflects on the affective dimensions of life-writing, including her own struggles in conducting this research, and the value of greater critical consideration of the connections between biographers and their subjects. Challis' moving description of the connections and echoes between her own life and Newton's offer insights into why and how scholars approach life-writing in practice, and might also need to step away again. Much life-writing is based on a sense of connection or kinship, and as Challis shows it can spark empathy but also grief and sadness. It remains for life-writing practices to better engage with these affective aspects, not least for their critical significance, and for the valuable perspectives that they shed on past lives.

New directions

Where next for archaeological life-writing? Many of the current trends are positive ones, including the search for forgotten or marginalised lives in archaeology and criticism of the focus on fieldwork and fieldworkers at the expense of other spheres of research and discovery. In our research we recently encountered files of printed emails from the 1990s, some reused as notepaper: an already-anachronistic material practice that points to the increasing value and necessity of natively digital sources and archives, alongside the widespread and commendable digitisation of archives and collections. As digital media are themselves becoming the subject of archaeological excavations, the shape of much future work comes into focus.[57]

An interesting recent trend in life-writing has been the rise of graphic novel biographies. Some of the best-known of these focus on the lives of ordinary people, such as Art Spiegelman's *Maus*, Marjane Satrapi's

Persepolis and Alison Bechtel's *Fun Home*.[58] Others have focused on important figures, such as the multi-volume *March* on the life of US politician and activist John Lewis, who co-authored the trilogy.[59] A growing number of these books are focused on the lives of scholars and scientists, and in most cases intertwine narratives of their intellectual and personal histories. An outstanding example of this is *Logicomix*, an exploration of Bertrand Russell's research into the philosophy of mathematics, an otherwise bone-dry topic brought to life through beautiful artwork and a layered narrative.[60] Naomi Miller's *Drawing on the Past* is a beautiful example of life-writing through artworks and text that draws on the distinctive visual cultures of archaeological fieldwork.[61]

From an academic perspective, the most significant recent research project in our field was the *Collective Biography of Archaeology in the Pacific* project based at Australian National University from 2015 to 2020.[62] This was a wide-ranging initiative intended to establish a field of scholarship around the history of Pacific archaeology, and with specific aims to highlight the forgotten and erased histories of women archaeologists and indigenous scholars and collaborators.[63] The project took an explicitly international perspective, ranging across the Pacific and studying the work of German, French and Russian archaeologists, amongst others. The outputs of this project represent a significant advance in the field of Pacific archaeology and in the historiography of archaeology more generally, and it would be good to see projects of similar scale and ambition, with explicitly biographical scope, elsewhere in the world.[64]

One of the pleasures of bringing together this book has been a greater appreciation for the vast number of fascinating lives in archaeology, across the centuries and around the world. Their stories shed light on times and places, intellectual currents and world events. Some of the most striking and rewarding parts of reading these studies comes from spotting points of connection between individuals. Overlaps in place and time, mutual friends or contacts, illicit relations, forgotten collaborations and small favours: the threads that connect individuals into social, economic and scholarly networks, which in turn set out the frameworks for disciplinary histories.

Notes

1 See, for example, Allison Mickel, 'Reasons for redundancy in reflexivity: the role of diaries in archaeological epistemology', *Journal of Field Archaeology* 40 (2015): 300–9; and for use as a source, see Polina Nikolaou, 'Authoring the ancient sites of Cyprus in the late nineteenth century: the British Museum excavation notebooks, 1893–1896', *Journal of Historical*

Geography 56 (2017): 83–100. Chris Naunton recently published an interesting collection of extracts of field notebooks as *Egyptologist's Notebooks* (London: Thames and Hudson, 2020).

2. Neal Ascherson, 'Archaeology and the British media', in *Public Archaeology*, ed. Nick Merriman (London: Routledge, 2004), 145–58; Nicholas Lanoie, 'Inventing Egypt for the emerging British travel class: Amelia Edwards' *A Thousand Miles up the Nile*', *British Journal of Middle Eastern Studies*, 40 (2013): 149–61.

3. C. W. Ceram, *Götter, Gräber und Gelehrte: Roman der Archäologie* (Hamburg: Rowohlt, 1949); Mary Chubb, *Nefertiti Lived Here* (London: Geoffrey Bless, 1954); Robert Eric Mortimer Wheeler, *Still Digging: Interleaves from an antiquary's notebook* (London: Michael Joseph, 1955). For a more detailed discussion of the relationships between publishing and popularisation of archaeology, see Amara Thornton, *Archaeologists in Print: Publishing for the people* (London: UCL Press, 2018).

4. See Marc-Antoine Kaeser, 'Biography, science studies and the historiography of archaeological research: managing personal archives', *Complutum* 24 (2013): 101–8; also discussed in William Carruthers, 'Introduction: thinking about histories of Egyptology', in *Histories of Egyptology: Interdisciplinary measures*, ed. William Carruthers (Abingdon: Routledge, 2015), 1–15.

5. Hermione Lee includes a good discussion of hostility to biography in *Biography: A very short introduction* (Oxford: Oxford University Press, 2009). For a history of science perspective on this scepticism, see Mary Jo Nye, 'Scientific biography: history of science by another means?', *Isis* 97 (2006): 322–9. R. G. Collingwood is an interesting example of a historian and archaeologist who sharply differentiates biography from true history in his *The Idea of History* (Oxford: Oxford University Press, 1946). This did not prevent him from publishing his own memoirs.

6. See, for example, Paola Govoni and Zelda Alice Franceschi, eds. *Writing about Lives in Science: (Auto)biography, gender, and genre* (Göttingen: Vandenhoeck & Ruprecht, 2014); Bart Moore-Gilbert, *Postcolonial Life-Writing: Culture, politics and self-representation* (London: Routledge, 2009).

7. Hans Renders, Binne De Haan, and Jonne Harmsma, eds. *The Biographical Turn: Lives in history* (Abingdon: Routledge, 2016).

8. David P. Miller, 'The Sobel effect', *Metascience* 11 (2002): 185–200.

9. Renders et al., *Biographical Turn*, 3.

10. Marc-Antoine Kaeser, 'Biography as microhistory: the relevance of private archives for writing the history of archaeology', in *Archives, Ancestors, Practices: Archaeology in the light of its history*, eds. Nathan Schlanger and Jarl Nordbladh (Oxford: Berghahn, 2008), 9–20. This should not be confused with the more technical meanings of internalism and externalism in the history and philosophy of science: see, for example, Steven Shapin, 'Discipline and bounding: the history and sociology of science as seen through the externalism–internalism debate', *History of Science* 30 (1992): 333–69.

11. A recent example of this is Wesam Mohammed's exhibition *El Reis* at the Misr Public Library in Luxor in 2021, telling the stories of local workmen in Egyptology. The overwhelming majority of the images exhibited were contributed by the workmen themselves.

12. Kaeser, 'Biography as microhistory', 9.

13. Thomas Söderqvist, *The History and Poetics of Scientific Biography* (Aldershot: Ashgate, 2007), 7.

14. Allison Mickel, *Why Those Who Shovel Are Silent: A history of local archaeological knowledge and labor* (Boulder: University Press of Colorado, 2021); Stephen Quirke, *Hidden Hands: Egyptian workforces in Petrie excavation archives, 1880–1924* (London: Duckworth, 2010); Alice Stevenson, *Scattered Finds: Archaeology, Egyptology and museums* (London: UCL Press, 2019); Malcom Reid, *Whose Pharaohs?* (Berkeley : University of California Press, 2002) and *Contesting Antiquity in Egypt: Archaeologies, museums, and the struggle for identities from World War I to Nasser*. (New York: The American University in Cairo Press, 2019). The Abydos Archive Project is a good example of research that shares these aims: see Nora Shalaby, Ayman Damarany, and Jessica Kaiser, 'Tewfik Boulos and the administration of Egyptian Heritage at the beginning of the twentieth century', *The Journal of Egyptian Archaeology* 106 (2020): 75–88.

15. For example, there is a notable silence around Petrie's eugenicist ideology in early biographical studies, although more recent work has begun to remedy this, such as Debbie Challis, *The Archaeology of Race: The eugenic ideas of Francis Galton and Flinders Petrie* (London: Bloomsbury, 2014).

16 See, for example, Carr's discussion of Hawkes' treatment of infidelity in her biography of Wheeler, in Lydia Carr, *Tessa Verney Wheeler: Women and archaeology before World War Two* (Oxford: Oxford University Press, 2012), 20.
17 George Stocking, *Glimpses into My Own Black Box: An exercise in self-deconstruction* (Madison: University of Wisconsin Press, 2010), 156.
18 Another interesting discussion on this topic is Söderqvist's exploration of crafting life-writing narratives and the need for care for 'one's scholarly self'. See Thomas Söderqvist, 'What is the use of writing lives of recent scientists?', in *The Historiography of Contemporary Science, Technology, and Medicine: Writing recent science*, eds. Ronald Doel and Thomas Söderqvist (London: Routledge, 2006), 99–127.
19 See, for example, Zachary Leader, ed., *On Life-Writing* (Oxford: Oxford University Press, 2015); Mary Besemeres and Maureen Perkins, 'Editorial', *Life Writing* 1 (2004): vii–xii.
20 Anthologised in Jeanne Schulkind, ed., *Moments of Being: Unpublished autobiographical writings of Virginia Woolf* (Brighton: Sussex University Press, 1976).
21 Sidonie Smith and Julia Watson, *Reading Autobiography: A guide for interpreting life narratives* (Minneapolis: University of Minnesota Press, 2010). The list of different forms grows in length with each new edition of the book: see David McCooey, 'The limits of life writing', *Life Writing* 14 (2017): 277–80.
22 Renders et al., *Biographical Turn*, 5. Jill Lepore, 'Historians who love too much: Reflections on microhistory and biography', *The Journal of American History* 88 (2001): 129–44.
23 Morris Bierbrier, ed., *Who Was Who in Egyptology*, fourth revised edition (London: Egypt Exploration Society, 2012), and, for comparison, see Bernard Lightman, ed. *Dictionary of Nineteenth-Century British Scientists* (Bristol: Thoemmes, 2004); for dictionaries of national biography, see Lawrence Goldman, 'A monument to the Victorian Age? Continuity and discontinuity in the dictionaries of national biography 1882–2004', *Journal of Victorian Culture* 11 (2006): 111–32. For criticisms of *Who Was Who in Egyptology*, see *inter alia* Carruthers, Introduction, 5.
24 This view is echoed by Jason Thompson in *Wonderful Things: A history of Egyptology 1: From antiquity to 1881* (Cairo: American University in Cairo Press, 2015).
25 Warren Dawson, 'Preface to the first edition', in *Who Was Who in Egyptology*, fourth revised edition, ed. Morris Bierbrier (London: Egypt Exploration Society, 2012), vii–viii.
26 Colin Wallace, 'Writing disciplinary history, or why Romano-British archaeology needs a biographical dictionary of its own', *Oxford Journal of Archaeology* 21 (2002): 381–92.
27 Evert Baudou, 'The problem-orientated scientific biography as a research method', *Norwegian Archaeological Review* 31 (1998): 79–96.
28 Tim Murray, ed., *Encyclopedia of Archaeology: The great archaeologists* (Santa Barbara: ABC Clio, 1999).
29 From Murray's epilogue to his encyclopaedia, republished as chapter 9 in Tim Murray, *From Antiquarian to Archaeologist: The history and philosophy of archaeology* (Barnsley: Pen & Sword Archaeology, 2014), 106.
30 Murray, *From Antiquarian*, 100.
31 Douglas Givens, 'The role of biography in writing the history of archaeology', in *Histories of Archaeology: A reader in the history of archaeology*, eds. Tim Murray and Christopher Evans (Oxford: Oxford University Press, 2008), 181.
32 Jacob Gruber, 'In search of experience: biography as an instrument for the history of anthropology', in *Pioneers of American Anthropology: The uses of biography*, ed. J. Helm (Seattle: University of Washington Press, 1966), 3–27; and see Murray, *From Antiquarian*, 99; Givens, *Role of Biography*, 182.
33 Givens, *Role of Biography*, 183.
34 Getzel Cohen and Martha Sharp Joukowsky, eds. *Breaking Ground: Pioneering women archaeologists* (Ann Arbor: University of Michigan Press, 2006); Brenna Hassett, Suzanne Pilaar Birch, Victoria Herridge, and Rebecca Wragg Sykes, 'TrowelBlazers: Accidentally crowdsourcing an archive of women in archaeology', in *Shared Knowledge, Shared Power: Engaging local and indigenous heritage*, ed. Veysel Apaydin (Cham: Springer, 2018), 129–41; Katherine Grillo and Daniel Contreras, 'Public archaeology's mammoth in the room: engaging Wikipedia as a tool for teaching and outreach', *Advances in Archaeological Practice* 7 (2019): 435–42.
35 Kathleen Sheppard, *The Life of Margaret Alice Murray: A woman's work in archaeology* (Lanham: Lexington Books, 2013); David Gill, *Winifred Lamb: Aegean prehistorian and museum curator* (Oxford: Archaeopress, 2018); Carr, *Tessa Verney Wheeler*.

36 See, for example, Stevenson, *Scattered Finds*; Sheppard, *Life of Margaret Alice Murray*.
37 Pamela Jane Smith, '*A Splendid Idiosyncrasy': Prehistory at Cambridge, 1915–50* (Oxford: Archaeopress, 2009); Amara Thornton, 'Social networks in the history of archaeology: placing archaeology in its context', in *Historiographical Approaches to Past Archaeological Research*, eds. Gisela Eberhardt and Fabian Link (Berlin: Edition Topoi, 2015), 69–94; Amara Thornton, 'The allure of archaeology: Agnes Conway and Jane Harrison at Newnham College, 1903–1907', *Bulletin of the History of Archaeology* 21 (2011): 37–56.
38 Nathan Schlanger, 'Ancestral archives: explorations in the history of archaeology', *Antiquity* 76 (2002): 127–31; Murray, *From Antiquarian*, 149.
39 Nathan Schlanger and Jarl Nordbladh, eds. *Archives, Ancestors, Practices: Archaeology in the light of its history* (Oxford: Berghahn, 2008).
40 The Oxford series began with Peter Rowley-Conwy, *From Genesis to Prehistory: The archaeological three age system and its contested reception in Denmark, Britain, and Ireland* (Oxford: Oxford University Press, 2007), and includes Leo Klejn's book, *Soviet Archaeology: Trends, schools, and history* (Oxford: Oxford University Press, 2013). The Archaeopress series includes the late Don Brothwell's memoir *A Faith in Archaeological Science: Reflections on a life* (Oxford: Archaeopress, 2016), and Aleksander Konopatskii's huge two-volume study *Aleksei P. Okladnikov: The great explorer of the past* (Oxford: Archaeopress, 2019 and 2021).
41 Bruce Trigger, *Gordon Childe: Revolutions in archaeology* (London: Thames and Hudson, 1980); Barbara McNairn, *The Method and Theory of V. Gordon Childe: Economic, social and cultural interpretations of prehistory* (Edinburgh: Edinburgh University Press, 1980); Sally Green, *Prehistorian: A biography of V. Gordon Childe* (Bradford-on-Avon: Moonraker Press, 1981); Terry Irving, *The Fatal Allure of Politics: The life and thought of Vere Gordon Childe* (Melbourne: Monash University Publishing, 2020). For the most substantial of Peter Gathercole's works on Childe, see '"Patterns in prehistory": an examination of the later thinking of V. Gordon Childe', *World Archaeology* 3 (1971): 225–32; and his chapter in Peter Gathercole, Terence Irving, and Gregory Melleuish, eds. *Childe and Australia: Archaeology, politics and ideas* (St Lucia: University of Queensland Press, 1995).
42 Joan L. Richards, 'Focus section. Introduction: Fragmented lives', *Isis* 97 (2006): 303.
43 Michael Shortland and Richard Yeo, 'Introduction', in *Telling Lives in Science: Essays on scientific biography*, eds. Michael Shortland and Richard Yeo (Cambridge: Cambridge University Press, 1996).
44 Stephen Leach, *A Russian Perspective on Theoretical Archaeology: The life and work of Leo S. Klejn* (Walnut Creek: Left Coast Press, 2015).
45 See, for example, Klejn, *Soviet Archaeology*.
46 Marc-Antoine Kaeser, *L'univers du préhistorien: Science, foi et politique dans l'oeuvre et la vie d'Éduard Desor (1811–1882)* (Paris: L'Harmattan, 2004).
47 Kaeser, 'Biography as microhistory'; Kaeser, 'Biography, science studies'.
48 Kaeser, 'Biography, science studies', 105.
49 Carr, *Tessa Verney Wheeler*; Jacquetta Hawkes, *Mortimer Wheeler: Adventurer in archaeology* (London: Weidenfeld and Nicolson, 1982).
50 Hawkes, *Mortimer Wheeler*, 1–2.
51 Carr, *Tessa Verney Wheeler*, 1.
52 Hawkes, *Mortimer Wheeler*, x.
53 See footnote 16.
54 Carr, *Tessa Verney Wheeler*, 18–22.
55 Bonnie Clark and Laurie Wilkie 'The prism of self: gender and personhood', in *Handbook of Gender in Archaeology*, ed. Sarah Milledge Nelson (Lanham: AltaMira, 2006), 333–64.
56 Carr, *Tessa Verney Wheeler*, 19.
57 Jennifer Baird and Lesley McFadyen, 'Towards an archaeology of archaeological archives', *Archaeological Review from Cambridge* 29 (2014): 14–32; Julian Richards, 'Digital preservation and access', *European Journal of Archaeology* 5 (2002): 343–66.
58 Art Spiegelman, *Maus: A survivor's tale* (New York: Pantheon Books, 1986); Marjane Satrapi, *The Complete Persepolis* (New York: Random House, 2007); Alison Bechdel, *Fun Home: A family tragicomic* (Boston: Houghton Mifflin, 2007).
59 John Lewis, Andrew Aydin, and Nate Powell, *March (Book One)* (Marietta: Top Shelf Productions, 2013).
60 Apostolos Doxiadēs, Christos Papadimitriou, Alekos Papadatos, and Annie Di Donna, *Logicomix* (New York: Bloomsbury, 2009).

61 Naomi Miller, *Drawing on the Past: An archaeologist's sketchbook* (Philadelphia: University of Pennsylvania Museum of Archaeology and Anthropology, 2002).
62 Hilary Howes and Matthew Spriggs, 'Writing the history of archaeology in the Pacific: voices and perspectives', *Journal of Pacific History* 54 (2019): 295–306.
63 Emilie Dotte-Sarout, 'Pacific Matildas: Finding the women in the history of Pacific archaeology', *Bulletin of the History of Archaeology*, 31 (2021): 2.
64 See, for example, special issues of *Journal of Pacific Archaeology* 8 (2017) on the 'History of Archaeology in the Pacific', and *Bulletin of the History of Archaeology* (2019–2021) on 'Histories of Asia-Pacific Archaeologies'.

Bibliography

Ascherson, Neal, 'Archaeology and the British media', in *Public Archaeology*, ed. Nick Merriman (London: Routledge, 2004), 145–58.
Baird, Jennifer and Lesley McFadyen, 'Towards an archaeology of archaeological archives', *Archaeological Review from Cambridge* 29 (2014): 14–32.
Baudou, Evert, 'The problem-orientated scientific biography as a research method', *Norwegian Archaeological Review* 31 (1998): 79–96.
Bechdel, Alison, *Fun Home: A family tragicomic* (Boston: Houghton Mifflin, 2007).
Besemeres, Mary and Maureen Perkins, 'Editorial', *Life Writing* 1 (2004): vii–xii.
Bierbrier, Morris, ed. *Who Was Who in Egyptology*, fourth revised edition (London: Egypt Exploration Society, 2012).
Brothwell, Don, *A Faith in Archaeological Science: Reflections on a life* (Oxford: Archaeopress, 2016).
Carr, Lydia, *Tessa Verney Wheeler: Women and archaeology before World War Two* (Oxford: Oxford University Press, 2012).
Carruthers, William, 'Introduction: thinking about histories of Egyptology', in *Histories of Egyptology: Interdisciplinary measures*, ed. William Carruthers (Abingdon: Routledge, 2015), 1–15.
Ceram, C. W., *Götter, Gräber und Gelehrte: Roman der Archäologie* (Hamburg: Rowohlt, 1949).
Challis, Debbie, *The Archaeology of Race: The eugenic ideas of Francis Galton and Flinders Petrie* (London: Bloomsbury, 2014).
Chubb, Mary, *Nefertiti Lived Here* (London: Geoffrey Bless, 1954).
Clark, Bonnie and Laurie Wilkie, 'The prism of self: gender and personhood', in *Handbook of Gender in Archaeology*, ed. Sarah Milledge Nelson (Lanham: AltaMira, 2006), 333–64.
Cohen, Getzel and Martha Sharp Joukowsky, eds. *Breaking Ground: Pioneering women archaeologists* (Ann Arbor: University of Michigan Press, 2006).
Collingwood, R. G., *The Idea of History* (Oxford: Oxford University Press, 1946).
Dawson, Warren, 'Preface to the first edition', in *Who Was Who in Egyptology*, fourth revised edition, ed. Morris Bierbrier (London: Egypt Exploration Society, 2012), vii–viii.
Dotte-Sarout, Emilie, 'Pacific Matildas: finding the women in the history of Pacific archaeology', *Bulletin of the History of Archaeology*, 31 (2021): 2.
Doxiadēs, Apostolos, Christos Papadimitriou, Alekos Papadatos, and Annie Di Donna, *Logicomix* (New York: Bloomsbury, 2009).
Gathercole, Peter, '"Patterns in prehistory":an examination of the later thinking of V. Gordon Childe', *World Archaeology* 3 (1971): 225–32.
Gathercole, Peter, Terence Irving, and Gregory Melleuish, eds., *Childe and Australia: Archaeology, politics and ideas* (St Lucia: University of Queensland Press, 1995).
Gill, David, *Winifred Lamb: Aegean prehistorian and museum curator* (Oxford: Archaeopress, 2018).
Givens, Douglas, 'The role of biography in writing the history of archaeology', in *Histories of Archaeology: A reader in the history of archaeology*, eds., Tim Murray and Christopher Evans (Oxford: Oxford University Press, 2008), 177–93.
Goldman, Lawrence, 'A monument to the Victorian Age? Continuity and discontinuity in the dictionaries of national biography 1882–2004', *Journal of Victorian Culture* 11 (2006): 111–32.
Govoni, Paola and Zelda Alice Franceschi, eds., *Writing about Lives in Science: (Auto) biography, gender, and genre* (Göttingen: Vandenhoeck & Ruprecht, 2014).

Green, Sally, *Prehistorian: A biography of V. Gordon Childe* (Bradford-on-Avon: Moonraker Press, 1981).
Grillo, Katherine and Daniel Contreras, 'Public archaeology's mammoth in the room: engaging Wikipedia as a tool for teaching and outreach', *Advances in Archaeological Practice* 7 (2019): 435–42.
Gruber, Jacob, 'In search of experience: biography as an instrument for the history of anthropology', in *Pioneers of American Anthropology: The uses of biography*, ed. J. Helm (Seattle: University of Washington Press, 1966), 3–27.
Hassett, Brenna, Suzanne Pilaar Birch, Victoria Herridge, and Rebecca Wragg Sykes, 'TrowelBlazers: accidentally crowdsourcing an archive of women in archaeology', in *Shared Knowledge, Shared Power: Engaging local and indigenous heritage*, ed. Veysel Apaydin (Cham: Springer, 2018), 129–41.
Hawkes, Jacquetta, *Mortimer Wheeler: Adventurer in archaeology* (London: Weidenfeld and Nicolson, 1982).
Howes, Hilary and Matthew Spriggs, 'Writing the history of archaeology in the Pacific: voices and perspectives', *Journal of Pacific History* 54 (2019): 295–306.
Irving, Terry, *The Fatal Allure of Politics: The life and thought of Vere Gordon Childe* (Melbourne: Monash University Publishing, 2020).
Kaeser, Marc-Antoine, 'Biography, science studies and the historiography of archaeological research: managing personal archives', *Complutum* 24 (2013): 101–8.
Kaeser, Marc-Antoine, 'Biography as microhistory: the relevance of private archives for writing the history of archaeology', in *Archives, Ancestors, Practices: Archaeology in the light of its history*, eds. Nathan Schlanger and Jarl Nordbladh (Oxford: Berghahn, 2008), 9–20.
Kaeser, Marc-Antoine, *L'univers du préhistorien: Science, foi et politique dans l'oeuvre et la vie d'Éduard Desor (1811–1882)* (Paris: L'Harmattan, 2004).
Klejn, Leo, *Soviet Archaeology: Trends, schools, and history* (Oxford: Oxford University Press, 2013).
Konopatskii, Aleksander, *Aleksei P. Okladnikov: The great explorer of the past* (Oxford: Archaeopress, 2019 and 2021).
Lanoie, Nicholas, 'Inventing Egypt for the emerging British travel class: Amelia Edwards' *A Thousand Miles up the Nile*', *British Journal of Middle Eastern Studies*, 40 (2013): 149–61.
Leach, Stephen, *A Russian Perspective on Theoretical Archaeology: The life and work of Leo S. Klejn* (Walnut Creek: Left Coast Press, 2015).
Leader, Zachary, ed., *On Life-Writing* (Oxford: Oxford University Press, 2015).
Lee, Hermione, *Biography: A very short introduction* (Oxford: Oxford University Press, 2009).
Lepore, Jill, 'Historians who love too much: Reflections on microhistory and biography', *The Journal of American History* 88 (2001): 129–44.
Lewis, John, Andrew Aydin, and Nate Powell, *March (Book One)* (Marietta: Top Shelf Productions, 2013).
Lightman, Bernard, ed., *Dictionary of Nineteenth-Century British Scientists* (Bristol: Thoemmes, 2004).
McCooey, David, 'The limits of life writing', *Life Writing* 14 (2017): 277–80.
McNairn, Barbara, *The Method and Theory of V. Gordon Childe: Economic, social and cultural interpretations of prehistory* (Edinburgh: Edinburgh University Press, 1980).
Mickel, Allison, *Why Those Who Shovel Are Silent: A history of local archaeological knowledge and labor* (Boulder: University Press of Colorado, 2021).
Mickel, Allison, 'Reasons for redundancy in reflexivity: the role of diaries in archaeological epistemology', *Journal of Field Archaeology* 40 (2015): 300–9.
Miller, David P., 'The Sobel effect', *Metascience* 11 (2002): 185–200.
Miller, Naomi, *Drawing on the Past: An archaeologist's sketchbook* (Philadelphia: University of Pennsylvania Museum of Archaeology and Anthropology, 2002).
Moore-Gilbert, Bart, *Postcolonial Life-Writing: Culture, politics and self-representation* (London: Routledge, 2009).
Murray, Tim, *From Antiquarian to Archaeologist: The history and philosophy of archaeology* (Barnsley: Pen & Sword Archaeology, 2014).
Murray, Tim, ed., *Encyclopedia of Archaeology: The great archaeologists* (Santa Barbara: ABC Clio, 1999).
Naunton, Chris, *Egyptologist's Notebooks* (London: Thames and Hudson, 2020).
Nikolaou, Polina, 'Authoring the ancient sites of Cyprus in the late nineteenth century: the British Museum excavation notebooks, 1893–1896', *Journal of Historical Geography* 56 (2017): 83–100.

Nye, Mary Jo, 'Scientific biography: history of science by another means?', *Isis* 97 (2006): 322–9.
Quirke, Stephen, *Hidden Hands: Egyptian workforces in Petrie excavation archives, 1880–1924* (London: Duckworth, 2010).
Reid, Malcolm, *Contesting Antiquity in Egypt: Archaeologies, museums, and the struggle for identities from World War I to Nasser*. (New York: The American University in Cairo Press, 2019).
Reid, Malcolm, *Whose Pharaohs?* (Berkeley: University of California Press, 2002).
Renders, Hans, Binne De Haan, and Jonne Harmsma, eds. *The Biographical Turn: Lives in history* (Abingdon: Routledge, 2016).
Richards, Joan L., 'Focus section. Introduction: Fragmented lives', *Isis* 97 (2006): 303.
Richards, Julian, 'Digital preservation and access', *European Journal of Archaeology* 5 (2002): 343–66.
Rowley-Conwy, Peter, *From Genesis to Prehistory: The archaeological three age system and its contested reception in Denmark, Britain, and Ireland* (Oxford: Oxford University Press, 2007).
Satrapi, Marjane, *The Complete Persepolis* (New York: Random House, 2007).
Schlanger, Nathan and Jarl Nordbladh, eds., *Archives, Ancestors, Practices: Archaeology in the light of its history* (Oxford: Berghahn, 2008).
Schlanger, Nathan, 'Ancestral archives: explorations in the history of archaeology', *Antiquity* 76 (2002): 127–31.
Schulkind, Jeanne, ed., *Moments of Being: Unpublished autobiographical writings of Virginia Woolf* (Brighton: Sussex University Press, 1976).
Shalaby, Nora, Ayman Damarany, and Jessica Kaiser, 'Tewfik Boulos and the administration of Egyptian heritage at the beginning of the twentieth century', *The Journal of Egyptian Archaeology* 106 (2020): 75–88.
Shapin, Steven, 'Discipline and bounding: the history and sociology of science as seen through the externalism–internalism debate', *History of Science* 30 (1992): 333–69.
Sheppard, Kathleen, *The Life of Margaret Alice Murray: A woman's work in archaeology* (Lanham: Lexington Books, 2013).
Shortland, Michael and Richard Yeo, 'Introduction', in *Telling Lives in Science: Essays on scientific biography*, eds. Michael Shortland and Richard Yeo (Cambridge: Cambridge University Press, 1996).
Smith, Pamela Jane, *'A Splendid Idiosyncrasy': Prehistory at Cambridge, 1915–50* (Oxford: Archaeopress, 2009).
Smith, Sidonie and Julia Watson, *Reading Autobiography: A guide for interpreting life narratives* (Minneapolis: University of Minnesota Press, 2010).
Söderqvist, Thomas, *The History and Poetics of Scientific Biography* (Aldershot: Ashgate, 2007).
Söderqvist, Thomas, 'What is the use of writing lives of recent scientists?', in *The Historiography of Contemporary Science, Technology, and Medicine: Writing recent science*, eds. Ronald Doel and Thomas Söderqvist (London: Routledge, 2006), 99–127.
Spiegelman, Art, *Maus: A survivor's tale* (New York: Pantheon Books, 1986).
Stevenson, Alice, *Scattered Finds: Archaeology, Egyptology and museums* (London: UCL Press, 2019).
Stocking, George, *Glimpses into My Own Black Box: An exercise in self-deconstruction* (Madison: University of Wisconsin Press, 2010).
Thompson, Jason, *Wonderful Things: A history of Egyptology 1: From Antiquity to 1881* (Cairo: American University in Cairo Press, 2015).
Thornton, Amara, *Archaeologists in Print: Publishing for the people* (London: UCL Press, 2018).
Thornton, Amara, 'Social networks in the history of archaeology: placing archaeology in its context', in *Historiographical Approaches to Past Archaeological Research*, eds. Gisela Eberhardt and Fabian Link (Berlin: Edition Topoi, 2015), 69–94.
Thornton, Amara, 'The allure of archaeology: Agnes Conway and Jane Harrison at Newnham College, 1903–1907', *Bulletin of the History of Archaeology* 21 (2011): 37–56.
Trigger, Bruce, *Gordon Childe: Revolutions in archaeology* (London: Thames and Hudson, 1980).
Wallace, Colin, 'Writing disciplinary history, or why Romano-British archaeology needs a biographical dictionary of its own', *Oxford Journal of Archaeology* 21 (2002): 381–92.
Wheeler, Robert Eric Mortimer, *Still Digging: Interleaves from an antiquary's notebook* (London: Michael Joseph, 1955).

Part I
Critical perspectives

1
Biography in science studies and the historiography of archaeology: Some methodological guidelines

Marc-Antoine Kaeser

Introduction

Over the last two or three decades, the field of history of archaeology has been characterised by a major development of historiographic endeavours. Considering the large number of theoretical arguments and justifications which have accompanied this long-term trend,[1] I do not consider it necessary or even useful to delve again into the grounds, motives and benefits of this development. Rather, I would like to focus on the important (and apparently ever growing) proportion of life-writing within this trend.[2] There are certainly multiple causes, which can account for this widespread growth of biographic approaches; one may, however, emphasise two main explanations, which appear relatively specific to the field.

Firstly, the archival turn successfully advocated, among others, by the influential European research project AREA (Archives of European Archaeology)[3], has led to the discovery of innumerable, often previously unknown or unnoticed, archival sources. Now, considering the late disciplinarisation of archaeology[4] and the ensuing deficiencies of institutional structures in the archiving of archaeological documentation, these newly discovered archives are most frequently private documents, whose quantity, scale and novelty, make them particularly suitable for implementing biographical approaches.

Secondly, one cannot overlook the impact of the complete reversal which has, in the long term, characterised authorship in the history of archaeology. Whereas it had long been the preserve of senior, dominant scholars who tended to instrumentalise historiography in order to legitimise the present shape of the discipline and to advocate future directions of research, the history of archaeology has now become a most popular area of specialisation among PhD students and young academics who, in contrast to their predecessors (and often quite accurately), see it as a convenient means to question the current theories and conceptual frameworks of archaeology. However, their lesser erudition diverts these junior scholars from engaging in overly ambitious syntheses or comprehensive approaches, in favour of monographic or more topic-oriented research. Thus, resorting to a collection of private archives in compiling a biographical essay logically appears as a particularly suitable choice, since it allows one to cover a welcome diversity of themes while clearly defining the scope and the boundaries of the object of research.

Since I had personally contributed to this trend towards biographical approaches prior to my PhD and before the launching of the AREA project, and still engage in research on individual scientists,[5] I am in no position to minimise the relevance and significance of life-writing, as well as their invaluable assets for the development of innovative perspectives and realistic approaches toward the past of archaeology. Nonetheless, I think it is vital to explicitly address, not only the practical grounds, but above all the theoretical underpinnings of scientific biographies, and to reflect on the meaning and the specific pitfalls of such approaches, on a methodological and epistemological, but also on a more psychological basis. Now, to this end, it appears necessary to broaden the scope of inquiry, and to assess the place of life-writing within science studies in general.

In fact, this is a reflection that I have already been led to conduct for my doctoral research on Édouard Desor (1811–1882). Desor was a palaeontologist and geologist of German origin who settled in Neuchâtel (Switzerland) after long stays in Paris (France) and Boston (USA). A politician, entrepreneur, businessman and religious reformer, he established himself as one of the main authorities in Swiss scientific research and exercised significant power over the development of scientific research policy in Switzerland in the second half of the nineteenth century. In 1860, he entered the field of archaeology and played a notable role in the institutionalisation of prehistoric sciences on an international scale, in particular by the founding the International Congress of Prehistoric Anthropology and Archaeology, in 1866. The multiplicity of Desor's fields of action and the obvious interconnection of his commitments represented a challenge for the contextualisation of his scholarly research, which actually motivated the interdisciplinary registration of my PhD, where the study conducted from the perspective of prehistoric archaeology

(University of Neuchâtel) had to be complemented by the expertise of science studies at the École des hautes études en sciences sociales, Paris.

Biography, history and science studies

The recent trend for life-writing is not restricted to the domain of the history of archaeology. Quite the contrary: a strong comeback in biography can indeed be observed within science studies in general, especially since the 1970s, with a particular increase from the beginning of the twenty-first century. What is new, however, is the academic legitimacy which has finally been recognised in life-writings. While biography had long been confined to public outreach publications, mainly due to the dilettantish endeavours of amateur historians, it is presently allowed to bask within the most respectable precincts of intellectual production.

Basically, the acceptance of biography relies on its theoretical and practical elasticity, and consequently, on its significant capacity for heuristic productivity.[6] For, in essence, biography has the potential to transcend schools of thought or paradigm clashes – scholarly conflicts which still strongly prevail within science studies, where they are fuelled by persistent disagreements as to the nature of science, the actual object of research. Considered from the singular perspective authorised by biography, the history, sociology and philosophy of sciences are not incompatible. And the respective inputs of intellectual, cultural, political and social history may even be combined without insuperable methodological contradictions.

Of course, the present trend of biographic essays still raises some ethical questions. Until proven otherwise, a biographer always remains suspected of a certain opportunism. In the context of theoretical disarray affecting the discipline of history,[7] and in the absence of widely acknowledged doctrines or references, one can easily capitalise on the genuine attraction of the biographical genre, without a meaningful heuristic objective. In this respect, and in order to identify the requirements of life-writing in the field of science, it is all the more necessary to explore the origins and the background of scientific biography. As a matter of fact, this is an undertaking with a heavy legacy.

Men of science: A prominent role in the origins and development of the biographical genre

Leaving aside literary or apologetic writings such as Plutarch's *Lives of the Noble Greeks and Romans*, or the Christian 'Life of Saints', it appears that accounts of scholars' and scientists' lives have played a decisive role in the establishment of the biographical genre as such.[8] As early as the beginning of the eighteenth century, the ritualised eulogies of the French Académie des Sciences have actually imposed the relevance of a retrospective view on scholarly work and performance, thus laying down the rules of biographical writing. In the nineteenth century, the extraordinary popularity of innumerable Victorian 'Life and Works' even raised scientific biography to the rank of a genre in its own right. During the twentieth century, scientific biography then gradually declined, and became relatively marginalised in parallel to the institutional establishment of the history of science. But it is mainly the rise of the philosophy of science which led to its progressive disregard, until its disqualification in the times of triumphant structuralism. While philosophers proclaimed the death of man and the consecutive demise of the author, life-writing appeared as futile, or even inane exercises, overvaluing the superficial and delusional 'creative act': as a matter of fact, scientific production was then viewed as the random expression of intrinsically anonymous knowledge conditions of possibility.[9]

Sociology and the equivocal comeback of the singular

Somewhat surprisingly, the progressive rehabilitation of biography has been carried out by sociology. Starting within social history in the 1970s, the comeback of individual perspectives was actually the outcome of the interest shown by sociologists in the collective *experience* hidden behind their quantitative data.[10] In science studies, two articles, the first by Steven Shapin and Arnold Thackray and the second by Thomas L. Hankins, both published during the 1970s in the distinguished periodical *History of Science*,[11] illustrate the pluri-individual detour through prosopography which was first needed to restore the legitimacy of biography: in the opinion of sociologists, life-writing adequately allowed one to grasp the concrete and human realities of the 'social context'.

Such equivocal expectations testify to the ambivalence of the first comeback of biography, which rested upon quite wobbly theoretical grounds: single lives were mainly investigated in order to enable a grasp of the background behind them. In other words, individual characteristics were only approached as they offered a pattern of what precisely lay beyond them.[12] Operating in the extrapolation mode, this alleged social 'representativeness' based the biographical undertakings on a methodological contradiction: the relevance and scope of a biography depended upon the 'ordinariness' of the individual under scrutiny. Now, since the subject of the biography was just a pretext for the illustration of their surroundings, the biographer was driven to either fabricate the illusion of collective biographies which his or her sources could actually not really provide for, or to resort to external, determinist causes as soon as his or her biographical data seemed to differ from the general picture inferred from social history.

Giovanni Levi and the dynamics of representativeness

All in all, the methodological contradiction of 'social' biographies resulted from an inappropriate, mechanistic notion of the 'context', which is in fact a plural reality of multiple interacting factors, also encompassing the human, individual perception. In this sense, there is no necessary contradiction between the study of the singular and that of the collective. Since the characterisation of the individuals lies somewhere between their social image and their own perception of their individuality, the biographer is forced, no matter what, to take the social context into consideration. Furthermore, the personal perception of the subject of a biography also stems from his or her own social representations; and in its turn, his or her social image depends upon the cultural definitions of identity prevailing in his or her society.

In fact, as Giovanni Levi has shown,[13] the relations between the social and the individual are to be understood as a dynamic: the character of a person is a construction in interaction with his or her social context, and it evolves with the changing of his or her environment as well as the development of his or her own representations. Needless to say, these principles can easily be transposed to the biographies of scientists. For scientific stances proceed equally from the interaction between individual, personal questionings on the one hand, and the evolution of the intellectual environment and the bibliographical landscape on the other hand.[14]

In sum, these dynamics between singular and collective resolve the false issue of representativeness. Contrary to some common wisdom popularised by the ideology of liberal thinking, the actual entanglement of social and individual rules out any simplistic antagonism between an a priori unlimited individual freedom on the one hand, and rigid social contingencies on the other hand. As Levi underlines,[15] the system generates its own interstices. Consequently, the study of social practices fostered by biographical approaches can precisely allow us to assess the elasticity of the social standards.

Biography as microhistory

As already mentioned, the comeback of biography in the field of history benefited from recognition of the limitations of both structuralist abstractions and quantitative approaches. But it also drew on the 'theoretical disarray' of the historical discipline referred to above: all categories commonly employed by historians (such as social classes, socio-professional classifications, etc.) have been denounced as academic constructs.[16]

In this respect, microhistory, as Jacques Revel has defined it,[17] emerged as the most productive answer to the potentially devastating consequences of the critical turn. Now, in our opinion, biography should and can be considered and practised as a kind of microhistory,[18] especially owing to the fact that biography also enables the objectification of these categories which remain of the utmost necessity for the operation of historical analysis. Accordingly, the biographer should resort to using categories derived from the conscience and the wording of his or her own object of study. In other words, concepts such as the 'clerical party' or the 'amateur archaeologists' in the biography of a nineteenth century prehistorian should be based on (or, at least, explicitly refer to) the actual language terms employed by the object of the study.

Ultimately, such a microhistorical perspective is best suited in order to explain the actions and the rationale of the subjects of biographies.[19] But it requires diving into the midst of their life experience (Figure 1.1), integrating their own individual perceptions and social representations, as well as the meaning given by them to the world they lived in. By relating science as it was lived and practised by the scholars themselves, the biographer is able to establish its effective place, within the actual entanglement of social factors that interact with all cognitive undertakings. Firstly, according to the diversity of the subject's activities and commitments, it is possible to highlight the dynamics which rule the connections between science, politics, religion, etc. And secondly, within science itself, the biographer can uncover the relations shared by applied research, basic research, politics of science and scientific popularisation: Louis Agassiz's research on the Ice Age provides an example. When Agassiz and his colleagues were studying the Aar Glacier, their camp was humorously referred to by its residents the 'Hôtel des Neuchâtelois': this makeshift shelter contributed to the reputation of his research on the Ice Age, as well as to Agassiz's popularity – a scientist quite well versed in the demands of self-promotion (Figure 1.2).

Of course, this comes at a price: even if microhistory leaves room for alternating depths of field,[20] the scaling down obviously precludes

Figure 1.1 Édouard Desor (1811–1882) posing at the photographer's studio with his dog Rino. Bibliothèque publique et universitaire, Neuchâtel, Switzerland.

hindsight. But in return, the minute processing of the details ensures an optimal autonomy of the biographer towards the existing body of knowledge. The importance of this heuristic autonomy will be addressed below, but I ought already to underline its particular relevance in the field of science studies: actually, it offers an ideal protection against the pitfalls of presentism, because the issues of the biography can be outlined in the light of the actual perceptions of its subject of study. Concisely put, the life of the individual serves as a mediator: his or her thoughts, actions and engagement with his or her environment provide access to 'science in action',[21] that is, to science as it was experienced and lived in the

HOTEL DES NEUCHATELOIS
sur la Mer de glace ou Lauteraar et Finsteraar
Tel Rhénéal

Figure 1.2 The base camp of Louis Agassiz and his companions' expeditions on the middle moraine of the Aar Glacier (ca. 1840). Drawing J. Bettanier, lithography H. Nicolet, Musée d'art et d'histoire de Neuchâtel, Switzerland (H 3706).

midst of intertwining social logics[22] which participated in its construction, thus doing justice to the original complexity of research issues and processes.

Undoubtedly, the assets of a microhistorical approach prove particularly adequate for biographies of archaeologists, especially prior to the mid-twentieth century, for reasons related to the complex character of the emergence of this field of research, as well as both its late and heterogeneous institutionalisation and disciplinarisation. As is well known, the archaeological discipline has actually been developed as the outcome of very diverse cognitive impulses – sometimes contradictory, sometimes combined. This is a fact that is still demonstrated by its quite eclectic institutional designation, differing from one country, or even from one university to the other (between art history, cultural anthropology, human palaeontology, 'national' history, natural sciences or even geography). Now, this testifies to the extreme diversity of the respective scientific traditions, but also to the vagaries of scientific competition and institutional rivalries in which the subjects of our biographies were involved, and whose outcome would indeed not become known to them.

Overriding the legacy of previous scholarship

The prolific production of life-writings of scholars over the last three centuries, and especially since the 1970s, has been mentioned above. Now, for the present biographer, the exploitation of the often abundant and indeed precious data gathered in previous biographies proves particularly problematic: considering their purpose, these life stories are often seriously biased. In a certain sense, they at least remind the biographer about the limitations of biographical writing.

Bourdieu and the 'biographic illusion'

When dealing with scientists, the habitual complacency of obituaries, eulogies, Victorian biographies and autobiographical essays is strengthened by their object. Considering the long-standing faith in the progress of science, these biographical undertakings had an inspirational role. With scientific discipline being perceived as an exemplary asceticism, the scientist took on the appearance of missionary, whose quite earthly task, however, pursued a transcendent ideal of natural truth.

Such biases do not necessarily impair the documentary value of these works: the reader just needs to put the range of the flattering assessments into perspective; between the lines they may also detect some flaws of the subject left implicit by the writer. Yet these secondary sources share another, more troublesome characteristic: a systematic tendency to retrospection, which leads to Pierre Bourdieu's disparaging sentence of the biographic illusion.[23] In short, the subject of the biography is perceived according to his or her ultimate achievements, while their earlier life is depicted as a linear path with deceptive coherence – leaving aside, if needed, everything which could have deviated from the straight line drawn between birth and death. All doubts, mistakes and wanderings of the subject are erased, even though such precious information could precisely serve to underscore his or her later achievements.

Besides, one may also point out the fact that the obituaries and the biographical essays written shortly after the death of the subject often present striking similarities. As a matter of fact, it appears that such similarities are not only the outcome of a lazy copying by their authors: they can even proceed from the tapping into a single source – a biographical sketch (some kind of a curriculum vitae) written by the subject shortly before his or her own death![24] This perfectly exemplifies the necessary reservations, less to the reality of the facts or even the objectivity of witnessing in such biographical works, than to the selection and the arrangement of these facts. In brief, obituaries and Victorian biographies appear to be more instructive about the image the subject wanted to leave for posterity than about the realities of his or her existence.

Pseudo-collective biographies

By force of circumstance, a biographer can find much useful information while going through the secondary documentation, especially in the ancient biographies of some of the colleagues or friends of his or her subject of study. Indeed, as stated above, such biographical essays were particularly plentiful in Victorian times, when Life and Works of scientists served an edifying purpose. Now, many such works claim a collective character, which is misleading because they actually remain organised around a key figure. The picture of the human environment surrounding this figure may be elaborate, but the collective still serves as a stooge – an admittedly detailed stage set for a scene where all action is determined in order to highlight the whereabouts of the protagonist. In short, the cohorts are relegated to the role of sidekick: they are depicted only in the presence of the lead role, and disappear backstage as soon as the contingencies of their lives and careers drive them to other arenas. In other words, they are perceived in a fragmentary way, as a composite of partial features frozen in biased perspectives.

The strengths and drawbacks of archival research

Considering the shortcomings and specific downsides of secondary documentation, resorting to primary sources appears all the more crucial. Leaving aside all material records, scientific collections (Figure 1.3) and personal objects, and notwithstanding the potential taking into account of relevant places and spaces, we shall focus here on the written, historical sources, which are indeed already manifold. They may include private and scientific correspondence as well as personal diaries, manuscript drafts of articles or oral communications and corrected proofs of publications, but also annotated books or offprints in the personal library of the subject of the biography. In their contextual diversity, these original documents

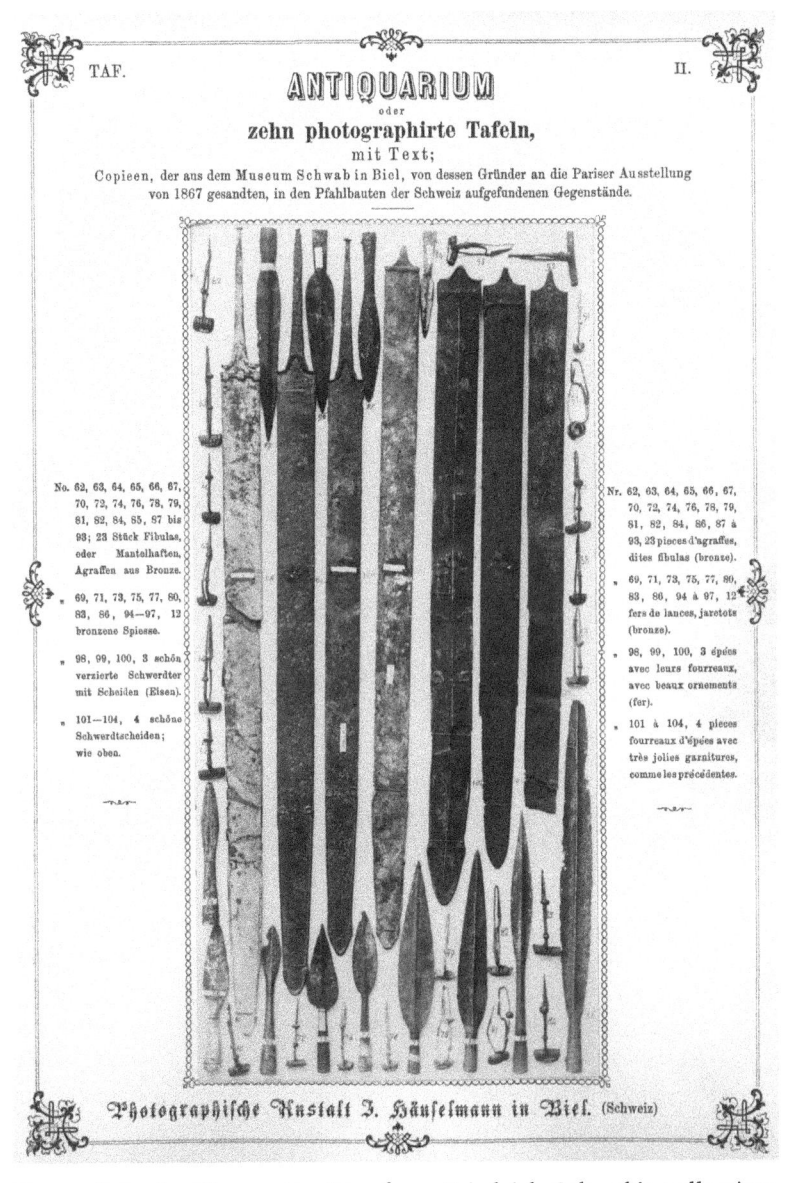

Figure 1.3 La Tène antiquities from Friedrich Schwab's collection: one of the displays produced for the Paris World Exhibition in 1867. The public presentation of the collection, as well as the diffusion of these phototypical prints, have greatly contributed to the notoriety of La Tène (Neuchâtel, Switzerland) and its subsequent election as the eponymous site of the Second European Iron Age. Archives Laténium, Hauterive, Switzerland.

offer a direct and invaluable access to the day-to-day activities of the subject of study. Such materials are often of an intimate and spontaneous character, and are generally little formalised, thus allowing the analyst to leave behind the overall *a posteriori* reconstructions of the secondary literature. All in all, the cross-checking of these various documents provides for a balanced understanding of the ambitions, goals, actions, positions and postures of the scientist under scrutiny.[25]

Now, despite all the advantages of the resorting to primary sources and original documents (private archives in particular), there are nevertheless some serious pitfalls to be avoided – especially in the case of life-writing, and all the more so when (as is often the case in the history of archaeology) the research is undertaken by archaeologists unfamiliar with, or insufficiently trained, in the skills of historical criticism.

The delusions of the 'reality effect'

Working on archives, one should, however, not credit the original documents with an immanent power of demonstration. Because direct testimonies never speak for themselves, they have to be confronted with critical exegesis and the available syntheses, within the scope of current theoretical understanding. In fact, biographers should guard themselves against the lure of the reality effect, such as defined by the French historian Arlette Farge.[26] And as proven by their systematic misuse in Victorian 'Life and Letters', the relevance of quotations should be assessed within their context of production.

As a matter of fact, exhuming an archival document, especially when one is the first to read it since it had been written by the subject of the biography, can easily give the biographer the illusion of touching a raw, inviolate truth. Now, such an illusion is significantly strengthened when dealing with documents such as letters, where the spontaneity of the writer seems to ensure the authenticity and honesty of the testimony.[27] The sometimes intense emotions[28] conveyed in private documents may even enhance the impact of such illusions: being placed in the position of a voyeur, the biographer tends to overestimate the sincerity and the significance of the words and statements he or she is encountering. Undoubtedly, the illusion of the reality effect is most blatant and challenging in private diaries. These documents actually unveil the most intimate dialogue possible: that of an individual with his or her own conscience, miles away from the stances of everyday, mundane social rituals. The reader may therefore consider each phrase worded in a diary as the candid expression of an inner truth. Introspection, however, is not a pledge of insight from the part of the diarist, for everyone may lie to themselves. Furthermore, it is admitted that the simple fact of writing his or her own ideas onto paper entails an unconscious desire of a reader – even a virtual one. As noted by Jean-Marie Goulemot 'each autobiographical text invents, by the mere process of writing, a fictitious reader which it calls and challenges';[29] and it is the advent of that reader (the biographer, in our case) which establishes the 'autobiographical pact' such as defined by Philippe Lejeune.[30] In a nutshell, private archives should therefore be handled with special care, because their authors may be fooled by their own feelings and urges. In other words, the biographer may confuse his or her subject with the character role the latter is playing for him- or herself.

Ultimately, beyond the undoubtedly fruitful awareness of these limits to the exploitation of private archives, the biographer should first and foremost be mindful of the fact that no single archival document can have informative value exclusively by itself on any matter. The relevance of the documentation is proportional to the plurality and diversity of the documents used, for each document is assigned its value through its critical confrontation with the rest of the archival materials gathered.

The ambiguities of the relation between biographer and subject

In the history of literature, the biographical genre has established itself through its exemplary function. Traditionally, the biography served as a mirror, whose reflection called for the self-improvement of the reader. Of course, this idealised function then also applies to the *writer* of a biography: life-writing experience inevitably brings the biographer to confront his or her own individuality with that of his or her subject. Now, when this process is based on the handling of private documents, especially of personal diaries, the close intimacy which develops between the biographer and the subject may turn out to be quite perilous: the confrontation may imperceptibly evolve into some kind of identification.[31]

As a matter of fact, since the writer of a diary writes for a fantasised reader, the biographer handling such documents is automatically designated as an ideal reader by their subject of study. The biographer is thus strongly tempted to appropriate the personality of the subject, and to put him- or herself in the subject's shoes. Such an ambiguous relation, commonly defined as 'counter-transference' in psychoanalysis, can drive the biographer to manipulate their subject as the privileged interlocutor of their own interior dialogue – thus granting their subject with their own personal and present view of the past world the subject had been living in.

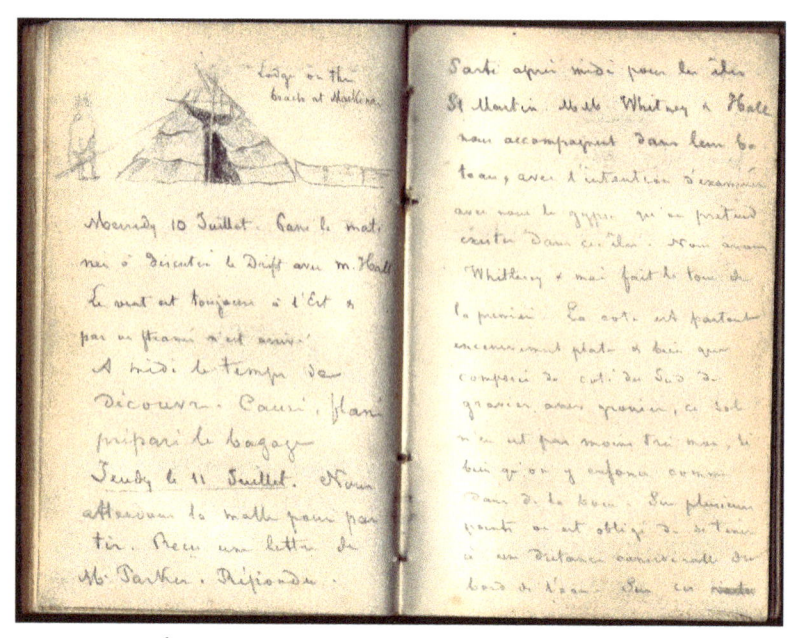

Figure 1.4 Édouard Desor's diary, July 10th–11th 1850, during the geological survey on the shores of Lake Mackinaw (Michigan, USA) – a difficult scientific terrain, where Desor had to retreat after his conflict with Louis Agassiz at Harvard University, which closed the doors of the American academic world to him. Bibliothèque publique et universitaire, Neuchâtel, Switzerland.

After all is said and done, the biographical approach is intrinsically ambiguous. To be honest, I have to admit that through my own biographical research, I have definitely been the (willing) victim of such mental projections – most notably during the time-consuming weeks and months when I was reading the numerous parts of Édouard Desor's diary (Figure 1.4).[32] And I confess it all the more readily, since the awareness of the equivocal relations is certainly the best remedy available to biographers in this process. Indeed, such projections are also productive. As Michael Shortland and Richard Yeo emphasised,[33] the biographical exercise requires the development of what they call a 'split vision': one must be able to feel the emotions of the subject of the biography, while alternately standing aside in order to observe the subject.

By all accounts, such an exercise may prove difficult. Here again, I can only advocate for the decisive usefulness of resorting to a wide variety of documentary sources. In order to avoid the risk of being smothered by the single voice of the subject of the biography, the biographer is well advised to seek out other sources – ideally, similar private documents but written by the hands of contemporary friends or colleagues sharing close contacts with the subject of study. For it is the intrusive gaze of these third parties, when introduced into the equivocal couple formed between the subject and the biographer, which helps the latter to break the charm of identification.

Epilogue

In practical terms, all the methodological, epistemological and psychological considerations developed above may certainly be applied with some flexibility – depending on the required level of each biographical investigation, on the wealth of the available body of archival material, but also on the thematic approach of the particular biographical research or the nature of the editorial project. For my part, I must accordingly admit that I have worked in very different ways and at quite different degrees of scrutiny, in the case of my 'totalising' and comprehensive monographic biography of Édouard Desor,[34] in the fictionalised biography I wrote on the natural scientist Louis Agassiz,[35] in the introduction to a collective book dedicated to the numerous research fields of the prehistorian Paul Vouga,[36] or in the many biographical notes I published on antiquarians, prehistorians and naturalists in diverse types of encyclopaedias and dictionaries. Similarly, some life-writings are undertaken mainly in the perspective of the delineation of one particular aspect of the work of a scientist, as has been the case, as far as I'm concerned, for Ferdinand Keller and the invention of the pile-dwelling theory, for Friedrich Schwab and the first explorations of the famous Celtic site of La Tène, or for Antoine Poidebard and the origins of aerial survey in archaeology (Figure 1.5).[37]

In that sense, in their diversity and with their markedly differing levels of ambition, all such life-writings obviously testify to the richness and the versatility of the biographical approach. But at any level, I remain convinced of the critical importance of a straightforward compliance with the methodological principles outlined here. Ultimately, although the main interest of biographies certainly lies in the diversity of possible insights into multiple realities, at times broad, other times quite slim, the author of a biography should never forget that such undertakings merely lead to the restitution of one plausible truth – that of the subject of study.

Figure 1.5 Antoine Poidebard (1878–1955), French pioneer of aerial detection in archaeology. Photothèque de la Bibliothèque orientale (Université Saint-Joseph), Beirut, Lebanon © Bibliothèque Orientale-USJ-Beyrouth.

Notes

1. Amongst many other references, cf. Bruce Trigger, 'Historiography', in *Encyclopedia of Archaeology: History and discoveries*, ed. Tim Murray (Oxford–Santa Barbara: ABC-CLIO Press, 2001), 630–9. Nathan Schlanger, 'Ancestral Archives: explorations in the history of archaeology', *Antiquity* 76 (2002): 127–31. Oscar Moro Abadía, *Arqueología prehistórica e historia de la ciencia* (Barcelona: Bellaterra arqueología, 2007). Tim Murray and Christopher Evans, eds., *Histories of Archaeology: A reader in the history of archaeology* (Oxford: Oxford University Press, 2008). Marc-Antoine Kaeser, 'Innovative alliances in the history of archaeology: Introduction to a new field of inquiry', in *History of Archaeology: International perspectives. Proceedings of the sessions of the 17th Congress of the International Union of Pre- and Protohistoric Sciences, Burgos (Spain)*, ed. Géraldine Delley et al. (Oxford: Archaeopress, 2016), 198–9.
2. Evert Baudou, 'The problem-orientated scientific biography as a research method', *Norwegian Archaeological Review* 31/2 (1998): 79–96 (as well as the comments by Jarl Nordbladh, 109–11, and her reply, 113–8). Tim Murray, 'Epilogue: The art of archaeological biography', in *Encyclopedia of Archaeology. The great archaeologists*, ed. Tim Murray (Oxford–Santa Barbara: ABC-Clio, 1999), 869–83.
3. Alain Schnapp et al. 'Archives of memory: a note on the Archives of European Archaeology (AREA) and its scientific seminars (1998–2008)', in *Sites of Memory: Between scientific research and collective representations. Proceedings of the 'Archives of European Archaeology' Seminar at Prague Castle, February 2006*, ed. Jana Marikova-Kubkova et al. (Prague: Institute of Archaeology, 2008), 6–22. Nathan Schlanger and Jarl Nordbladh, 'Preface and Acknowledgements', in *Archives, Ancestors, Practices: Archaeology in the light of its history*, eds., Nathan Schlanger and Jarl Nordbladh (Oxford–New York: Berghahn Books, 2008), XVII–XIX.
4. Johan Callmer et al., eds., *Die Anfänge der ur- und frühgeschichtlichen Archäologie als archäologisches Fach (1890–1930) im europäischen Vergleich. Internationale Tagung an der*

Humboldt-Universität zu Berlin vom 13.–16. März 2003 (Rahden: M. Leidorf, 2006) – especially my own contribution: Marc-Antoine Kaeser, 'The first establishment of prehistoric science. the shortcomings of autonomy', 149–60.

5 For example, Marc-Antoine Kaeser, 'Nachwort. Ferdinand Keller und die moderne Archäologie', in Bernhard von Arx, *Die versunkenen Dörfer. Ferdinand Keller und die Erfindung der Pfahlbauer* (Zürich: Unionsverlag – Schweizerisches Landesmuseum, 2004), 161–71. Marc-Antoine Kaeser, *L'univers du préhistorien. Science, foi et politique dans l'œuvre et la vie d'Edouard Desor, 1811–1882* (Paris: L'Harmattan, 2004). Marc-Antoine Kaeser, ed., *De la mémoire à l'histoire: L'œuvre de Paul Vouga (1880–1940). Des fouilles de la Tène au 'néolithique lacustre'* (Neuchâtel: Service et musée d'archéologie, 2006). Marc-Antoine Kaeser, *Un savant séducteur. Louis Agassiz (1807–1873), prophète de la science* (Vevey: L'Aire, 2007). Marc-Antoine Kaeser, 'Epilogue: Histoire de la collection et du Musée Schwab (1852–2012)', in *La Tène: La collection du Musée Schwab (Bienne)*, ed. Thierry Lejars (Lausanne: Cahiers d'archéologie romande, 2013), 469–87. Levon Nordiguian and Marc-Antoine Kaeser, *De l'Asie mineure au ciel du Levant. Antoine Poidebard, explorateur et pionnier de l'archéologie aérienne* (Hauterive: Laténium, 2016).

6 Marc-Antoine Kaeser, 'La science vécue. Les potentialités de la biographie en histoire des sciences', *Revue d'Histoire des Sciences Humaines* 8 (2003): 139–60.

7 Gérard Noiriel, *Sur la 'crise' de l'histoire* (Paris: Belin, 1996), 123–71. Victoria E. Bonnel and Lynn Hunt, eds., *Beyond the Cultural Turn: New directions in the study of society and culture* (Berkeley: University of California Press, 1999). Don Kalb and Herman Tak, eds., *Critical Junctions: Anthropology and history beyond the cultural turn* (New York: Berghahn Books, 2005).

8 Michael Shortland and Richard Yeo, 'Introduction', in *Telling Lives in Science. Essays in scientific biography,* eds., M. Shortland and R. Yeo (Cambridge: Cambridge University Press, 1996), 1–44.

9 Claude Blanckaert, 'L'histoire générale des sciences de l'homme: Principes et périodisation', in *L'histoire des sciences de l'homme. Trajectoire, enjeux et questions vives*, eds. Claude Blanckaert et al. (Paris, L'Harmattan, 1999), 29 *sqq.*

10 Bernard Lepetit, 'L'histoire prend-elle les acteurs au sérieux?', *Espaces-Temps*, 59–61 (1995): 112–22. Sabina Loriga, 'La biographie comme problème', in *Jeux d'échelles. La micro-analyse à l'expérience,* ed. Jacques Revel (Paris: EHESS Gallimard-Seuil, 1996), 209–31.

11 Steven Shapin and Arnold Thackray, 'Prosopography as a research tool in history of science: The British scientific community 1700–1900', *History of Science* 12 (1974): 1–28. Thomas L. Hankins, 'In defence of biography: the use of biography in the history of science', *History of Science,* 17 (1979): 1–16.

12 Thomas Söderqvist, 'Existential projects and existential choice in science: science biography as an edifying genre', in *Telling Lives in Science,* eds. Shortland and Yeo, 45–84.

13 Giovanni Levi, 'Les usages de la biographie', *Annales E.S.C.* 6 (1989): 1325–36.

14 Douglas R. Givens, 'The role of biography in writing the history of archaeology'. In *Rediscovering Our Past: Essays on the history of American archaeology,* ed. Jonathan E. Reyman, (Avebury: Ashgate, 1992), 51–66.

15 Levi, 'Les usages de la biographie', 1333–5. Cf. also Loriga, 'La biographie comme problème'.

16 Roger Chartier, *Au bord de la falaise. L'histoire entre certitudes et inquiétude* (Paris: Albin Michel, 1997).

17 Jacques Revel, 'Micro-analyse et construction du social', in *Jeux d'échelles. La micro-analyse à l'expérience,* ed. J. Revel (Paris: EHESS-Gallimard-Seuil, 1996), 15–36.

18 Giovanni Levi, 'On microhistory', in *New Perspectives on Historical Writing,* ed., Peter Burke (University Park: Penn State University Press, 1992), 93–113. Marc-Antoine Kaeser, 'Mikrohistorie und Wissenschaftsgeschichte. Über die Relevanz der Biographie in der Forschungsgeschichte der Archäologie', *Archäologisches Nachrichtenblatt* 11/4 (2006): 307–13. Marc-Antoine Kaeser, 'Biography as microhistory: the relevance of private archives for writing the history of archaeology', in *Archives, Ancestors, Practices,* eds., N. Schlanger and J. Nordbladh, 9–20.

19 Roger Chartier, 'Histoire intellectuelle et histoire des mentalités. Trajectoires et questions', *Revue de synthèse* 104 (1983): 277–307. Roger Chartier, 'Le monde comme représentation', *Annales E.S.C.* 6 (1989): 1505–20.

20 Loriga, 'La biographie comme problème'.

21 Bruno Latour, *Science in Action* (Cambridge: Harvard University Press, 1987). Bruno Latour, *Pasteur, une science, un style, un siècle* (Paris: Perrin, 1994).

22 Revel, 'Présentation', in *Jeux d'échelles. La micro-analyse à l'expérience,* 13.
23 Pierre Bourdieu, 'L'illusion biographique', *Actes de la recherche en sciences sociales* 62/63 (1986): 69–72. For a reevaluation of his critique, cf. Loriga, 'La biographie comme problème'.
24 Kaeser, *L'univers du préhistorien,* 22.
25 Kaeser, 'La science vécue'. Kaeser, Marc-Antoine. 'Biography, science studies, and the historiography of archaeological research: managing the personal archives'. In *Speaking Materials: Sources for the history of archaeology,* eds., Oscar Moro Abadia and Christoph Huth. *Complutum* 24/2 (2013): 101–8.
26 Arlette Farge, *Le goût de l'archive* (Paris: Seuil, 1989).
27 Cécile Dauphin, Pierrette Lebrun-Pézerat, and Danièle Poulban, *Ces bonnes lettres. Une correspondance familiale au XIXe siècle* (Paris: Albin Michel, 1995).
28 In the history of science, taking into account the emotions of the scientists, albeit tricky, is actually necessary, since emotions undoubtedly are part of the intellectual process and the construction of knowledge; cf. for instance Laurent Mucchielli, 'Autour de la "révélation d'Emile Durkheim". De l'inscription biographique des découvertes savantes à la notion de "névrose créatrice"', in *La découverte et ses récits en sciences humaines. Champollion, Freud et les autres,* eds. Jacqueline Carroy and Nathalie Richard (Paris: L'Harmattan, 1998), 57–96.
29 Jean-Marie Goulemot, 'Les pratiques littéraires ou la publicité du privé', in *Histoire de la vie privée. Tome 3,* eds., Philippe Ariès and Georges Duby (Paris: Seuil, 1986), 405 (our translation).
30 Philippe Lejeune, *Le pacte autobiographique* (Paris: Seuil, 1975).
31 Shortland and Yeo, 'Introduction', 31 *sqq.*
32 Kaeser, *L'univers du préhistorien,* 537–8.
33 Shortland and Yeo, 'Introduction', 34 *sqq.*
34 Kaeser, *L'univers du préhistorien.*
35 Kaeser, *Un savant séducteur.*
36 Kaeser, *De la mémoire à l'histoire.*
37 Kaeser, 'Nachwort'. Kaeser, Marc-Antoine. *Les Lacustres: Archéologie et mythe national* (Lausanne: Presses polytechniques et universitaires, 2004). Marc-Antoine Kaeser, 'La Tène, de la découverte du site à l'éponymie du second âge du Fer européen. Les prospections de Friedrich Schwab et les recherches archéologiques antérieures à la Correction des Eaux du Jura'. In *La Tène: La collection du Musée Schwab (Bienne),* ed., Thierry Lejars (Lausanne: Cahiers d'archéologie romande, 2013), 21–53. Marc-Antoine Kaeser, 'Epilogue', in *La Tène: La collection du Musée Schwab,* 469–87. Nordiguian and Kaeser, *De l'Asie mineure au ciel du Levant.*

Bibliography

Baudou, Evert, 'The problem-orientated scientific biography as a research method', *Norwegian Archaeological Review* 31.2 (1998): 79–96.
Blanckaert, Claude, 'L'histoire générale des sciences de l'homme: Principes et périodisation', in *L'histoire des sciences de l'homme. Trajectoire, enjeux et questions vives. Actes du colloque international des dix ans de la Société Française pour l'Histoire des Sciences de l'Homme, 5–7 décembre 1996,* eds. Claude Blanckaert et al. (Paris: L'Harmattan, 1999), 23–60.
Bonnel, Victoria E. and Lynn Hunt, eds., *Beyond the Cultural Turn: New directions in the study of society and culture* (Berkeley: University of California Press, 1999).
Bourdieu, Pierre, 'L'illusion biographique', *Actes de la recherche en sciences sociales* 62/63 (1986): 69–72.
Callmer, Johan et al., eds. *Die Anfänge der ur- und frühgeschichtlichen Archäologie als archäologisches Fach (1890–1930) im europäischen Vergleich. Internationale Tagung an der Humboldt-Universität zu Berlin vom 13.–16. März 2003* (Rahden: M. Leidorf, 2006).
Chartier, Roger, 'Histoire intellectuelle et histoire des mentalités. Trajectoires et questions', *Revue de synthèse* 104 (1983): 277–307.
Chartier, Roger, 'Le monde comme représentation', *Annales E.S.C.,* 6 (1989): 1505–20.
Chartier, Roger, *Au bord de la falaise. L'histoire entre certitudes et inquiétude* (Paris: Albin Michel, 1997).
Dauphin, Cécile, Pierrette Lebrun-Pézerat and Danièle Poulban, *Ces bonnes lettres. Une correspondance familiale au XIXe siècle* (Paris: Albin Michel, 1995).

Farge, Arlette, *Le goût de l'archive* (Paris: Seuil, 1989).
Givens, Douglas R., 'The role of biography in writing the history of archaeology', in *Rediscovering Our Past: Essays on the history of American archaeology*, ed. Jonathan E. Reyman (Avebury: Ashgate, 1992), 51–66.
Goulemot, Jean-Marie, 'Les pratiques littéraires ou la publicité du privé', in *Histoire de la vie privée. Tome 3*, eds. Philippe Ariès and Georges Duby (Paris: Seuil, 1986), 371–405.
Hankins, Thomas L., 'In defence of biography: The use of biography in the history of science', *History of Science*, 17 (1979): 1–16.
Kaeser, Marc-Antoine, 'La science vécue. Les potentialités de la biographie en histoire des sciences', *Revue d'Histoire des Sciences Humaines* 8 (2003): 139–60.
Kaeser, Marc-Antoine, 'Nachwort. Ferdinand Keller und die moderne Archäologie', in Bernhard von Arx, *Die versunkenen Dörfer. Ferdinand Keller und die Erfindung der Pfahlbauer* (Zürich: Unionsverlag/Schweizerisches Landesmuseum, 2004): 161–71.
Kaeser, Marc-Antoine, *L'univers du préhistorien. Science, foi et politique dans l'œuvre et la vie d'Edouard Desor, 1811–1882* (Paris: L'Harmattan, 2004).
Kaeser, Marc-Antoine, *Les Lacustres: Archéologie et mythe national* (Lausanne: Presses polytechniques et universitaires, 2004).
Kaeser, Marc-Antoine, 'The first establishment of prehistoric science. The shortcomings of autonomy', in *Die Anfänge der ur- und frühgeschichtlichen Archäologie als archäologisches Fach (1890–1930) im europäischen Vergleich*, eds. Johan Callmer et al. (Rahden: M. Leidorf, 2006), 149–60.
Kaeser, Marc-Antoine, ed., *De la mémoire à l'histoire : L'œuvre de Paul Vouga (1880–1940). Des fouilles de la Tène au 'néolithique lacustre'* (Neuchâtel: Service et musée d'archéologie (Archéologie neuchâteloise, 35): 2006).
Kaeser, Marc-Antoine, 'Mikrohistorie und Wissenschaftsgeschichte. Über die Relevanz der Biographie in der Forschungsgeschichte der Archäologie', *Archäologisches Nachrichtenblatt* 11/4 (2006): 307–13.
Kaeser, Marc-Antoine, *Un savant séducteur. Louis Agassiz (1807–1873), prophète de la science* (Vevey: L'Aire, 2007).
Kaeser, Marc-Antoine, 'Biography as microhistory: the relevance of private archives for writing the history of archaeology', in *Archives, Ancestors, Practices: Archaeology in the light of its history*, eds. Nathan Schlanger and Jarl Nordbladh (Oxford–New York: Berghahn Books, 2008), 9–20.
Kaeser, Marc-Antoine, 'La Tène, de la découverte du site à l'éponymie du second âge du Fer européen. Les prospections de Friedrich Schwab et les recherches archéologiques antérieures à la Correction des Eaux du Jura', in *La Tène: La collection du Musée Schwab (Bienne)*, ed. Thierry Lejars (Lausanne: Cahiers d'archéologie romande, 2013), 21–53.
Kaeser, Marc-Antoine, 'Epilogue: Histoire de la collection et du Musée Schwab (1852–2012)', in *La Tène: La collection du Musée Schwab (Bienne)*, ed. Thierry Lejars (Lausanne: Cahiers d'archéologie romande, 2013), 469–87.
Kaeser, Marc-Antoine, 'Biography, science studies, and the historiography of archaeological research: managing the personal archives', in *Speaking Materials: Sources for the history of archaeology*, eds. Oscar Moro Abadia and Christoph Huth. *Complutum* 24/2 (2013): 101–8.
Kaeser, Marc-Antoine, 'Innovative alliances in the history of archaeology: Introduction to a new field of inquiry', in *History of archaeology: International perspectives. Proceedings of the sessions of the 17th Congress of the International Union of Pre- and Protohistoric Sciences, Burgos (Spain)*, eds. Géraldine Delley et al. (Oxford: Archaeopress, 2016), 197–206.
Kalb, Don, and Herman Tak, eds., *Critical Junctions: Anthropology and history beyond the cultural turn* (New York: Berghahn Books, 2005).
Latour, Bruno, *Science in Action* (Cambridge: Harvard University Press, 1987).
Latour, Bruno, *Pasteur, une science, un style, un siècle* (Paris: Perrin, 1994).
Lejeune, Philippe, *Le pacte autobiographique* (Paris: Seuil, 1975).
Lepetit, Bernard, 'L'histoire prend-elle les acteurs au sérieux?', *Espaces-Temps*, 59–61 (1995): 112–22.
Levi, Giovanni, 'Les usages de la biographie', *Annales E.S.C.* 6 (1989): 1325–36.
Levi, Giovanni, 'On microhistory', in *New Perspectives on Historical Writing*, ed. Peter Burke (University Park: Penn State University Press, 1992), 93–113.
Loriga, Sabina, 'La biographie comme problème', in *Jeux d'échelles. La micro-analyse à l'expérience*, ed. Jacques Revel (Paris: EHESS-Gallimard-Seuil, 1996), 209–31.

Moro Abadía, Oscar, *Arqueología prehistórica e historia de la ciencia* (Barcelona: Bellaterra arqueología, 2007).

Mucchielli, Laurent, 'Autour de la "révélation d'Emile Durkheim". De l'inscription biographique des découvertes savantes à la notion de "névrose créatrice"', in *La découverte et ses récits en sciences humaines. Champollion, Freud et les autres,* eds. Jacqueline Carroy and Nathalie Richard (Paris: L'Harmattan, 1998), 57–96.

Murray, Tim, 'Epilogue: The art of archaeological biography', in *Encyclopedia of Archaeology. The great archaeologists,* ed. Tim Murray (Oxford–Santa Barbara: ABC-Clio, 1999), 869–83.

Murray, Tim and Christopher Evans, eds., *Histories of Archaeology: A reader in the history of archaeology* (Oxford: Oxford University Press, 2008).

Noiriel, Gérard, *Sur la 'crise' de l'histoire* (Paris: Belin, 1996).

Nordiguian, Levon and Marc-Antoine Kaeser, *De l'Asie mineure au ciel du Levant. Antoine Poidebard, explorateur et pionnier de l'archéologie aérienne* (Hauterive: Laténium, 2016).

Revel, Jacques, 'Présentation', in *Jeux d'échelles. La micro-analyse à l'expérience,* ed. Jacques Revel (Paris: EHESS-Gallimard-Seuil, 1996), 7–14.

Revel, Jacques, 'Micro-analyse et construction du social', in *Jeux d'échelles. La micro-analyse à l'expérience,* ed. Jacques Revel (Paris: EHESS-Gallimard-Seuil, 1996), 15–36.

Schlanger, Nathan, 'Ancestral archives: explorations in the history of archaeology', *Antiquity* 76 (2002): 127–31.

Schlanger, Nathan and Jarl Nordbladh, 'Preface and acknowledgements', in *Archives, Ancestors, Practices: Archaeology in the light of its history,* eds. Nathan Schlanger and Jarl Nordbladh (Oxford–New York: Berghahn Books, 2008), XVII–XIX.

Schnapp, Alain et al., 'Archives of memory: A note on the Archives of European Archaeology (AREA) and its scientific seminars (1998–2008)', in *Sites of Memory: Between scientific research and collective representations. Proceedings of the 'Archives of European Archaeology' Seminar at Prague Castle, February 2006,* eds. Jana Marikova-Kubkova et al. (Prague: Institute of Archaeology, 2008/Castrum Pragense, 8), 6–22.

Shapin, Steven and Arnold Thackray, 'Prosopography as a research tool in history of science: The British scientific community 1700–1900', *History of Science* 12 (1974): 1–28.

Shortland, Michael and Richard Yeo, 'Introduction', in *Telling Lives in Science. Essays in scientific biography,* eds. Michael Shortland and Richard Yeo (Cambridge: Cambridge University Press, 1996), 1–44.

Söderqvist, Thomas, 'Existential projects and existential choice in science: science biography as an edifying genre', in *Telling Lives in Science. Essays in scientific biography,* eds. Michael Shortland and Richard Yeo (Cambridge: Cambridge University Press, 1996), 45–84.

Trigger, Bruce, 'Historiography', in *Encyclopedia of Archaeology: History and discoveries,* ed. Tim Murray (Oxford–Santa Barbara: ABC-CLIO Press, 2001), 630–9.

2
A plea for 'higher criticism' in disciplinary history: Life-writing sources in the history of German-speaking Egyptology

Thomas L. Gertzen

Introduction: German Egyptology and German history

In contrast to other major players in the field, German Egyptology is characterised by intensive interdependency between academic institutions and the state.[1] Whereas French or British Egyptology emerged from a distinctively colonial or imperialist setting, German Egyptology developed within the framework of domestic or federal politics, mainly of the kingdom of Prussia.[2] From the beginning, German Egyptological research was perceived and advertised as a means to achieve *ulturmacht* (roughly, cultural power) and *eltgeltung* (roughly, international standing) for German *Wissenschaft*.[3] As a consequence the upheavals of German history, from the revolution of 1848, through the Franco-Prussian War (1870/71) and the subsequent foundation of the German *Reich*, the First World War (1914–1918) and the Weimar Republic, to the seizure of power by the Nazis in 1933 and the Second World War (1939–1945), had an enormous impact on disciplinary history. The close ties between German academia and the state, on the one hand, and the totalitarian character, on the other, of two phases in German history – the Third Reich and the (East-) German Democratic Republic (GDR) – render the history of German Egyptology and the life-writing of its representatives a special case.[4]

The interconnection of scholarship and totalitarianism – often framed in a 'binary' concept of politics and scholarship as the determining cornerstones – distinguishes the history of Egyptology in the German-speaking world from that of other western nations.[5] Even more than in the case of post-colonial issues, this field of research is influenced by moral judgements and consequently a 'personal' approach – not only to the subjects of study, but sometimes also to the researchers themselves.[6] This chapter will (re-)present the history of German Egyptology with some individual case studies of sources and source criticism, including individual biographies and methodical approaches in life-writing and disciplinary history.

Biographies within a 'dwarf discipline'

From the 1960s onwards, the genre of historic biography was widely rejected by the representatives of modern history in Germany. It was considered outdated, a remnant of German historicism. The Bielefield School therefore proposed a structuralist approach, based on the methods of social sciences.[7] Interestingly, the history of German Egyptology became subject to study according to these new principles. Hans-Josef Trümpener attempted a sociological analysis of the 'conditions of existence' of German Egyptology.[8] Although most Egyptologists ignored his study, some reactions are worth mentioning because they pinpoint the fundamental difficulties of the disciplinary history of Egyptology. John Baines, professor of Egyptology at Oxford, commented on Trümpener's study:

> A revealing feature of this work is its title, terming the subject a 'dwarf discipline', which implies that special conditions apply to orthodoxy within it. It is difficult to say whether this is correct beyond the obvious point that personal feeling may surface more than in a larger and more anonymous group. […] Although criticism of the fieldworker by his data is awkward, it can be said that Trümpener's essay is based on limited fieldwork.[9]

Since the number of Egyptologists is comparatively small, Trümpener interviewed only 15 (!) and based his findings on the information gathered in this process. Additionally, he also consulted some of the literature on the history of the subject, mostly autobiographies of Egyptologists. Although this approach seems rather 'personalised', Trümpener tried to squeeze the information into a theoretical chronological framework of three phases: 'initiation', 'establishment' and 'institutionalisation', which seems only superficially applicable to the discipline at best.[10] Baines, who relied heavily on the concepts of Thomas Kuhn, clearly pointed out these shortcomings or lack of interconnection between theory and Egyptological practice, which in his view was also insufficiently defined by Trümpener, and others:[11]

> Near Eastern studies are not a 'science' or a discipline in the Kuhnian sense. Rather, they are the sum of a range of methods and approaches applied to a great variety of materials from a particular geographical region and period; even definitions of the area and period are open to revision.[12]

And as to Egyptology in particular:

> As I have indicated, the Egyptological argument is not finally in terms of 'Egyptological Method', which does not exist as such, but in terms of the range of general methods and approaches that are brought to bear upon materials from ancient Egypt.[13]

Baines recently even went so far as to define Egyptology as an entirely individualistic endeavour:

> Egyptology is not a single discipline, but a branch of 'Area Studies'. Egyptologists study all the aspects of ancient Egypt that they can, across periods from about 7,000 BC to the early middle ages. [...]. No two Egyptologists have the same interests and focuses.[14]

Without an 'Egyptological method'[15] we are confronted with the question 'What defines an Egyptologist?' – Trümpener made a suggestion: '[Egyptian] Grammar and the command of language [in other words, the ability to read Hieroglyphs] are substituted for the function of scientific theory.'[16] Although this might be contested in the cases of British and French Egyptology – the French rejecting 'German' grammar in the first place and the British, under the auspices of William Mathew Flinders Petrie, focussing on material culture, i.e. archaeology – I adopt this working definition for German Egyptology here, nonetheless.[17] The limited number of practitioners and the lack of a clearly defined theoretical framework naturally increase the importance of individual scholars and their biographies in the history of the discipline.[18] Or, as the historian Jason Thompson wrote: 'But in the end the story of Egyptology is the story of the people who created Egyptology.'[19] It is very important, however, to note that this microanalytical approach results from the limitations cited above.

In fact, Thompson presents a very 'Anglo-Saxon' perspective on the history of Egyptology, relying mainly on English-speaking secondary literature and disregarding the importance of academic as well as national institutions (which indeed were of less importance to the development of Egyptology in Britain).[20] In the case of German Egyptology the state and state-funded institutions provide a wider reference for macroanalysis in disciplinary history. The relationship between individual scholars and the institutional framework of German academia, however, is very often perceived as binary, not least because many Egyptologists did not and do not want to be identified with contemporaneous German government policies.

German scholarship and politics as two stable worlds

Research into the history of Egyptology during the Third Reich and the GDR has only just begun.[21] Biographies of individual scholars clearly indicate the necessity to include the 'pre-history' as well as the aftermath of these particular periods.[22] The British historian of science William Carruthers made a striking general observation about German publications dealing with Egyptology under Nazi-rule, describing the binary concept, mentioned above:

> This binary is manifest in a recent [...] lengthy piece by Thomas Schneider[23] on the relationship between German Egyptologists and the Nazi regime. [...]. Schneider details the biographies of these individual [Egyptologists] with view to understanding the relationship between their scholarly work and the wider political discourse [...] in Germany.
> What emerges from this discussion [...], is a recounting of the evidence for and against the links between two stable worlds: [...] of German Egyptology [...] and another of National Socialism. In this frame, the implication [...] is that Egyptology is at heart a 'pure' discipline.[24]

This assessment was seconded by his colleague David Gange, who wrote in the same volume:

> In studies of the history of Egyptology, the discipline can often appear to have been created and developed in a hermetic compartment, separated cleanly from its surroundings and isolated in purely disciplinary space. Text without context, it seems to require theorizing

only in its own terms, amenable to explanation only through its internal dynamics irrespective of the complex relations between Egyptology and society.[25]

The interdependency of (German) politics and academia is definitely more complex, of course, though the two observations cited sadly apply to many of even the more recent studies of the subject. There are several reasons for this: (1) Most of the publications on disciplinary history are written by Egyptologists, not historians, although the latter also show some deficiencies when it comes to the details or 'internal dynamics' of the subject, the lack of historical training takes its toll when Egyptologists have to deal with 'the outside world'. (2) Believing in the purity of Egyptological research enables scholars to distance their discipline (and themselves as well) from the more problematic or negative aspects. (3) The investigators belong to the same group as the subject(s) of study. This might arouse sympathy or antipathy for the Egyptologist(s) under scrutiny, but not only is the former more likely – decorum demands a certain 'respect for' and 'trust in' the predecessors or 'fathers' of the discipline.

This has dramatic effects on the way Egyptologists, when conducting research in disciplinary history, deal with their sources: (1) Very often they limit their research to 'internal' sources, written by other Egyptologists. (2) They try to maintain the alleged non-political or neutral character of their discipline. (3) If, however, one Egyptologist seems to be too compromised, he or she might be ostracised. Interestingly, in these cases, the Egyptological competence of these outcasts is also questioned during the process. This leads to three major patterns of assessing political infringement on the pure world of scholarship. (1) Individual scholars seem (personally) compromised or were forced 'to compromise', *but* their scholarship remained untainted or (2) Egyptologists actively engaged with politics, in order to gain personal advantage and so willingly exploited their subject, to the disadvantage of the quality of their work. (3) Scholars acted under false presumptions but 'in good faith' so that the temporary entanglement of their work with politics seems only marginal.

To illustrate how these interpretative patterns work, I would like to cite three examples. In a recent assessment of the activities of the Göttingen Egyptologist Hermann Kees (1886–1964)[26] during the Nazi period, Thomas Schneider stated:

> Kees' antisemitic attitude can be derived not only from his leading position in the programmatic anti-Semitic DNVP [= German National People's Party] until 1933. It is also to be found in his contemporaneous Egyptological writings.[27]

But finally Schneider came to the conclusion, that:

> The political incrimination of Kees contrasts with his formidable scholarly achievement, particularly in the area of Egyptian religious history. [...] As in the cases of other Egyptologists during [the time of] National Socialism [it] reveals a discrepancy between academic grandeur and political as well as personal behaviour.[28]

Although, according to Schneider, anti-Semitism can be detected in Kees's Egyptological publications, his scholarly achievements must be separated from his personal behaviour. This certainly illustrates Carruthers' binary concept but is also outright contradictory.

Another example is Schneider's verdict on Hermann Grapow (1885–1967),[29] whom he describes as a 'convinced National Socialist' and a 'National-Socialistic Egyptologist' with 'absolute loyalty to the National-Socialistic state',[30] without providing proper definitions. What constitutes 'absolute loyalty'? What characterises Egyptological research as National-Socialist? What defines a National-Socialist conviction? Although Schneider maintains a certain reserve towards the critical evaluation of Grapow's Egyptological competence by some of his peers, he implicitly associates his professional advancement with his political activities, rather than his scholarly achievements.[31] In this context it must be pointed out that Schneider has incriminated Erika Endesfelder and questioned her reliability in disciplinary history research. Citing her assessment of Grapow's conduct during the Third Reich, Schneider called attention to the fact 'that Endesfelder, prior to her professorship in Egyptology at East Berlin, had herself been an official of the totalitarian state of the German Democratic Republic'.[32] Would Schneider accept someone questioning his scholarly integrity in view of his role as Senior Advisor for Global Education (2020) and Associate Vice President (2018) for the Southern University of Science & Technology,[33] a public university founded in the Shenzhen Special Economic Zone of the People's Republic of China – considered by some to conform to the definition of a totalitarian state?

Finally, I would like to introduce a rather bizarre example of (re-)interpreting the political entanglement of a German Egyptologist with Nazism: Alfred Grimm described the political engagement of Baron Friedrich Wilhelm von Bissing (1873–1956):[34]

> who, during World War I (1914–1918) took an unequivocal German-nationalist stand, joined the NSDAP [National Socialist German Worker's Party] already in 1925; and this solely because of [his] political convictions but not out of opportunism.[35]

In this way von Bissing's political incrimination is explicitly addressed; however, emphasis is placed on his upright political conviction and the denial of any kind of opportunism. In other words: von Bissing was a 'Nazi', but for 'good' reason.[36]

A plea for higher criticism[37] – the Steindorff list

Aside from the reasons mentioned above for sometimes contradictory or even contorted black-and-white judgements, separating German Egyptologists in to two or three groups – (1) personally compromised but scholarly above suspicion; (2) personally and scholarly compromised; (3) compromised but well-intentioned – the approach to the subject can be directly traced to the role played by sources.

In 1945 Georg Steindorff (1861–1951; Figure 2.1) wrote a letter to his colleague John A. Wilson (1899–1976) in which he assessed the charge of political incrimination against his former German colleagues,[38] after he had been driven into exile, because of his Jewish descent.[39]

The letter was intended for circulation among his colleagues and not written at anyone's request (Figure 2.2).[40] Steindorff himself chose the title '*J'accuse*'[41] and grouped his former colleagues into the following categories: (1) 'Men of honour'; (2) 'the other side of the picture' and

Figure 2.1   Georg Steindorff. Ägyptisches Museum – Georg Steindorff – der Universität Leipzig, Archiv.

J'accuse. Rundschreiben Juni 1945.

I have been asked on several occasions to furnish a list of German Egyptologists who have been actively affiliated with the Nazi party and to tell to what extent they have violated the rules of international scholarship. I have hesitated to do so. But now that the party has broken down and the problem of building anew the educational and scientific life of Germany confronts us, it seems to me my duty to provide a list of those men who are unfit, in the light of their past activities, to have a part in the scolarly life of the post-war world.

There are a few German Egyptologists who have proved themselves men of honor.

1) Dr. Alexander Scharff, professor of Egyptology at the University of Munich, who has been during all his life a democrat and anti-Nazi.

2) Dr. Rudolf Anthes, assistant curator at the Berlin Museum, a former Freemason, who was persecuted by his Nazi colleagues and who always courageously stood by his anti-Nazi friends and colleagues.

3) Dr. Hans Bonnet, professor of Egyptology at the University of Bonn, one of the finest personalities I have ever known. He was my pupil, and later my assistant at Leipzig, and I proved him as a gentleman without fear and without reproach. During my darkest days at Leipzig, some weeks after the pogrom of November 1938, he came to our house in Leipzig and invited me and my wife to go with him and find asylum in his house at Bonn, though to give us sanctuary might well have resulted in his confinement in a concentration camp.

4) Dr. Hans Wolfgang Müller, formerly attached to the Berlin Museum, who is, in my opinion, one of the most able Egyptologists of the younger generation, a reliable anti-Nazi.

5) Dr. Ing. Herbert Ricke, a pupil of Borchardt and an expert in the history of Egyptian architecture. He lives in exile in Zurich, Switzerland, with his family in the house of Mrs. Borchardt, and after Borchardt's death was the administrator of the "Deutsches Institut für ägyptische Bauforschung".

6) Dr. Ludwig Keimer, lecturer on Egyptology at the German University of Prague, a fanatical anti-Nazi, born in Westphalia, and educated in Germany, for many years resident of Cairo, known as a specialist in ancient Egyptian botany and zoology and an expert in Egyptian antiquities.

7) Bernhard von Bothmer, formerly for a number of years attached to the Berlin Museum, who left Germany of his own volition, and together with his brother came to America, because he would not live in a Nazi Germany. He is now a private in the United States Army, his greatest wish to fight and conquer Nazidom.

Now I must present the other side of the picture:

1) Dr. Hermann Grapow, professor of Egyptology and member of the Berlin Academy of Science, a man of truly base character. You know him by name as a pupil and collaborator of Erman. So long as Erman lived, he posed as a democrat. Later however, especially after Sethe passed away, he showed his true colors as an arch-Nazi, and used every means to be Erman's and Sethe's successor in the professorship at the University. He persecuted everybody who did not say "Heil Hitler", and did not follow the Nazi flag. Finely he succeeded. In my opinion there is no one who excelled Grapow in meanness, hatefulness and denunciation of those who were not of his political opinion.

2) Grapow's counterpart and closest follower: Dr. Alfred Hermann. To caracterize him, I need only repeat, what I have said about Grapow.

Figure 2.2 Steindorff's 'J'accuse'-letter, (a) page 1/2 and (b) 2/2. Ägyptisches Museum – Georg Steindorff – der Universität Leipzig, Archiv.

2.

3) Dr. Hermann Kees, professor of Egyptology, University of Göttingen, a member of an old Saxon land-owning family, a militarist and Junker. He was an army officer in the First World War, and fought later by all means in his power, openly and secretly the Weimar Republic. He is anti-democratic from the bottom of his soul. A conservative, he at first opposed Hitlerism, but afterwards became a Nazi. Though I do not know whether he actually joined the party, I would not trust him, even if he should say that he became Nazi only from compulsion.

4) Dr. Hermann Junker, formerly professor of Egyptology at the University of Vienna, later director of the "Deutsches Institut für ägyptische Altertumskunde" in Cairo. It is very difficult to describe the character of this man, because he has none. I have heard that it was rumored in England that Junker acted as a spy in Egypt. I do not believe it. He was too clever to compromise himself by such activity. He played safe. However he used his position and the State Institute to promote Nazi propaganda. The Institute was always available for Nazi meetings. Junker's house was always open to Nazi guests, chiefly Austrian. Every Nazi found a cordial reception in the German Institute in Cairo. I appreciate Junker as a scholar of first order. More than that, I am sorry I cannot say. At best, his actions and opinions have always been ambiguous.

5) Dr. Cermak, Junker's successor at Vienna. I do not know him very well, but I know him sufficiently to say that he is a Nazi of first order.

6) Dr. Siegfried Schott, to whom was entrusted the professorship at Heidelberg formerly held by Professor Ranke. He has always been an admirer of Hitler, so he did not have to change when Hitler came into power. He is a gentleman and I do not think that he approved of the atrocities perpetrated under the Hitler regime.

7) Dr. Herbert Schädel, assistant of Wolf at the Leipzig University and a political follower of his boss. Not a great Egyptological genius.

8) and 9) About Gunther Roeder's and Uvo Hölscher's political position, I am not accurately informed. However, I suspect that both of them joined the Nazis. Roeder became Director of the Berlin Egyptian Museum---too important a job for a non-Nazi.

There are some younger good Egyptologists in Berlin, Göttingen, Leipzig and Vienna, whom I know too little to say anything about their political opinions.

I do not include in this list three scholars:

1) Heinrich Schäfer, whom you all know as a scholar and as a representative of pan-Germanism. He is now in his late seventies. I do not think he joined the Nazi party, but I know that it was his ardent wish to attend the Nazi rally at Nürnberg and to watch the parade of the storm-troopers. He was once among my best friends, but later he abandoned me. I will not further criticise my old friend.

2) Dr. Walter Wolf, formerly my assistant and later my successor at Leipzig. I am told that he was killed in action. He was a terrible Nazi!

3) Friedrich Wilhelm von Bissing, who joined the Nazi party in its beginning. He was a very good friend of Rudolf Hess, to whom he dedicated his History of Egyptian Art. He was decorated by Hitler with a golden party-symbol, but later he sent it back and left the party. After the pogrom he came personally to me to show his sympathy and was very sorry not to be able to improve my situation with the help of his former party colleagues. Belonging to an old Prussian family, a grandson of Mathilda Wesendonck, a man of great culture, he detests the low level of the Nazi ideology. However, he is very nervous and hysterical and not young enough to play further part in politics.

Dixi et salvavi animan meam,
Very sincerely yours,

Figure 2.2 (Continued)

(3) those he excluded ('I do not include these scholars') out of piety.[42] The second group includes both Kees and Grapow. Steindorff wrote about Kees:

> Dr Hermann Kees, professor of Egyptology, University of Göttingen, a member of an old Saxon land-owning family, a militarist and Junker. He was an army officer in the First World War, and fought later by all means in his power, openly and secretly, the Weimar republic. He is anti-democratic from the bottom of his soul. A conservative, he at first opposed Hitlerism, but afterwards became a Nazi. Though I do not know whether he actually joined the party, I would not trust him, even if he should say that he became Nazi only from compulsion.

This is clearly a severe judgement. However, Steindorff made some allowances: Kees would have been a conservative right-wing anti-democratic nationalist, at first opposing the Nazi-movement and then perhaps only joining the party under duress.

The case of Hermann Grapow by contrast appears very different:

> Dr. Hermann Grapow, professor of Egyptology and member of the Berlin Academy of Science, a man of truly base character. You know him by name as a pupil and collaborator of [Adolf] Erman.[43] So long as Erman lived, he posed as a democrat. Later however, especially after [Kurt] Sethe passed away, he showed his true colors as an arch-Nazi, and used every means to be Erman's and Sethe's successor in the professorship at the University. He persecuted everybody who did not say, 'Heil, Hitler!' and did not follow the Nazi flag. Finally he succeeded. In my opinion there is no one who excelled Grapow in meanness, hatefulness and denunciation of those who were not of his political opinion.

Grapow is presented as a 'truly base character', who 'posed as a democrat' and succeeded his predecessors through political persecution. He is named an 'arch-Nazi'.

Friedrich Wilhelm von Bissing belongs to the third category in Steindorff's assessment:

> Friedrich Wilhelm von Bissing, who joined the Nazi party in its beginning. He was a very good friend of Rudolf Hess, to whom he dedicated his History of Egyptian Art. He was decorated by Hitler

with a golden party-symbol, but later he sent it back and left the party. After the pogrom⁴⁴ he came personally to me to show his sympathy and was very sorry not to be able to improve my situation with the help of his former party-colleagues. Belonging to an old Prussian family, a grandson of Mathilda [sic] Wesendonck,⁴⁵ a man of great culture, he detests the low level of the Nazi ideology. However, he is very nervous and hysterical and not young enough to play much further part in politics.

Bissing's Nazi connections are mentioned, but he has shown personal loyalty towards his colleague. Allegedly, he had no inclination for politics or the Nazi ideology, due to his 'great culture'.

Now, one might argue that the statements cited in the previous section seem congruent with the information provided in the primary source presented here: that is so, but it is exactly this which constitutes the fundamental problem. Apart from the fact that Thomas Schneider structured his study on Egyptologists during the Third Reich according to the Steindorff-list,⁴⁶ he also adopted Steindorff's interpretative judgements. The list is taken as positive proof and all the other archival material – so diligently collected by Schneider and his collaborators – serves but one purpose: to prove Steindorff right. Neither he, his intentions and motivation, nor the circumstances of the production of his list are in any way scrutinised. That is partly because Steindorff is primarily perceived as a victim of Nazi persecution: to doubt him, might be considered improper but actually is relevant from a methodological point of view.

Dietrich Raue has shown that Steindorff's biography can be told in at least three different ways: (1) the persecuted academic; (2) the extremely successful scholar and (3) the revered patriarch or head of his family.⁴⁷ The religious background, Steindorff's *Weltanschauung*, which clearly reflected a highly problematic attitude, oscillates after his conversion to Protestant Christianity between 'Jewish self-hatred' and outright anti-Semitism.⁴⁸ Susanne Voss documented his pivotal role in reshaping German Egyptology into a *völkisch* discipline, based on anthropological, or rather 'racial' studies.⁴⁹ The intention was not to 'besmirch' Steindorff's assessment of his colleagues, but the necessity to conduct a 'background check' is clearly mandated before using his statements as published and interpreted by Schneider.

Not only do the author of the document and the colleagues he mentions have to be dealt with separately and independently, but so do their respective personal relationships, comprising such issues as simple personal animosity, generational conflicts and scholarly competition.⁵⁰

Furthermore, Steindorff had left Germany in 1939: even as a well-connected leading scholar in the field, he had no direct access to any information thereafter, relying instead on hearsay and information provided by third parties. For example, he did not know that Hermann Kees actually joined the NSDAP or that his unit of the Stahlhelm (German right-wing militia) was incorporated into the Sturmabteilung (Brownshirts). He was also unaware that von Bissing did not leave the party on his own volition but was thrown out and afterwards desperately tried to rejoin its ranks.[51] Historical or higher criticism has to be applied to reconstruct 'the world behind the text',[52] in this case behind the primary sources for the history of German Egyptology or life-writing of its representatives.

Comparative analysis of similar primary sources

Primary sources are not necessarily prime sources: they are at least as biased and subjective as others, and the simple fact that their authors very often (but not always) wrote from a contemporaneous perspective does to not render them more reliable or more accurate. Furthermore, they were originally addressed to a different audience or served another purpose than historic documentation. Unfortunately, this is very often ignored in disciplinary history. In the field of German ancient Near Eastern Studies, there are at least two texts or sources comparable to the Steindorff list, representing similar as well as specific challenges to the researcher.

When the German Archaeological Society was to be re-established after World War II, Rudolf Anthes (1896–1985; Figure 2.3) was asked by the president of the German Archaeological Institute, Carl Weickert (1885–1975)[53] to provide or rather supplement a list of German Egyptologists and their addresses.[54] Anthes had been discriminated against during the Third Reich, allegedly because of his membership of a Masonic Lodge, but even more so because of his political convictions.[55] As in Steindorff's case, this persecution gave him a certain credibility, when providing not only contact details but also an assessment of the political charges against his colleagues.

The list is structured as a table, presenting the scholars in alphabetical order (with handwritten additions), providing their postal addresses and, in an extra column, information on the degree of their political incrimination. Anthes employed the categories 'not incriminated', 'denazification planned', 'denazified', 'unknown' and finally 'incriminated'.

Figure 2.3 Rudolf Anthes. University of Pennsylvania Museum of Archaeology and Anthropology, Archive.

Anthes did not provide his sources or criteria for his assessments. Hermann Kees and Hermann Grapow appear likewise incriminated, whereas in the case of Friedrich Wilhelm von Bissing 'denazification' was planned. Interestingly, Anthes clearly indicated the cases about which he was not informed whether the respective individual was politically entangled with the Nazis or not. In contrast to Steindorff, he believed it possible that a person might be 'cured' of Nazism. But like Steindorff, however, he also provides a special category for colleagues who, like Bissing, might simply be termed incriminated, but appear 'on the road to salvation'. Anthes's list of German Egyptologists is certainly sketchy and was not intended for either historical or juridical usage (Figure 2.4). It illustrates the highly subjective character of this kind of source, which must be evaluated nonetheless – but with caution!

Another example of the assessment of political incrimination of German Oriental scholars dates from 1993.[56] It was composed by Hans Gustav Güterbock (1908–2000; Figure 2.5), a Hittitologist, son of the

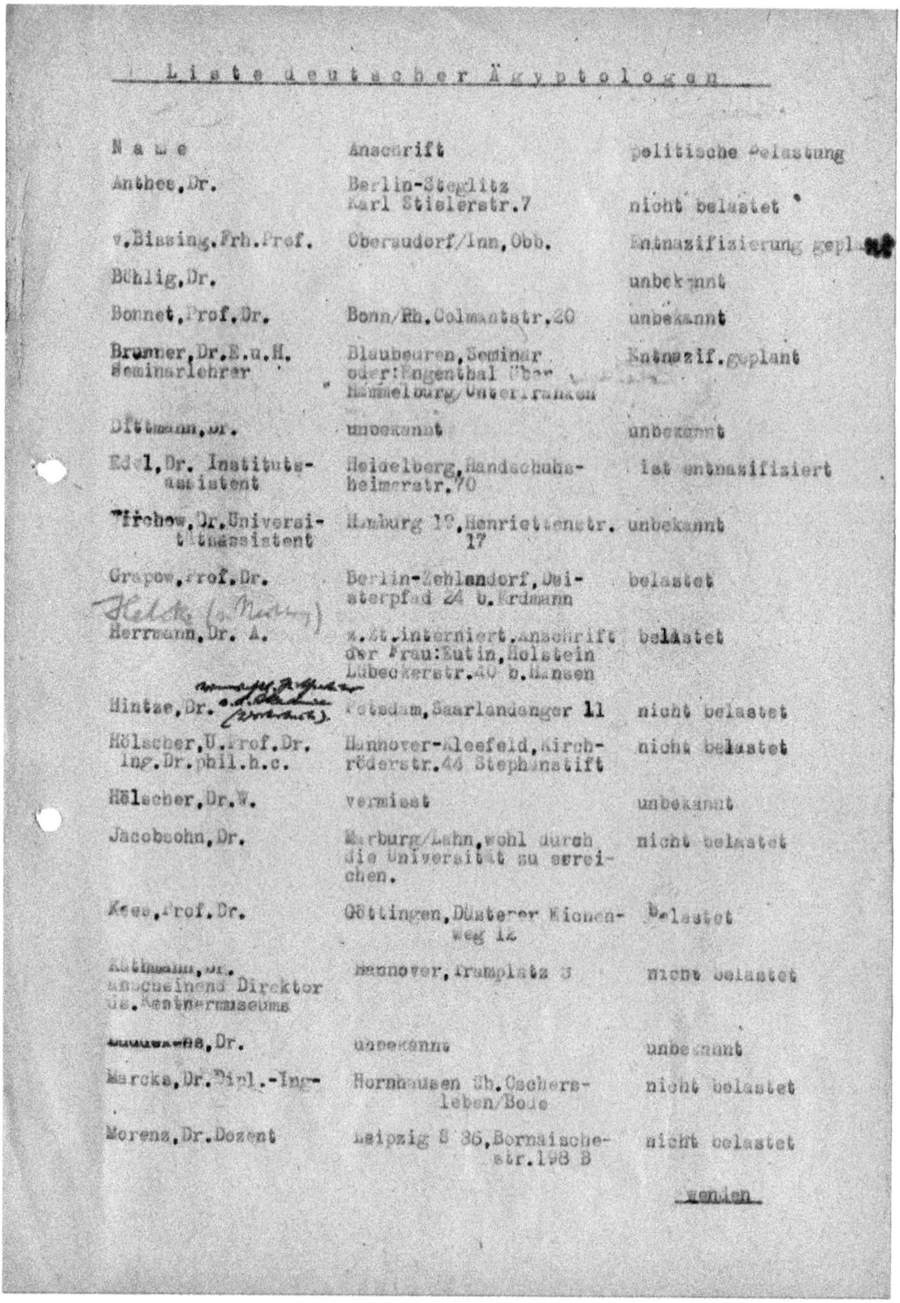

Liste deutscher Ägyptologen

Name	Anschrift	politische Belastung
Anthes, Dr.	Berlin-Steglitz, Karl Stielerstr. 7	nicht belastet
v. Bissing, Frh. Prof.	Obersudorf/Inn, Obb.	Entnazifizierung gepl.
Böhlig, Dr.		unbekannt
Bonnet, Prof. Dr.	Bonn/Rh. Colmantstr. 20	unbekannt
Brunner, Dr. E. u. H. Seminarlehrer	Blaubeuren, Seminar oder: Engenthal Über Hammelburg/Unterfranken	Entnazif. geplant
Dittmann, Dr.	unbekannt	unbekannt
Edel, Dr. Institutsassistent	Heidelberg, Handschuhsheimerstr. 70	ist entnazifiziert
Firchow, Dr. Universitätsassistent	Hamburg 19, Henriettenstr. 17	unbekannt
Grapow, Prof. Dr.	Berlin-Zehlendorf, Beisterpfad 24 b. Erdmann	belastet
Herrmann, Dr. A.	z. Zt. interniert, Anschrift der Frau: Eutin, Holstein Lübeckerstr. 40 b. Hansen	belastet
Hintze, Dr.	Potsdam, Saarlandanger 11	nicht belastet
Hölscher, U. Prof. Dr. Ing. Dr. phil. h.c.	Hannover-Kleefeld, Kirchröderstr. 44 Stephanstift	nicht belastet
Hölscher, Dr. W.	vermisst	unbekannt
Jacobsohn, Dr.	Marburg/Lahn, wohl durch die Universität zu erreichen.	nicht belastet
Kees, Prof. Dr.	Göttingen, Düsterer Eichenweg 12	belastet
Kuthmann, Dr. anscheinend Direktor des Kestnermuseums	Hannover, Trammplatz 3	nicht belastet
Luddeckens, Dr.	unbekannt	unbekannt
Marcks, Dr. Dipl.-Ing.	Hornhausen Üb. Oschersleben/Bode	nicht belastet
Morenz, Dr. Dozent	Leipzig S 36, Bornaischestr. 198 B	nicht belastet

wenden

Figure 2.4 Anthes' list of German Egyptologists, (a) page 1/3, (b) page 2/3, (c) page 3/3. Zentralarchiv der Staatlichen Museen zu Berlin: SMB-ZA, II/VA 283.

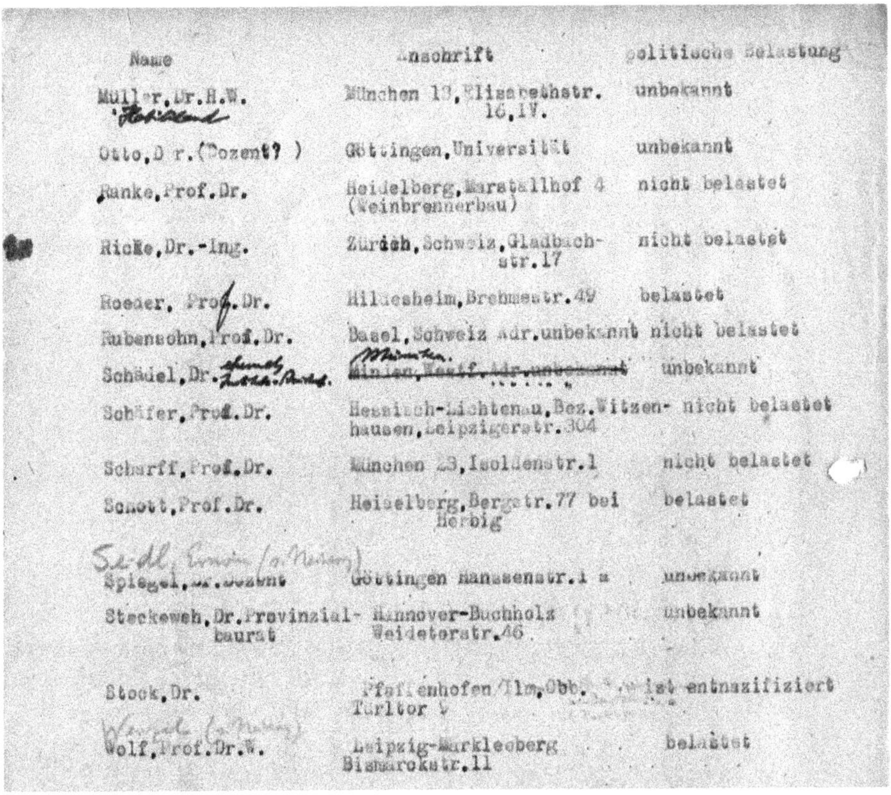

Name	Anschrift	politische Belastung
Müller,Dr.H.W.	München 19,Elisabethstr. 16.IV.	unbekannt
Otto,Dr.(Dozent?)	Göttingen,Universität	unbekannt
Ranke,Prof.Dr.	Heidelberg,Marstallhof 4 (Weinbrennerbau)	nicht belastet
Ricke,Dr.-Ing.	Zürich,Schweiz,Gladbach-str.17	nicht belastet
Roeder, Prof.Dr.	Hildesheim,Brehmstr.49	belastet
Rubensohn,Prof.Dr.	Basel,Schweiz Adr.unbekannt	nicht belastet
Schädel,Dr.	Minden,Westf.Adr.unbekannt	unbekannt
Schäfer,Prof.Dr.	Hessisch-Lichtenau,Bez.Witzenhausen,Leipzigerstr.304	nicht belastet
Scharff,Prof.Dr.	München 23,Isoldenstr.1	nicht belastet
Schott,Prof.Dr.	Heidelberg,Bergstr.77 bei Herbig	belastet
Spiegel,Dr.Dozent	Göttingen Hanssenstr.1 a	unbekannt
Steckeweh,Dr.Provinzialbaurat	Hannover-Buchholz Weideterstr.46	unbekannt
Stock,Dr.	Pfaffenhofen/Ilm,Obb. Turltor 5	ist entnazifiziert
Wolf,Prof.Dr.W.	Leipzig-Markleeberg Bismarckstr.11	belastet

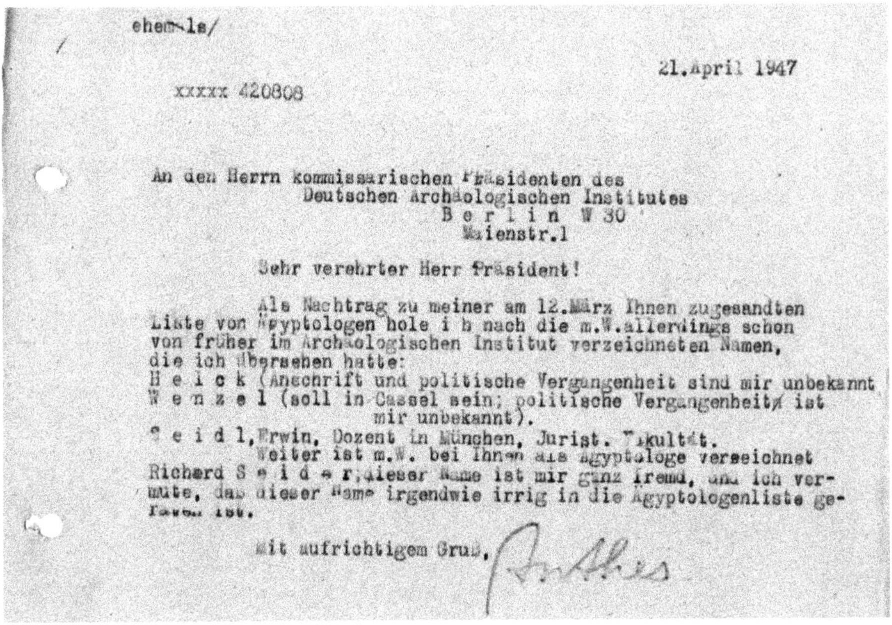

ehemals/

xxxxx 420808

21.April 1947

An den Herrn kommissarischen Präsidenten des
Deutschen Archäologischen Institutes
B e r l i n W 30
Maienstr.1

Sehr verehrter Herr Präsident!

Als Nachtrag zu meiner am 12.März Ihnen zugesandten Liste von Ägyptologen hole i h nach die m.W.allerdings schon von früher im Archäologischen Institut verzeichneten Namen, die ich übersehen hatte:
H e i c k (Anschrift und politische Vergangenheit sind mir unbekannt
W e n z e l (soll in Cassel sein; politische Vergangenheit ist mir unbekannt).
S e i d l,Erwin, Dozent in München, Jurist. Fakultät.
Weiter ist m.W. bei Ihnen als Ägyptologe verzeichnet Richard S e i d e r,dieser Name ist mir ganz fremd, und ich vermute, das dieser Name irgendwie irrig in die Ägyptologenliste geraten ist.

Mit aufrichtigem Gruß,

Figure 2.4 (Continued)

Figure 2.5 Hans Gustav Güterbock. The Oriental Institute Chicago, Museum Archives. Reproduced under a CC BY-NC-ND 4.0 licence.

Indo-European scholar and secretary of the German Oriental Society, Bruno Güterbock (1858–1940).[57] Obviously, the son reiterated the views of his father but it is not possible to tell which information stems from whom. To further complicate the genesis of the document, it was dictated by Hans Gustav Güterbock to his wife, Franziska (née Hellmann, 1919–2014) and published online by Charles E. Jones within the Ancient Near East mailing list of the Oriental Institute in Chicago.[58]

The text begins by citing Güterbock's statement: 'I am glad to contribute my recollections of Nazis in our fields.' The first question here, as already remarked, should be whose recollections are these? Immediately after that, the reference to Wolfram von Soden (1908–1996) as 'older co-student' makes it clear that this information was provided by Hans Gustav Güterbock. The entire statement reads:

> The case of Wolfram von Soden is generally known. I know that he joined the party and I heard that he personally took part in the burning of synagogues on the so called 'Kristallnacht' November 9, 1938. He was an older co-student of mine at Leipzig […]. I found von Soden rather naïve about real life so that I am ready to believe that he really believed in National Socialism.

Analysis of the structure here is worthwhile: The statement begins with the assertion that the case 'is generally known'. Güterbock 'knows' that von Soden joined the NSDAP and 'heard' that he took part in the November pogrom. A personal relationship (whatever the intensity) is established ('co-student') and an explanation provided as to why von Soden could have actually 'believed' in Nazism. Aside from the fact that the last part in particular reads like an excuse (cf. Alfred Grimm's 'excuse' for Friedrich Wilhelm von Bissing, above), the foundation for the assessment seems rather shaky. The only fact provided is that von Soden joined the party.

In another example, Güterbock – in this case obviously Hans Gustav, writing about his father – explicitly refers to the Steindorff list:

> Heinrich Schafer [sic, read: Schäfer] was a close friend of my father's until 1933. Supplementing the statement of Steindorff I would say that it was my impression that Schafer [sic] joined the party.

Güterbock is not supplementing Steindorff's statement here, although emulating the tone; he actually presents an outright contradictory assessment. Steindorff wrote:

> Heinrich Schäfer, whom you all know as a scholar and as a representative of Pan-Germanism. He is now in his late seventies. I do not think he joined the Nazi party, but I know that it was his ardent wish to attend the Nazi rally at Nurnberg [sic, read Nuremberg] and to watch the parade of storm-troopers. He was once among my best friends, but later he abandoned me. I will not further criticize my old friend.

The last sentence probably presents one of the reasons why Steindorff assigned 'his friend' Schäfer to the group of scholars he did not include out of piety in his black-and-white assessment. Schäfer, by that time, had lost his two sons (Heinz in 1924, in a boating accident, and Diederich in 1936, who took his own life). Sylvia Peuckert recently took up the challenge to analyse Schäfer's attitude towards Nazism, clearly pointing out that mere party membership or non-membership is not indicative.[59] However, the two primary sources presented here, the latter one even explicitly relying on the former, convey totally different positions when it comes to this single item of factual information.

Apart from that, the diverse lists convey a rather personal, subjective assessment. Before making use of such information, the researcher has to compare other sources to determine the veracity or falsity of statements and to establish possible reasons or motivations for particular assessments.

Of course, this could only be indicated within the framework of this contribution. Different kind of sources as well as different issues require different methodological approaches. However, what – hopefully – has become apparent is that there is no such thing as an 'authoritative source' beyond doubt.

Epilogue: '*Law & Order*.[60] Disciplinary History'?

Carlo Ginzburg, inspired by the writings of Thomas Kuhn, developed the 'paradigm of circumstantial evidence' (or *Indizienparadigma* in German) drawing parallels between the work of criminal investigators and scholars.[61] Although the concept seems rather distant,[62] historians, art historians and archaeologists frequently refer to the metaphor of being 'detectives of the past', collecting evidence and drawing conclusions. Even the method of deduction, at first sight, seems similar in both cases, although I do not wish to discuss the consistency of that paradigm in more detail here.[63] However, the image of 'historical investigators', from my point of view, should be supplemented by that of 'historical prosecutors'. Many studies dealing with the history of Egyptology during the Nazi era tend to have a judgemental tone, trying to 'prove' Egyptologists guilty or not guilty. There are several reasons for this: (1) the sources, not least influenced by contemporary (juridical) processes of denazification already tried to separate the sheep from the goats; (2) because the question of political incrimination during that particular era is perceived as a moral one, definite results are sought and (3) the researcher, being a German, very often wants to distance him- or herself clearly from Nazism and alleged Nazi Egyptologists. But for a 'trial' you would also need a 'lawyer' (sometimes literally a 'Devil's advocate'), defending the accused, a 'judge' granting a fair procedure and finally it might also help to imagine the scientific community as a 'jury'.

Now what has that to do with life-writing sources and higher criticism? Although the written documents employed by the historians cannot be compared with testimonies in court, it sometimes helps to close one's eyes and imagine the situation: The prosecutor calls his witnesses: Georg Steindorff, Rudolf Anthes and Hans Gustav Güterbock. Their statements are recorded. After that, the defence lawyer rises and begins the cross-examination. He will already have objected to any statements based on hearsay; he will also doubt the accuracy of the witnesses' accounts and he will certainly scrutinise their integrity. (Are there any reasons why their statements might be biased? Is there a 'hidden agenda'?) In the case of Hans Gustav Güterbock, the lawyer might even appeal to the judge to disallow his statements altogether, because his assessments cannot be differentiated from those of his father. If the prosecution provides sufficient other evidence and convinces the jury, the accused might be convicted. Maybe the defence can spread serious doubts about the plausibility of the charges laid before the court and the accused is acquitted for lack of (sufficient) evidence. Of course, the accused has every right to refuse to give evidence, a case, which might very well apply to those Egyptologists who did not prepare a written apology. However, if they had, these sources should not *a priori* be disqualified as 'apologetic'. Hermann Grapow, for instance, compiled his own 'History of the Berlin Academy'[64] during the Third Reich, to complement the official version. But his draft was rejected by the president of the Academy. As in court, the statement might also harm the defence – for example, Grapow's boast that after the failed 20th July plot against Hitler in 1944, he would have rescued the entire staff of the Academy from arrest and maybe execution, single-handedly.[65]

When it comes to the actual sentence, the metaphor should no longer be employed, for it is not for historians to hand down moral or juridical judgements.

The procedure of presenting evidence for and against a certain hypothesis, to question and cross-examine sources, to consider possible alternatives and, when in doubt, not to formulate a definitive conclusion seems to me to be a highly advisable mandate for the historian. The likelihood of someone shouting 'objection!' and someone else declaring 'sustained' must always be kept in mind. Leading disciplinary historians, like Stefan Rebenich have advised German Egyptologists not to assume the role of a criminal judge but rather of an examining magistrate.[66] Adopting this role includes certain prerequisites: (1) accepting the interdependency of politics and scholarship – the latter being always (including today) influenced by the Zeitgeist; (2) considering the cases of single scholars individually, against the background of general historical research to incorporate all accessible sources impartially but critically; (3) recognising the limits of one's own perspective and acknowledging that all scholars are human beings with human weaknesses – which also applies to the researcher, who should not hand down moral judgements but present the case instead.

The assessment of political incrimination of German Egyptology during the Third Reich has only just begun. More important than the isolated examination of that era in particular within disciplinary history, however, is the realisation that history never ends, that analysis cannot be finalised and that many of the relevant factors in the past remain relevant today and for the future as well.

Notes

1. Cf. Thomas L. Gertzen, '"Germanic" Egyptology? Scholarship and politics as resources for each other and their alleged binary relationship', in *Towards a History of Egyptology. Proceedings of the Egyptological Section of the 8th ESHS Conference in London, 2018*, eds., Hana Navratilova et al. (Münster: Zaphon, 2019).
2. Cf. Thomas L. Gertzen, *École de Berlin und Goldenes Zeitalter (1882–1914) der Ägyptologie als Wissenschaft. Das Lehrer-Schüler-Verhältnis zwischen Ebers, Erman und Sethe* (Berlin: De Gruyter, 2013); Thomas L. Gertzen, Susanne Voss and Maximilian Georg, 'Prussia and Germany', in *A History of World Egyptology*, eds. Andrew Bednarski, Aidan Dodson and Salima Ikram (Cambridge: Cambridge University Press, 2021), 210–58.
3. The term cannot be equated with English 'science', since it also comprises the humanities, such as Egyptology.
4. This is not to say that the naive assertion of Edward W. Said, *Orientalism* (New York: Random House, 1978), p. 19: 'the German Orient was almost exclusively a scholarly [...] Orient, but it was never actual,' would be true. The post-colonial or 'Orientalist' discourse, however, is comparatively less important for German Egyptologists than for British and French scholars. In this context it should also be mentioned that this does not apply to the same degree to German Near Eastern Studies, cf. Stefan Hauser, 'Deutsche Forschungen zum Alten Orient und ihre Beziehungen zu politischen und ökonomischen Interessen vom Kaiserreich bis zum Zweiten Weltkrieg', in *Deutschland und der Mittlere Osten*, ed. Wolfgang G. Schwanitz (Leipzig: Leipziger Universitätsverlag, 2004), 46–65; Stefan Hauser, 'History, races, and orientalism – Eduard Meyer, the organization of Oriental research, and Herzfeld's intellectual heritage', in *Ernst Herzfeld and the Development of Near Eastern Studies, 1900–1950*, eds. Ann C. Gunter and Stefan R. Hauser (Leiden: Brill, 2005), 505–59.
5. Germany became part of the 'West' only during the second half of the twentieth century; cf. Heinrich August Winkler, *Der lange Weg nach Westen. Deutsche Geschichte*, Vol. 2, second edition, (Munich: Beck, 2020).
6. Meanwhile, ill-informed, polemic and totally undifferentiated assertions obfuscate serious discussion about the role of post-colonialism in the history of Egyptology; cf. Thomas L. Gertzen, 'Some remarks on the "de-colonization" of Egyptology', *Göttinger Miszellen. Beiträge zur ägyptologischen Diskussion* 261 (2020): 189–203.
7. Bettina Hitzer and Thomas Welskopp, eds., *Die Bielefelder Sozialgeschichte. Klassische Texte zu einem geschichtswissenschaftlichen Programm und seinen Kontroversen* (Bielefeld: Transcript, 2010).
8. Hans-Josef Trümpener, *Die Existenzbedingungen einer Zwergwissenschaft. Eine Darstellung des Zusammenhanges von wissenschaftlichem Wandel und der Institutionalisierung einer Disziplin am Beispiel der Ägyptologie* (Bielefeld: Kleine, 1981).
9. John Baines, 'Restricted knowledge, hierarchy and decorum. Modern perceptions and ancient institutions', *Journal of the American Research Center in Egypt* 27, 1990: 5 (n. 32).
10. Cf. Gertzen, *École de Berlin*, 13–4; 44–6.
11. Thomas S. Kuhn, *The Structure of Scientific Revolutions*, (Chicago: University of Chicago Press, 1969).
12. John Baines, 'On the methods and aims of Black Athena', in *Black Athena Revisited*, eds. Mary R. Lefkowitz and Guy MacLean Rogers (Chapel Hill NC: The University of North Carolina Press, 1997), 42.
13. *Ibid.*, 47.
14. John Baines, 'What is Egyptology?', in The British Academy Blog, last modified March 27th 2020, https://www.thebritishacademy.ac.uk/blog/what-is-egyptology/.
15. The complex interrelationship between Egyptology and its application of methods and theoretical concepts from other disciplines was recently assessed in Alexandra Verbovsek, Burkhard Backes and Catherine Jones, eds., *Methodik und Didaktik in der*

Ägyptologie: Herausforderungen eines kulturwissenschaftlichen Paradigmenwechsels in den Altertumswissenschaften, (München: Wilhelm Fink, 2011).

16　Trümpener, *Die Existenzbedingungen*, 101: 'Grammatik und Sprachbeherrschung erfüllen hier stellvertretend die Funktion von Wissenschaftstheorie.' [Translations if not otherwise indicated by TLG.]

17　For a detailed argument, cf. Gertzen, *École de Berlin*, 20–40; 248–60; 382–94.

18　German Egyptologists as well as Assyriologists might also be considered a part of the history of German Oriental studies, though the importance of their respective disciplines seems somewhat marginal; cf. Suzanne Marchand, *German Orientalism in the Age of Empire. Religion Race and Scholarship*, (Cambridge: Cambridge University Press, 2009), 196–206; 236–51.

19　Jason Thompson, *Wonderful Things. A History of Egyptology*, Vol. 1: *From Antiquity to 1881* (Cairo: The American University in Cairo Press, 2015), 12.

20　Cf. Thomas L. Gertzen, 'Review of *A History of Egyptology*, Vol. 1: *From Antiquity to 1881*, by Jason Thompson', *Bibliotheca Orientalis* 72.5–6 (2015), 626–32 (in German) and particularly: Gertzen, 'Review of *A History of Egyptology*, Vol. 2: *The Golden Age 1881–1914*', by Jason Thompson, *Bibliotheca Orientalis* 73.3–4 (2016), 360–65 (in English).

21　For the Third Reich: Thomas Beckh, 'Das Institut für Ägyptologie der LMU München im Nationalsozialismus', in *Die Universität München im Dritten Reich*, ed. Elisabeth Kraus (München: Herbert Utz, 2006), 249–97; Thomas Schneider and Peter Raulwing, eds., *Egyptology from the First World War to the Third Reich. Ideology, Scholarship and Individual Biographies*, (Leiden: Brill, 2013); Hannelore Kischkewitz, 'Die Jahre 1933–1945 im Ägyptischen Museum' in *Zwischen Politik und Kunst. Die Staatlichen Museen zu Berlin in der Zeit des Nationalsozialismus*, eds. Jörn Grabowski and Petra Winter (Berlin: Böhlau, 2013), 303–16; Klaus Finneiser, 'Auslagerung des Ägyptischen Museums in Sophienhof. Der Zweite Weltkrieg und die Folgen', *ibid.*, 287–301; Susanne Voss, 'Der lange Arm des Nationalsozialismus. Zur Geschichte der Abteilung Kairo des DAI im "Dritten Reich"' in *Ägyptologen und Ägyptologien zwischen Kaiserreich und Gründung der beiden deutschen Staaten. Reflexionen zur Geschichte und Episteme eines altertumswissenschaftlichen Fachs im 150. Jahr der Zeitschrift für ägyptische Sprache und Altertumskunde*, eds. Susanne Bickel et al. (Berlin: De Gruyter, 2013), 267–98; Julia Budka and Claus Jurmann, 'Ein deutsch-österreichisches Forscherleben zwischen Pyramiden, Kreuz und Hakenkreuz' *ibid.*, 299–331; Thomas Schneider, '"Eine Führernatur, wie sie der neue Staat braucht!". Hermann Kees' Tätigkeit in Göttingen 1924–1945 und die Kontroverse um Entnazifizierung und Wiedereinstellung in der Nachkriegszeit', *Studien zur Altägyptischen Kultur* 44 (2015): 333–81; Susanne Voss, *Die Geschichte der Abteilung Kairo des DAI im Spannungsfeld deutscher politischer Interessen*, Vol. 2: *1929–1966*, (Rahden i. Westf.: Marie Leidorf, 2017); Susanne Voss, 'Ein "österreichischer" Gelehrter im Dienst des deutschen Staates. Hermann Junkers Amtszeit als Direktor des DAI-Kairo im "Dritten Reich"' in *Hermann Junker – eine Spurensuche im Schatten der österreichischen Ägyptologie und Afrikanistik*, ed. Clemens Gütl (Wien: Cuvillier, 2017), 131–79; Julia Budka and Claus Jurmann, 'Ägyptologische Forschung zwischen Christentum und Nationalsozialismus', *ibid.*, 181–219; for the GDR: Thomas L. Gertzen, 'Strukturgefängnis und exotischer Freiraum: Die Wissenschaftsgeschichte der Ägyptologie in der DDR', *Göttinger Miszellen. Beiträge zur ägyptologischen Diskussion* 251 (2017), 149–57; and *idem.* at the conference: 'BERLIN-SUDAN. The history of Berlin-based research on Northeast Africa. Change, continuity and scientific "Zeitgeist" from the Kingdom of Prussia until the end of the GDR', Archäologie und Kulturgeschichte Nordostafrikas (AKNOA); Humboldt Universität zu Berlin, last modified July 15th, 2017, https://www.archaeologie.hu-berlin.de/de/aknoa/veranstaltungen/konferenzen/berlin-sudan.

22　A biography covering almost the entire time-span from the *Kaiserreich* to the GDR: Thomas L. Gertzen, *Die Berliner Schule der Ägyptologie im 'Dritten Reich'. Begegnung mit Hermann Grapow* (Berlin: Kadmos, 2015) and, ground breaking for the developments in the inter-war-period: Susanne Voss and Dietrich Raue, eds., *Georg Steindorff und die deutsche Ägyptologie im 20. Jahrhundert* (Berlin: De Gruyter, 2016).

23　Thomas Schneider, 'Ägyptologen im Dritten Reich: Biographische Notizen anhand der sogenannten "Steindorff-Liste"', *Journal of Egyptian History* 5 (2012), 120–247; re-published without changes in Schneider and Raulwing, *Egyptology from the First World War to the Third Reich*, 120–247.

24　William Carruthers, 'Thinking about histories of Egyptology' in *Histories of Egyptology. Interdisciplinary measures*, ed. William Carruthers (London: Routledge, 2015), 3–4.

25 David Gange, 'Interdisciplinary measures: beyond disciplinary histories of Egyptology', in *Histories of Egyptology. Interdisciplinary measures*, ed. William Carruthers (London: Routledge, 2015), 64–77.
26 Cf. 'Virtuelle Ausstellung Hermann Kees (1886–1964). Ein Ägyptologe zwischen Wissenschaft und Politik', Seminar für Ägyptologie und Koptologie der Universität Göttingen, https://www.uni-goettingen.de/de/8222virtuelle-ausstellung8221-hermann-kees/487302.html.
27 Schneider, 'Eine Führernatur', 350: 'Kees' antisemitische Haltung lässt sich allerdings nicht nur durch seine führende Stellung in der programmatisch antisemitischen DNVP bis 1933 belegen. Sie findet sich auch in seinem zeitgenössischen ägyptologischen Schrifttum.'
28 *Ibid.*, 381: 'Mit Kees' politischer Belastung kontrastiert seine überragende wissenschaftliche Leistung insbesondere im Bereich der ägyptischen Religionsgeschichte. [...] Wie bei anderen Ägyptologen während des Nationalsozialismus offenbart sich eine Diskrepanz zwischen wissenschaftlicher Größe und politisch-menschlichem Verhalten.'
29 Cf. Gertzen, *Die Berliner Schule*, and particularly the critique of Schneider and others on pp. 18–25.
30 Schneider, 'Ägyptologen im Dritten Reich', 130; 157; 159; Schneider continues to believe that Grapow 'embraced National Socialist agendas as a pathway for future research and teaching'; Thomas Schneider, 'Hermann Grapow, Egyptology, and National Socialist Initiatives for the Humanities', in *The Betrayal of the Humanities. The university during the Third Reich*, Bernard M. Levinson and Robert P. Erickson eds., (Bloomington, IN: IUP, 2022), 297.
31 Schneider, 'Ägyptologen im Dritten Reich', 158–60.
32 Schneider, 'Hermann Grapow', 290.
33 According to his profile on LinkedIn: https://ca.linkedin.com/in/thomas-schneider-401306191.
34 Cf. Peter Raulwing and Thomas L. Gertzen, 'Friedrich Wilhelm Freiherr von Bissing im Blickpunkt ägyptologischer und zeithistorischer Forschungen: Die Jahre 1914 bis 1926', in *Egyptology from the First World War to the Third Reich. Ideology, scholarship, and individual biographies*, eds. Thomas Schneider and Peter Raulwing (Leiden: Brill, 2013), 34–119.
35 *Friedrich Wilhelm Freiherr von Bissing. Ägyptologe, Mäzen, Sammler*, eds. Alfred Grimm and Sylvia Schoske (München: Staaliches Museum Ägyptischer Kunst, 2010), 40: 'der während des Ersten Weltkrieges (1914–1918) in einer Reihe von Veröffentlichungen eine ganz entschieden deutschnationale Stellung bezogen hatte, war bereits 1925 der NSDAP beigetreten, und zwar einzig und allein aus politischer Überzeugung, nicht jedoch aus Opportunismus.'
36 Von Bissing was indeed a multi-faceted personality, for his political entanglements were further complicated due to his homosexuality; cf. Thomas L. Gertzen, 'Wie sich eben nur ein hysterischer Mensch benehmen kann'. 'Homophobie und Antisemitismus in der Geschichte der Ägyptologie. Der Fall Friedrich Wilhelm Freiherr von Bissing (1873–1956)', in *Winckelmann and his Passionate Followers: Queer archaeology, Egyptology and the history of arts since 1750*, eds. Wolfgang Cortjaens and Christian E. Loeben (Rhaden i. Westf.: Marie Leidorf, 2022).
37 Of course, this is nothing new: Phillipp Müller, 'Understanding history. Hermeneutics and source-criticism in historical scholarship', in *Reading Primary Sources. The interpretation of texts from nineteenth- and twentieth-century history*, eds. Miriam Dobson and Benjamin Ziemann (London: Routledge, 2009), 21–36.
38 The textual basis here is kept at the archive of the Egyptological Institute in Leipzig: ÄMULA, NL Georg Steindorff, Korrespondenz, G. Steindorff, Juni 1945; reproduced in Voss and Raue, *Georg Steindorff und die deutsche Ägyptologie*, 546–47; also reproduced in Thomas L. Gertzen, *Einführung in die Wissenschaftsgeschichte der Ägyptologie* (Berlin: LIT, 2017), 372–5; another but mostly identical version from the archives of the Oriental Institute, Chicago published in Schneider, 'Ägyptologen im "Dritten Reich"', 145–7; with reproduction on 231–3.
39 Thomas L. Gertzen, '"In Deutschland steht Ihnen Ihre Abstammung entgegen" – zur Bedeutung von Judentum und Konfessionalismus für die wissenschaftliche Laufbahn G. Steindorffs und seiner Rolle innerhalb der École de Berlin', in *Georg Steindorff und die deutsche Ägyptologie im 20. Jahrhundert*, eds. Susanne Voss and Dietrich Raue (Berlin: De Gruyter, 2016), 333–400; *idem.*, *Judentum und Konfession in der Geschichte der deutschsprachigen Ägyptologie* (Berlin: De Gruyter, 2017), in particular 156–8.
40 Susanne Voss, '"J'accuse": Die sogenannte Steindorff-Liste von 1945, ihre historische Einordnung und deren Wert bei der Einschätzung der Urteile', in *Georg Steindorff und die deutsche Ägyptologie im 20. Jahrhundert*, eds., Susanne Voss and Dietrich Raue (Berlin: De Gruyter, 2016), 303; cf. Gertzen, *Einführung in die Wissenschaftsgeschichte*, 372–5.

41 An allusion to the open letter by Émile Zola to the president of France protesting against the unjust imprisonment of the Jewish officer Alfred Dreyfus.
42 Cf. Raulwing and Gertzen, 'Friedrich Wilhelm Freiherr von Bissing', 93.
43 For Erman and Sethe cf. Gertzen, *École de Berlin*, 93–153; 153–93 and 326–31; for Grapow's relationship to both: Gertzen, *Die Berliner Schule*, 56–61; 61–7.
44 Reichskristallnacht (Night of Broken Glass), pogrom on 9th to 10th November 1938 carried out by Sturmabteilung paramilitary forces and German civilians.
45 Mathilde Wesendonck (1828–1902), the 'muse' of Richard Wagner; cf. Judith Cabaud, *Mathilde Wesendonck ou le reve d'isolde* (Paris: Actes Sud, 1992).
46 Cf. Schneider, 'Ägyptologen im Dritten Reich'.
47 Dietrich Raue, 'Der "J'accuse"-Brief an John A. Wilson. Drei Ansichten von Georg Steindorff', in *Ägyptologen und Ägyptologien zwischen Kaiserreich und Gründung der beiden deutschen Staaten. Reflexionen zur Geschichte und Episteme eines altertumswissenschaftlichen Fachs im 150. Jahr der Zeitschrift für ägyptische Sprache und Altertumskunde*, eds. Susanne Bickel et al. (Berlin: De Gruyter, 2013), 345–76.
48 Thomas L. Gertzen, '"To become a German and nothing but a German …". The role of Paul de Lagarde in the conversion of Egyptologist Georg Steindorff', *Leo Baeck Institute Yearbook* 60 (2015), 79–89.
49 Susanne Voss, 'Wissenshintergründe – die Ägyptologie als "völkische" Wissenschaft vom Ersten Weltkrieg bis zum "Dritten Reich" am Beispiel des Nachlasses Georg Steindorffs' in *Georg Steindorff und die deutsche Ägyptologie im 20. Jahrhundert*, eds. Susanne Voss and Dietrich Raue (Berlin: De Gruyter, 2016), 105–332.
50 In the case of both Steindorff and Grapow cf. Gertzen, *Die Berliner Schule*, 67–72; idem., 'In Deutschland steht Ihnen Ihre Abstammung entgegen', 365–89.
51 Raulwing and Gertzen, 'Friedrich Wilhelm von Bissing', 98–9.
52 Richard N. Soulen and R. Kendall Soulen, *Handbook of Biblical Criticism* (third revised and expanded edition, Louisville KY: Westminster John Knox Press, 2001), 21; 78–80.
53 Michael Krumme and Marie Vigener, 'Carl Weickert (1885–1975)', in *Lebensbilder. Klassische Archäologen und der Nationalsozialismus*, eds. Martin Maischberger and Gunnar Brands (Rahden i. Westf.: Marie Leidorf, 2016), 203–22.
54 Reproduced and transcribed in Gertzen, *Einführung in die Wissenschaftsgeschichte*, 377–83.
55 Thomas L. Gertzen, '"Hochgradig humanistisch" – Der Ägyptologe Rudolf Anthes (1896–1985)', in *O Isis und Osiris. Ägyptens Mysterien und die Freimaurerei*, eds. Florian Ebeling and Christian Loeben (Rahden i. Westf.: Marie Leidorf, second revised edition, 2019), 475–89.
56 The document will be discussed extensively in a new biography: Peter Raulwing, Theo van den Hout and Lars Petersen, *Hans Gustav Güterbock. Ein Leben für die Hethitologie: Berlin, Ankara, Uppsala, Chicago*, (Münster: Zaphon, forthcoming). I am indebted to Peter Raulwing and his co-authors for providing me with their manuscript.
57 Cf. the memoir of his wife: Grete Auer, *Wenn ich mein Leben betrachte … Wien, Bern, Marokko, Berlin*, (Berlin: Stapp, 1995).
58 Cf. Ancient Near East Digest, Friday, 29th October 1993, Vol. 1, no. 24, http://oi-archive. uchicago.edu/research/library/ane/digest/v01/v01.n024; also reprinted and commented upon in Gertzen, *Einführung in die Wissenschaftsgeschichte*, 383–6.
59 Sylvia Peuckert, 'Überlegungen zu Heinrich Schäfers "Von ägyptischer Kunst" und zu Hedwig Fechheimers Plastik der Aegypter', *Zeitschrift für Ägyptische Sprache und Altertumskunde* 144.1 (2017), 117–23; see also p. 117: 'Die Mitgliedschaft in der NSDAP ist allerdings nicht ein derart aussagekräftiges Kriterium […].' In the very same sense, Stefan Rebenich, 'Zwischen Verweigerung und Anpassung. Die Altertumswissenschaften im "Dritten Reich"', in *Ägyptologen und Ägyptologien zwischen Kaiserreich und Gründung der beiden deutschen Staaten. Reflexionen zur Geschichte und Episteme eines altertumswissenschaftlichen Fachs im 150. Jahr der Zeitschrift für ägyptische Sprache und Altertumskunde*, eds. Susanne Bickel et al. (Berlin: De Gruyter, 2013), 17: 'Parteimitgliedschaft allein [ist] kein exklusives Kriterium für die Bestimmung des Grades der Anpassung an die NS-Ideologie.'
60 Refers to the American police procedural and legal drama television series, created by Dick Wolf (1990–2010).
61 Carlo Ginzburg, *Clues, Myths, and the Historical Method* (Baltimore: Johns Hopkins University Press, 2013).
62 Cf., e.g. the critical assessment of Christian Bachhiesl, *Zwischen Indizienparadigma und Pseudowissenschaft. Wissenschaftshistorische Überlegungen zum epistemischen Status

kriminalwissenschaftlicher Forschung (Wien: LIT, 2012), 11–14, i.a. pointing out that Ginzburg modelled his paradigm on fictitious characters such as Sherlock Holmes.
63   And I certainly do not claim any criminological or juridical competences.
64   Grapow, Hermann, *Zur Geschichte der Akademie in den Jahren 1938–1945*, reproduced in: Gertzen, *Die Berliner Schule*, 145–61.
65   Grapow held Claus Schenk Graf von Stauffenberg in low regard. In an official statement to the Academy from 1959 he expressed his opinion that if you are serious about killing someone, you do not plant a bomb inside a room, you just shoot him in the head; cf. *ibid.*, 160–1: 'wenn man es wirklich ernst meine, dann stelle man nicht auf umständliche Art eine Bombe in ein Zimmer, sondern gehe auf Hitler zu und schieße ihm eine Kugel durch den Kopf'.
66   In the keynote address at the annual meeting in 2011 of German-speaking Egyptologists in Leipzig; cf. *Idem.*, 'Zwischen Verweigerung und Anpassung. Die Altertumswissenschaften im "Dritten Reich"' in *Ägyptologen und Ägyptologien zwischen Kaiserreich und Gründung der beiden deutschen Staaten. Reflexionen zur Geschichte und Episteme eines altertumswissenschaftlichen Fachs im 150. Jahr der Zeitschrift für ägyptische Sprache und Altertumskunde*, eds. Susanne Bickel et al. (Berlin: De Gruyter, 2013), 14: 'Dabei sollte sich der Historiker allerdings nicht die Rolle des Strafrichters anmaßen, sondern sich mit der des Untersuchungsrichters bescheiden.'

Bibliography

Auer, Grete, *Wenn ich mein Leben betrachte … Wien, Bern, Marokko, Berlin: Erinnerungen* (Berlin: Stapp, 1995).
Bachhiesl, Christian, *Zwischen Indizienparadigma und Pseudowissenschaft. Wissenschaftshistorische ische Überlegungen zum epistemischen Status kriminalwissenschaftlicher Forschung* (Wien: LIT, 2012).
Baines, John, 'Restricted knowledge, hierarchy, and decorum. Modern perceptions and ancient institutions', *Journal of the American Research Center in Egypt* 27, (1990): 1–23.
Baines, John, 'On the methods and aims of Black Athena', in *Black Athena Revisited*, eds., Mary R. Lefkowitz and Guy MacLean Rogers, (Chapel Hill, NC: The University of North Carolina Press, 1997), 27–48.
Baines, John, 'What is Egyptology?', in The British Academy Blog, last modified 27 March 2020. Last accessed 6 February 2022. https://www.thebritishacademy.ac.uk/blog/what-is-egyptology/
Beckh, Thomas, 'Das Institut für Ägyptologie der LMU München im Nationalsozialismus', in *Die Universität München im Dritten Reich*, ed., Elisabeth Kraus (München: Herbert Utz, 2006), 249–97.
Budka, Julia and Claus Jurmann, 'Ein deutsch-österreichisches Forscherleben zwischen Pyramiden, Kreuz und Hakenkreuz', in *Ägyptologen und Ägyptologien zwischen Kaiserreich und Gründung der beiden deutschen Staaten. Reflexionen zur Geschichte und Episteme eines altertumswissenschaftlichen Fachs im 150. Jahr der Zeitschrift für ägyptische Sprache und Altertumskunde*, eds., Susanne Bickel et al. (Berlin: De Gruyter, 2013), 299–331.
Budka, Julia and Claus Jurmann, 'Ägyptologische Forschung zwischen Christentum und Nationalsozialismus', in *Hermann Junker – eine Spurensuche im Schatten der österreichischen Ägyptologie und Afrikanistik*, ed., Clemens Gütl (Wien: Cuvillier, 2017), 181–219.
Cabaud, Judith, *Mathilde Wesendonck ou le reve d'isolde* (Paris: Actes Sud, 1992).
Carruthers, William, 'Thinking about histories of Egyptology', in *Histories of Egyptology. Interdisciplinary Measures*, ed., William Carruthers (London: Routledge, 2015), 1–15.
Finneiser, Klaus, 'Auslagerung des Ägyptischen Museums in Sophienhof. Der Zweite Weltkrieg und die Folgen', in *Zwischen Politik und Kunst. Die Staatlichen Museen zu Berlin in der Zeit des Nationalsozialismus*, Vol. 2, eds., Jörn Grabowski and Petra Winter (Berlin: Böhlau Verlag, 2013), 303–16.
Gange, David, 'Interdisciplinary measures: beyond disciplinary histories of Egyptology', in *Histories of Egyptology. Interdisciplinary measures*, ed., William Carruthers (London: Routledge, 2015, 64–77.
Gertzen, Thomas L., *École de Berlin und Goldenes Zeitalter (1882–1914) der Ägyptologie als Wissenschaft. Das Lehrer-Schüler-Verhältnis zwischen Ebers, Erman und Sethe* (Berlin: De Gruyter, 2013).

Gertzen, Thomas L., *Die Berliner Schule der Ägyptologie im 'Dritten Reich'. Begegnung mit Hermann Grapow* (Berlin: Kadmos, 2015).

Gertzen, Thomas L., '"To become a German and nothing but a German ...". The role of Paul de Lagarde in the conversion of Egyptologist Georg Steindorff', *Leo Baeck Institute Yearbook* 60 (2015), 79–89.

Gertzen, Thomas L., 'Review of *A History of Egyptology*, Vol. 1: *From Antiquity to 1881*, by Jason Thompson', *Bibliotheca Orientalis* 72.5–6 (2015): 626–32.

Gertzen, Thomas L., '"In Deutschland steht Ihnen Ihre Abstammung entgegen" – zur Bedeutung von Judentum und Konfessionalismus für die wissenschaftliche Laufbahn G. Steindorffs und seiner Rolle innerhalb der École de Berlin', in *Georg Steindorff und die deutsche Ägyptologie im 20. Jahrhundert*, eds., Susanne Voss and Dietrich Raue (Berlin: De Gruyter, 2016), 333–400.

Gertzen, Thomas L., 'Review of *A History of Egyptology*, Vol. 2: *The Golden Age 1881–1914*, by Jason Thompson', *Bibliotheca Orientalis* 73.3–4 (2016): 360–365.

Gertzen, Thomas L., *Einführung in die Wissenschaftsgeschichte der Ägyptologie* (Berlin: LIT, 2017).

Gertzen, Thomas L., *Judentum und Konfession in der Geschichte der deutschsprachigen Ägyptologie* (Berlin: De Gruyter, 2017).

Gertzen, Thomas L., 'Strukturgefängnis und exotischer Freiraum: Die Wissenschaftsgeschichte der Ägyptologie in der DDR', *Göttinger Miszellen. Beiträge zur ägyptologischen Diskussion* 251 (2017): 149–57.

Gertzen, Thomas L., '"Hochgradig humanistisch" – Der Ägyptologe Rudolf Anthes (1896–1985)', in *O Isis und Osiris. Ägyptens Mysterien und die Freimaurerei*, eds. Florian Ebeling and Christian Loeben (Rahden/Westf.: Marie Leidorf, second and revised edition 2019), 475–89.

Gertzen, Thomas L., '"Germanic" Egyptology? Scholarship and politics as resources for each other and their alleged binary relationship', in *Towards a History of Egyptology. Proceedings of the Egyptological Section of the 8th ESHS Conference in London*, 2018, eds. Hana Navratilova et al. (Münster: Zaphon, 2019).

Gertzen, Thomas L., 'Some remarks on the 'de-colonization' of Egyptology', *Göttinger Miszellen. Beiträge zur ägyptologischen Diskussion* 261 (2020): 189–203.

Gertzen, Thomas L., Susanne Voss and Maximilian Georg, 'Prussia and Germany', in *A History of World Egyptology*, eds., Andrew Bednarski, Aidan Dodson and Salima Ikram, (Cambridge: CUP, 2021), 210–58.

Gertzen, Thomas L., '"Wie sich eben nur ein hysterischer Mensch benehmen kann". Homophobie und Antisemitismus in der Geschichte der Ägyptologie. Der Fall Friedrich Wilhelm Freiherr von Bissing (1873–1956)', in *Winckelmann and His Passionate Followers: Queer archaeology, Egyptology and the history of arts 1750–2018*, eds., Wolfgang Cortjaens and Christian E. Loeben, (Rhaden/Westf: Marie Leidorf 2022), 388–408.

Ginzburg, Carlo, *Clues, Myths, and the Historical Method* (Baltimore, MD: Johns Hopkins University Press, 2013).

Grimm, Alfred and Sylvia Schoske, eds., *Friedrich Wilhelm Freiherr von Bissing. Ägyptologe, Mäzen, Sammler*, (München: Staatliches Museum Ägyptischer Kunst, 2010).

Hauser, Stefan, 'Deutsche Forschungen zum Alten Orient und ihre Beziehungen zu politischen und ökonomischen Interessen vom Kaiserreich bis zum Zweiten Weltkrieg', in *Deutschland und der Mittlere Osten*, ed., Wolfgang G. Schwanitz (Leipzig: Leipziger Universitätsverlag, 2004), 46–65.

Hauser, Stefan, 'History, races, and orientalism – Eduard Meyer, the organization of Oriental research, and Herzfeld's intellectual heritage', in *Ernst Herzfeld and the Development of Near Eastern Studies, 1900–1950*, eds., Ann C. Gunter and Stefan R. Hauser (Leiden: Brill, 2005), 505–59.

Hitzer, Bettina and Thomas Welskopp, eds., *Die Bielefelder Sozialgeschichte. Klassische Texte zu einem geschichtswissenschaftlichen Programm und seinen Kontroversen* (Bielefeld: Transcript, 2010).

Kischkewitz, Hannelore, 'Die Jahre 1933–1945 im Ägyptischen Museum', in *Zwischen Politik und Kunst. Die Staatlichen Museen zu Berlin in der Zeit des Nationalsozialismus*, eds., Jörn Grabowski and Petra Winter (Berlin: Böhlau Verlag), 303–16.

Krumme, Michael and Marie Vigener, 'Carl Weickert (1885–1975)', in *Lebensbilder. Klassische Archäologen und der Nationalsozialismus*, eds., Martin Maischberger and Gunnar Brands (Rahden/Westf.: Marie Leidorf, 2016), 203–22.

Kuhn, Thomas S., *The Structure of Scientific Revolutions*, (Chicago IL: University of Chicago Press, 1969).

Magen, Barbara and Waldemar Wolze, 'Virtuelle Ausstellung Hermann Kees (1886–1964). Ein Ägyptologe zwischen Wissenschaft und Politik', Seminar für Ägyptologie und Koptologie der

Universität Göttingen. Last accessed 6 February 2022. https://www.uni-goettingen.de/de/8222virtuelle-ausstellung8221-hermann-kees/487302.html
Marchand, Suzanne, *German Orientalism in the Age of Empire. Religion, Race and Scholarship* (Cambridge: CUP, 2009).
Müller, Phillipp, 'Understanding history. Hermeneutics and source-criticism in historical scholarship', in *Reading Primary Sources. The interpretation of texts from nineteenth- and twentieth-century history*, eds., Miriam Dobson and Benjamin Ziemann (London: Routledge, 2009), 21–36.
Peuckert, Sylvia, 'Überlegungen zu Heinrich Schäfers 'Von ägyptischer Kunst' und zu Hedwig Fechheimers Plastik der Aegypter', in *Zeitschrift für Ägyptische Sprache und Altertumskunde* 144.1 (2017): 117–23.
Raue, Dietrich, 'Der 'J'accuse'-Brief an John A. Wilson. Drei Ansichten von Georg Steindorff', in *Ägyptologen und Ägyptologien zwischen Kaiserreich und Gründung der beiden deutschen Staaten. Reflexionen zur Geschichte und Episteme eines altertumswissenschaftlichen Fachs im 150. Jahr der Zeitschrift für ägyptische Sprache und Altertumskunde*, eds., Susanne Bickel et al. (Berlin: De Gruyter, 2013), 345–76.
Raulwing, Peter and Thomas L. Gertzen, 'Friedrich Wilhelm Freiherr von Bissing im Blickpunkt ägyptologischer und zeithistorischer Forschungen: Die Jahre 1914 bis 1926', in *Egyptology from the First World War to the Third Reich. Ideology, Scholarship, and Individual Biographies*, eds., Thomas Schneider and Peter Raulwing (Leiden: Brill, 2013), 34–119.
Raulwing, Peter, Theo van den Hout and Lars Petersen, *Hans Gustav Güterbock. Ein Leben für die Hethitologie: Berlin, Ankara, Uppsala, Chicago* (Münster: Zaphon, forthcoming).
Rebenich, Stefan, 'Zwischen Verweigerung und Anpassung. Die Altertumswissenschaften im "Dritten Reich"', in *Ägyptologen und Ägyptologien zwischen Kaiserreich und Gründung der beiden deutschen Staaten. Reflexionen zur Geschichte und Episteme eines altertumswissenschaftlichen Fachs im 150. Jahr der Zeitschrift für ägyptische Sprache und Altertumskunde*, eds. Susanne Bickel et al. (Berlin: De Gruyter, 2013), 13–35.
Said, Edward W., *Orientalism* (New York: Random House, 1978).
Schneider, Thomas, 'Ägyptologen im Dritten Reich: Biographische Notizen anhand der sogenannten "Steindorff-Liste"', *Journal of Egyptian History* 5 (2012), 120–247; re-published without changes in Schneider and Raulwing, *Egyptology from the First World War to the Third Reich. Ideology, Scholarship and Individual Biographies* (Leiden: Brill, 2013), 120–247.
Schneider, Thomas, '"Eine Führernatur, wie sie der neue Staat braucht!". Hermann Kees' Tätigkeit in Göttingen 1924–1945 und die Kontroverse um Entnazifizierung und Wiedereinstellung in der Nachkriegszeit', *Studien zur Altägyptischen Kultur* 44 (2015): 333–81.
Schneider, Thomas, 'Hermann Grapow, Egyptology, and National Socialist initiatives for the humanities', in *The Betrayal of the Humanities. The university during the Third Reich*, eds. Bernard M. Levinson and Robert P. Erickson, (Bloomington, IN: IUP, 2022), 263–305.
Schneider, Thomas and Peter Raulwing, eds., *Egyptology from the First World War to the Third Reich. Ideology, scholarship and individual biographies* (Leiden: Brill, 2013).
Soulen, Richard N. and R. Kendall Soulen, *Handbook of Biblical Criticism* (third revised and expanded edition, Louisville KY: Westminster John Knox Press, 2001).
Thompson, Jason, *Wonderful Things. A History of Egyptology*, Vol. 1, *From Antiquity to 1881* (Cairo: The American University in Cairo Press, 2015).
Trümpener, Hans-Josef, *Die Existenzbedingungen einer Zwergwissenschaft. Eine Darstellung des Zusammenhanges von wissenschaftlichem Wandel und der Institutionalisierung einer Disziplin am Beispiel der Ägyptologie* (Bielefeld: Kleine, 1981).
Verbovsek, Alexandra, Burkhard Backes and Catherine Jones, eds., *Methodik und Didaktik in der Ägyptologie: Herausforderungen eines kulturwissenschaftlichen Paradigmenwechsels in den Altertumswissenschaften*, (München: Wilhelm Fink, 2011).
Voss, Susanne, 'Der lange Arm des Nationalsozialismus. Zur Geschichte der Abteilung Kairo des DAI im "Dritten Reich"', in *Ägyptologen und Ägyptologien zwischen Kaiserreich und Gründung der beiden deutschen Staaten. Reflexionen zur Geschichte und Episteme eines altertumswissenschaftlichen Fachs im 150. Jahr der Zeitschrift für ägyptische Sprache und Altertumskunde*, eds., Susanne Bickel et al. (Berlin: De Gruyter, 2013), 267–98.
Voss, Susanne, 'Wissenshintergründe – die Ägyptologie als "völkische" Wissenschaft vom Ersten Weltkrieg bis zum 'Dritten Reich' am Beispiel des Nachlasses Georg Steindorffs', in *Georg Steindorff und die deutsche Ägyptologie im 20. Jahrhundert*, eds., Susanne Voss and Dietrich Raue (Berlin: De Gruyter, 2016), 105–332.

Voss, Susanne, '"J'accuse": Die sogenannte Steindorff-Liste von 1945, ihre historische Einordnung und deren Wert bei der Einschätzung der Urteile', in *Georg Steindorff und die deutsche Ägyptologie im 20. Jahrhundert*, eds., Susanne Voss and Dietrich Raue (Berlin: De Gruyter, 2016), 302–17.

Voss, Susanne, *Die Geschichte der Abteilung Kairo des DAI im Spannungsfeld deutscher politischer Interessen*, Vol. 2: *1929–1966*, (Rahden/Westf.: Marie Leidorf, 2017).

Voss, Susanne, 'Ein "österreichischer" Gelehrter im Dienst des deutschen Staates. Hermann Junkers Amtszeit als Direktor des DAI-Kairo im "Dritten Reich"', in *Hermann Junker – eine Spurensuche im Schatten der österreichischen Ägyptologie und Afrikanistik*, ed., Clemens Gütl, (Wien: Cuvillier, 2017), 131–79.

Voss, Susanne and Dietrich Raue eds., *Georg Steindorff und die deutsche Ägyptologie im 20. Jahrhundert* (Berlin: De Gruyter, 2016).

Winkler, Heinrich August, *Der lange Weg nach Westen. Deutsche Geschichte*, 2 volumes, second edition (Munich: Beck, 2020).

3
Toward a prosopography of archaeology from the margins
Thea De Armond

Introduction

'Pardon me for the liberty I take in addressing these lines to you, without having the honour of being known to you,' begins Gisela Weyde's first letter to the classicist Antonín Salač.[1] 'It seems that fate is involved – for I cannot manage without disturbing you—and, since one should not resist destiny, I am writing to bother you.'[2] If fate was involved in Weyde's correspondence with Salač, that fate was not favourable to her – or, rather, it proved so, only after her death. Fate was the fortuitous preservation of Weyde's correspondence with Salač in the latter's personal archive at the Academy of Science of the Czech Republic; fate was my unearthing of that correspondence, 90 years after it was written.

My research on Antonín Salač (1885–1960), a philologist, epigrapher and archaeologist in early twentieth-century Czechoslovakia, has been motivated by interests in margins, minor figures and untold stories. However, Salač is only 'marginal' vis-à-vis the geopolitical centre; during his lifetime, he stood at the centre of classical studies in Czechoslovakia. Stories like that of Weyde, whose correspondence with Salač might have inaugurated an illustrious archaeological career but did not: failures, false starts, dead ends, the stories of those at the margins of archaeological practice – *these* untold stories truly expand our histories of archaeology.

This chapter is a call for a prosopography of archaeology in the margins. I begin with a brief discussion of the status of biography among academic historians, considering the potential of microhistory, coupled with a diversification of our histories' narrative arcs, to expand our histories of archaeology. I follow with an account of the life of Gisela

Weyde, a figure whose biographical trajectory is ill-suited to most of our narratives about the history of archaeology – ill-suited because it is not a straightforward, ascending arc – though it nevertheless adds to our understanding of archaeology, by revealing its contours in the negative. Finally, I close with a reconsideration of the potential of microhistory – particularly, biographies of truly micro figures – to give much-needed depth to our histories of archaeology.

History and biography

Apologias for biography are practically de rigueur among scholars whose work might reasonably be characterised as biographical. In his introduction to a roundtable on biography in the *American Historical Review*, David Nasaw observes, 'Biography remains the [history] profession's unloved stepchild.'[3] Much of what makes biography popular with the lay public – its exaltation of 'great men', its predilections toward historical 'closeness' – render it suspect among historians.[4] Many 'biography-adjacent' scholars do not self-identify as biographers. Judith M. Brown, the author of works on Gandhi and Nehru (and a contributor to the aforementioned *American Historical Review* roundtable), describes herself 'not as a biographer but as a historian of a time and region…who uses the medium of "life histories" of individuals and groups of individuals to seek for evidence to probe many key historical issues'.[5]

Mark-Antoine Kaeser's unambiguously positive assessment of biography's standing ('Biography has now clearly achieved academic recognition and scientific legitimacy') is, thus, striking.[6] But the new wave of biographies in histories of science that Kaeser praises as inspiration for historians of archaeology 'definitely has nothing to do with a comeback of…simplistic and apologetic perspectives'.[7] Rather, these works use biography as a venue to explore broader historical questions. After all, scholarship – and scholars – are not insulated from society.[8] Therefore, histories of scholarship – and biographies of scholars – ought to be anchored in broader, social history.

For historians of archaeology like Kaeser, these wide-ranging, deeply contextual approaches to biography have a particular benefit. Not only do they militate against hagiography, they also expand the significance of histories of archaeology. '[I]t appears that the past of [archaeology] did not and still does not arouse much interest among professionals within Science studies,' Kaeser observes.[9] This is partly because histories of archaeology tend to be 'internalist', produced for and by archaeologists, and, concomitantly, narrowly presentist.[10] But the history of archaeology is not solely about archaeology; it brings together a whole host of intellectual, cultural, political and sociological currents.[11] This is Kaeser's biography as microhistory.

Microhistory and biography

The term 'biography' may be warily policed by historians, but the term 'microhistory' remains only loosely defined. For the most part, microhistorians are unified by the micro scale of their inquiries. According to Carlo Ginzburg and Carlo Poni's programmatic account of the genre, microhistory comprises the 'analysis, at extremely close range, of highly circumscribed phenomena – a village community, a group of families, even an individual person'.[12] How does a microhistorical analysis of an individual person differ from a biography? In part, in its deployment of life histories as windows upon the past or, as Jill Lepore writes, as 'allegor[ies] for broader issues affecting the culture as a whole'.[13] Microhistory is a narrative device, a starting point for a historical account that expands outward in both scope and signification. In addition, microhistorians, in contrast to traditional biographers, are often interested in 'micro people', rather than 'great men'. Carlo Ginzburg's *The Cheese and the Worms* centres on a miller Menocchio, who might have remained unknown but for his execution by the Inquisition; Robert Darnton's 'The Great Cat Massacre' analyses a very different witchcraft trial, a mock trial of cats by a printer's apprentices; Jill Lepore's *Book of Ages: The Life and Opinions of Jane Franklin* considers the life of Benjamin Franklin's little-known sister.[14]

Kaeser's biography as microhistory tends to be more micro in scale than in biographical subject. The central figure in Kaeser's *L'univers du préhistorien*, Édouard Desor – though 'an obscure figure in the history of biology' – was a professor and a politician.[15] He is sufficiently well known as to have had a street named after him (Edouard-Desor-Straße, in his birthplace Friedrichsdorf, Germany). Of course, Desor's privilege – his income, social standing and so on – relative to Menocchio, is simply the privilege of most scholars, relative to most peasants. Desor is micro ('an obscure figure') among scholars – and, indeed, scholars' eminence (and the standards whereby eminence is assessed are lofty) continues to dictate their worthiness of study. Mary Terrall acknowledges that, as she began her research on the Enlightenment polymath Pierre-Louis Moreau de Maupertuis, she wondered whether 'lesser lights…deserved that kind of attention'.[16] But Terrall's lesser light was only lesser vis-à-vis his contemporary Isaac Newton. Maupertuis was director of the French Academy of Sciences, president of the Prussian Academy of Sciences, and eponym of a physical principle. Similarly, my research on Antonín Salač – a lesser light in his milieu than Maupertuis in his own, but, nevertheless, a professor, deacon, prorector and founding member of the Czechoslovak Academy of Science – has been questioned on the basis of Salač's relative obscurity. 'Is Salač so great?' a colleague asked me recently.

Michael Polanyi cautions us that 'The example of great scientists is the light which guides all workers in science, but we must guard against being blinded by it.'[17] The lives of 'great scientists' can only show us so much about how science works, and they cannot be isolated from larger social and intellectual currents. Ironically, Polanyi's injunction prefaces and justifies an overmodest account of his contributions to the study of X-ray diffraction – Polanyi, a nominee for the Nobel Prize in Physics and a two-time nominee for the Nobel Prize in Chemistry, was a great scientist by most metrics. But if Desor, Salač and Polanyi remain questionable biographical subjects, nevertheless, there is nothing especially micro about them, not in the sense of Ginzburg's Menocchio.[18]

Narrative and biography

The problem is partly one of narrative. 'Does the world really present itself to perception in the form of well-made stories with central subjects, proper beginnings, middles, and ends, and a coherence that permits us to see "the end" in every beginning?' asks Hayden White.[19] This is not to say that narrative is artificial or unproductive (certainly, this is not White's conclusion); its ubiquity testifies to its utility. Nevertheless, coherent narratives – thematically unified narratives that proceed in a linear, chronological fashion – are often the province of the privileged. Matti Hyvärinen et al. write, '[…] the coherence paradigm privileges middle-class conventionality and marginalizes the experiences of artistically creative as well as politically traumatized people'.[20] Hyvärinen et al.'s *Beyond Narrative Coherence* is particularly interested in the value accorded to coherence in natural, oral narratives – in the speech of an aphasic man or the testimony of the survivor of a terrorist attack – but the above observation holds for our histories, too.[21] At a basic level, a full, narrative arc – a beginning, middle and end – demands primary source materials, materials that may be lacking for all but the most privileged. Thematic coherence, too – White's '"end" in every beginning' – is the stuff of *Bildungsroman*, or, perhaps, of a life with little in the way of rupture or displacement.

Our predisposition toward narrative coherence accounts for the fact that the central subjects in our histories of scholarship tend to be scholars, and that the hierarchy of values that dictates figures' worthiness of biography mostly plays out among scholars of varying eminence (that is, among the relatively privileged). On the one hand, this is fairly logical. Shouldn't scholars be the central subjects of our histories of scholarship? On the other hand, scholarly knowledge is not solely produced by scholars. What of those people labouring at the margins of scholarly production? What of those whose forays into scholarship were brief, abortive or tangential, but nonetheless vital to or at least broadly illustrative of the shape of a discipline?

History is not solely a matter of what happened. It is also a matter of what did not happen – of hypotheticals, precluded possibilities and roads not taken. Nor is history solely created at its centre, that is, by notables (if second-tier notables) like Édouard Desor and Antonín Salač. With this in mind, and with an imperative to tell novel stories of micro people, let us turn to the life of Gisela Weyde.

Gisela Weyde and Antonín Salač[22]

In February 1923, when she introduced herself to Antonín Salač (1885–1960), Gisela Weyde (1894–1984) was 28 years old.[23] She was born in Košice/Kaschau to Franz Weyde, an engineering professor at a local vocational school, and Genoveva, née Perolini.[24] Following Franz's death in 1902, Gisela and her mother moved to Bratislava/Pressburg, where Gisela attended elementary and secondary school. She spent the 1910s and early 1920s wandering through central European secondary and post-secondary institutions. In Budapest, Weyde studied fine arts and completed her secondary education (in that order).[25] In Munich, she studied archaeology and art history under the art historian Heinrich Wölfflin (1864–1945), his former student Paul Frankl (1878–1962), the classical archaeologist Paul Wolters (1858–1936) and the Egyptologist Friedrich Wilhelm von Bissing (1873–1956). In 1920, Weyde transferred to the University of Vienna, where she took classes with the art historian Max Dvořák (1874–1921) and the classical archaeologists Emanuel Löwy (1857–1938) and Emil Reisch (1863–1933).[26] It bears emphasising that Weyde's university education is practically a 'Who's Who' of archaeological and art historical (particularly, art historical) eminence – Wölfflin, Frankl and Dvořák are regarded as foundational figures in the development of art history; Reisch was the sometime-director of the Austrian Archaeological Institute at Athens (Österreichisches Archäologisches Institut Athen). In December 1921, Weyde successfully defended her doctoral dissertation, *Problems of Early Greek Vase-Painting* (*Probleme der frühgriechischen Vasen malerei*). Shortly thereafter, she returned to Bratislava.

In February 1923, when he received Weyde's letter, Antonín Salač was a docent at Charles University in Prague. He had spent the decade following the 1909 conferral of his doctorate (likewise, at Charles University) as a gymnasium professor in Bohemia. In 1920, shortly after his habilitation in classical philology (and shortly after the establishment of an independent Czechoslovak state), Salač travelled to Greece for the first time.[27] He spent more than a year and a half there, cultivating the connections – mostly with the French School at Athens (École française d'Athènes), of which he became a foreign member – that would facilitate his next project. That project brought Weyde to write to him.

'I am an archaeologist', Weyde introduced herself to Salač. 'A Czechoslovak citizen (from Bratislava)'.[28] Having heard via her former professor Emil Reisch that Salač planned to excavate the Sanctuary of the Great Gods on the Greek island Samothraki, Weyde sought to ascertain 'if I might join the excavations, which I ardently desire, believing myself to have a certain aptitude for this work.'[29] Before writing to Salač, Weyde had exhausted her connections. She'd contacted Salač's senior colleague at Charles University, the archaeologist Hynek Vysoký (1860–1935), as well as the director of the French School at Athens, Charles Picard (1883–1965). Both Vysoký and Picard had referred her to Salač.

Picard's letter to Weyde had been chiefly occupied with the possibility of Weyde's admission to the French School's Foreign Section. He was encouraging but cautious: 'I personally have no serious objection, in principle, to the admission of girls to our school.'[30] He encouraged Weyde to write to Salač for information about accommodation and the admissions process to the school. Weyde drafted an effusive response to Picard: 'You ask me if I would be prepared to participate in excavations, but I am prepared to sell my soul ~~to the devil~~ for the opportunity.'[31]

By contrast, Salač's letter to Weyde was discouraging. He wrote little of the French School (perhaps because Weyde's original request for information was somewhat unclear); instead, he wrote of Weyde's request to join his upcoming excavations: The Samothraki excavation was only 'a beginning, alas, a very modest beginning'.[32] Given the expedition's limited resources, it would not be possible for a woman to join it.

Salač added: '[Y]our imagination is deceived, I am sure of it; Life here is hard and even dangerous, particularly right now, after the war.'³³

Weyde's response of 12 February 1923 response to Salač's cautions is worth quoting at length: 'I am in no way a young girl dreaming of adventure – I am already 28 years old, have earned my living for many years, and have travelled around the world. I, too, know the difficulties of excavations because I have had many conversations about the topic with [Paul] Wolters [1858–1936], [Paul] Arndt [(1865–1937)], [Georg] Karo [(1872–1963)], [Camillo] Praschnicker [(1884–1949)] and others.'³⁴ She had similarly staved off Picard's concerns about the French School's lack of accommodation for young women with the declaration that – given her age and life experience – Weyde was practically 'an old bachelor'.³⁵ Nevertheless, to Salač, she acknowledged that 'there exist situations in which a woman might be out of place' (like Salač's 'modest beginning' on Samothraki) before irritably reiterating her request for information about the French School.³⁶ Weyde wrote: 'You do not say one word about what I asked you to communicate to me…concerning life and conditions at the French School at Athens, as well as the necessary steps to secure admission.'³⁷

If Salač and Weyde exchanged further correspondence about Samothraki or the French School, it is not extant. In April 1923, more than two months after Weyde had written her second letter to Salač, the French School director Charles Picard wrote to him, indicating that he understood Weyde to be interested in joining the school in the indefinite future (that is, not soon) and that, at any rate, the school was not presently equipped or authorised to admit women.³⁸ That indefinite future was less distant than Picard thought – according to Didier Viviers, during the 1922–1923 academic year, the Dutch government nominated Weyde for admission to the school as a foreign member.³⁹ However, the French School would not admit its first female foreign member – a 'Mademoiselle' Van Leeuwen-Boomkamp – until December 1926.⁴⁰ The school's first female French member was admitted nearly 30 years later. In this respect, the French School lagged significantly behind Athens' other foreign archaeological institutes – Annie Smith Peck enrolled at the American School of Classical Studies in 1885; the British School at Athens began to admit women five years later; and Margarete Bieber became a member of the German Archaeological Institute in 1912.

This is the extent of Weyde's intersection with Salač – an unsuccessful attempt to join his first archaeological expedition to the Sanctuary of the Great Gods and an (as best as we can tell) unanswered request for information about the French School at Athens. These failures mark the point at which Weyde's story diverges from that of Salač – or nearly. Salač's review of his colleague Alois Gotsmich's 1930 *Studies of the Oldest Greek Art* (*Studien zur ältesten griechischen Kunst*) cites Weyde's 1926 *Problems of Greek Geometric Style* (*Probleme der griechischen geometrischen stils*).⁴¹

These failures also mark the point at which Weyde's narrative arc shifts. Weyde had been trained as an art historian and archaeologist by some of central Europe's best known university professors. It is tempting to imagine that, given these promising beginnings, she might have embarked upon an illustrious career as a classical archaeologist – as a Slovak Margarete Bieber or Hetty Goldman – had Salač or the French School supported her attempts to join an excavation. But we should remember the fate that has brought Weyde's correspondence with Salač to our notice. That we know about Weyde's attempts to join the French School is due to the scope of her efforts (at least three different archives in three different countries contain traces of those efforts), as well as historical and historiographical contingency: the fact that I located Weyde's correspondence with Salač among the latter's vast, unprocessed archive (more than forty metres of miscellany), and that, serendipitously, it spoke to me.⁴² Accordingly, we might extrapolate this counterfactual – that is, what if Weyde had managed to join an archaeological excavation? – more broadly: a host of unknown women, as well as other marginalised people, have been and continue to be summarily excluded from archaeological excavations. What might our histories of archaeology look like, if we were willing to populate them with these people, as well as 'success stories'? What might we glean from a prosopography of failed applicants to archaeological excavations?

Gisela Weyde in Bratislava

Gisela Weyde recalled the early 1920s as presenting her with two possibilities.⁴³ The first possibility was that she, supported by a stipend from the Italian government, join an archaeological expedition.⁴⁴ Weyde's second possibility was that she accept a position with Bratislava's Beautification Society (Okrášlovací spolok), which was tasked with the curation and management of the city's museum. Weyde had been offered the position on the strength of independent research she had conducted in the city archives of Bratislava.⁴⁵ In 1922 – less than a year after the conferral of her doctorate and several months before she introduced herself to Salač – Weyde published the fruits of that research, a study of Bratislava's Baroque Church and Convent of St. Elisabeth.

Weyde's hopes of joining an archaeological expedition must have been disappointed, though not stymied, by her failure to secure support from Salač or the French School. But it was '[b]ecause of my mother', not for lack of support (after all, she had secured support from the Italian government), that Weyde chose to remain in Bratislava.[46] She accepted a fixed-term position as a curator with the City Museum of Bratislava (Múzeum mesta Bratislavy). There, she applied herself to a whole cohort of little-acknowledged curatorial duties – accession, classification, exhibition – work that Mária Orišková has characterised as an extension of women's housework – practical, hidden, detail-oriented.[47] Weyde was likely responsible for the first catalogue of the museum's collections, as well as a booklet about the museum's first exhibition.[48]

Had she joined an archaeological excavation, Weyde would have been relegated to 'archaeological housework', too.[49] Given her fine arts education, she had assumed that she would be tasked with the excavation's drawing; this work rarely – if ever – earns its practitioner a place in archaeology's canon of saints.[50] Many women tasked with archaeological housework in archaeology's early years have been disregarded or forgotten; sometimes, their work has been co-opted. The case of Mary Ross Ellingson (1906–1993), whose work at Olynthos (a study of its figurines) was published by her mentor David Robinson under his own name, is notorious.[51] But there are other, less well-known and more routine cases, like that of Libuše Jansová (1904–1996), an eminent prehistorian who, as a student, illustrated a catalogue of Thasian amphora stamps for Salač; this work was remunerated but not otherwise acknowledged.[52] Consider, likewise, Madeleine Charléty and Yvonne Dupuy, who appear to have assisted several French School projects as architects and illustrators but about whom we can otherwise say relatively little.[53] Indeed, consider those women admitted to the French School as foreign members, shortly after Weyde's rejection: Van Leeuwen-Boomkamp, A. Wentzel, Ch. Brøndsted, Anna Roes(-Vollgraff) and Emilie Haspels, of whom only Roes and Haspels appear to have published under their own names.[54] Weyde herself executed drawings for Camillo Praschniker's oft-cited 1928 *Parthenon Studies* (*Parthenonstudien*), but, except in reviews of the publication, she is rarely identified as one of its illustrators.

During her tenure at Bratislava's City Museum, Weyde published dozens of scholarly articles. Her *Problems of Greek Geometric Style*, which derived from her doctoral dissertation, was an exception in this oeuvre. The vast majority of Weyde's publications were occupied with central

European, rather than classical, art history. After all, Bratislava had little to offer the classical archaeologist, but it had a great deal to offer the Baroque art historian. Moreover, Baroque art history was far less rarefied – and, so, more accessible – than classical archaeology. Weyde, with her Vienna School art historical education, was well-equipped to apply herself to the study of a wide range of times and places. 'My love of the beauties of the old town [of Bratislava] grew with my interest', she wrote.[55]

Gisela Weyde in Halle

In 1928, Gisela Weyde asked for a permanent position at the Bratislava City Museum. Her manifold national and ethnic affiliations had stood her in good stead when it came to classical archaeology: Weyde's mother Genoveva hailed from Romandy ('being French on my mother's side', wrote Weyde, she had thought she might apply to the French School at Athens) but was of Italian origin (hence, presumably, the stipend from the Italian government).[56] Weyde's surname likely accounts for the Dutch government's support of her admission to the French School. But Weyde – despite deep roots in Bratislava (her father's family had settled in Bratislava 250 years before she was born) – was not 'Slovak' or 'Czechoslovak' enough for the new state of Czechoslovakia.[57] Habsburg Pressburg, Bratislava's predecessor, had been a majority German city. German, Hungarian and Italian were more familiar to Weyde than Slovak (to say nothing of Czech).[58] But Czechoslovak nation- and statehood had deep roots in linguistic nationalism – that is, in the Czech and Slovak languages.[59] Weyde's successor at the Bratislava museum, Alžbeta Günther-Mayer (1905–1973), likewise, a long-time resident of Bratislava, wrote of Czechoslovak Bratislava's stance toward Pressburg's multilingualism: 'Trilingualism [German, Hungarian, and Slovak] became fatal to the city, for it was politically abused…[It] became a dangerous divider and the germ of blind hatred.'[60] Thus, Weyde – who had written to Salač in French because she was not fluent in Czech or Slovak – was not granted a permanent position at the museum.

On the advice of her former professors in Munich, Weyde travelled to Halle for a course in restoration. She never returned to Bratislava (her mother joined her in Halle). In 1929, Weyde married Fritz Leweke, likewise an artist and conservator ('our shared professional interests have contributed to our happy, harmonious, 40-year marriage') with whom she had two children.[61] Leweke-Weyde spent the rest of her life in Halle, working as a freelance artist and conservator. She continued to publish scholarly works in Halle and, following her teacher Max Dvořák's 1916 *Catechism of Preservation* (*Katechismus der Denkmalpflege*), to intervene in discussions of the restoration of Bratislava.[62] She died in 1984.

Toward a prosopography of archaeology from the margins

Gisela Weyde's biography is part of the history of classical archaeology, but chiefly as a narrative of failure – at least, failure in traditional, biographical terms. Such failures should not be consigned to the ash heap of history: rather, they should push us to reconsider the arc of our disciplinary histories, particularly, the inequities that have shaped them. Continuous, factual narratives elide unfulfilled possibilities, failed attempts and figures like Weyde. Without these, our histories of archaeology inevitably become prosopographies of the privileged, as well as occasional 'pioneers'. By writing about figures who did not attain an intellectual or academic apotheosis (whatever that may have meant in their time) or, indeed, figures who never sought to become 'professional' scholars, we expand our understanding of how archaeological practice works. After all, the policing of archaeology's boundaries shapes archaeology as much as its internal developments do.

Weyde's story is that of a woman, who, despite the advantages of education and audacity, was consigned to the margins of archaeology. She never became a field archaeologist. She never secured a permanent museum appointment. At the same time, she is relatively rare among the figures whose lives share her narrative arc – one of 'failure' or discontinuity – not just because of her impressive credentials but because she has been the object of some interest among Slovak art historians.[63] Indeed – further testament to her significance – Weyde has a relatively extensive personal archive, housed in Dresden (although that archive is not referenced in any of the aforementioned publications about Weyde). Thus, in many respects, Weyde is only a bit more micro than is Salač. Of course, given that Salač's valorisation through biography is still contestable, even that incremental reduction in status between Salač and Weyde is significant.

Ginzburg and Poni advocate a 'prosopography from below', analogous to E. P. Thompson's 'history from below', a genre combining qualitative and quantitative strains of prosopography.[64] Accordingly, the preceding account of Weyde's life and career is an injunction to produce more – and more micro – case studies, to flesh out a prosopography of archaeology from below. Such studies are imperative in histories of archaeology, particularly given archaeology's cross-cutting of social and economic strata. The average 'academic' archaeological expedition employs dozens of people whose paths might not otherwise intersect – for example, professors, students, agricultural labourers – whose tenures as archaeologists might last a summer or a lifetime. Weyde, as I have already indicated, possessed many of the distinctions valorised by historians of archaeology. What of the other figures whose lives – if only briefly – intersect with and facilitate archaeologists' work? What of students, diggers, museum workers and government officials? What of the support staff – guides, cooks, security guards – who make archaeology possible? That their stories are missing from most histories of archaeology is not simply a regrettable accident. It is, in part, a product of archaeology's long-held ties with imperialism and colonialism; the archaeologist is figured as an intrepid explorer, for whom local officials and workers are mere annoyances. Even in non-imperialist, non-colonial contexts, archaeologists-cum-scholars tend to be relatively privileged, certainly vis-à-vis the historically marginalised, archaeologically adjacent.[65]

Weyde's story ceases to be 'about' classical archaeology – except inasmuch as classical archaeology remains a road not taken – relatively early in her lifetime. In the case of some of the archaeological workers mentioned above, archaeology's tenure as preeminent biographical current might be still briefer. But scholarship need not be the driving force of a life for that life to shape scholarship. Weyde's sketches of the Parthenon contributed to classical archaeology's knowledge about the Parthenon, even though Weyde did not devote her life to classical archaeology.

Moreover, microhistory hardly necessitates cradle-to-grave biography. Quite the opposite – microhistory allows for (and, indeed, calls for) novel narrative arcs. The above cradle-to-grave biography of Weyde might be easily broken down into a series of more micro narratives. I might have solely related Weyde's attempts to join a classical archaeological excavation, attempts that suggest a great deal about the geopolitics and gender politics underpinning classical archaeology. That these were abortive attempts – that Weyde failed – also tells us a great deal about classical archaeology, a discipline that has long defined itself by its exclusivity. Similarly, we might learn a great deal from a fine-grained account of a student or an agricultural labourer's single season with an archaeological excavation; so, too, do we learn a great deal from their persistent absence from archaeology's accounts of itself.

The erasure of students, diggers and so on from our histories of archaeology reflects and perpetuates their marginalisation, both in the past and today. Consider the paradoxical status of fieldwork in archaeology, a *sine qua non* for 'legitimate' archaeologists, but, in practice, laboured at by 'non-professionals' – students or agricultural labourers – or poorly remunerated cultural resource management specialists. Both groups (the non-professional and the professional) are, not coincidentally, excluded from most of our histories of archaeology. But 'materiality' is at the centre of archaeology's self-conceptualisation. How can we exclude those people at the forefront of archaeology's confrontation with the material from our narratives about archaeology?

Like Kaeser, I welcome the advent of biography as microhistory in our histories of archaeology. I likewise hope that, inspired by microhistory, we might broaden our notions of the sorts of narratives that shape archaeology. These fuller, more diverse narratives – diverse in their arcs and in their main players – give depth to our accounts of the shape of archaeology and of archaeological practice. If fate brought Weyde to write to Salač, that fate dictated that she not be forgotten.

Notes

1. This chapter is dedicated to my father M. Keith De Armond. Thanks to Anja Krieger for her assistance securing German archival materials and to Peter Pavúk for correcting my Slovak. Thanks to Mark Pyzyk, Gabriel Moshenka and Clare Lewis for comments on drafts. All errors are mine.
2. 'Pardonnez moi la liberté que je prends en vous adressant ces lignes sans avoir l'honneur d'être connue de vous. Il semble que le sort s'en mêle—car je ne puis me débrouiller sans vous importuner—et comme il ne faut pas résister à la déstinée je viens vous embêter.'
Masaryk Institute and Archives of the Academy of Sciences of the Czech Republic, Prague (hereafter, MÚA AV ČR), Antonín Salač, inventory no. 410, box no. 6, letter from Gisèle (Gisela/Gizela) (Leweke-)Weyde to Antonín Salač, 3 Feb. 1923.
3. David Nasaw, 'Introduction to *AHR Roundtable*: Historians and biography', *American Historical Review* 114 (2009): 573.
4. See Mark Salber Phillips, 'Distance and historical representation', *History Workshop Journal* 57 (2004): 123–41 for a thoughtful discussion of distance in historical writing.
5. Judith M. Brown, 'Life histories and the history of modern South Asia', *American Historical Review* 114 (2009): 587.
6. Marc-Antoine Kaeser, 'Biography, science studies and the historiography of archaeological research: managing personal archives', *Complutum* 24 (2013): 102.
7. Kaeser, 'Biography', 102.
8. See Steven Shapin, 'Placing the view from nowhere: historical and sociological problems in the location of science', *Transaction of the Institute of British Geographers* 23 (1998): 1–8.
9. Marc-Antoine Kaeser, 'Biography as microhistory: the relevance of private archives for writing the history of archaeology', in *Archives, Ancestors, Practices: Archaeology in the light of its history*, eds., Nathan Schlanger and Jarl Nordbladh (New York: Berghahn Books, 2008), 11.
10. See Kaeser, 'Biography as microhistory', 10–11.
11. Kaeser, 'Biography as microhistory', 12.

12 Carlo Ginzburg and Carlo Poni, 'The name and the game: Unequal exchange and the historical marketplace', in *Microhistory and the Lost Peoples of Europe*, eds. Edward Muir and Guido Ruggiero, trans. Eren Branch (Baltimore: Johns Hopkins University Press, 1991), 3.
13 Jill Lepore, 'Historians who love too much: reflections on microhistory and biography', *Journal of American History* 88 (2001): 133.
14 Carlo Ginzburg, *The Cheese and the Worms*, trans. John Tedeschi and Anne C. Tedeschi (Baltimore: Johns Hopkins University Press, 1992); Robert Darnton, 'The great cat massacre', in *The Great Cat Massacre and Other Episodes in French Cultural History* (New York: Basic Books, 1984), 75–106; Jill Lepore, *Book of Ages: The life and opinions of Jane Franklin* (New York: Alfred A. Knopf, 2013).
15 Marc-Antoine Kaeser, *L'univers du préhistorien. Science, foi et politique dans l'œuvre et la vie d'Édouard Desor (1811–1882)* (Paris: L'Harmattan, 2004); Michael Chazan, 'Review of L'univers du préhistorien. Science, foi et politique dans l'œuvre et la vie d'Édouard Desor (1811–1882)', by Marc-Antoine Kaeser', *Isis* 97 (2006): 365.
16 Mary Terrall, 'Biography as cultural history of science', *Isis* 97 (2006): 308.
17 Michael Polanyi, 'My time with X-rays and crystals', in *Fifty Years of X-Ray Diffraction*, ed. Paul Peter Ewald (Utrecht: A. Oosthoek, 1962), 629–36.
18 Though each (particularly, Polanyi) has been given the biographical treatment.
19 Hayden White, 'The value of narrativity in the representation of reality', *Critical Inquiry* 7 (1980): 27.
20 Matti Hyvärinen et al., 'Beyond narrative coherence: an introduction', in *Beyond Narrative Coherence*, eds. Matti Hyvärinen et al. (Philadelphia: John Benjamins Publishing Company, 2010), 2.
21 See Tarja Aaltonen, '"Mind-reading", a method for understanding the broken narrative of an aphasic man', in *Beyond Narrative Coherence*, eds., Matti Hyvärinen et al. (Philadelphia: John Benjamins Publishing Company, 2010), 49–66; Alison Stern Perez, Yishai Tobin, and Shifa Sagy, '"There is no fear in my lexicon" vs. "You are not normal if you won't be scared": A qualitative semiotic analysis of the "broken" discourse of Israeli bus drivers who experienced terror attacks', in *Beyond Narrative Coherence*, eds., Matti Hyvärinen et al. (Philadelphia: John Benjamins Publishing Company, 2010), 121–46.
22 Weyde's personal archive at the State and University Library in Dresden, as well as Antonín Salač's personal archive at the Academy of Science of the Czech Republic in Prague, were key sources for this study. *100 Rokov Mestského Múzea v Bratislave, 1868–1968*, which celebrates the centennial of the Bratislava City Museum, where Weyde worked as a curator, includes Weyde's reminiscences; it was likewise an important source for this study.
23 'Gisela' is also written as 'Gizela' (in Slovak-language materials) and 'Gisèle' (in French-language materials). I use 'Gisela' because it is the spelling Weyde used for most of her publications (likely, because those publications were in German).
24 See State and University Library, Dresden (Staats- und Universitätsbibliothek Dresden; hereafter, SLUB), Mscr.Dresd.App. 2482, 1, curriculum vitae by Gisela (Gizela/Gisèle) Leweke-Weyde, undated.
MÚA AV ČR, Antonín Salač, inventory no. 410, box no. 6, letter from Gisèle (Gisela/Gizela) (Leweke-)Weyde to Antonín Salač, 3 Feb. 1923.
25 Weyde attended the first six grades of secondary school in Bratislava. She completed the final two grades of secondary school (which qualified her for university study) in Budapest, following (and perhaps even during) her tenure at Budapest's art academy.
26 See SLUB, Mscr.Dresd.App. 2482, 1, curriculum vitae by Gisela (Gizela/Gisèle) Leweke-Weyde, undated.
27 See Thea De Armond, 'A romance and a tragedy: Antonín Salač and the French School at Athens', in *Communities and Knowledge Production in Archaeology*, eds., Julia Roberts, et al. (Manchester: Manchester University Press, 2020), 88–108; Idem., '"One thousand pieces of eyes": A few notes on Antonín Salač's 1920–1921 trip to Greece', *Eirene* LIV (2018): 169–91.
28 'Je suis archéologue, citoyenne Tchécoslovaque (de Bratislava)'.
MÚA AV ČR, Antonín Salač, inventory no. 410, box no. 6, letter from Gisèle (Gisela/Gizela) (Leweke-)Weyde to Antonín Salač, 3 Feb. 1923.
29 'si je ne pouvais pas participer aux travaux de fouilles, ce que je désire ardemment, croyant avoir quelques aptitudes pour ces travaux.'
MÚA AV ČR, Antonín Salač, inventory no. 410, box no. 6, letter from Gisèle (Gisela/Gizela) (Leweke-)Weyde to Antonín Salač, 3 Feb. 1923.

Salač had written to Reisch to ensure that the Austrian Archaeological Institute, which had led excavations on Samothraki at the turn of the century, was not planning future excavations on the site.
MÚA AV ČR, Antonín Salač, inventory no. 410, box no. 14, draft of letter from the State Archaeological Institute (written by Antonín Salač) to the Ministry of Ecclesiastical Affairs and Education in Athens, undated.
Reisch's response to Salač is at the Institute of Classical Archaeology at Charles University.

30 'Je n'ai personnellement aucune objection grave, de principe, contre l'admission des jeunes filles à notre École.'
SLUB, Mscr.Dresd.App. 2482, 55, letter from Charles Picard to Gisèle (Gisela/Gizela) (Leweke-)Weyde, 10/23 January 1923.

31 'Vous me demandez, Monsieur, si je serais disposée à participer à des travaux de fouilles, mais je suis prête à vendre mon âme au diable pour avoir cette possibilité-là.'
The crossing-out is in the original.
SLUB, Mscr.Dresd.App. 2482, 54, draft of letter from Gisèle (Gisela/Gizela) (Leweke-)Weyde to Charles Picard, undated.

32 'un début, hélas, un très modeste début'.
MÚA AV ČR, Antonín Salač, inventory no. 410, box no. 14. Draft of letter from Antonín Salač to Gisèle (Gisela/Gizela) (Leweke-)Weyde, undated.
Judging by Weyde's 12 Feb. 1923 letter to Salač, this draft is at least broadly consonant with the letter Salač sent to Weyde.

33 'Enfin, votre imagination serait déçue, j'en suis sûr; la vie y est dure et même dangereuse, surtout maintenant, après la guerre'.
MÚA AV ČR, Antonín Salač, inventory no. 410, box no. 14. Draft of letter from Antonín Salač to Gisèle (Gisela/Gizela) (Leweke-)Weyde, undated.

34 'Je ne suis nullement une jeune fille qui rêve à l'aventure, ayant déjà 28 ans, gagnant ma vie depuis bien des années et ayant beaucoup voyagé de par le monde. Je connais aussi très bien les désagréments des fouilles, car j'en ai beaucoup parlé avec MM. Wolters, Arndt, Karo, Praschniker et d'autres.'
MÚA AV ČR, Antonín Salač, inventory no. 410, box no. 6, letter from Gisèle (Gisela/Gizela) (Leweke-)Weyde to Antonín Salač, 12 Feb. 1923.

35 'un vieux garcon'.
SLUB, Mscr.Dresd.App. 2482, 54, draft of letter from Gisèle (Gisela/Gizela) (Leweke-)Weyde to Charles Picard, undated.

36 'il aie des cas où une femme n'est pas à sa place'.
MÚA AV ČR, Antonín Salač, inventory no. 410, box no. 6, letter from Gisèle (Gisela/Gizela) (Leweke-)Weyde to Antonín Salač, 12 Feb. 1923.

37 'vous ne me dites pas un mot de ce que je vous priais de me communiquer…sur la vie et les circonstances de l'École française d'Athènes ainsi que sur les démarches nécessaires à faire pour obtenir l'admission'.
MÚA AV ČR, Antonín Salač, inventory no. 410, box no. 6, letter from Gisèle (Gisela/Gizela) (Leweke-)Weyde to Antonín Salač, 12 Feb. 1923.

38 MÚA AV ČR, Antonín Salač, inventory no. 410, box no. 36, letter from Charles Picard to Antonín Salač, 26 Apr. 1923.

39 Didier Viviers, 'Un enjeu de politique scientifique: La Section étrangère de l'École française d'Athènes', *Bulletin de correspondance hellénique* 120 (1996): 182.

40 Viviers, 'Un enjeu', 182.

41 Antonín Salač, 'Review of *Studien zur ältesten griechischen Kunst* by Alois Gotsmich', *Listy filologické* 57 (1930): 444–6.

42 These archives include that of Salač in Prague, that of Weyde in Dresden, as well as the French National Archives in Paris, which were consulted by Viviers for 'Un enjeu'.

43 Gizela Leweke-Weyde, 'Spomienky bývalých pracovníkov', in *100 rokov Mestského múzea v Bratislave, 1868–1968*, ed. Mestské múzeum v Bratislave (Bratislava: OBZOR, 1968), 300.

44 The Italian government awarded Weyde a grant to support archaeological and art historical studies at the University of Rome. While there, she presumably hoped to join an archaeological expedition.
SLUB, Mscr.Dresd.App. 2482, 63, letter from the Italian diplomatic mission to Prague to Ghisela (Gisela/Gizela/Gisèle) (Leweke-)Weyde, 4 Apr. 1924.

45 Ingrid Ciulisová, 'Spomienka na Gizelu Weyde (6.8.1894 - ca. 1974)', *ARS: Časopis Ústavu dejín umenia Slovenskej akadémie vied* 38 (2005): 67.
46 'Kvôli matke'.
    Leweke-Weyde, 'Spomienky', 300.
47 Mária Orišková, 'Naše staršie sestry: kustódky a kurátorky na Slovensku v prvej polovici 20. storočia', in *Artemis a Dr. Faust, Ženy v českých a slovenských dějinách umění*, eds. Milena Bartlová and Martina Pachmanová (Prague: Akademie, 2008), 54–5.
48 Ciulisová, 'Spomienka', 68.
49 Joan Gero, 'Socio-politics and the woman-at-home ideology', *American Antiquity* 50 (1985): 344.
    For Gero, 'archaeological housework' is, for the most part, non-field research. However, even in the field, the task of documentation has more in common with the stereotyped female archaeologist, ordering and systematizing in the lab, than with the stereotype of 'the practicing [male] field archaeologist who himself conquers the landscape, brings home the goodies, and takes his data raw!' (Gero, 'Socio-Politics', 345).
50 Leweke-Weyde, 'Spomienky', 300.
51 See Alan Kaiser, *Archaeology, Sexism, and Scandal: The long-suppressed story of one woman's discoveries and the man who stole credit for them* (New York: Rowman & Littlefield, 2014).
52 See MÚA AV ČR, Antonín Salač, inventory no. 410, box no. 6, letter from Charles Picard to Antonín Salač, 23 Oct. 1922; MÚA AV ČR, Antonín Salač, inventory no. 410, box no. 6, letter from Charles Picard to Antonín Salač, 26 Apr. 1923.
    The catalogue of amphora stamps, which is housed in the archive of the French School at Athens, remains unpublished. The French School's archives list Salač as its sole author.
53 Marie-Christine Hellmann, 'Les architectes de l'École française d'Athènes', *Bulletin de correspondance hellénique* 120 (1996): 208–9.
54 See Viviers, 'Un enjeu', 182.
55 'Sa záujmom rástla aj moja láska ku krásam Starého mesta.'
    Leweke-Weyde, 'Spomienky', 301.
56 'étant française par ma mère'.
    MÚA AV ČR, Antonín Salač, inventory no. 410, box no. 6, letter from Gisèle (Gisela/Gizela) (Leweke-)Weyde to Antonín Salač, 3 Feb. 1923.
57 Leweke-Weyde, 'Spomienky', 299.
58 Ciulisová, 'Spomienka', 68.
59 See, for example, Vladimír Macura, *Znamení zrodu: české obrození jako kulturní typ* (Prague: Československý spisovatel, 1983); Hugh L. Agnew, *Origins of the Czech National Renascence* (Pittsburgh: University of Pittsburgh Press, 1993); Tara Zahra, 'Reclaiming children for the nation: Germanization, national ascription, and democracy in the Bohemian Lands, 1900–1945', *Central European History* 37 (2004): 501–43.
    The separateness of the two languages continues to be a subject of debate.
60 'Trojjazyčnost' sa však stala osudovou pre mesto len čo bola politicky zneužitá a…sa stala nebezpečným delidlom zárodkom zaslepenej nenávisti'.
    Alžbeta Güntherová-Mayerová, 'Spomienky bývalých pracovníkov', in *100 rokov Mestského múzea v Bratislave, 1868–1968*, ed. Mestské múzeum v Bratislave (Bratislava: OBZOR, 1968), 307.
61 'spoločné záujmy povolania prispeli k tomu, že naše manželstvo je takmer 40 rokov šťastné a harmonické.'
    Leweke-Weyde, 'Spomienky', 301.
    The preponderance of woman scholars married to other scholars – if married at all – merits remark. Consider the first university-educated Czech woman art historians, Alžbeta Birnbaumová (née Šourková) and Hana Volavková (née Frankensteinová), both of whom have been overshadowed by their husbands, Vojtěch Birnbaum and Vojtěch Volavka.
    See Milena Bartlová and Martina Pachmanová, 'Ženy v českých a slovenských dějinách umění', in *Artemis a Dr. Faust, Ženy v českých a slovenských dějinách umění*, eds. Milena Bartlová and Martina Pachmanová (Praha: Akademie, 2008), 18.
62 See Jan Bakoš, 'A corrupt past: The case of Bratislava Castle', *RIHA Journal* 0141 (15 Oct. 2016): n.p.; Ingrid Ciulisová, 'Gizela Weyde a ochrana bratislavských pamiatok', *Pamiatky a múzeá* 1 (1994): 30–1.
63 See Bartlová and Pachmanová, 'Ženy'; Orišková, 'Naše staršie sestry'; Ingrid Ciulisová, 'Lesk a bieda slovenskej kunsthistórie I. (Slovenský dejepis umenia 1918–1938)', *ARS: Časopis Ústavu*

dejín umenia Slovenskej akadémie vied 1 (1993): 66–68; *Idem.*, 'Gizela Weyde'; *Idem.*, 'Spomienka'.
64 Ginzburg and Poni, 'Name', 7.
65 For the archaeologically adjacent in imperialist contexts, see, e.g., Stephen Quirke, *Hidden Hands: Egyptian Workforces in Petrie Excavation Archives* (London: Duckworth, 2010); Wendy Doyon, 'The History of Archaeology through the Eyes of Egyptians', in *Unmasking Ideology in Imperialist and Colonialist Archaeology: Vocabulary, Symbols, and Legacy* (Los Angeles: UCLA Cotsen Institute of Archaeology Press, 2018), 173–200.

Bibliography

Aaltonen, Tarja, '"Mind-reading": a method for understanding the broken narrative of an aphasic man', in *Beyond Narrative Coherence*, eds., Matti Hyvärinen, Lars-Christer Hydén, Marjo Saarenheimo, and Maria Tambouko (Philadelphia: John Benjamins Publishing Company, 2010), 49–66.
Agnew, Hugh L., *Origins of the Czech National Renascence* (Pittsburgh: University of Pittsburgh Press, 1993).
Bakoš, Jan, 'A corrupt past: The case of Bratislava Castle', *RIHA Journal* 0141 (2016): n.p.
Bartlová, Milena and Martina Pachmanová, 'Ženy v českých a slovenských dějinách umění', in *Artemis a Dr. Faust, Ženy v českých a slovenských dějinách umění*, eds., Milena Bartlová and Martina Pachmanová (Praha: Akademie, 2008), 13–27.
Brown, Judith M., 'Life histories and the history of modern South Asia', *American Historical Review* 114 (2009): 587–95.
Chazan, Michael, 'Review of *L'univers du préhistorien. Science, foi et politique dans l'œuvre et la vie d'Édouard Desor (1811–1882)*, by Marc-Antoine Kaeser', *Isis* 97 (2006): 365.
Ciulisová, Ingrid, 'Spomienka na Gizelu Weyde (6.8.1894 - ca. 1974)', *ARS: Časopis Ústavu dejín umenia Slovenskej akadémie vied* 38 (2005): 67–9.
Ciulisová, Ingrid, 'Gizela Weyde a ochrana bratislavských pamiatok', *Pamiatky a múzeá* 1 (1994): 30–1.
Ciulisová, Ingrid, 'Lesk a bieda slovenskej kunsthistórie I. (Slovenský dejepis umenia 1918-1938)', *ARS: Časopis Ústavu dejín umenia Slovenskej akadémie vied* 1 (1993): 66–75.
Darnton, Robert, 'The great cat massacre', in *The Great Cat Massacre and Other Episodes in French Cultural History* (New York: Basic Books, 1984), 75–106.
De Armond, Thea, 'A romance and a tragedy: Antonín Salač and the French School at Athens', in *Communities and Knowledge Production in Archaeology*, eds., Julia Roberts, Kathleen Sheppard, Ulf R. Hansson, and Jonathan Trigg (Manchester: Manchester University Press, 2020), 88–108.
De Armond, Thea, '"One thousand pieces of eyes": A few notes on Antonín Salač's 1920–1921 trip to Greece', *Eirene* LIV (2018): 169–91.
Doyon, Wendy, 'The history of archaeology through the eyes of Egyptians', in *Unmasking Ideology in Imperialist and Colonialist Archaeology: Vocabulary, symbols, and legacy* (Los Angeles: UCLA Cotsen Institute of Archaeology Press, 2018), 173–200.
Gero, Joan, 'Socio-politics and the woman-at-home ideology', *American Antiquity* 50 (1985): 342–50.
Ginzburg, Carlo, *The Cheese and the Worms*, trans. John Tedeschi and Anne C. Tedeschi (Baltimore: Johns Hopkins University Press, 1992).
Ginzburg, Carlo and Carlo Poni, 'The name and the game: Unequal exchange and the historical marketplace', in *Microhistory and the Lost Peoples of Europe*, eds., Edward Muir and Guido Ruggiero, trans. Eren Branch (Baltimore: Johns Hopkins University Press, 1991), 1–10.
Güntherová-Mayerová, Alžbeta, 'Spomienky bývalých pracovníkov', in *100 rokov Mestského múzea v Bratislave, 1868–1968*, ed., Mestské múzeum v Bratislave (Bratislava: OBZOR, 1968), 299–319.
Hellmann, Marie-Christine, 'Les architectes de l'École française d'Athènes', *Bulletin de corrrespondance hellénique* 120 (1996): 208–9.
Hyvärinen, Matti, Lars-Christer Hydén, Marjo Saarenheimo, and Maria Tambouko, 'Beyond narrative coherence: an introduction', in *Beyond Narrative Coherence*, eds., Matti Hyvärinen,

Lars-Christer Hydén, Marjo Saarenheimo, and Maria Tambouko (Philadelphia: John Benjamins Publishing Company, 2010), 1–15.

Kaeser, Marc-Antoine, 'Biography, science studies and the historiography of archaeological research: managing personal archives', *Complutum* 24 (2013): 101–8.

Kaeser, Marc-Antoine, 'Biography as microhistory: the relevance of private archives for writing the history of archaeology', in *Archives, Ancestors, Practices: Archaeology in the light of its history*, eds., Nathan Schlanger and Jarl Nordbladh (New York: Berghahn Books, 2008), 9–20.

Kaeser, Marc-Antoine, *L'univers du préhistorien. Science, foi et politique dans l'oeuvre et la vie d'Édouard Desor (1811–1882)* (Paris: L'Harmattan, 2004).

Kaiser, Alan, *Archaeology, Sexism, and Scandal: The long-suppressed story of one woman's discoveries and the man who stole credit for them* (New York: Rowman & Littlefield, 2014).

Lepore, Jill, *Book of Ages: The life and opinions of Jane Franklin* (New York: Alfred A. Knopf, 2013).

Lepore, Jill, 'Historians who love too much: Reflections on microhistory and biography', *Journal of American History* 88 (2001): 129–44.

Leweke-Weyde, Gizela, 'Spomienky bývalých pracovníkov', in *100 rokov Mestského múzea v Bratislave, 1868–1968*, ed., Mestské múzeum v Bratislave (Bratislava: OBZOR, 1968), 299–301.

Macura, Vladimír, *Znamení zrodu: české obrození jako kulturní typ* (Prague: Československý spisovatel, 1983).

Nasaw, David, 'Introduction to *AHR Roundtable*: Historians and biography', *American Historical Review* 114 (2009): 573–8.

Orišková, Mária, 'Naše staršie sestry: kustódky a kurátorky na Slovensku v prvej polovici 20. Storočia', in *Artemis a Dr. Faust, Ženy v českých a slovenských dějinách umění*, eds., Milena Bartlová and Martina Pachmanová (Prague: Akademie, 2008), 48–60.

Perez, Alison Stern, Yishai Tobin, and Shifa Sagy, '"There is no fear in my lexicon" vs. "You are not normal if you won't be scared": A qualitative semiotic analysis of the "broken" discourse of Israeli bus drivers who experienced terror attacks', in *Beyond Narrative Coherence*, eds., Matti Hyvärinen, Lars-Christer Hydén, Marjo Saarenheimo, and Maria Tambouko (Philadelphia: John Benjamins Publishing Company, 2010), 121–46.

Phillips, Mark Salber, 'Distance and historical representation', *History Workshop Journal* 57 (2004): 123–41.

Polanyi, Michael, 'My time with X-rays and crystals', in *Fifty Years of X-Ray Diffraction*, ed., Paul Peter Ewald (Utrecht: A. Oosthoek, 1962), 629–36.

Quirke, Stephen, *Hidden Hands: Egyptian workforces in Petrie excavation archives*. (London: Duckworth, 2010).

Salač, Antonín, 'Review of *Studien zur ältesten griechischen Kunst*, by Alois Gotsmich', *Listy filologické* 57 (1930): 444–6.

Shapin, Steven, 'Placing the view from nowhere: historical and sociological problems in the location of science', *Transaction of the Institute of British Geographers* 23 (1998): 1–8.

Terrall, Mary, 'Biography as cultural history of science', *Isis* 97 (2006): 306–13.

Viviers, Didier, 'Un enjeu de politique scientifique: La Section étrangère de l'École française d'Athènes', *Bulletin de correspondance hellénique* 120 (1996): 173–90.

White, Hayden, 'The value of narrativity in the representation of reality', *Critical Inquiry* 7 (1980): 5–27.

Zahra, Tara, 'Reclaiming children for the nation: Germanization, national ascription, and democracy in the Bohemian Lands, 1900-1945', *Central European History* 37 (2004): 501–43.

4
Crafting an institution, reshaping a discipline: Intellectual biography, the archive and philanthropic culture

Jeffrey Abt

Introduction: What the search for archaeological funding might tell us

Archaeology has always been expensive. A familiar feature of archaeology's history is its practitioners' reliance on individual and institutional patrons – aristocrats, royalty, associations, governments, museums, universities. Less well known are the appeals by which archaeologists inspired their sponsors' support. The history of archaeology offers only glimpses of mutually beneficial interests: individual donors, like early venture capitalists, wagered on obtaining great treasures; governments and museums validated treasure hunting in the context of international and inter-institutional rivalries.[1] Yet there is far more to glean from the philanthropic culture surrounding archaeology, especially during the nineteenth and early twentieth centuries when archaeologists relied on a variety of backers to advance their research.

Why might this type of investigation be useful? When archaeologists sought donors' backing, they had to explain their objectives and why they were important. During the nineteenth and early twentieth centuries archaeologists' appeals were in effect grant applications and, alongside their sponsors' replies, constituted discourses of archaeological patronage that offer valuable insights regarding archaeologists' perceptions of the field, standards of practice and scholarly visions.[2] However, the richest veins of this information, which can be indispensable for studying how archaeology evolved from a playground of dilettantes into a rigorous academic discipline, are rarely published. Rather they are found in the personal papers of the individuals involved, tucked away in archival repositories documenting the lives of archaeologists and their patrons. But, within the archive, it's not so much in archaeologists' field notes or season reports that one finds reflections on the contours and validation of disciplines; instead, those matters are more commonly addressed in requests for financial support. It was there that the most ambitious researchers were compelled to articulate their projects to non-specialists. This is because potential funders typically possessed little prior knowledge of increasingly specialised fields, the nature of advanced research, its intellectual standards or means of validation. By historical coincidence, the same period witnessed a gradual change in cultural philanthropy. It began changing from small, usually impulsive and random gifts to large-scale, multi-year grants guided by ever higher standards implemented with increasingly rigorous evaluation methods, sometimes employing the advice of expert reviewers.[3] As disciplines became more exacting, so too did their philanthropic counterparts, a phenomenon increasingly evident in the archival records left by all involved.

An unusually extensive example is the three decades of proposals authored by the once-prominent American Egyptologist, James Henry Breasted, many directed to American oilman and philanthropist John D. Rockefeller and his son, and to the multiple foundations they established. During his partnership with them, Breasted obtained funding for what grew into a network of archaeological expeditions, numerous publications and – eventually – a permanently endowed institution: the Oriental Institute at the University of Chicago. Early in his career, Breasted began learning how to cultivate support by utilising the web of social relations that connected individual and institutional donors, scholarly associations and the public sphere. As Rockefeller's son, John D. Jr., assumed ever greater responsibilities for the family's business activities, he transformed its charitable giving from personal and often spontaneous donations into 'scientific philanthropy', requiring ever more detailed proposals, independent vetting and follow-up reports. Although the Breasted–Rockefeller philanthropic relationship was comparatively rare in its scale and duration, its archival trail exemplifies the insights to be gained about discipline formation from the unpublished records of scholars and their patrons. It is possible as well to trace through these unpublished documents, not only the formation of Breasted's ideas, but to gain insights into the interpenetration of his ideals and lived experiences, revealing how his private failures altered the course of a career seemingly marked only by public successes.[4]

First forays

Breasted (1865–1935, Figure 4.1) grew up in Rockford and Downers Grove, Illinois, then small towns in America's rural Midwest, the latter about 20 miles southwest of Chicago. After briefly exploring a career in the ministry, he turned to ancient Semitic languages and literatures at Yale University. He was drawn to Yale by William Rainey Harper (1856–1906), a leading Hebraist and academic entrepreneur whose intellectual acumen and personal charisma inspired Harper's selection as the founding president of the University of Chicago in 1890. Recognising Breasted's gift for ancient and modern languages, Harper endorsed his pursuit of a doctorate in Egyptology at the University of Berlin, promising Breasted a faculty appointment at Chicago upon his degree's completion.

Figure 4.1 'Orientalist', from the Bristol, Pennsylvania, *Courier*, 14 September 1932. Source: Public domain, reproduction by author.

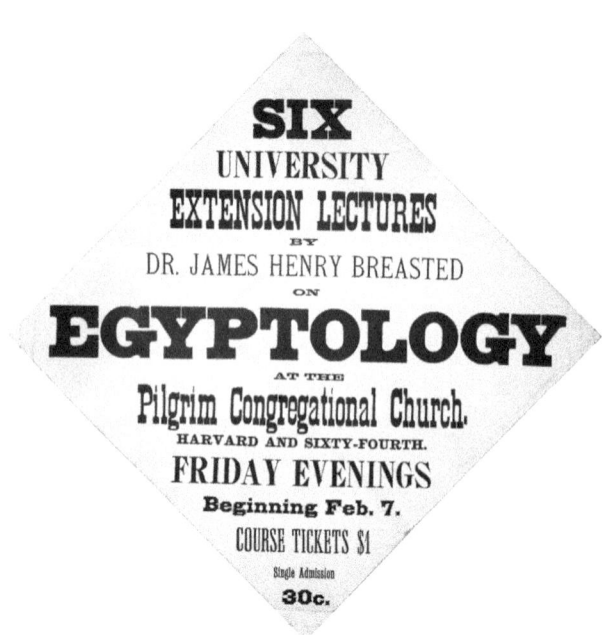

Figure 4.2 Poster, ca. January–February 1896. Source: Courtesy of the Oriental Institute Museum Archives at the University of Chicago. Reproduced under a CC BY-NC-ND 4.0 licence.

After earning the degree, and a brief honeymoon excursion to Egypt that doubled as Breasted's first research trip there, he arrived in Chicago in 1895 and threw himself into research and teaching. To supplement his modest salary as a newly minted professor, Breasted lectured to a variety of community groups, honing his skills at translating the complexities of ancient Egyptian history into terms accessible to a general public (Figure 4.2).[5] Harper modelled the University of Chicago on German research universities, including their arrangements as constellations of relatively autonomous academic departments, and he populated it with scholars capable of joining him in building top programmes and research facilities.[6] The university was established and developed in its early years with generous grants from John D. Rockefeller (1839–1937), by then one of the nation's wealthiest men, and a number of Chicago business leaders and philanthropists – all assiduously cultivated by Harper.[7] But there were limits to that backing and faculty members were encouraged to find other funding sources to supplement their departments and personal research. And so Breasted did, learning from Harper and other successful academic fund-raisers how to articulate scholarly ambitions, relate them to improving the world of learning and society, and thereby obtain grants to underwrite personal research.[8]

Breasted's first fund-raising efforts were in conjunction with his additional duties as assistant director and curator of Egyptology for the university's Haskell Oriental Museum, opened in 1896. He pursued gifts from Chicago collectors and created the Chicago Society of Egyptian Research to collect, via membership dues, modest sums to acquire objects being excavated in Egypt.[9] Within a few years, however, he aspired to raise far more money for his own research. It was a good time for fund-raising in America because the nation was still enjoying the extraordinary economic expansion of the Gilded Era in the late 1800s which boosted the incomes of many citizens and made a number of industrious individuals very wealthy. Some, led by Andrew Carnegie (1835–1919), turned their fortunes to philanthropy. Born in Scotland and brought to America as a youngster, Carnegie's benefactions included the creation of municipal libraries across the nation, museums, a university and several research institutions. The announcement of one, the Carnegie Institution of Washington in December 1901, prompted Breasted to send its founding director a proposal.[10]

He began with an appeal to the institution's American purposes, noting the nation was missing from the 'great field of Egypt' in contrast to the 'larger governments of Europe' that were supporting expeditions there. What American funds had been spent were sent to the Egypt Exploration Fund in England. Breasted argued the other expeditions' work was inaccurate and incomplete, a problem that carried over to their publications. His disciplinary position was informed by his initial specialisation within Egyptology – epigraphy, or the study of ancient inscriptions – and the discovery, during his doctoral studies and subsequent research, that the majority of published hieroglyphic transcriptions, when compared to original sources, often overlooked grammatically significant subtleties in hieroglyphic orthography or left out entire inscriptions essential to a monument's textual import. Further, Breasted observed, his proposed programme was urgent as a means of preservation: 'Weather, the [annual] inundation [of the Nile], other causes of natural decay, and modern vandalism' were degrading these records. It was feasible 'for America to step in and rescue' them because his plan focused on recording known Egyptian inscriptions, rather than excavations to discover more, and he would employ photography to speed the process. He claimed the efficiency and 'epigraphic accuracy' of modern photographic techniques he had innovated made it possible to complete the project in 10–12 years, working nine months per year.[11] Breasted's photographic method was worked out a few years prior while documenting inscriptions in European collections – first for his own research and later for the *Wörterbuch der aegyptischen Sprache*, or Egyptian dictionary project, sponsored by several German academies. Breasted's Carnegie proposal was not funded, however. His proposal arrived just as the institution was forming its board of trustees and narrowing its mission to the natural sciences, the rejection alerting him to the inferior position of the humanities in comparison to the sciences among potential funders, especially those attempting to address societal needs in America.[12]

Breasted's next try, written in 1903 on behalf of colleagues in Chicago's Semitic languages and literatures department, was addressed to John D. Rockefeller Jr. (1874–1960) who by then was helping manage his father's charitable giving.[13] The proposal borrowed from Breasted's previous one a sense of urgency driven by the 'daily perishing' of monuments and the application of modern archaeological methods to preserve the knowledge they contained. To accommodate his colleagues' interests, however, he broadened his geographical scope to include 'Babylonia and Assyria' and 'Syria-Palestine' alongside Egypt. Breasted envisioned a two-step approach to each region that began with exploratory surveys to prepare a 'careful system of preliminary plans' that would be followed by ongoing excavation and epigraphic recording programmes conducted from 'permanent archaeological missions[s] or institute[s]' in Beirut and Cairo. The surveys would be documented in bulletins published annually or semiannually, and excavations annually in 'elaborate' volumes. The other noteworthy difference in this proposal was Breasted's shift from an American to a religious context. He characterised the regions to be studied as 'Bible Lands' and seasoned his argument with references to Old Testament notables, sites and events.[14] The shift likely reflects Breasted's awareness of the Rockefellers' Christian faith and his desire to capture the project's significance in terms familiar to them. Rockefeller backed the proposal and Breasted pursued his share, two years of explorations along the Nile in Nubia (now northern Sudan). During this time he was able to refine his field photography techniques, employing a portable darkroom, special cameras, films, flashes for dark interiors (Figure 4.3) and photographic papers conducive to field annotations over images printed on site that failed to capture essential details, necessitating hand-drawn corrections to fully capture the inscriptions and reliefs.[15]

While on his second Nubia expedition, Breasted was invited by Rockefeller advisor Frederick T. Gates (1853–1929) to request additional

Figure 4.3 Nubian expedition photographer Friedrich Koch, with unidentified Egyptian assistant, Great Hypostyle Hall, Temple of Ramses II, Abu Simbel, late January–early February 1906, P. 2403. Source: Courtesy of the Oriental Institute of the University of Chicago. Reproduced under a CC BY-NC-ND 4.0 licence.

funding for his research.[16] He responded with a plan to record all the ancient monuments and inscriptions in Egypt with detailed line drawings based on photographs and to publish the resulting images with a scholarly apparatus. They were to be issued in 100 'stately volumes', each containing about 100 plates probably printed in elephant folio size (about 24" x 19"), in an edition of 300 sets, ideally to be distributed free of charge to major research institutions and museums. The goal was 'perpetuating for all time both the fast perishing monuments of Egypt, and the memory' of the donor whose generosity made their documentation and publication 'accessible to all the civilized world forever': John D. Rockefeller.[17] To exemplify what Breasted had in mind, he cited the publication by German Egyptologist Richard Lepsius (1810–1884) of his *Denkmäler*, 12 magisterial volumes containing 894 plates recording the findings of his 1842–1845 expeditions in Egypt and Nubia – all underwritten by

Prussian King Friedrich Wilhelm IV.[18] Breasted's plan, which included construction of a 'floating headquarters and working laboratory', a large and elaborately equipped barge to house the project on the Nile as it proceeded from site to site, would have required 15 years to complete. He estimated it would cost US$434,450, or about US$12.2 million today.[19] The proposal's scale and expense dampened Gates's enthusiasm, however, and it didn't help that the Rockefellers avoided the kind of donor recognition Breasted offered. But preparing the proposal compelled him to think through potential methods and field resources for his programme more fully. This included translating photographs into publishable line drawings and the types of additional materials – such as a small research library for field use – necessary to speed the analysis and collation of inscriptions with those at other sites.[20]

From Egyptology to ancient Near Eastern studies

In the years following his plan's failure, Breasted's disciplinary horizons began widening as he strove to bridge the divisions between linguistics and archaeology in ancient Near Eastern research. He adopted what, today, would be called an area studies approach to the cultures around the eastern Mediterranean and Near East – especially the interrelations of ancient Greece and the regions south and east of it, examined other disciplines to round out his understanding of ancient history and utilised historical narrative as a means of rendering the findings of advanced research accessible to the general public.

Breasted's training, like many of his peers, was essentially in ancient languages and thus 'too narrow and restricted'. Whether 'Hebraists, or Assyriologists, or Egyptologists', they were essentially 'philologists rather than historians'. He felt most scholars, as a result, were ill prepared to learn from material culture, a fate he escaped via his doctoral research in museum collections. Further, the approach to history inherited by his generation emphasised major figures and decisive events, overlooking the day-to-day experiences of common people. 'There is a vast category of economic questions like the distribution of land, sources of royal income ...; and social questions like relations between classes, relation of classes to fiscal system, [and the] effect of foreign immigration' to be investigated.[21] To get at that information, Breasted imagined an expansion of ancient Near Eastern research to include anthropology, psychology, comparative religions, sociology, political economy and 'even the later periods of geology ... before wh[ich] Paleolithic man lived'.[22] Through his teaching, lectures and scholarly essays during the 1910s, Breasted fleshed out his ideas. But it was in two high school textbooks that he reified the potential benefits of the disciplinary breadth he envisioned. By this point Breasted had become a captivating writer with a keen eye for telling illustrations and colourful narratives, and his second textbook – *Ancient Times* – attracted a large adult readership as well. It was there that he coined the expression 'Fertile Crescent' to characterise the shape and nature of the 'borderland between desert and mountains' where ancient Near Eastern civilisations arose.[23]

While Breasted was rethinking the methodological foundations of his research, he was also contemplating ways of supporting it. If the challenges of funding known fields like Egyptology were formidable, those for a field still being adumbrated were even greater. Further, Breasted lacked a model for structuring a research enterprise that both embraced area studies and was multidisciplinary. A valuable sounding board in his search for examples, validation and money was Breasted's one-time Chicago colleague and lifelong friend, George Ellery Hale. An astronomer, scientific impresario and opinion leader, Hale (1868–1938) was well connected among the major philanthropic institutions – he obtained support from the Carnegie Institution of Washington – and had become a prominent voice in American science policy.[24] During the 1910s, Hale was attempting to transform America's once sleepy and reclusive National Academy of Sciences into a vital advisory body for the federal government. Valuing Breasted's expertise and breadth, Hale asked his friend for ideas about increasing the Academy's relevance. Breasted replied with a plan to enlarge the Academy's scope by adding a new 'Historico-Philosophical Section' for certain humanities disciplines. Although nothing came of it, the collaboration engaged Hale in Breasted's search for funding.[25] Hale mentored his friend with questions such as: 'Possible donors may ask how many inscriptions not previously known or deciphered would be copied. Also how much the work would contribute to new knowledge instead of recording what is already known.' In responding Breasted not only clarified his ideas, he bolstered them with science analogies to validate the rigour and novelty of his research. Recognising the differences between experimental and observational science, and drawing on his knowledge of Hale's work, Breasted favoured astronomy comparisons:

> The difference between an old and a modern photograph of a nebula may suggest ... the vast difference between a copy of an inscription made today and a copy made twenty-five years ago. Although in both the case of the nebula and that of the inscription, the original has long been known, only the modern reproduction of it furnishes any adequate basis for study.[26]

Their colloquy led to a proposal drafted by Breasted and forwarded by Hale to an individual donor with a cover letter advocating the plan – for an 'Egyptian Institute of the National Academy of Sciences' – and suggesting it be named for the donor. Breasted's plan revived his floating archaeological laboratory (Figure 4.4), but with a new rationale reflecting his expanding vision. He stood by his concept of the recording project as a means of preservation, but argued its value by asserting the revelation of new information from hitherto unknown inscriptions, more accurately recording those that were previously misinterpreted and clearing partially buried ones. Significantly, Breasted now argued for Egypt's seminal place in the development of ancient civilisation prior to the rise of ancient Greece and, because of Egypt's contacts with cultures further east in Asia Minor and the Fertile Crescent, its crucial role in the origins of European civilisation: 'The floating laboratory could be made a great archaeological institute' which scholars worldwide would consult 'for authoritative … research in the early history of civilization.'[27] Although the donor declined the proposal because it was beyond his means, Hale encouraged Breasted to keep trying, adding he should focus more on excavations 'as it is so much easier to interest people in this'. Breasted later conceded that 'we must always carry on some kind of excavation, although I should always regard it as merely a means to an end – a kind of sop, if you will – a concession to popular interest'.[28]

About a year later, in 1916, Hale was cultivating yet another donor for a project that could include Breasted's initiative within a larger research entity. Hale shared his idea with Breasted and in response the latter suggested it be called an academy and its sub-sections be structured as institutes, his to be 'The Oriental Institute'. Breasted's adoption of the term 'Oriental' signalled another step in his broadening objectives, from an emphasis on Egyptology alone to an area-studies embrace of the entire ancient Near East. Although Hale's initiative failed, he pushed Breasted to further articulate the latter's widening vision. Responding to a query from Hale about 'pending Oriental research', Breasted distilled his aims into four objectives: The 'Rise of Civilization', exploring the 'fundamental processes in the evolution of mankind' from the Stone Age to the advent of classical antiquity; 'The Decipherment of Hittite', building on a 1915 advance in translating Hittite to compile inscriptions relevant to the history of the eastern Mediterranean; 'An Assyrian and Babylonian Dictionary', expediting the translations of Assyrian and Babylonian cuneiform inscriptions; and 'Egyptian Documents and the Mediterranean Situation', completing Breasted's epigraphic survey to reveal the Mediterranean context of ancient Egypt.[29] His expanding historical and

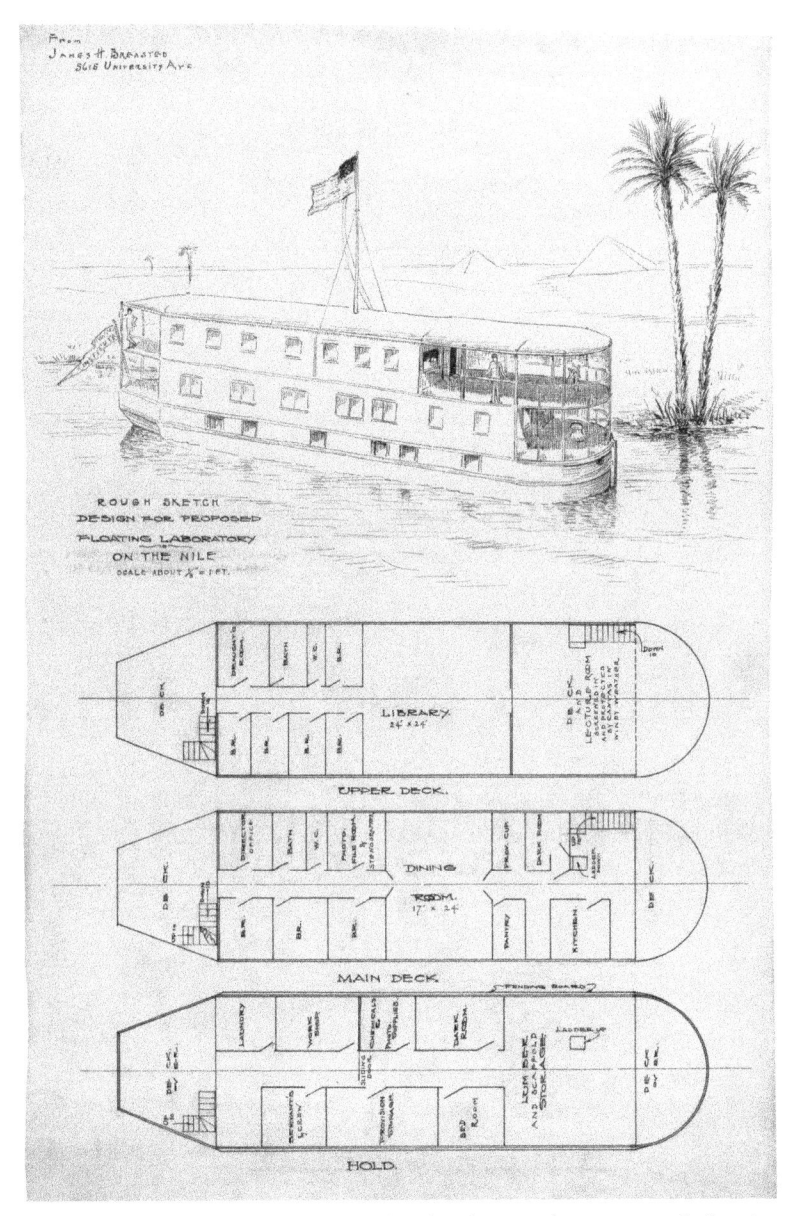

Figure 4.4 Breasted's 'Rough sketch: design for proposed floating laboratory on the Nile', prepared ca. April 1907 and revised ca. April 1914. Source: Courtesy of the Oriental Institute Museum Archives at the University of Chicago. Reproduced under a CC BY-NC-ND 4.0 licence.

regional outlook grew out of his textbook writing and Breasted's collaboration with a Chicago colleague, John Merlin Powis Smith (1866–1932), who specialised in ancient Near Eastern, especially Old Testament, studies. 'As the years passed', Breasted recalled, the two 'saw more and more clearly that our ultimate task was historical interpretation' realised by broadening their curriculum and marked by changing its name to the Department of *Oriental* Languages and Literatures, substituting 'Oriental' (as representing the entire range of ancient Near Eastern languages and locales) for what was formerly 'Semitic' (as confined to Hebraic, Arabic and cognate languages).[30]

Breasted likely proposed the 'institute' structure to Hale based on the former's familiarity with the German model, one that could thrive either in a university environment or as an independent organisation. For scholars in American research universities, the 'institute had a particular appeal' because the vision of their founders was being compromised as higher education professionalised, bureaucracies grew and swelling student populations diluted institutional resources. At several of America's leading universities, including Johns Hopkins, Princeton and Stanford, efforts to 'revive the research ideal and preserve the integrity of "real" university work' found expression in proposals like Breasted's. The research institute 'promised a refuge from teaching obligations and the prospect of undisturbed time and funding for investigation' while also protecting specialised projects from competing demands. Although Breasted's plan was not unique in American higher education, it was unusual in the realm of ancient Near Eastern studies as he modelled an institutional approach to advancing the field.[31]

From answers to questions, from the known to the unknown

Public acclaim for *Ancient Times* exemplified by former American president Theodore Roosevelt's enthusiastic review and private praise from Frederick Gates and John D. Rockefeller Jr.'s wife, Abby Aldrich Rockefeller (1874–1948), both influential in the family's philanthropic endeavours, emboldened Breasted in 1917 to again seek Rockefeller support.[32] But the family's philanthropy had been fundamentally altered during the years following his proposal a decade earlier. In the interim, Gates persuaded Rockefeller to reorganise his donations according to 'the principle of scientific giving'. Several Rockefeller foundations, each specialising in a separate area of charitable interests, were created with the objective of establishing 'efficiency in giving' by improving 'underlying conditions' rather than responding piecemeal to society's myriad problems. Rather than supporting numerous hospitals to care for the ill, for example, the Rockefellers would now fund medical research and education to *prevent* illnesses.[33] The foundations, each with its own staff and trustees, operated out of the Rockefellers' corporate headquarters in New York.[34] Their priorities were guided by John D. Rockefeller Jr. who by this point had fashioned himself into a 'consciously modern' foundations manager and the first 'to make his career as a "professional philanthropist"'.[35] Breasted travelled to New York and launched his new campaign by meeting with Rockefeller foundation officials who warmly received him, in part because several had read *Ancient Times*. Thus encouraged, he followed up with a written proposal.

Breasted's 'Plan for an Institute of Oriental Archaeology' knitted together many of his most recent ideas, but within a framework that emphasised 'gaps in our knowledge' of certain 'epochs': 'the origin of civilization', the 'transition of man from barbarism to civilization', 'the development of the great civilized societies' and 'the transmission of civilization to Europe'. Those gaps could only be filled, he argued, by research at the sites where civilisation arose, 'on the spot' as with 'the geology or botany of a given region'. Noting the Carnegie Institution's support of those kinds of natural sciences research, Breasted argued that archaeology had never enjoyed comparable backing: 'Just as chemistry or astronomy would be helpless without their laboratories and instruments, so permanent archaeological research in the Near East would be impossible without a fully equipped archaeological laboratory.' To pursue this work, Breasted proposed two 'headquarters', one for 'Asia' in Beirut, Damascus or Aleppo, the other for 'Africa' in Cairo – the latter relying on his floating laboratory. He would begin with a preliminary survey of 'the almost untouched buried cities of Syria' to preserve what is above ground and plan excavations of the 'most promising places'; and in Egypt he would undertake a similar approach, but with greater priority to documenting the many monuments above ground. Breasted underscored the compilation of records for the benefit of scholars worldwide and the prompt and frequent dissemination of findings by a well-staffed publications department. Cooperation with American universities and museums was highlighted as well, principally by sharing with them objects discovered during excavations so that, over time, 'collections of world-wide importance … would grow up in America'.[36]

Echoing his earlier proposal's attention to American interests, this one shifted from a concern over intellectual parity with Europe to the country's international responsibilities in place of Europe. America had declared war on Germany just a few days before Breasted's visit and he anticipated the Ottoman Empire's collapse after war's end and America's expanded role in Middle Eastern affairs:

> Delivered from Turkish misrule, the lands around the eastern end of the Mediterranean are about to be opened up for the first time to unrestricted exploration and excavation.... It is but obvious scientific statesmanship ... to do what European governments will feel too financially hampered to do after the war is over.... The great opportunity can be seized and the work efficiently done by the establishment of an ORIENTAL INSTITUTE.[37]

Breasted's reference to international responsibilities echoed concerns of Rockefeller officials at the time. American foundations were exploring new approaches involving private–public partnerships to address large needs. The First World War accelerated discussions about how foundations might perform services the U.S. government did not provide. In calling upon Rockefeller officials to consider America's opportunities and obligations in the Middle East, Breasted was aligning his objectives with the foundations' expanding purview.[38] Of the visit with Rockefeller officials and his ensuing proposal, Breasted concluded, 'I shall have to wait until after the war before they can undertake my plans, – but I have their attention, their interest & their confidence.'[39]

Institutionalising multidisciplinary and area studies

About a year later, in April 1918, Breasted was elected president of the American Oriental Society. By tradition, the society's president addressed its annual meeting at the conclusion of his or her year-long term, the subject to be 'some phase of the progress and significance of Oriental studies'.[40] When Breasted's turn came, he drew together his ideas about the geographical reach, multidisciplinary requirements and historical purposes of the field in 'The Place of the Near Orient in the Career of Man and the Task of the American Orientalist'. A call for change, the address was also his first *public* discussion of the ideas he expressed privately in grant applications over the previous 15 years. The timing, just months after the First World War's end, also invited a fresh look at the Middle East as a land of scholarly 'responsibility' and 'opportunity'. By 'responsibility', Breasted meant his audience's obligations to current and previous generations of European scholars to whose findings Americans were indebted and who, impoverished by war, deserved assistance just as weary Allies were aided by American troops on Europe's battlefields. The 'opportunity' Breasted envisioned was 'the correlation of the whole ancient Near East with the development of early Europe' leading, in turn, to an understanding of 'mankind viewed *as a whole*'.[41]

Breasted lamented society's ignorance of the ancient Near East's seminal place 'in the career of man', a problem he attributed to scholars' failure to make 'the Near East intelligible'. In his own efforts to do so, Breasted was inspired by anthropologists studying the pre-Columbian period in the Americas, exemplified by Clark Wissler's *The American Indian: An introduction to the anthropology of the New World*, especially the concept of 'culture traits': clusters of evidence associated with the cultivation of maize, the 'cotton complex', pottery, rudimentary metallurgical skills and the transition 'from the pictographic to the phonetic stage' in ancient writing. Breasted admired the Americanists' linking of culture traits at widely dispersed sites to trace 'lines of diffusion' back to their points of origin and their use of that information to reveal the antiquity and role of the 'great inter-continental bridge' connecting the North and South American continents. Breasted also admired the anthropologists' integration of evidence from many disciplines enabling them to transcend divisions impeding research in the eastern Mediterranean. Breasted bemoaned the 'watertight compartments' that separated researchers studying ancient Greece and Rome from those working on the ancient Near East, or that kept the findings of philologists/epigraphers separate from those of archaeologists. In the Americanists' example, Breasted found a model for drawing together philologists and archaeologists over questions of common interest, as well as a way to integrate the history of Western antiquity, from the upper Nile to ancient Greece and Rome, and from the eastern Mediterranean to western India, from the prehistoric period to the dawn of European civilization (Figure 4.5).[42] Breasted likened the origins and central role of ancient Near Eastern peoples to those of the ancient peoples of Central America by proposing an 'Egypto-Babylonian culture-nucleus' that spanned the 'inter-continental bridge connecting Africa and Eurasia'. The 'Egypto-Babylonian group' thus provided both a crucible for and source of the advances that led from 'prehistoric man' to 'civilized Europe'. Yet, Breasted declared, research on this 'cultural synthesis' had 'hardly begun' because of disciplinary parochialism.[43]

Overcoming his long-standing aversion to archaeology in favour of epigraphy, Breasted admitted that philologists and epigraphers would have to closely collaborate with archaeologists. But to fully explore the

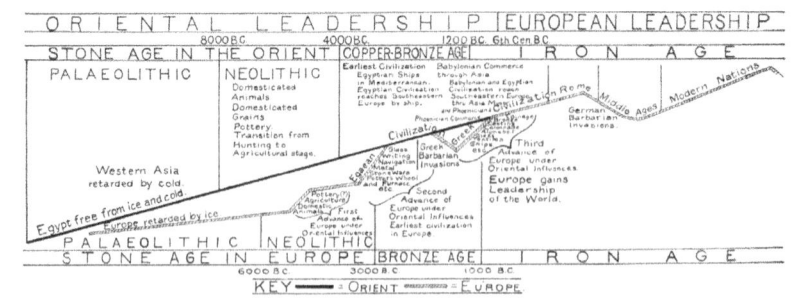

Figure 4.5 'Diagram Visualizing the Rise of Civilization in the Orient and Its Transition Thence to Europe', from Breasted's 'Origins of Civilization', *Scientific Monthly* 10, no. 3 (March 1920): 267. Source: Public domain, reproduction by author.

'culture traits' distinctive to the ancient Near East, they must also draw on the expertise of other disciplines. Physical anthropologists had discovered evidence of circumcision and the consumption of certain grains in prehistoric Egypt. Revealing evidence for the latter along with other cereals eaten in the Near East required the assistance of botanists. Suggestions of animal husbandry demanded the expertise of palaeontologists and zoologists. Finds of human bones and artefacts on the 'Pleistocene river terraces of Egypt' called for geologists' participation. Evidence of attempts to collect, store and redirect rainfall for irrigation would best be understood with the assistance of hydrographers. Add a host of other culture traits such as the potter's wheel, the composite bow or ceramic glazing, and it was abundantly clear that only by integrating the expertise of many disciplines 'shall we accomplish in the Old World what the Americanists are so successfully doing for the New'.[44]

To efficiently assemble the resulting evidence into the 'vast cultural synthesis', Breasted envisioned was beyond the capacities of the individual scholar. Staff and a 'properly equipped building ... a veritable laboratory of systematic oriental research' were required. It is, Breasted argued, 'as necessary to a proper study of the career of man as an astronomical observatory with its files of observations, computations, and negatives [is] to an investigation of the career of the universe'. The 'historical laboratory' Breasted imagined was, of course, an institute to be associated with a university so as to 'maintain close relations with [its] scientific departments' and draw upon the many disciplines they represented. His references to the sciences and, in particular, his use of scientific imagery, enlarged upon his colloquies with Hale about the nature of Breasted's field in comparison with the astronomer's, as well as their mutual effort to validate research in the humanities as comparable to that in the sciences in social value and intellectual import. The laboratory analogy reflected a trend in American popular culture as well.[45]

In sketching out his historical laboratory – to be called the Oriental Institute – Breasted proposed 'liberal provision' be made for postdoctoral research fellows, support staff, darkrooms, drafting rooms and all the other accoutrements necessary so that 'not only the methods but especially the equipment of natural science should be applied to our study'. Breasted aligned ancient Near Eastern studies, as a 'humanistic science', with the natural sciences and connected results of the former with discoveries of the latter: 'The stages which carried man out of savagery and far along into the age of civilization, can be recovered' for 'a great synthesis of the developing universe which the progress of scientific research is now making it possible to build up.' His Oriental Institute would complement and extend research in the natural sciences to reach that great synthesis. Ought not, Breasted concluded, 'the worth and dignity of our great task ... move us to claim all that is conceded to the natural sciences. Are we not engaged upon later phases of the same vast process of development which they are investigating?'[46]

A recognised branch of science

Several passages of Breasted's address that transformed it from an essay on methodology to a call for action were drawn from a fresh institute grant proposal he circulated among Rockefeller officials a few months earlier. As before, Breasted focused on America's 'obligation', in the wake of the First World War and the Ottoman Empire's collapse, this time to supplement the scholarly initiatives of 'Allies in Europe ... financially too exhausted to take advantage of the great opportunity' for presumably unhindered research throughout the ancient Near East. Where, in his address, Breasted underscored American scholars' imperative and opportunity to gather evidence for a 'history of mankind viewed *as a whole*', in his Rockefeller proposal, Breasted took a different path. He highlighted the preservation of precious archaeological sources from the threats of post-war development – such as 'exploitation in mining, railroad-building, manufactures and agriculture' – and 'illicit native diggings'. Appealing to the Rockefeller group's entrepreneurial ethos, Breasted spoke to his plan's business values such as efficiency, systematic administration and financial economy, adding that the proposed institute was not 'an excavation organization and hence [could operate on a] modest budget'. There were also ancillary socioeconomic benefits of his plan such as how institute reports on 'present-day conditions in the Near East might also be of value to our government, to our educational and relief organizations, and even to our business men'. Breasted sought enough money to endow a small, ongoing field operation, originating in America but perhaps with a couple of small, satellite 'headquarters' in Aleppo and Cairo to store records and equipment. The focus was on recording information and, to an extent, collecting objects. If excavations were deemed necessary at some point, hopefully they could be funded by other sources on a site-by-site basis.[47]

Though there was considerable interest in Breasted's goals among Rockefeller officials, and they held him in high regard, he had sent the proposal without first clearing it with the University of Chicago's president. The Rockefeller foundation most appropriate for Breasted's proposal did not give grants based on individual faculty requests, but only for university-authorised initiatives. Breasted hastily presented his plan to Chicago's president, obtained the latter's endorsement and continued to lobby Rockefeller officials, but to no avail.[48] His patience growing thin, Breasted sent the proposal directly to John D. Rockefeller Jr., hoping he might break the logjam. Rockefeller was inclined to endorse the project but asked an advisor to evaluate it and Breasted's ability to achieve the stated aims. After consultations with several others, the advisor suggested Rockefeller personally fund the project because it fell outside the purview of his various foundations. The advisor also recommended, however, the donation be sufficient for five years' work only so 'the thing can be tested' – the endowment question could be revisited later. Rockefeller followed the recommendation and Breasted promptly launched the Oriental Institute.[49]

As promised, he began with a survey of sites to be documented or excavated in Egypt and along the Fertile Crescent. Breasted soon produced results, published reports, and kept Rockefeller and his advisors apprised of the Institute's progress at every step.[50] As its fifth anniversary and the depletion of its funding approached, Breasted again sought an endowment to fund the Institute in perpetuity, as well as a new building to house its growing collection of objects, field records and – ideally – an enlarged staff to conduct research, process incoming materials and issue publications. Again, one of Rockefeller's advisors was persuaded by the significance of Breasted's objectives and his exceptional ability. And again, Rockefeller personally donated money for five years of Institute work, this time for an expanded programme. But he declined to endow the Institute or erect a building for it, adding 'he was supporting a

Figure 4.6 Oriental Institute building from the northwest, designed by Oscar Harold Murray and completed in 1931, ca. 1931, P. 18730/N. 10872. Source: Courtesy of the Oriental Institute of the University of Chicago. Reproduced under a CC BY-NC-ND 4.0 licence.

man, not a recognized branch of science' – a comment that confirmed Breasted's fears about perceptions of his field's validity in comparison to the natural sciences.[51] It would take another five years and numerous grant requests to Rockefeller foundations for smaller Institute projects, before Rockefeller officials concluded: 'The work has been supported in that way long enough. These details are without end.'[52] The result, in 1928, was two Rockefeller foundations' grants erecting a new building (Figure 4.6), endowing its maintenance and museum operations, endowing the Institute's teaching programme and funding 10 years of research, fieldwork and publications. Those grants, along with subsequent ones, would result in the Oriental Institute that remains to this day. Ever restless, Breasted continued to refine his priorities of geographical breadth, chronological depth, multidisciplinary reach and technological innovation – all evident in his last and most complete statement of the Institute's activities and aims published in 1933, just two years before his death. He remained faithful to the call he issued in 1919 and, remarkably, the institution he created remains a permanent feature in the landscape of ancient Near Eastern research, sustaining Breasted's vision of scholarly innovation, multidisciplinarity and productivity, its findings regularly disseminated by an in-house publication programme.[53]

Coda: what archaeologists may study

Near the beginning of Bruce Trigger's *A History of Archaeological Thought*, in the chapter on 'Studying the History of Archaeology', he explored factors shaping the questions archaeologists pursue in their research and how they do it. He added that:

> What archaeologists can study is also influenced by the resources that are made available for archaeological research, the institutional and public contexts in which research is carried out, and the kinds of investigations societies or governments are prepared to let archaeologists undertake. To obtain support archaeologists must please their sponsors, whether these be wealthy patrons, colleagues and politicians managing the allocation of public funds, or the general public.[54]

Trigger's observation stops short of addressing a more subtle but ultimately more consequential historiographical consideration: What might the negotiations between archaeologists and their backers, as archaeology's history unfolded, tell us about the evolution of its aims and approaches? In fairness to Trigger, the task of surveying archaeological history and theory usually relies on published sources that command attention because they represent successfully backed projects and the work of accomplished scholars – that is, ones that left a mark.[55] There is a lack of evidence of archaeologists either unable to find patrons or of their sidelining valuable ideas in favour of lesser ones to successfully earn sponsors' approval, as did Breasted when he agreed to pursue excavations as a 'sop' to donors and 'concession to popular interest'. Without a history of such failures and reversals, one has at best only a partial understanding of the forces affecting those archaeological initiatives that succeeded.

Were one to search through Breasted's dozens of publications to learn of the ideas that shaped the Oriental Institute's creation, the first published evidence would be his 1919 American Oriental Society address. Without the information contained in his unpublished records the Institute's particular configuration would seem to have come out of the blue. With those materials, however, it's possible to trace Breasted's nearly two decades of proposals, rejections, revised plans, personal and professional relationships, and other factors that contributed to his eventually successful drive for the Oriental Institute. Because he was indefatigable in his pursuits, he was a prolific correspondent and he preserved all his writings, the archival record of Breasted's career as a scholar and academic entrepreneur is nearly comprehensive. The records of several of his scholarly collaborators, Hale, and the Rockefellers and their associates are equally extensive. Taken together, these materials afford opportunities to explore not only the formation of Breasted's ideas, but to gain insights into the development of his and cognate disciplines. The records also suggest possibilities for exploring the interpenetration of ideals and lived experience, illuminating how Breasted's private failures altered the course of a biography seemingly marked only by public successes.

While the unpublished records left by Breasted and others whose lives he touched are unusually complete and well preserved, they are hardly unique. What might the archival materials left by other archaeologists and their backers convey about the discipline's reversals as well as its accomplishments, the paths from false starts to eventual successes and broader societal perceptions of archaeology informing the decisions of private and institutional funders? The unpublished and often unstudied records of archaeologists' efforts to coax support from potential backers offer veins of knowledge yet to be mined, insights that are likely to both complicate and enlarge our understanding of the field's history.

Archival sources

California Institute of Technology Archives, Pasadena, California, USA
Carnegie Institution of Washington Archives, Washington, DC, USA
Oriental Institute Archives (now the Institute for the Study of Ancient Cultures Archives, see note 4 below), University of Chicago, Chicago, Illinois, USA
Rockefeller Archive Center, Sleepy Hollow, New York, USA
Special Collections Research Center, University of Chicago Library, Chicago, Illinois, USA

Notes

1 Examples of these glimpses include: Margaret S. Drower, *Flinders Petrie: A life in archeology* (London: Victor Gollancz Ltd, 1985); Peter Der Manuelian, Walking Among Pharaohs: George Reisner and the dawn of modern Egyptology (Oxford: Oxford University Press, 2023); T.G.H. James, *Howard Carter: The path to Tutankhamun* (London: Taurus Parke, 2001). For institutional perspectives, see, for example, Nancy Thomas, 'American institutional fieldwork in Egypt, 1899–1960', in *The American Discovery of Ancient Egypt*, ed. Nancy Thomas (Los Angeles: Los Angeles County Museum of Art, 1995), 49–72; Amara Thornton, '"… a certain faculty for extricating cash": Collective sponsorship in late 19th and early 20th century British archaeology', *Present Pasts* 5 (2013): 1–12. As for rivalries: James F. Goode, *Negotiating for the Past: Archaeology, nationalism, and diplomacy in the Middle East, 1919–1941* (Austin: University of Texas Press, 2007).
2 These discourses are at best only suggested in archaeologists' biographies. A colourful example is the exchange between Howard Carter and his patron, Lord Carnarvon, in the run up to the King

Tut tomb discovery: James, *Howard Carter*, 250–51; Charles Breasted, *Pioneer to the Past: The Story of James Henry Breasted, archaeologist* (Chicago: University of Chicago Press, 1943), 328–9.

3   The shift began with policy changes among American charitable organisations providing health and social support for the indigent: Robert H. Bremner, '"Scientific philanthropy", 1873–93', *Social Service Review* 30, No. 1, March (1956): 168–73; Barbara Howe, 'The emergence of scientific philanthropy, 1900–1920: Origins, issues, and outcomes', in *Philanthropy and Cultural Imperialism: The foundations at home and abroad*, ed., Robert F. Arnove (Boston: G. K. Hall & Company, 1980), 25–54.

4   Regarding the expression 'scientific philanthropy', see the previous note. In spring 2023 the Oriental Institute changed its name to 'Institute for the Study of Ancient Cultures' (ISAC). As this essay was typeset prior to the change, all subsequent mentions of the Oriental Institute should be understood as referring to ISAC. 'Name change information', ISAC. Accessed April 2023. https://isac.uchicago.edu/about/name-change-information.

5   Biographical information on Breasted (hereafter JHB) is from research for: Jeffrey Abt, *American Egyptologist: The life of James Henry Breasted and the creation of his Oriental Institute* (Chicago: University of Chicago Press, 2011) (hereafter *AE*). Earlier biographies of JHB, cited in *AE*, include the colorful Breasted, *Pioneer to the Past*, which is essentially JHB's son's memoir.

6   On the University's founding and intellectual environment during that era: Richard J. Storr, *Harper's University: The beginnings* (Chicago: University of Chicago Press, 1966). See also, Thomas Wakefield Goodspeed, *William Rainey Harper: First president of the University of Chicago* (Chicago: University of Chicago Press, 1928) and Goodspeed's, *A History of the University of Chicago: The first quarter-century*, third edition (Chicago: University of Chicago Press, 1972).

7   Ron Chernow, *Titan: The life of John D. Rockefeller, Sr.* (New York: Random House, 1988).

8   On public outreach: Merle Curti, 'Scholarship and popularization of learning', in *The Growth of American Thought* (New York: Harper and Row, 1943), 564–87. The philanthropic context of this essay is distinctly American, see Robert H. Bremner, *American Philanthropy*, second edition (Chicago: University of Chicago Press, 1988).

9   JHB became familiar with museum work during his doctoral studies in Berlin: *AE*, 29–30; on the Haskell Oriental Museum and his efforts there: *AE*, 62–71. Regarding Chicago's philanthropic environment at the time: Helen Lefkowitz Horowitz, *Culture and the City: Cultural philanthropy in Chicago from the 1880s to 1917* (Lexington: University of Kentucky Press, 1976).

10 David Nasaw, *Andrew Carnegie* (New York: Penguin Press, 2006). On the Carnegie Institution's founding: Nathan Reingold, 'National science policy in a private foundation: The Carnegie Institution of Washington', in *The Organization of Knowledge in Modern America, 1860–1920*, ed. Alexandra Oleson and John Voss (Baltimore: Johns Hopkins University Press, 1979), 313–41; David Madsen, 'Daniel Coit Gilman at the Carnegie Institution of Washington', *History of Education Quarterly* IX, (1969): 154–86.

11 JHB to Daniel C. Gilman, 17 February 1902, JHB File, Carnegie Institution of Washington Archives. The Egypt Exploration Fund was renamed the Egypt Exploration Society in 1919, *Excavating in Egypt: The Egypt Exploration Society, 1882–1982*, ed. T. G. H. James (Chicago: University of Chicago Press, 1982).

12 On JHB's photographic methods up to this point and his work for the Egyptian dictionary: *AE*, 73–80.

13 Raymond B. Fosdick, *John D. Rockefeller, Jr.: A portrait* (New York: Harper and Brothers, 1956).

14 JHB et al. to John D. Rockefeller, Jr. (hereafter JDR, Jr.), 20 May 1903, and William R. Harper to Frederick T. Gates, w/attachment: 'Estimate of expense… for exploration and excavation in Bible Lands', 8 June 1903, Rockefeller Family Archives (hereafter RFA)/Record Group (hereafter R.G.) 2 (Office of Messrs. Rockefeller (hereafter OMR))/Educational Interests series, box 108, folder: Pledge - Bible Land Exploration, Rockefeller Archive Center, (hereafter RAC); John D. Rockefeller to JDR Jr., 25 June 1903, RFA/R. G. 2 (OMR)/Educational Interests series, University of Chicago, box 104, RAC.

15 John D. Rockefeller's gift establishing the University of Chicago resulted from a community of shared religious beliefs: Storr, *Harper's University* and John W. Boyer, '"Broad and Christian in the fullest sense": William Rainey Harper and the University of Chicago', *University of Chicago Record* 40, No. 2, 5 January (2006): 2–26. Concerning JDR, Jr.'s religious beliefs and charitable activities: Albert F. Schenkel, *The Rich Man and the Kingdom: John D. Rockefeller, Jr., and the*

Protestant establishment, Harvard Theological Studies (Minneapolis: Fortress Press, 1995). While JHB was conversant with biblical archaeology, he never subscribed to its purposes. Yet, when the Old and New Testaments furnished an effective means of contextualising his work, he readily drew on his deep familiarity with them. On the place of JHB's religious beliefs in his work: *AE*, 372–74. Regarding biblical archaeology in general: Neil Asher Silberman, 'Desolation and restoration: The impact of a biblical concept on Near Eastern archaeology', *Biblical Archaeologist* 54 (1991): 76–87; Thomas W. Davis, *Shifting Sands: The rise and fall of biblical archaeology* (Oxford: Oxford University Press, 2004). On this grant proposal and its relation to JHB's epigraphic methodology: *AE*, 120–23, 126–53.

16 Frederick T. Gates, *Chapters in My Life* [with Robert S. Morison, 'Frederick Taylor Gates Lectures'] (New York: Free Press, 1977). For the invitation's inception and outcome, *AE*, 153–59.

17 JHB, Draft letter/proposal [addressed to Frederick T. Gates], 13 April 1907, Director's Office Correspondence (hereafter DOC), Oriental Institute Archives (hereafter OIA). When JHB obtained funding for what became the Oriental Institute's Epigraphic Survey and its first volumes were published, they were all elephant folio size or larger. See, for example, The Epigraphic Survey (directed by Harold H. Nelson), *Earlier Historical Records of Ramses III*, Medinet Habu–vol. I, Oriental Institute Publications, vol. VIII, ed. JHB (Chicago: University of Chicago Press, 1930).

18 *Who Was Who in Egyptology*, s.v. 'Karl Richard Lepsius', Karl Richard Lepsius, *Denkmäler aus Ägypten und Äthiopien nach den Zeichnungen der von Seiner Majestät dem Könige von Preußen Friedrich Wilhelm IV nach diesen Ländern gesendeten und in den Jahren 1842–1845, ausgeführten wissenschaftlichen Expedition auf Befehl Seiner Majestät herausgegeben und erläutert*, 12 vols. (Berlin: Nicolaische Buchhandlung, 1859).

19 JHB, Draft letter/proposal [addressed to Frederick T. Gates], 13 April 1907, DOC, OIA. The cost in today's terms is based on the online calculator at: Samuel H. Williamson, 'Seven Ways to compute the relative value of a U.S. dollar amount, 1774 to present'. Accessed June 2021. https://www.measuringworth.com/calculators/uscompare/.

20 The epigraphic techniques first envisioned here evolved into the 'Chicago House method': *AE*, 281–99; on why it is so exacting: *AE*, 265–76.

21 JHB's training was primarily in hieroglyphics and Egyptian demotic, but he was also proficient in seven other ancient languages and fluent in four modern ones, including Arabic. JHB, 'Oriental History as a Field of Investigation', Unpublished manuscript, December 1912, James Henry Breasted Papers (hereafter JHBP), OIA.

22 JHB, 'The Old Historical Method', Unpublished manuscript, 21 January 1911, JHBP, OIA.

23 On JHB's teaching: *AE*, 167–69; on the textbooks and their reception: *AE*, 182–206. The first textbook is: JHB and James Harvey Robinson, *Outlines of European History, Part I* (Boston: Ginn and Company, 1914). JHB, *Ancient Times: A history of the early world, an introduction to the study of ancient history and the career of early man* (Boston & New York: Ginn and Company, 1916), 100–101.

24 Walter S. Adams, 'George Ellery Hale, 1868–1938', *Biographical Memoirs* (National Academy of Sciences) XXI, No. 5 (1940): 181–241; Helen Wright, *Explorer of the Universe: A biography of George Ellery Hale* (New York: E. P. Dutton and Company, 1966).

25 On the National Academy of Sciences initiative: *AE*, 208–11; it was briefly revived a few years later when JHB proposed creation of a 'National Academy of Humanistic Science': *AE*, 225–28.

26 George Ellery Hale (hereafter GEH) to JHB, 15 April 1914 and JHB to GEH, 18 April 1914, GEH Papers, California Institute of Technology Archives (hereafter CITA, emphases JHB's).

27 JHB to GEH, 1 May 1914, CITA; GEH to N. W. Harris, 8 May 1914, JHBP, OIA.

28 N. W. Harris, to GEH, 29 June 1914, CITA; GEH to JHB, 14 July 191[4] JHBP, OIA. The sop to popular interest quote is from: JHB to GEH, 24 June 1915, JHBP, OIA.

29 JHB to GEH, 18 January 1916, JHBP, OIA.

30 The historical interpretation quote is from: JHB, 'John Merlin Powis Smith', *University [of Chicago] Record* 19 [new series], No. 1, January (1933): 69–73. On the departmental name change: University of Chicago Board of Trustees, Minutes, 13 April 1915, Board of Trustees Minutes vol. 9, 55–66, Special Collections Research Center (hereafter SPRC). The nomenclature of 'Oriental' and 'Orientalism' in this context represents a topic too complex to unpack here. For a discussion of JHB's usages: *AE*, 59–60.

31 The quotes are from: Daniel Lee Meyer, 'The Chicago Faculty and the University Ideal, 1891–1929' (Unpublished Ph.D. dissertation, Department of History, University of Chicago,

1994), 334–5; 398–401. On the German model: Charles E. McClelland, *State, Society, and University in Germany, 1700–1914* (Cambridge: Cambridge University Press, 1980), 275. See also Robert E. Kohler, *Partners in Science: Foundations and natural scientists, 1900–1945* (Chicago: University of Chicago Press, 1991), 217–9. JHB's institute focus on the ancient Near East differed from subsequent similarly named research institutions like the School of Oriental and African Studies, University of London (founded in 1917, which Edward Said discusses in *Orientalism* [New York: Random House, 1978], 214–5) and the Oriental Institute of Oxford University (established in 1957). Those are geographically broader or chronologically more inclusive – going from antiquity to the present to embrace the modern (Islamic) period: C. H. Phillips, *The School of Oriental and African Studies, University of London, 1917–1967: An introduction* (London: School of Oriental & African Studies, University of London, 1967); and G. R. Driver, 'Oriental Studies and the Oriental Institute', *Oxford* 17, No. 2 May (1961): 56–67. See also Jerrold S. Cooper, 'From Mosul to Manila: Early approaches to funding Ancient Near Eastern Studies research in the United States', *Culture and History* 11 (1992): 133–7.

32 Theodore Roosevelt, 'The dawn and sunrise of history', *The Outlook* 115, No. 7, 14 February (1917): 272–75; Frederick T. Gates to JHB, [ca. September 1916] and Abby Aldrich Rockefeller to JHB, 18 May 1917, DOC, OIA. Mary Ellen Chase, *Abby Aldrich Rockefeller* (New York: Avon Books, 1966). On the reception of *Ancient Times* more generally: *AE*, 202–6.

33 Howe, 'Emergence of scientific philanthropy', 27–8; Barry D. Karl and Stanley N. Katz, 'Donors, trustees, staffs: An historical view, 1890–1930', in *The Art of Giving: Four views on American philanthropy* (North Tarrytown: RAC, 1979), 3.

34 On the newly created foundations, Daryl L. Revoldt, 'Raymond B. Fosdick: Reform, Internationalism, and the Rockefeller Foundation' (Unpublished Ph.D. dissertation, University of Akron, 1982), 376–77; Raymond B. Fosdick, *Adventures in Giving: The story of the General Education Board* (New York: Harper and Row, 1962); Raymond B. Fosdick, *The Story of the Rockefeller Foundation*, reprint of 1952 edition and introduction by Steven C. Wheatley (New Brunswick: Transaction Publishers, 1989); George W. Gray, *Education on an International Scale: A history of the International Education Board* (New York: Harcourt, Brace, 1941).

35 Karl and Katz, 'Donors, trustees, staffs', 9.

36 JHB, 'Plan for an Institute of Oriental Archaeology in the Eastern Mediterranean World', 19 May 1917, CITA.

37 JHB, 'Plan for an Institute of Oriental Archaeology in the Eastern Mediterranean World', 19 May 1917, CITA (emphasis JHB's).

38 Karl and Katz, 'Donors, trustees, staffs', 6, 10.

39 For the quote on JHB's Rockefeller visit: JHB to Frances (Hart) Breasted, 10 April 1917, Letters to Frances Hart Breasted, JHBP, OIA.

40 'Proceedings of the American Oriental Society', *Journal of the American Oriental Society* 38, April (1918): 334. Nathaniel Schmidt, 'Early Oriental Studies in Europe and the work of the American Oriental Society, 1842–1922', *Journal of the American Oriental Society* 43 (1923): 1–14, quote regarding annual addresses from p. 1.

41 JHB, 'The place of the Near Orient in the career of man and the task of the American Orientalist', *Journal of the American Oriental Society* 39 (1919): 159–84, quotes from pp. 159–60, 183 (emphasis JHB's). Some of the material closely parallels JHB's ideas advanced in National Academy of Sciences lectures delivered the same spring: JHB, 'The origins of civilization', *The Scientific Monthly* 9, Nos. 4–6, October–December (1919) and 10, Nos. 1–3, January–March (1920).

42 JHB, 'Place of the Near Orient', 160–63, 165. Clark Wissler, *The American Indian: An introduction to the anthropology of the New World* (New York: Douglas C. McMurtrie, 1917). Some of Wissler's notions related to cultural diffusion have not stood the test of time: George W. Stocking, in *Dictionary of American Biography*, supplement 4: 1946–50, s.v. 'Clark Wissler'. For the larger contexts of 'diffusion' and 'diffusionism' as archaeological concepts: Bruce G. Trigger, *A History of Archaeological Thought*, second edition (Cambridge: Cambridge University Press, 2006), 217–23; 284–8; 307–8.

43 JHB, 'Place of the Near Orient', 161; 165; 168–9; 170–1.

44 JHB, 'Place of the Near Orient', 163; 169–7; 174–80.

45 JHB, 'Place of the Near Orient', 180–81. JHB later used 'historical laboratory' as an analogy of the historical-research field in a promotional booklet for his textbooks: [JHB], *A Historical Laboratory: How the expert historian does his work* (Boston: Ginn and Company, 1922).

On JHB's conversations with GEH about the sciences and humanities: *AE*, 214–15, 224–28. On science in American popular culture: Marcel C. LaFollette, *Making Science Our Own: Public images of science, 1910–1955* (Chicago: University of Chicago Press, 1990).

46 JHB, 'Place of the Near Orient', 180–84.

47 JHB, 'Plan for the Organization of an Oriental Institute at the University of Chicago', 16 January 1919, General Education Board (hereafter GEB)/2324.2 Oriental Inst./series I, sub-series 4, box 659, folder 6851, RAC. JHB, 'Place of the Near Orient', 159–60 (emphasis JHB's).

48 JHB to Harry Pratt Judson, 25 January 1919, Office of the President, Harper, Judson and Burton Administrations Records (hereafter OP), 9:19, SPRC; Wallace Buttrick to JHB, 28 January 1919, GEB/2324.2 Oriental Inst./series I, sub-series 4, box 659, folder 6851, RAC.

49 JHB to JDR Jr. w/enc: 'Plan for the Organization of an Oriental Institute at the University of Chicago', 16 February 1919; Starr J. Murphy to Harry Pratt Judson, 5 March 1919; Harry Pratt Judson to Starr J. Murphy, 7 March 1919; Starr J. Murphy (the source of the project-test idea) to JDR Jr., 14 and 19 April 1919; JDR Jr. to JHB, 2 May 1919, RFA/R.G. 2 (OMR)/JDR Jr. series, Educational Interests sub-series, box 112, University of Chicago, Oriental Institute, 3 yr. pledge - 5 yr. pledge, RAC. JHB formally announced the Institute's creation in: JHB, 'The Oriental Institute of the University of Chicago', *American Journal of Semitic Languages and Literatures* XXXV, No. 4, July (1919): 196–204.

50 On the Fertile Crescent survey: *AE*, 231–48; see also *Pioneers to the Past: American archaeologists in the Middle East, 1919–1920*, ed. Geoff Emberling (Chicago: Oriental Institute, University of Chicago, 2010). Upon learning of JHB's Institute grant, GEH advised him to compile detailed reports to cultivate future support: GEH to JHB, 17 May 1919, JHPB, OIA. JHB followed that advice: JHB to JDR Jr., 16 August 1919 and 29 December 1922, DOC, OIA. For JHB's first published report: JHB, *The Oriental Institute of the University of Chicago: A beginning and a program* (Chicago: University of Chicago Press, 1922), Preprint from *American Journal of Semitic Languages* 38 (July 1922): 233–328.

51 On the renewal of OI funding: JHB, Memorandum of Conversation with Martin A. Ryerson, 30 October 1923, OP, 51:8, SPRC; JHB, 'Future and Development of the Oriental Institute', 23 November 1923, OP, 51:9, SPRC; JHB to JDR Jr., 24 November 1923, RFA/R.G. 2 (OMR)/JDR Jr. series, Educational Interests sub-series, box 111, University of Chicago, Oriental Institute, Env. 1, RAC; JDR Jr. to Ernest D. Burton, 26 November 1923, RFA/R.G. 2 (OMR)/JDR Jr. series, Educational Interests sub-series, box 112, University of Chicago, Oriental Institute, 3 yr. pledge - 5 yr. pledge, RAC; JHB to Ernest D. Burton, 30 November 1923, OP, 9:20, SPRC; Ernest D. Burton to JDR Jr., 1 December 1923, RFA/R.G. 2 (OMR)/JDR Jr. series, Educational Interests sub-series, box 112, Univ. of Chicago, Oriental Inst., 3 yr. pledge - 5 yr. pledge, RAC; JDR Jr. to Ernest D. Burton, 4 and 29 December 1923, OP, 51:8, SPRC. For the man-not-science quote: JHB to GEH, 31 December 1923, CITA (emphasis JHB's).

52 Wickliffe Rose to Raymond B. Fosdick, 25 May 1928, GEB/2324.2 Oriental Institute/series 1, sub-series 4, box 659, folder 6852, RAC. The health, natural and social sciences remained a Rockefeller priority, and when the General Education Board eventually allocated funds for the OI, it was as an exception to policy: Merle Curti and Roderick Nash, *Philanthropy in the Shaping of American Higher Education* (New Brunswick: Rutgers University Press, 1965), 236–7.

53 On the proposal that resulted in the endowments: *AE*, 337–41. Over his lifetime, JHB raised nearly US$11.2 million for the Institute and his personal research programme: Dana S. Creel, 'Dr. Breasted's Work and the Oriental Institute', Memorandum to JDR Jr., 23 March 1959, RFA/R.G. 2 (OMR)/series JDR Jr., sub-series Educational Interests, box 111, University of Chicago, Oriental Institute, Env. 3, RAC. That sum would equal about US$248 million at the time of writing: Samuel H. Williamson, 'Seven ways to compute the relative value of a U.S. dollar amount, 1774 to present'. JHB, *The Oriental Institute*, The University of Chicago Survey, Vol. XII (Chicago: University of Chicago Press, 1933). For the Institute's projects today: 'Research at the Oriental Institute'. Accessed June 2021. https://oi.uchicago.edu/research.

54 Trigger, *A History of Archaeological Thought*, 21–2.

55 Trigger's 'Bibliographical Essay' and references comprised, at the time, an admirably thorough and critical survey of such publications: Trigger, *A History of Archaeological Thought*, 549–680.

Bibliography

Abt, Jeffrey, *American Egyptologist: The life of James Henry Breasted and the creation of his Oriental Institute* (Chicago: University of Chicago Press, 2011).

Adams, Walter S., 'George Ellery Hale, 1868–1938', *Biographical Memoirs* (National Academy of Sciences) XXI, no. 5 (1940): 181–241.

Boyer, John W., '"Broad and Christian in the fullest sense": William Rainey Harper and the University of Chicago', *University of Chicago Record* 40, No.2 (2006): 2–26.

Breasted, Charles, *Pioneer to the Past: The story of James Henry Breasted, archaeologist* (Chicago: University of Chicago Press, 1943).

Breasted, James Henry, *Ancient Times: A history of the early world, an introduction to the study of ancient history and the career of early man* (Boston & New York: Ginn and Company, 1916).

Breasted, James Henry, 'The Oriental Institute of the University of Chicago', *American Journal of Semitic Languages and Literatures* XXXV, no. 4, July (1919): 196–204.

Breasted, James Henry, 'The place of the Near Orient in the career of man and the task of the American Orientalist', *Journal of the American Oriental Society* 39 (1919): 159–84.

Breasted, James Henry, 'The origins of civilization', *The Scientific Monthly* 9.4 – 6 (1919) and 10.1 – 3 (1920).

Breasted, James Henry, *The Oriental Institute of the University of Chicago: A beginning and a program* (Chicago: University of Chicago Press, 1922). Preprint from *American Journal of Semitic Languages* 38, July (1922): 233–328.

Breasted, James Henry, *A Historical Laboratory: How the expert historian does his work* (Boston: Ginn and Company, 1922).

Breasted, James Henry, 'John Merlin Powis Smith', *University [of Chicago] Record* 19 [new series], no. 1, January (1933): 69–73.

Breasted, James Henry, *The Oriental Institute*. The University of Chicago Survey, vol. XII. (Chicago: University of Chicago Press, 1933).

Breasted, James Henry, ed., The Epigraphic Survey (directed by Harold H. Nelson), *Earlier Historical Records of Ramses III*, Medinet Habu–Vol. I, Oriental Institute Publications, Vol. VIII, (Chicago: University of Chicago Press, 1930).

Breasted, James Henry and James Harvey Robinson, *Outlines of European History, Part I* (Boston: Ginn and Company, 1914).

Bremner, Robert H., '"Scientific philanthropy", 1873–93', *Social Service Review* 30, No. 1, March (1956): 168–73.

Bremner, Robert H., *American Philanthropy*, second edition (Chicago: University of Chicago Press, 1988).

Chernow, Ron, *Titan: The life of John D. Rockefeller, Sr.* (New York: Random House, 1988).

Cooper, Jerrold S., 'From Mosul to Manila: early approaches to funding Ancient Near Eastern Studies research in the United States', *Culture and History* 11 (1992): 133–37.

Curti, Merle, 'Scholarship and popularization of learning', in *The Growth of American Thought* (New York: Harper and Row, 1943), 564–87.

Curti, Merle and Roderick Nash, *Philanthropy in the Shaping of American Higher Education* (New Brunswick: Rutgers University Press, 1965).

Davis, Thomas W., *Shifting Sands: The rise and fall of biblical archaeology* (Oxford: Oxford University Press, 2004).

Der Manuelian, Peter, *Walking Among Pharaohs: George Reisner and the dawn of modern Egyptology* (Oxford: Oxford University Press, 2023).

Driver, G. R., 'Oriental studies and the Oriental Institute', *Oxford* 17, No. 2, May (1961): 56–67.

Drower, Margaret S., *Flinders Petrie: A life in archeology* (London: Victor Gollancz Ltd, 1985).

Emberling, Geoff, ed., *Pioneers to the Past: American archaeologists in the Middle East, 1919–1920* (Chicago: Oriental Institute, University of Chicago, 2010).

Fosdick, Raymond B., *John D. Rockefeller, Jr.: A portrait.* (New York: Harper and Brothers, 1956).

Fosdick, Raymond B., *Adventures in Giving: The story of the General Education Board* (New York: Harper and Row, 1962).

Fosdick, Raymond B., *The Story of the Rockefeller Foundation*. Reprint of 1952 edition, with introduction by Steven C. Wheatley. (New Brunswick: Transaction Publishers, 1989).

Gates, Frederick T., *Chapters in My Life* [with Robert S. Morison, 'Frederick Taylor Gates Lectures'] (New York: Free Press, 1977).

Gray, George W., *Education on an International Scale: A history of the International Education Board* (New York: Harcourt, Brace, 1941).

Goode, James F., *Negotiating for the Past: Archaeology, nationalism, and diplomacy in the Middle East, 1919–1941* (Austin: University of Texas Press, 2007).

Goodspeed, Thomas Wakefield, *William Rainey Harper: First president of the University of Chicago* (Chicago: University of Chicago Press, 1928).

Goodspeed, Thomas Wakefield, *A History of the University of Chicago: The first quarter-century*, third edition (Chicago: University of Chicago Press, 1972).

Horowitz, Helen Lefkowitz, *Culture and the City: Cultural philanthropy in Chicago from the 1880s to 1917* (Lexington: University of Kentucky Press, 1976).

Howe, Barbara, 'The emergence of scientific philanthropy, 1900–1920: origins, issues, and outcomes', in *Philanthropy and Cultural Imperialism: The foundations at home and abroad*, ed. Robert F. Arnove (Boston: G. K. Hall & Company, 1980), 25–54.

James, T. G. H., *Howard Carter: The path to Tutankhamun* (London: Taurus Parke, 2001).

James, T. G. H., ed., *Excavating in Egypt: The Egypt Exploration Society, 1882–1982* (Chicago: University of Chicago Press, 1982).

Karl, Barry D. and Stanley N. Katz, 'Donors, trustees, staffs: an historical view, 1890–1930', in *The Art of Giving: Four views on American philanthropy* (North Tarrytown: Rockefeller Archive Center, 1979).

Kohler, Robert E. *Partners in Science: Foundations and natural scientists, 1900–1945* (Chicago: University of Chicago Press, 1991).

LaFollette, Marcel C., *Making Science Our Own: Public images of science, 1910–1955* (Chicago: University of Chicago Press, 1990).

Lepsius, Karl Richard, *Denkmäler aus Ägypten und Äthiopien nach den Zeichnungen der von Seiner Majestät dem Könige von Preußen Friedrich Wilhelm IV nach diesen Ländern gesendeten und in den Jahren 1842–1845, ausgeführten wissenschaftlichen Expedition auf Befehl Seiner Majestät herausgegeben und erläutert*, 12 vols. (Berlin: Nicolaische Buchhandlung, 1859).

Madsen, David, 'Daniel Coit Gilman at the Carnegie Institution of Washington', *History of Education Quarterly* IX 2 (1969): 154–86.

McClelland, Charles E., *State, Society, and University in Germany, 1700–1914* (Cambridge: Cambridge University Press, 1980).

Meyer, Daniel Lee., 'The Chicago Faculty and the University Ideal, 1891–1929' (Unpublished Ph.D. dissertation, University of Chicago, 1994).

Nasaw, David, *Andrew Carnegie* (New York: Penguin Press, 2006).

Phillips, C. H., *The School of Oriental and African Studies, University of London, 1917–1967: An introduction* (London: School of Oriental & African Studies, University of London, 1967).

'Proceedings of the American Oriental Society at the Meeting in New Haven, Conn., 1918', *Journal of the American Oriental Society*, 38 (1918): 320–37.

Reingold, Nathan, 'National science policy in a private foundation: The Carnegie Institution of Washington'. In *The Organization of Knowledge in Modern America, 1860–1920*, eds. Alexandra Oleson and John Voss (Baltimore: Johns Hopkins University Press, 1979), 313–41.

Revoldt, Daryl L., 'Raymond B. Fosdick: Reform, Internationalism, and the Rockefeller Foundation', (Unpublished Ph.D. dissertation, University of Akron, 1982).

Roosevelt, Theodore, 'The dawn and sunrise of history', *The Outlook* 115, no. 7, 14 February (1917): 272–75.

Said, Edward, *Orientalism* (New York: Random House, 1978).

Schenkel, Albert F., *The Rich Man and the Kingdom: John D. Rockefeller, Jr., and the protestant establishment*, Harvard Theological Studies (Minneapolis: Fortress Press, 1995).

Schmidt, Nathaniel, 'Early Oriental Studies in Europe and the work of the American Oriental Society, 1842–1922', *Journal of the American Oriental Society* 43 (1923): 1–14.

Silberman, Neil Asher, 'Desolation and restoration: The impact of a biblical concept on Near Eastern Archaeology', *Biblical Archaeologist* 54 (1991): 76–87.

Stocking, George W., 'Clark Wissler', in *Dictionary of American Biography*, supplement 4: 1946–50 (New York: Scribner and Sons, 1958).

Storr, Richard J., *Harper's University: The beginnings* (Chicago: University of Chicago Press, 1966).

Thomas, Nancy, 'American institutional fieldwork in Egypt, 1899–1960', in *The American Discovery of Ancient Egypt*, ed. Nancy Thomas (Los Angeles: Los Angeles County Museum of Art, 1995), 49–72.

Thornton, Amara, '". . . a certain faculty for extricating cash": Collective sponsorship in late 19th and early 20th century British archaeology', *Present Pasts*, 5 (2013): 1–12, doi: http://dx.doi.org/10.5334/pp.55.

Trigger, Bruce G., *A History of Archaeological Thought*, second edition (Cambridge: Cambridge University Press, 2006).

Williamson, Samuel H., 'Seven ways to compute the relative value of a U.S. dollar amount, 1774 to present'. Accessed June 2021, https://www.measuringworth.com/calculators/uscompare/.

Wissler, Clark, *The American Indian: An introduction to the anthropology of the New World* (New York: Douglas C. McMurtrie, 1917).

Wright, Helen, *Explorer of the Universe: A biography of George Ellery Hale* (New York: E. P. Dutton and Company, 1966).

5
An epistolary corpus: beyond the margins of 'official' archives: T. E Peet's First World War correspondence
Clare Lewis

When researching individuals, we are sometimes lucky and family archives collide with institutional ones. This chapter focuses on the case of Thomas Eric Peet (1882–1934, known as T. Eric Peet), a highly influential figure in the history of British Egyptology and its formation as an academic field.[1] During the course of my research, which explores the development of Egyptology as an academic discipline in Britain through the lens of Egyptological inaugural lectures (EILs), I was privileged to have access to the family archive of Peet spread across three members of the family in Cambridge, Harrogate and Oxford.[2] This encounter provided me with a rare insight into both the public and private self (atypical in the treatment of male lives)[3] and thus an unusual opportunity to combine the public and private lives of one key protagonist in the formation of Egyptology as an academic field in Britain.

In particular these family archives include a striking set of stories Peet wrote to his young daughter during active service in the First World War (WW1).[4] The antics of a group of personified hieroglyphs that these stories feature – a highly personal and compelling form of life-writing – catapult the reader into Peet's imaginary world. They are unlike any other form of life-writing that I have encountered across 11 different archival sites. On careful reading with the two other (and more conventional) archival strands of Peet's WW1 correspondence – at the Egypt Exploration Society (EES) in London and Griffith Institute, University of Oxford (GI) – they give insight into the locales and some of the conditions Peet faced on active service during WW1 which he could not discuss explicitly. These letters from a father to a daughter also scale WW1 back to a very human dimension. Sitting on a bus from the family's home in Oxford back to London, holding Peet's briefcase lent to me so kindly by his family and looking through these letters written to his very young daughter – born in March 1914[5] – it was hard not to form an emotional engagement. Indeed I felt uncomfortably like a voyeur, sneaking unauthorised into an intense period of a life lived.

Albeit highly valuable in the study of WW1, my emotional engagement with these letters initially drove my view of this source as falling outside of the remit of the research on EILs that led to this encounter. With a microhistorical approach and a concern more with the social and institutional constructions of knowledge, I felt that my research was perhaps more distanced from the type of engagement with the authors of the EILs that can be problematic in the writing of biographies.[6]

Equally Fulbrook and Rublack reminded me that ego documents do not have to be used in the pursuit of a historical individual, rather:

> Ego documents may also be used for the light they shed on persons whose identities are shaped in relation to changing networks of interpersonal relations, with the 'self' at the intersection of different sets of roles and expectations, while a monitoring 'inner eye' records experiences, expectations and norms in the literary vehicles and conventions available and acceptable at any given time…they can also provide clues to the ways in which the 'social self', thus constructed, may change in certain respects over longer stretches of time.[7]

With this in mind, I returned to these letters interested in how the heavily coded expression of the self compared and contrasted to the version (also heavily coded albeit in different ways) presented to the public and colleagues in EILs. Here, therefore, I test the potential insight that contextual understandings and reading of these letters in conjunction with the WW1 era letters held at the EES and GI can offer for my research deciphering the development of Egyptology through EILs. In Peet's case this relates to his EIL at Oxford in 1934.[8] As yet I can locate no evidence of an EIL when Peet took on his role as the second Brunner Professor of Egyptology at the Institute of Archaeology, University of Liverpool (other than one possible mention in a letter).[9]

Approach to the analysis of EILs

In order to test the potential for the three strands of Peet's WW1 epistolary corpus in deciphering some of the statements in Peet's 1934 EIL, it is useful briefly to outline my approach to EILs as these are an unusual source in themselves.

They also sit as a genre of life-writing, nested within personal, institutional and disciplinary histories. As a highly constrained form of celebratory academic discourse, they are often viewed as ephemera. However, I believe that they can be used as a powerful tool with which to take into account ideas, individuals, structures and socio-economic forces, and their interactions within institutional contexts. They offer a route to a middle path of historiography, that is between the extremes of the history of people or organisations and the history of ideas. For example, the institutional setting both constrains and enables these lectures, and the genealogy of the Chair sets the lectures as part of a series. Destabilising a purely diachronic analysis of the corpus on an individual basis, they represent a tripartite transition rite with content reflecting the research interests of the individual seeking to make an impact at that institutional site.[10] Furthermore, as Waquet observes, 'the rhetorical schema of the lecture and its ritual character … involve personal introspection'.[11] Some go as far as to observe '[it] is a bit like writing one's own obituary … with the obvious difference that I'm not dead yet'[12] and as such inaugural lectures can be viewed as a constituent element of an intellectual autobiography.

My approach to the autobiographical element of EILs is microhistorical rather than biographical, drawing on Lepore's distinctions between biography and microhistory, and in particular her first proposition:

> If biography is largely founded on a belief in the singularity and significance of an individual's contribution to history, microhistory is founded upon almost the opposite assumption: however singular a person's life may be, the value of examining it lies in how it serves as an allegory for the culture as a whole.[13]

Rather than trying to recapture a life history, my research uses a fine-grained analysis to explore why particular statements are made in the context of EILs and the functioning of the Egyptological community around these events. Indeed, the micro-decisions individuals make create social macrostructure, although I do not advocate a purely constructivist position since institutional and social structures, and the constrained nature of EILs as a genre, mean individual agency is not unlimited.[14]

This fine-grained approach is analogous to the 'Morelli method' in fine art where 'one should abandon the convention of concentrating on the most obvious characteristics of the paintings, for these could most easily be imitated … Instead one should concentrate on minor details'.[15]

It is argued that these details provide the authenticity of a work, or for the purposes of this research provide a means of exploring knowledge practices and their contingencies, with the 'idiosyncrasies of the subject … [helping] to shed light on the characteristics of the collective'.[16]

As part of this analysis, it is necessary to build up a sense of the key individual's networks. Considering the array of networks functioning around individuals helps to build up a more complex and nuanced picture, as Thornton suggests.[17] Exploring the development and workings of Peet's networks pre-WW1 also offers an introduction to – and a more informed contextual understanding of – the two main correspondents in the GI and EES WW1 archival strands. These two individuals are the highly influential Egyptologist Sir Alan Gardiner (1879–1963)[18] and the first Brunner Professor of Egyptology at Institute of Archaeology, University of Liverpool, Percy Newberry (1869–1949).[19] I therefore turn to the development of Peet's career and his networks in the next section, before introducing the letters themselves.

T. Eric Peet's entry into Egyptology and the development of his networks

Peet grew up in Liverpool[20] and attended Merchant Taylors' School in Crosby. He sparked his interest in archaeology through listening to a lecture on Cretan archaeology at University College Liverpool[21] as it was then called, prior to the formation of the Institute of Archaeology in Liverpool in 1904. Peet began his studies at Queen's College Oxford some five months after the first reader of Egyptology, Francis Llewellyn Griffith's EIL, but at that stage archaeology and Egyptology were not degree subjects and Peet studied classics and maths (Table 5.1).[22] This shared locale might suggest the nascent development of Peet's Egyptological network, but it was inactive at this stage. Archives tell us that Griffith was to have 'no part in his [Peet's] Egyptological education'[23] and there is no evidence as yet to suggest they intersected during Peet's studies in Oxford.

Instead, contingencies and chance encounters emerge in a study of the development of Peet's archaeological and Egyptological network. A chance meeting with archaeologist and anthropologist David Randall-MacIver[24] over the dinner table at Queen's in Peet's final year as an undergraduate is identified as rekindling Peet's interest in archaeology.[25] This information, deriving from a letter that Randall-MacIver wrote to Gardiner, introduces an issue within biography and microhistory – that of representation and the construction of collective memory. These recollections were written by Randall-MacIver after Peet's death in 1934

Table 5.1　T. E. Peet's career.

1901	Jodrell scholarship Queen's, Oxford to read Maths and Classics
1903–5	Second Class Classics and Maths Mods, Second Class Lit. Hum. Finals
1906	Craven Fellowship
1909	Pelham Student, British School Rome
1909	Garstang excavation Abydos; Newberry Cairo & Delta
1909–13	Excavation at Abydos (with the EEF from 1911)
1914–28	Lectureship, University of Manchester
1915–19	Active service, WW1, Lieutenant 14th Battalion (King's Regiment Liverpool)
1920–33	Brunner Professor of Egyptology, Liverpool
1920–21	Excavation at Amarna
1921–33	Editor of *Liverpool Annals of Archaeology*
1923	Laycock Studentship, Oxford
1923–34	Editor of *The Journal of Egyptian Archaeology* (JEA)
1933–34	Reader (professor designate) Egyptology, Oxford

Source: Author

and at present no archival information corroborates these recollections. There is no extant record from Peet as to what stimulated his interest, but Randall-MacIver's recollections are reproduced in three key biographical sources: Gardiner's obituary of Peet, Peet's entry in the *Oxford Dictionary of National Bibliography* and in *Who Was Who in Egyptology*.[26]

Initially Peet concentrated on Italian prehistoric archaeology, but by 1907 there are indications that he had decided that he could not hold out hope for a post in this field. By 1908 Peet turned to Newberry, then the Brunner Professor of Egyptology at Liverpool, for help and was dispatched to excavate in Egypt with John Garstang, the founder of the Liverpool Institute of Archaeology, at Abydos in 1909. He moved to work with Newberry himself in Egypt later that season, and first encountered Gardiner in the library of Cairo Museum in the autumn of that year. Newberry, unlike Garstang, was employed by the Egypt Exploration Fund (EEF) and in 1910 Peet transferred his services to the EEF excavations at Abydos. By 1911, Peet devoted himself full time to Egyptology and the EEF at Abydos until 1913, firstly with the Swiss archaeologist Édouard Naville and then independently.[27]

Here a concern expressed by Telling highlights another issue with a microhistorical focus such as this. She warns that a focus on the small 'mundane' decisions, made on a day-to-day basis, has the potential to empty a concept of its political content.[28] In particular Egyptian agency is notably absent from this account of Peet's entry into Egyptian archaeology. The exclusion of Egyptians from Egyptology during this period is powerfully encapsulated in a 1923 retort by Ahmed Kamal, a pioneer of Egyptian Egyptology, to Pierre Lacau, the then head of the antiquities service (which was controlled by the French under the terms of the Entente Cordiale until Egypt's full independence in 1952): 'in the sixty-five years you French have directed the Service, what opportunities have you given us?'.[29] This quote also draws attention back to the issue of the construction of collective memory, as the source of this quotation in western histories of Egyptology is John Wilson's 1964 English language history of Egyptology and it would be interesting to explore the original source (and language) of the quote.[30]

Build up to WW1

Differences in excavation approaches and publication aims, and in particular Peet's desire for more scientific methodologies, caused increasing animosity between Naville and Peet. Thus, in the first edition of *The Journal of Egyptology* (*JEA*) two separate articles appeared on Abydos, one by Naville and one by Peet, albeit covering different aspects of the site, with Naville focusing more broadly on Abydos and the Osireion whereas Peet confines himself to discussing that year's excavation activity.[31]

The launch of the *JEA* in 1914 by the EEF was intended to transform the way that the EEF communicated with its subscribers. Previously dig reports had been sent to subscribers in return for their donations. Through the launch of the *JEA*, dig reports were freed to become 'models of scientific authority'[32] and, with this in mind, subscribers became members who were to receive, for their membership dues, the *JEA*, whose aims were announced in its first editorial:

> To give all information obtainable regarding excavations that are being conducted in Egypt, and will contain articles, some, specialized and technical, intended mainly for experts, others, simpler in character, such as will be intelligible for all who care for Egypt and its marvelous interests.[33]

The outbreak of WW1 was to limit this scope for the next five years. Although the *JEA* continued to be published throughout the hostilities the EEF ceased to excavate in Egypt from 1915 until 1920–21.[34] Nonetheless, the EEF Committee did continue to meet, using this time to reorganise the Fund, which would be renamed the Egypt Exploration Society in 1919, and discuss its scheme of work after WW1 and how the objectives of the Fund should be reshaped explicitly to 'promote the knowledge of Ancient Egypt and the Science of Egyptology'.[35]

By 1915, as part of this process, Peet had not only been identified as the prospective lead excavator for the Fund – '[w]hen the time comes for renewing active operations … I do not think we shall find a better man than Peet' – but also as potential future editor of the *JEA*.[36] But Peet had other ideas. In 1915 with signs that WW1 was escalating, and fiercely patriotic, he signed up – receiving his commission as Lieutenant (Army Service Corps) in October 1915 – despite the attempts of friends and colleagues to encourage him into administrative work in Britain.[37]

Initially Peet joined the King's Regiment (Liverpool) 1st and 2nd Battalion (Regular) Army Service Corps and was deployed to Salonika in late 1915. But, discontent with this posting, he requested a transfer to the Western Front in 1918. Ultimately assigned to the 14th Battalion King's Regiment (Liverpool), he arrived in France in July 1918 and was engaged on the Western Front in various actions including the Hundred Days Offensive (the series of Allied offensives in the final hundred days of WW1).[38]

Reflecting once more on Telling's caution regarding microhistories and their exclusion of other narratives, it is worth observing here that the Egyptian Labour Corps (ELC) were also deployed in Salonika and on the Western Front. However their experience was to be very different from British volunteers. Members of the ELC were never given military ranks, uniforms or training. Consisting of over 300,000 individuals classified as 'peasants' (one third of the male 18–35-year-old Egyptian population), these men were 'volunteered' into this corps in often questionable circumstances. Fahmy has drawn attention to the highly problematic representation of the ELC by the modern Egyptian Army over the 2014–18 centenary, and their very poor treatment during WW1.[39] He also argues convincingly that this poor treatment, compounded with that of their compatriots in Egypt, was a key factor contributing to the 1919 Egyptian Revolution.

The three archival strands

Throughout Peet's career he did not have the financial freedom that some of his contemporaries enjoyed and, keen not to lose Peet altogether from Egyptology, a memorandum was drawn up by the EEF in November 1915.[40] In this the EEF formally agreed to contribute to his army salary to maintain it at a pre-defined level, in effect paying him what they understood to be a retaining fee throughout WW1 to ensure his return to them after the war. This contribution was split with Robert (later Sir Robert) Mond[41] contributing two-thirds, and the EEF and Gardiner contributing one-sixth each. Letters relating to these payments form the *first strand* of the correspondence archives of Peet during the war. All but one of these letters were written whilst Peet was not on active service, but during times spent in Britain, or in Ireland whilst transferring between regiments. They date from 1915 and 1916 and his return to Britain following his early decommission.

Peet's regiment was not demobilised fully until March 1919. However, Newberry, who was instrumental in Peet's initial entry into Egyptological excavations prior to WW1, secured his early decommission. Thus Peet was back in the UK working for the EEF in January 1919 and lecturing in Manchester by May that year.[42] Peet's letters to Newberry over the duration of WW1 form the *second archival strand*. These cover the entire duration of WW1, both whilst Peet was on active service and during times back in Britain and Ireland.

The letters of the *third strand* were all written whilst Peet was on active service. Spanning 1917–1919, these letters are from Peet to his young daughter, Patricia (Figure 5.1). As alluded to in the introduction to this chapter, these are a highly unusual set of ego-documents.

Reading the three strands

Peet, highly active on the lecturing circuit prior to WW1, gave his second public lecture for the EEF during 1915 on 22 June speaking about the 'Shepherd Kings of Egypt'.[43] However, less than a month later he was to write to Henry Hall, the Secretary of the EEF, about his desires for a commission 'but only if the Fund can make it possible for me, since I shall have my work cut out to live on an officer's pay'.[44] Re-emphasising three days later that he felt unable to 'do anything definite' until the EEF made its decision, the EEF committee resolved to pay 'him a small retaining fee to help him along in addition to his military pay and to carry on the

Figure 5.1 Portrait of Patricia (daughter of T. E. Peet) aged two years; no location stated [1916]. Peet MS5.5. © Griffith Institute, University of Oxford.

editorial work as best we can without him'.[45] His anxieties thus resolved, he received his commission in October[46] and by 26 December 1915 he was in Salonika where he wrote to Newberry describing his activities:

> What can I tell you except that I am very fit and have never regretted my decision. Anything else that would interest you would come under the ban. We came out on the Olympic and saw something of Moudros harbour – a wonderful sight at present – on the way. Here though still a long way from the firing line, we see exciting events and it is interesting to guess at political movements from the signs we see at the base here.
>
> We are under canvas and suffer no hardships and few discomforts, tho' of course, the men do not come off so easily. Still they are very cheerful and considering half of them are over 45 they stand it very well.[47]

There is no extant correspondence until four months later, when Peet wrote again to Newberry:

> Life passes very quietly. The enemy don't attack and I am convinced they never will. It would be simply throwing away men. On the other hand we don't attack either and I can't say whether we intend to or not. My own work is now on the quay in connection with Greek labourers used in mending the ships. We have few excitements except occasionally a visit from enemy airplanes and once from a Zeppelin. I am just spending my fifth successive day in bed, the result of a chill, but apart from that I have been in excellent health throughout. At first I was in camp with my company, in glorious air in the fields 5 miles out, but I hadn't enough to do then they brought me down to the quay where my Greek is useful and gave me a good billet in a Greek house, and an allowance for meals. Lastly they moved me into this new officers' camp, which is pleasantly situated in a public garden, but ... when spring comes soon deserve [sic] its name of Mosquito Camp.[48]

A letter from this time was also written to Joseph Milne, the then Treasurer of EEF. Sent 'as from' his home address, this is the only letter Peet sent to the EEF during his active service.[49] Largely transactional, it detailed his military pay and asked for the shortfall of just under £109 to the agreed £300 p.a. to be paid. However, he ended his letter with a comment in Greek as to the Greek view of the British presence, thus implicitly revealing details, albeit imprecise, as to his location.

The mosquitoes Peet referenced were a constant feature and problem of the Salonika campaign, leading the Official Correspondent with the Allied Forces to later observe '[t]he only forces to hold the Struma Valley in strength are the mosquitoes, and their effectives may be counted by thousands of millions'.[50] Throughout the three-year duration of the Salonika Campaign the British force suffered severely from malaria, with over 162,000 casualties in total, over six times the level of battle casualties.[51]

One of the other environmental challenges of the Salonika Front was the terrain.[52] A mountainous region overlapping the border between Greece and Bulgaria, the front was made up of a combination of trenches and mountain top strongholds. Lying within the boundaries of Alexander the Great's Macedonia, it was soon discovered by the troops digging trenches that the area was rich in archaeology, with records noting a rifle bomber's comment that 'you could hardly turn a shovel of earth without a piece of old pot coming out'.[53]

Whitworth observes '[a]t first the soldiers on the ground dumped them into sandbags with other rubble, though the more enterprising would pocket items they felt of value to sell to local traders or to their officers later'.[54] However, a number of men and officers with pre-war archaeological experience realised the importance of what was being found and by December 1915 an order protecting antiquities was issued by the British. An intervention by the Greek government meant an order was issued in early 1916 that the British and French forces were to take responsibility for upholding the Greek antiquities laws.[55]

Thus British and the French forces set up specialist archaeology units whose job it was to locate, catalogue and save these artefacts. The British unit was initially under Lieutenant Commander Ernest Gardner who established the British Salonika Force Museum.[56] From February 1916 this museum was based in the White Tower in Salonika harbour, while field teams were formed to retrieve and record finds. These were commanded by officers with archaeological backgrounds.[57] Peet, given his experience, was originally recruited as a field section commander, and in March 1917 when Gardner was recalled to London Peet took over command, remaining as curator of the museum until the autumn of that year. By Peet's own admission he was not an active curator of the museum and did not contribute to the finds or indeed publish on the finds after WW1.[58]

Prior to Peet taking his curatorship he returned briefly to the UK, reviving his Egyptological network. In late October he wrote from Gardiner's house to invite himself to visit Newberry, and during November and early December responded to various EEF questions surrounding guarding the Abydos dig house and ghaffirs in the absence of excavations.[59]

One can only speculate as to how this visit stimulated his letters to his daughter, but it was on his return to Salonika, and his curatorship of the White Tower Museum, that his third strand of wartime correspondence begins. These 15 letters begin with birthday wishes for her third birthday in March 1917.[60] The corpus indicates reciprocation by (and/or on behalf of) his daughter, but none of these letters have come to light.

His second letter, in July 1917, was longer and represents the start of the literary vehicle of personification he was to use for all bar one of the remaining 14 letters. This contains a story to his daughter about her toy horse Anver, who took on the persona of a 'real' horse and went with her to a merry-go-round in Margate. The letter ends rather poignantly:

> And little Marnie was pleased with the bucking of the horses & wrote to Father in his little tent in Salonica. And Father was glad when he read the letter & saw the stamp & the post mark done with real ink. And he said 'Truly my games are not forgotten by my little one.'[61]

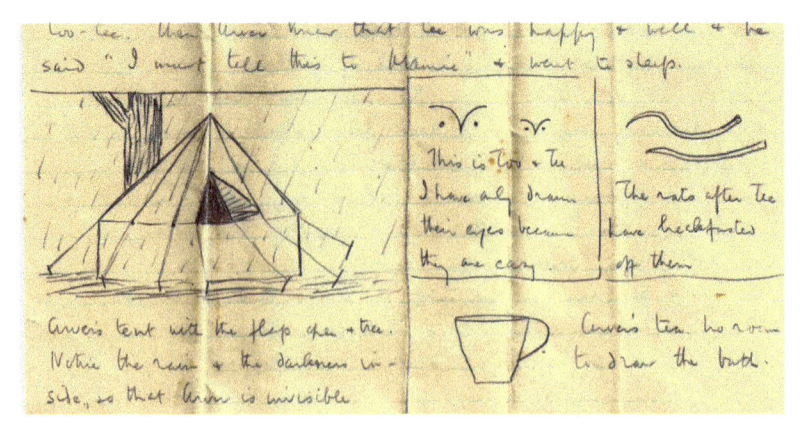

Figure 5.2 Peet's first drawing to his daughter, Peet MSS 4.2.11. T. E. Peet letter to Patricia (undated). © Griffith Institute, University of Oxford.

For the duration of the war Anver appeared in the stories Peet sent back to his daughter, transformed into a soldier serving in Salonika and then the Western Front. The other two key protagonists of these stories were two owls Too and Tee. These characters are first introduced to us in an undated letter written before 31 August 1917 (Figure 5.2).[62] These two owls, who said 'too-tee' at night outside Anver's tent had to be saved one night because of heavy rain. They were sheltered by Anver in his tent and returned the favour by gorging themselves on rats in the tent, which Peet drew at the end of the letter giving us a glimpse, albeit somewhat idealised, into the conditions he was facing.

Too and Tee make their first full first appearance as illustrations in the next letter.[63] As Figure 5.3 shows they have an uncanny likeness to the hieroglyph *m*.[64] For comparison, I show this illustration alongside a transcription by Peet, a transcription from Gardiner, influential in the development in Peet's language skills, and *m* in Gardiner's sign list in Gardiner's *Egyptian Grammar*. After the two men had encountered each other in Cairo Museum in 1909, Peet had begun to study Ancient Egyptian with Gardiner in 1911. Peet subsequently published his first book based around translation work, *The Stela of Sebekkhu*, in 1914, and had begun to publish philologically focused papers in the same year.[65]

Returning to the letter in question, and the further adventures of Too and Tee, we read that the owls went to wake up Anver, and through a series of adventures they found that he had been relocated from 'the Gardens' to 'Marsh Pier'. Peet could well have been relocated at this time as we know that he was located in the 'Camp in the Gardens' in his letter to Newberry in November 1916 (see page 129), and the White Tower,

Figure 5.3 Too and Tee, Peet's Turin Papyrus notes, Gardiner's handwritten hieroglyph m and G17, Gardiner's Sign List. Peet MSS 4.2.3 Letter from T. E. Peet to Patricia (undated); Gardiner Correspondence AHG/42.230.55 Letter from T. E. Peet to A. H. Gardiner (26 November 1928); Griffith MSS 21 Letter from Gardiner to Griffith 22 May 1896; A. H. Gardiner, Egyptian Grammar (Oxford: Griffith Institute, 1957) G17, p.469. © Griffith Institute, University of Oxford.

where the archaeology collection was kept, was at the harbour. Indeed, this White Tower site served a double purpose, being also useful for various intelligence activities – all the archaeologists working closely with the museum over the duration of the war worked in intelligence, with the possible exception of Peet where no archival evidence exists.[66]

Whilst the British authorities recognised the various values of this role with the collection, there were no full-time posts at the White Tower. Peet was not excused from military duties with a contemporary noting that: '[t]heir military duties, it is true, had nothing in common with their special studies, and the late Professor Peet was detailed to count empty petrol tins'.[67]

Peet himself provided a less idealised version of conditions than those in his letter to his daughter in a letter to Newberry in August 1917, almost exactly one month after his letter to his daughter:

> From time to time I realise what a poor correspondent I am and I make good resolutions. These, at least so I excuse myself, are broken in summer by the heat (and letter writing is hot) and in the winter by the cold which benumbs ones [sic] fingers. And I fear the war

> has so dulled my consciousness that I really believe these excuses. The result is that the home letters are the only ones I do not regret. You will have heard that Salonica, or at least the best part of it, has ceased to exist except as a heap of ruins. This leaves us with about 100,000 homeless creatures on our hands, who seem to be unable to lift a finger to help themselves…[68]

This letter also made no direct mention of the White Tower – indeed there is no mention of this throughout the archive – but in a highly patriotic section (Peet's obituaries were to recall his sense of patriotism) it emerges through the letter that Peet was applying for a transfer to the Infantry, ideally on the Western Front, discontent with his tasks in Salonika:

> Since I came out here again 6 months ago I have been doing about one hour's work a day and that could have been done by an NCO… I have applied for transfer to the Infantry. First I tried Machine Guns, but it was full and being a poor houseman I rather fight shy of Artillery, tho' I really think that is the place for a mathematician… the only thing which is any use to the country is ones all … Whether this will come through or not I can't say but I hope so. I shd like to get to France, so much nearer home, but I believe one transfers direct here. In any case I'll let you hear…[69]

A letter to Patricia less than three months after this letter to Newberry was written also gives us a little more insight into conditions. In this letter Too and Tee went to meet the Adjutant's dog for tea in one of the dug-outs. In this tale it transpired that the dug-out had not been bailed out by the fatigue party and was flooded two feet deep with water and dark, although Anver managed to get candles through mysterious means with the rhetorical question of 'do people who have been in the army 2 years buy candles?' In another intersection with 'reality' in this letter it appeared that the Adjutant had promised a photo of the dog 'to send home to… Marnie so that she may know what [the dog is] like' – a promise which Peet, as the 'editor' of the story sincerely hoped he would keep.[70]

The sequence breaks with the next letter. The curatorship of the museum had been transferred to Alexander Wade[71] and on 2 January 1918 Peet wrote a short letter to Patricia, telling her that Too and Tee 'have been very quiet recently …. because they are pleased because the war will not last very long now'.[72] It reveals a homesick Peet, wishing for the end of the war and a return to Egypt, which he described as an idyll for the family unit:

> And I think we will go to Egypt where there is no rain & the sun shines all day long & the sky is blue. And we will live in our little house there & you will not be able to go to school because there is no school to go to and perhaps we shall have a kitten, & 2 little white rabbits & some fowls & a turkey & a goose. And we will make a little pond for the geese to play in. But first we have to finish the war & beat the wicked Hun & I don't think that will take very long now.[73]

One wonders if these sentiments had been driven by the EEF's attempts to interest him in Egyptology at this time, as he comments to Newberry later the same month that 'of Egyptology I know nothing except the Egyptian Journal which Gardiner sent out to me regularly. He keeps it up to an excellent standard under these difficult conditions.'[74]

However welcome the *JEA* was during this time, in 1920 Peet was to convey to Newberry the problems its editorial stance during the war had created:

> When in France I had some copies of our Journal with me, and two brother officers who looked them over both made the same comment. For they both asked me how my paper could on one page appeal for subscriptions and on the next print obituaries of slain Germans with, and this was the point, expressions of regret for their deaths. I had no answer. Now these men were not fools, but rather typical British readers, and what occurred to them has, as I have heard more than once, struck and offended other readers. The irony of it to people whose sons and husbands and brothers were in the trenches was a little too fine to be relished.[75]

This letter also revealed that Gardiner, the then editor of the *JEA*, was a pacifist. Gardiner did not fight in WW1 and had lived in Berlin from 1902–1911 working on the Wörterbuch (the German-based but internationally co-operative Ancient Egyptian dictionary project initiated by Adolf Erman in 1897).[76] Indeed one of the German obituaries referred to relates to the son of Erman, under whom Gardiner had studied in Berlin (the other relates to Dr Gerhard Plaumann who was killed on the German side of the Belgium front, 3 October 1917).[77]

The unusual form of the 2 January 1918 letter to Patricia – it is the only letter of the corpus (bar the initial birthday wishes) without Anver and his friends – also hinted at a change in location for Peet.[78] A letter written on 22 January 1918 to Newberry addressed this issue. Written from Peet's home address, it discussed that his transfer had come into effect, and described his route back to the UK which culminated in 'disturb[ing] a sleepy but delighted family' who believed him to still be in Salonika, early on Christmas morning.[79] It also appears that his January letter to Patricia was written from Cork, as this was where the 3rd Battalion were then located, and he met them on 27 December. This change in circumstances, away from the front – but also still away from his family – may account for the difference in this letter.

He spent six months in Cork, before joining the 14th Battalion in France in mid 1918.[80] Peet explained this location to his daughter through the use, once more, of the trio of Anver, Too and Tee.[81] He had originally been re-dispatched back to Salonika, diverting to the Western Front on his arrival at the interim staging post of Italy.[82] In this July 1918 letter, Too and Tee discovered that Anver had been relocated to France after dealing with a very formidable Colonel at Salonika. Too and Tee conveniently had two cousins – Ta and To – living close to the relocated Anver. Thus a message was sent through the owl network, and Anver danced in delight upon hearing Ta and To. This letter also explains the six-month pause in this correspondence chain, as it appears that his wife and child came to visit him in Cork sometime after 22 January 1918 as he wrote: '[n]ow one evening Anver was going for a little walk, thinking about Rita and Patricia & how happy they all used to be in Cork and he also thought about far Salonica & wondered whether Too & Tee were grieved because he had not gone back there'.[83]

At this stage another hieroglyph character is introduced to us in the form of Buzbug[84] a very irritating wasp who accompanied Anver to target practice on the French coast in what are the last drawings to Peet's daughter in August 1918. Again, the similarities to hieroglyphs are striking (Figure 5.4).

The 14th Battalion, as part 66th Division, was heavily involved in the Hundred Days Offensive and in these later letters to his daughter some descriptions of conditions around the Western Front emerge, albeit sanitised for his daughter and the censors. For example, on 2 October 1918, eight days ahead of the battle of Cambrai, Peet wrote to his daughter again, saying that Anver was going to strafe 'the Huns':

> So at last they came to a place miles from any-where, where there used to be hundreds & hundreds of Huns. And the place was dreadful to see because the guns of the Huns had killed all the grass & flowers

Figure 5.4 Buzbug and Gardiner's sign list L2 compared. Peet MSS 4.2.7. Letter from T. E. Peet to Patricia (8th August 1918); A. H. Gardiner, Egyptian Grammar (Oxford: Griffith Institute, 1957) L2, p.477. © Griffith Institute, University of Oxford.

> & knocked all the leaves & branches off the trees, so that they look just like telegraph poles cut off in the middle. And all the houses had been smashed to bits by the guns & were just like heaps of brick & wood & plaster & all the French people who lived in them had had to go away and leave them taking their cows & horses & carts.[85]

On 15 October, in a pause between the battles of Cambrai and Selle, Peet wrote again. He described how Anver had been chasing the retreating 'Huns': 'In the middle of the night you will get up, take food for 2 days & chase the naughty Huns'.[86] He also depicted the joy of the liberated French, and some of the troop tactics emerge quietly in the letter:

> And when Anver and his men were tired of chasing the Hun other men came up from behind & chased them further. And all the little animals who are Anver's friends & Patricia's too helped to chase the Hun, & Anver cannot write a letter about them because they were all so tired of chasing with their little legs that they have all gone to sleep, & refuse to get up again until they are rested.[87]

In what one can reasonably assume is extreme fatigue Peet signed this letter Anver (the only instance of this in the corpus).

By 11 November the Battalion was in Belgium, which marks the final two letters in this archival strand. Anver's last appearance was in a letter of 2 December 1918, in the longest letter written to his daughter during his wartime service. In this story Anver's servant rescued a frightened, thin puppy from the villages the men were liberating, and tried to hide it from Anver. Ultimately Anver adopted the dog, calling it Tok [*sic*] Emma Beer, which Peet explained as the army vernacular for Trench Mortar Battery.[88]

Perhaps caught up in the exhilaration of the end of the War, Peet wrote a highly patriotic description of the Western Front in a letter written the same day to Newberry in a striking contrast to the conditions suffered by the ELC as described by Fahmy:

> good friends, fairly decent living conditions, and also success have all gone to make it a pleasant though exciting time. I have had phenomenally good luck all through and never been touched, and in addition I have lost very few friends…The last battles … to the Belgium Frontier where we were at the moment when the Armistice began were a wonderful experience…[89]

Peet's mind turned to Egyptology once more, which he referenced in only two of his letters to Newberry during the war:

> Reading is a difficulty because of the book problem. I can carry no large books & am mainly restricted to pamphlets which can be thrown away as read. If you have any of these in hand, old or new I should be only too pleased to have them. Those with anything hieroglyphic in them are what I most need as I feel very badly out of touch with the language.[90]

After the Armistice, the 66th Division secured eastern Belgium and remained in the region until disbanded 24 March 1919, but Newberry secured Peet's early demobilisation, and in his final, undated, letter to Patricia, Peet announced that he would be coming home after telling the 'true story of Jerry the Hun' to his now 4-year-old daughter:

> And with them [the British soldiers] came the big guns & howitzers that nearly shook the house down when they shoot from anywhere near it, & other nasty weapons, & last but not least Anver's Trench Mortars, all packed up on mules. And they all began to give Jerry a bad time (otherwise known as Hell).
>
> And Jerry said This [sic] is no good we have very little to eat & if we stay here we shall certainly all be killed. So he wrote a letter & said 'If you stop shooting & let us go home we will never be wicked again & we will give up all our guns & ships, & there will be no more war. And the British Army said Right-oh.
>
> So Jerry went off back home to try to be good & gave up his ships & his guns … When Anver, Uncle Raymond come marching home again we'll all have crackers for tea and so we will.[91]

And with this, the adventures of Anver and his friends were brought to a close.

These three archival strands, when read together in this way, illustrate how Peet worked his way through conflicting demands during WW1 and the narrative forms his self-representation took over this time. It also helps us to explore the networks of social relationships and systems of meaning that contribute to constituting what might be called the 'social self' over this period. For example, his letters to his daughter, and to his Egyptological colleagues and friend provide insights into his locations and the conditions he faced in some perhaps surprising levels of detail (given the censorship). Despite the level of detail in some aspects, in others it was absent. He made no reference to the White Tower and his archaeological activities, and seemed somehow disengaged from this activity, neither adding to the collection nor actively curating or publishing on it. However, he did choose to use hieroglyphs in his images to his daughter, and his last letter to Newberry from the Front expressed concern as to his lack of engagement in this sphere over the War. This engagement in one sphere, but not in another, suggests an implicit shift in his Egyptological interests during this time.

Fulbrook and Rublack suggest that this microhistorical approach can be extended further, arguing it provides clues to the ways in which the individual's construction of the 'social self' changes over a longer period of time.[92] With this in mind, I now turn to Peet's return to Egyptology on the cessation of hostilities and what these letters add to our understandings of his EIL.

Return to Britain

On Peet's return from WW1, Gardiner and other members of the EES (as it had been renamed) believed that the retaining fee meant that Peet was destined to work for them. However, concerned that the EES could not provide him with the steady income he sought, Peet refused to relocate, believing that he had been paid a salary through WW1, rather than a retaining fee, and that his commitment to the EES had been honoured through publication.[93]

Thus Peet's concern over his family's financial stability emerged as it did prior to his commission in 1915 (and was to re-emerge again prior to his appointment at Oxford). Family, Gardiner, the EES and Newberry intertwine once more. This time Gardiner and the EES were more intransigent than in 1915, and the ensuing impasse was resolved by Newberry. He resigned his Chair at Liverpool University in Peet's favour, with Peet receiving the news in December 1919 just under 12 months after returning from the front.[94]

Commitments for this role rose as Peet sought to increase interest in Egyptology at his Liverpool institutional base where the war had 'killed off interest, more especially financial'.[95] This, combined with Peet's increasing focus on philology, implicitly evident in his wartime correspondence, meant that the 1920–21 EES season at Amarna became his last excavation. Peet initially explained this decision to Gardiner in terms of his career plans: 'I always intended to try to give up regular excavation at 40 or thereabouts. The war and circumstances have hastened the moment.'[96]

The granting of the Amarna concession to the EES was to create ruptures in the Anglo-German Egyptological network, and between Erman and Gardiner in particular, as it had been a German concession prior to the outbreak of WW1.[97] These conflicts also reveal Peet's sense of patriotism once more and hint at his view of Gardiner's WW1 stance:

> Does the Committee realize that this pro-Germanism ... for with which its policy is at present affected is doing it a great deal of harm. We all know the real reasons why poor Gardiner's excellent designs in Egypt fell to the ground. You can't be a pacifist in England and at the same time pull strings at the Foreign office or in Egypt. To the same cause I am inclined to attribute our original failure to get El Amarna. ... Now I do not want to see our Journal full of intentional insults to Germany, but ... our policy must be purged of this pro-German taint.[98]

Interestingly, however, in 1926 Peet was to correspond with Neugebauer (a veteran from the opposing side in WW1) regarding the latter's work on the Rhind Papyrus, and he appears to have divided his belief in the 'internationalism in science' from his post WW1 sentiments, hinting at the complexities of the Anglo-German Egyptological interwar networks.[99]

On Peet's return to England from this excavation, Gardiner and others involved in the EES continued to press him to lecture on their behalf, and to visit London. In 1921 Peet no longer used his views of career trajectory to explain his lack of engagement – blurring the public/private divide with more personal reasons, with an indication of poor health as a consequence of WW1:

> ... that the doctor describes as ... not uncommon in older men from the army, a reaction after what he calls with a smile 'the healthy open life of the trenches' and calls for regular exercise... But looking

back I see that I did overwork and underplay in 1919 and 1920, and in consequence the work has to suffer a little now.[100]

By 1922, after again being chastised by Gardiner, Peet opened up further, describing his condition more fully, shifting from professional discourse to a very personal letter describing what would probably now be recognised as shell-shock or PTSD (post-traumatic stress disorder):

> ... the truth is that for some time I have been in a very curious mental condition. I suppose I had, or nearly had, during the winter, what those who can afford it call a nervous breakdown, due entirely to working through from 1919 without proper holidays. By going away for long weekends on walking tours I managed to stave off the worst, and even keep a certain amount of work and research going. But it was at the cost of considerable mental struggle, mostly shown in curious dislikes for certain people, or still more certain places. For a term I couldn't enter the University Club, and for about a fortnight I had to avoid my own study. Altogether I had a great feeling of nervousness about meeting numbers of people, even those whom I know, which hasn't quite worn off yet. So you can imagine I could hardly have faced London ... At present I have thrown over all pretence of work ... I am a little anxious about next winter, but am taking the precaution of cutting out practically all my free lectures to local societies. I think these were part of the cause of the trouble, and anyhow as soon as they find you can give a popular sort of lecture they begin to impose on your good nature, and though I believe in popularizing my subject I do think there are limits.[101]

Increasingly focusing on philology, as a concession to Gardiner and the EES, Peet began editing the *JEA*, the editorials of which he had so objected to during WW1.

With this compromise in place, Peet largely withdrew from his role as an active public lecturer, increasingly basing himself at the University of Liverpool and building his reputation in philology where publication rather than public presentation and engagement was key. As a prominent individual in Egyptology in the UK at the time, this was to impact the public presentation of Egyptology at a time of disproportionate press interest in the wake of the 'discovery' of the tomb of Tutankhamun. This was particularly relevant for the EES since its funding model meant it was dependent in part upon popular interest generating subscribers for the funding of excavations (Figure 5.5).

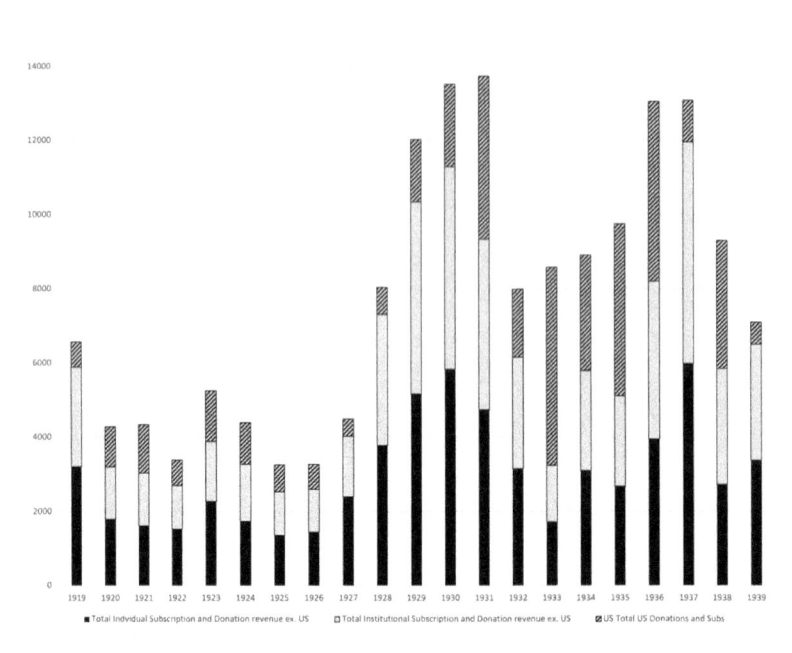

Figure 5.5 EES Income by type 1919–1939 (£). Source: Author's own calculations derived from EES Annual Reports 1919–1939.

The move to Oxford and *The Present Position of Egyptological Studies*, 1934

Peet progressively viewed Oxford, with the subject's locus within what was then called the Oriental Languages and Literature faculty, as ideal for his philological studies and the culmination of his ambitions. Griffith's retirement in 1933 provided him with this opportunity, although once more Gardiner's financial support became key in Peet's career path. Initially Peet viewed the stipend at Oxford as unacceptable. It was only when this was more than doubled by contributions from The Queen's College, the locus of the Chair, and anonymously by Gardiner, that he accepted the post in 1933.[102]

I suggest that an aversion to travel and crowds of people, enunciated in the 1922 letter to Gardiner, also impacted Peet's decision to cease excavating. This is both in terms of the excavations themselves and also the associated public engagement demands driven by the need for public funding for the next year's excavations. Philology had a less explicit driver for regular and material public engagement. This positively reinforced

Peet's decisions to increasingly focus on this aspect, which is reflected in his positioning of Egyptological studies in his EIL at Oxford in 1934. Here one finds statements rejecting the primacy of objects in the study of Egyptology such as 'we are not likely to learn very much more Egyptian history from excavation in Egypt', and instead he argued 'the philological side of Egyptology … there is most reason for hope'.[103]

Returning to the tensions between an institutional and personal reading of inaugurals alluded to earlier in this chapter, from an institutional perspective these can be viewed as an iconic public articulation of the disciplinary divorce process that was underway during the 1920s–1930s. During this era, as Stevenson has discussed, British Egyptology, anthropology and archaeology strove to define and distinguish their fieldwork and methodologies as these fields of study sought to professionalise in their British university settings.[104] As part of this process of disciplinary definition 'Egyptology, faced with more restricted opportunities for new fieldwork, looked increasingly inwards towards its most uniquely distinguishing feature: the ancient language'.[105]

Equally, these EIL sentiments could be viewed as curious for a man who had entered Egyptology – and built up his authority and status – through excavation. However, the microhistorical approach taken in this chapter using the archives held at the EES, the GI and the family archive combine to provide a more personal perspective around one man's experiences. It suggests that during WW1, Peet implicitly shifted his interest towards philology. This is inferred (for example) by his lack of active engagement – or reference to – the White Tower Museum but continued use of hieroglyph animals in his stories to his daughter. Initially, on return to Egyptology after WW1, he presented his decision to cease excavating in terms of career trajectory, before disclosing some three years after the cessation of hostilities that ill health – as a direct result of WW1 – impacted his ability to travel and deal with large crowds. This in all likelihood reinforced his decision to shift focus to philology, compounded with concerns as to family finances, which further guided his decisions around his career choices and focus.

Conclusion

The WW1 archive of Peet allowed me to explore the different sets of roles, expectations and choices that he faced alongside a number of the more personal decisions that led to his appointment as Reader, professor designate, at Oxford in 1934. It also provides some more personal perspectives on several of the choices behind the Egyptological academic community's increasingly philological focus in British academia after WW1. It returns our attention back to certain of the contingences and compunctions that surrounded this trajectory and 'to the place of human beings, with all their wonderful quirks and crankiness, in the development of the great human enterprise that is science'.[106]

There are, however, limits of this approach which extend beyond the banalities of word count.[107] There is a risk that the nature of Peet's letters to his daughter beguiles the researcher into narrowing the scope of the enquiry to a very detailed narrow historical focus. Such a focus does not invariably provide better explanatory power, or to return to the analogy of a painting, 'if examined too closely the blotches of blended pigment … obscure its coherence as a work of art'.[108] In particular, as Telling highlights, it can risk removing possibilities to see a bigger picture and the structures at work.[109] As such, Lepore's claim of the use of microhistory as an allegory to culture (see page 121) seems overstated, as in this case a microfocus overlooks the imperial and national politics (and subsequent power inequalities) in which Egyptology and Egyptians operated. I have referenced two such instances in the discussions above: the restriction of opportunities for Egyptian Egyptologists, and the treatment of Egyptians in the ELC during WW1. But these are only two instances. I have not, for example, discussed the Egyptian uprising of 1919, or the tensions around the contents of Tutankhamun's tomb in 1924.[110]

However, if one acknowledges that a microhistorical approach, such as the one taken in this chapter, offers an 'understanding that consists of seeing connections' but not *all* connections, a systematic microhistory such as this has value.[111] It highlights the dense social networks, and in this case the impact of personal living conditions and the contingencies around people's career trajectories. Rethinking historical developments in this way not only helps draw attention to how Egyptology is constituted in and of its time, but also the individual nature of the enterprise and the disproportionate influence of single personalities. It also reveals the role of happenstance in the development of networks, in this case in terms of chance encounters with both Randall-MacIver and Gardiner. Peet's self-presentation as financially insecure at times of change, and the nascent attempts to provide him with the security he needed, also highlight the workings of the invisible college over this time.

Peet's letters home to his daughter also evoke a vivid sense of lived experience and his patriotic descriptions of the Front at the cessation of hostilities sit in sharp contrast to his later discussions of his ill health. Equally this corpus demonstrates the private/public divide that we all have. Gardiner regarded Peet as a reticent conversationalist. Upon his premature death in 1934 Gardiner was to record that he was 'slightly lacking in imagination', could be 'glum, nay almost sepulchral in appearance' and was prone 'not to mince his words'.[112] This is not the impression one is left with when one has the privilege of reading the stories of Anver, Too and Tee, and their friends.

Acknowledgements

I am grateful to Stephen Quirke, Gabriel Moshenska and the anonymous reviewer for their insightful comments and observations on this chapter; the Peet family for their hospitality, kindness and generously sharing their family archive with me; and the archivists at the EES and the Griffith Institute, University of Oxford.

Notes

1. For example, Alan H. Gardiner, 'Thomas Eric Peet', *Journal of Egyptian Archaeology*, Volume XX, No.1–2 (1934): 66–70.
2. I would like to thank the members of the Peet family who were so generous with their time and access to this archive.
3. Paola Govoni, 'Crafting scientific (auto)biographies', in *Writing About Lives in Science: (Auto) biography, gender and genre*, eds. Paula Govoni and Zelda Alice Franeschi (Göttingen: V&R unipress, 2014), 17.
4. These letters were in the family's possession when I first encountered them. Twelve of them were transferred to the Griffith Institute, University of Oxford in 2014 (see Griffith Institute, University of Oxford. 'Accessions of the Griffith Institute Archive 1990–2020, 2014'. Accessed 9 September 2021. http://www.griffith.ox.ac.uk/archive/accessions/#2014) and are held as Peet MSS 4.2. All bar three of these letters are dated, although the stories in the letters provide a chronology to the corpus. The remaining letters have been retained by the family.
5. She was born 3 March 1914. Britain declared war on 4 August 1914.
6. Jill Lepore, 'Historians who love too much: reflections on microhistory and biography', *The Journal of American History* 88 (2001): 141.
7. Mary Fulbrook and Ulinka Rublack, 'In relation: The 'social self' and ego-documents', *German History* 28, No. 3 (2010): 268.
8. T. Eric Peet, The Present Position of Egyptological Studies. Inaugural lecture delivered before the University of Oxford on 17 January 1934 (Oxford: Oxford University Press, 1934).
9. Griffith Institute University of Oxford. Newberry Correspondence, 23/10, Letter from H. R. Hall to Percy Newberry (1 April 1920).
10. For a fuller discussion of some of the various methodological limitations and approaches that emerge when considering this genre, see Clare Lewis, 'Inaugural Lectures in Egyptology: T. E. Peet and his pupil W. B. Emery', *Bulletin of the History of Archaeology*, Vol 26, Issue 1, November: Art 9 (2016).
11. Françoise Waquet, 'Academic Homage and Intellectual Genealogy: Inaugural Lectures at the College de France (1949–2003)', *History of Universities* Volume XXI/2 (2006): 203.
12. Eleanor Robson, 'In Nisaba's House of Wisdom and Nabu's True House: Social Geographies of Cuneiform Scholarship in Ancient Iraq', Inaugural Lecture, UCL, London (3 February, 2015).

Recording accessed 14 September 2021. https://soundcloud.com/ucl-arts-social-science/in-nisabas-house-of-wisdom-and-nabus-true-house-professor-eleanor-robson-ucl-history
13 Lepore 'Historians who love too much', 134–8.
14 See, for example, Kathryn Telling, 'Bourdieu and the problem of reflexivity: recent answers to some old questions', *European Journal of Social Theory* 19 (2016): 149.
15 Carlo Ginzburg and Anna Davin, 'Morelli, Freud and Sherlock Holmes: clues and scientific method', *History Workshop* No. 9, Spring (1980): 7.
16 Elizabeth Garber, 'Introduction', in *Beyond History of Science: Essays in honor of Robert E. Schofield,* ed. Elizabeth Garber (Bethlehem and Cranbury: Lehigh University Press; London: Associated University Press, 1990), 9.
17 Amara Thornton 'Social networks in the history of archaeology: placing archaeology in its context', in *Historiographical Approaches to Past Archaeological Research*, eds. Gisela Eberhardt and Fabian Link (Berlin: Edition Topoi, 2015), 69–94.
18 For the influence and reach of Sir Alan Gardiner over British Egyptology see Raymond Falconer, 'Sir Alan Henderson Gardiner', *The Journal of Egyptian Egyptology* 50 (1964): 170–2.
19 For Newberry, see Warren Dawson, 'Percy Edward Newberry, M.A., O.B.E.' *The Journal of Egyptian Archaeology* Vol. 36 (1950): 101–3
20 Family archives include T. Eric Peet's birth certificate, registered in the Walton subdistrict, now part of Liverpool North, Bootle, and Crosby. See UK Births Marriages, Deaths and Censuses on the Internet. Accessed 10 September 2021. https://www.ukbmd.org.uk/reg/districts/west%20derby.html.
21 Griffith Institute, University of Oxford. Gardiner Correspondence, AHG/42.230.1, Unsigned letter, 'Thomas Eric Peet' (no date). This testament, written by a school friend of T. E. Peet's describes the lecture as being in 1899–1900 'by Hogarth or Evans – I forget which'. Given that Evans embarked on a series of public lectures in the summer of 1900, it is probable that it is reference to these. See Susan Sherratt, 'Representations of Knossos and Minoan Crete in the British, American and Continental Press 1900 – C.1930', *Creta Antica* 10/II, (2009): 622.
22 Gardiner, 'Thomas Eric Peet', 66; Frances Ll. Griffith, The Study of Egyptology: inaugural lecture delivered in the Ashmolean Museum on May 8, 1901. (Oxford: H. Hart, printer to the University, 1901); Alice Stevenson, 'The object of study: Egyptology, archaeology, and anthropology at Oxford, 1860–1960' in *Histories of Egyptology: Interdisciplinary measures,* ed. William Carruthers (London and New York: Routledge, 2015), 24–25. For F Ll. Griffith (1862–1934) see Alan H. Gardiner, 'Francis Llewellyn Griffith', The Journal of Egyptian Archaeology, Vol. 20, No. 1/2 (1934): 71–77.
23 Peet Library, The Queen's College, University of Oxford. Letter from F. Ll. Griffith addressed to Driver (6 June 1932).
24 For Randall-MacIver, see T. C. Hencken, revised by S. Stoddart, 'MacIver, David Randall (1873–1945)', Oxford Dictionary of National Biography (published online 24 September 2004). https://doi.org/10.1093/ref:odnb/35667.
25 Around the time he met Peet, David Randall-MacIver was excavating at Abydos (from 1899–1901) for the EEF and was the Laycock Scholar, which Peet himself went on to become in 1923. Peet, as a senior undergraduate, was invited for dessert either by Grove or Clark (Randall-MacIver was a permanent member of the common room at this time). See also Griffith Institute, University of Oxford, Gardiner Correspondence AHG/42.230.2. Letter from Randall-MacIver to A. H. Gardiner (13 March 1934).
26 Gardiner, 'Thomas Eric Peet'; Battiscombe Gunn, revised by R. S. Simpson, 'Peet, (Thomas) Eric' *Oxford Dictionary of National Biography,* (published online 23 September 2004). https://doi.org/10.1093/ref:odnb/35456; Morris L. Bierbrier, ed., *Who Was Who in Egyptology* (London: Egypt Exploration Society, fifth edition. 2019), 357.
27 T. Eric Peet published *The Stone and Bronze Ages in Italy* (Oxford: The Clarendon Press) in 1909 which was viewed as a canonical text for some time. See, for example, Gardiner, 'Thomas Eric Peet': 68; J. L. M. 'Thomas Eric Peet', *The Oxford Magazine,* March 1 (1943): 531. For Percy Newberry, see Bierbrier, *Who Was Who in Egyptology*, 341; and for John Garstang, see Bierbrier, *Who Was Who in Egyptology,* 177. For Gardiner's encounter with Peet, see Gardiner, 'Thomas Eric Peet': 68. At the time Gardiner was working with Weigall at Sheikh Abd el-Kurna to survey tombs (the results of which would be published in 1913). Gardiner recollects that this encounter in Cairo Museum led to Peet asking Gardiner to teach him hieroglyphs, but by the time this happened Peet had taught himself Middle Egyptian, and thus Gardiner confined

himself to 'starting him in Late Egyptian'. For Édouard Naville, see Bierbrier *Who Was Who in Egyptology*, 338–9.
28 Telling, 'Bourdieu and the problem of reflexivity', 155.
29 See Donald M. Reid, *Whose Pharaohs? Archaeology, museums, and Egyptian national identity from Napoleon to World War I* (Berkeley: University of California Press, 2002), 172–212; Donald M. Reid 'Indigenous Egyptology: The decolonization of a profession?', *Journal of the American Oriental Society*, 105, (1985): 233–46; Fekri Hassan, 'Conserving Egyptian Heritage: seizing the moment', in *British-Egyptian Relations from Suez to the Present Day*, eds. Noel Brehony and Ayman El-Desouky (Berkeley, London and Beirut: SAQI, 2007), 209–33.
30 John A Wilson, *Signs & Wonders upon Pharaoh: A history of American Egyptology* (Chicago: University of Chicago Press, 1964), 192–3. For Kamal see Bierbrier, Who Was Who in Egyptology, 246.
31 T. Eric Peet, 'The year's work at Abydos', *The Journal of Egyptian Archaeology*, Vol. 1, No. 1, Jan. (1914): 37–9.
32 David Gange, *Dialogues with the Dead: Egyptology in British culture and religion, 1822–1922* (Oxford: Oxford University Press, 2013), 153–5.
33 Anon, 'Editorial Statement', *The Journal of Egyptian Archaeology*, Vol. 1, No. 1 Jan. (1914): 1.
34 The 1915 EEF expedition to Balabish, the only one undertaken by the EEF during the war, was requested by American members of the EEF and directed by Thomas Whittemore. See EES Correspondence Archives London. Box 14c, Letter from HR Hall to Emily Paterson (4 July 1915); also Thomas Whittemore, 'Preface' in *Balabish*, Gerald A. Wainwright and Thomas Whittemore (London: George Allen & Unwin, 1920), v.
35 EES Correspondence Archives, London. EES XVIII.32, EEF Report of Sub-committee (3 October 1916).
36 The quote derives from EES Correspondence Archives, London. EES.XIV.c, Letter from F. G. Kenyon to H. R. Hall (25 July 1915). Discussion as to his potential editorship emerges in related correspondence for example, EES Correspondence Archives, London. EES.XIV.c, Letter from F. G. Kenyon to H. R. Hall (25 May 1915).
37 Gardiner, 'Thomas Eric Peet', 69; EES Archives London. EES.XIV.h, T. E. Peet letter to H. R. Hall (19 October 1915); Griffith Institute, University of Oxford. Gardiner Correspondence, AHG/42.230.1, Unsigned letter, 'Thomas Eric Peet' (no date).
38 See Forces War Records, 'Record Details for T. E. Peet' (21 October 1915). Accessed 19 September 2019. https://www.forces-war-records.co.uk/records/4143514/lieutenant-t-e-peet-british-army-kings-liverpool-regiment/. The 14th Battalion arrived in France June 1918 from Salonika where they joined the 66th (2nd East Lancashire) Division on 23 July. Actions on the Western Front included the Battle of Cambrai, the Pursuit to the Selle, the Battle of the Selle, and the Final Advance in Picardy. On 13 August 1918 the Battalion were absorbed by the 18th Battalion of the 199th Brigade in the 66th Division. See Forces War Records, 'Unit History: King's (Liverpool Regiment)' (2019). Accessed 19 September 2019. https://www.forces-war-records.co.uk/units/259/kings-liverpool-regiment; also The Wartime Memories Project, '14th Battalion, Kings Regiment (Liverpool)' https://wartimememoriesproject.com/greatwar/allied/battalion.php?pid=6417. Accessed 14 September 2021. For correspondence relating to Peet's deployment and subsequent discontent with his posting see, for example, Griffith Institute University of Oxford. Newberry Correspondence 36/41, Letter from T. E. Peet to P. E. Newberry (26 December 1915); Griffith Institute University of Oxford. Newberry Correspondence, 36/44, Letter from T. E. Peet to Percy Newberry (25 August 1917).
39 Khaled Fahmy, 'The Great Threat of History', recording of conference paper (27 March 2019). Accessed 19 September 2019. https://khaledfahmy.org/en/2019/04/06/the-great-theft-of-history/. In this paper Fahmy discusses the problem of lack of access to Egyptian primary sources. The memoir of Ismat Sayft al-Dawa details the poor treatment experienced on the Western Front, and the work of Alia Mossallam tracing the popular song 'Ya Aziz Einy' provides information as to the ELC locations. For the problematic representation of the ELC by the Egyptian Army over 1914–18 see, for example, Egypt Today Staff, Egypt's Army celebrates end of World War I, *Egypt Today* online (12 November 2017). Accessed 20 September 2019. https://www.egypttoday.com/Article/1/32176/Egypt's-Army-celebrates-end-of-World-War-I. No Victoria Crosses have been awarded to Egyptians.
40 EES Archives London. EES.XI.h.21, EEF Committee contract between the EEF and T. E. Peet (12 November 1915). Also, EES Archives London, EES Correspondence Archive Box 14f, Letter from Milne to Miss Paterson (16 March 1916).

41. Robert Mond (1867–1938) was a generous supporter of excavations in the Middle East and Egypt in particular, defraying the cost of publications, and presenting antiquities to museums. He became President of the EES in 1929. See Bierbrier, *Who Was Who in Egyptology*, 323.
42. For the demobilisation of the regiment, see Chris Baker, 'The 66th (2nd East Lancashire) Division', *The Long Trail* (2019). Accessed 11 September 2019. https://www.longlongtrail.co.uk/army/order-of-battle-of-divisions/66th-2nd-east-lancashire-division/. Regarding Peet's early decommission, see Gardiner, 'Thomas Eric Peet', 70; and regarding his return to work for the EEF, see Griffith Institute, University of Oxford. Newberry Correspondence 36/48, Letter from T. E. Peet to Percy Newberry (6 January 1919). For his lecturing in Manchester, see Griffith Institute, University of Oxford. Gardiner Correspondence, AHG/42.230.220, Letter from T. E. Peet to Gardiner (2 May 1919). He had been appointed lecturer at Manchester in 1914, following Gardiner's resignation (see Table 5.1).
43. Egypt Exploration Fund, *Report of the Annual General Meeting* (London: Kegan Paul, Trench Trubner & Co, 1915), 16.
44. EES Archives London. Box 14c, Letter from T. E. Peet to H. R. Hall (20 July 1915). For Henry Hall see Bierbrier Who Was Who in Egyptology, 203.
45. EES Archives London. Box 14c, Letter from T. E. Peet to H. R. Hall (23 July 1915); EES Archives London. Box 14c, Letter from Kenyon to H. R. Hall (25 July 1915).
46. War Forces Records Record, Details for T. E. Peet (King's (Liverpool Regiment)) *War Forces Record* 21 October 1915. Accessed 20 May 2019. https://www.forces-war-records.co.uk/records/4143514/lieutenant-t-e-peet-british-army-kings-liverpool-regiment/
47. Griffith Institute University of Oxford. Newberry Correspondence 36/41, Letter from T. E. Peet to P. E. Newberry (26 December 1915).
48. Griffith Institute University of Oxford. Newberry Correspondence 36/42, Letter from T. E. Peet to P. E. Newberry (11 February 1916).
49. EES Correspondence Archive, EES, London. Box 14f, letter from T. E. Peet to Milne (20 February 1916). For Milne see Bierbrier Who Was Who in Egyptology, 319.
50. I noticed in researching this paper that the Salonika Campaign Society newsletter is called *The New Mosquito*. Salonika Campaign Society, 'Salonika Campaign Society, 1915–1918'. Accessed 20 November 2020. https://salonikacampaignsociety.org.uk/publications-and-dvds/the-new-mosquito/. See also George Ward Price, *The Story of the Salonica Army* (London: Hodder and Stoughton, 1918), 206.
51. Alan S. Wakefield, 'Mountains, mules and malaria: the British frontline soldier's experience of campaigning in Macedonia, 1915–1918', *Journal of the Society for Army Historical Research* 82 (2004): 333.
52. Wakefield, 'Mountains, mules and malaria', 329–33.
53. Michael Llewellyn-Smith, *Archaeology Behind the Battle Lines*, eds. Andrew Shapland and Evangelia Stefani (London and New York: Taylor and Francis. Kindle Edition, 2017), xv. Also M. Whitworth, 'Thomas Eric Peet University of Manchester and Manchester Museum', *University of Manchester* (n.d.). Accessed 11 September 2019. http://www.ww1.manchester.ac.uk/thomas-eric-peet/.
54. Whitworth, 'Thomas Eric Peet'.
55. Andrew Shapland, 'The British Salonika Force Collection at the British Museum', in *Archaeology Behind the Battle Lines*, eds. Andrew Shapland and Evangelia Stefani (London and New York: Taylor and Francis. Kindle Edition, 2017), 85.
56. Ernest Gardner shared Egyptian fieldwork experience and interest with Peet having also worked for the EEF during 1885–6 excavating at Naucratis. See Bierbrier, *Who Was Who in Egyptology*, 176. For the British Salonika Forces Museum, see Llewellyn-Smith, 'Foreword', xxii; Shapland, 'The British Salonika Force Collection at the British Museum'.
57. This account does not reflect Greek views as to the formation of the White Tower Collection. See the papers in Shapland, Andrew and Evangelia Stefani (eds.), *Archaeology Behind the Battle Lines*. (London and New York: Taylor and Francis Kindle Edition, 2017) for more perspectives on this issue.
58. Shapland, 'The British Salonika Force Collection at the British Museum', 85–7.
59. Griffith Institute, University of Oxford. Newberry Correspondence 36/43, Letter from T. E. Peet to P. E. Newberry (26 October 1916). Examples of EEF correspondence over this period include EES Correspondence Archive, EES, London. Miscellaneous Correspondence, letter from T. E. Peet to Miss E. Paterson (5 November 1916) and letter from T. E. Peet to Milne (20 November 1916).
60. Family private archives. Letter from T. E. Peet to his daughter (3 March 1917).

61 Griffith Institute, University of Oxford. Peet MSS 4.2.1, Letter from T. E. Peet to Patricia (27 July 1917).
62 Griffith Institute, University of Oxford. Peet MSS 4.2.11, Letter from T. E. Peet to Patricia (undated but identifiable from series as coming before 4.2).
63 Griffith Institute, University of Oxford. Peet MSS 4.2.3, Letter from T. E. Peet to Patricia (undated but in envelope dated 30 September 1917).
64 Alan H. Gardiner, *Gardiner's Egyptian Grammar* (Oxford: Griffith Institute, 1957), 469, G17.
65 T. Eric. Peet, *The Stela of Sebekkhu* (Manchester: Univ. Pr., 1914); T. Eric Peet, 'An unrecognized meaning of the verb 𓅓.', *Journal of Egyptian Archaeology* Vol. I, (1914): 209–11; T. Eric Peet, 'Can ⇌ be used to negative *sdmt.f*?' *ZAS* 52 (1914): 109–11.
66 Shapland, 'The British Salonika Force Collection at the British Museum', 88.
67 Malcom Burr, *Slouch Hat* (London: MW Books, 1935), 212; also Shapland, 'The British Salonika Force Collection at the British Museum', 87.
68 Griffith Institute, University of Oxford. Newberry correspondence 36/44, Letter from T. E. Peet to Percy Newberry (25 August 1917).
69 *Ibid.*
70 Griffith Institute, University of Oxford. Peet MSS 4.2.5, Letter from T. E. Peet to Patricia, 'How Too and Tee had Tea in a Dug-out' (12 November 1917).
71 Shapland, 'The British Salonika Force Collection at the British Museum', 87; for a discussion of Wade and his role, see Shapland, 'The British Salonika Force Collection at the British Museum', Richard Clogg, 'Foreign archaeologists in Greece in time of war', in *Archaeology Behind the Battle Lines*, eds. Andrew Shapland and Evangelia Stefani (London and New York: Taylor and Francis. Kindle Edition, 2017), 40–57
72 Griffith Institute, University of Oxford, Peet MSS 4.2.6, Letter from T. E. Peet to Patricia (2 January 1918).
73 *Ibid.* Other letters do offer perspectives on Peet's view of Egyptians. For example within these archival threads he believed that Arabic proficiency was necessary for an excavator in order to communicate effectively – Griffith Institute, University of Oxford. Gardiner Correspondence, AHG/42.230.181, Letter from T. E. Peet to Alan Gardiner (1 June 1921); he defended the local guards in an instance where the EEF and Naville thought they were to blame with the comment that no 'Arab will sleep alone, especially on the desert' – EES Correspondence Archive, EES, London. Miscellaneous Correspondence, letter from T. E. Peet to Miss E Paterson (5 November 1916); and was keen for Egyptians to study Egyptology at Liverpool, believing this to be the 'signal service to Archaeology and also to Egypt itself' – Griffith Institute, University of Oxford. Gardiner Correspondence, AHG/42.230.144, Letter from T. E. Peet to Alan Gardiner (16 October 1923) Gardiner; Liverpool University, *Annual Report 1922 and Prospectus 1922–23 of the Institute of Archaeology* (Liverpool: C. Tinling & Co, 1922), 14.
74 Griffith Institute, University of Oxford. Newberry Correspondence, 36/45, Letter from T. E. Peet to Percy Newberry (22 January 1918).
75 Griffith Institute, University of Oxford. Newberry Correspondence, 36/68, Letter from T. E. Peet to Percy Newberry (28 September 1920).
76 For more on the Wörterbuch see, for example, Thomas Gertzen, *École de Berlin und "Goldenes Zeitalter" (1882–1914) der Ägyptologie als Wissenschaft* (Berlin and Boston: de Gruyter, 2013), 194–258.
77 Editor JEA, 'Notes and news', *The Journal of Egyptian Archaeology* 4, No. 1, Jan. (1917): 64; Editor JEA, 'Notes and news,' *The Journal of Egyptian Archaeology* 5, No. 4 Oct. (1918): 304.
78 Griffith Institute, University of Oxford, Peet MSS 4.2.6, Letter from T. E. Peet to Patricia (2 January 1918).
79 Griffith Institute, University of Oxford. Newberry Correspondence, 36/45, Letter from T. E. Peet to Percy Newberry (22 January 1918).
80 On 11 June 1918 the 14th Battalion left Salonika. The Battalion was attached to the reconstituted 66th Division at Forges les Eaux on the Western Front on 23 July 1918. See Forces War Records, 'Unit History: King's (Liverpool Regiment)'.
81 Private family archives. Letter from T. E. Peet to Patricia (14 July 1918).
82 Griffith Institute, University of Oxford. Newberry Correspondence 36/46, Letter from T. E. Peet to Professor Newberry (14 July 1918).
83 Griffith Institute, University of Oxford, Peet MSS 4.2.6, Letter from T. E. Peet to Patricia (2 January 1918).

84 Griffith Institute, University of Oxford, Peet MSS 4.2.7, Letter from T. E. Peet to Patricia (8 August 1918).
85 Griffith Institute, University of Oxford, Peet MSS 4.2.9, Letter from T. E. Peet to Patricia (2 October 1918).
86 Griffith Institute, University of Oxford, Peet MSS 4.2.12, Letter from T. E. Peet to Patricia (15 October 1918).
87 *Ibid.*
88 Griffith Institute, University of Oxford, Peet MSS 4.2.13, Letter from T. E. Peet to Patricia (2 December 1918); for WW1 army vernacular, see Peter Doyle and Julian Walker, *Trench Talk: Words of the First World War* (Stroud: The History Press, 2011).
89 Fahmy, 'The Great Threat of History'; Griffith Institute, University of Oxford. Newberry Correspondence 36/67, Letter from T. E. Peet to Percy Newberry (2 December 1918).
90 Griffith Institute, University of Oxford. Newberry Correspondence 36/67, Letter from T. E. Peet to Percy Newberry (2 December 1918).
91 Griffith Institute, University of Oxford, Peet MSS 4.2.4, Letter from T. E. Peet to Patricia (undated letter to Patricia held with dated letter envelope dated 30 September 1917).
92 Fulbrook and Rublack, 'In relation: the 'social self' and ego-documents', 268; 271.
93 Griffith Institute, University of Oxford. Gardiner Correspondence AHG/42.230.198, Letter from T. E. Peet to A.H Gardiner (7 April 1920).
94 Although intransigent in this instance, Gardiner was to contribute to the funding of the Readership at Oxford to bring the salary up to a level which Peet felt financially secure. Griffith Institute, University of Oxford. Gardiner Correspondence AHG/42.230.8, Letter from A. H. Gardiner to T. E. Peet (27 May 1933); University of Oxford, Central University administrative ('Registry') correspondence files UR 6/ER/2/1 Professorship of Egyptology. 1934–64, Letter from Gardiner to Veale (2 June 1934). For Newberry and Peet's appointment to the Chair at the Institute of Archaeology, Liverpool, see Griffith Institute, University of Oxford. Newberry Correspondence 36/58, Letter from P. E. Newberry to T. E. Peet (16 December 1919).
95 This Chair was originally founded as a research chair – Griffith Institute, University of Oxford. Newberry Correspondence 31/74, Letter from Mountford to P. E. Newberry (no date); Liverpool University, *Preliminary Prospectus of the Institute of Archaeology* (Liverpool: University Press of Liverpool, 1904), 4; but Peet was to develop teaching here, working on the Diploma and MA, see Griffith Institute, University of Oxford. Gardiner Correspondence AHG/42.230.65, Letter from T. E Peet to Gardiner (25 January 1928); Thomas Kelly, *For Advancement of Learning* (Liverpool: Liverpool University Press, 1981), 219.
96 Griffith Institute, University of Oxford. Gardiner Correspondence AHG/42.230.202, Letter from T. E Peet to Gardiner (27 February 1920).
97 See Thomas L. Gertzen, 'The Anglo-Saxon branch of the Berlin School. The interwar correspondence of Adolf Erman and Alan Gardiner and the loss of the German Concession at Amarna' in *Histories of Egyptology: Interdisciplinary measures,* ed., William Carruthers (New York and London: Routledge, 2015), 34–49.
98 Griffith Institute, University of Oxford. Newberry Correspondence, 36/68. Letter from T. E. Peet to Percy Newberry (28 September 1920).
99 Christopher Hollings and Richard B. Parkinson, 'Two letters from Otto Neugebauer to Thomas Eric Peet on ancient Egyptian mathematics', *Historia Mathematica*, Volume 52, August (2020): 66–98; Griffith Institute, University of Oxford. Gardiner Correspondence AHG/42.230.180, Letter from T. E. Peet to A. H. Gardiner (23 October 1925).
100 Griffith Institute, University of Oxford. Gardiner Correspondence AHG/42.230.180, Letter from T. E. Peet to A. H. Gardiner (1 June 1921).
101 Griffith Institute, University of Oxford, Gardiner Correspondence AHG/42.230.171, Letter from T. E. Peet to A. H. Gardiner (11 July 1922). See B. Christopher Freuh et al., *Assessment and treatment planning for PTSD* (Hoboken, NJ: John Wiley & Sons, 2012), 71–89 for a discussion of the symptoms of PTSD.
102 Peet's view of Oxford becomes increasingly apparent in Peet's letters, for example, Griffith Institute, University of Oxford Gardiner Correspondence AHG/42.230.25, Letter from T. E. Peet to A. H. Gardiner (5 January 1932); Griffith Institute, University of Oxford. Gardiner Correspondence AHG/42.230.19, Letter from T. E. Peet to A. H. Gardiner (16 November 1932). Details as to Peet viewing the stipend as unacceptable to fund an individual without private means include Griffith Institute, University of Oxford. Gardiner Correspondence

AHG/42.230.25, Letter from T. E. Peet to A. H. Gardiner (5 January 1932); Griffith Institute, University of Oxford. Gardiner Correspondence AHG/42.230.19A, Letter from T. E. Peet to A. H. Gardiner (10 November 1932). The correspondence detailing Gardiner's contribution to the stipend can be found in Griffith Institute, University of Oxford. Gardiner Correspondence AHG/42.230.8, Letter from T. E. Peet to T. E. Gardiner (27 May 1933); University of Oxford. UR 6/ER/2/1 Professorship of Egyptology. 1934–64, Letter from Gardiner to Veale (2 June 1934); University of Oxford, Central University administrative ('Registry') correspondence files UR 6/ER/2/1 Professorship of Egyptology. 1934–75, Letter from M. Shearer to Sir Alan Gardiner (24 March 1950).
103 Peet, *The Present Position of Egyptological Studies*, 11.
104 For example Alice Stevenson, *Scattered Finds: Archaeology, Egyptology and Museums* (London: UCL Press, 2019), 181–216; Alice Stevenson, 'The object of study: Egyptology, archaeology, and anthropology at Oxford, 1860–1960', 19–33; see also William Y. Adams, 'Anthropology and Egyptology: divorce and remarriage?' in *Anthropology and Egyptology: A developing dialogue,* ed. J. Lustig (Sheffield: Sheffield Academic Press, 1997), 28.
105 Stevenson, *Scattered Finds*, 201
106 Joan L Richards, 'Introduction: Fragmented Lives', *ISIS*, vol. 97, no. 2 (June 2006): 305.
107 See David McCooey, 'The limits of life writing', *Life Writing*, 14:3 (2017): 280 for a discussion of this issue.
108 See Brad S. Gregory, 'Review: is small beautiful? Microhistory and the history of everyday life', *History and Theory*, 38 (1999): 100.
109 Telling, 'Bourdieu and the problem of reflexivity', 155.
110 I explore this in the context of examining statements in Peet's inaugural lecture in Lewis, 'Inaugural lectures in Egyptology: T. E. Peet and His Pupil W. B. Emery', 8.
111 In contrast to episodic – that is, the scrutiny of a specific encounter. See Gregory, 'Review: is small beautiful?', 102.
112 Gardiner wrote to Peet suggesting he was a reticent conversationalist: Griffith Institute, University of Oxford. Gardiner Correspondence AHG/42.230.77, Letter from T. E. Gardiner to Peet (26 August 1927). The quotes derive from Gardiner, 'Thomas Eric Peet', 70.

Bibliography

Adams, William Y., 'Anthropology and Egyptology: Divorce and remarriage?', in *Anthropology and Egyptology: A developing dialogue,* ed., J. Lustig (Sheffield: Sheffield Academic Press, 1997), 25–32.
Anon., 'Editorial statement', *The Journal of Egyptian Archaeology* 1, No. 1, Jan. (1914): 1.
Baker, Chris, 'The 66th (2nd East Lancashire) Division', *The Long Trail* (2019). Accessed 11 September 2019. https://www.longlongtrail.co.uk/army/order-of-battle-of-divisions/66th-2nd-east-lancashire-division/.
Bierbrier, Morris L. ed., *Who Was Who in Egyptology*, fifth revised edition (London: Egypt Exploration Society, 2019).
Burr, Malcolm (author) and Milne of Salonica (foreword), *Slouch Hat* (London: MW Books, 1935).
Clogg, Richard, 'Foreign archaeologists in Greece in time of war', in *Archaeology Behind the Battle Lines*, eds., Andrew Shapland and Evangelia Stefani (London and New York: Taylor and Francis. Kindle Edition, 2017), 40–57.
Dawson, Warren, R., 'Percy Edward Newberry, M.A., O.B.E.' *The Journal of Egyptian Archaeology* 36 (1950): 101–3.
Doyle, Peter and Julian Walker, *Trench Talk: Words of the First World War* (Stroud: The History Press, 2011).
Editor JEA, 'Notes and news', *The Journal of Egyptian Archaeology* 4, No. 1, Jan. (1917): 63–4.
Editor JEA, 'Notes and news', *The Journal of Egyptian Archaeology* 5, No. 4, Oct. (1918): 303–4.
Egypt Exploration Fund, *Report of the Annual General Meeting* (London: Kegan Paul, Trench Trubner & Co., 1915).
Egypt Today Staff, Egypt's Army celebrates end of World War I, *Egypt Today* online (12 November 2017). Accessed 20 September 2019. https://www.egypttoday.com/Article/1/32176/Egypt's-Army-celebrates-end-of-World-War-I.

Fahmy, Khaled, 'The Great Threat of History', recording of conference paper (27 March 2019). Accessed 19 September 2019. https://khaledfahmy.org/en/2019/04/06/the-great-theft-of-history/
Falconer, Raymond, 'Sir Alan Henderson Gardiner', *The Journal of Egyptian Egyptology* 50 (1964): 170–2.
Forces War Records, 'Record Details for T. E. Peet' (21 October 1915). Accessed 19 September 2019. https://www.forces-war-records.co.uk/records/4143514/lieutenant-t-e-peet-british-army-kings-liverpool-regiment/.
Forces War Records, 'Unit history: King's (Liverpool Regiment)' (2019) Accessed 20 September 2019. https://www.forces-war-records.co.uk/units/259/kings-liverpool-regiment.
Frueh, B. Christopher, Anouk L. Grubaugh, Jon D. Elhai, and Julian D. Ford, *Assessment and Treatment Planning for PTSD* (Hoboken, NJ: John Wiley & Sons, 2012).
Fulbrook, Mary and Ulinka Rublack, 'In relation: The 'social self' and ego-documents', *German History* 28 (2010): 263–72.
Gange, David, *Dialogues with the Dead: Egyptology in British culture and religion, 1822–1922* (Oxford: Oxford University Press, 2013).
Garber, Elizabeth, 'Introduction', in *Beyond History of Science: Essays in honor of Robert E. Schofield*, ed. E. Garber (Bethlehem and Cranbury: Lehigh University Press; London: Associated University Press, 1990), 7–20.
Gardiner, Alan H., 'Thomas Eric Peet', *Journal of Egyptian Archaeology* XX, No.1–2 (1934): 66–70.
Gardiner, Alan H., *Gardiner's Egyptian Grammar* (Oxford: Griffith Institute, 1957).
Gertzen, Thomas L., *École de Berlin und "Goldenes Zeitalter" (1882–1914) der Ägyptologie als Wissenschaft* (Berlin and Boston: de Gruyter, 2013), 194–258.
Gertzen, Thomas L, 'The Anglo-Saxon branch of the Berlin School. The interwar correspondence of Adolf Erman and Alan Gardiner and the loss of the German concession at Amarna', in *Histories of Egyptology: Interdisciplinary methods,* ed. William Carruthers (New York and London: Routledge, 2015), 34–49.
Ginzburg, Carlo and Anna Davin, 'Morelli, Freud and Sherlock Holmes: Clues and scientific method', *History Workshop* No. 9, Spring (1980): 5–36.
Govoni, Paola, 'Crafting scientific (auto)biographies', in *Writing About Lives in Science: (Auto) biography, gender and genre*, eds. Paula Govoni and Zelda Alice Franeschi (Göttingen: V&R unipress, 2014), 7–30.
Gregory, Brad S., 'Review: is small beautiful? Microhistory and the history of everyday life', *History and Theory* 38, No. 1 (1999): 100–10.
Griffith, Frances Ll., The Study of Egyptology: Inaugural lecture delivered in the Ashmolean Museum on May 8, 1901. (Oxford: H. Hart, printer to the University, 1901).
Gunn, Battiscombe, revised by R. S. Simpson, 'Peet, (Thomas) Eric (1882–1934)' in *Oxford Dictionary of National Biography* (published online 23 September 2004). https://doi.org/10.1093/ref:odnb/35456.
Hassan, Fekri, 'Conserving Egyptian heritage: seizing the moment', in *British-Egyptian Relations from Suez to the Present Day*, eds., Noel Brehony and Ayman El-Desouky (Berkeley, London and Beirut: SAQI, 2007), 209–33.
Hencken, T. C., revised by S. Stoddart, 'MacIver, David Randall (1873–1945)', in *Oxford Dictionary of National Biography* (published online 23 September 2004). https://doi.org/10.1093/ref:odnb/35667.
Hollings, Christopher D. and Richard B. Parkinson, 'Two letters from Otto Neugebauer to Thomas Eric Peet on ancient Egyptian mathematics', *Historia Mathematica* 52, August (2020): 66–98.
J. L. M., 'Thomas Eric Peet', *The Oxford Magazine,* 1 March (1943): 531.
Kelly, Thomas, *For Advancement of Learning* (Liverpool: Liverpool University Press, 1981).
Lepore, Jill, 'Historians who love too much: reflections on microhistory and biography', *The Journal of American History* 88, (2001): 129–44.
Lewis, Clare, 'Inaugural lectures in Egyptology: T. E. Peet and his pupil W. B. Emery', *Bulletin of the History of Archaeology* 26, Issue 1, Art 9, November (2016): 1–15.
Liverpool University, *Preliminary Prospectus of the Institute of Archaeology* (Liverpool: University Press of Liverpool, 1904).
Liverpool University, *Annual Report 1922 and Prospectus 1922–23 of the Institute of Archaeology* (Liverpool: C. Tinling & Co, 1922).

Llewellyn-Smith, Michael, 'Foreword', in *Archaeology Behind the Battle Lines*, eds. Andrew Shapland and Evangelia Stefani (London and New York: Taylor and Francis. Kindle Edition, 2017), xv–xvii.

McCooey, David, 'The limits of life writing', *Life Writing* 14:3 (2017): 277–80.

Peet, T. Eric, *The Stone and Bronze Ages in Italy* (Oxford: The Clarendon Press, 1909).

Peet, T. Eric, 'The year's work at Abydos', *The Journal of Egyptian Archaeology* 1, No. 1, Jan. (1914): 37–39.

Peet, T. Eric, 'An unrecognized meaning of the verb 𓐍𓏲.', *Journal of Egyptian Archaeology* I, No 3 (1914): 209–11.

Peet, T. Eric, *The Stela of Sebekkhu* (Manchester: University Press, 1914).

Peet, T. Eric, 'Can ≏ be used to negative *sdmt.f*?' *ZAS* 52 (1914): 109–11.

Peet, T. Eric, The Present Position of Egyptological Studies. Inaugural lecture delivered before the University of Oxford on 17 January 1934. (Oxford: Oxford University Press, 1934).

Reid, Donald M., 'Indigenous Egyptology: The decolonization of a profession?', *Journal of the American Oriental Society* 105, (1985): 233–46.

Reid, Donald M., *Whose Pharaohs? Archaeology, museums, and Egyptian national identity from Napoleon to World War I* (Berkeley: University of California Press, 2002).

Richards, Joan L., 'Introduction: Fragmented lives', *ISIS* 97 (2006): 302–5.

Robson, Eleanor, 'In Nisaba's House of Wisdom and Nabu's True House: Social Geographies of Cuneiform Scholarship in Ancient Iraq', Inaugural Lecture, UCL, London (3 February, 2015). Recording accessed 14 September 2021. https://soundcloud.com/ucl-arts-social-science/in-nisabas-house-of-wisdom-and-nabus-true-house-professor-eleanor-robson-ucl-history

Salonika Campaign Society, 'Salonika Campaign Society, 1915–1918'. Accessed 20 November 2020. https://salonikacampaignsociety.org.uk/publications-and-dvds/the-new-mosquito/.

Shapland, Andrew, 'The British Salonika Force Collection at the British Museum', in *Archaeology Behind the Battle Lines*, eds. Andrew Shapland and Evangelia Stefani (London and New York: Taylor and Francis. Kindle Edition, 2017), 85–120.

Shapland, Andrew and Evangelia Stefani, eds., *Archaeology Behind the Battle Lines*. (London and New York: Taylor and Francis Kindle Edition, 2017).

Sherratt, Susan, 'Representations of Knossos and Minoan Crete in the British, American and continental press 1900–C.1930', *Creta Antica* 10/II (2009): 619–49.

Stevenson, Alice, 'The object of study: Egyptology, archaeology, and anthropology at Oxford, 1860–1960', in *Histories of Egyptology: Interdisciplinary measures*, ed., William Carruthers (London and New York: Routledge, 2015), 19–33.

Stevenson, Alice, *Scattered Finds: Archaeology, Egyptology and museums* (London: UCL Press, 2019).

Telling, Kathryn, 'Bourdieu and the problem of reflexivity: recent answers to some old questions', *European Journal of Social Theory* 19 (2016): 146–156.

Thornton, Amara, 'Social networks in the history of archaeology: placing archaeology in its context', in *Historiographical Approaches to Past Archaeological Research*, eds., Gisela Eberhardt and Fabian Link (Berlin: Edition Topoi, 2015), 69–94.

The Wartime Memories Project, '14th Battalion, Kings Regiment (Liverpool)'. Accessed 14 September 2021. https://wartimememoriesproject.com/greatwar/allied/battalion.php?pid=6417.

Wakefield, Alan S., 'Mountains, mules and malaria: the British frontline soldier's experience of campaigning in Macedonia, 1915–1918', *Journal of the Society for Army Historical Research* 82 (2004): 325–340.

Waquet, Françoise, 'Academic Homage and Intellectual Genealogy: Inaugural Lectures at the College de France (1949-2003)', *History of Universities*, Volume XXI/2 (2006): 202–27.

War Forces Records Record, Details for T. E. Peet (King's (Liverpool Regiment)) 21 October 1915. Accessed 20 May 2019. https://www.forces-war-records.co.uk/records/4143514/lieutenant-t-e-peet-british-army-kings-liverpool-regiment/

Ward Price, Gerald, *The Story of the Salonica Army* (London: Hodder and Stoughton, 1918).

Whittemore, Thomas, 'Preface', in *Balabish*, Gerald A. Wainwright and Thomas Whittemore (London: George Allen & Unwin, 1920).

Whitworth, Mike, 'Thomas Eric Peet University of Manchester and Manchester Museum', *University of Manchester* (n.d.). Accessed 11 September 2019. http://www.ww1.manchester.ac.uk/thomas-eric-peet/.

Wilson, John A., *Signs & Wonders upon Pharaoh: A history of American Egyptology* (Chicago: University of Chicago Press, 1964).

6
Archaeology, social networks and lives: 'Dig writing' and the history of archaeology
Bart Wagemakers

Dig writing versus life-writing

In the last six decades many studies on the history of archaeology have focused on the development of archaeology as a discipline.[1] One of the approaches used for describing the archaeological development in the past is life-writing; a generic term which became current in the 1980s and which meant 'to encompass a range of writings about lives or parts of lives, or which provide materials out of which lives or parts of lives are composed'.[2] This methodology – which includes among other things memoirs, letters, retrospects, diaries, journals, newspapers, film, photos, wills and virtual communications[3] – has already resulted in numerous biographies about renowned archaeologists.[4] After three decades of discussion about its scientific validity and value for writing the history of science, the biography nowadays gets academic recognition and scientific legitimacy, and is considered as an analytical tool.[5]

Using the genre of life-writing in the history of archaeology has several advantages. It charts individual contributions to the overall archaeological development, the focus on the individual's life enables the scholar to incorporate all kinds of factors that interact in the construction of archaeological knowledge, and the biographer must submit to the views presented by the subject's records.[6] It has even been suggested that the scientific biography would be the best way to approach the ideal goal of historicism in the history of science.[7]

On the other hand, life-writing has also to deal with some concerns. The biographer's modern perception, concept and way of thought can be – whether deliberately or not – a trap as it may result in a practice which analyses the past from the present point of view: a phenomenon which is called 'presentism'.[8] Secondly, as the biographer chooses their subject for a reason, such as the strong personality of the archaeologist or his or her valuable contribution to the archaeological discipline, there is a risk that the distance between the writer and their subject is too small. There is even a serious risk that biographers identify themselves with their subjects or appropriate them – especially when the biographers of archaeologists are archaeologists themselves.[9]

The question is also what elements life-writing should encompass for creating a complete image of the concerning character. The late Douglas R. Givens suggested incorporating three data sets when writing the life of an archaeologist.[10] According to Givens, the biography should include the outline of the subject's life, that is, his/her intellectual and professional background. Secondly, life-writing should pay attention to the lifelong professional and personal relationships between the subject and his/her colleagues and supporting institutions. Finally, it is important to focus on the subject's role in expanding professional and public knowledge of archaeological results and the work of archaeologists.

Although these essential data sets for life-writing proposed by Givens could create a balanced picture of the archaeologist concerned, the question could be raised to what extent this method provides a view of the development of the archaeological discipline in the past. Too much focus on a certain character can lead the attention away from actors of importance on a macro level.[11] Besides, the dubious bond between the biographer and his or her subject keeps demanding our attention, as discussed above.

Instead of concentrating on individuals, one could focus on archaeological sites. By analysing the ins and outs of the excavations that took place in the past at a specific site, we can avoid having all attention centred on a single or a few individuals. Therefore I would like to put forward an alternative method for studying the history of archaeology: 'dig-writing'. As the term already implies, this method focuses on a specific archaeological campaign in the past, in the broader sense. The general aim of both life- and dig-writing is the same – they just use a different angle. In contrast with the principles of life-writing, leading personalities in the archaeological world are not the main subjects of the analyses in dig-writing; that is the expedition itself.

The data sets used by the approach of dig-writing – which follow in a sense those suggested by Givens, as will be discussed in the next section – will represent a cross-section of the teams involved in the excavations, instead of focusing on the main archaeologist(s); not just the co-ordinating staff, but also the field assistants; and not to forget – if the campaign took place abroad – the local labourers involved. The multi perspective view includes not only the archaeological results of the campaign, but also the organisation of the expedition, the relationships between people and institutes, and the experiences and impressions of the participants.

Dig-writing not only gives a balanced view of a particular excavation in the past, it is also significant for the history of archaeology in another way. If a site has been visited by different archaeological expeditions over a longer time span, comparing the analyses of those campaigns will provide insight into the development of the archaeological discipline in that region for the era of interest. One may conclude that the ultimate objective of dig writing is similar to that of life-writing where the 'subject of the biography is actually not the subject of the study, so much as a 'key' that leads to the wider reality of past archaeology'.[12]

Dimensions and sources for dig-writing

Studies of excavations carried out in the past often cover two of the data sets mentioned by Givens; in the case of dig writing I referred to these sets as 'dimensions'. Whereas Givens emphasised the importance of dissemination of archaeological information by the biographer's subject, dig writing encompasses the 'archaeological dimension', that is aspects such as the aims of the expedition, methods and techniques used on site, the entire processing of artefacts – from excavating to restoration – documenting, etc. Further, Givens' interest in the professional and personal relationships of the biographer's subject can be found in the 'social dimension' of dig writing which involves the documentation of social networks that refer to (work)relations between people as well as to people's affiliation to institutions or organisations.

Since it is hard to obtain a comprehensive picture of a past archaeological campaign on the basis of just these two dimensions, I would like to introduce the 'emotional dimension'. While life-writing should focus on the outline of the subject's life, according to Givens, the emotional dimension of dig writing pays a lot of attention to excavation life. It describes aspects such as the participants' personal reflections on archaeological activities, the way of life at a dig camp and the impact of the excavation on the participants' lives. The individual's perception is significant for acquiring real insight into the experiences, opinions and reflections regarding the expedition.

In order to gain a representative impression of an excavation carried out in the past, embedded in its historical context, we must examine and define a balanced combination of these dimensions.[13] The quality of the definition depends on the availability and type of sources. On the one hand, scholars use official publications such as annual field reports, articles and final reports. On the other hand, they depend on unpublished records which are usually stored in the archives of, for example, museums, libraries and (archaeological) institutes. Although these are useful sources for framing past excavations, one should be aware of their limitations. The professional staff involved in the excavation usually take the decisions concerning the data collected during the dig and any publications afterwards. Developments in archaeological recording over the years appear to suggest that there might be a difference between what staff members actually recorded at past excavations and what we today expect them to have documented at the time.[14]

Therefore, next to the published sources and unpublished archival records, scholars should use a third category, referred to as 'informal' sources. In contrast to the first two types of source, which primarily describe the archaeological and social dimensions of the excavation, the informal records not only reinforce the archaeological and social dimensions, but they are also able to supply the required data for the emotional dimension.

Firstly, the informal documentation refers to records created by former participants of excavations who were not part of the trained staff but who supported the dig as part of their continuing education or out of interest, such as students, volunteers, reporters and sponsors.[15] Secondly, this category of documentation includes the private documentation of staff members which is not kept in the excavation archives, but in the private sphere. Because of this, these records are excluded from the selection procedure regarding the *formal* (un)published records.[16]

Informal documentation is able to provide us with new aspects of an excavation which at the time did not seem important to the staff, or about which the staff were unwilling or did not deem worth divulging.[17] Besides, these new aspects give insight into the development of the scholar's thoughts which tend to only appear in publication once they have been finalised.[18] The informal records provide a valuable contribution to archaeological, social and emotional dimensions, and have a significant role in dig writing for that reason.

In conclusion, to obtain a comprehensive and balanced view of a past excavation, it is crucial for dig writing to include all three dimensions, by obtaining as many published sources, unpublished archival records and informal documentation as possible (Figure 6.1). This point will be

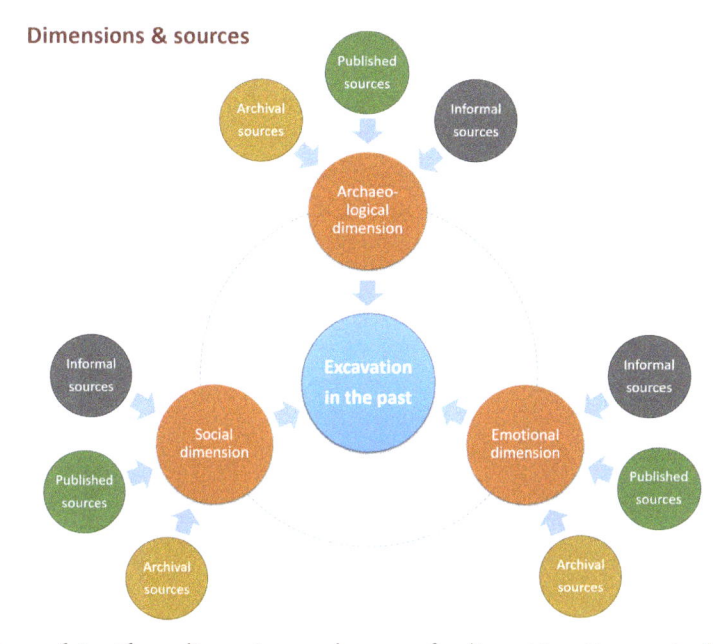

Figure 6.1 Three dimensions and sources for dig writing. Source: Author.

demonstrated by a case study on the archaeological campaign at Tell es-Sultan, ancient Jericho.[19]

The second British expedition to Tell es-Sultan

The second British expedition to Tell es-Sultan ran from 1952–1958 and was directed by Kathleen Kenyon on behalf of the British School of Archaeology in Jerusalem, the University of London and the Palestine Exploration Fund. As usual, the progress of the excavation was recorded by officially appointed draughtsmen and photographers. The surveyors and field assistants recorded the stratigraphy and the finds in their notebooks, which were then collected by Kenyon at the end of every season.[20] Kenyon used all these official notes, photographs, slides and drawings for her publication of the annual excavation reports, numerous articles and the final report *Excavations at Jericho*, a five-volume magnum opus published between 1960 and 1983.

Besides the official records made and collected as ordered by Kenyon, team members of the expedition produced many private records of the excavation, on their own initiative. As these informal documents, which include photographs, slides, film, drawings, notes, letters and diaries, have been neglected in the past, I initiated a new project a few years ago: *Jericho off the Record*. The project traced former participants of the dig, or their heirs, and gathered their records that were made at the site and in its surroundings. The search has located 707 black and white photographs, 52 colour slides, 63 letters, a diary which describes the archaeological progress and camp life in detail and even one unknown 16mm colour film. Furthermore, nine former participants have been interviewed about their time at Tell es-Sultan, some of whom were British, Americans, Canadians and Palestinians.[21] Thanks to the combination of the published sources, unpublished archival records and informal documentation the three dimensions of the expedition to Tell es-Sultan can be analysed. This case study aims to demonstrate the opportunities of dig writing.

The archaeological dimension

The first dimension that will be discussed here concerns the archaeological features of Tell es-Sultan. The archaeological data will be presented in the consecutive order of published, unpublished and informal records.

The published sources

The archaeological features of the expedition are well represented by the published sources. Apart from the annual reports on the progression of the dig, which Kenyon published in the *Palestine Exploration Quarterly* between 1952–1960, numerous other publications on the excavation have appeared since the first spade touched the tell. In 1957 the preliminary report *Digging up Jericho* saw the light of day; it describes the main results of the field seasons from 1952 until 1956[22] and the final report *Excavations at Jericho*, mentioned above, was published in five volumes between 1960 and 1983.[23]

It is not surprising that these publications paid a lot of attention to all kinds of archaeological features of the expedition. They describe the archaeological approach, the methods and techniques used, the architectural structures that were exposed, the stratigraphy, the artefacts that were encountered and the habitation history of the tell based on the findings of the expedition. These aspects are illustrated by dozens of images and drawings which enrich the publications. Due to the general aim of the reports, articles and volumes, the character of the selected sources for these publications is formal and the focus lies on the archaeological process and the results of the expedition.[24]

The unpublished archival sources

The records stored at the archives of the Museum of Archaeology and Anthropology (MAA) in Cambridge and the Institute of Archaeology (IoA) of UCL do give us more background information about the archaeological procedure during and after the expedition. For instance, there are numerous photographs and slides that can be divided into published and unpublished ones. By comparing the two collections it becomes clear what the selection procedure was like after every field season. The published images display well-prepared squares, artefacts *in situ* and show the measuring rod or the artefacts that have already been processed and are about to be registered.[25] If people appear in the pictures, they are usually (local) labourers who had to pose in front of the camera in order to indicate the scale of the architectural structures.[26] The aim of the images seems to have been to inform the reader about the state of work and the main results so far. In contrast, the unpublished photographs and slides display fewer static compositions and provide an impression of work in progress: people caught on camera during archaeological activities (Figure 6.2). There are panoramic views of the excavation, showing the

Figure 6.2 Kathleen Kenyon (standing in the centre) supervising local labourers at Tell es-Sultan. Photo by expedition photographer Peter Dorrell. Source: Institute of Archaeology, UCL/Kenyon Archive: Unmarked 022.

large number of labourers and archaeological features before their preparation to be recorded and registered.

Other interesting unpublished records found at the archives are the field notes written by the field assistants. Kenyon expected the field assistants to record the progress they made on their square space, to note down the exposed finds and to draw up plans and sections. At the end of the field season Kenyon gathered the notebooks and produced an archaeological overview of the tell.[27] The notes made by the field assistants are more comprehensive than the publications for which they were used and provide information about the way features were recorded, provisional conclusions were drawn and revisited, and techniques were used for processing artefacts, including evaluation.[28] Apart from writing about the progress of the digging and the processing of the finds, field assistants also described the way in which the excavation of a locus was organised.[29]

Another aspect found in the unpublished archival sources is the administration of the expedition materials used. It includes overviews of the tools they needed for excavation, which provide information about the way they used to dig; they show the scale of the campaign and imply that the expedition was well organised.[30]

Finally, the unpublished sources make clear that every season Kenyon took quite a number of archaeological key publications to the excavation camp at Tell es-Sultan. She needed the literature to use as references for the finds that were made at the dig. These lists reveal Kenyon's scholarly keystones that she depended on in those days.

The informal sources

Although the published sources and unpublished archival records combined seem to present the archaeological dimension of the expedition quite clearly, informal data are able to add valuable information. One example is the tremendous 16mm colour footage, taken by a biology student who was on her first trip outside the UK, thanks to the participation in the expedition. For this occasion she had bought a camera and filmed the journey all the way up to Jericho and the excavation. The footage frames all phases of archaeological research in a very natural way and provides information about the methods and techniques used at Tell es-Sultan.[31]

Other informal records can clarify the context in which artefacts were found, such as the discovery of the Neolithic rush mats in Square E in 1955. While the published sources just mention the discovery and interpretation of the rush mats,³² Canadian PhD student Bill Power describes comprehensively how the first mats were found:

> So on that particular day there was very little movement and the whole crew was unusually silent. It was Miss Kenyon's practice to visit our trench mid-morning and I liked to be prepared for her coming so that I could spell out quickly what we had done and what we were going to do. So I asked Muhammed what was going on. He didn't want to tell me. I insisted, so finally he said, "Come and see." I was fascinated, he had found two little reed mats, overlapping and kicked up in the corner of the little room. They were similar to the little mats that are still used in Jericho today. You could clearly see the fibers!! When Miss Kenyon came she was very pleased. It was the first time that such a thing had been found in Neolithic Jericho, even though people had been working there for a couple of years. So she brought in all the site supervisors to see what we had and she complimented me on my discovery. So I had to tell her that I had had nothing to do with it, Muhammed had done the work. She was dubious about that because he had a reputation as a trouble maker and never-do-well. Of course, from then everybody found mats.³³ (Figure 6.3)

Informal records also show the archaeological challenges an expedition had to face. As the conservation of artefacts was still in its infancy in those days, Cecil Western, who was responsible for 'conservation and repair' in the seasons 1953–54, encountered several challenges at the site. She had to figure out how to mend exposed pots and to conserve the wooden objects found in the tombs before they crumbled in to powder after the opening of the tomb. They had no experience with working with organic material at the time and she had to experiment with paraffin wax, which was the only thing they could get hold of at the time. And it seemed to work!³⁴ She also proved to be inventive – out of necessity – when one of the skulls found at the wall of a trench in 1953 was broken into four pieces during transport to London. She put the pieces together, filled the skull up with clay and restored the broken jaw.³⁵ Another example of this inventiveness can be seen in the way a rush mat was lifted from the soil. While the published sources only mention the find of several Neolithic mats in Square E,³⁶ a letter written by team member Henk Franken – including a sketch (Figure 6.4) – gives an insight into the way the excavators had to improvise when the mats had to be raised without damage.³⁷

Figure 6.3 Bill Power (right) and Muhammed exposing a Neolithic skeleton in Square E. Source: David Spurgeon (NPAPH Project repository).

Figure 6.4 Drawing made by Henk Franken of the construction to lift the rush mat. Source: Heirs of Henk Franken (NPAPH Project repository).

Now and then informal records reveal incidents at the dig that were not mentioned – possibly with intent – in the published or archival sources, but which can add interesting information to the archaeological dimension. For instance, when they tried to make a gypsum plaster cast of the Neolithic rush mats in Square E I, the linen tore. The plaster fell on the mats and the latter were broken into many pieces.[38] At the tell participants never paid much attention to the health and safety at work policy; as some of the former participants recalled, Kenyon sometimes had difficulty in judging the extent of the risks faced by workers there. One day foreman Ali Abu Said discovered a large crack in the soil on the surface of the slope in the northern trench, which was 30 metres long and 6 metres wide. The crack, about 10 centimetres wide, was running parallel to the trench edge over a length of 10 metres. It was reported to Kenyon immediately, but she said to ignore it, as it would do not any damage. The next day the crack had widened and the workmen softly touched the crack with their shovels and within seconds the entire slope collapsed. Tons of fallen debris had to be dug away. A similar incident happened at Trench I, which, in some places, was even 15 metres deep. Fortunately, there were no casualties, because it collapsed overnight, but it had a deep impact on the team members; Kenyon told them not to talk about it to anyone.[39]

The social dimension

The social dimension involves social networks and can be divided into three categories.[40] The organisational category incorporates formal and informal membership in an organisation, such as those serving on a board of trustees, a committee or council, and being an employee within an organisation. Furthermore, it concerns a relationship of participation, rather than it being merely a paid service. The transactional category includes the exchange or transfer of resources, knowledge and/or connections, such as sponsorship/funding, employment/training and logistical/practical assistance. Finally, the personal category which deals with the individual, familial and friendship relations that were part of, or the result of, the expedition.[41] Due to lack of space, the three categories will not be discussed separately; the information discussed here represents the social dimension as a whole.

The published sources

In the case of Kathleen Kenyon, the director of the expedition, we know that in the 1950s she served on the executive committee of the Palestine Exploration Fund, was Chairman of the Council of the British School of Archaeology in Jerusalem and Trustee of the Palestine Archaeological Museum in Jerusalem.[42]

In general, the transactions regarding the expedition to Tell es-Sultan involved financial support, manpower, equipment and exposure in the media. The authors usually start their publications with expressing gratitude to the partners and sponsors of the expedition.[43] In the first annual reports the two sponsors are mentioned by name, but as the number of sponsoring institutes and museums increased gradually, Kenyon decided to name only the most important sponsors, and added the remark that 'a large number of other museums and universities also made generous grants'.[44] As this remark already indicates, the greater part of the partners and sponsors were universities and museums. In exchange for their support they were given the opportunity to buy excavated artefacts for their own collections at the end of the field season.[45] Physical assistance was usually by the participation of scholars and (PhD) students in the dig. The material in kind received by the expedition varied from tents to an electric generator providing light for the dig house; from the loan of a station-wagon to a gift and free air transport of a supply of acetone.[46]

In the published sources the social networks also become visible thanks to the list of institutions or organisations that acquired artefacts from the expedition.[47] At the end of a field season the excavated artefacts were divided between the Jordanian Department of Antiquities and the expedition. Subsequently, the sponsors had the opportunity to acquire artefacts from the expedition. Participant Margaret Wheeler expresses very explicitly the significance of the division of artefacts, in order to satisfy the sponsors:

> Treasures are necessary to *us* too, because we have to satisfy hungry museums and universities all over the world who have financed our endeavours. Their generosity is for the high ideal of knowledge, we know; but few of them exist in such a rarefied atmosphere that they do not respond to material returns. A good tomb group, or a Neolithic plastered skull, is an aid to generosity.[48]

Another important feature of the social dimension is the media.[49] Kenyon gave regular radio broadcasts on archaeological topics, including Jericho.[50] In the field season of 1956 journalist David Spurgeon reported from the site, on behalf of the Toronto *Globe and Mail*, in connection with the financial contribution to the dig by the Royal Ontario Museum, Toronto. The newspaper reported on various themes related to the site, the community of Jericho and the adjacent refugee camp (Figure 6.5).[51] Subsequently accounts appeared in many other newspapers and magazines, such as *The Times*, the *Illustrated London News*, the *New York Times* and *National Geographic Magazine*.[52]

Figure 6.5 View from the excavation camp. Women from the refugee camp and the United Nations Relief and Works Administration truck near Elisha's Fountain. Tell es-Sultan in the background. Source: David Spurgeon (NPAPH Project repository).

Probably the most noteworthy media contribution was provided by the BBC. During the 1956 season, a BBC film crew – under the direction of Paul Johnstone – arrived at Tell es-Sultan in order to record an episode of the *Buried Treasure* series.[53] Thanks to this broadcast, the expedition to Tell es-Sultan was introduced to the British public (at least to those people who owned a television at that time).

The unpublished archival sources

The unpublished sources in the Jericho archives strengthen the image of these social networks and also provide new details about them. From the published sources, for example, it becomes clear that some institutes supported the expedition by providing equipment. The unpublished sources in the archives list explicitly the type and number of utensils on loan to the excavation. At the end of each field season the number of items missing or broken were recorded and the wares that were returned were also listed.[54]

The social dimension becomes not only visible due to the delivery of goods, but also thanks to the order of photographic records. Although the unpublished catalogue of photographic records that was found at the archives mostly dates from decades after the expedition took place, it provides us with information concerning the spin-off from the archaeological campaign. From this catalogue we may conclude that the network of the expedition included institutes, organisations, museums, publishers and scholars.[55]

Other details provided by the archival sources concern the local labourers. The published staff list[56] mentions the participating scholars and (PhD) students but does not refer to the local villagers and inhabitants of the adjacent refugee camp who joined the excavation. Several notebooks of the field assistants contain lists with names of local labourers. In this way we have an idea of the size and composition of this group.[57] In addition, expedition photographer Peter Dorrell (1956–1958) created several categories in his huge colour slide collection of the expedition, including 'Jericho locals'. Thanks to these slides, the local community who was involved in the excavation is given a face.

To ensure that work relations between field assistants and labourers would run smoothly, the assistants had to speak some words of Arabic as the labourers usually could not communicate in English. Vocabulary lists with the Arabic translation of English words and short phrases were found on the flap of several notebooks.[58] The vocabularies contain a variety of word sets such as numerals, colours, tools, limbs, food products and phrases like, 'What do you want?', 'I don't understand', 'be careful' and 'hurry up'. Apparently, these vocabulary lists were sufficient for communication with the labourers – along with the presence of a foreman of local origin who spoke English.

The informal sources

The (un)published (archival) sources manage to give an impression of the social dimension, but the informal sources can provide us with even more content. It has already been noted that the organisers of the expedition were in contact with several institutions for financial, material and physical support. However, the support could be of yet another kind. As Kenyon mentions in the annual report of the 1956 season, the American School provided the expedition with assistance at a time of political unrest in Jordan, including East Jerusalem. Although she retains a formal writing style in the report by noting that 'during this period, members of the expedition received most kind hospitality from the American School in Jerusalem'[59] Kenyon explains the situation in detail in a letter to her sister Nora:

> On the morning of the 5th, he [the British Consul General] reported that it [travel to Jericho] was considered inadvisable. That was a nuisance for us, though could stay quite comfortable at the American School, together with the 3 other men of the party who have arrived by various routes… The American School is in a large garden, with a good iron railing round it, and we had a platoon of the Arab Legion established in the garden… The American School was most noble and offered to put a whole wing of the School at our disposal, where we could put up our dig camp beds, and a kitchen where we could cook… Anyway, don't worry about us. We are well looked after, and probably in a few days things will be quiet again.[60]

The understanding Kenyon had with other institutes and their scholars also becomes clear when she and her team paid visits to their excavations, and she received guests at Tell es-Sultan. The best example is Père Roland de Vaux of the École Biblique et Archéologique française de Jérusalem. He and his students were regular visitors at the dig in Jericho and in turn Kenyon went to visit his excavations at Khirbet Qumran and Tell el-Farah (N) every year (Figure 6.6). At the site the visitors were shown around by the excavator. Gerald Lankester Harding, the Director-General of the Jordanian Department of Antiquities, was a frequent visitor to the excavation too.[61]

Sometimes informal records can alter the general opinion of a feature of an expedition. The enormous list of sponsors published in the annual and final reports gives the impression that the expedition was financially sound, but that assumption turned out to be faulty. Several expedition members wrote in private letters about the consequences of the poor financial situation for the expedition. A participant in 1956 informed his parents he might return home sooner than expected: 'Rather depressing news from Jericho. The excavation is going to have to close down early as they are short of cash…'[62] Another expedition member described the consternation in the final season and Kenyon's search for a solution:

> There is considerable excitement in the camp. For weeks now it has been known that the purse is empty – some mistake was made in the organisation sometime. All sorts of appeals have been written to try and raise cash. Somehow they will carry on to the finish – perhaps in overdraft (this does not mean I don't get my money).[63]

Figure 6.6 Kathleen Kenyon (left) and her team visit Roland de Vaux at his site Tell el-Far'ah (North). Source: Heirs of Vivienne Catleugh (NPAPH Project repository).

His account is confirmed by a letter written by Kenyon to her sister which makes clear that she needed £1,500 to be able to finish the dig.[64] According to the recollection of staff member Henk Franken, 'finance was always the great headache and the whole enterprise, both at Jericho and at Jerusalem, were run on a shoestring'.[65] Kenyon was well aware of the continuing financial 'challenges': 'I am just getting to my usual seasonal scare about finance.'[66]

In general, working relations between the local labourers and the staff were good and expedition members even attended local weddings and funerals and organised a film party at the cinema for the labourers.[67] However, informal sources also pay relatively significant attention to the way in which staff failed to have a good understanding with the local workers on the tell and the people living in the vicinity of the expedition camp. On the site there was a clear distinction between staff and the local labourers. While the staff enjoyed their meals in the dig house, prepared by a cook, the labourers brought their own meals from home. The groups of workers in the different areas on the site used to have their meals together.[68] The workers usually received their instructions from the foreman in Arabic, although Kenyon also used to walk around the tell, inspecting any progress the men had made and giving them commands in Arabic. Kenyon's presence made an impression on the men as they 'just started to work very hard' whenever she approached the place they were working at.[69]

Besides, informal sources record incidents, frequently caused by the politically turbulent events of the day. Due to the Arab–Israeli War of 1948 the Jericho Oasis housed numerous Palestinian refugees in the 1950s. Ain es-Sultan, one of the refugee camps present in the oasis, was even situated at the foot of the tell. The combination of local citizens, Palestinian refugees and archaeologists who – in the eyes of the locals and refugees – represented the Western powers who were responsible for the bad circumstances they were living in sometimes caused explosive situations.

A good example of the tension occurred when expedition photographer Dennis Corbett had decided to grow a beard. Because it looked like he had ringlets, it caused a stir and unrest among the local labourers who constantly shouted 'Jahudi' (Jew) at him.[70] A bigger incident took place in March 1956 when Glubb Pasha, British commander of the Arab Legion since 1939, was relieved from his duties. While the Jordanian people were given a day off to celebrate his departure, the expedition members found themselves in a rather difficult position, as draughtsman John Carswell wrote to his parents:

> … we had arranged a party for all our workers that night that couldn't easily be cancelled as we had roasted 7 sheep. The whole of Jericho naturally thought that we also were celebrating the same cause as themselves and although the meal itself went off all right, as soon as the dancing started the whole affair got completely out of hand. A couple of hundred of outsiders appeared from nowhere and wrecked the party and ended up by throwing stones at any of us that they could see… The party was further complicated by the fact that the workers on the Tell are from Jericho proper and hate the workers that Lady W. [Wheeler] employs in the tombs, who are refugees. The whole affair was a great misfortune and I am afraid, a moral victory for the troublemakers.[71]

In the informal records several kinds of (working-)relations can be observed. The long time span people spent at Tell es-Sultan sometimes resulted in temporary or lasting friendships.[72] The exchange of photographs also suggests active personal contact after the excavation. By studying informal photo albums, it is possible to deduce that particular photos were distributed within a circle of friends.[73] The stay at the dig could even weaken cultural borders. Towards the end of the 1956 season a Canadian PhD student decided to cycle to the Dead Sea with his team of local labourers and have an end-of-season picnic there:

> It was a lovely night of a full moon. After we had lit a fire and eaten our food, we sat there looking at the moon carving a path across the water right up to where we were. One of the boys said to me after a while, 'Do you have a moon like that in Canada?' When I affirmed that we did, he asked, 'Isn't it bigger?' I assured him that it was the same moon and no bigger. 'Do you mean to say that the same moon shines on people in Canada that shines on villagers in Jericho?' I nodded in agreement and then he said, 'Well if it's the same moon, whenever you see it would you please remember those of us who are your friends in Jericho?' We had a full moon the other night and I remembered.[74]

On the other hand, someone's cultural background could also evoke sentiments in others. One day a swastika had been excavated from a Pre-Pottery Neolithic layer, when a field assistant wrote: 'This will make the forthcoming German anthropologist glad.'[75] A colleague of his, who understood this Second World War sentiment, placed a board with a skull drawn onto it and the text 'Achtung' next to skeleton, on the spot where he was working. The next morning the board had vanished.[76]

However, in general the relationships among the team members were good. Indeed, the fact that young people spent some months together in a relatively remote place, far away from their family, resulted in affairs from time to time.[77] Sometimes a romance, which had started at Tell es-Sultan, grew into a steady relationship or even resulted in a marriage.[78] Beside friendships and romances, the expedition was also responsible for other kinds of long-lasting relationships: for most of the team members at Tell es-Sultan participation in the dig generated an archaeological network which proved useful for future appointments.[79]

The emotional dimension

The third dimension concerns the way in which the expedition members experienced their time at the dig and the excavation camp.

To fully understand an expedition of the past embedded in its historical context, it is necessary to discover the impact the excavation has had on the participants. For that reason, the emotional dimension incorporates personal impressions, emotions and life experiences. The records in this category – entirely informal – show how the stay at Tell es-Sultan affected people's view of archaeology, friendships and even life.

First of all, from the records it becomes clear that joining an expedition could have a great impact on one's future profession, and consequently, one's life. For several team members this expedition was in effect their first real experience with archaeology, having had no archaeological background at all.[80] Apparently, many of them enjoyed the archaeological experience at Tell es-Sultan so much so that they went on to pursue a career in this field and they were grateful to Kenyon for the knowledge, experience and inspiration they had gained.

Sometimes people would feel overwhelmed immediately after arrival on the site. For instance, a British draughtsman, who joined the dig in 1954 for the first time, wrote:

> I was woken by a blinding light – it was the sun! Through the window I could see palm trees, flowers and birds all against a brilliant blue sky. Coming from the drab greyness of post-war England, I felt as if the lights had turned on for the first time in my life.[81]

Someone else also described the exciting setting of the excavation camp in a letter he wrote to his parents while lying in his tent – amongst the banana plants and palm trees – listening to the sound of crickets, frogs and the flowing stream next to his tent; from his bed he looked across to the 'glorious mountains, which are bathed in pink at evenings'.[82] And while Europe was anxious about the deteriorating political situation in Jordan, expedition members reassured their family at home that there was no need to worry.[83]

Even after 60 years, former participants, when interviewed, still define their stay at Tell es-Sultan as a joyful time, which they enjoy recalling.[84] The combination of several aspects made the stay unforgettable for them. The memories can be very diverse, as the then Canadian PhD student indicates:

> I have lasting memories not so much from the tell but from the evenings spent in Jericho. I can still see KK [Kathleen Kenyon] smoking a cigarette, and sitting in my trench examining the strata, Henk [Franken] beginning his relationship with Ann [Battershill]…

I can still see the light changing on the hills of Moab, hear the boys' voices, and the children playing outside the Refugee school. I've gone back there several times but of course the old magic is not there because that magic derived from my colleagues and the others who worked there.[85]

However, these nostalgic memories must also be expounded to some extent. Even persons who enjoyed the expedition in hindsight, sometimes faced hard times when they were at the excavation. The pre-eminent example is that of draughtsman Terry Ball, who, in his letters from the excavation camp to his parents, admits that he was depressed for a while in Jericho. He sat inside the dig house all day and when he had finished work, the sun had already set. Ironically, the other team members congratulated Ball on 'being out of the sun and dust, and away from the constant chattering and noise of the Arab boys employed to labouring'. Ball just sighed: 'I wish to God, I could be out there sometimes, for it is very hot inside also.'[86] After a period of depression, he decided to only focus on the good points.

A stay at the excavation camp not only required mental resilience, the hard work and poor living conditions could also have an impact on one's physical health. It is not surprising that team members suffered from sore throats, bad colds or dysentery. Some of the participants even ended up in hospital.[87]

One of the aspects the expedition members really enjoyed were the evenings spent at the dig house filled with discussions, drinks, card games, singing and laughter (Figure 6.7). The conversations, which could last for hours, were on a broad range of topics. Sometimes Kenyon would join the group in the evening, but often retired to her room and worked until late.[88] From time to time the evenings were filled with singing and liquor was bought at the camp canteen, which was open after lunch and supper. The team members had their own supply: the bottles were labelled by name and paid off each second week. When, of an evening, too much liquor was consumed, the next morning Dorothy Marshall – who was responsible for general medical treatment at the camp – would provide the 'victims' with the necessary aspirins.[89]

Dig writing and the history of archaeology

This chapter aimed to demonstrate the advantages of dig writing. In contrast to life-writing, the approach of dig writing can avoid too much focus on a certain character which draws attention away from other

Figure 6.7 Sometimes there was time for relaxation. Team member Awni Dajani – later Director of the Department of Antiquities – invited the team to his property at Ain Duke for a picnic in 1952. Kenyon in the middle right, Dajani on the lower left. Source: Sarah Hennessy (NPAPH Project repository).

important actors: one of the challenges which life-writing has to face. Also, the question marks we should place alongside the excessive fascination a biographer might have for his or her subject, are less relevant in the case of dig writing.

As it combines several dimensions and is based on published sources, archival records and informal documentation, dig writing provides us with a more balanced view of an archaeological expedition carried out in the past. The data gathered comes from a considerable number and variety of sources, which makes cross-checking possible and can determine the historicity and reliability of the records. As dig writing includes several perspectives, it leads to a more representative account of what happened at a site decades ago: not just the views of the main characters present at the dig, but also the story of the 'quiet forces' such as students and local labourers. It offers not just the published results of the archaeological campaigns, it gives also insights into the uncertain paths they followed in order to reach those results, including wrong assumptions and methodologies. While traditional sources generally imply that a campaign was always successful and happy, the uncensored records make us aware of the downside of work and life at an excavation.

When more expeditions that took place at the same site (or region) over a wider time span are analysed in the way described in this chapter, dig writing can offer us unique insights into the developments that took place in the archaeological discipline in that specific period and region. For that reason, dig writing can be considered as a good alternative to life-writing when studying the history of archaeology.

Acknowledgements

I am grateful to the Council for British Research in the Levant for awarding me the CBRL Centennial Award which enabled me to go on a research visit to the archives of the MAA and IoA. The support of Rachael Sparks, Ian Carroll (IoA), Imogen Gunn and Wendy Brown (MAA) during the visits to these archives was indispensable. I am also indebted to Hamdan Taha and Miriam Saleh for interviewing Khalil Ahmad Darwish Jalyta and Mohammed Adawi respectively, and to all participants of the *Jericho off the Record* project for providing documentation to me. Last but not least, I would like to thank the anonymous reviewers for their constructive comments and suggestions.

Notes

1 For instance, Glyn Daniel, *One Hundred and Fifty Years of Archaeology* (London: Duckworth, 1975); William Stiebing Jr., *Uncovering the Past: A history of archaeology* (New York–Oxford: Oxford University Press, 1993); Bruce Trigger, *A History of Archaeological Thought* (Cambridge: Cambridge University Press, rev., 2006); Paul Bahn, ed., *The History of Archaeology: An introduction* (Abingdon-New York: Routledge, 2014).

2 Zachary Leader, ed., *On Life-Writing* (Oxford: Oxford University Press, 2015), 1.

3 Hermione Lee, '"From memory": literary encounters and life-writing', in *On Life-Writing*, ed. Leader, 125; Paola Govoni, 'Crafting scientific (auto)biographies', in *Writing about Lives in Science: (Auto)biography, gender, and genre*, eds., Paola Govoni and Zelda Alice Franceschi (Göttingen: V&R unipress, 2014), 10.

4 For example Mark C. B. Bowden, *Pitt Rivers: The life and archaeological work of Lieutenant-General Augustus Henry Lane Fox Pitt Rivers, DCL, FRS, FSA.* (Cambridge: Cambridge University Press, 1991); Miriam Davis, *Dame Kathleen Kenyon. Digging up the Holy Land* (Walnut Creek: Left Coast Press, 2008); Margaret S. Drower, *Flinders Petrie: A life in archaeology* (London: Gollancz, 1985); Jacquette Hawkes, *Mortimer Wheeler: Adventurer in Archaeology* (London: Weidenfeld and Nicholson, 1982); Bruce Trigger, *Gordon Childe: Revolution in archaeology* (New York: Columbia University Press, 1980).

5 Govoni, 'Crafting scientific (auto)biographies', 10; Marc-Antoine Kaeser, 'Biography, science studies and the historiography of archaeological research: managing personal archives', *Complutum* 24 (2013): 102.

6 Douglas R. Givens, 'The role of biography in writing the history of archaeology', in *Rediscovering Our Past: Essays on the history of American archaeology*, ed., Jonathan E. Reyman (Aldershot: Avebury, 1992), 54; Marc-Antoine Kaeser, 'Biography as microhistory: the relevance of private archives for writing the history of archaeology', in *Archives, Ancestors, Practices: Archaeology in*

the light of its history, eds. Nathan Schlanger and Jarl Nordbladh (New York-Oxford: Berghahn Books, 2008), 9, 12.
7 Kaeser, 'Biography as microhistory', 12. For a discussion on historicism, see Serge Reubi, 'Why is the dialogue so difficult between the historiography of the social sciences and the historiography of science?', in *Historiographical Approaches to Past Archaeological Research*, eds., Gisela Eberhardt and Fabian Link (Berlin: Edition Topoi, 2015), 229.
8 See, for instance, Kaeser, 'Biography as microhistory', 11 and Govoni, 'Crafting scientific (auto) biographies', 11–12.
9 Givens, 'The role of biography', 59–60; Kaeser, 'Biography, science studies', 104. Nathan Schlanger warns authors against venerating achievements of the 'genial founding fathers' of archaeology (Nathan Schlanger, 'The past is in the present: on the history and archives of archaeology', *Modernism/Modernity* 11.1 (2004): 165–6). Others suggest that self-analysis would be a necessary process before starting with life-writing or to recognise idealisation, ego distortion and transference (Michael Shortland and Richard Yeo, 'Introduction', in *Telling Lives in Science: Essays on scientific biography*, eds., Michael Shortland and Richard Yeo (Cambridge: Cambridge University Press, 1996), 32, 34).
10 Givens, 'The role of biography', 56–9.
11 Regarding the history of archaeology it is necessary to move beyond the narrative of great excavators, sites and objects. Amara Thornton, 'Social networks in the history of archaeology. placing archaeology in its context', in *Historiographical Approaches*, eds. Eberhardt and Link, 71; Schlanger, 'The past is in the present', 165.
12 Kaeser, 'Biography as microhistory', 9.
13 In order to be able to discuss the significance of combining different perspectives when analysing a past excavation, I have attempted to categorise the sources into clear, distinct dimensions. One should be aware that there might be overlap between these dimensions and that it is not always possible to assign an item to only a single dimension.
14 Bart Wagemakers, 'The digital non-professional archaeological photographs archives: private photographs of past excavations for current archaeological research', *The Archaeological Review from Cambridge* 29, no. 2 (2014): 50–68.
15 Bart Wagemakers, 'The Non-Professional Archaeological Photographs-Project', *The Antiquity Project Gallery* 87 Issue 338 (2013); http://antiquity.ac.uk/projgall/wagemakers338.
16 Wagemakers, 'Digital non-professional archaeological photographs archives', 50–68.
17 In private records such as diaries and letters, participants are able to express their thoughts and feelings which they would not dare to utter publicly on the site. Nathan Schlanger stresses the importance of seeking for the history of 'half-forgotten controversies and errors of yesteryear, of the routine operations so fundamental as to be self-evident, and indeed of all these episodes and practices deemed unfit for inclusion in the official or authorized histories of the discipline.' (Schlanger, 'The past is in the present', 166).
18 Kaeser, 'Biography, science studies', 105.
19 Several expeditions have been organized to the site of Tell es-Sultan in the last 150 years, so this site is very suitable for the study of the history of the archaeological discipline. However, because the aim of this chapter is to introduce the approach of dig writing, only one of these expeditions will be discussed here.
20 Most of these records are now stored at two depositories: the Museum of Archaeology and Anthropology in Cambridge and the Institute of Archaeology of UCL.
21 Bart Wagemakers, 'Jericho-off-the-record: tracing "new" records of the 1950s excavations at Tell es-Sultan', *Research Data Journal for the Humanities and Social Sciences* (2016), https://doi.org/10.1163/24523666-01000005.
22 Kathleen Kenyon, *Digging up Jericho* (London: Ernest Benn Limited, 1957).
23 Kathleen Kenyon, *Excavations at Jericho*. 5 Volumes (London: The British School of Archaeology in Jerusalem, 1960–1983). Results of the campaign have also been discussed in Kathleen Kenyon, *Archaeology in the Holy Land* (London: Benn, 1960).
24 An exception to the formal nature and the archaeological focus of the published sources is Margaret Wheeler's *Walls of Jericho* (London: Chatto & Windus, 1956) which pays a lot of attention to the daily life at the dig and the surroundings of the site.
25 A method also preferred by Mortimer Wheeler, Kenyon's mentor (Mortimer Wheeler, *Archaeology from the Earth* (Harmondsworth: Penguin Books, 1956), 200.
26 For possible colonial connotation of these settings with local labourers, see Jennifer Baird, 'Framing the past: situating the archaeological in photographs', *Journal of Latin American*

Cultural Studies 26 (2017): 12–16; *idem*., 'Photographing Duro-Europos, 1928–1937: An Archaeology of the Archive', *American Journal of Archaeology* 115 (2011): 433.

27 Letter from Henk Franken to Miriam Davis, 15 February 2004.
28 For instance, the methods they used for packing combs. While Wheeler, in *Walls of Jericho*, mentions the accepted way to process these objects, the unpublished notes give a glimpse of the courses pursued before they came to a conclusion (London: Readers Union and Chatto & Windus, 2nd, 1958, 154; Notebooks of the MAA archive BR6/3/1).
29 In field season 1957–58, for example, a field assistant listed the names of his team members, including their rank. From this list we may conclude that the field assistant concerned was accompanied by three pick men, three hoe men and 19 basket boys (MAA archive BR6/3/1).
30 The overview of expedition materials includes all field seasons and is divided into the following sections: surveying and drawing; camping; cooking and messing; tools; pottery shed equipment; technical equipment and materials; stationery; photographic equipment and materials; medical (MAA archive BR6/3/1).
31 In contrast to the BBC film recorded in 1956 (*Buried Treasure: The Walls of Jericho*, BBC, accessed 4 July 2021, http://www.bbc.co.uk/programmes/p01819yv) the informal footage was not edited to a tight script. It just shows all the features the student was interested in.
32 Kathleen Kenyon, 'Excavations at Jericho, 1955', *Palestine Exploration Quarterly* 87 (1955): 110–1 and Plate XVI.2; Kenyon, *Excavations at Jericho*, Vol. III.1, Text, 295 and Vol. III.2, Plates, Plate 161a.
33 Personal communication between Bill Power and the author, November 2014.
34 Interview with Cecil Western, 6 November 2016.
35 Interviews with Cecil Western, 30 April 2014 and 6 November 2016.
36 Kenyon, 'Excavations at Jericho, 1955', 110–1 and Plate XVI.2; Kenyon, *Excavations at Jericho*, Vol. III.1, Text, 295 and Vol. III.2, Plates, Plate 161a.
37 Letter from Henk Franken to Piet de Boer, 9 April 1955.
38 Letter from Henk Franken to Piet de Boer, 17 February 1955.
39 Letter from Henk Franken to Miriam Davis, 15 February 2004; Letter from John Carswell to his parents, 1955. At another time one of the basket boys was less lucky and fell 5.5 metres off the staircase down into the main trench (Letter from John Carswell to his parents, 4 March 1954).
40 The division into these categories follows Thornton, 'Social networks', 74.
41 Thornton, 'Social networks', 74. It must be acknowledged that the (artificial) divisions between the categories are not always explicitly clear.
42 Davis, *Dame Kathleen Kenyon*, 103; BSAJ Minute Book, 5 December 1950; 'Annual Report, 1956–1957', *Proceedings of the British Academy* XLIII (1957): 5.
43 *Palestine Exploration Quarterly* 85 (1953): 81; 86 (1954): 45; 87 (1955): 108; 88 (1956): 67. The volumes of *Excavations at Jericho* also start with listing the 'supporting organisations'. The last annual report also listed the amounts of money donated by every sponsor ('Appendix II, Jericho Accounts', *Palestine Exploration Quarterly* 92 (1960): 112–13).
44 *Palestine Exploration Quarterly* 88 (1956): 67.
45 See the distribution list in Kenyon, *Excavations at Jericho*, Vol. V, 825–56.
46 *Palestine Exploration Quarterly* 86 (1954): 45; 87 (1955): 108; 88 (1956): 67.
47 The introduction to the distribution list states that a large proportion of the almost 4000 artefacts recorded in the main Tell Excavation Register had been allocated to 27 museums and institutions (Kenyon, *Excavations at Jericho*, Vol V, 825).
48 Wheeler, *Walls of Jericho*, 145.
49 For an overview of how Tell es-Sultan was presented in the media and the role archaeologists played in creating media impressions, see Rachael Thyrza Sparks, 'Jericho in the media', in *Digging up Jericho: Past, present and future*, eds. Rachael Thyrza Sparks, Bill Finlayson, Bart Wagemakers, and Josef Briffa (Oxford: Archaeopress, 2020), 21–37.
50 Davis, *Dame Kathleen Kenyon*, 135–36.
51 *Palestine Exploration Quarterly* 88 (1956): 67; David Spurgeon in Toronto *Globe and Mail*, 6 February 1956, 19; 13 February 1956, 21; 17 February 1956, 17; 22 February 1956, 15; 3 March 1956, 25; 21 March 1956, 21; 3 April 1956, 17.
52 Sparks, 'Jericho in the Media', 22–4.
53 *Buried Treasure: The Walls of Jericho*, BBC, accessed 4 July 2021, http://www.bbc.co.uk/programmes/p01819yv.
54 MAA archive BR6/3/1.
55 Jericho Archives IoA.

56 Kenyon, *Excavations at Jericho*, Vol. III.1 Text, ix-x.
57 These records also show that sometimes a labourer got punished. In 1956 Mohammed Ismail and Ahmet Khalil, for instance, were registered for only half a day because of stone throwing. A certain Ghasim and Dhiab Mohammed received the same punishment for fighting (MAA archive BR6/3/1).
58 MAA archive BR6/3/1.
59 *Palestine Exploration Quarterly* 88 (1956): 67.
60 Letter Kathleen Kenyon to Nora Kenyon, 10 January 1956.
61 Diary Leo Boer, 10 March 1954; Letter Henk Franken to Piet de Boer, 23 January, 15 February and 25 March 1955; Letter John Carswell to his parents, 15 March 1955.
62 Letter from John Carswell to his parents, 1 December 1956.
63 Letter Terry Ball to his parents, 28 November 1957.
64 Letter Kathleen Kenyon to Nora Kenyon, 24 December 1957.
65 Letter Henk Franken to Miriam Davis, 15 February 2004.
66 Letter Kathleen Kenyon to Nora Kenyon, 15 February 1955.
67 Interview with former participant Khalil Ahmad Darwish Jalyta on 14 December 2015; Letter John Carswell to his parents, 6 April 1955.
68 Interview with Khalil Ahmad Darwish Jalyta, 14 December 2015.
69 Interview with Khalil Ahmad Darwish Jalyta, 14 December 2015; interview with former participant Mohammed Adawi on 20 June 2016.
70 Letter from Henk Franken to Piet de Boer, 21 January 1955.
71 Letter from John Carswell to his parents, 4 March 1956.
72 Interview with Mohammed Adawi, 20 June 2016; Interview Ann Knowles, 27 July 2015; Interview Cecil Western, 6 November 2016; Interview Martin Biddle, 21 July 2015.
73 For instance, photographs in the private collection of Nancy Lord were also found at the homes of Basil Hennessee and Maggie Tushingham, and also in a photo album at the MAA.
74 Personal communication between Bill Power and the author, November 2014.
75 Letter Henk Franken to Piet de Boer, 3 February 1955. Franken here refers to anthropologist Gottlieb Kurth from Göttingen, who studied the human remains at Tell es-Sultan from 1955–1958.
76 Letter Henk Franken to Piet de Boer, 3 February 1955.
77 Interview with John Carswell (30 November 2014) and Martin Biddle (21 July 2015).
78 Like Ann Battershill and Henk Franken, who met each other at Tell es-Sultan for the first time in 1955 (Personal communication between Bill Power and the author, November 2014).
79 Letters John Carswell to his parents, 19 and 31 January 1955; Letters from Terry Ball to his parents, 1961–1964; Interview with Mohammed Adawi, 20 June 2016; Mohammed Adawi, 'Mohammed Adawi Remembers', *ACOR Newsletter* 20, no. 1 (2008): 20–21; Letters Hendrik Brunsting to his parents, 9 and 19 January 1960.
80 Such as artists John Carswell and Terry Ball, or conscripted soldier Martin Biddle, theology PhD student Bill Power, missionary Henk Franken and biology student Ann Knowles.
81 John Carswell, 'In Honour of Honor: the Birth of Underwater Archaeology'. *The Honor Frost Foundation Lecture*, 11 June 2014. The British Academy, London; interview with John Carswell, 30 November 2014; Letter John Carswell to his parents, 5 January 1954.
82 Letter Terry Ball to his parents, 22 October 1957.
83 Letter Kathleen Kenyon to Nora Kenyon, 10 January 1956; Letter John Carswell to his parents, 10 March 1956; Letter Terry Ball to his parents, 22 and 31 October 1957. On the other hand, the political circumstances in the region sometimes did in fact cause some worries among the team members (Letter John Carswell to his parents, 18 January 1956).
84 Interview Martin Biddle, 21 July 2015; Personal communication between Bill Power and the author, November 2014; Interview Ann Knowles, 27 July 2015.
85 Personal communication between Bill Power and the author, November 2014.
86 Letter Terry Ball to his parents, 22 October 1957.
87 Letter Henk Franken to Piet de Boer, 12 March 1955; Letters Terry Ball to his parents, 28 November and 4 December 1957; Interview Ann Knowles, 27 July 2015.
88 Interview Ann Knowles, 27 July 2015. In a letter to her husband, the mother of registrar Maggie Tushingham wrote on 6 April 1953: 'Miss Kenyon is with us, but you would hardly know it, she appears at meals, back to the office and works there 17 or 18 hours every day.'.
89 Letter Terry Ball to his parents, 28 November 1957; Interview Ann Knowles, 27 July 2015; Interview Cecil Western, 6 November 2016.

Bibliography

Adawi, Mohammed, 'Mohammed Adawi Remembers'. *ACOR Newsletter* 20, no. 1 (2008): 20–1.
Bahn, Paul, ed., *The History of Archaeology: An introduction* (Abingdon–New York: Routledge, 2014).
Baird, Jennifer, 'Photographing Duro-Europos, 1928–1937: an archaeology of the archive', *American Journal of Archaeology* 115, (2011): 427–46.
Baird, Jennifer, 'Framing the past: situating the archaeological in photographs', *Journal of Latin American Cultural Studies* 26 (2017): 165–86.
Bowden, Mark C. B., *Pitt Rivers: The life and archaeological work of Lieutenant-General Augustus Henry Lane Fox Pitt Rivers, DCL, FRS, FSA* (Cambridge: Cambridge University Press, 1991).
Daniel, Glyn, *One Hundred and Fifty Years of Archaeology* (London: Duckworth, 1975).
Davis, Miriam, *Dame Kathleen Kenyon. Digging up the Holy Land* (Walnut Creek: Left Coast Press, 2008).
Drower, Margaret S., *Flinders Petrie: A life in archaeology* (London: Gollancz, 1985).
Givens, Douglas R., 'The role of biography in writing the history of archaeology', in *Rediscovering our Past: Essays on the history of American archaeology*, ed. Jonathan E. Reyman (Aldershot: Avebury, 1992).
Govoni, Paola, 'Crafting scientific (auto)biographies', in *Writing about Lives in Science: (Auto) biography, gender, and genre*, eds. Paola Govoni and Zelda Alice Franceschi (Göttingen: V&R Unipress, 2014).
Hawkes, Jacquette, *Mortimer Wheeler: Adventurer in archaeology* (London: Weidenfeld and Nicholson, 1982).
Kaeser, Marc-Antoine, 'Biography as microhistory: the relevance of private archives for writing the history of archaeology', in *Archives, Ancestors, Practices: Archaeology in the light of its history*, eds. Nathan Schlanger and Jarl Nordbladh (New York–Oxford: Berghahn Books, 2008).
Kaeser, Marc-Antoine. 'Biography, science studies and the historiography of archaeological research: managing personal archives', *Complutum* 24 (2013): 101–8.
Kenyon, Kathleen M., 'Excavations at Jericho, 1953', *Palestine Exploration Quarterly* 85 (1953): 81–95.
Kenyon, Kathleen M., 'Excavations at Jericho, 1954', *Palestine Exploration Quarterly* 86 (1954): 45–63.
Kenyon, Kathleen M., 'Excavations at Jericho, 1955', *Palestine Exploration Quarterly* 87 (1955): 108–17.
Kenyon, Kathleen M., 'Excavations at Jericho, 1956', *Palestine Exploration Quarterly* 88 (1956): 67–82.
Kenyon, Kathleen M., *Digging up Jericho* (London: Ernest Benn Limited, 1957).
Kenyon, Kathleen M., 'Excavations at Jericho, 1957–58', *Palestine Exploration Quarterly* 92 (1960): 88–108; 111–3.
Kenyon, Kathleen M., *Archaeology in the Holy Land* (London: Benn, 1960).
Kenyon, Kathleen M., *Excavations at Jericho*. 5 Volumes (London: The British School of Archaeology in Jerusalem, 1960–1983).
Leader, Zachary, ed., *On Life-Writing* (Oxford: Oxford University Press, 2015).
Lee, Hermione, '"From memory": literary encounters and life-writing', In *On Life-Writing*, ed., Zachary Leader (Oxford: Oxford University Press, 2015).
Reubi, Serge. 'Why is the dialogue so difficult between the historiography of the social sciences and the historiography of science?', in *Historiographical Approaches to Past Archaeological Research*, ed. Gisela Eberhardt and Fabian Link (Berlin: Edition Topoi, 2015).
Schlanger, Nathan. 'The past is in the present: on the history and archives of archaeology'. *Modernism/Modernity* 11 (2004): 165–7.
Shortland, Michael and Richard Yeo, 'Introduction', in *Telling Lives in Science: Essays on scientific biography* eds., Michael Shortland and Richard Yeo (Cambridge: Cambridge University Press, 1996).
Sparks, Rachael Thyrza, 'Jericho in the media', in *Digging up Jericho: Past, present and future*, eds., Rachael Thyrza Sparks, Bill Finlayson, Bart Wagemakers and Josef Briffa (Oxford: Archaeopress, 2020).
Stiebing Jr., William, *Uncovering the Past: A history of archaeology* (New York–Oxford: Oxford University Press, 1993).

Thornton, Amara, 'Social networks in the history of archaeology: placing archaeology in its context', in *Historiographical Approaches to Past Archaeological Research*, eds., Gisela Eberhardt and Fabian Link (Berlin: Edition Topoi, 2015).

Trigger, Bruce, *Gordon Childe, Revolution in Archaeology* (New York: Columbia University Press, 1980).

Trigger, Bruce, *A History of Archaeological Thought,* revised (Cambridge: Cambridge University Press, 2006).

Wagemakers, Bart, 'The Non-Professional Archaeological Photographs-Project', *The Antiquity Project Gallery* 87, issue 338 (2013): http://antiquity.ac.uk/projgall/wagemakers338.

Wagemakers, Bart, 'The digital non-professional archaeological photographs archives: private photographs of past excavations for current archaeological research' *The Archaeological Review from Cambridge* 29 (2014): 50–68.

Wagemakers, Bart, 'Jericho-off-the-record: tracing 'new' records of the 1950s excavations at Tell es-Sultan', *Research Data Journal for the Humanities and Social Sciences* (2016): 1–13.

Wheeler, Margaret, *Walls of Jericho* (London: Chatto & Windus, 1956).

Wheeler, Mortimer, *Archaeology from the Earth*, second edition (Harmondsworth: Penguin Books, 1956).

Part II
Sources and networks

7
The accidental linguist: Herbert Thompson's contribution to Egyptian language studies traced through his archive

Catherine Ansorge

Introduction

Sir Herbert Thompson's working papers and correspondence held as an archive at Cambridge University Library present a comprehensive record of his achievements in Egyptology made over more than 40 years. Thompson's dedication to his work can be traced here from the time his interest in the subject was first sparked around 1898, until his death in 1944. The notes and transcripts in the archive relate to early Egyptian texts, mostly in Demotic and Coptic, which, instead of excavation work, he had made his personal focus. The correspondence reveals the diversity of his academic contacts and provides evidence, both of the assistance he provided to colleagues and the respect he received from them for his learning and advice.

    The aim of this chapter is to show how such an archive can demonstrate the trajectory of an individual career and how the efforts of a single individual can make a significant contribution to a wider field of scholarship. Douglas Givens has, in the context of biographical studies, argued that the analysis of past events and the contributions of specific individuals, through time, is best appreciated through biography. He suggests that this should focus on the available evidence from the work produced, of the individual's existence in space and time, as well as their position and contribution in the current intellectual climate.[1] Thompson, through his archive, provides evidence in both senses.

The importance of collections of private papers as a resource for biographical studies is also demonstrated by Marc-Antoine Kaeser, in his study of the archive of Édouard Desor (1811–1882). Desor was a Swiss-German prehistorian, from a generation prior to Thompson, but as his archive also consists of correspondence, notes and a personal library, it shares many similarities with the Thompson material. Kaeser also remarks on the increase in recent decades, of biographical studies and their acceptance as a valuable resource in historiography.[2] The significance of the Thompson archive rests not only on reconstructing his life, but also on the evidence it provides of progress made by British Egyptology in the early twentieth century and the network of scholarship within which Thompson is gradually revealed to be a critical figure. Yet, because the archive was handed from scholar to scholar in Cambridge, its contents have been little known and the contents unaddressed in the broader context of the times. Thompson, along with his colleagues F. Ll. Griffith and W. E. Crum, made a significant contribution to the study of Demotic and Coptic and in a sense, provided the third, and least known, side of the triangle formed by them. But Thompson was not only an Egyptologist, he also had a fascinating personal life with interests in the visual arts, music and natural history and there is evidence that these also influenced the course of his career.

Egyptology in Cambridge before Thompson's time

Although a separate issue from the archive and its contents, it was a legacy from Thompson which later founded, in 1946, the Chair of Egyptology in Cambridge.[3] His intentions in this respect gradually become clear through evidence from the archive and his actions later in life. It is important to note, though, that there had been connections between Egyptology and Cambridge long before Thompson. The polymath Thomas Young (1773–1829), noted for his pioneering work on the decipherment of hieroglyphs and Demotic, as well as his work as a physicist, studied at Emmanuel College. William John Bankes (1786–1855) studied at Trinity College (where he became a firm friend of Lord Byron) before his years as a traveller and collector in Egypt.[4] Another Cambridge pioneer was Charles Goodwin (1817–1878), Fellow of St Catharine's College. Although a lawyer by profession, Goodwin had many private interests, including an enthusiasm for reading ancient Egyptian texts and he produced many articles on his studies made on the papyri in the British Museum collections.[5]

There was also a Cambridge connection with Wallis Budge (1857–1934), Keeper of the Department of Egyptian and Assyrian Antiquities of the British Museum, so noted for his antiquities acquisitions and many publications. Budge studied at Christ's College in Cambridge and bequeathed funds to the College to establish a research scholarship there. He also left his library to Christ's and provided the Fitzwilliam Museum in Cambridge with a large collection of Egyptian artefacts which he also catalogued.[6] Many other distinguished Egyptologists have their discoveries represented in the collection in the Fitzwilliam Museum, including Flinders Petrie, Frederick William Green, James Quibell, Guy Brunton, and Stephen Glanville. So even before Thompson's endowment of the Chair at Cambridge, there was already a significant subject presence within the University, but no official teaching post had ever been established.

The Thompson archive and its contents

The Thompson archive arrived at Cambridge University Library in two batches in 2012 and in 2014 from the Faculty of Asian and Middle Eastern Studies, consequent on a decision to transfer the Egyptology books collection to the Faculty of Archaeology and Anthropology Library (Haddon Library) in line with the transfer of the teaching Department. The Haddon Library was unable to make provision for archive storage or consultation, so the archival material was deposited in the Manuscripts Department of the University Library where the relevant reader facilities were already in place.

The Thompson archive is extensive, comprising a hundred files of papers containing detailed notes on original texts (including transcriptions and translations), preparatory notes for publications and correspondence.[7] There are several boxes of index cards, photographic positives and negatives, some newspaper cuttings and small number of artefacts, and in total, the archive occupies around 6m of shelving. The notes are written on paper, either in notebooks or on single sheets, often clipped together. However, as they are mainly undated, the historical sequence is often unclear. No Thompson material appears to exist in archives elsewhere, apart from a file of correspondence in the Griffith Institute in Oxford.[8]

There are files in the archive that consist only of correspondence, although letters and postcards are sometimes found in other files when they relate to the subject content.[9] There is no private correspondence from his family and friends: his will states that this was bequeathed to his family.

It is the very comprehensive nature of the archive, with so much material together in one place, which makes the Thompson archive such a satisfying subject for biographical research. The working notes reflect a lifetime's endeavour and the correspondence indicates the scope of his contacts and the extent of his influence. Also, the writing of a biography of a single individual opens up the possibility of considering the wider social context of his times, but from the interior life of a single existence.[10]

Background to the study of Egyptology in England

The contents of the archive relate to the first four decades of the twentieth century, a crucial time for the development of Egyptology in England. Although the archive is now held in Cambridge, Thompson's work in Egyptology did not begin there, but in London. When Thompson began his studies around 1898, only one established post in the subject existed in England, the Chair at University College, London (UCL), founded in 1892 by the bequest of Amelia Edwards (1831–1892); her great friend and protégé Flinders Petrie became the first holder of the position.[11] She also donated her own collection of Egyptian antiquities and her library to UCL, forming the founding collections of a teaching department. Petrie also brought his own expertise and antiquities collections to add to these.[12]

In 1901, F. Ll. Griffith founded the readership in Egyptology (later chair) at Oxford, in 1906 a professorship was founded at Liverpool and in 1912–1914, a readership in Manchester.[13] With so few official positions, the subject was very reliant on the skills and dedication of private scholars, museum staff and individual enthusiasts. These individuals were from varied backgrounds, some quite modest origins, others from a wealthy, even aristocratic, background. Thompson came from a wealthy and well-connected family, the 'Bart', often printed after his name in some of his publications, denoting the baronetcy he inherited from his father. But Thompson was never reliant on the world of Egyptology for his income; he also lived a busy and varied private life away from that world. He remains a rather an enigmatic character, reticent by nature and a relative unknown in the world of Egyptology, in contrast to other prominent names of his generation. Yet there are indications dating back to the early part of his life as to why this might have been his own choice. The influence of his family of birth remained significant throughout his life, so a description of his early years, and the way in which he came to the world of Egyptology, is important.

Thompson's early life

Born in London in 1859 into a wealthy family, Herbert Thompson never needed to strive for the necessities of life, but there is evidence of personal struggles in both his family situation and his professional life. His father, Sir Henry Thompson (1820–1904), was an eminent urologist and professor of surgery at University College Hospital in London.[14] The family house at 35 Wimpole Street in London served both as a home and as Sir Henry's professional practice. Sir Henry had weathered a difficult struggle against his own father's wishes to follow his chosen profession in which he had become a leading expert, even treating patients from royalty. He was knighted in 1867 and created a baronet in 1899.

Thompson's mother, Kate Loder (1825–1904), born in Bath, was an accomplished pianist and composer. She studied the piano from the age of six and in 1844 performed Mendelssohn's G minor concerto in the composer's presence. In the same year she was appointed professor of harmony at the Royal Academy of Music and among her musical compositions were chamber music and works for the piano and songs.[15] In 1851 she married Henry Thompson with whom she had two daughters and a son. The son was also named Henry, but preferred to be known by his last forename, Herbert. After her marriage, his mother was persuaded to give up her musical profession, or at least the public aspects, to concentrate on family duties.

The Thompsons were a respected and well-connected family, and among their social circle, were eminent scientists, artists and musicians. Apparently, the Thompsons gave fashionable dinner parties with eight guests, known as 'octaves'.[16] Concerts were also a regular occurrence, and it was at 35 Wimpole Street that the first UK performance of the Brahms Requiem, in the adaptation for piano duet, took place in 1871, and in which Lady Thompson played one of the piano parts. Sir Henry was also an accomplished artist, producing paintings which were displayed at the Royal Academy of Arts; among his teachers was the noted artist Sir Lawrence Alma-Tadema (1836–1912). His own portrait was painted by his friend John Everett Millais and now hangs in the Tate Gallery.[17] It is very likely that the Thompsons were acquainted with other members of the Pre-Raphaelite Brotherhood, and it is said that Herbert Thompson himself was a good friend of Jane Morris, the wife of William Morris.[18] So the young Herbert moved among some of the most noted artistic, musical and social circles in London, and this cultural background remained with him throughout his life, forming a parallel thread to his work in Egyptology. In 1904, Sir Henry Thompson died, followed in the same year by his wife, resulting in significant changes for their son, who inherited the Baronetcy and a considerable personal fortune. The Wimpole Street house appears to have been sold, but London and Bath, the two cities with parental connections, remained significant to Thompson throughout his life.

Thompson's early career

The Thompsons sent their son to school at Marlborough College and then, in 1876, to Trinity College, Cambridge. He is said to have been quite unhappy at both, nor was he well-liked, but he achieved a first in history at Cambridge, graduating in 1881.[19] Presumably it was at school that he first studied the classics, for which he retained a life-long enthusiasm, and his expertise in Greek proved to be of immense value in his later work, especially with Coptic studies. It appears that Sir Henry had great ambitions for his only son and his father's constant interference in his career plans proved to be a major problem. Henry was keen for his son to study law and Herbert was admitted to the Inner Temple in 1878. Four years later he was called to the Bar, but although he followed a legal career for a number of years, he felt no affinity or enthusiasm for it.

In 1889, Herbert met Thomas Huxley, by that time a well-known and established scientist; both he and Sir Henry Thompson were members of the Royal College of Surgeons. Huxley was a man who had received little formal education but who had, by his own endeavours, risen to a position of public respect and acclaim for his scientific understanding of the natural world.[20] Influenced by Huxley, and once more at his father's prompting, Herbert entered UCL in 1896 to study biology. He had always had an interest in the natural world and had previously studied botany and entomology. A portrait of him, painted at age 17, is said to be of him reading an entomology book.[21] But this occupation brought him further problems: use of the microscope resulted in serious eye trouble, and its further use was out of the question. But during this time, he had met the archaeologist Flinders Petrie, already famous for his archaeological excavations and new methodology in his fieldwork. Petrie, only a few years older than Thompson, was the holder of the chair of Egyptology at UCL.[22]

Thompson's introduction to Egyptology

It was this meeting with Petrie, then at the peak of his career, which proved to be life-changing for Thompson. A lesser-known aspect of

Petrie's work was his close collaboration, with colleagues Francis Galton and Karl Pearson, on the study of eugenics.[23] This had brought Petrie into the world of biology and anthropometrics as early as 1883. From his excavations in Egypt, Petrie sent back human skeletons, bones and skulls to the Anthropometrics Laboratory at UCL where their analysis provided original research data.[24] It was on a visit to here that Petrie first met Thompson, from whom he requested a report on some Egyptian skeletal remains. Thompson was caught up by Petrie's enthusiasm and charisma, perhaps also seeing here the possibility of escape from his father's influence, and he gradually became absorbed by the world of Egyptology. So, at the age of 40, his interest in the subject took hold and was to last for the rest of his life. Thompson had approached the study of Egyptology by a very indirect route, characterised by chance encounters and by failures in other projects. His fierce resistance to his father's influence resulted in him forming his own path in life; his financial independence providing him with considerable freedom. Such were the influences on Thompson at the start of his career in Egyptology, but gradually his focus began to change, and it was a very different group of individuals who subsequently became his colleagues.

Thompson as an Egyptology student

The study of Egyptology at UCL, as directed by Petrie, had attracted an impressive group of gifted scholars, including both archaeologists and language specialists. New to the discipline, Thompson concentrated initially on a general grounding in Egyptology but his interests focused increasingly on language studies. He became part of a close-knit group which included F. Ll. Griffith, the Demotic specialist and W. C. Crum who focused on Coptic. Both were younger than Thompson by a few years, but as both had studied Egyptology from much earlier in life, and already developed a greater expertise, they became Thompson's first teachers.

Francis Llewellyn Griffith (1862–1934) developed an early enthusiasm for Egyptology and gained a position with the Egypt Exploration Fund (EEF) enabling him to visit Egypt as Petrie's assistant for several winter excavation seasons. From 1893–1901, Griffith also acted as Petrie's assistant at UCL teaching the linguistic aspects of the Egyptology course.[25] Years later it was the Griffith bequest, including his very fine library, which founded the Griffith Institute putting Egyptology on a firm footing in Oxford. Walter Ewing Crum (1865–1944) became interested in Egyptology from studying monuments and museum objects and later studied in Paris with Gaston Maspero and in Berlin with Adolf Erman. Family wealth enabled him to be a private scholar and he was attracted to Coptic studies through publications he saw on the subject, including those by Petrie. From 1893, Crum assisted Petrie with the teaching of Coptic at UCL, so becoming Thompson's teacher.[26] At UCL, Thompson began by learning hieroglyphs, but subsequently, under the tutelage of Griffith and Crum, developed a mastery of Demotic and Coptic. Though all three of them later left UCL to work elsewhere, they remained firm friends and colleagues throughout the rest of their lives and collaborated on projects and publications. Eventually they became the accepted leaders of expertise in these languages in the UK.

Thompson's early publications

Thompson continued his language studies at UCL, improving his knowledge by working on texts at the British Museum. With Griffith he worked on a collection of Demotic papyri, particularly on one dating from the third century CE and containing texts on magic and medicine.[27] Together they edited and published it in 1904–9, Thompson's first published work.[28] The papyrus in question had been discovered in Thebes in the early nineteenth century, torn into two halves and subsequently separated, with one half in Leiden and the other in the British Museum. The Leiden half had been studied in the early nineteenth century and published by Caspar Reuvens.[29] The British Museum half had remained unknown until later in the century when part of it was published by Jean-Jacques Hess; it was recognised as an important text in the decipherment of Demotic script.[30] Griffith and Thompson produced the first complete translation of the text, revealing its full content. The papyrus is especially interesting for the language in which it is written, a very late form of Demotic; also its extensive vocabulary contributed significantly to the decipherment of Demotic. Around the same time Thompson also assisted Petrie by writing the chapters on the Demotic texts in his excavation report *Gizeh and Rifeh* to which Crum also contributed chapters on the Coptic finds.[31] Once Thompson begins to publish, a direct link to the papers in the archive becomes apparent. It is possible to trace the original notes that Thompson made on the texts, both the transcription and transliteration, for this publication.[32]

It is not clear where Thompson lived during his years working at UCL, but he remained unmarried, so it is quite possible that he continued to live in the family home at 35 Wimpole Street. There are letters in the archive written as late as 1899 addressed to him there.

Thompson continued to collaborate with Griffith and Crum, although Griffith had left London to live in his wife's family home in Ashton-under-Lyne, and later on, in Oxford. Crum subsequently left his post at UCL for personal reasons as he had made an unhappy marriage and through his work had met Margaret Hart-Davies, with whom he lived for the rest of his life. They lived for a time in Austria but were forced to flee at the outbreak of the First World War, and after their return to England, lived first near to Bristol and later, in 1927, moved to Bath. During the whole of this time, and especially while abroad, Crum was visiting museums to work on Coptic manuscripts as preparatory work on his Coptic dictionary, a life-long project in which Thompson would later become closely involved.

Further progress and a visit to Egypt

From these modest beginnings at UCL, Thompson's expertise grew and more publications followed. He also left Wimpole Street for a new address at 9 Kensington Park Gardens, a large and lavish house where he lived for some years. There are letters in the archive addressed to him there around 1915; possibly he lived there for around 10 years.

It was also during the UCL years that Thompson made his one and only visit to Egypt, an extended visit to excavations at Saqqara in 1907–1908, working with J.E. Quibell, also a pupil of Petrie. It is unclear why he never visited Egypt again, but what seems most likely is that he found that he preferred reading texts, a skill that could just as well be satisfied by visits to museums and libraries. Thompson contributed chapters on the Coptic texts in Quibell's *Excavations at Saqqara, 1907–1908*, and his presence at the excavation is recorded in the volume's introduction.[33] There are notes on his findings at Saqqara in the archive.[34]

Also contributing to this volume was Wilhelm Spiegelberg, writing on the hieroglyphic texts from the excavations. Spiegelberg (1870–1930) was also a specialist in Demotic and Coptic, perhaps the foremost German scholar in these subjects at the time, and in 1921, published a Coptic dictionary.[35] In 1925 he also published a Demotic grammar.[36] Thompson's archive contains closely written notes taken from Spiegelberg's works and the two remained in contact.[37] With their shared language interests and expertise, it is recorded in a biography of Spiegelberg that they became established colleagues.[38] Thompson's preparatory notes for his own Demotic dictionary can also be found in the archive consisting of 12 files of notes, the result of considerable effort on his part, but which were never published.[39]

The archive also houses a photostat copy, stored in 25 blue binders of a microfilm of Spiegelberg's manuscript notes for an unpublished Demotic dictionary.[40] These were obtained in 1953 or 1954 by Stephen Glanville in return for the offer by him of a copy of Thompson's lexicological files from the archive to George Hughes and William F. Edgerton, for incorporation the Chicago Demotic Dictionary Project.[41] These photostat copies are now shelved with the Thompson archive.[42]

A decade of publications

From his first publication in 1904, Thompson continued to produce text-based studies for another 10 years until disruptions to his life were caused by the outbreak of the First World War in 1914. During these pre-war years he developed a special interest in the Coptic Bible and in 1908 he published on the Coptic texts of the Old Testament from papyri in the British Museum.[43] The idea to study this text originally came from Crum and the preparatory notes for this can be identified in the archive.[44] In 1911, he edited a work on a palimpsest text based on a seventh century text of books of the Old Testament where the Coptic under text is overwritten by Syriac.[45] He also contributed, in 1912, to a second volume of texts from Saqqara, containing work on the Coptic inscriptions (see Figure 7.1). The Apa Jeremias monastery at Saqqara had also been excavated by Quibell and the Coptic texts recovered from the site merited a separate volume.[46] In 1913, Thompson also published a further volume of Coptic Biblical texts from the British Museum papyrus manuscript. This describes a Coptic codex dating earlier than 350 CE and on which Wallis Budge had previously published an edited version.[47] Thompson was also a great collaborator, and in 1913 with Sir Alan Gardiner and J. G. Milne contributed to a descriptive volume on ostraca from Thebes.[48] Thompson describes here a collection of 44 Demotic ostraca from a much larger collection of over 400 specimens acquired in 1906 and the notes for these can be identified in the archive.[49]

By the beginning of the First World War, and after a later start in his studies than most of his contemporaries, Thompson had produced a steady stream of substantial publications on Demotic and Coptic texts, also numerous papers in journals. However, Thompson then took on the role of special constable to aid the war effort in London, and during this period there is a noticeable break in the sequence. Around this time, aged almost 60, he also expressed his intention to retire and move to the country and with this plan in mind, he donated books from his personal

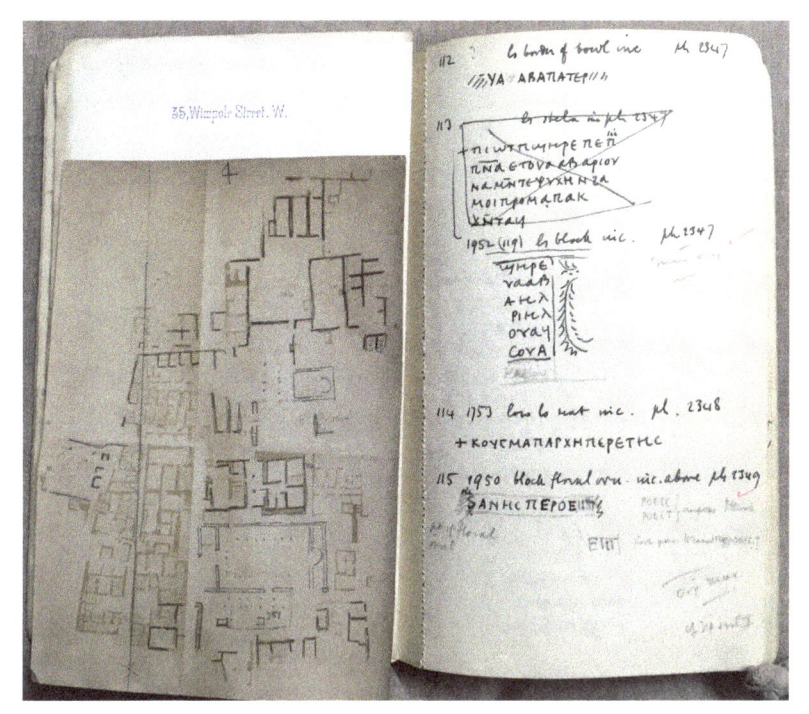

Figure 7.1 Page from a notebook containing notes from various sources including the Cairo Museum and Saqqara and a photograph of a hand-drawn plan of the Monastery of Apa Jeremias at Saqqara. Source: GBR/0012/MS Thompson, HT 88 and reproduced by kind permission of the Syndics of Cambridge University Library.

Egyptology library to the EEF in 1919.[50] These were mainly works on hieroglyphs; books on Demotic and Coptic he retained in his possession. Although he possibly intended to distance himself from his work with Egyptology, this was far from the scenario which subsequently unfolded. After the war there were further calls on his time and expertise which opened up a second career for him.

Thompson's personal interests

Quite apart from his work on ancient Egyptian texts, Thompson also professed a deep interest in the Classics and in the arts. He travelled frequently, visiting museums, art galleries and attending concerts and operatic performances. It is said that he made a visit to Rome every year and regularly travelled in other parts of Europe. He had a keen interest in painting and collected original works of art, some of which he later donated to the Fitzwilliam Museum in Cambridge. These include a small collection of early Italian paintings and a larger collection of prints and artefacts. Also, in the Fitzwilliam Museum there are two portraits of Herbert Thompson and one of his father, Sir Henry, painted by Sir Lawrence Alma-Tadema (1836–1912), the Anglo-Dutch artist, who became fashionable in England, especially for his classical scenes and portraits. The two paintings of Herbert Thompson include one portrait painted in 1877, when he was aged 18, and another painting entitled *94 Degrees in the Shade*, painted in the previous year, which depicts a young Herbert lying in a field of corn, reading a book on entomology (see Figure 7.2). The clothing he wears appears to be rather unseasonal

Figure 7.2 Lawrence Alma-Tadema (1836–1912) *94 Degrees in the Shade*, a young Herbert Thompson painted in 1876 in a cornfield in Godstone, Surrey. Oil on canvas, 35.3cm × 21.6cm. Source: © The Fitzwilliam Museum, Cambridge.

for such a high temperature. Both pictures were donated by Thompson. Alma-Tadema also painted a portrait of Thompson's mother which hangs in the Royal Academy of Music.[51]

Thompson's notes and correspondence

As Thompson's travels and artistic interests made museum visits a regular occupation, it is very likely that these would include the first-hand study of texts. The archive contains notes made in the British Museum, in Oxford, Manchester and Dublin, and in Europe, in the museums in Turin, Berlin, Paris, Rome, Leiden, Copenhagen, Vienna and Brussels (see Figure 7.3). There are also notes from Cairo where he visited the museum at the time of his visit to Saqqara in 1907.[52] From the evidence of Thompson's working life, it is easy to comprehend how his archive became an immense repository of notes painstakingly gathered in museums and private collections. Regular work over the years resulted in an archive with a wealth of material in transcription, transliteration and translation, many of which have never been published and some others which have since been lost. In a sense, Thompson had formed himself into a Demotic and Coptic text library and others working in the same field became well aware of this.

The correspondence in the archive provides evidence to the extent to which his expertise was valued by colleagues (see Figure 7.4). As might be expected, there are many letters here from Thompson's collaborators, also many requests from other specialists for Thompson's language expertise on translation and grammatical problems. Some enquiries are in search of a copy of a particular text, such as a correspondence with Wallis Budge in 1912. There are letters from colleagues at UCL and beyond, including Francis and Nora Griffith, Margaret Murray, Rosalind Moss and from his pupil Stephen Glanville. There are letters from A. S. Hunt, the Oxyrhynchus excavator, dated 1912 requesting help with the translation of a Demotic text. Frederic Kenyon from the British Museum requests an opinion on the dating of Coptic texts. Another bundle of letters is from the specialist in Greek papyri and ostraca, John Gavin Tait.[53] Some of the letters are long and detailed; others quite short and some are brief notes on postcards.

Other queries from collaborators abroad include letters from Jean Capart, Kurt Sethe, Wilhelm Spiegelberg, and Ulrich Wilcken the German papyrologist. With the Italian Demotist, Giuseppe Botti, he corresponded late in life (the letters are dated 1940) and with Ernesto Schiaparelli, the

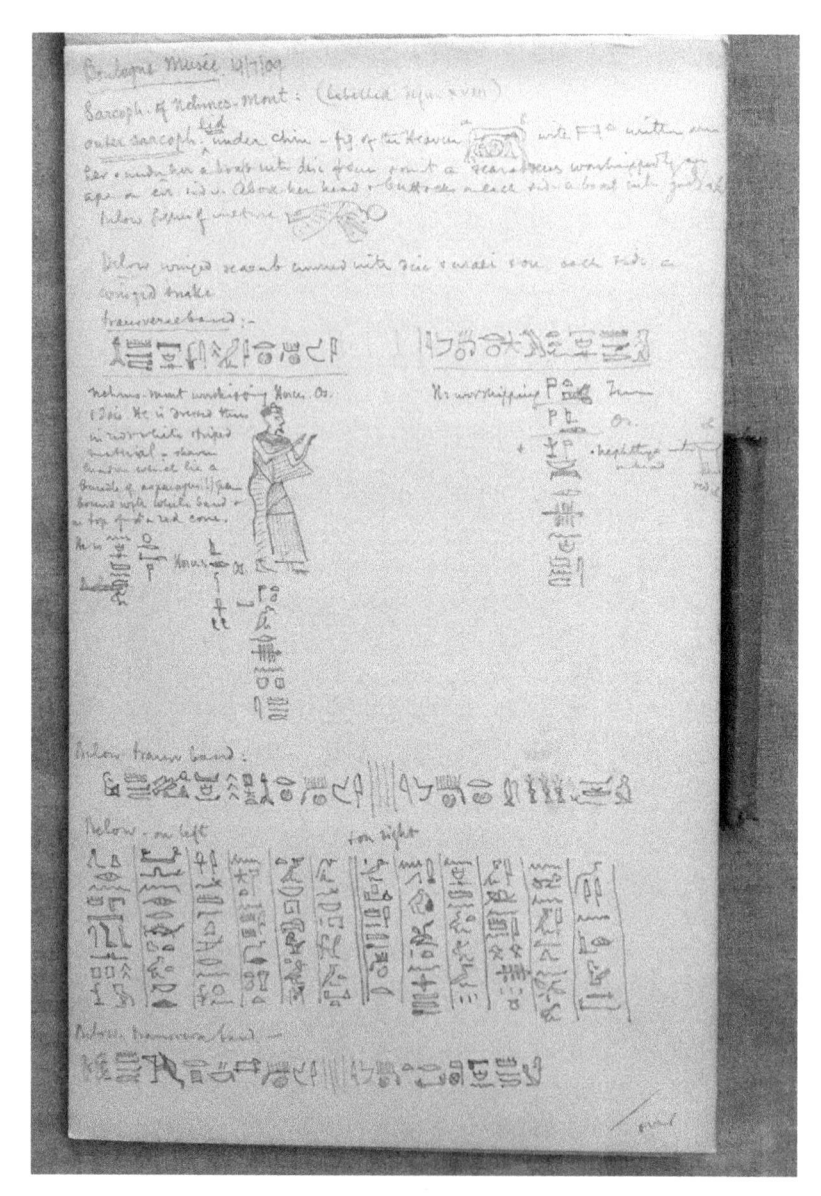

Figure 7.3 Notebook containing sketches and hieroglyphic texts from a visit to the Musée de Boulogne in 1909. Source: GBR/0012/MS Thompson, HT 87 and reproduced by kind permission of the Syndics of Cambridge University Library.

Figure 7.4 Notes and letters to Thompson from colleagues both local and abroad. Source: GBR/0012/MS Thompson, HT 95 and reproduced by kind permission of the Syndics of Cambridge University Library.

Director of the Turin Museum, where Thompson made a detailed study of the papyrus collection, there is a long correspondence.[54] In 1923 Thompson and Griffith had visited the museum in Turin together to examine Demotic texts and letters between them elucidate their discussions.

There are many lengthy letters from the Danish Egyptologist H.O. Lange and from Adolphe Hebberlynck (1859–1939), the Belgian theologian and Coptic scholar, dated 1921.[55] American correspondents include Nathaniel Reich in Philadelphia, dating from 1931–1933, containing queries on papyrus texts and he introduces to Thompson one of his students with a request for his advice and assistance. From contacts in Egypt there are letters from Girgis Mattha, the Egyptian Demotist, and a bundle of letters from G. P. Sobhy, the Egyptian Coptic scholar, containing photographs of artefacts with inscriptions on which he requests Thompson's advice.[56] The correspondence is a rich source of information on the day-to-day working methods of these specialists and more detailed research on it would reveal much more of interest.

During the 1930s, Thompson had a long correspondence with the book binder Douglas Cockerell, who had rebound the celebrated fourth-century biblical text the Codex Sinaiticus for the British Museum, and whose knowledge of the bookbinding traditions found in manuscripts originating from the Middle East was much valued by Thompson. The correspondence contains a discussion on the structure and origins of Coptic binding style, as well as details about repairs to bindings and to papyri on which Cockerell was evidently working for Thompson.[57] The most prolific correspondence by far is, however, with Walter Crum with whom Thompson maintained a friendship for over 40 years.[58] The earliest letters from Crum are dated 1912, at the time when he was living in Austria, and they continue through the 1920s and 1930s in Crum's characteristic but almost unreadable handwriting. Crum remained one of Thompson's closest friends and the letters contain a personal warmth as well as discussions and comments on texts and translations on which they shared so many common interests. The correspondence in the Thompson archive deserves further study in itself, as it demonstrates the variety and breadth of his contacts and the level of expertise he shared freely with his colleagues.

His move to country life

From 1921, there are many letters in the archive addressed to Thompson at 'The Old House, Aspley Guise', near Bletchley in Bedfordshire, where Thompson lived for around ten or fifteen years. This house did not belong to Thompson himself, it was the property of George Herbert Fowler (1861–1940), a zoologist at UCL and a specialist in marine biology.[59] Thomas Huxley had been president of the Marine Biological Association from 1884–1890 and had supported the effort to build a marine station at Plymouth. Fowler was an interim director at Plymouth in 1890–1891, and subsequently returned to be a lecturer at UCL. Presumably Thompson had met Fowler through the UCL connection, or possibly, through Huxley. 'The Old House' is one of the oldest properties in the village of Aspley Guise, a remarkable structure dating back to 1575 and with many original architectural features still in place. Fowler purchased the house in 1906 and carried out restoration work there. Fowler also took a leading role in local history research, local archives and parish affairs in the area. Thompson had not, however, escaped from Egyptology at Aspley Guise and was drawn back to its study constantly, his colleagues regularly making requests for his special skills. Evidence of this can be traced through the archive of letters, more of which are addressed to him while he lived here than at any other residence. Possibly this move to rural

Bedfordshire, where he could enjoy country walks and follow his interests as a naturalist, was an attempt at retirement on Thompson's part. However, this rural idyll did not go as planned, work followed him there, and further discoveries of papyri made a life of ease impossible to contemplate.

Once again, Thompson was approached by Petrie for his help, this time with the decipherment of a manuscript which had been excavated in 1923 by Guy Brunton near the village of Hemamieh, close to Asyut, for the British School of Archaeology in Egypt. A broken pot had been discovered containing a small linen bag in which a roll of papyrus was hidden. A small censer was also uncovered nearby, perhaps indicating that a church once stood on the site. These were sent to London for further examination, and the papyrus in the pot was found to contain the almost complete text of St John's Gospel written in Coptic. The papyrus consisted of 43 leaves written on both sides; it was in a remarkably good state of preservation and estimated to date to the fourth century. In 1924, Thompson published this text, with a preface by Petrie.[60] The papyrus, the linen bag and the censer were given to the British and Foreign Bible Society in return for a contribution to the funds of the British School of Archaeology. In 1985, the Society's library came on permanent loan to Cambridge University Library so these items are now housed in the Library's collections.[61]

Nor was this the only publication from this period of Thompson's life; he continued to publish texts in both Coptic and Demotic. In 1932, he published a second Biblical text from a papyrus copy in the Chester Beatty and the University of Michigan collections. The text was said to date from around 600 CE and was originally discovered at the monastery of Apa Jeremias at Saqqara.[62] In the following year he edited, with H. I. Bell and A. D. Nock, a work on the Demotic texts in a bilingual Greek/Demotic papyrus in the British Museum collection.[63]

It was also from this time that Thompson, although now in his seventies, produced *A Family Archive from Siut,* the work for which he is probably best known. It was published in 1934 and is now recognised as a classic work of scholarship and a major contribution to Demotic studies.[64] Purchased by the British Museum in 1923, the texts were probably discovered at Asyut and tell of a complex family history concerning marriage, inheritance and property rights and Thompson's early career in the legal profession might possibly have provided him with some useful expertise relating to legal documents[65] (see Figure 7.5). The proposal that Thompson should edit these texts came from the Director of the British Museum, Frederic Kenyon and the copious notes Thompson made for this study can be found in the archive.[66] However, this

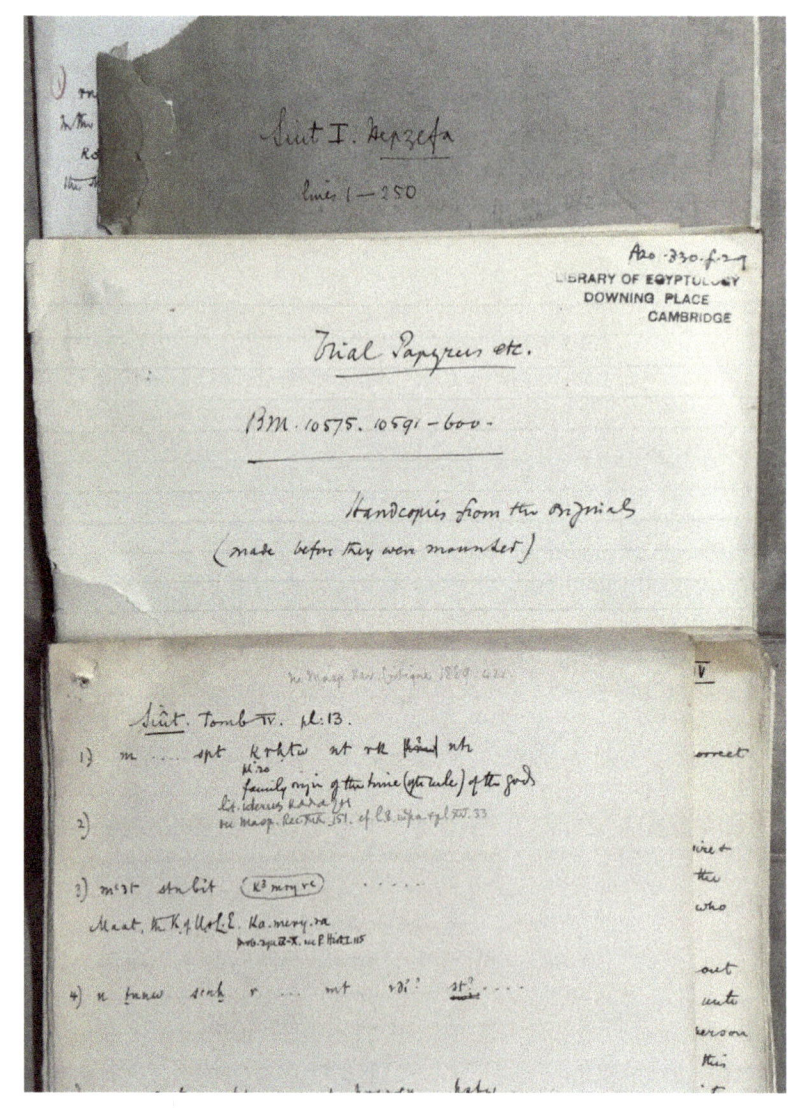

Figure 7.5 Notes for Thompson's publication on 'The archive of Siut' and on Tomb IV at Siut. Source: GBR/0012/MS Thompson, HT 77 and reproduced by kind permission of the Syndics of Cambridge University Library.

publication was the subject of a very critical review by Battiscombe Gunn, Egyptology professor at Oxford, 1934–1950.[67] Thompson was apparently very hurt by this criticism and apparently vowed to give up Demotic studies.[68]

The criticism levelled at Thompson might very well have had a significant influence on the course of his work as in the 1930s he made a new departure by developing an interest in Manichaeism. In the archive there are seven files of notes relating to texts found at Medinet Madi in the Fayyum, where, in 1928, Coptic texts had been found near the site.[69] Among them were Manichaean texts which included the Psalm-book studied by the Cambridge Manichaean scholar Charles Allberry (1911–1943).[70] Thompson made a preliminary study on the Coptic writings of Mani, part of which was later published by Allberry in *'A Manichaean Psalm-Book; Part II'* (1938). Correspondence between Thompson and Allberry relating to this can be found in the Allberry archive which is also held in the Library's collections.[71] Possibly it was his connection to Allberry which encouraged Thompson's interests to develop in this direction, but Allberry was a great loss to Coptic studies when he was killed in action in the Second World War near Nedeweert, Holland, on 3 April 1943.

Around this time, perhaps even before the publication of '*A Family Archive from Siut'*, Thompson made another attempt at retirement, a further bid to make his escape from his work on Egyptian texts. He left Aspley Guise to live in Bath in the early 1930s, where he remained for the rest of his life. Herbert Fowler remained in his Aspley Guise home for the remainder of his life; he died there in 1940.

Thompson's move to Bath

Thompson's move to Bath was possibly a reflection of his family connections with the city, where he very likely felt at home. His mother's wider family there included other musical members: her father who had been a flautist and her brother, George Loder, a composer and conductor. Thompson lived at 1 Bathwick Hill on the south-east side of the city in a large, elegant, four-storey house built of the cream stone common to finer buildings in Bath. However, in a rather less lavish house at 19 Bathwick Hill lived the Crums, who had moved there in 1927. Was this move really another attempt by Thompson at retirement or was it done with the express intention of assisting Crum with the work on his *Coptic Dictionary*? The dictionary project had been initiated by Crum many years previously during his stay in Austria before the First World War, and from this time forward it became the major focus of Thompson's effort. Crum's *'Dictionary'* was eventually published in 1939, and collaboration on the work included many others as well as

Thompson. In the preface to the dictionary Crum specifically acknowledges Thompson's help, especially for his assistance on the compilation of the Greek index.[72]

Later years

At the outbreak of the Second World War, Thompson placed his house on Bathwick Hill at the disposal of the Admiralty for the war effort, and in 1940 he moved to 17 Macaulay Buildings situated some distance away, a smaller residence with perhaps only half the living space. There are many letters in the archive are addressed to him there. He contributed to the war effort by taking his full share of duties as a firewatcher until his health began to fail in 1944. This smaller residence was too limited a space to house all his books and papers and he began to consider ways of disposing of them. After the completion of the *Coptic Dictionary*, Crum's energy also began to fail but he spent much of his time acting as next-of-kin to Thompson who was no longer in good health. Crum suffered a sudden heart attack at his home in Bath and died on 18 May 1944. Thompson himself died only a week later on 26 May, bringing to an end the long and fruitful collaboration and friendship which had lasted over many years since their first meeting as teacher and pupil at UCL. Along with the death of Charles Allberry in the previous year, it ended an era of significant progress in Coptic studies.

Thompson's legacy to Cambridge

As Thompson had no close family, he had at some point, made the decision to direct his resources towards securing the future of Egyptology studies. He had supported the subject financially during his lifetime, but his most significant contribution was the endowment of a post in Egyptology at Cambridge, with the aim of focusing specifically on language study. The first incumbent was Stephen Glanville, a pupil of both Petrie and Thompson, who was appointed not only Cambridge's first professor of Egyptology (1946–1956) but later also the provost of King's College (1954–1956). What was the reason behind Thompson's decision to leave such a generous bequest to Cambridge? By tracing Thompson's other donations, which began in the 1920s, the answer to this question gradually becomes clear.

Donations of ostraca and manuscripts

In 1921, possibly around the time of his move from London to Aspley Guise, Thompson donated to Cambridge University Library a collection of 110 ostraca, most of which are in Demotic but around 30 are in Greek and five in Coptic. Thompson published eight short papers in the *Proceedings of the Society of Biblical Archaeology* in 1912 and 1913 on ostraca from this collection.[73] A supplementary set of a 185 items donated later brought the total number of ostraca to 295. A letter found with them indicates that six of the Demotic items had formerly belonged to Sir Alan Gardiner who gave them to Thompson in 1916 and a further 20 items had been given to him by Crum. Some 30 of the Demotic ostraca had been acquired by Flinders Petrie, possibly from Thebes, in 1908–1909. Thompson had made some notes on these, preliminary to making a catalogue but it was left unfinished.[74]

On 29 April 1939, perhaps around the time of his move to his final home in Bath, Thompson presented to Cambridge University Library a collection of Coptic texts on vellum.[75] Originally these were from Shenute's White Monastery near Sohag in Upper Egypt and consist of literary fragments, mainly in Coptic, but also some in Greek. Several texts appear to date to between the sixth and eighth centuries, but most are from later dates. These were bound into a large flat folder and some are stored in two additional boxes of smaller fragments with some of Thompson's own transcripts. There is also correspondence between Thompson and the Coptic scholar Henri Hyvernat from whom he had purchased the manuscripts in 1914.

Donations of books

From Thompson's own library, by far the greatest number of volumes came to Cambridge University Library and, as well as his Egyptology books, there are others relating to his private interests, such as travels and music. But some of the Egyptology volumes were duplicates of works already held by the University Library and, as a result, the University Librarian offered these to the Egyptology teaching library situated not far away, in Downing Place. Finding room in the Library's existing premises for this now substantial collection eventually resulted in the teaching library gaining larger premises, becoming part of the Faculty of Oriental Studies Library (now Faculty of Asian and Middle Eastern Studies) on its move to Sidgwick Avenue in 1968.[76] More recently, in 2012, the collection was moved once again to the Library of the Faculty of Archaeology and Anthropology (Haddon Library).

So, at the time of his death, Thompson had already donated the ostraca and the vellum manuscripts to the University Library and the books followed soon after. Considering his actions in hindsight it becomes obvious that Thompson may have deliberately planned the establishment of a collection of library materials which would support Egyptology teaching in Cambridge. Did he, perhaps, make this plan from early in his time as an Egyptologist? Confirmation of this intention can be found in a letter from Thompson to Glanville, found not in his own archive, but in the Glanville archive, also held in the Library. Here Thompson's intentions are clear:

> I owe a far greater part of my education to Cambridge' … 'the Univ. of Camb. has been named as my residuary legatee (having no great family claims on me) under my will for the last 40 years …that it may partly secure the foundation for an Egyptology Chair or lectureship, as I have always felt that Cambridge made a very poor show therein as compared with Oxford.[77]

It appears, therefore, that Thompson may have resolved to make this bequest many years previously, very possibly at the time he received his inheritance in 1904. He noted how UCL had benefited so much from the legacy of Amelia Edwards and Oxford from Griffith, but that Cambridge had had no such great fortune. Amelia Edwards had wanted Petrie to be the first holder of the UCL post, Oxford had appointed Griffith, and Thompson intended Glanville to have the post in Cambridge. So apart from the work which Thompson himself achieved, his influence through his gifts and bequests continued. The study of the distribution of donations of books, manuscripts and artefacts such as this could in itself provide the subject of a study on the long-term influence of a legacy; certainly this is true in the case of the Thompson collection.

The archive after Thompson's death

Thompson had, in his later years, become close to Stephen Glanville, perhaps perceiving him as his protégé. He reached an understanding with Glanville that his archive should be passed to him for research purposes and Glanville retained ownership of the papers during his lifetime.

However, his sudden death in 1956 left his family in a quandary. Glanville's daughter asked I. E. S. Edwards, Keeper of Egyptian Antiquities at the British Museum, to act a literary executor and a decision was made to deposit the Thompson archive in the Department of Egyptology in Downing Place in Cambridge, and subsequently it was transferred, along with the Department, to the Faculty of Oriental Studies in Sidgwick Avenue.[78] Here it remained for many years away from the public eye, and perhaps it is for this reason that the archive has been relatively unknown until this most recent move to Cambridge University Library which has provided reader access to the archive and a listing of its contents.

Within the archive, found after its recent transfer to the University Library, was one final exciting and unexpected find. Two sets of fragmentary texts, some on small papyrus fragments and others on vellum, were discovered. One set was hidden in an envelope and another between sheets of *The Oxford Gazette* dating from 1912–1914. From these details it was possible to trace a letter in the archive from John de Monins Johnson of the EEF indicating their origins from the Antinöe excavations of 1912 and being sent to Thompson in 1914. Thompson's own notes on these exist in the archive.[79]

Thompson's contribution to Egyptology and public recognition

Thompson's working life in Egyptology encompassed four decades of the twentieth century, yet he is far from being one of the best-known names from that era. Little has been written about him, but Stephen Glanville, in his obituary, paid tribute to Thompson as his teacher, to his generosity of spirit and to the many contributions he had made to the subject.[80] In terms of official positions, Thompson was a member of the EEF from 1898, (and served on its Committee from 1901–1908), but otherwise played rather little part in its affairs. His only official positions at UCL were also rather limited; he lectured there for a single academic year in 1915–1916 and held an honorary position as a Fellow from 1930. In 1926, he received a Hon. D.Litt. from Oxford, and became a Fellow of the British Academy in 1933.

Yet Thompson's era was a crucial time in the development of the understanding of ancient Egyptian languages when the study of Demotic and Coptic made significant progress. A lack of reliable reference works such as dictionaries, and of published works on texts, was noticeable at the time, and discussions on standards of transliteration practice for Demotic were on-going. Thompson's work, along with that of Griffith and Crum, changed this and there can have been few students working on these languages at this time who did not owe a debt to Thompson in terms of advice. From his private fortune he was able to support the subject financially, and in his generous donations of books and manuscripts he was able to strengthen library collections. The limitations of space mean that the description of the archive given here is brief; there is much more material of significance and interest to be researched.

It has been suggested that the value of writing biography is as a tool to help us to understand, as well as its actual content, the social and cultural elements of the information it provides. In addition, biography can give unique access to the structures in which work is carried out and can provide useful access points to these.[81] Writing about Thompson and his life has not been a simple task: he was a reticent character whose personal problems and struggles remain unknown. Also, as he was not a practical archaeologist, he left no traces of his efforts through excavations or artefacts discovered. Not being a scientist either, he left no traces of experimental work or resulting data: his language notes were his data. All the evidence of his many years of productive work are in the archive itself and through the gifts of personal wealth, manuscripts and books to Cambridge where his influence continues long after his death.

Possibly many more fascinating details remain to be discovered in the Thompson archive for those with an interest in language studies, in Thompson's network of colleagues or in the development of the study of Egyptology during this era. The archive has been relatively unexplored and this chapter provides only a general description, there are many more possibilities for research here. The archive provides numerous possibilities for those with an interest in life-writing and further exploring Thompson's significance in the wider context of Egyptology in this era.

Looking back over Thompson's life from 75 years since his death, it is possible to trace a pattern: the early part, until his meeting with Petrie was a period of finding his way after various false starts. From his first publication with Griffith in 1904-5, he continued to study texts and publish (for the most part as a single author) until 'A Family Archive from Siut' in 1934. After that he ceased to publish but continued his collaborative work with Crum on the *Coptic Dictionary*, which he must have considered to be the best use of his skills at that time. How far these were very conscious decisions he made, it is impossible to tell, but in retrospect it does appear to show a consistent thread of a personal direction running through his lifetime. Thompson appears to have avoided official positions and their responsibilities, preferring work stemming from personal enthusiasm to give him direction. He seems to have been a man of dedication, but not all of his time was dedicated to his work. In his travels his work on texts must have been interleaved with attending concerts, opera and visits to art galleries: perhaps Thompson remained, always, the perfect English gentleman.

Acknowledgements

The author would like to thank Professor W. J. Tait, emeritus professor of Egyptology, at UCL for his helpful comments on this chapter, also to thank Dr Anna Johnson, Book and Paper Conservator at Cambridge University Library, for her investigations into the provenance of the papyrus fragments from Antinöe. She is also currently working on their conservation.

Notes

1. Douglas R. Givens, 'The role of biography in writing the history of archaeology', in *Rediscovering Our Past: Essays on the history of American archaeology*, ed. Jonathan E. Reyman (Aldershot: Avebury, 1992), 51–2.
2. Marc-Antoine Kaeser, 'Biography, science studies and the historiography of archaeological research: managing personal archives', *Complutum,* 24 (2013): 101–4.
3. An acknowledgement of Thompson's bequest and its subsequent acceptance appears in the *Cambridge University Reporter* 3407 (25 July 1944): 711, 738.
4. Patricia Usick, *Adventures in Egypt and Nubia: The travels of William John Bankes (1786–1855)* (London: British Museum, 2002).
5. There is a more detailed account of the early history of Egyptology in Cambridge by John D. Ray, 'The Marquis, the urchin and the labyrinth: Egyptology and the University of Cambridge' in *Proceedings of the 7th International Congress of Egyptologists*, ed. Christopher Eyre (Leuven: Peeters, 1988), 1–17.
6. Ernest A. W. Budge, *A Catalogue of the Egyptian Collection in the Fitzwilliam Museum, Cambridge* (Cambridge: Cambridge University Press, 1893).
7. Cambridge University Library. 'Henry Francis Herbert Thompson: Correspondence and papers', GBR/0012/MS Thompson. Accessed 1 July 2021. https://archivesearch.lib.cam.ac.uk/repositories/2/resources/13405.
   All subsequent references to archive files are subdivisions of this collection.
8. The Griffith Institute Archive 'Collection Thompson MSS'. Accessed 1 July 2021. http://archive.griffith.ox.ac.uk/index.php/thompson-sir-henry-francis-herbert-2.
9. GBR/0012/MS Thompson/HT11 General academic correspondence, with notes, manuscript and typescript, 1912–1937.
10. This role of archival material is discussed in more detail in Marc-Antoine Kaeser, 'Biography as microhistory: the relevance of private archives for writing the history of archaeology' in *Archives, ancestors, practices: Archaeology in the light of its history*, eds., Nathan Schlanger and Jarl Nordbladh (New York: Berghahn Books, 2008), 9–20.
11. John D. Wortham, *British Egyptology 1549–1906* (Newton Abbot: David and Charles, 1971), 118.

12 A more detailed history of Egyptology at UCL can be found in Rosalind M. Janssen, *The First Hundred Years: Egyptology at University College London 1892–1992* (London: Petrie Museum, 1992).
13 The development of Egyptology studies in the UK is outlined in Stephen R. K. Glanville, The growth and nature of Egyptology; an inaugural lecture (Cambridge: Cambridge University Press, 1947).
14 Alex Paton, 'Thompson, Sir Henry, first baronet (1820–1904)', in *Oxford Dictionary of National Biography*. Last accessed 1 July 2021 https://doi.org/10.1093/ref:odnb/36490.
15 Julie Anne Sadie and Rhian Samuel, eds., *The New Grove Dictionary of Women Composers* (London: Macmillan, 1994), 285–6.
16 A painting by Solomon Joseph Solomon 'An octave for Mr Ernest Hart at Sir Henry Thompson's house', dated c. 1897 can be found in the Wellcome Collection.
17 'Sir Henry Thompson, Bt' by Sir John Everett Millais (1829–96) in the Tate Britain collection, bequeathed by the sitter in 1904.
18 A copy of 'Goblin Market' by Christina Rossetti in the Fitzwilliam Museum Library, Cambridge, contains the note on a label 'bequeathed to Cambridge University by Sir H. F. Herbert Thompson, 2nd Baronet, of Trinity College 26 May 1944'. Also inscribed 'Jane Morris June 1862', and by Thompson 'This volume was bequeathed to me by May Morris in 1938. It belonged to her mother, Mrs. William Morris.'
19 Walter W. Rouse Ball and John A. Venn, eds., *Admissions to Trinity College, Cambridge* (London: Macmillan, 1913), 549–50.
20 Adrian Desmond 'Thomas Henry Huxley (1825–1895)', in *Oxford Dictionary of National Biography*. Last accessed 1 July 2021. https://doi.org/10.1093/ref:odnb/14320.
21 In Fig. 7.2, the portrait painted by Lawrence Alma-Tadema *94 Degrees in the Shade*, a young Herbert Thompson is lying in a cornfield in Godstone, Surrey.
22 Margaret S. Drower, *Flinders Petrie: A life in archaeology* (London: Gollancz, 1985), 199–231.
23 Kathleen L. Sheppard, 'Flinders Petrie and eugenics at UCL', *Bulletin of the History of Archaeology* 20.1 (2010): 16–29.
24 Debbie Challis, *The Archaeology of Race: The eugenic ideas of Francis Galton and Flinders Petrie* (London: Bloomsbury 2013).
25 Morris L. Bierbrier, ed., *Who Was Who in Egyptology*, fourth edition (London: Egypt Exploration Society, 2012), 227–8.
26 Jennifer Cromwell, 'Walter Ewing Crum (1865–1944): a Coptic scholar "sui generis"' in *Christlicher Orient im Porträt: Wissenschaftsgeschichte des christlichen Orients*, ed. Predrag Bukovec (Tubingen: Kovac, 2014), 407–22.
27 BM. EA10070,2.
28 Francis L. Griffith and Herbert Thompson, *The Demotic Magical Papyrus of London & Leiden* (London: H. Grevel, 1904–9).
29 Jacob C. Kaspar, *Lettres à M. Letronne, sur les papyrus bilingues et grecs et sur quelques autres monumens gréco-égyptiens du Musée d'antiquités de l'Université de Leide* (Leiden: Chez S. et J. Luchtmans, imprimeurs de l'université, 1830). After the death of Reuvens the work was completed by Conradus Leemans and published in 1839.
30 Jean J. Hess, *Der gnostische Papyrus von London: Einleitung, Text und demotisch-deutsches Glossar* (Freiburg: Universitätsbuchhandlung, 1892).
31 W. M. Flinders Petrie, *Gizeh and Rifeh: With chapters by Sir Herbert Thompson and W.E. Crum* (London: School of Archaeology in Egypt, 1907).
32 GBR/0012/MS Thompson/HT1 Notes on Demotic papyri from Rifeh, 1906–07.
33 James E. Quibell, with sections by Sir Herbert Thompson and Prof. W. Spiegelberg, *Excavations at Saqqara (1907–1908)* (Cairo: Imprimerie de l'Institut français d'archéologie orientale, 1909), vi.
34 GBR/0012/MS Thompson/HT93 Notes on Coptic texts, 1900–1935.
35 Wilhelm Spiegelberg, *Koptische Handworterbuch* (Heidelberg: Carl Winters, 1921).
36 Wilhelm Spiegelberg, *Demotische Grammatik* (Heidelberg: Carl Winters, 1925).
37 GBR/0012/MS Thompson/HT23 Notes on Demotic texts, 1900–1935.
38 Richard Spiegelberg 'Biography: Wilhelm Spiegelberg' Accessed 1 July 2021. https://oi.uchicago.edu/research/projects/chicago-demotic-dictionary-cdd-0/biography-wilhelm-spiegelberg.
39 GBR/0012/MS Thompson HT 37–48 Notes on a Demotic dictionary.

40 GBR/0012/MS Thompson/HT 109 Spiegelberg's dictionary, 1900–1930.
41 The Chicago Demotic Dictionary (CDD)Accessed 1 July 2021. https://oi.uchicago.edu/research/projects/chicago-demotic-dictionary-cdd-0.
42 A further explanation of this can be found in *Liber amicorum demoticorum in honour of Prof. H. S. Smith on the occasion of his 90th birthday by many friends and colleagues in various countries 14 June 2018*, 74.
43 Herbert Thompson, *The Coptic (Sahidic) Version of Certain Books of the Old Testament, From a Papyrus in the British Museum* (London: Henry Frowde, 1908).
44 GBR/0012/MS Thompson/HT 84 Notes on Coptic texts, 1900–1935.
45 Herbert Thompson, ed., *A Coptic Palimpsest containing Joshua, Judges, Ruth, Judith and Esther in the Sahidic Dialect* (London: Oxford University Press, 1911).
46 James E. Quibell, *Excavations of Saqqara, 1908–9, 1909–10: The monastery of Apa Jeremias; the Coptic inscriptions by Sir Herbert Thompson* (Cairo: Imprimerie de l'Institut français d'archéologie orientale, 1912).
47 Herbert Thompson, ed., *The New Biblical Papyrus: A Sahidic version of Deuteronomy, Jonah and the Acts of the Apostles, from MS. Or.7594 of the British Museum* (London: Printed for private circulation, 1913).
48 Alan H. Gardiner et al., *Theban ostraca: edited from the originals, now mainly in the Royal Ontario Museum of Archaeology, Toronto, and the Bodleian Library, Oxford. (Hieratic texts: by A. H. Gardiner.pt. II. Demotic texts: by H. Thompson.pt. III. Greek texts: by J. G. Milne.pt. IV. Coptic texts: by H. Thompson)* (London: University of Toronto library, 1913).
49 GBR/0012/MS Thompson/HT 25–26 Notes on Demotic and Coptic ostraca.
50 R.S. Simpson. 'Thompson, Sir (Henry Francis) Herbert, second baronet (1859–1944)', in *Oxford Dictionary of National Biography*. Accessed 1 July 2021 https://doi.org/10.1093/ref:odnb/36491.
51 Portrait of Kate Loder [Lady Thompson] by Sir Lawrence Alma Tadema. Accessed 1 July 2021. https://collections.ram.ac.uk/IMU/#/details/ecatalogue/10691.
52 GBR/0012/MS Thompson/HT 90 Notes on Demotic texts, 1900–1935.
53 GBR/0012/MS Thompson/HT 18 Correspondence with John Gavin Tate, 1921–1931.
54 GBR/0012/MS Thompson/HT 95 Correspondence, 1900–1935.
55 GBR/0012/MS Thompson/HT 16 Correspondence with A. Hebberlynck, manuscript and typescript, 1921.
56 GBR/0012/MS Thompson/HT 17 Letters from G. P. Sobhy; with photographs and notes, 1911–24.
57 GBR/0012/MS Thomson/HT 13 Letters from Douglas Cockerell, 1931–33.
58 GBR/0012/MS Thompson/HT 14 Letters from Walter Crum.
59 Margaret Deacon, 'George Herbert Fowler (1861–1940)', in *Oxford Dictionary of National Biography*. Accessed 1 July 2021. https://doi.org/10.1093/ref:odnb/53910.
60 Herbert Thompson, ed., *The Gospel of St John, According to the Earliest Coptic manuscript* (London: British School of Archaeology in Egypt, 1924).
61 British and Foreign Bible Society MS 137.
62 Herbert Thompson, *A Coptic Version of the Acts of the Apostles, and the Pauline Epistles in the Sahidic Dialect* (Cambridge: Cambridge University Press, 1932).
63 Harold I. Bell, Arthur D. Nock and Herbert Thompson, eds., *Magical Texts from a Bilingual Papyrus in the British Museum* (London: Humphrey Milford, 1933?).
64 Herbert Thompson, *A Family Archive from Siut: From papyri in the British Museum. Including an account of a trial before the Laocritae in the year B.C. 170* (Oxford: Oxford University Press, 1934).
65 BM. EA01575, 10091-16000.
66 GBR/0012/MS Thompson/HT 77 Notes on Demotic texts, 1900–1935.
67 Battiscombe Gunn, 'A Family Archive from Siut': From Papyri in the British Museum', *Journal of Egyptian Archaeology* 20 (1934): 223–8.
68 This is referred to in *Liber amicorum demoticorum*, 70.
69 GBR/0012/MS Thompson HT/55-60 Notes on the Fayum papyri.
70 Cambridge University Library. 'Charles Allberry: Correspondence and papers', GBR/0012/MS Allberry. Accessed July 01, 2021. https://archivesearch.lib.cam.ac.uk/repositories/2/resources/9269.
71 Cambridge University Library. Herbert Thompson notes on 'A Manichaeian Psalm-Book; Part II (1938), 1940. GBR/0012/MS Allberry/CA36/. Accessed 1 July, 2021. https://archivesearch.lib.cam.ac.uk/repositories/2/archival_objects/582802.

72 Walter E. Crum, *A Coptic Dictionary* (Oxford: Clarendon Press, 1939), ix.
73 *Proceedings of the Society of Biblical Archaeology* 34–35 (1912–13).
74 An unpublished listing of the ostraca has been made by Professor J. W. Tait. This is shelved in the Library's manuscript collection at CUL MS Or.2549.
75 CUL MS Or.1699 and Or.1700.
76 Catherine Ansorge, 'The Oriental Studies Faculty Library: a history of the early years' *South Asia Archive & Library Group Newsletter* 1 (2004): 24–34.
77 Letter from the Glanville Archive dated January 28 1942, written by Thompson from 17 Macaulay Buildings.
78 Personal communication to the author in 1994, from H.S. Smith, Emeritus Professor of Egyptology at UCL.
79 GBR/0012/MS Thompson/HT 81 Notes on Coptic texts, 1900–1935.
80 Stephen K. R. Glanville, 'Sir Herbert Thompson', *Journal of Egyptian Archaeology* 30 (1944): 67–8.
81 Tim Murray, ed., *Encyclopedia of Archaeology: The great archaeologists* (Santa Barbara, CA: ABC Clio, 1999) 877–9.

Bibliography

Ansorge, Catherine, 'The Oriental Studies Faculty Library: a history of the early years'. *South Asia Archive & Library Group Newsletter* 1 (2004): 24–34.
Ball, Walter W. Rouse and John A. Venn, eds., *Admissions to Trinity College, Cambridge* (London: Macmillan, 1913).
Bell, Harold I., Arthur D. Nock and Herbert Thompson, eds., *Magical Texts from a Bilingual Papyrus in the British Museum* (London: Humphrey Milford, 1933?).
Bierbrier, Morris L., ed., *Who Was Who in Egyptology,* fourth edition (London: Egypt Exploration Society, 2012).
Budge, Ernest A. W., *A Catalogue of the Egyptian Collection in the Fitzwilliam Museum Cambridge* (Cambridge: Cambridge University Press, 1893). *Cambridge University Reporter* 3407, 25 July 1944, 711, 738.
Crum, Walter E., *A Coptic Dictionary* (Oxford: Clarendon Press, 1939), ix.
Deacon, Margaret, 'George Herbert Fowler (1861–1940)' in *Oxford Dictionary of National Biography*. Accessed 1 July 2021. https://doi.org/10.1093/ref:odnb/53910.
Desmond, Adrian, 'Thomas Henry Huxley (1825–1895)' in *Oxford Dictionary of National Biography*. Accessed 1 July 2021 https://doi.org/10.1093/ref:odnb/14320.
Drower, Margaret S., *Flinders Petrie: A life in archaeology* (London: Gollancz, 1985).
Gardiner, Alan H. et al., *Theban ostraca: edited from the originals, now mainly in the Royal Ontario Museum of Archaeology, Toronto, and the Bodleian Library, Oxford. Hieratic texts: by A. H. Gardiner, pt. II. Demotic texts: by H. Thompson, pt. III. Greek texts: by J. G. Milne, pt. IV. Coptic texts: by H. Thompson* (London: University of Toronto library, 1913).
Givens, Douglas R., 'The role of biography in writing the history of archaeology', in *Rediscovering our Past: Essays on the history of American archaeology*, ed. Jonathan E. Reyman (Aldershot: Avebury, 1992): 51–2.
Glanville, Stephen R. K., *The growth and nature of Egyptology: An inaugural lecture* (Cambridge: Cambridge University Press, 1947).
Glanville, Stephen R. K., 'Sir Herbert Thompson', *Journal of Egyptian Archaeology* 30 (1944): 67–8.
Griffith, Francis L. and Herbert Thompson, *The Demotic Magical Papyrus of London & Leiden* (London: H. Grevel, 1904–9).
Gunn, Battiscombe, '"A Family Archive from Siut" from papyri in the British Museum', *Journal of Egyptian Archaeology* 20 (1934): 223–8.
Hess, Jean J., *Der gnostische Papyrus von London: Einleitung, Text und demotisch-deutsches Glossar* (Freiburg: Universitätsbuchhandlung, 1892).
Janssen, Rosalind M., *The First Hundred Years: Egyptology at University College London 1892–1992* (London: Petrie Museum, 1992).
Kaeser, Marc-Antoine, 'Biography as microhistory: the relevance of private archives for writing the history of archaeology', in *Archives, ancestors, practices: Archaeology in the light of its history*, eds. Nathan Schlanger and Jarl Nordbladh (New York: Berghahn Books, 2008).

Kaeser, Marc-Antoine, 'Biography, science studies and the historiography of archaeological research: managing personal archives', *Complutum,* 24, (2013): 101–4.

Kaspar, Jacob C., *Lettres à M. Letronne, sur les papyrus bilingues et grecs et sur quelques autres monumens gréco-égyptiens du Musée d'antiquités de l'Université de Leide.* (Leiden: Chez S. et J. Luchtmans, imprimeurs de l'université, 1830).

Murray, Tim, ed., *Encyclopedia of Archaeology: The great archaeologists* (Santa Barbara, CA: ABC Clio, 1999): 877–9.

Paton, Alex, 'Thompson, Sir Henry, first baronet (1820–1904)' in *Oxford Database of National Biography*. Accessed 1 July 2021 https://doi.org/10.1093/ref:odnb/36490.

Petrie, W. M. Flinders, *Gizeh and Rifeh: With chapters by Sir Herbert Thompson and W.E. Crum* (London: School of Archaeology in Egypt, 1907).

Proceedings of the Society of Biblical Archaeology 34–5 (1912–13).

Quibell, James E., with sections by Sir Herbert Thompson and Prof. W. Spiegelberg, *Excavations at Saqqara (1907–1908)* (Cairo: Imprimerie de l'Institut français d'archéologie orientale, 1909).

Quibell, James E. *Excavations of Saqqara, 1908–9, 1909–10: the Monastery of Apa Jeremias; the Coptic inscriptions by Sir Herbert Thompson.* (Cairo: Imprimerie de l'Institut français d'archéologie orientale, 1912).

Ray, John D., 'The Marquis, the urchin and the labyrinth: Egyptology and the University of Cambridge', in *Proceedings of the 7th International Congress of Egyptologists*, ed. Christopher Eyre (Leuven: Peeters, 1988).

Sadie, Julie Anne and Rhian Samuel, eds., *The New Grove Dictionary of Women Composers* (London: Macmillan, 1994).

Sheppard, Kathleen L., 'Flinders Petrie and eugenics at UCL', *Bulletin of the History of Archaeology,* 20, no. 1 (2010): 16–29

Simpson, R. S., 'Thompson, Sir (Henry Francis) Herbert, second baronet (1859–1944)' in *Oxford Dictionary of National Biography*. Accessed 1 July 2021 https://doi.org/10.1093/ref:odnb/36491.

Spiegelberg, Richard, 'Biography: Wilhelm Spiegelberg' Accessed 1 July 2021 https://oi.uchicago.edu/research/projects/chicago-demotic-dictionary-cdd-0/biography-wilhelm-spiegelberg.

Spiegelberg, Wilhelm, *Demotische Grammatik* (Heidelberg: Carl Winters, 1925).

Spiegelberg, Wilhelm, *Koptische Handworterbuch* (Heidelberg: Carl Winters, 1921).

Thompson, Herbert, ed., *A Coptic Palimpsest containing Joshua, Judges, Ruth, Judith and Esther in the Sahidic Dialect* (London: Oxford University Press, 1911).

Thompson, Herbert, *The Coptic (Sahidic) Version of Certain Books of the Old Testament, from a Papyrus in the British Museum* (London: Henry Frowde, 1908).

Thompson, Herbert, *A Coptic Version of the Acts of the Apostles, and the Pauline Epistles in the Sahidic Dialect* (Cambridge: Cambridge University Press, 1932).

Thompson, Herbert, *A Family Archive from Siut: From papyri in the British Museum, including an account of a trial before the Laocritae in the year B.C. 170* (Oxford: Oxford University Press, 1934).

Thompson, Herbert, ed., *The Gospel of St John, According to the Earliest Coptic manuscript* (London: British School of Archaeology in Egypt, 1924).

Thompson, Herbert, ed., *The New Biblical Papyrus: A Sahidic version of Deuteronomy, Jonah and the Acts of the Apostles, from MS. Or.7594 of the British Museum* (London: Printed for private circulation, 1913).

Usick, Patricia, *Adventures in Egypt and Nubia: The travels of William John Bankes (1786–1855)* (London: British Museum, 2002).

Wortham, John D., *British Egyptology 1549–1906* (Newton Abbot: David and Charles, 1971).

8
Margerie Venables Taylor (1881–1963): An unsung heroine of Roman Britain?

Martha Lovell Stewart

Introduction

It is difficult not to be curious about Miss Taylor, as she was almost universally known. On the one hand, a quarter of a century after her death, the eminent archaeologist Sheppard Frere paid tribute to her as a key figure in the study of Roman Britain in the mid-twentieth-century, an opinion which was widely shared during her lifetime.[1] Other accounts of the development of the subject, however, omit any mention of her at all.[2] There is no doubt that she was someone who, for 50 years or more, worked at the heart of the British archaeological establishment as it was then calibrated. In 1925, she became the first woman to be elected an 'ordinary' (rather than honorary) Fellow of the Society of Antiquaries, and later served as the first female vice-president of that Society. Not only did she publish extensively herself,[3] but as editor of the *Journal of Roman Studies* (*JRS*) from 1923–1963, she set high standards in academic publishing, and undoubtedly wielded enormous influence in controlling the access of others to publication. In 1948, she was designated CBE, in recognition of her services to scholarship. This chapter aims both to explore aspects of her long and interesting career, and to try and assess her significance in the history of Romano-British archaeology.

Issues of historiography

Before turning to Miss Taylor herself, it may be helpful to consider why it might be that the subsequent recognition of her role has been so patchy.

Figure 8.1 Portrait of Miss M. V. Taylor at 80, illustrating an article in *The Times*, 31 July 1961: 'The Happy Scholar'. Source: Reproduced by permission of Bodleian Libraries, University of Oxford.

In 1998, Sara Champion published an essay demonstrating that women archaeologists from the late nineteenth and early twentieth century have surprisingly often become 'invisible' in the historical record, despite being well-recognised in their chosen field while they were alive.[4] She also suggested that this was even more likely to be the case for women who pursued amateur careers under the auspices of local archaeological societies, often the only avenue open to them.[5] Taking an example from British archaeology, this theme was developed more recently in a piece about Clare Fell, prehistorian and member of the Cumberland and Westmorland Society, highlighting the importance of appreciating the position of such societies and their journals as arenas for research and publication of real quality.[6] In an era when a professional, institutionally sponsored career in archaeology was hardly a possibility for many women (or men, either, for that matter), this is surely unsurprising.[7] Both essays argue that, for as long as disciplinary history is written from the perspective of the (still male-dominated) world of university departments, a version of events concentrating disproportionately on those who held salaried academic posts, or easily identifiable professional roles, will continue to emerge.

In pursuit of Miss Taylor, the level of historiographical challenge is heightened because her career has most often, and with some justice, been defined in relation to the historian Francis Haverfield, her sponsor and employer for many years. In a subject with strong historiographical leanings towards academic genealogies and the 'great man' tradition,[8] it is reasonable to argue that her contribution has been minimised partly because she was (and still is) described as Haverfield's 'assistant' or 'secretary', as well as choosing a *modus operandi* which now seems perversely self-effacing, leaving little trace except in the writings of those who were considerably less modest. As one powerful supporter of her election to the Society of Antiquaries admitted, in 1924: 'She has always merged her work in other people's, notably F. H.'s, and hasn't got credit for it.'[9] This essay will suggest that continuing to introduce her as 'Haverfield's assistant' and 'Haverfield's secretary', while factually accurate, may have hindered a keener understanding of the role Miss Taylor had begun to develop, and the contributions to scholarship she made, even prior to his death in 1919. Philip Freeman in particular has argued that she may have been strongly motivated by a calculated *need* to create a position for herself, rather than considering whether she might already have earned one.[10] Freeman seems perplexed by Frere's assessment of her achievements, commenting: 'Frere went as far as to group her contribution to Roman studies with that of Haverfield and Collingwood although she was not to produce the sort of work that made Haverfield's name or to undertake major excavation.'[11]

Nor does the use of life-writing in a historiographical context itself evade scrutiny. In 1992, Douglas Givens, founding editor of *The Bulletin of the History of Archaeology,* published an inspiring and practical essay on the role of biography in writing the history of archaeology. He makes reference to R. G. Collingwood's view that biography had no place in writing the history of any discipline, likening the biographer to 'a scissors-and-paste historian repeating statements that other people have made before him',[12] but argues, on the contrary, that key to understanding a discipline is seeking to understand the background, influences and development of practitioners of it.[13] Since the 1990s, indeed, the use of biography as a tool of disciplinary history has even acquired a historiography of its own.[14] On the one hand, there is a reasonable 'historicist' justification for a biographical approach, since 'plunging into the life experience of a scientist forces the historian to submit himself to the otherness of the past, instead of imposing, knowingly or not, his own perspectives onto it'.[15] But it has also been suggested that historians of science have had to grapple with a long legacy of eulogistic 'lives', which arguably have the effect of isolating the subject socially and intellectually, rather than contextualising his or her achievements.[16] Its rehabilitation has resulted in (and from) a crop of creative and self-reflexive experiments in science life-writing, from which any attempt to create a narrative account of a scholar's life and work now benefits.[17]

The intensely subjective nature of any biographical writing, both in terms of selection of subject, and the approaches the writer chooses to adopt, nevertheless remains an ethical anxiety for researchers. While there is broad agreement that 'There is no such thing as an entirely neutral biographical narrative',[18] there is less consensus on the question of whether to ignore or embrace the inevitability of moral and cultural affinities between 'biographer' and subject. At one end of the scale, Paola Govoni makes a strong case for positively welcoming and incorporating the 'author bias' inherent in the relationship, as do several of the papers her essay introduces.[19] This approach has been shown to produce very effective results, perhaps especially where Lyndall Gordon's mantra that 'the real subject of biography is always going to be yourself' is most explicitly realised.[20] Givens instead chooses to emphasise the importance of acknowledging bias, in order to achieve a proper distance from the subject of the research. This approach seems most appropriate when biography is the chosen tool of the history of archaeology, and certainly sits more comfortably with the inherently 'contextual' perspective of the essay.[21] While the story of Miss Taylor's career is arguably interesting in itself, as a biographical subject she also becomes a 'key' to a period in the development of British archaeology, and part of a historiographical discussion about the study of the Roman occupation.[22] In the spirit of Givens, I should admit that my interest in Miss Taylor began with the recognition of certain aspects of her world: the Haverfield Library in the Ashmolean where she worked (now long gone), her house on the Woodstock Road in Oxford and countless undergraduate hours reading articles of every vintage in the *JRS*.[23] There are also indications that Miss Taylor took a particular interest in the educational achievements of women at the University.[24] While a superficial sense of identification of this sort should not make it impossible to discuss her career judiciously, neither can the possibility of unconscious bias be ignored.

Sources

In the months leading up to her death, aware that her life was drawing to a close, Miss Taylor seems to have disposed of personal papers, leaving no personal archive as such.[25] Nevertheless, there are two boxes of 'miscellaneous papers' in the Sackler Library in Oxford – probably the contents of her desk – and some correspondence in the Haverfield Archive, also in the Sackler Library.[26] There is material relating to her work at the Roman Society (1923–1963) stored in the Secretary's office in the Senate House in Bloomsbury. As Miss Taylor never based herself in London, and indeed ran the Society from Oxford until 1954, the archive from before this time is sparse. There is, however, a separate file relating to 'The Triennial' (Classics conference) initiated by Miss Taylor in 1942, which contains some of the planning and administration of the inaugural wartime meeting.[27] Other sources include an obituary evidently written by a close colleague,[28] and a *Times* article based on an interview with Miss Taylor following the success of the Roman Art in Britain exhibition, staged at Goldsmith's Hall in London, to mark the Roman Society's Golden Jubilee in 1961.[29] Additionally, quotations from Miss Taylor correspondence, and the personal testimony of colleagues, appear in the memoirs of several archaeological contemporaries.[30]

Early life and career

Miss Taylor was born in 1881, second daughter of Henry Taylor, a solicitor in Chester, but also a keen local historian and Fellow of the Society of Antiquaries of London. As an 80th birthday 'Tribute' in the *JRS* records: 'She came… from a family and environment immersed in Roman antiquity, inheriting these tastes from her father and her native Chester.'[31] In 1889, Francis Haverfield became involved in a scheme to excavate the city's north wall, where a cluster of inscribed stones had been discovered. He was still a master at Lancing College, rather than the university professional he was to become, but already making his name as an expert in Roman epigraphy. Throughout the 1890s, as Miss Taylor wrote in his obituary, 'He was constantly at Chester, not only supervising the excavations, but attending meetings of our Society, and reading papers on the inscriptions and on other subjects.' She added, 'He made many personal friends in Chester then and later…',[32] including, we infer, the Secretary of the Excavation Committee Henry Taylor, and his young daughter.³³ Inspired by the episode, and by Haverfield's approach, she is said to have determined on Romano-British archaeology as a career.³⁴

From this background, in early 1900 she went up to Somerville College, Oxford, sitting final exams in Modern History in 1903.³⁵ A recent biography of the novelist Rose Macaulay, a close friend, draws on an album produced by the 1903 leavers, and some early correspondence from Macaulay's archive, to describe their time at Somerville. Here we learn that in the going-down pageant staged by the leavers (in which each girl represented herself as her totem animal), Miss Taylor chose to be a frog, reflecting her enthusiasm for punting and rowing on the river. The book also reproduced a cartoon sent by Macaulay to Taylor in 1903, with the caption 'The Flamingo and the Hedgehogs: A Story of Schools' (as the final exams are called at Oxford). The picture shows an Alice in Wonderland-style croquet game controlled by their history tutor, Miss Lees, a flamingo with a huge beak. The game is being played using two hedgehogs, but whereas 'MVT' is rolled into a ball, and poised to pass through one of the hoops, 'ERM' (Macaulay) is being prevented from doing so by Miss Lees's beak. Rose Macaulay had apparently begun to suffer from poor mental health and had not been allowed to sit the exams, which was evidently a source of frustration. Despite her early success as a writer, in letters to her friend written during the next few years, she continued to express doubt in her own abilities, as well as her admiration for Taylor's achievements as a serious scholar and academic.³⁶

Following her undergraduate studies, the Chester connection with Francis Haverfield provided Miss Taylor, it seems, with a suitable channel for such academic aspirations. From 1903, she was employed to assist him in researching and writing the Roman-period chapters of the *Victoria County History*, an ambitious commercial publishing venture to present a new historical survey of the counties of England in 160 volumes.³⁷ Haverfield was involved in the project from its early days as the editor of the 'Roman' section for each county, and is considered to have been particularly industrious, and personally productive, in the role.³⁸ Miss Taylor completed several more 'Roman' chapters in the years following his death, and continued making contributions to the *VCH* until 1939.³⁹ In an interview in the *Times* in 1961, she recalled starting her working life in a women's hostel near the British Museum 'on 45s. a week', which may suggest she was employed directly by the *VCH*, even if she worked exclusively on the Roman material.⁴⁰ At some point, however, she became Haverfield's 'secretary' and moved back to Oxford, possibly by 1906.⁴¹ In the following year, Haverfield married Winifred Breakwell, another of the Somerville 1903-ers, which may even have been prompted by a mingling of their social circles.⁴² A friendly personal relationship between Miss Taylor and Mrs Haverfield is attested by a letter of September 1911 in which Winifred alluded, with gentle humour, to a potential conflict between Haverfield and Hadrian's Wall archaeologist F. G. Simpson. Meanwhile, a series of 1913 diary entries by G. L. Cheesman, a colleague (and former pupil) of Haverfield's far nearer to their age than to his, contains several references to accompanying the pair on picnics.⁴³

The absence of personal papers means we otherwise know too little of Miss Taylor's life and development in the crucial years of her late twenties and early thirties. Membership lists from the Roman Society tell us that from 1912 she lived at 44 St. Giles, Oxford for about 10 years, very close to the libraries and Brasenose College, where Haverfield held his Chair. More surprisingly, it appears that she took a leading role in the folk dancing revival which became a craze in the University in the years before the First World War, acting first as treasurer and then secretary to the Committee. Society records also confirm snippets of information we have from elsewhere, suggesting that Miss Taylor left Oxford for a time from early summer 1913, but was back in July 1914, when the dancing teacher's diary reported: 'Morris Class at 5 o'clock in St Giles for Miss Taylor, as she had no dancing in Rome and was pining for a little…'⁴⁴Although her *Times* obituary suggests that she was in Rome only in order to work for antiquities expert John Marshall, we do know that the initial reason for her presence there was to take up a studentship at the fledgling British School,⁴⁵ following in the recent footsteps of several other Haverfield protegés.⁴⁶ Over the course of 15 months, she may well have done both things. The more interesting point is that Haverfield presumably supported her application to study in Rome, suggesting both that he rated the quality of her scholarship, and that they both considered she had independent work to pursue.⁴⁷

After her return to England, and the start of the war, Miss Taylor again took up her work for Haverfield, but change was on the way. It is widely accepted that he suffered a mental and physical decline precipitated by the death in 1915 of G. L. Cheesman, and died in October 1919, without ever having regained sound health.⁴⁸ That he was as productive as he was during these difficult years surely bears testimony to the working partnership which he and Miss Taylor had been developing over the previous decade, and which now came into its own.⁴⁹ It should be noted, indeed, that she was given due credit by his contemporaries in their tributes to Haverfield.⁵⁰ A newspaper report of January 1917 relating to their work may also indicate the level of his reliance on her more generally. It consists of a précis of a paper prepared by Haverfield (but with Miss Taylor's assistance, it states), which she then delivered to the intended audience, as Haverfield was unable to make the journey himself.[51]

She was, by this stage in her career, well-practised in the skills of research, academic writing, editing and presenting, and clearly respected by colleagues in the field of Romano-British studies. Following the death of Haverfield in 1919, the question was, what would Miss Taylor do now?

The Haverfield bequest

In 1987 Sheppard Frere, by then the retired Oxford professor of the archaeology of the Roman Empire, gave a lecture in that University entitled 'Roman Britain since Haverfield and Richmond'. In it he ascribed the existence of Roman Britain as a subject for study in the University '…to Francis Haverfield and his twin successors Robin Collingwood and Margerie Venables Taylor.'[52] Collingwood's main contribution, according to Frere, apart from being the dominant (Oxford) figure in the subject in the 1920s and 1930s, was the report on work on Roman Britain, published annually in the *JRS* from 1922 onwards, which he prepared with the assistance of Miss Taylor, and his continued work on material for a corpus of Roman inscriptions from Britain, also a project of Haverfield's.[53] Most of the credit, however, in Frere's estimation, should go to Miss Taylor herself, particularly after Collingwood withdrew from his non-philosophical activities in the later 1930s:

> It was her devotion to Haverfield's memory and principles, her stern scholarship and intellectual prestige – exercised through the annual report, through the administration of the Haverfield Bequest for the furtherance of Romano-British studies, and through the editorship of the JRS for so many years – that was largely responsible for keeping the subject on course through the '40s, '50s, and '60s.[54]

Collingwood took the opportunity to explain his understanding of his obligations following the death of Haverfield in an autobiography he wrote in 1938.[55] By contrast, not only did Miss Taylor opt not to leave an account of her life and work at all, she also took care to dispose of papers, letters and perhaps diaries, from which her version of events could have been reconstructed. This has left space not only for the 'great men' to fight it out posthumously, but also, as she may not have foreseen, for her position to be misunderstood. In the absence of any explanation from

Miss Taylor herself, Phil Freeman, for instance, has argued that the chief motivation for the zeal and tenacity with which she prosecuted her late employer's wishes was self-interest, and that her influence resulted not only in a distorted version of Haverfield's significance, but in the stunted development of Romano-British studies for decades.[56] The scope of Freeman's theme is too great for this necessarily brief engagement with Miss Taylor, but in an effort to disentangle cause and effect, it is certainly possible to look more closely at what she did after the death of Francis Haverfield, how and why.

A document key to understanding what happened next is the Haverfield obituary Miss Taylor wrote for the *Journal of the Chester Archaeological Society* in August 1920 (almost a year after his death), by which time the terms of his bequest were in the public domain.[57] She outlined the philosophy behind Haverfield's interest in Roman Britain, inspired directly, she explained, by Mommsen's appreciation of the importance of Roman provincial archaeology. This had shown him how to take finds such as the inscribed altars at Chester '…out of the sphere of local archaeology, and fit them into their proper place in the history of the empire'. The comparative, contextual approach was the crucial element.[58] Once he became Camden Professor of Ancient History in 1907, he had begun to advance his ideas 'by training a school of Romano-British archaeologists, and by promoting excavations in every part of Britain', and under the terms of his will, '…he left to the University of Oxford a sum of money for the excavation of Romano-British sites under proper direction, in the hope of bringing together ancient historians and local archaeologists'. She concluded that although the two pupils Haverfield had identified as his potential successors had been killed in the war:

> One may only hope that the means he has provided for excavation and for the study of the Roman empire, more especially of Roman Britain, by the impulse he gave to those studies, and by the bequest to the University of Oxford both of money and of his very complete library, may in time produce the effect he desired, and that others may appear to follow in his footsteps.[59]

It is not too much to say that the principles and future hopes laid out here were the credo to which Miss Taylor harnessed her energy and considerable talents for the next 40 years, with the unswerving 'devotion to Haverfield's memory and principles' alluded to by Frere. In this sense it might be described as a joint venture between one living partner, and one dead.

In practical terms, she achieved 'their' ends chiefly by acting as Secretary to the Administrators of the Bequest from 1921. In 1923 she took on the running of the Roman Society, begun by Haverfield in 1910, and the editing of its journal.[60] These were the two 'pillars' on which Miss Taylor built what was to be her life's work. Her work for the Bequest included much travel to inspect the sites of excavations they were funding: '...and her always trenchant views on the progress, or otherwise, of projects supported by the Bequest were an invaluable source of informed comment'.[61] Meanwhile, back in Oxford she talent-spotted potential archaeologists among the undergraduates who visited the Ashmolean Library. Christopher Hawkes, who first met her there in the autumn of 1924, was one such, and described her as 'a tremendous help to him throughout his time at Oxford; for when she learnt that he wanted to be an excavator, she wrote at once to a Dr Wheeler, who would be digging, in the summer of 1925, at the Roman fort of Brecon Gaer'.[62] The following year, using money from the Bequest, she set him up with an excavation project (with hired labourers) at Alchester, north east of Oxford, which R. G. Collingwood visited to inspect how matters were progressing.[63] The undergraduate Ian Richmond, similarly, was recruited onto the Wheelers' excavation at Segontium in 1921–1922, which was funded by the Bequest, and also encouraged by Collingwood and Taylor to apply for a string of studentships to fund his time at the British School at Rome, after graduating in 1924.[64]

In some ways, however, the funding of excavation was a secondary matter, or perhaps a means to several different ends. Haverfield had been clear in his wishes that the production of a corpus of Roman inscriptions in Britain should be 'a prime and particular objective of the Bequest'.[65] This was the task taken on by Collingwood, who was one of the Administrators from 1921–1938. Next, in 1922, and of far greater immediate use to students of Roman Britain, Collingwood and Taylor jointly undertook to produce a regular annual report on Roman sites around the country, to be published in the *JRS*. The first report duly appeared in Miss Taylor's debut edition,[66] with a preface explicitly making the connection between the objectives of the Haverfield Bequest fund, the role of the Haverfield Library as a reference library and repository of information, the *JRS* reports on Roman Britain and 'the new *corpus* of Roman inscriptions in Britain.'[67] Based in the Haverfield Library, Miss Taylor had clearly embarked on coordinating an ambitious programme to build Roman Britain up into a larger and more serious area of Roman studies. These were also intensive years of collaboration on Roman Britain, during which she worked steadily to support Collingwood[68] and to keep Wheeler on board, partly by sanctioning successive grants to fund his excavations.[69] The level of her involvement in their own projects is indicated by the prominent acknowledgement both made of her in their publications,[70] and her presence in the organisation of their archaeological work at a local level. She was, for instance, a member of the excavation committee at Brecon Gaer in 1926 and on the committee of Collingwood's Hadrian's Wall 'Pilgrimage' in 1930, a week-long archaeological guided tour of the frontier works. Their respect for her influence, and the level of her contribution to Roman Britain, is reflected in her election to the Society of Antiquaries in 1925, with the support of both these men.[71]

Archaeology in wartime

'When you get to my age', Miss Taylor is reported to have reflected in 1961, 'and have lived through wars, you realise that though wars come and go, work and learning do and must go on. It is no use being unduly anxious.'[72] In July 1941, Miss Taylor wrote at length to Ronald Syme, who spent most of the war active in diplomacy or intelligence for the British in Turkey.[73] She described the privations and upheavals of Oxford in wartime, and passed on some University gossip. But mostly, the letter reflects her efforts to ensure that 'work and learning' should indeed go on, including the latest edition of *JRS,* and her plans for a 'joint conference', to be held in Oxford in August or September of 1942: 'Nothing like being ambitious, but conferences of all kinds here are very well attended… so why should not we have one. The President and I thought it a good idea…' Despite the war, not only had the Roman Society broached discussions with the Hellenic Society about a classics conference in Oxford, but it was very much Miss Taylor's venture.

The week-long 'Joint Meeting', which was duly organised for 29 August to 5 September 1942, has since achieved iconic status as it was attended, astonishingly given the date, by almost 'everyone who was anyone' in classics and archaeology, and set in train a determination to ensure that archaeology should be a properly conducted part of the post-war reconstruction and development of Britain.[74] In his memoir, the ancient historian Frank Walbank remembered the conference as 'the brilliant and confident initiative of Miss M. V. Taylor, the formidable editor of the *Journal of Roman Studies*… It was a tremendous display of talent and all who were there felt amazingly encouraged and excited at such a gesture. It looked as if every British scholar who was not prevented by war work had taken part.'[75] It should be noted that even without the benefit of historical perspective, her commitment to performing the necessary negotiations and driving the scheme to a successful conclusion was acknowledged and widely admired.[76]

Miss Taylor's hand can moreover be detected in the process of translating the discussions which took place at the Joint Meeting to action. In November 1942, she wrote to the President of the Society of Antiquaries, outlining the determination of the recent conference, and proposing that an organisation should be created 'for the recording and rescuing of antiquities wherever threatened, and where possible for securing their preservation.'[77] The next move was a letter to the Council of the Society of Antiquaries signed by the President of the Roman Society,[78] requesting that it should help to organise a representative body to speak for archaeology to the government. A steering group met to consider the scope of the new body and to draft a constitution and, as a result of its recommendations, a provisional Council for British Archaeology was formed. In summary, this led to the Conference for the Future of Archaeology, held in London in August 1943, out of which emerged the permanently constituted Council for British Archaeology in 1944.[79]

Partly, no doubt, in recognition of her role in this remarkable and forward-thinking train of events, Cyril Fox appointed Miss Taylor Vice-President of the Society of Antiquaries in 1944, the first woman to occupy the position. And in this case, it was no mere *sinecure*: as Fox was Director of the National Museum of Wales in Cardiff, and therefore at some distance from London, in practice Miss Taylor frequently presided over ballots and meetings in his absence.[80]

The 'iron hand in the chiffon glove'[81]

In an article to mark the centenary of the Roman Society in 2010, Christopher Stray judged Miss Taylor's contribution to have been exceptional by any standards, commenting: 'Not only did she reign as Secretary and of Editor of *JRS* for many decades; she also crossed the conventional boundary between the male academic and his female secretary to become a one-woman administrative and editorial power-house.'[82] This essay has argued that a partnership, which Miss Taylor found to be a way of working that suited her, took root in the period leading up to the death of Francis Haverfield and developed rapidly in the first few years afterwards. This facility for collaboration and apparent willingness to subsume her own academic identity in that of others, as noted by R. G. Collingwood,[83] certainly makes it no less difficult to appreciate the full weight of her achievement today, beyond the expectations she imposed and upheld at the Roman Society. Additionally, the vigilance with which she maintained Haverfield's (and by extension, her own) vision of Roman Britain as a province of a great empire, and the Mommsenite methodologies by which this should be explored, have inevitably diminished, to the twenty-first century gaze, her significance in the history of British archaeology.[84] Even in the restricted context of an institutional memoir, Stray has noted somewhat discrepant assessments of Miss Taylor's attitude to Roman Britain. To Frere, she 'had her finger on [its] pulse', tirelessly verifying and re-crafting excavation reports for the *JRS*. To Mary Bennett, Hon. Secretary of the Society 1960–1985:

> … during Miss Taylor's lifetime the lid was firmly kept on Roman Britain. The orthodoxy was that those who enjoyed a good dig should be led, via the archaeological survey in the JRS, to read further, and come to see their subject in a wider context, while Miss Taylor herself did not admit the possibility of diverting energies or funds from her own cherished Journal. This position became increasingly hard to hold as archaeological interest spread…[85]

It is also possible that these two versions are not necessarily contradictory, but rather bear remarkable witness to Miss Taylor's loyal and devoted adherence to a set of principles which had inevitably become outmoded. This essay represents an attempt to explore one person's contribution to a strand of scholarship which blossomed, during her lifetime, from being the amateur pursuit of an educated middle class, to a professionalised, institutionally sponsored discipline. We have touched on some of the challenges of understanding the power and influence Miss Taylor wielded in the British archaeological establishment from the 1920s onwards. As we have seen, she forged a unique 'career' as administrator, editor and facilitator of opportunities for young hopefuls, which convenient badges such as 'secretary' and 'assistant' cannot begin to describe.

It is worth re-emphasising two particular circumstances which make the task more difficult. The first is the straightforward point that academic disciplines, and the institutional structures within which they are pursued, move on. However striking the developments in Roman archaeology between the 1890s and the 1960s, the shifts and turns in the 55 years since Miss Taylor's death, though of a different nature, have been just as great. On first acquaintance, almost everything about the academic world in which she operated seems alien – narrower, smaller, more bounded, certainly rather privileged – which can easily provoke impatient or dismissive judgement of her achievement. The second, not unrelated, point, is what we don't know about her. As she neared the end of her life, Miss Taylor presumably felt her work and her reputation to be secure to her own satisfaction. At any rate, she chose to make no arrangements for the archiving of letters and diaries, or even papers relating strictly to her work; and in his obituary notice for the *JRS*, Ian Richmond implied that she destroyed much material deliberately in the months before her death. This was her decision to make, clearly, but has had certain consequences. For in the absence of more substantial publications in her own name, a reputation as an excavator or pupils through whom her influence can be traced, the impact of her work in archaeology has often been underestimated and overlooked. It has also been a deliberate policy on the part of the author to avoid ascribing to Miss Taylor motivation and reflections which can only be a matter of conjecture. There are surely, however, more of her letters to friends and colleagues carefully buried in various archives: the reference to correspondence kept by Rose Macaulay, and now at Trinity College, Cambridge, for instance, was one such lucky find.

Some targeted archival research, to add more flesh to the industrious bones of Miss Taylor's career, is an aspiration for the future. In the meanwhile, it is hoped that this chapter has at least made a case for paying tribute to a figure who charted her course, however controversially, through the most turbulent years of the twentieth century, and fulfilled her calling with such vigour and satisfaction. As she is reported to have said in 1961: 'It has been a happy life, for I have enjoyed my work... When you get to my age, and have lived through wars, you realize that though wars come and go, work and learning do and must go on.'[86]

Acknowledgements

Many thanks to Fiona Haarer at the Roman Society, to Chris Stray for his valuable comments and to the late Anthony Birley, who kindly shared unpublished material from the Syme archive. Tony was also one of the few people I have known who actually met Miss Taylor – most probably in the Haverfield Library, of course.

Notes

1 Sheppard Frere, 'Roman Britain since Haverfield and Richmond', *History and Archaeology Review* 3 (1988): 32. For contemporary endorsements, cf. Ian Richmond, *The Archaeology of the Roman Empire (An Inaugural Lecture delivered before the University of Oxford)*

(Oxford: Clarendon Press, 1957), 18; Eric Birley, *Research on Hadrian's Wall* (Kendal: Titus Wilson & Son, 1961): 36, 40, described her as a 'distinguished visitor' to the Hadrian's Wall Pilgrimage in 1930, and one of several 'leading archaeologists' attending the Centenary Pilgrimage in 1949.
2   Richard Jones, 'The archaeologists of Roman Britain', *Bulletin of the Institute of Archaeology* 24 (1987): 84–97; Martin Millett, 'Roman Britain since Haverfield', in *The Oxford Handbook of Roman Britain*, eds. Martin Millett, Louise Revell, and Alison Moore (Oxford: Oxford University Press, 2016), 22–42.
3   Margerie V. Taylor, 'A bibliography of the published writings of Margerie Venables Taylor', *Journal of Roman Studies* 54 (1964): 2–6.
4   Sara Champion, 'On women in archaeology: visible and invisible', in *Excavating Women: A history of women in European archaeology*, eds. Margarita Díaz-Andreu and Marie-Louise Stig Sørensen (London: Routledge, 1998), 175–97.
5   Champion, 'Visible and invisible': 175–77.
6   Kate E. Sharpe, 'The Lady of the Lakes: Clare Isobel Fell and the role of local societies for women in archaeology', in *Studies in Northern Prehistory: Essays in memory of Clare Fell*, ed. P. J. Cherry (Kendal: Cumberland & Westmorland Archaeological & Architectural Society, 2007), 1–23.
7   On the rarity of professional jobs in archaeology in the 1920s and 1930s: J. N. L. Myres, 'Anniversary Address', *Antiquaries Journal* 55 (1975): 1.
8   Philip Freeman, *The Best Training-Ground for Archaeologists: Francis Haverfield and the invention of Romano-British archaeology* (Oxford: Oxbow Books, 2007): 586; cf. Millett, 'Roman Britain', 22.
9   Robin George Collingwood, letter to Mortimer Wheeler, 9 January 1924, in *R. G. Collingwood: A research companion*, eds. James Connelly, Peter Johnson and Stephen Leach (London: Bloomsbury Academic, 2014), 187.
10 Freeman, *Best Training-Ground*, 589: 'Margerie Taylor was forced to create her own niche in the vacuum created by Haverfield's demise. Certainly in her case, keeping alive the Haverfield reputation benefited her, possibility [sic] at the expense of aspects of Haverfield's work.'
11 Freeman, *Best Training-Ground*, 380; cf. Frere, 'Roman Britain', 32.
12 Robin George Collingwood, *The Idea of History* (Oxford: Oxford University Press, 1946), 247.
13 Douglas Givens, 'The role of biography in writing the history of archaeology', in *Histories of Archaeology: A reader in the history of archaeology*, eds. Tim Murray and Christopher Evans (Oxford: Oxford University Press, 1992), 181: 'The role of biography in explaining archaeology's past is to describe the place of individual contributions to the development of archaeology within the intellectual climate in which they were made.'
14 E.g. Thomas Söderqvist, 'Existential projects and existential choice in science: science biography as an edifying genre', in *Telling Lives in Science: Essays on scientific biography*, eds. Michael Shortland and Richard Yeo (Cambridge: Cambridge University Press, 1996), 45–84; idem., 'What is the use of writing lives of recent scientists?' in *The Historiography of Contemporary Science, Technology, and Medicine: Writing recent science*, eds. Ronald E. Doel and Thomas Söderqvist (London & New York: Routledge, 2006), 99–127; idem., 'Introduction: A new look at the genre of scientific biography', in *The History and Poetics of Scientific Biography*, ed. Thomas Söderqvist (Aldershot: Ashgate, 2007), 1–15.
15 Marc-Antoine Kaeser, 'Biography as microhistory: the relevance of private archives for writing the history of archaeology', in *Archives, Ancestors, Practices: Archaeology in the light of its history*, eds. Nathan Schlanger and Jarl Nordbladh (New York–Oxford: Berghahn Books, 2008), 12.
16 Cf. Paula Findlen, 'Listening to the archives: searching for eighteenth-century women of science', in *Writing about Lives in Science: (Auto)biography, gender and genre*, eds. Paola Govoni and Zelda A. Franceschi (Göttingen: V&R unipress, 2014), 93.
17 E.g. Michael Shortland and Richard Yeo, eds., *Telling Lives in Science: Essays on scientific biography* (Cambridge: Cambridge University Press, 1996); Ronald E. Doel and Thomas Söderqvist, eds., *The Historiography of Contemporary Science, Technology, and Medicine: Writing recent science*, (London–New York: Routledge, 2006); Govoni and Franceschi, *Writing*.
18 Hermione Lee, *Biography: A very short introduction* (Oxford: Oxford University Press, 2009), 134; cf. Shortland and Yeo, *Telling lives in science*, 31.
19 Paola Govoni, 'Crafting science (auto)biographies', in Govoni and Franceschi, *Writing*, 7–30.
20 E.g. Elizabeth Gowing, *Edith and I: On the trail of an Edwardian traveller in Kosovo* (Cornwall: Elbow Press, 2013); cf. Govoni, 'Crafting', 11.

21 Douglas Givens, 'The role of biography', 187–8: '[T]he biographer *must not* fall in love with his or her subject. Instead the biographer must develop a serious identification with the person… Everything during this time comes together: the character's time, place, intellectual climate; the subject's friends, enemies, and appetites… This is the time when the biographer must remain detached *from* the archaeologist being written about. Such detachment allows the biographer to assess fully the intellectual climate that surrounds and affects his or her subject's life and, therefore, this person's contributions to archaeology.'
22 Cf. Kaeser, 'Biography as microhistory'; Marc-Antoine Kaeser, 'Biography, science studies and the historiography of archaeological research: Managing personal archives', *Complutum* 24 (2013): 101–8.
23 In the pre-digital age, it was *the* readily accessible resource, and rather heavily relied-upon by generations of Oxford tutors as a result.
24 Margerie Taylor, letter to Ronald Syme, 13 July 1941 (Syme archive, Bodleian library): 'The term is over and Greats list out on Friday last with 4 women firsts, three of them philosophers, one J. Reynolds (Somerville) a historian…'
25 Freeman, *Best Training-Ground*, 19; cf. Ian Richmond, 'Margerie Venables Taylor', *Journal of Roman Studies* 54 (1964): 1.
26 The Haverfield Archive was moved from the Ashmolean (Haverfield) Library in the early 2000s, and it has not been possible to locate, for example, items of Miss Taylor's correspondence consulted by Freeman in his research on Haverfield (Philip Freeman, Email to author, 5 June 2017). A 1970s report, with Haverfield Library locations, effectively suggests there must be material elsewhere, as it is not all currently in evidence at the Sackler: J. E. S. & R. D. A., *Haverfield Archive* (unpublished report, Roman Society archive, July 1976).
27 Use was made of the archive in the preparation of an institutional memoir for the Society's centenary, including a section on Miss Taylor: Christopher Stray, '"Patriots and professors": A century of Roman Studies, 1910–2010', *Journal of Roman Studies* 100 (2010), 1–31.
28 'Miss M. V. Taylor', *Times,* 27 December 1963, 10, *The Times Digital Archive.* Accessed May 24, 2018. http://tinyurl.galegroup.com/tinyurl/63mAC9. Ian Richmond was probably the author.
29 'The happy scholar', *Times*, 31 July 1961, 13, *The Times Digital Archive.* Accessed 24 May 2018., http://tinyurl.galegroup.com/tinyurl/63mTV9.
30 E.g. Glen Bowersock, 'Ronald Syme 1903–1989', *Proceedings of the British Academy* 84 (1994), 550; Diana Bonakis Webster, *Hawkeseye: The early life of Christopher Hawkes* (Stroud: Alan Sutton, 1991), 118–20, 146.
31 'To Miss M. V. Taylor, CBE, MA, FSA, A Tribute', *Journal of Roman Studies* 50 (1960): xi.
32 Margerie Taylor, 'F. J. Haverfield', *Journal of the Chester & North Wales Archaeological & Historical Society* 23 (1920), 69.
33 Cf. Freeman, *Best Training-Ground,* 380.
34 P. H. Lawson, 'Miss Margerie Venables Taylor', *Journal of the Chester & North Wales Archaeological & Historical Society* 51 (1964), 77–8. After his death, she described his impact on the Chester Archaeological Society as follows: 'His common sense and sound judgement, his wide grasp and sense of proportion, his comparative knowledge and appreciation of historical value of the finds enabled him to take them out of the sphere of local archaeology, and fit them into their proper place in the history of the empire.' (Taylor, 'Haverfield', 67).
35 Women were eligible to receive degrees at Oxford only from 1920, the year she took an MA, according to College Records.
36 Sarah LeFanu, *Rose Macaulay* (London: Virago Press 2003), 50, 55–67.
37 Cf. *Happy Scholar*, 13; *Tribute*, xi. The 'Romano-British' section of the Shropshire volume (1908), is jointly credited to Haverfield and Taylor, her first publication (cf. Taylor, 'Bibliography', 2).
38 John Beckett, Matthew Bristow and Elizabeth Williamson, *The Victoria County History 1899–2012: A Diamond Jubilee celebration* (London: University of London Institute of Historical Research, 2013), 11–8. The project soon hit financial difficulties, and the production of volumes slowed, but in the early years, the *Victoria County History* was remarkable for two things: firstly, that it 'put the study of archaeology and architecture alike on newly professional footing. It avoided rehashing second-hand interpretations, insisting on active fieldwork by well-trained investigators.' (*ibid.*, 21). The second remarkable feature was that 1904–8, it was largely researched and written by young woman scholars such as Miss Taylor, employed

directly by the publisher on a contract basis (*ibid.*, 27–8). *Tribute,* xi notes how Haverfield's sections of the *VCH* 'did so much to set the tone of Romano-British studies'.
39 Freeman, *Best Training-Ground,* 380–81; cf. Taylor, 'Bibliography', 2–4. The authors of the *Haverfield Archive* report comment: 'It proved impossible to separate out the work of Miss Taylor from that of Professor Haverfield (for example, in work for the *Victoria County Histories*) and for this reason much work by Miss Taylor is included here'.
40 The happy scholar, 13.
41 Freeman, *Best Training-Ground,* 380, n. 41. She was certainly fulfilling the role in June 1910, cf. The happy scholar, 13, on the foundation of the Roman Society.
42 Christopher Hawkes, perhaps mischievously, told his biographer that 'there was much speculation at the time that [Miss Taylor] was hoping to become Mrs Haverfield' (Webster, *Hawkeseye*, 119). But his information would surely be second-hand at best. Even Collingwood (Haverfield's pupil, Hawkes' tutor) only arrived in Oxford in 1908, so cannot himself have witnessed what happened.
43 Freeman, *Best Training-Ground,* 419, n.89; *ibid.*, 361.
44 Ian Hall and Gerald Robinson, *The Ancient Men: The OUMM and its background*, 1993, 6–16. When she retired from the committee in 1920, a vote of thanks was reported in the *Oxford Times* including, as follows: 'Not only was Miss Taylor largely responsible for the early spadework which gave the branch its great success in pre-war days, but it is owing in great measure to her energy and enthusiasm that the even more arduous task of restarting after the war has been accomplished.' (*ibid.*, 16).
45 Andrew Wallace-Hadrill, *The British School at Rome: One hundred years* (London: British School at Rome, 2001), 53.
46 Freeman, *Best Training-Ground,* 331.
47 Her only publication for 1914 was a *Topographical Index* for one of the Hertfordshire volumes of the *VCH*, which surely cannot have been the subject of her study in Rome.
48 Freeman, *Best Training-Ground,* 425–6; cf. Robert Carr Bosanquet, 'Francis John Haverfield', *Archaeologia Aeliana 3rd series,* 17 (1920), 140: 'He worked on, but in 1916 a paralytic seizure was followed by a long illness from which he never wholly recovered.'
49 Cf. Macdonald, 'Professor Haverfield: A bibliography', *Journal of Roman Studies* 8 (1918).
50 Cf. Macdonald, 'Haverfield', 184: Miss Taylor *sine qua non*; Bosanquet, 'Haverfield', 141: his debt to 'Miss M. V. Taylor, the skilled researcher who was Dr. Haverfield's assistant for so many years'.
51 'War Lessons from Ancient Rome – archive, 11 January 1917', *The Guardian,* 11 January 2017, https://www.theguardian.com/education/2017/jan/11/war-lessons-from-ancient-rome-archive-1917.
52 Frere, 'Roman Britain Since Haverfield', 31.
53 Malcolm Todd, 'The Haverfield Bequest, 1921–2000, and the study of Roman Britain', *Britannia* 34 (2003), 38.
54 Frere, 'Roman Britain since Haverfield', 32.
55 Robin George Collingwood, *An Autobiography* (Oxford: Clarendon Press, 1939), 120; cf. David Boucher and Teresa Smith, 'Introduction: The biography of *An Autobiography*', in *An Autobiography and Other Writings,* eds. David Boucher and Teresa Smith (Oxford: Oxford University Press, 2013), xxi–xxiv.
56 Freeman, *Best Training-Ground,* 494–95. *Ibid.*, 250–53; 280; 295, 427: Freeman analyses letters between Taylor and Eric Birley, written in February 1962, in the wake of a review in *Antiquity* by Wheeler, criticising the way Haverfield's legacy had been promulgated and enshrined, and the negative impact of this on Romano-British studies (from which the thesis of Freeman's book draws fire power). Even here, Miss Taylor chooses to defend and analyse *Haverfield's* reputation, ignoring Wheeler's impugning of her own. Freeman read the letters in the Haverfield Archive when it was housed in the Ashmolean Library (Phil Freeman, Email to author, 5 June 2017), although it has not been possible to find them more recently.
57 Taylor, 'Haverfield', 64–71.
58 *Ibid.*, 66–67.
59 *Ibid.*, 69; 71.
60 Stray, 'Patriots and professors', 8: Both were in a poor way following the war and a string of short-term appointments to both roles, and in sore need of the administrative efficiency and editorial acumen which Miss Taylor was able to supply.

61 Todd, 'Haverfield Bequest', 38: 'Apart from the work of successive Chairmen, no one did more to ensure the effective operation of the Bequest than Margery [sic] Taylor.'
62 Webster, *Hawkeseye,* 120; cf. Jacquetta Hawkes, *The Biography of Sir Mortimer Wheeler: Adventurer in archaeology* (London: Weidenfeld & Nicolson, 1982), 90.
63 Webster, *Hawkeseye,* 146; cf. Todd, 'Haverfield Bequest', 38.
64 Todd, 'Haverfield Bequest', 39; Freeman, *Best Training Ground,* 566.
65 Todd, 'Haverfield Bequest', 35.
66 *Journal of Roman Studies* 11 (1921), published in 1923, as the Journal had, at that point, fallen so far into arrears, cf. Stray, 'Patriots and professors', 8.
67 Margerie Venables Taylor and Robin George Collingwood, 'Roman Britain in 1921 and 1922', *Journal of Roman Studies* 11 (1921), 200.
68 It was never any secret that for Collingwood, Roman Britain was always a means to an end. As he wrote in 1938, his philosophical work demanded that he should be 'the acknowledged master' in a historical field of study: 'The field had, accordingly, to be a small one, and ripe for intensive cultivation. For this purpose, Roman Britain was very suitable.' (*Autobiography,* 120).
69 Todd, 'Haverfield Bequest', 38. Dynamic, charismatic, and always an enthusiastic self-publicist, Wheeler was seemingly keen both to make his mark as an excavator of Roman period sites, and to train a new generation of archaeologists in the field, and eventually via his new 'Institute of Archaeology' in London. He was undoubtedly an asset to her 'cause'.
70 For example, R. E. Mortimer Wheeler, *Prehistoric and Roman Wales* (Oxford: Clarendon Press, 1925), 6; Robin George Collingwood, *The Archaeology of Roman Britain* (London: Methuen, 1930), vii.
71 Cf. n. 9, above. Lydia Carr, *Tessa Verney Wheeler* (Oxford: Oxford University Press, 2012), 126–28 discussed the earliest admssions of women to the *Society,* although she identified Mrs Reginald Poole as the first woman member to be ordinarily proposed, in 1926.
72 The happy scholar, 13.
73 Margerie Venables Taylor, Letter to Ronald Syme, 13 July 1941 (Syme archive, Bodleian Library); cf. Bowersock, 'Ronald Syme', 550–51.
74 Joan Evans, *A History of the Society of Antiquaries* (Oxford: Oxford University Press, 1956), 427.
75 Stray, 'Patriots and professors', 19 n. 68.
76 Martin P. Charlesworth, *Report of the Joint Meeting of the Hellenic and Roman Societies* (London, 1943), 3; 16.
77 Margerie Venables Taylor, Letter to the President and Secretary of *SAL,* 21 November 1942, in Pearce, *Visions,* 427.
78 Cf. Mortimer Wheeler, review of *Journal of Roman Studies* 50, *Antiquity* 35 (1961), 157: '… the distinguished line of Presidents whom she has controlled…'
79 Evans, *Antiquaries,* 427–28; cf. Stray, 'Patriots and professors', 28. For the context and significance of the 1943 Conference, cf. Gabriel Moshenska, 'Reflections on the 1943 "Conference on the Future of Archaeology"', *Archaeology International* 16 (2012–13), 128–39.
80 Evans, *Antiquaries,* 432.
81 Stray, 'Patriots and professors', 20 n. 75.
82 *Ibid.,* 28. Her exceptional capacity for detail remained with her into old age. The Roman Society archives show that she exercised executive oversight of every part of organising the admired Exhibition of Art in Roman Britain, staged at Goldsmith's Hall in London, to mark the Roman Society's Golden Jubilee in 1961. From running the funding appeal, to negotiating the insurance and transport for 202 unique and priceless objects, to masterminding the publicity and ensuring that the public and educational remit was fulfilled, Miss Taylor maintained her grasp.
83 Cf. n.9, above. In an unpublished 1938 letter to his Editor at the Clarendon Press, Collingwood (knowing he is gravely ill) suggests individuals who might be approached to complete various outstanding projects and commissions, including in one instance Miss Taylor, but in partnership with another colleague, as 'She is very good at spade work & each would supply just what the other lacks.' Cf. James Connelly, Peter Johnson and Stephen Leach, eds., *R. G. Collingwood: A research companion* (London: Bloomsbury, 2015), 87.
84 Freeman, *Best Training-Ground,* 591.
85 Stray, 'Patriots and professors', 21.
86 The happy scholar, 13.

Bibliography

Anon, 'To Miss M. V. Taylor, CBE, MA, FSA, A Tribute', *Journal of Roman Studies* 50 (1960): xi.
Beckett, John, Matthew Bristow and Elizabeth Williamson, *The Victoria County History 1899–2012: A Diamond Jubilee celebration* (London: University of London Institute of Historical Research, 2013).
Birley, Eric, *Research on Hadrian's Wall* (Kendal: Titus Wilson & Son, 1961).
Bosanquet, Robert Carr, 'Francis John Haverfield', *Archaeologia Aeliana* 3rd series, 17 (1920): 137–43.
Boucher, David and Teresa Smith, 'Introduction: the biography of *An Autobiography*', in *An Autobiography and Other Writings*, eds. David Boucher and Teresa Smith (Oxford: Oxford University Press, 2013), xxi–xlix.
Bowersock, Glen, 'Ronald Syme 1903–1989', *Proceedings of the British Academy* 84 (1994): 539–63.
Carr, Lydia C., *Tessa Verney Wheeler: Women and archaeology before World War Two* (Oxford: Oxford University Press, 2012).
Champion, Sara, 'On women in archaeology: visible and invisible', in *Excavating Women: A history of women in European archaeology*, ed. Margarita Díaz-Andreu and Marie-Louise Stig Sørensen (London: Routledge, 1998), 175–97.
Charlesworth, Martin P., *Report of the Joint Meeting of the Hellenic and Roman Societies* (London, 1943).
Collingwood, Robin George, *The Archaeology of Roman Britain* (London: Methuen, 1930).
Collingwood, Robin George, *An Autobiography* (Oxford: Clarendon Press, 1939).
Collingwood, Robin George, *The Idea of History* (Oxford: Clarendon Press, 1946).
Connelly, James, Peter Johnson and Stephen Leach, *R. G. Collingwood: A research companion* (London: Bloomsbury Academic, 2014).
Evans, Joan, *A History of the Society of Antiquaries* (Oxford: Oxford University Press, 1956).
Findlen, Paula, 'Listening to the archives: searching for eighteenth-century women of science', in *Writing about Lives in Science:(Auto)biography, gender and genre,* eds. Paola Govoni and Zelda A. Franceschi (Göttingen: V&R unipress, 2014), 87–116.
Freeman, Philip, *The Best Training-Ground for Archaeologists: Francis Haverfield and the invention of Romano-British archaeology* (Oxford: Oxbow Books, 2007).
Frere, Sheppard, 'Roman Britain since Haverfield and Richmond', *History and Archaeology Review* 3 (1988): 31–6.
Givens, Douglas, 'The role of biography in writing the history of archaeology', in *Histories of Archaeology: A reader in the history of archaeology,* eds. Tim Murray and Christopher Evans (Oxford: Oxford University Press, 1992), 177–93.
Govoni, Paola and Zelda A. Franceschi, eds., *Writing about Lives in Science: (Auto)biography, gender and genre* (Göttingen: V&R unipress, 2014).
Govoni, Paola, 'Crafting science (auto)biographies', in *Writing about Lives in Science: (Auto) biography, gender and genre,* eds. Paola Govoni and Zelda A. Franceschi (Göttingen: V&R unipress, 2014), 7–30.
Gowing, Elizabeth, *Edith and I: On the trail of an Edwardian traveller in Kosovo* (Cornwall: Elbow Press, 2013).
Guardian Archive, 'War lessons from Ancient Rome – archive, 11 January 1917', *The Guardian*. Accessed 11 January 2017. https://www.theguardian.com/education/2017/jan/11/war-lessons-from-ancient-rome-archive-1917.
Hall, Ian, and Gerald Robinson, *The Ancient Men: The OUMM and its background* (revised 1993), Accessed 5 February 2022, https://oxforduniversitymorris.files.wordpress.com/2016/12/oummhist.pdf.
Hawkes, Jacquetta, *The Biography of Sir Mortimer Wheeler: Adventurer in archaeology* (London: Weidenfeld & Nicolson, 1982).
Jones, Richard, 'The archaeologists of Roman Britain', *Bulletin of the Institute of Archaeology* 24 (1987): 84–97.
Kaeser, Marc-Antoine, 'Biography as microhistory: the relevance of private archives for writing the history of archaeology', in *Archives, Ancestors, Practices: Archaeology in the light of its history,* eds., Nathan Schlanger and Jarl Nordbladh (New York–Oxford: Berghahn Books, 2008), 9–20.
Kaeser, Marc-Antoine, 'Biography, science studies and the historiography of archival research: Managing personal archives', *Complutum* 24 (2013): 101–8.

Lawson, P. H., 'Miss Margerie Venables Taylor', *Journal of the Chester & North Wales Archaeological & Historical Society* 51 (1964): 77–8.
Lee, Hermione, *Biography: A very short introduction* (Oxford: Oxford University Press, 2009).
LeFanu, Sarah, *Rose Macaulay* (London: Virago Press, 2003).
Macdonald, George, 'Professor Haverfield: A bibliography', *Journal of Roman Studies* 8 (1918): 184–98.
Millett, Martin, 'Roman Britain since Haverfield', in *The Oxford Handbook of Roman Britain*, ed. Martin Millett, Louise Revell, and Alison Moore (Oxford: Oxford University Press, 2016), 22–42.
Moshenska, Gabriel, 'Reflections on the 1943 "Conference on the Future of Archaeology"', *Archaeology International* 16 (2012-13): 128–39.
Myres, J. N. L., 'Anniversary address', *Antiquaries Journal* 55 (1975): 1–10.
Richmond, Ian, The Archaeology of the Roman Empire (An Inaugural Lecture delivered before the University of Oxford) (Oxford: Clarendon Press, 1957).
Richmond, Ian, 'Margerie Venables Taylor', *Journal of Roman Studies* 54 (1964): 1.
Sharpe, Kate E., 'The Lady of the Lakes: Clare Isobel Fell and the role of local societies for women in archaeology', in *Studies in Northern Prehistory: Essays in memory of Clare Fell*, ed. P. J. Cherry (Kendal: Cumberland & Westmoreland Archaeological & Architectural Society, 2007), 1–23.
Shortland, Michael and Richard Yeo, *Telling Lives in Science: Essays on scientific biography* (Cambridge: Cambridge University Press, 1996).
Söderqvist, Thomas, 'Existential projects and existential choice in science: science biography as an edifying genre', in *Telling Lives in Science: Essays on scientific biography*, eds. Michael Shortland and Richard Yeo (Cambridge: Cambridge University Press, 1996), 45–84.
Söderqvist, Thomas, 'What is the use of writing lives of recent scientists', in *The Historiography of Contemporary Science, Technology, and Medicine: Writing recent science,* eds. Ronald E. Doel and Thomas Söderqvist (London–New York: Routledge, 2006), 99–127.
Söderqvist, Thomas, 'Introduction: A new look at the genre of scientific biography', in *The History and Poetics of Scientific Biography*, ed. Thomas Söderqvist (Aldershot: Ashgate, 2007), 1–15.
Stray, Christopher, '"Patriots and Professors": a century of Roman studies, 1910–2010', *Journal of Roman Studies* 100 (2010): 1–31.
Taylor, Margerie Venables, 'F. J. Haverfield', *Journal of the Chester & North Wales Archaeological & Historical Society* 23 (1920): 64–71.
Taylor, Margerie Venables, 'A bibliography of the published writings of Margerie Venables Taylor', *Journal of Roman Studies* 54 (1964): 2–6.
Taylor, Margerie Venables and Robin George Collingwood, 'Roman Britain in 1921 and 1922', *Journal of Roman Studies* 11 (1921): 200–44.
Times Archive, 'Miss M. V. Taylor', *The Times,* December 27, 1963, 10, *The Times Digital Archive.* Accessed May 24, 2018. http://tinyurl.galegroup.com/tinyurl/63mAC9.
Times Archive, 'The happy scholar', *The Times,* July 31, 1961, 13, *The Times Digital Archive.* Accessed May 24, 2018. http://tinyurl.galegroup.com/tinyurl/63mTV9.
Todd, Malcolm, 'The Haverfield Bequest, 1921–2000, and the study of Roman Britain', *Britannia* 34 (2003): 35–40.
Wallace-Hadrill, Andrew, *The British School at Rome: One hundred years* (London: British School at Rome, 2001).
Webster, Diana Bonakis, *Hawkeseye: The early life of Christopher Hawkes* (Stroud: Alan Sutton, 1991).
Wheeler, R. E. Mortimer, *Prehistoric and Roman Wales* (Oxford: Clarendon Press, 1925).
Wheeler, R. E. Mortimer, 'Review of *The Journal of Roman Studies* Vol. L (1960)', *Antiquity* 35 (June 1961): 157–59.

9
Father Alfred-Louis Delattre (1850–1932) versus Paul Gauckler (1866–1911): The struggle to control archaeology at Carthage at the turn of the twentieth century

Joann Freed

Introduction: The problem of a nationalist bias

Father Alfred-Louis Delattre (1850–1932) excavated Punic, Roman and Early Christian sites at Carthage in Tunisia for 50 years and preserved his finds in his own museum, today the Musée National de Carthage.[1] During his lifetime he was a respected member of the French academic community and his publications in scholarly and popular journals brought him fame. Yet today his massive contribution to the archaeology of Carthage is denigrated and to a great extent his publications are ignored. Reputable scholars today perpetuate this negative attitude thoughtlessly, as they do not understand its origin, while the first history of the archaeology of Carthage considered Delattre, whose contributions were fundamental, a problem too difficult to tackle.[2] My subject is the story behind Delattre's negative reception by modern archaeologists and historians.

Between 1892 and 1904, Paul Gauckler (1866–1911), the young head of the Tunisian Antiquities Service, faced off against Delattre, who was by then an experienced archaeologist excavating the Punic cemeteries of Carthage. Gauckler's attempts to unseat Delattre ended in disaster for Gauckler, although the political context would not have predicted this outcome. But today French scholars try to vindicate Gauckler and imply that Delattre was somehow in the wrong. This chapter responds to the claims of Gilbert Charles-Picard that Gauckler was the first scientific archaeologist in Tunisia and was driven out of his job because of his homosexuality,[3] and to the claims of Clémentine Gutron that Delattre as a Catholic priest was 'not really French', and that by doing archaeology in Tunisia, Delattre 'placed himself above the law'.[4] In fact, Delattre's rights were written into the Tunisian laws.[5] Charles-Picard, head of the Tunisian Antiquities Service from 1942–1955, repeated gossip from half a century earlier, but Gauckler's sexuality, for which there is no objective evidence, is a red herring. There is no evidence for Picard's claim that Gauckler used superior methodology, much less for the claim that Gauckler's sexual identity cost him his position: homosexuality was not illegal in France at the time.

Once the relevant events had been laid out chronologically, I found 'everything yet to explain'.[6] Where does this modern prejudice against Delattre originate? French nationalism was a major impetus for the archaeology of North Africa in the nineteenth century,[7] but certainly not all distortions in the history of archaeology stem from simple nationalism,[8] which Delattre and Gauckler both served. The French conflict between church and state was a crucial issue in the conflict between Delattre and Gauckler, but it does not completely explain the ongoing resentment against Delattre. In their day, colonialism united many interests; it was the last French national adventure in which the Catholic Church and the traditionally aristocratic army could equally participate.[9] Because colonialism increased France's international status and gave opportunities for the propagation of Catholic Christianity, certain churchmen, like Archbishop Lavigerie of Algiers, the founder of the White Fathers, of which Delattre was an early recruit, warmly supported it.[10] Today French colonialism seems unjustifiable, but both Delattre and Gauckler participated equally in that system.

Janet Malcolm stated that the biographer stands in quicksand, since new evidence, but even more 'the coming into fashion of a new ideology' may 'transform any character into a bad one'.[11] I argue that the resentment against Delattre originates in fixed ideas with such deep roots in French secular and republican identity that they ensure a negative evaluation of Delattre's work today.[12] The French Revolution attempted to destroy both the aristocratic level of French society and the Catholic Church. A century later the Third Republic, which followed the ousting of Emperor Napoleon III in 1870, imposed a moderate version of the ideals of the French Revolution. The new ideal of the meritocracy of French bureaucracy against the old aristocratic system necessarily led to denigration of the achievements of a Catholic priest in comparison to a properly appointed bureaucrat: this is an intensely French prejudice, questionable in societies that value religious freedom.

My theoretical approach to life-writing in archaeology

Biography 'provides a unique and powerful point of access' to the social structures that determine and affect archaeological work.[13] Biography is based on the concept that *individuals* do the work,[14] a concept that has survived heavy philosophical attack.[15] I agree with Marc-Antoine Kaeser that biography is microhistory.[16] The rules of historiography must apply, but I do not agree that history can be 'scientific'. Because as a biographer I must select and interpret, the history I write can only be *methodologically correct*. Biography tries to capture the subject's point of view, but it unavoidably superimposes the biographer's, which is also culturally determined. This chapter presents *my* view of a particular historical contretemps. No biography can be considered the final word, but life-writing can be more or less sophisticated and more or less aware of pitfalls.

Archaeological biography is a necessarily lengthy process that involves many layers of knowledge and judgment, including, at least implicitly, a grasp of research methodology and current theory. There is no professional programme of preparation in the history of archaeology.[17] Yet the required skill set is demanding and the work cannot be undertaken lightly. I have an ongoing research interest in Carthage as an archaeological site. Language training in French, Greek and Latin gave me an essential base. My dissertation prepared me to be a pottery analyst at Carthage in Tunisia with one of the Canadian UNESCO archaeological teams. Beginning in 1985, more than 20 years of six-week summer seasons at Carthage with several different excavations made me aware that Delattre's excavations over the half-century of his life as an archaeologist (from 1875–1932) formed the basis of most of what we then knew about Punic, Roman and Early Christian Carthage. In 1990 I participated in the reorganisation of the galleries of the Musée National de Carthage and, with the permission of then Site and Museum Director Abdelmajid Ennabli, I catalogued the amphoras that Delattre had excavated and preserved. This project gave me an insider's view of Delattre's museum and an understanding of how Delattre's finds relate to his publications.[18] Intrigued by the claim that Delattre's publications were unavailable, I began an annotated bibliography of his work, demonstrating that hundreds of Delattre's publications were in the best French academic journals.[19] I differ from Delattre in that I am not French, not a man, do not have a religious vocation, do not know Arabic, and do not have Delattre's prodigious energy and lifelong dedication to one place. These differences protect me from the temptation of confusing my subject with myself.[20]

No one has previously attempted a biography of Delattre.[21] The French reviewers of an early paper of mine on Delattre's archaeological methods encouraged me to consult the archives of the White Fathers in Rome. Delattre's publications both in professional journals and popular Catholic publications, as well as mission diaries he kept, his personal correspondence and obituaries in the archives, and notices in internal papers, formed the basis of a chronological timeline of his life. Delattre's life fell into three periods: his early life at Carthage, which ended with the death of Archbishop and Cardinal Lavigerie, was that of a young priest/adventurer (1875–1892). A middle phase as a mature, respected and popularly famous scholar (1892–1904) was followed by a third phase of almost 30 years committed to the excavation of Early Christian sites at Carthage (1904–1932).[22] Delattre's excavations built on the work of earlier archaeologists at Carthage, about which I wrote a book based on papers in the British National Archives. That work included a study of the topography of Carthage;[23] knowing the topography is essential to understanding Delattre's excavation results.

The importance of Delattre and Gauckler for the archaeology of Carthage

Delattre had the powerful advantage of living in the centre of the ruins of the ancient city of Carthage, the capital of the Punic Empire, the second city of the western Roman Empire, and the city that was home to Tertullian and Augustine. The site had been intensively robbed after the Arab conquest of AD 698 and was still being robbed when Delattre arrived. Much of his earliest archaeological work at Carthage had the character of rescue excavation – he was the first to know if a stone robber's pick hit something of special significance. His work on sites that were being destroyed or damaged preserved information and finds that would otherwise have been irretrievably lost. Delattre's excavations provided unique insights on elite Punic burials in shaft tombs; on the construction of the Roman city and on the slave administrators of the emperor, and finally on the layout of the church complexes of Early Christian Carthage.

Delattre is important, not for advances in methodology, although his methodology improved over his long career, but for the tremendous amount of evidence he unearthed, published and preserved in his museum – much of which would be impossible to excavate today, because the sites are covered by suburban housing. Delattre was a Catholic priest, an early member of the Society of Missionaries of Africa ('White Fathers'), but, largely due to the guidance of the founder of the society, Charles Martial Allemand-Lavigerie, Archbishop of Algiers, Delattre saw no conflict between science and religion. Lavigerie had the contacts in Paris, in scholars Ernest Renan and Léon Renier, for example, to get Delattre a grounding in epigraphic method;[24] ancient inscriptions had joined sculpture as the central interest in ancient material culture by the time Delattre arrived at Carthage in 1875. Delattre eventually provided thousands of inscriptions from his excavations (many of them epitaphs) to the editors of the major *corpora*,[25] which allowed many later scholars to use his finds and insights without crediting him. In his 'middle period', he carried on long-term excavation of sites such as the Punic cemeteries of Douïmès and 'near Sainte-Monique'. Delattre preserved his finds in the Musée National de Carthage, the museum he founded.[26]

In contrast, Gauckler, as director of the Tunisian Antiquities Service from 1892–1904, was responsible for the archaeology of the entire country. Gauckler began work at Carthage in 1895 and he and his subordinates excavated Punic, Roman and Early Christian sites in the city, often sites that had already been partially excavated by Delattre. Gauckler used the same methods as Delattre, published in the same scholarly journals, including the *Comptes rendus* of the Academy of Inscriptions, issued annual reports on the work of the Antiquities Service and preserved his finds in the Musée du Bardo in Tunis.

Three periods in Delattre's life as an archaeologist at Carthage

The young Delattre was a devout and obedient adventurer, who came to Carthage somewhat oblivious of the political use that Lavigerie was making of him. Lavigerie stationed Delattre at Carthage, where the Chapel of Saint Louis on 'the' Byrsa Hill was already a potent symbol of French and Catholic influence in Tunisia.[27] 'The' Byrsa was a historically over-determined site: Saint Louis, King Louis IX of France, a failed Crusader against Islam, met his death from plague there in AD 1270. The site was also the centre of Punic Carthage and, as we now know, it was the centre of the Roman city street grid.[28] The French, who had already controlled

Algeria for 50 years, seized Tunisia with minimal military losses during the invasion of 1881, and the government they imposed was a Protectorate, so Tunisia continued to be a sovereign country under a Bey.[29]

My subject is Delattre's middle period, from 1892–1904, in which his constant discoveries at Carthage provided the base for Punic archaeology. Although still a missionary, Delattre was also a diocesan priest and an archaeologist, excavating, publishing his finds in professional and popular journals, and running his museum. He was already famous, with many renowned, wealthy, and even royal visitors. In 1891 Delattre contributed 2,000 inscriptions to René Cagnat's North African supplement to the Corpus of Latin Inscriptions.[30] By the time his mentor Lavigerie died in 1892, Delattre was a mature professional of 42 and was planning an ambitious excavation on the south side of 'the' Byrsa at Carthage.[31]

Paul Gauckler arrived at Carthage as Inspector for the Tunisian Antiquities Service that same year. He was the second person in that role, appointed by the Bey of Tunis, subject to the French Resident General in Tunisia and to René du Coudray de la Blanchère, the first Director of the Tunisian Antiquities Service, with ties to the French Ministry of Public Instruction in Paris, which oversaw education and museums in Tunisia. Although Gauckler was just 26, he was a graduate of the prestigious École Normale Supérieure in Paris. A 'normal school' for the preparation of high-school teachers, it was in fact a cloistered institution for a very small number of academically elite young men preparing to teach in French lycées (academic high schools), who also had the best available preparation for writing a doctoral thesis. Gauckler was a practising Protestant and a leftist Republican, strongly opposed to the dominance of the Catholic Church in French political life.[32] His job gave him authority over Delattre and he was determined to carry on his own excavations at Carthage.[33]

By 1890 the French Third Republic, the first Republican government in Europe, had survived for two decades. Catholicism was seen as its major internal enemy, since French Catholics and surviving aristocrats often made common cause. During the years that Gauckler headed the Antiquities Service a rising wave of anticlericalism – that is, anti-Catholicism – in France encouraged Gauckler to believe that Delattre and the White Fathers could literally be expelled from Tunisia.[34]

Delattre's struggle with Gauckler wore him out during a period in which his archaeological discoveries increased exponentially while his missionary society gave him decreasing support. After more than a decade of conflict with Gauckler, Delattre decided in 1904 to narrow his field of endeavour, devoting himself to the early Christian Church at Carthage. This began the third and longest phase of his life as an archaeologist at Carthage, and the one with which he is most strongly identified.[35] By the time Delattre died in 1932, more than a quarter century later, many scholars were not aware of the earlier phases of his career.

Delattre's role as archaeologist and missionary

Lavigerie was no ordinary archbishop; a former professor of religion at the Sorbonne, he had a command of the political situation on an international scale. After France invaded Tunisia in 1881, Lavigerie controlled Catholic administration there as Cardinal, Archbishop of Carthage and Primate of Africa.[36] By 1892 the White Fathers had bought up about half of the ancient site of Carthage;[37] they built a seminary with space for Delattre's museum and a huge cathedral on the summit of the Byrsa. Lavigerie had appointed Delattre archpriest of the Cathedral well before construction was complete. The Cathedral of Carthage was a French and aristocratic as well as a Catholic symbol, paid for by Saint Louis's direct descendants.[38] Delattre's enterprise was in flagrant opposition to the ideals of the French Revolution and to the secular rule of a bourgeois meritocracy, the ideal of the Third Republic.

Delattre wanted to devote significant time to archaeology and convinced Lavigerie to mobilise the necessary resources.[39] Lavigerie's decision was not made out of pure reverence for 'science'. A museum or collection was a modern European concept, and Lavigerie wanted to plant French culture in this Muslim country. Lavigerie also saw that the mission at Saint Louis could earn a fame that would support his other projects, the most important of which was converting sub-Saharan Africa to Catholic Christianity.[40] Archaeology also gave Lavigerie's men another outlet for their energies, since, although White Fathers were missionaries, in Tunisia they could not legally proselytise. Some of his fellow missionaries resented Delattre's intellectual interest in Carthage. Throughout his life, Delattre struggled to keep two conflicting identities in balance: the modest Catholic missionary persona he never abandoned and the circumstantially determined persona of famous archaeologist. As an archaeologist, he acted in his own interest. He built a museum with fabulous finds,[41] and he wanted to keep those finds under his own control. Since spiritual self-evaluation was a regular part of his priestly life, and even of his day, he was well aware of an internal conflict.[42]

The organisation of archaeological research in colonial Tunisia

Even before the French controlled Tunisia, Lavigerie brought Delattre's interest in archaeology to the attention of the Academy of Inscriptions in Paris. As soon as the French invasion was underway, he published a 64-page 'letter' that asked their support for Delattre at Carthage, which a committee headed by Ernest Renan was happy to approve.[43] Nearly all of the French intellectuals Delattre regularly worked with were eventually elected to one of the 55 chairs of the Academy of Inscriptions, an exclusive self-elected club of the highest ranking Parisian academics, which met weekly to hear presentations on academic work. Academicians had extraordinary status in France; they are the 'Immortals', guaranteed a substantial obituary by a fellow Academician. About one-quarter of the members of the Academy were Classicists, ancient historians or archaeologists; they all supported Delattre, whose work appeared regularly in their *Comptes rendus*.

Already in the 1880s, the French established an infrastructure that supported archaeology in Tunisia from Paris. During the first years following the French invasion of Tunisia in 1881, young French archaeologists René Cagnat and Salomon Reinach, both graduates of the École Normale, advised Paul Cambon, the French Resident General in Tunisia, and Xavier Charmes, a brilliant young bureaucrat at the French Ministry of Public Instruction, on the creation of laws protecting antiquities in Tunisia.[44] With the approval of the Bey, Resident Cambon founded an Antiquities Service in Tunisia, 67 years before France got something similar in 1942.[45] He also appointed its first Director, the young René du Coudray de la Blanchère, another graduate of the École Normale.[46] Cagnat, Reinach and La Blanchère were members of the new Commission for North Africa in Paris, which organised and encouraged publication of archaeology in Tunisia, whether by professionals or amateurs, including soldiers and priests.[47] Delattre had avoided directing the newly created Bardo Museum in Tunis, although he was acting head until La Blanchère's appointment, preferring to concentrate on Carthage, the 'pearl' of Tunisian sites. The year 1888 was a particularly brilliant one for Delattre; his friend Antoine Héron de Villefosse, curator at the Louvre and newly elected to the Academy of Inscriptions, brought three distinguished Academicians to see Delattre when they attended the opening of the Bardo Museum: they were Henri Wallon, known as the 'Father of the Republic' for his contribution to the constitution of the Republic; archaeologist of the Holy Land and diplomat, the Marquis de Vogüé, and Georges Perrot, Director of the École Normale.[48]

Education in Republican France and the role of the École Normale

After the defeat of Napoleon III in the Franco-Prussian War in 1870, followed by the revolutionary 'Paris Commune', France was governed by the Third Republic, a moderate and constitutional version of the ideals of the French Revolution. The Third Republic prioritised individual merit and secular education to improve the intellectual level of the citizenry and provide a structure in which individual excellence could be demonstrated. From 1883, Minister of Public Instruction Jules Ferry imposed compulsory secular primary education for all French children. His drive to educate the French nation in accordance with Republican ideals hit the Catholic Church hard; the Jesuits were driven out of France and many Catholic teaching orders were forced to disband.[49]

Under the Third Republic an elite system of education was established for the top one per cent of students. The middle class ('bourgeois') young men who came through this rigid system to achieve a bureaucratic or teaching post by personal merit strongly identified with the Republican system.[50] Most of Delattre's archaeological colleagues were graduates of the École Normale. René Cagnat, who had the greatest influence on French archaeology in Tunisia in this period, was a *normalien*, as were Academician Georges Perrot, and other colleagues of Delattre: Salomon Reinach; La Blanchère, and younger scholars Paul Gauckler, Paul Monceaux, Stéphane Gsell and Jules Toutain. These young men had the best preparation in France for the doctorate and university teaching in Classics, history or geography. In Delattre's day the École Normale also produced a high proportion of French government ministers, journalists and bureaucrats.[51]

About 25 brilliant young men entered the arts programme of the Normale annually, publicly ranked by exam both on entry and graduation. The Normale gave a three-year university course in a closed boarding school – a hothouse for intellectual development, with a tradition that graduates supported each other without question. The atmosphere also supported homosexual interests: Salomon Reinach's youthful journal described his emotional love affairs there (although he described himself as a virgin), as well as those of his fellow *normalien* René de la Blanchère.[52]

Discreet homosexuality was not a criminal offence in France and did not preclude a successful career.

In the period when Delattre was in conflict with Gauckler, Delattre's warmest and most loyal friend in Paris was Antoine Héron de Villefosse, conservator at the Louvre and a devout Catholic. Villefosse had trained at the École des Chartes: when Delattre's problems with Gauckler erupted, Villefosse feared the powerful cabal that the École Normale represented. Delattre, in contrast, had attended Catholic seminary in Rouen. A seminary education at the time was the equivalent of a three-year undergraduate degree, oriented to the Classics, like the École Normale, but at a lower standard; on the other hand, it was a much higher education than the national norm. This was not the end of Delattre's education: in the 1880s Delattre was also coached by Archbishop and Cardinal Lavigerie, and by Léon Renier, an Academician who had made the first collection of Latin inscriptions in Algeria.[53] René Cagnat, two years younger than Delattre but already in 1887 professor at the Collège de France, the most prestigious university in Paris, also advised Delattre.

Competition and conflict between Delattre and Gauckler

The events of the conflict between Gauckler and Delattre play like a tennis match with equally matched opponents. Paul Gauckler had worked under La Blanchère for two years in Algeria before La Blanchère sent him to Tunisia in 1892. I believe La Blanchère chose the 26-year-old Gauckler over Jules Toutain, La Blanchère's able assistant and the natural incumbent, because he thought of Gauckler as not likely to accomplish much. Gauckler's opinion of himself, as third in his graduating class at the École Normale, was much higher. In the letter accepting his new post he also declared himself a Protestant, a coded way of announcing his radical Republican sympathies. Gauckler arrived in Tunisia as Inspector, still under the thumb of La Blanchère and with a ridiculously tiny budget of 2,400 francs per annum to cover archaeological expenses for the entire country.[54] When La Blanchère headed the Service, from 1884 until his departure in 1892, he had had a budget of 30–40,000 francs, paid for by France.[55] During Salomon Reinach and Ernest Babelon's major excavations at Carthage in March and April of 1884, their workmen cost them 8,000 French francs.[56] Gauckler might have been able to hire 10 unskilled men full-time on this annual budget, but he needed a draftsman, site supervisors, museum guards and conservators as well. Gauckler soon found he could not excavate at Carthage because the

Catholic diocese owned the land and Delattre was entrenched there, and this greatly displeased him. He immediately ordered a map of Carthage from the Tunisian topographic services with diocesan ownership marked.[57] But Gauckler had the good sense to get experience as an archaeologist before directly confronting Delattre. From 1893–1895 he excavated at Oudna, where he acquired a passionate but then unfashionable interest in mosaics.[58]

Delattre's unbelievably successful excavations at Carthage in 1893 include the discovery of bas-reliefs of Victory and Abundance on Byrsa Hill;[59] the 'First Amphora Wall', which dated completion of the Roman re-engineering of the Byrsa Hill to post 15 BCE,[60] and new excavations in the Archaic period Punic necropolis of Douïmès. In November 1894, Delattre read a paper on his excavations at Douïmès at the Academy of Inscriptions in Paris;[61] during these years he received between 3,000 and 6,000 francs from the Academy every year for excavations at Carthage.

Already in May 1893, after six months as Inspector, Gauckler instituted a pattern of ungracious behaviour. He did not inform Delattre about a visit from Raymond Poincaré, the Minister of Public Instruction and later twice Prime Minister of France. Poincaré and his entourage visited Delattre's museum anyway and honoured Delattre by making him an Officer of the Ministry of Public Instruction.[62] Gauckler spent his summers in France; in the summer of 1893 a series of negative articles about Catholic dominance in the archaeology of Tunisia appeared in the Tunisian press. The articles reflected ideas Gauckler shared with Salomon Reinach, who had excavated at Carthage 10 years earlier, but had little effect on public opinion.[63]

In 1894 Gauckler presented a list of 19 monuments at Carthage, 10 owned by the Catholic diocese, to be controlled by the Antiquities Service. Xavier Charmes at the French Ministry of Public Instruction did not approve, and a year later just three of the 19 sites Gauckler had proposed for classification at Carthage were approved by the Tunisian government: the summit of 'the' Byrsa; the basilica of Damous el-Karita, and the Punic necropolis on Bordj-Djedid, but this did not impede Delattre's excavation on these sites. Meanwhile a group of French and Tunisian intellectuals founded the Institut de Carthage at Tunis and a scholarly journal, *Revue tunisienne*; Gauckler's support for this group was less than lukewarm. Salomon Reinach, Gauckler's friend and fellow graduate of the École Normale, visited Tunis and lectured at the Institut de Carthage, expressing his annoyance that the White Fathers owned 'the' Byrsa Hill and had built on it,[64] but again, this protest had no effect.

A new French Resident General, René Millet, arrived in January 1895. Millet, also a *normalien*, was influenced by Gauckler's arguments against Delattre, but wanted Gauckler to publish on hydrology, applying ancient science to modern colonial problems. Gauckler objected, and his insubordination stressed his relations with Millet.[65] When Resident Millet then visited Delattre's museum, Millet not only promised Delattre his total support, but made it clear he did so as a good Catholic.

In 1895 the new Archbishop of Carthage, Monsignor Combes, dedicated a chapel in the central trench of the amphitheatre to commemorate the martyrdom of Perpetua and Felicity; Delattre approved this Catholic misuse of an archaeological site. Gauckler was in trouble with the French Ministry of Public Instruction in April for 'temporising' over Resident Millet's demand that he produce reports on Roman hydrology, but the Resident defended him.[66] At the end of April, Gauckler apologised to René Cagnat for some unguarded outburst. Perhaps Gauckler had learned that Cagnat was planning an official publication of Delattre's museum; by the time it appeared, in 1899, Delattre's museum contained more than 100,000 objects.[67]

Delattre was at the apogee of his worldly success in 1895. The Centenary of the Institut de France, the home of all five French Academies, took place on 25 October 1895 and Delattre was invited. He saw many friends in Paris, as he had at least 14 academic patrons at the Academy of Inscriptions. He was invited to the Chateau of Chantilly, home of the Duke d'Aumale,[68] who had presented his chateau to the Institute. Meanwhile, Gauckler opened his first excavation at Carthage at Bir es-Zitoun, near where Delattre had dug cemeteries of Roman slave administrators on the west side of the ancient city. After working there briefly, Gauckler irritably returned the site to Delattre early in 1896, saying Delattre had more money for excavation.[69] Jules Toutain, Gauckler's contemporary at the École Normale, finished his two doctoral theses on North Africa in 1895; Gauckler never finished his doctorate, which wasn't required of him, but would have spoken in his favour.

In April 1896 the French Learned Societies met in Tunis, and Gauckler organised the sessions on archaeology. Many distinguished French Academicians attended. Gauckler, working hard to make a good impression, wrote a brief guide to the Bardo Museum at this time.[70] The Bardo had consisted of only two rooms until 1896, but Gauckler now opened three new rooms with mosaics. But Delattre was made a Knight of the Legion of Honour at the opening of the Congress and Gauckler had to make the congratulatory speech.[71]

In June 1896, a military doctor, Louis Carton, who had a strong publication record as an amateur archaeologist in Tunisia, wrote to

Resident Millet that Gauckler's qualifications were weak and offered to take over his position. This is the earliest sign of Carton's active opposition to Gauckler. Although Carton's offer never became generally known, Gauckler knew of it, because Resident Millet showed him the letter.[72]

Gauckler becomes Director of the Tunisian Antiquities Service

Then came a stunning event: La Blanchère, the absentee Director of the Tunisian Antiquities Service, died unexpectedly in Paris, the victim of a sore throat. With the support of René Cagnat, Gauckler was appointed Director, and also got control of the Bardo. The 30-year-old Gauckler now had the base to achieve his ambitions, and he immediately sent his first *Marche du Service* report to the printer; in it he said that Delattre's museum did not have room for the objects Delattre was finding.[73]

At the end of 1896, the Academy of Inscriptions and the Ministry of Public Instruction began work on an accurate topographic map of Carthage, known today as the Bordy map. The project was entrusted to Delattre, but by January Gauckler had hijacked it. Engineer Bordy, a good Catholic, consulted with both, but became a devoted friend to Delattre. René Cagnat collaborated on the map from Paris as Secretary of the Commission for North Africa. In 1898 Gauckler and Delattre were sent copies to add their notes; Gauckler announced that he would add all the information necessary. Fortunately Cagnat knew better, and Bordy, a determined supporter of Delattre, ensured that Delattre's name and notes were also on the plan when it finally appeared.[74]

In January 1897, Delattre's close friend Antoine Héron de Villefosse was elected annual President of the Academy of Inscriptions. Paul Monceaux, a *normalien* and rising young scholar, began to collaborate with Delattre on early Christian North Africa and Monceaux's brilliance made early Christianity an attractive subject to other scholars.[75] Gauckler immediately dug at Delattre's old excavations at the Christian basilica of Damous el-Karita and lifted mosaics from another basilica, Bir Ftouha. In the autumn Jules Toutain catalogued the Roman lamps at Delattre's museum; Toutain became a firm friend of Delattre.

The threat to move Delattre's museum

Delattre experienced Gauckler's third major effort to undermine him in 1898, when Resident Millet announced that he wanted to move Delattre's museum from the mission's headquarters on Byrsa Hill to the quarantine hospital near the ports at Carthage.[76] Millet argued this would be a good thing since Delattre could die at any time; Delattre was only 47, but, after all, La Blanchère had recently died suddenly at 43. Delattre was very worried for the first six months of this year. Because Gauckler said Delattre's museum was too crowded, Delattre got backing from his Superior, Mgr Livinhac, to take over the old refectory, doubling his museum's size. In June Resident Millet visited, and a week later he assured Delattre that he had given up his plan of moving the museum.

Gauckler's budget improved greatly in 1898; the Tunisian government increased his grant and the French Ministry of Public Instruction gave him 10,000 francs per year. In his *Marche du Service*, Gauckler claimed credit for Delattre's new discoveries at the Punic necropolis on Bordj-Djedid, as well as the subvention Delattre had received to excavate the amphitheatre, and repeated that Delattre's museum was so crowded that his finds could not be catalogued. Gauckler meanwhile told fellow administrators that he intended to impose 'a spirit of subordination' on archaeology in Tunisia.[77]

Delattre complained about Gauckler's machinations to his friend Héron de Villefosse. In May 1898, Delattre received a magisterial letter from René Cagnat, who wrote:

> Our rule has always been to leave you master of the terrain of Carthage, because it was yours before any of us set foot in Tunisia, because you have conquered it by your labour, and because we think the land is large enough that it is not useful to get in one another's way.[78]

Delattre had the right man on his side, because Cagnat was able to control the situation from Paris. But despite Cagnat's awareness that Gauckler was not behaving in a reasonable or even normal way, he continued to support him. In the meantime Delattre was able to excavate and Gauckler had not succeeded in taking Delattre's museum from him.[79] But after six years of psychological warfare, Delattre had built up a backlog of incomprehension, resentment and fear, evident from his disturbed handwriting and inarticulate and incomplete drafts of appeals to his friends.[80]

It is not hard to understand why Gauckler resented Delattre's control over archaeology at Carthage. Furthermore Gauckler ordinarily arrogated the work of all archaeologists in Tunisia to himself and could be forgiven for doing so in his *Marche du Service*. His quick work at getting his name on the Bordy map might be construed positively by those who admire a 'smooth operator'. But his desire to destroy Delattre and take over Delattre's museum had no chance of approval from Ali Bey and his family members, who knew and supported Delattre, from the French administration in Tunisia, members of the Academy of Inscriptions and the Commission for North Africa, or from the larger public in both Tunisia and France, especially those French Catholics who read *Missions catholiques* and *Cosmos*, in which Delattre published constantly. Gauckler's support came from a narrower base: he had friends at the École Normale, the Academy of Inscriptions and the Commission for North Africa, and his funding came from the French Ministry of Public Instruction, but he owed his job to the Bey, and was supervised by the Resident General, which made him a direct concern of the French Ministry of Foreign Affairs.

In the autumn of 1898 Gauckler requested money from the Academy of Inscriptions, competing directly with Delattre, who had already received 5,000 francs for excavation in the amphitheatre. Happily, the Academy was able to give each of them 3,000 francs. While Delattre worked in peace for the rest of 1898, Gauckler was complaining bitterly about his restricted budget, although it was now almost ten times larger than it had been in 1892. In January 1899, Gauckler moved into excavation at Carthage on a larger scale, opening a long trench beside Delattre's old trench at Douïmès. He soon discovered a treasure of Roman sculpture under the 'Maison de la Cachette' and excavated other Roman houses, a Christian basilica and a late Punic kiln.[81] His assistants dug on the Odeon Hill and at Roman tombs south of the Carthage ports.

In February Gauckler invited Delattre to tour the Bardo Museum with him and a visiting Cardinal. Although Gauckler had headed the Tunisian Antiquities Service for the past seven years, he had never previously invited Delattre to the Bardo. Delattre had sent Gauckler a friendly letter on his first appointment, and Gauckler sent Delattre his annual letters of permission and visited the Museum of Saint Louis occasionally, but there was no friendship between Gauckler and Delattre, and not even a good facsimile of collegiality.

For the rest of 1899 Gauckler was planning Tunisian exhibits for the Universal Exposition in Paris, but Delattre now shied away from cooperating with him. Gauckler's health was poor and he was often home in bed. But he had help from his assistants Louis Drappier at Carthage and Eugène Sadoux and Louis Poinssot at Dougga, while Bertrand Pradère was excavating the Temple of Caelestis and the Capitolium at Dougga. The competitive Dr Carton was also excavating the theatre there, to Gauckler's disgust.[82] Young volunteers, whom Gauckler encouraged, especially military men, were excavating as many as 20 other sites in Tunisia.

Gauckler's career successes

In 1899 Gauckler got full control of funds for excavation in Tunisia,[83] but the Academy funded Delattre directly after Héron de Villefosse pointed out that it was humiliating for the older and more experienced Delattre to have to ask Gauckler for funding. Villefosse pressured Delattre for exciting finds. In January 1900 Gauckler visited Delattre's museum with Resident Millet and his wife, both now Delattre's firm friends; they were accompanied by historian Gabriel Hanotaux, recently French Minister of Foreign Affairs.[84] Gauckler was still at odds with Millet and probably wanted to be there for damage control. Delattre was digging in the Punic necropolis 'near Sainte-Monique' on Bordj-Djedid, and Gauckler was worried that his own finds were not spectacular enough. But early in 1900 Gauckler was able to remove Dr Carton from Dougga, having convinced Louis Liard at the Ministry of Public Instruction that Dougga was an excellent site for students from the French School at Rome, who could not dig in Italy, Greece or Turkey because these countries sharply limited foreign excavation.[85]

The Paris Exposition opened in April 1900 and Gauckler's exhibits were impressive.[86] Gauckler's annual funding just from the French Ministry of Public Instruction was doubled to 20,000 francs because the Tunisian exhibition earned so much money. But Gauckler was more arrogant and insubordinate than ever; Resident Millet was so angry with him that he removed him from the Tunisian governing council and tried to cut him off from the Ministry of Public Instruction in Paris.[87] Through Gauckler's deliberate negligence no one got credit for their contributions to the Paris exhibition but Gauckler – who won a major grand prize, a silver medal for his workshop that produced traditional Arab stucco, a grand prize for scientific missions and a gold medal as collaborator. Gauckler wrote a defensive letter to Delattre: it was not just Delattre, but also Stéphane Gsell in Algeria; amateur archaeologists Dr Carton and Captain Hannézo in Tunisia; architect Henri Saladin, who was Cagnat's close friend, and others, who got no recognition.[88] But Gauckler's skin was saved for the moment, when Resident Millet was recalled from Tunisia over an unrelated issue.

French separation of Church and State

In 1901 there was a tremendous political backlash against the Catholic Church in France as fallout from the Dreyfus Affair. An innocent Jewish army officer, Lieutenant-Colonel Alfred Dreyfus, had been convicted of treason through the duplicity of a fellow officer inside the traditionally Catholic French army. When in 1898 Zola's newspaper story 'J'accuse' aroused international attention, it divided French public opinion. France could not afford to discredit her army. Many Catholics had attacked Dreyfus as a traitor before all the facts were known, and a leftist Republican government now made the Catholic Church the scapegoat.[89] In March Gauckler wrote an impromptu angry letter to the centrist *Dépêche tunisienne* attacking the Catholics, and the newspaper published it. He then apologised to Delattre, saying that illness had caused him to be intemperate.

In 1901 Gauckler's assistant Louis Drappier discovered an impressive cache of Roman statues in the cisterns of the Odeon, while Delattre started finding late Classical marble sarcophagi in Punic graveshafts on Bordj-Djedid. In July French Prime Minister Waldeck-Rousseau proposed the 'Law of Associations', aimed to remove Catholic religious congregations from all teaching. As if in response, Delattre was promoted to Commander of Nicham-Iftikhar (the Tunisian 'Order of Glory') by Ali Bey, an honour approved by the French Resident. The White Fathers had to request authorisation for their existence from the French government and the decision hung fire for six months. Looking for popular validation, Fathers Delattre and Vellard wrote a new edition of their Carthage guidebook and Delattre published a memoir of his work.[90] Delattre was still excavating at Bordj-Djedid, and Villefosse again pressed him for spectacular finds.

At the end of 1901 a new and highly competent Resident General, Stephen Pichon, another *normalien* and a radical Republican, arrived in Tunisia and immediately visited Delattre's museum. In January 1902 only five male Congregations, including the White Fathers, were authorised to exist in France; more than 50 Congregations were not authorised and 20,000 men with religious vocations were expelled from France.[91] But the White Fathers were protected because their work supported France in colonial Africa.

By this time Alfred Merlin, a graduate of the École Normale, Fellow at the French School at Rome, and soon to marry René Cagnat's daughter, was excavating at Dougga, nominally under Gauckler's supervision, while amateur archaeologists were working all over Tunisia. Then Dr Louis Carton had his military posting changed from France to Sousse in Tunisia. In June 1902 Carton organised the Sousse Archaeological Society, establishing himself as the expert archaeologist in the south of the country.[92] And after Villefosse's emphasising that Delattre needed extraordinary finds because of the competition, Delattre discovered eight

Hellenistic marble sarcophagi in the late Punic necropolis on Bordj-Djedid in 1902, including four spectacular anthropoid sarcophagi.[93]

President of France Émile Loubet visited Delattre at Carthage in April 1903, and Minister of Foreign Affairs Théophile Delcassé also visited the Bardo. Meanwhile the new Prime Minister of France Émile Combes,[94] a former Catholic seminarian, but now a leftist radical, was trying to break the century-old French Concordate with the Vatican,[95] by which, in 1801, Napoleon had agreed to the free practice of Catholicism and to paying bishops and clergy, in return for a veto on the appointment of bishops and the agreement of the clergy to a civil oath of allegiance to him.[96] Rumours again said the White Fathers might be expelled from Tunisia. In the summer Gauckler, in France on vacation, sent a confidential report to Salomon Reinach proposing a hostile takeover of Delattre's museum.[97] In the autumn a journalist attacked the White Fathers' ownership of their museum in the French press, but a member of the Chamber of Deputies in Paris rose up to accuse Gauckler of being behind the attack; naturally Gauckler felt persecuted. In December Gauckler visited Delattre, telling him openly that his museum was easily worth a million francs and *must* belong to the state.[98]

Gauckler's removal and the White Fathers' renewed authorisation

The story now hurried to its climax. In January 1904 Gauckler sent Delattre a letter of authorisation as usual, but to both, expropriation of Delattre's museum seemed likely. But then Gauckler learned that the Tunisian government had slashed his budget, despite the fact that in his 12 years in Tunisia he had increased the Bardo's exhibition space from two to 23 rooms, many filled with mosaics. Undaunted, Gauckler proposed the expropriation of the Roman theatre of Carthage, which belonged to the Catholic Diocese. But Gauckler continually ignored the autonomy of Tunisia, offending the Bey and the Resident. Resident Pichon now informed the French Ministry of Public Instruction that the Residency had given Gauckler 36,000 francs over the past five years; this was clearly a protest. Louis Liard and Charles Bayet in Paris immediately expressed their continued support for Gauckler. By March 1904, both Gauckler and Delattre were showing signs of severe strain: Gauckler's comments in a letter to Louis Liard suggested mental illness[99] and for the first time Delattre felt overburdened with work and increased his spiritual reliance on the Virgin.

In June 1904, Dr Carton's military unit was moved from Sousse to La Goulette, five kilometres from Carthage; from then until his death in 1924 Carton too focused on excavation at Carthage.[100] In July France and the Vatican broke off the Napoleonic Concordate. Fathers Delattre and Vellard made a strategic visit to their friend and neighbour, the new Bey Mohammed.[101] Young scholar Alfred Merlin, who was cataloguing inscriptions at Delattre's museum, began a warm friendship with Delattre. At the end of August the White Fathers received authorisation for the second time, a blow to Gauckler's hopes for their expulsion from Tunisia. In November Delattre was in Rome for a Catholic congress on the Virgin Mary, as 1904 was the fiftieth anniversary of the dogma of her immaculate conception. There Cardinal Rampolla urged Delattre to finish a book on the earliest evidence for the Virgin in North Africa.[102] This was the beginning of the third and longest phase of Delattre's career, in which the early Christian church became his major concern.

By the end of 1904 Gauckler feared that Cagnat and Saladin, his fellow *normaliens*, as well as the influential Héron de Villefosse, had turned against him.[103] Gauckler sent Delattre his annual authorisation and a collegial letter on 31 December 1904, but Gauckler was in fact ill with exhaustion, abdominal upset and laryngitis. In mid-January Émile Combes's violently anti-Catholic government was forced to resign, but Combes's legislation remained under discussion. At the same moment, Gauckler was asked to justify the large subventions he had received from the Ministry of Public Instruction. In February, attacks on Gauckler's archaeological administration appeared in newspapers at Sousse, almost certainly planted by Dr Carton.

Now Gauckler really began to behave badly. Dr Carton announced a jaunt to the Christian Basilica at Uppenna with his Sousse Archaeological Society; Gauckler flatly denied permission. On Valentine's Day 1905, Gauckler prevented Resident Pichon and French Minister of Justice Ernest Vallé from meeting with Delattre. Not long after, Gauckler arranged a meeting between his assistant Ernest Sadoux and Delattre and Catholic administrator Monsignor Tournier at Uppenna, 100 kilometres from Carthage by an all-day train trip; the Fathers prepared a backup plan, which came in handy, because Sadoux did not meet them, and Gauckler's apology, blaming Sadoux, made no sense.[104]

At the end of February 1905, an attack on Gauckler appeared in *L'Avenir du centre*, a newspaper in Sousse. Another newspaper reported a vote of censure against the Tunisian Antiquities Service, sent to Resident Pichon in Tunisia and to the Learned Societies in France, that is, to Héron de Villefosse, the organiser that year.[105] This attack was probably written by Dr Carton; Villefosse already knew Carton was deeply bitter about Gauckler's control of archaeology in Tunisia. But on 19 March the government debate on the separation of church and state began; Gauckler still had reason to hope that he would prevail against Delattre.

In April 1905 the French Learned Societies, chaired by Héron de Villefosse, met in Algiers. Gauckler headed a session and his patrons from the French Ministry of Public Instruction were there. On 3 May Héron de Villefosse was at Carthage visiting Delattre; Dr Carton and his wife had asked to be included. Just in time for many visiting Parisian dignitaries to see it, an attack on Gauckler appeared in *La Tunisie française*, with another in the moderate *Dépêche tunisienne* the next day. These stories attacked Gauckler's arrogance in running the Antiquities Service; they said nothing about his sexual preferences.[106] To demonstrate their support, Gauckler's friends in the Ministry of Public Instruction at Paris immediately sent him his annual subvention of 20,000 francs.[107]

Gauckler left Tunisia for Paris before the end of May 1905, perhaps a bit earlier than usual for his annual summer vacation. In June he presented a paper to the Commission for North Africa in Paris, and in July he addressed the Academy of Inscriptions, still as Director of the Tunisian Antiquities Service. In July the 'Law of Separation' was ratified, concluding the separation of the Catholic Church from the republican state of France: good news for Gauckler. But meanwhile one of Gauckler's archaeological volunteers, Commander Ordioni, learned that Gauckler had been confronted in Paris with some misdemeanour; Ordioni hoped 'nothing more will come up'. The draft of a letter of Charles Bayet in the French National Archives suggests that Gauckler had already been asked to resign.[108]

During the months in which Gauckler's status was in limbo, only Georges Perrot, of his fellow *normaliens*, wrote a letter of support for him;[109] *normaliens* Cagnat, Reinach, Toutain, Gsell and Monceaux did nothing. In October René Cagnat's son-in-law, Alfred Merlin, replaced Gauckler as Director of the Tunisian Antiquities Service; the announcement came from Resident Pichon. The appointment was approved by Prime Minister of France Maurice Rouvier, who was also Minister of Foreign Affairs. Rouvier knew both Delattre and Gauckler personally as he had been Resident General in Tunisia from 1892–1894. The appointment of Merlin forced Gauckler to resign.

Resident Pichon had written to Prime Minister Rouvier saying: 'Following incidents about which I verbally informed the department ...', implying it was unsuitable to put these into writing.[110] So the decisive matter in Gauckler's downfall is unknown. As far as we can tell, his misdemeanours were not criminal. The fact that he was not appointed elsewhere is disturbing, however, as he had a right to an appropriate appointment as a graduate of the École Normale. His use of his funding may have been an issue. Gauckler was not helped by his difficult personality: charming with supporters on a good day, he could range from being obnoxious, to making those around him fear he was mentally ill, and perhaps stress caused him to devolve into clinical paranoia. When Alfred Merlin arrived as the new Director, Tunisians were delighted, if confused by Gauckler's unexplained departure. Merlin supported Delattre and his museum and continued to excavate at Carthage in the context of a warm friendship between the two men.

On 9 December 1905 the separation of church and state was enforced in France, and because of the new Pope's intransigence, all Catholic Church property, including Delattre's former seminary in Rouen, was confiscated, and 42,000 French priests were no longer paid by the state.[111] In France today, the principal of *'laïcité'* ('secularism' in the special French sense of freedom *from* religion in the public domain) is defended by law.[112] Yet because of political expediency, in Tunisia in 1905 no church property was confiscated, none of the remaining members of religious orders and societies were expelled, and diocesan priests were paid as before. What actually occurred in Tunisia was not what 'should' have occurred; the events that had such long-term effects for Delattre and Gauckler require very close analysis.[113]

Conclusion: A fairer evaluation

In this chapter my subject is a conflict between an archaeologist whose primary identification was religious (Delattre), who was supported by an international religious institution (the Catholic Church) and an international public, against an archaeologist of primarily nationalist identification (Gauckler), who fought for his peculiarly French view of professionalism within a bureaucratic system that selects for excellence. Both men were generously funded by institutions of their national government for political reasons. Their work supported the colonialist cause, which aggrandised France by exploiting the resources of a weaker country. Both men were intensely committed to building museums and conserving and interpreting their finds, and both were intellectually supported by prestigious intellectual associations and published by prestigious national academic journals. Both men used the same rather slapdash excavation methods of their times and both could be accused of antiquarianism in their enthusiasm for objects.

The conflict between Gauckler and Delattre was a French conflict that took place on Tunisian soil. Gauckler was ambitious to control the archaeology of Tunisia, but his conflict with Delattre was more basic. Gauckler fiercely upheld the secular principles of the French Third Republic. He never accepted that Tunisia was a sovereign country with different interests from those of France. The existence of Delattre's museum suggested that French Catholics could make an important intellectual contribution outside the bureaucratic system, an idea that Gauckler rejected. The final outcome was a tragic defeat for Gauckler, whose life and career were ruined by his dismissal; he took his own life in Rome in December 1911.

Gauckler excavated multiple sites in Tunisia and filled the Bardo Museum with mosaics, but he did not do the job he was hired to do, which was to coordinate the work of *all* amateur and professional archaeologists in Tunisia and facilitate publication of their finds. Father Delattre survived because everybody – scholars, ministers of government, and a raft of the rich and famous – knew and liked him personally. In addition, he was there first, six years before the French occupation; his museum and his discoveries were famous; his work supported that of other scholars; his work enhanced the image of France, and the Catholic Church was crucial to French colonial control in Tunisia. But Delattre did his greatest volume of work in the period in which he was under constant pressure from Gauckler. Both made tremendously important finds and the archaeology of Carthage owes a great deal to both.

Why then do the French today praise Gauckler and denigrate Delattre? The opinions I cited in the introduction of this chapter come from Gilbert Charles-Picard and Clémentine Gutron, both successful French bureaucrats, and their opinions are highly politicised. Over the past two centuries, the French have suffered many blows to their national identity and amour-propre. In the twentieth century imperialism and colonialism were discredited. While the Revolution had violently rejected monarchy, aristocracy and the Catholic Church a century before the conflict between Delattre and Gauckler, these threats to revolutionary ideals continually resurfaced. France actively rejected the Empire of Napoleon III when Delattre was a very young man; the separation of church and state at the turn of the twentieth century was another win for the ideals of the Revolution. The French Revolution is the great watershed that led to republicanism, secularism and the reward of individual merit. Under the Third Republic this meant the ascendancy of the bourgeoisie in a bureaucratic government based on a meritocracy of intellect. For the highly educated French, Gauckler is on the right side of history and Delattre, a Catholic priest, is not.

The conflict between priest and bureaucrat had a reputational winner in the short run (Delattre) and a reputational winner in the long run (Gauckler), but for both men their achievements have largely fallen into oblivion despite the importance of their discoveries, because archaeologists have avoided using their body of work. Gauckler produced important publications on Carthage after his forced departure. Delattre's and Gauckler's publications are no longer difficult to find,[114] and are supported by the accessibility of their finds in their respective museums. And, as Givens pointed out, 'the depth of the archaeological past is relatively shallow';[115] the discoveries of these earlier archaeologists are still relevant. Theories of biography in archaeology have emphasised the importance of individuals, the pressure of nationalist agendas and the guidance of international congresses in deciding the histories that will prevail. But biography also reveals the factor of complicated human interactions, with mixed motives, philosophical, political and personal, and with repercussions that encourage disregard of archaeological data.[116] Archaeologists are not historians: they can benefit from the biographer's revelation of this type of historical bias.

Notes

1 I have used Delattre's papers in the Archives of the White Fathers (Archivio dei Missionari d'Africa), on the Via Aurelia in Rome. I also presented a version of this chapter to a Classics Colloquium at Bryn Mawr College on 6 May 2016, at the invitation of Alicia Walker, who, with Christine Atiyeh, is digitising materials on Delattre from the Archives of the White Fathers. Much is now available on Artstor under "The White Fathers at Carthage", https://library.artstor.org/#/collection/87731690. I presented a version of this paper at the White Fathers' headquarters in Rome on 19 October 2016, at the invitation of archivist Father Dominique Arnauld and late librarian Father Fritz Stenger. I owe special thanks to the late Father Ivan Page, archivist at my earliest visit in 2000, and to Father François Richard and Fathers Arnauld and Stenger.
2 Iván Fumadó Ortega, *Cartago. Historia de la investigación*, Consejo Superior de Investigaciones Científicas (Madrid: Escuela Española y Arqueologia en Roma, 2009); reviewed by Joann Freed, 'The unvarnished story of archaeology in Carthage and Tunisia', *Journal of Roman Archaeology* 25 (2012): 988–95, with a review of Clémentine Gutron, *L'archéologie en Tunisie (XIXe–XXe siècles). Jeux généalogiques sur l'antiquité* (Paris-Karthala-Tunis: IRMC, 2010).
3 Gilbert Charles-Picard, 'La recherche archéologique en Tunisie des origines à l'indépendance', *Cahiers des Études Anciennes* 16 (1983), 17.
4 Gutron, *L'archéologie*, 84.
5 A complete set of laws establishing the Tunisian Antiquities Service appeared between 8 March 1885 and 7 March 1886; Christian Landes, 'À propos d'un rapport "confidentiel" sur le musée de Carthage rédigé en juillet 1903 par Paul Gauckler, directeur des Antiquités et Arts de la Régence de Tunis, conservé aux archives du Musée d'Archéologie Nationale', *Antiquités nationales* 40 (2009): 245. Delattre had earlier been assured by Resident Paul Cambon that his rights to excavate and preserve finds in his Museum would not be affected; Pierre Gandolphe, 'Origines et débuts du Musée Lavigerie', *Cahiers de Byrsa* 2 (1952): 165–6.
6 Nathan Schlanger, 'Introduction', in *Archives, Ancestors, Practices. Archaeology in the light of its history* eds. Nathan Schlanger and Jarl Nordbladh (Oxford–New York: Bergbahn Books, 2008), 2.

7   Éve Gran-Aymerich, *Naissance de l'archéologie moderne, 1798–1945* (Paris: CNRS Éditions, 1998).
8   Marc-Antoine Kaeser, 'Talking about readings of the past: a delusive debate', *Archaeological Dialogues* 7 (2009), 34–6.
9   Monique Dondin-Payre, 'La découverte de l'Afrique romaine: L'influence des acteurs et de l'idéologie sur l'élaboration de l'histoire', *Pallas* 68 (2005), 35–48.
10 Joseph D. O'Donnell, *Lavigerie in Tunisia: The interplay of imperialist and missionary* (Atlanta, GA: University of Georgia Press, 1979).
11 Janet Malcolm, 'A house of one's own', *The New Yorker*, 5 June 1995, 75.
12 For another view similarly prejudiced against Delattre: Landes, 'À propos d'un rapport'.
13 Tim Murray, 'The art of archaeological biography', in *Encyclopedia of Archaeology: History and Discoveries*, ed. Tim Murray, vol. 2, *E–M* (Santa Barbara: ABC-CLIO, 2001), 879.
14 Douglas R. Givens, 'The role of biography in the writing the history of archaeology', in *Rediscovering Our Past: Essays on the history of American archaeology*, ed. Jonathan E. Reyman (Aldershot: Avebury, 1992), 51–7.
15 Marc-Antoine Kaeser, 'Biography, science studies and the historiography of archaeological research: managing personal archives', *Complutum* 24 (2013), 102.
16 Marc-Antoine Kaeser, 'Biography as microhistory. the relevance of private archives for writing the history of archaeology', in *Archives, Ancestors, Practices. Archaeology in the light of its history*, eds., Nathan Schlanger and Jarl Nordbladh (Oxford–New York: Bergbahn Books, 2008), 9–20.
17 Kaeser, 'Biography as Microhistory', 10–11.
18 Joann Freed, 'Early Roman amphoras in the collection of the Museum of Carthage', *Échos du Monde Classique/Classical Views* 40 (1996), 119–55.
19 Joann Freed, 'Bibliography of publications by Alfred-Louis Delattre (1850–1932)', *CEDAC Carthage* 20 (2001), 2–60.
20 Kaeser, 'Biography, science studies', 104.
21 Specifically on Delattre before my own work, I have found only an article by Ève and Jean Gran Aymerich, 'Les grands archéologues: A.-L. Delattre', *Archeologia* 208 (1985), 74–80.
22 Joann Freed, 'Le père Alfred-Louis Delattre (1850–1932) et les fouilles archéologiques de Carthage', *Histoire et missions chrétiennes* 8 (2008), 67–100 (tr. Jean-Claude Ceillier).
23 Joann Freed, *Bringing Carthage Home. The excavations of Nathan Davis, 1856–1859*, University of British Columbia Studies in the Ancient World 2 (Oxford: Oxbow Books, 2011); especially 50–68 on the topography.
24 William H. C. Frend, *The Archaeology of Early Christianity. A history* (London: Geoffrey Chapman, 1996), 69–72.
25 *Corpus Inscriptionum Latinarum*, vol VIII, 1881-, especially sections on Carthage (*CIL* VIII 999–1169; 12462–14286; 24516–25361) and on *instrumentum domesticum* (stamps on pottery, lamps and amphoras); for example, Greek amphora stamps recorded by Delattre = *CIL* VIII, 22639, 1–196. Delattre also has important entries in the *Corpus Inscriptionum Semiticarum*, vol. I, 1881.
26 Delattre's Musée National de Carthage, a precious resource for archaeologists and historians, has been closed 'for renovation' since the autumn of 2019, with some access for scholarly research in 2022.
27 Pierre Gandolphe, 'Saint-Louis de Carthage, 1830–1850', *Cahiers de Byrsa* 1 (1950), 269–307 and pls 6–22.
28 Jean Deneauve, 'Le centre monumental de Carthage. Un ensemble cultuel sur le colline de Byrsa', in *Histoire et archéologie de l'Afrique du Nord. 1. Carthage et son territoire dans l'antiquité*, ed. Claude Lepelley, vol. 1, Actes du IVe colloque international réuni dans le cadre du 113e Congrès national des Sociétés savantes (Strasbourg, 5–9 avril 1988) (Paris, 1990), 143–55; Iván Fumadó Ortega, *Cartago fenicio-púnica. Arqueología de la forma urbana* (Seville: Universidad de Sevilla, 2013).
29 Jean Ganiage, *L'Expansion coloniale de la France sous la troisième République, 1871–1914* (Paris: Payot, 1968).
30 Johannes Schmidt and René Cagnat, eds., *Corpus Inscriptionum Latinarum* vol. VIII: *Inscriptiones Latinae Africae*, part 4 (Berlin: Reimer, 1891).
31 Alfred-Louis Delattre, 'Fouilles archéologiques dans le flanc sud-ouest de la colline de Saint-Louis en 1892', *Bulletin archéologique du comité des travaux historiques et scientifiques* (1893): 94–123 and pls 11–12, figs 1–6.

32 My account of the conflict between Gauckler and Delattre depends heavily on the intensive archival research of the late Dominique Raynal (1944–88): Dominique Raynal, *Archéologie et histoire de l'Église d'Afrique. Uppenna I, Les fouilles 1904–1907*, vol. 1 (Toulouse: Presses Universitaires de Mirail, 2005), especially 171–81.
33 For the details, Landes, 'À propos d'un rapport'.
34 Théodore Zeldin, ed., *Conflicts in French Society. Anticlericalism, education and morals in the 19th century* (London: George Allen and Unwin, 1970).
35 For Delattre's excavations of Christian sites at Carthage, see Joann Freed, 'Louis-Alfred Delattre', in Stefan Heid and Martin Dennert, eds., *Personenlexikon zur christlichen Archäologie, Forscher und Persönlichkeiten vom 16. bis 21. Jahrhundert, aus über 30 Ländern Europas, Asiens, Nordafrikas und Nordamerikas*, 2 vols. (Regensburg: Schnell & Steiner, 2012).
36 François Renault, *Cardinal Lavigerie: Churchman, prophet and missionary* (London: Athlone Press, 1994), tr. from François Renault, *Le Cardinal Lavigerie. Visions d'hier, orientations d'aujourd'hui* (Paris: Fayard, 1992).
37 Landes, 'À propos d'un rapport', 237–40. Gauckler ordered a map from the Tunisian topographic services with diocesan properties marked; he got this in 1893. The Diocese owned 208 hectares, especially around Byrsa Hill and the north. The whole ancient site covers about 400 hectares.
38 Deux Pères Blancs du Cardinal Lavigerie [André Vellard, and A.-L. Delattre], *Carthage autrefois, Carthage aujourd'hui. Description et guide* (Tunis: J. Barlier, 6th ed., 1927), 40–1.
39 Charles M. Lavigerie, *Lettre à M. le Sécretaire perpetuel de l'Académie des Inscriptions et Belles-Lettres de l'utilité d'une mission archéologique permanente à Carthage*, 17 avril 1881 (Algiers: Adolphe Jourdan, 1881); reprinted in Lavigerie's *Oeuvres choisies*, (Paris: Poussièlgue, 1884), vol. 2, 397–431.
40 François Renault, *Lavigerie, l'esclavage africain, et l'Europe*, 1868–1892, 2 vols. (Paris: Boccard, 1971); also Aylward Shorter, *Cross & Flag in Africa: the 'White Fathers' during the colonial scramble (1892–1914)* (Maryknoll: Orbis Books, 2007).
41 The collection of the Musée National de Carthage in Carthage, Tunisia, is still largely based on Delattre's finds: Gandolphe, 'Origines et débuts', 151–78. For a view that I consider prejudiced and ill-informed: Clémentine Gutron, 'Mise en place de l'archéologie en Tunisie: le Musée Lavigerie de Saint Louis de Carthage (1875–1932)', *IBLA* 194 (2005), 169–80.
42 A proper description of Delattre's spiritual life would require another paper. As a member of the White Fathers, he attended and/or celebrated religious services every day, regularly engaged in 'examination of conscience', and participated in regularly scheduled retreats whose purpose was religious contemplation and self-examination.
43 Frend, *The Archaeology of Early Christianity*, 67–73.
44 Xavier Charmes, *Le comité des travaux historiques et scientifiques (histoire et documents)*, 3 vols. (Paris: Imprimerie nationale, 1886); François Arnoulet, *Résidents générauxde France en Tunisie—ces mal-aimés* (Marseilles: Narration Éditions, 1995).
45 Ève Gran-Aymerich, 'L'archéologie française au Maghreb de 1945 à 1962', in *Savoirs historiques au Maghreb. Constructions et usages*, eds. Sami Bargaoui and Hassan Ramaoun (Oran: Éditions CRASC, 2006), 243–65.
46 Hervé Duchêne, *Notre École Normale* (Paris: Les Belles Lettres, 1994), 157 and note 1; for La Blanchère's obituary, Stéphane Gsell, 'Chronique archéologique africaine', *Mélanges d'archéologie et d'histoire* 16 (1896), 489–90.
47 Jehan Desanges, 'La commission dite de l'Afrique du Nord au sein du CTHS: origine, evolution, perspectives', in *Afrique du Nord antique et medieval. Numismatique, langues, écritures et arts du livre, specificité des arts figurés. Actes du VIIe colloque international sur l'histoire et l'archéologie de l'Afrique du Nord*, ed. Serge Lancel (Paris: Éditions du CTHS, 1999), 11–24.
48 *Chroniques trimestrielles* 1888-07-00.39-4, 2.11, 6 mai 1888. *Chroniques trimestrielles* was an internal paper of the White Fathers, now an online database at Archivio dei Missionari d'Africa website, 'Chroniques et Rapports Annuels': http://www.msv3.org/Main.aspx?BASEID=MDACH.
49 Zeldin, *Conflicts in French Society*.
50 Christophe Charle, *Les Élites de la République, 1880-1900* (Paris: Fayard, 1987).
51 Robert J. Smith, *The École Normale Supérieure and the Third Republic* (Albany: SUNY Press, 1982).
52 Duchêne edited and published three memoirs: 'Notre École Normale', by Émile Zola; 'Rapport sur l'ENS', by Ernest Bersot; and 'Types de normaliens', by Salomon Reinach, in Duchêne, *Notre École Normale*.

53 Léon Renier, *Mélanges d'épigraphie* (Paris: Firmin Didot, 1854).
54 Raynal quoted a statement of Gauckler of 13 December 1904, Archives Nationales de France F17/2969A; Raynal, *Uppenna I*, 29, note 6.
55 Raynal, 'Autres enjeux', 571–2; Landes, 'À propos d'un rapport', 232.
56 Salomon Reinach and Ernest Babelon, 'Recherches archéologiques en Tunisie (1883–1884)', *Bulletin archéologique du comité des travaux historiques et scientifiques* (1886), 8. Gauckler's 2400 francs could buy 600 days of skilled construction labour in Paris in 1892; John McMackin (ed.), 'International Labor Statistics', *Bulletin, State of New York Department of Labor* 6 (1904), 328–29. Wages in Tunisia were much lower; Reinach and Babelon were evidently grossly overcharged for labour.
57 Landes, 'À propos d'un rapport', 237.
58 Paul Gauckler, 'Le domaine des Laberii à Uthina', *Monuments Piot* 3 (1897), 177–230 with plates XX–XXIII; Paul Gauckler, *Inventaire des mosaïques de la Gaule et de l'Afrique*, vol. 2, 1. *Tunisie* (Paris: Ernest Leroux, text 1910 and plates 1913).
59 Antoine Héron de Villefosse, 'Rapport de M. Héron de Villefosse sur des découvertes faites à Carthage par le R. P. Delattre pendant les premières mois de l'année 1894', *Comptes rendus de l'Académie des inscriptions et belles-lettres* 38.3 (1894): 197–201. For discussions of these finds: Iris Tillesssen, *Die Triumphalreliefs von Karthago* (Unpublished Ph.D. dissertation, Westfälische Wilhelms-Universität, Münster, 1978); Gilbert Charles-Picard, 'Le monument aux Victoires de Carthage et l'expédition orientale de Lucius Verus', *Karthago* 1 (1950), 65–94.
60 Alfred-Louis, Delattre, 'Fouilles archéologiques dans le flanc sud-ouest de la colline de Saint-Louis en 1892', *Bulletin archéologique du comité des travaux historiques et scientifiques* (1893): 94–123 and pls 11–12, figs 1–6. For discussion of these finds: Stefanie Martin-Kilcher, 'Amphoren der späten Republik und der frühen Kaiserzeit in Karthago: Zu den Lebensmittelimporten der Colonia Iulia Concordia', *MDAI(R)* 100 (1993): 269–320, especially 286–96, and Joann Freed and Jennifer Moore, 'New observations on the earliest Roman amphoras from Carthage: Delattre's first amphora wall', *CEDAC Carthage* 15 (1996), 19–28.
61 Alfred-Louis Delattre, 'Notes sur la nécropole punique voisine du Serapeum, à Carthage', *Comptes rendus de l'Académie des Inscriptions et Belles-Lettres* 38.6 (1894), 430–42. This was the beginning of the excavation of an archaic Punic cemetery (Douïmès) that continued for three years.
62 Archivio dei Missionari d'Africa, Diaire of Saint Louis, 29 May 1893, with a long description of the events; *Chroniques trimestrielles* 1893-07-00.59-2,2.30, for 29 May 1893 (online database at AGMAfr website, see note 48); other details from an anonymous author, 'Carthage', *Missions catholiques* 25 (1893): 255.
63 Jacques Alexandropoulos, 'Paul Gauckler (1866–1911): une evocation de son passage à Tunis d'après les fonds des archives départementales de l'Arièges', *Pallas* 56 (2000): 119–37.
64 Lucien Bertholon, 'Salomon Reinach: Recherches archéologiques en Tunisie', *Revue tunisienne* 2 (1895): 85.
65 Landes, 'À propos d'un rapport', 241.
66 Raynal, *Uppenna I*, 45, note 31, citing Archives Nationales de France F17 /13059.
67 *Description de l'Afrique du Nord. Musées et collections archéologiques de l'Algérie et de la Tunisie*. Vol. 8. *Musée Lavigerie de Saint-Louis de Carthage. Collection des Pères blancs formée par le R. P. Delattre*. Part 1: P. Berger (with an introduction by A. Héron de Villefosse), *Antiquités puniques*, 1900; Part 2: E. Babelon, H. Saladin, and R. Cagnat, *Époque romaine*, 1899; Part 3: R. P. Delattre, *Archéologie chrétienne*, 1899 (Paris: Ernest Leroux, 1899–1900).
68 Delattre, who was wearing hobnail boots, slipped and fell on the parquet floors; Archivio dei Missionari d'Africa, 'Y I, I Anecdotes', in Cahier V. These anecdotes are memories of Delattre's friend Augustin-Fernand Leynaud (1865–1953), Archbishop of Algiers, although he is not named.
69 Paul Gauckler, 'Découvertes archéologiques en Tunisie. I. Fouilles dans le premier cimetière des officiales à Carthage', *Mémoires de la Société Nationale des Antiquaires de France* 56 (1894 [1897]), 83–124.
70 Paul Gauckler, 'Guide du visiteur au musée du Bardo', *Revue tunisienne* 3 (1896): 309–26.
71 Archivio dei Missionari d'Africa, *Notices necrologiques* IV, for Delattre, 52*; documents collected for the Legion of Honour can be consulted in the Base de données Léonore, https://www.leonore.archives-nationales.culture.gouv.fr/ui/, under the name 'Delattre, Louis-Alfred'. A detailed account, largely in Delattre's handwriting, dated 2 April 1896, was written for *Chroniques trimestrielles* 1896-07-00.71-7,1.1 (2 avril 1896) (online database of Archivio dei Missionari d'Africa, see note 48).

72 Alexandropoulos, 'Paul Gauckler', 131, note 40.
73 Gauckler's eight *Comptes rendus de la Marche du Service* were privately published in Tunis (Imprimerie rapide) for 1896–1903 (1897–1904); for this comment, 1896 (1897), 10.
74 Ingénieur Bordy, *Carte topographique et archéologique des environs de Carthage, avec le concours de MM. le R. P. Delattre, le général Dolot and P. Gauckler*, scale 1/5,000 (Paris: Service Géographique de l'Armée, [c1900]).
75 Leila Ladjimi Sebaï, 'Introduction', in *Histoire littéraire de l'Afrique chrétienne depuis les origines jusqu'à l'invasion arabe*, vol. 1, Paul Monceaux, (Brussels: Culture et civilisation, 1966), 16–18.
76 Archivio dei Missionari d'Africa, 'Y3, I, Musée', letter from Delattre to Mgr Livinhac (January 5, 1898).
77 Paul Gauckler, 'Le service des antiquités', in MM. Anterrieu, Berge, Boulle et al., *Conférences faites en 1898 sur les administrations tunisiennes*, 467–95, copy consulted at the Institut des Belles Lettres Arabes (IBLA), Tunis, June 2014; Raynal, *Uppenna I*, 46 and note 34, cited Gauckler's paper from a copy in the French National Archives, 'Sur l'utilité du Service des Antiquités et Arts', Archives Nationales de France F17/17236. See also Landes, 'À propos d'un rapport', 232, note 26, citing the same paper of 1888–9 as 'Présentation du Service des Antiquités'.
78 Archivio dei Missionari d'Africa, letter of Cagnat to Delattre (22 May 1898); cited in Raynal, *Uppenna I*, 174, note 12; further cited Raynal, *Uppenna I*, 175, note 15; Raynal, *Uppenna I*, 177, note 22.
79 Raynal noted that Gauckler's activities were not 'decisive'; Raynal, *Uppenna I*, 175.
80 Kaeser noted this type of evidence of psychological distress; Kaeser, 'Biography, science studies', 107, n. 5.
81 Paul Gauckler, 'Découvertes à Carthage', *Comptes rendus de l'Académie des Inscriptions et Belles-lettres* 43.2 (1899), 156–62.
82 Myriam Bacha, *Patrimoine et monuments en Tunisie* (Rennes: Presses Universitaires de Rennes, 2013), 158–64.
83 Archivio dei Missionari d'Africa, letter of Héron de Villefosse to Delattre (5 January 1900).
84 Archivio dei Missionari d'Africa, diaire de Saint-Louis, Carthage (13 January 1900); Arnoulet, *Résidents*, 64–6.
85 Jean-Pierre Laporte, 'Un archéologue en Tunisie, Louis Carton (1861–1924)', *Bulletin archéologique du comité des travaux historiques et scientifiques* 39 (2009): 246–7.
86 Paul Gauckler, *Marche du Service* for 1900 (dated 15 April 1901), 17–19; Landes, 'À propos d'un rapport', 236.
87 Letter of Gauckler to Bernard Roy (26 July 1900), written from the Gauckler home in Paris, quoted in Landes, 'À propos d'un rapport', 241 and note 73, citing INHA (Institut National d'Histoire de l'Art, Paris), Fonds Poinssot.
88 Archivio dei Missionari d'Africa, letter of Gauckler to Delattre (19 October 1900).
89 Eric Cahm, *The Dreyfus Affair in French Society and Politics*, tr. Eric Cahm (London: Longman, 1966); Mary McAuliffe, *Dawn of the Belle Époque. The Paris of Monet, Zola, Bernhardt, Eiffel, Debussy, Clemenceau and their Friends* (Lanham: Rowman & Littlefield Publishers, 2011), passim.
90 Alfred-Louis Delattre, *Un pèlerinage aux ruines de Carthage et au Musée Lavigerie*, (Lyons: X. Jevain, 1902).
91 Patrick Cabanel, ed., *Une France en Méditerranée: écoles, langue et culture françaises, XIXe-XXe siècles*, Colloque international, Toulouse, 10–12 mars 2005 (Grane: Créaphis, 2006), 15, 24; Frank Tallett and Nicholas Atkin, *Religion, Society and Politics in France since 1789* (London: Hambledon Press, 1991), 151–3.
92 Laporte, 'Louis Carton', 248.
93 Published by Villefosse; Antoine Héron de Villefosse, 'Les sarcophages peints trouvés à Carthage', *Monuments Piot* 12 (1905): 79–111.
94 No relation to the Archbishop of Carthage at that time, although they shared the same last name.
95 Catherine Salles, *La IIIe République au tournant du siècle, 1893–1914* (Paris: Librairie Larousse, 1985): 103-4.
96 Lewis Rayapen and Gordon Anderson, 'Napoleon and the Church', *International Social Science Review* 66 (1991): 125–6.
97 Landes, 'À propos d'un rapport'.
98 Archivio dei Missionari d'Africa, letter of Delattre to Maison-Carrée in Algiers [probably to Livinhac] (18 December 1903).

99 'Justice confounds my enemies! Everything is well in the best of all possible worlds. Until the day that they can strangle us in a corner, in silence'. Letter of Gauckler to Louis Liard, 18 March 1904, cited by Alexandropoulos, 'Paul Gauckler', 136–7.
100 Laporte, 'Louis Carton.'
101 *Chroniques trimestrielles*, see note 48, 1904-12-00.111-1, 3.5; 17 juillet 1904.
102 Alfred-Louis Delattre, *Le culte de la Sainte-Vierge en Afrique d'après les monuments archéologiques* (Lille and Paris: Société de St-Augustin, 1907), preface and 232.
103 Letter from Gauckler to Toutain, quoted by Alexandropoulos, 'Paul Gauckler', 131, who gives no closer date.
104 Archivio dei Missionari d'Africa, letter of Delattre to a friend in Rouen (21 February 1905), Y1, I, 'fragments biographiques'; letter of Delattre to Abbé Catteville, an old friend at the Grand-Seminaire de Rouen (24 February 1905), which is unclear as to whether Delattre visited Uppenna on Sunday, 19 February, but stated that he went on to Sousse to visit the Catacombs and Leynaud; also cited by Raynal, *Uppenna I*, 254. Archivio dei Missionari d'Africa, letter from Gauckler to Delattre (21 February 1905).
105 26 February 1905: 'Mesquinerie administrative', in *L'Avenir du Centre*, a paper published at Sousse, cited by Dominique Raynal, 'Autres enjeux et contraintes de l'archéologie en Tunisie aux débuts du Protectorat', in *La Tunisie mosaïque: diasporas, cosmopolitisme, archéologies de l'identité*, eds. Jacques Alexandropoulos and Patrick Cabanel, (Toulouse: Presses universitaires de Mirail, 2000), 580, note 22; the articles were attributed to Louis Carton in Raynal, *Uppenna I*, 51.
106 Raynal, *Uppenna I*, 62–3 and notes 72 (letters of Carton to Delattre in April) and 73 (article of April 30, repeated in *Dépêche tunisienne*, May 4, 1905).
107 Raynal, *Uppenna I*, 64, note 77, citing Archives Nationales de France F17/17238 and memo in the Tunisian Institut National du Patrimoine for a payment to Sadoux.
108 Draft of a letter by a Minister of Public Instruction, 17 July 1905, quoted in Raynal, *Uppenna I*, 65–6, and note 80, citing Archives Nationales de France F17/17236; the document is reproduced in Raynal, *Uppenna I*, 242, fig. 44.
109 Raynal, *Uppenna I*, 178, note 27, citing telegram of 24 June 1904, Archives Nationales de France F17/17236; letter of Perrot as Secretary General of the Academy of Inscriptions to the Ministry of Public Instruction, 7 July 1904, cited by Raynal, *Uppenna I*, 178, note 27, from the same archival folder.
110 Letter of Resident Stephen Pichon to the President of the Council, Ministry of Foreign Affairs, Rouvier, quoted by Raynal, *Uppenna I*, 60 and note 66, Archives Nationales de Tunisie, Section d'État, Series E, Direction de Service, Dossier of Alfred Merlin.
111 Maurice Larkin, *Religion, Politics and Preferment in France since 1890. La Belle Époque and its legacy* (Cambridge: Cambridge University Press, 1995), 60.
112 For an intelligent discussion of the resulting problems, Constant Méheut, interviewed by Michael Barbaro, 'France, Islam and "Laïcité"', Friday, 12 February 2021, podcast, New York Times/The Daily: https://www.nytimes.com/2021/02/12/podcasts/the-daily/france-secularism-laicite-samuel-paty.html
113 Kaeser, 'Biography, science studies', 105.
114 Freed, 'Bibliography of Delattre'. In the summer of 2022 I placed a complete (unpublished) bibliography of Gauckler's publications on my page at Academia.edu: https://www.academia.edu/73346897/Paul_Gauckler_publications. More than 90% of the full publications of these men can be found online today, largely on the French online sites Gallica and Persée.
115 Givens, 'The role of biography', 55.
116 Bruce G. Trigger, 'Historiography', in *Encyclopedia of Archaeology: History and discoveries*, ed., Tim Murray, vol. 2, E–M, (Santa Barbara: ABC- CLIO, 2001), 638.

Bibliography

Alexandropoulos, Jacques, 'Paul Gauckler (1866–1911): Une évocation de son passage à Tunis d'après les fonds des archives départementales de l'Arièges', *Pallas* 56 (2000), 119–37.
Anonymous, 'Carthage', *Missions catholiques* 25 (1893): 255.
Arnoulet, François, *Résidents généraux de France en Tunisie—ces mal-aimés* (Marseilles: Narration Éditions, 1995).

Bacha, Myriam, *Patrimoine et monuments en Tunisie* (Rennes: Presses Universitaires de Rennes, 2013).
Bertholon, Lucien, 'Salomon Reinach: Recherches archéologiques en Tunisie', *Revue tunisienne* 2 (1895): 84–7.
Bordy, Ingénieur, *Carte topographique et archéologique des environs de Carthage, avec le concours de MM. le R. P. Delattre, le général Dolot and P. Gauckler*, scale 1/5,000 (Paris: Service Géographique de l'Armée, [c1900]).
Cabanel, Patrick, ed., *Une France en Méditerranée: écoles, langue et culture françaises, XIXe–XXe siècles, Colloque international, Toulouse, 10–12 mars 2005* (Grane: Créaphis, 2006).
Cahm, Eric, *The Dreyfus Affair in French Society and Politics*, tr. Eric Cahm (London: Longman, 1966).
Charle, Christophe, *Les Élites de la République, 1880–1900* (Paris: Fayard, 1987).
Charles-Picard, Gilbert, 'Le monument aux Victoires de Carthage et l'expédition orientale de Lucius Verus', *Karthago* 1 (1950), 65–94.
Charles-Picard, Gilbert, 'La recherche archéologique en Tunisie des origines à l'indépendance', *Cahiers des études anciennes* 16 (1983): 11–20.
Charmes, Xavier, *Le comité des travaux historiques et scientifiques (histoire et documents)*, 3 vols. (Paris: Imprimerie nationale, 1886).
Delattre, Alfred-Louis, 'Fouilles archéologiques dans le flanc sud-ouest de la colline de Saint-Louis en 1892', *Bulletin archéologique du comité des travaux historiques et scientifiques* (1893): 94–123 and pls 11–12, figs 1–6.
Delattre, Alfred-Louis, 'Le mur à amphores de la colline de Saint-Louis à Carthage', *Bulletin archéologique du comité des travaux historiques et scientifiques* (1894): 89–119 and pls 3–4.
Delattre, Alfred-Louis, 'Notes sur la nécropole punique voisine du Serapeum, à Carthage', *Comptes rendus de l'Académie des Inscriptions et Belles-Lettres* 38.6 (1894): 430–42.
Delattre, Alfred-Louis, *Un pèlerinage aux ruines de Carthage et au Musée Lavigerie* (Lyons: X. Jevain, 1902).
Delattre, Alfred-Louis, *Le culte de la Sainte-Vierge en Afrique d'après les monuments archéologiques* (Paris: Société de St-Augustin, 1907).
Deneauve, Jean, 'Le centre monumental de Carthage. Un ensemble cultuel sur le colline de Byrsa', in *Histoire et archéologie de l'Afrique du Nord. 1. Carthage et son territoire dans l'antiquité*, vol. 1, Actes du IVe colloque international réuni dans le cadre du 113e Congrès national des Sociétés savantes (Strasbourg, 5–9 avril 1988) (Paris, 1990), 143–55.
Desanges, Jehan, 'La commission dite de l'Afrique du Nord au sein du CTHS: origine, évolution, perspectives', in *Afrique du Nord antique et medieval. Numismatique, langues, écritures et arts du livre, specificité des arts figurés. Actes du VIIe colloque international sur l'histoire et l'archéologie de l'Afrique du Nord*, ed. Serge Lancel (Paris: Éditions du CTHS, 1999), 11–24.
Description de l'Afrique du Nord. Musées et collections archéologiques de l'Algérie et de la Tunisie. Vol. 8. *Musée Lavigerie de Saint-Louis de Carthage. Collection des Pères blancs formée par le R. P. Delattre.* Part 1: Berger, Philippe (with an introduction by A. Héron de Villefosse), *Antiquités puniques*, 1900; Part 2: Babelon, Ernest, H. Saladin, and R. Cagnat, *Époque romaine*, 1899; Part 3: Révérend Père Delattre, *Archéologie chrétienne*, 1899 (Paris: Ernest Leroux, 1899–1900).
Dondin-Payre, Monique, 'La découverte de l'Afrique romaine: L'influence des acteurs et de l'idéologie sur l'élaboration de l'histoire', *Pallas* 68 (2005): 35–48.
Duchêne, Hervé, *Notre École Normale* (Paris: Les Belles Lettres, 1994).
Freed, Joann, 'Early Roman amphoras in the collection of the Museum of Carthage', *Échos du Monde Classique/Classical Views* 40 (1996): 119–55.
Freed, Joann, 'Bibliography of publications by Alfred-Louis Delattre (1850–1932)', *CEDAC Carthage* 20 (2001): 3–60, online on the website of the Tunisian Institut National du Patrimoine (INP): https://www.inp2020.tn/cedac/cedac_20.pdf.
Freed, Joann (tr. Jean-Claude Ceillier), 'Le père Alfred-Louis Delattre (1850–1932) et les fouilles archéologiques de Carthage', *Histoire et missions chrétiennes* 8 (2008): 67–100.
Freed, Joann, *Bringing Carthage Home. The excavations of Nathan Davis, 1856–1859*, University of British Columbia Studies in the Ancient World 2 (Oxford: Oxbow Books, 2011).
Freed, Joann, 'Louis-Alfred Delattre', in *Personenlexikon zur christlichen Archäologie, Forscher und Persönlichkeiten vom 16. bis 21. Jahrhundert, aus über 30 Ländern Europas, Asiens, Nordafrikas und Nordamerikas*, eds., Stefan Heid and Martin Dennert, 2 vols. (Regensburg: Schnell & Steiner, 2012).

Freed, Joann, 'The unvarnished story of archaeology in Carthage and Tunisia', [review of Fumadó Ortega 2009 and Gutron 2010], *Journal of Roman Archaeology* 25 (2012): 988–95.
Freed, Joann, and Jennifer Moore, 'New observations on the earliest Roman amphoras from Carthage: Delattre's first amphora wall', *CEDAC Carthage* 15 (1996): 19–28.
Frend, William H. C., *The Archaeology of Early Christianity. A history* (London: Geoffrey Chapman, 1996).
Fumadó Ortega, Iván, *Cartago. Historia de la investigación*, Consejo Superior de Investigaciones Científicas (Madrid: Escuela Española y Arqueologia en Roma, 2009).
Fumadó Ortega, Iván, *Cartago fenicio-púnica. Arqueología de la forma urbana* (Seville: Universidad de Sevilla, 2013).
Gandolphe, Pierre, 'Saint-Louis de Carthage, 1830–1850', *Cahiers de Byrsa* 1 (1950): 269–307 and plates.
Gandolphe, Pierre, 'Origines et débuts du Musée Lavigerie', *Cahiers de Byrsa* 2 (1952): 151–78 and plates.
Ganiage, Jean, *L'Expansion coloniale de la France sous la troisième République, 1871–1914* (Paris: Payot, 1968).
Gauckler, Paul, 'Découvertes archéologiques en Tunisie. I. Fouilles dans le premier cimetière des officiales à Carthage', *Mémoires de la Société Nationale des Antiquaires de France* 56 (1895 [1897]): 83–124.
Gauckler, Paul, 'Régence de Tunis, Direction des Antiquités et des Beaux-arts', *Comptes rendus de la marche du Service* (Tunis: Imprimerie rapide [8 issues for 1896–1903], 1897–1904).
Gauckler, Paul, 'Guide du visiteur au musée du Bardo', *Revue tunisienne* 3 (1896): 309–26.
Gauckler, Paul, 'Le domaine des Laberii à Uthina', *Monuments Piot* 3 (1897): 177–229, plates XX–XXIII.
Gauckler, Paul, 'Le service des antiquités', in *Conférences faites en 1898 sur les administrations tunisiennes* (Sousse: Imprimerie française, 1898), 467–95.
Gauckler, Paul, 'Découvertes à Carthage', *Comptes rendus de l'Académie des Inscriptions et Belles-lettres* 43.2 (1899): 156–62.
Gauckler, Paul, *Inventaire des mosaïques de la Gaule et de l'Afrique*, vol. 2, 1. Tunisie (Paris: Ernest Leroux, text 1910 and plates 1913).
Givens, Douglas R., 'The role of biography in writing the history of archaeology', in *Rediscovering our Past: Essays on the history of American archaeology*, ed. Jonathan E. Reyman (Aldershot: Avebury, 1992), 51–66.
Gran-Aymerich, Ève, 'L'archéologie française au Maghreb de 1945 à 1962', in *Savoirs historiques au Maghreb. Constructions et usages*, eds., Sami Bargaoui and Hassan Ramaoun (Oran: Éditions CRASC, 2006), 243–65.
Gran-Aymerich, Ève, *Naissance de l'archéologie moderne, 1798–1945* (Paris: CNRS Éditions, 1998).
Gran Aymerich, Ève and Jean Gran Aymerich, 'Les grands archéologues: A.-L. Delattre', *Archeologia* 208 (1985): 74–80.
Gsell, Stéphane, 'Chronique archéologique africaine', *Mélanges d'archéologie et d'histoire* 16 (1902): 441–90.
Gutron, Clémentine, 'Mise en place de l'archéologie en Tunisie: le Musée Lavigerie de Saint Louis de Carthage (1875–1932)', *IBLA* [Revue de l'Institut des Belles-Lettres Arabes] 194 (2005): 169–80.
Gutron, Clémentine, *L'archéologie en Tunisie (XIXe–XXe siècles). Jeux généalogiques sur l'antiquité* (Paris–Karthala–Tunis: IRMC, 2010).
Héron de Villefosse, Antoine, 'Rapport de M. Héron de Villefosse sur des découvertes faites à Carthage par le R. P. Delattre pendant les premières mois de l'année 1894', *Comptes rendus de l'Académie des inscriptions et belles-lettres* 38.3 (1894): 195–201.
Héron de Villefosse, Antoine, 'Les sarcophages peints trouvés à Carthage', *Monuments Piot* 12 (1905): 79–111.
Kaeser, Marc-Antoine, 'Biography as microhistory: the relevance of private archives for writing the history of archaeology', in *Archives, Ancestors, Practices: Archaeology in the light of its history*, eds. Nathan Schlanger and Jarl Nordbladh (Oxford–New York: Bergbahn Books, 2008), 9–20.
Kaeser, Marc-Antoine, 'Talking about readings of the past: a delusive debate', *Archaeological Dialogues* 7 (2009): 34–6.
Kaeser, Marc-Antoine, 'Biography, science studies and the historiography of archaeological research: managing personal archives', *Complutum* 24.2 (2013): 101–8.

Ladjimi Sebaï, Leila, 'Introduction' in *Histoire littéraire de l'Afrique chrétienne depuis les origines jusqu'à l'invasion arabe*, Paul Monceaux, vol. 1 (Brussels: Culture et civilisation, 1966).

Landes, Christian, 'À propos d'un rapport "confidentiel" sur le musée de Carthage rédigé en juillet 1903 par Paul Gauckler, directeur des Antiquités et Arts de la Régence de Tunis, conservé aux archives du Musée d'Archéologie Nationale', *Antiquités nationales* 40 (2009): 227–48.

Laporte, Jean-Pierre, 'Un archéologue en Tunisie, Louis Carton (1861–1924)', *Bulletin archéologique du comité des travaux historiques et scientifiques* 39 (2009): 239–64.

Larkin, Maurice, *Religion, Politics and Preferment in France since 1890: La Belle Époque and its legacy* (Cambridge: Cambridge University Press, 1995).

Lavigerie, Charles M., *Lettre à M. le Sécretaire perpetuel de l'Académie des Inscriptions et Belles-Lettres par l'Archevêque d'Alger de l'utilité d'une mission archéologique permanente à Carthage*, 17 avril 1881 (Algiers: Adolphe Jourdan, 1881); reprinted in Lavigerie's *Oeuvres choisies*, (Paris: Poussièlgue, 1884), vol. 2, 397–431.

McMackin, John, ed., 'International Labor Statistics,' *Bulletin, State of New York Department of Labor* 6 (1904), 304–29 (on HathiTrust).

Malcolm, Janet, 'A house of one's own', *The New Yorker*, June 5, 1995, 58–79.

Martin-Kilcher, Stefanie, 'Amphoren der späten Republik und der frühen Kaiserzeit in Karthago: Zu den Lebensmittelimporten der Colonia Iulia Concordia', *Mitteilungen des Deutschen Archäolgischen Instituts (Abteilung Roma)* 100 (1993): 269–320.

McAuliffe, Mary, *Dawn of the Belle Époque. The Paris of Monet, Zola, Bernhardt, Eiffel, Debussy, Clemenceau and their Friends* (Lanham: Rowman & Littlefield Publishers, 2011).

Murray, Tim, 'The art of archaeological biography', in *Encyclopedia of Archaeology: History and Discoveries*, ed. Tim Murray, vol. 2, *E–M* (Santa Barbara: ABC-CLIO, 1999), 869–83.

O'Donnell, Joseph D., *Lavigerie in Tunisia: The interplay of imperialist and missionary* (Atlanta: University of Georgia Press, 1979).

Rayapen, Lewis, and Gordon Anderson, 'Napoleon and the Church', *International Social Science Review* 66 (1991), 117–27.

Raynal, Dominique, 'Autres enjeux et contraintes de l'archéologie en Tunisie aux débuts du Protectorat', in *La Tunisie mosaïque: diasporas, cosmopolitisme, archéologies de l'identité*, eds. Jacques Alexandropoulos and Patrick Cabanel (Toulouse: Presses universitaires de Mirail, 2000).

Raynal, Dominique, *Archéologie et histoire de l'Église d'Afrique. Uppenna I, Les fouilles 1904–1907*, vol. 1 (Toulouse: Presses Universitaires de Mirail, 2005).

Reinach, Salomon and Ernest Babelon, 'Recherches archéologiques en Tunisie (1883–1884)', *Bulletin archéologique du comité des travaux historiques et scientifiques* (1886), 4–79.

Renault, François, *Lavigerie, l'esclavage africain, et l'Europe*, 1868–1892, 2 vols. (Paris: Boccard, 1971).

Renault, François, *Cardinal Lavigerie: Churchman, prophet and missionary* (London: Athlone Press, 1994), tr. from F. Renault, *Le Cardinal Lavigerie. Visions d'hier, orientations d'aujourd'hui* (Paris: Fayard, 1992).

Renier, Léon, *Mélanges d'épigraphie* (Paris: Firmin Didot, 1854).

Salles, Catherine, *La IIIe République au tournant du siècle, 1893–1914* (Paris: Librairie Larousse, 1985).

Schlanger, Nathan, 'Introduction', in *Archives, Ancestors, Practices. Archaeology in the light of its history*, eds. Nathan Schlanger and Jarl Nordbladh (Oxford–New York: Bergbahn Books, 2008).

Schmidt, Johannes and René Cagnat, eds., *Corpus Inscriptionum Latinarum* vol. VIII: *Inscriptiones Latinae Africae*, part 4 (Berlin: Reimer, 1891).

Shorter, Aylward, *Cross & Flag in Africa: The 'White Fathers' during the colonial scramble (1892–1914)* (Maryknoll: Orbis Books, 2007).

Smith, Robert J., *The École Normale Supérieure and the Third Republic* (Albany: SUNY Press, 1982).

Tallett, Frank, and Nicholas Atkin, *Religion, Society and Politics in France since 1789* (London: Hambledon Press, 1991).

Tillessen, Iris, Die Triumphalreliefs von Karthago (Unpublished Ph.D. dissertation, Westfälische Wilhelms-Universität, Münster, 1978).

Trigger, Bruce G., 'Historiography', in *Encyclopedia of Archaeology: History and discoveries*, ed., Tim Murray, vol. 2, *E–M* (Santa Barbara: ABC-CLIO, 2001), 630–9.

Vellard, André, and Alfred-Louis Delattre [Deux Pères Blancs du Cardinal Lavigerie], *Carthage autrefois, Carthage aujourd'hui. Description et guide* (Tunis: J. Barlier, 6th edition, 1927).

Zeldin, Théodore, ed., *Conflicts in French Society. Anticlericalism, education and morals in the 19th century* (London: George Allen and Unwin, 1970).

10
Hugh Falconer: Botanist, palaeontologist, controversialist
Tim Murray

What a glorious privilege it would be, could we live back – were it but for an instant – into those ancient times when these extinct animals peopled the earth! To see them all congregated together in one grand natural menagerie – these Mastodons and Elephants, so numerous in species, toiling their ponderous forms and trumpeting their march in countless herds through the swamps and reedy forests: to view the giant Sivatherium, armed in front with four horns.... We have only to light the torch of philosophy, to seize the clue of induction, and ... to proceed into the valley of death, when the graves open before us ... the dry and fragmented bones run together, each bone to his bone; the sinews are laid over, the flesh is brought on, the skin covers all, and the past existence - to the mind's eye – starts again into being, decked out in all the lineaments of life.[1]

This brief sketch stems from long-running preparations for a biography of the Scottish scientist Hugh Falconer (1808–1865), and cuts across several significant elements of his life as a researcher committed to uncovering the history of life on earth.[2] Most famous among archaeologists for his work at Brixham Cave (but also in Gibraltar and Sicily) and his debunking of the 'ancient' jaw from Moulin Quignon, Falconer's extraordinary range of research interests extended from documenting the Tertiary fauna of the Himalayas to overseeing the introduction of tea to India (and are very well represented in the banners produced by the Falconer Museum in Forres, Scotland)[3]. Who else would have species as diverse as the Markhor of Central Asia (the spiral horned goat *Capra Falconer*), the bamboo (*Himalayacalamus falconeri*) and the rhododendron (*Rhododendron Falconeri*) named after them?

In many ways Falconer was a typical Scottish recruit to the Medical Corps of the East India Company – well educated at home and forced to find his living abroad. He was also typical of the many young men with indifferent prospects at home (such as Henry Creswicke Rawlinson [1810–1895]) who found their *metier* in foreign service, and in doing so transformed British science and culture. In other ways he was an archetypical Victorian scientist, sufficiently well-connected through memberships of the most important scientific societies to successfully raise funds to seriously prosecute research into high human antiquity (a highly controversial undertaking). Falconer was a man with friends (and enemies) in high places.

Though mostly based on the analysis of Falconer's work and that of his contemporaries such as Sir Charles Lyell (1797–1876), Sir Joseph Prestwich (1812–1896), Sir John Evans (1823–1908) and Sir John Lubbock (1834–1913), my very brief observations sample some of Falconer's letters, and those of his niece (and companion) Grace Milne (1832–1899), later Lady Prestwich, and the correspondence of scientific luminaries such as Charles Darwin (1809–1882) and Sir Joseph Hooker (1817–1911), to gain a clearer picture of his complex social and cultural milieu. Given the range of Falconer's interests, this chapter represents only a very brief portrayal of what really amounts to the *several* lives of a Victorian polymath.

Falconer was very deeply engaged in the evolving politics of Darwinism and knew many of its various supporters and detractors.[4] He was a mainstay of major scientific societies (such as the Royal Society of London and the Geological Society of London), and a fiercely proud (and combative) servant of the search for scientific truth. Above all, Falconer was a practical natural historian capable of achieving extraordinary discoveries in the field, applying his great forensic skill to exploring the evolution of human beings, while at the same time engaging in fundamental contributions to economic botany in India.

Notwithstanding his staunch support for Darwin and Prestwich, and his love of family, Falconer clearly could behave in a curmudgeonly way, frequently spoiling for a fight about matters great and small. He is a fascinating figure – luminously intelligent and riven with personal contradictions. Falconer, like so many of his contemporaries such as Prestwich, Evans, Lubbock and indeed Sir Proby Cautley (1802–71), was the epitome of well-spent leisure, at a time before career pathways in science became clear.[5] In his case his employment as a medical doctor with the East India Company provided wonderful opportunities for palaeontological and botanical research.[6]

Early life and work at the British East India Company (1808–1855)

The youngest son of David Falconer, Hugh was born at Forres, Elginshire, on 29 February 1808. He was educated at the Forres grammar school and at the University of Aberdeen, where he graduated with an MA in 1826. Shortly afterwards he began his medical studies in Edinburgh, graduating in 1829 (Figure 10.1). An appointment as assistant-surgeon in the Bengal establishment of the East India Company quickly followed. During his time at Edinburgh he was a keen student of botany and geology, gaining skills which were soon put to use when he moved to London to act as assistant to Dr Nathaniel Wallich (1786–1854) in his work on the Indian Herbarium.[7] Falconer also pursued his interests in geology (and Indian fossils), by working with William Lonsdale (1794–1872) at the museum of the Geological Society of London. Both Wallich and Lonsdale are

Figure 10.1 Dr Hugh Falconer, 1844, Salted paper print from a paper negative. 37.3 × 26.7 cm (14 11/16 × 10 1/2 in.), 88.XM.57.40. Reproduced with permission. The J. Paul Getty Museum, Los Angeles.

further examples of researchers who grasped the opportunities for doing science while on active service away from England.[8]

Falconer arrived in at Calcutta in September 1830. Shortly afterwards he published the fossil bones from Ava which were held in the Asiatic Society of Bengal, which was to become his favourite place for publication and scientific disputation in India.[9] In early 1831 Falconer was sent to Meerut (a major base of the British East India Company in the northwest of the sub-continent, and the site where the Revolt of 1857 began). While there he travelled to the nearby city of Sahāranpur, the site of a botanic garden established by the Company and managed by John Forbes Royle (1798–1858) whose focus was on the application of economic botany to India – both as a source of revenue for the Company, but also a basis on which to prevent food shortages among the people. He and Royle got along famously, botanising together while Falconer pursued research in palaeontology with his friend, the engineer of the Ganges Canal, Captain (afterwards Sir) Proby Cautley.[10] In 1831 Royle returned to England and Falconer, who had begun his major palaeontological fieldwork in the Siwalik Hills of northern India, was appointed his successor. Falconer made spectacular discoveries in the Tertiary deposits of the Hills, establishing a globally significant collection of fossil vertebrate fauna, and from 1832 onwards the *Journal of the Asiatic Society of Bengal* and *Asiatic Researches* contained numerous memoirs on their discoveries. The importance of Falconer and Cautley's researches was recognised in 1837 when the Geological Society of London awarded the Wollaston medal to both of them.[11]

However the practical needs of the Company could not be long forgotten and in 1834 a commission was appointed by the Bengal government to report on the fitness of India for the growth of tea, and Falconer set up the field trials at locations spread across Bengal and adjacent provinces. Barely pausing for breath, Falconer seized the opportunity provided by the extension of British interest in the western Himalayas (especially Afghanistan) to botanise in Kashmir, Tibet and present day western Nepal. After all this frenetic activity Falconer became seriously ill in 1840 and was sent back to England (along with 70 large chests of dried plants and five tons of fossil bones) in 1842.

Falconer remained in England between 1843 and 1847 and published his work on Indian botany and the fossils of the Siwaliks (aided by a government grant of £1000 procured on the advice of the Royal Society and the British Association for the Advancement of Science). It was proved to be a very wise investment, allowing Falconer sufficient support to make good progress on the analysis. Sadly, his work was never completed as he was compelled by the Company to return to India in 1847 to take up the posts of director of Calcutta Botanic Garden and professor of botany in the Calcutta Medical College. He remained in India until 1855, when he retired to England in poor health.

A return to Europe: life as an itinerant natural historian (1855–1865)

The last ten years of Falconer's life were spent almost entirely in motion as he pursued his interests in palaeontology and archaeology to the exclusion of all else (particularly botany). These were the years when he engaged in almost constant disputation with scientific friends and foes, especially about the processes of the evolution of life on Earth, and the most scientifically reputable ways of first describing and then understanding transformations in physical form and in material culture. Falconer's particular skill was in exploring the evidence that pointed to high human antiquity – gauged most effectively by demonstrating the presence of material culture with the bones of extinct animals, particularly (but not exclusively) in caves.

Falconer and his associates, such as Prestwich, Evans, Lubbock and Boucher de Perthes (1788–1868), Edouard Lartet (1801–1871), George Busk (1807–1808) and Henry Christy (1810–1865) concerned themselves with empirical evidence and developed effective networks that fostered the open discussion of claims for and against high human antiquity.[12] Much of Falconer's last decade was spent visiting museums and sites throughout Europe (with his fieldwork focused on southern Europe during the European winter), and he maintained direct contact with an ever-expanding network of natural historians and antiquaries. Indeed his return to Europe allowed him to firmly focus on the task of demonstrating a high human antiquity which he had begun to consider a strong likelihood while working in the Siwaliks.[13]

This quest cut across most of the still-forming disciplines devoted to understanding the history of life on earth, particularly anthropology, ethnology and archaeology, that were now being forced to contemplate a much longer human history.[14] Indeed Falconer was intimately connected with the major discoveries at Brixham Cave and in Sicily and Gibraltar, as well as being much involved in bringing to public prominence the work of Boucher de Perthes in the Somme gravels. Typically of Falconer, he was also instrumental in debunking the antiquity of the

Moulin-Quignon Jaw claimed by Boucher and his supporters, one of the earliest of many fakes that have been forced on credulous scientists and lay-persons alike.[15]

Falconer was also connected to other centres of power and influence within mainstream Victorian science. His close friendship with fellow Scot Mary Somerville (1780–1872), whom he used to visit in Florence after she removed there from England, and Baroness Burdett-Coutts (1814–1906) gave Falconer even greater access to the elite of British science and society. This became particularly beneficial when Falconer sought to raise funds for the initial work at Brixham. The Baroness was an enthusiastic and generous subscriber.

However, Falconer's relationship with his niece Grace Milne is of particular interest in understanding how a bachelor scientist of means could participate in society outside his professional space. Grace had long been a favourite of Falconer's and he used to write to her often while in India discussing his life and work there. He also shared with her his thoughts on the relationship between science and religion, particularly as it related to a search for the history of human beings.[16] After the death of her husband she became Falconer's constant companion and hostess until his death – after which she married Falconer's close friend Prestwich. Milne's letters chart Falconer's many visits to Europe and give us a great deal of information about the scientific networks cultivated by him which became a foundation of his detailed understanding of European palaeontology, geology and natural history.

Historians of the establishment of high human antiquity have rightly focused on the significance of Brixham Cave and the Somme (and Falconer's central role in both discoveries).[17] However, historians of geology and of evolution as it came to be practised in mid-Victorian Britain have broadened discussion to include his participation in debates that coincided with establishing its implications. Among the most important of these debates was that between Falconer and Huxley about the place of Cuvier's approach to understanding the process of anatomical transformation in evolution. The issues were complex and highly technical, but they were regarded by all participants (and observers such as Darwin) as having significant implications for the viability of Darwin's account of the evolution of life on earth. Correspondence between the major players (who most often regarded themselves as friends) revealed the extent of personal and professional conflicts exposed by such debates (and the responses of Darwin and Hooker to them).[18]

Indeed on occasion this correspondence reveals that some players (particularly Hooker) were keen to take the opportunity to pay Falconer back for old slights, and to improve their position with Darwin. This from Hooker in Calcutta to Darwin is an example:

> C. Bot Gardens. April 7th. 1850 Dear Darwin Here I am staying with Falconer! he played me another sad trick since last mid summer keeping all my letters & overland parcels for 5 months: deaf to all my letters whether written from Camp or prison till I had to come down on him after due warning by the intervention of powerful friends in Calcutta. He sent 7 of Miss Henslows letters, of as many months—& various overland parcels— he had no excuse to offer & plead none— I flared up & forgave all, & visited him immediately on my arrival in Calcutta. Here I find him in capital health & spirits, living by rule enthusiastic in his pursuits as Botanist horticulturalist & Landscape Gardener—He is fat & looks far better than he did in England—is as great a favorite as ever & most liberal with his garden duplicates. His conduct—dilatoriness in the affairs I allude to incomprehensible as it was arose from nothing but insane procrastination. I never mentioned it to any one at home but you—& now we are together it is never alluded to in any way— His society is as ever delightful & a more amiable fellow never lived. He never goes to the As. Soc. & has dropped all his interference with their ways & doings. for the better or worst.
> (Letter from J. D. Hooker, 6 and 7 April 1850)

Much the same kind of jockeying for Darwin's good opinion was revealed in Falconer's second great conflict; this was with Lyell, his old friend and fellow Scot. The cause of the dispute was Falconer's reaction to what he regarded as being Lyell's ungenerous treatment of the role played by himself and Prestwich in the discovery of high human antiquity. Correspondence between Lyell and Darwin, William Pengelly (1812–1894) and others clearly indicates that Darwin was particularly worried about infighting among his supporters (thereby potentially damaging the prospects of his theory), even though Lyell himself was only a very recent convert to those theories. In essence the response of the most powerful members of Darwin's circle worked in much the same ways that Barton described for the management of the Royal Society and the British Association for the Advancement of Science – to close ranks and to control debate.[19]

Death

Having returned hastily from Gibraltar to support Darwin being awarded the Copley medal of the Royal Society, in January 1865 Falconer suffered an attack of acute rheumatism and what looks to be pneumonia. He died in London on 31 January and was buried at Kensal Green on 4 February. Falconer's death at such a young age (no doubt in part at least the product of his time in India) disturbed many of his closest colleagues, not least Charles Darwin:

> My dear Hooker
>
> I heard this morning of Falconer's death. Poor fellow I am much grieved; It will be a great loss to science. What a lot of knowledge of all kinds has perished with him. He was always a most kind friend to me. So the world goes.
> (Letter to J. D. Hooker, 2 February [1865])

Hooker responded the next day:

> Kew
> Feby 3rd/65.
>
> My dear Darwin
>
> I hope you are better—I am pretty well, but somehow not over strong & bothered with eczema in the lobes of the ear, for which I am put upon Mercury & Iodide of Iron by Startin.
> Poor old Falconer! how my mind runs back to those happiest of all my days, that I used to spend at Down 20 years ago.—when I left your house with my heart in my mouth like a school-boy. We had heard he was ill on Wednesday or Thursday & sent daily to enquire, but the report was so good on Saturday that we sent no more, & on Monday night he died. We had dined together at the Athenaeum just 10 days before. He took cold on the day of that awful fog—Rheumatic fever & Bronchitis. From the first his heart did not act, & his attendant, Dr Murchison, took a gloomy view of his case— still on Friday he rallied & Dr M. thought the worst was over, or at least said so: on Saturday the heart again gave way & no stimulant sufficed to get it to act— on Sunday there was no more hope. He suffered terribly— he was fixed with pain, could not move a muscle, & the sweat rolled down his face & ears with agony. Poor dear old Falconer he had led the worst life for his temperament that was possible— At Post. Mort. his heart was found choked with fatty deposits. I go to the grave tomorrow with Thomson Bentham & many friends.

> What a mountainous mass of admirable & accurate information dies with our dear old friend.— I shall miss him greatly not only personally, but as a scientific man of unflinching & uncompromising integrity—& of great weight in Murchisonian & other counsels where ballast is sadly needed.
>
> The inconceivability of our being born for nothing better than such a paltry existence as ours' is, gives me some hope of meeting in a better world. What does it all mean.– When we think what millions upon millions of lives & intellects it has taken to work up to a knowledge of gravity & Natural selection, we really do seem a contemptible creation intellectually & when we feel the death of friends more keenly the older we grow, we do strike me as being corporeally most miserable, for we have no pleasures to compensate fully for our griefs & pains: these alone are unalloyed.
>
> Ever Yrs affec | J D Hooker.
>
> (Letter from J. D. Hooker, 3 February 1865)

Grim stuff indeed, prompting further sad reflections on the transience of life by Darwin. However both Hooker and Darwin were practical men and very adept at sensing the mood of their colleagues. The matter of a memorial to Falconer was widely canvassed among the geological and botanical communities in Britain, and Darwin wrote to Hooker seeking guidance on the issue:

> Can you give me any notion what to subscribe for poor dear Falconer's bust: would 5 guineas be too much or not enough?
>
> (Letter to J. D. Hooker, 15 February 1865)

Hooker responded in a way that laid bare some of the conflicts between botany and geology at the time, which Falconer managed to serve as a kind of lightning rod:

> I am puzzled about the Falconer affair, not what to subscribe, for I have no hesitation in thinking that £1"1. or £2"2 would be ample, adding if necessary afterwards to £5.5.0 the object being to secure a bust only—for which £100 or £150 should be enough. But I like to see these subscriptions confined to definite objects & bodies—as far as possible, & especially in Falconers case, because I suspect that Botanists will not subscribe with enthusiasm.—for this simple reason, that though he enjoyed for nearly 25 years the most

magnificent pay as a Botanist, he did nothing Botanical for it— his collections he let go to ruin, his mss he shut up & would let no one see.— As Superintendent of the Gardens his name was a byeword in Calcutta & a scandal elsewhere. Poor dear old F. these are very hard things for a friend to say—but so it is— it is impossible to exaggerate the mischief he did. He very nearly brought about the abandonment of the Calcutta Gardens, & to all my appeals at the India House for something to be done for Botany, *Falconer* was thrown in my teeth. So my idea is that the Geolog. Soc. should form the subscription & confine it to their own Members, & his friends afterwards subscribe for a copy of the bust if so disposed. I will subscribe to both.

(Letter from J.D. Hooker 17th February 1865)

Tough love from Hooker who, according to Desmond and McCracken (doubtless benefiting from a lack of direct involvement in the matter), overstated his case. They give a different, more generous, view of Falconer's behaviour, but there is little doubt that botany very much took a back seat to geology and palaeontology after his discoveries in the Siwaliks. It is also clear this was much resented by the botanists who regarded Falconer's tenure of what was supposed to be a botanist's post as a waste of scarce resources and opportunities.[20] This was not the view of the people who paid his salary. It is worth noting that Falconer certainly handsomely repaid the investment of the East India Company with his work on the domestication of tea and the establishment of Cinchona bark forests that created significant new sources of revenue for the Company.[21] Notwithstanding Hooker's unhappiness about Falconer as a botanist, his eminence in geology and palaeontology could hardly be questioned. Darwin duly contributed some £10 to the nearly £2000 collected. This allowed the carving of a bust for the Royal Society, and yet more funds were contributed to purchase a bust for the Asiatic Society of Bengal. A Falconer memorial fellowship for medical or natural science graduates of not more than three years' standing was also founded in the University of Edinburgh for the encouragement of the study of palaeontology and geology.

Concluding remarks

From what has been said, it is obvious that Falconer did enough during his life-time to render his name as a palaeontologist immortal in science; but the work which he published was only a fraction of what he accomplished. The amount of scientific knowledge which perished with him was very great for he was always cautious to a fault; he always feared aligning himself to an opinion until he was sure that he was right; and he died in the prime of life and in the fulness of his power. Lovers of science and those who knew him well can best appreciate his fearlessness of opposition when truth was to be evolved, his originality of observation and depth of thought, his penetrating and discriminating judgment, his extraordinary memory, the scrupulous care with which he ascribed to every man his due, and his honest and powerful advocacy of that cause which his strong intellect led him to adopt: they also have occasion to deplore the death of a staid adviser, a genial companion, and a hearty friend.[22]

No full-scale biography of Falconer currently exists. Instead he remains at the margins of the biographies of other luminaries such as Lyell, Darwin, Hooker and Huxley, which essentially means that we see him through their eyes rather than as the outcome of a detailed engagement with every aspect of his life and work – whether it be in England, India or on the continent of Europe. Researching a biography of Falconer that would seek to capture the complexities of his genius and his milieu in Europe and India, is a major undertaking, requiring a detailed understanding of the history of archaeology, palaeontology, geology and botany – to say nothing of the operations of the East India Company and the social and cultural context of mid-Victorian science. Falconer was an assiduous correspondent, a controversialist who was not afraid to 'speak truth to power', a person who inspired strong feelings of affection and loathing, and a scientist whose work continues to inspire the development of evolutionary theory long after his death.

Notwithstanding these significant challenges, a detailed engagement with Falconer can provide a fresh point of access into the development of disciplines such as archaeology and palaeontology at a critical point in their histories when they began to take the shapes we came to know in the twentieth century. Falconer's life also tells us much about the social and cultural contexts of scientific practice at the time when the Darwinian revolution had begun to transform our understanding of the natural world and the place of humanity in it, and all the jealousies, feuds, infighting and conflicts that were pursued with such intensity, because the stakes were so high.

Acknowledgements

I gratefully acknowledge the permission granted by the Falconer Museum, Forres, Scotland to allow reproduction of images that could unfortunately not be included in this publication, http://falconermuseum.co.uk/. Thanks also to Gabe Moshenska for the invitation to contribute to this volume and for his editorial suggestions.

Archives

Falconer's papers are held in the Falconer Museum, Forres, Scotland. Other major sources are: Asiatic Society of Bengal; Geological Society of London; Royal Society of London; *Gleanings in Science* (later journal of the Asiatic Society of Bengal). British Library Asian and African Studies for the East India Company. The Darwin Correspondence Project (https://www.darwinproject.ac.uk) presents a slice though his voluminous correspondence with Falconer and many others, and the letters quoted here are sourced to that archive. Other major sources can be found in the papers of Sir Joseph Prestwich, Sir Joseph Hooker, Sir John Evans and Sir John Lubbock held in the National Archive, the British Library and the Royal Botanic Gardens, Kew.

Notes

1 Falconer in Charles Murchison, *Palaeontological Memoirs and Notes of the Late Hugh Falconer, Edited, with a Biographical Sketch* (London: R. Hardwicke, 1868), note 97, volume 1: 22–23.
2 Major sources for biographical information about Falconer are Patrick J. Boylan, *The Falconer Papers, Forres* (Leicester: Leicestershire Museums, Art Galleries and Records Service, 1977); Idem., 'The controversy of the Moulin-Quignon jaw: the role of Hugh Falconer', in *Images of the Earth: Essays in the History of the Environmental Sciences*, eds. Ludmilla J. Jordanova and Roy S. Porter (Chalfont St. Giles: British Society for the History of Science, 1979); William F. Bynum, 'Charles Lyell's "Antiquity of Man and Its Critics"', *Journal of the History of Biology* 7 (1984): 153–87.; Gowan Dawson, '"The great O. versus the Jermyn St. pet": Huxley, Falconer, and Owen on paleontological method', in *Victorian Scientific Naturalism*, eds. Gowan Dawson and Bernard Lightman (Chicago: University of Chicago Press, 2014), 27–52; Gowan Dawson, *Show Me the Bone: Reconstructing prehistoric monsters in nineteenth-century Britain and America* (Chicago: University of Chicago Press, 2016); Ray Desmond, *The European Discovery of the Indian Flora* (Oxford: Oxford University Press, 1992); Grace Anne Prestwich, *Essays Descriptive and Biographical* (Edinburgh–London: William Blackwood, 1901); D. T. Moore, 'Falconer, Hugh (1808–1865)' in *Dictionary of National Biography*. https://doi.org/10.1093/ref:odnb/9110; Murchison, *Palaeontological Memoirs*; Anne O'Connor, 'Hugh Falconer, Joseph Prestwich and the Gower caves', *Studies in Speleology* 14 (2006): 75–9; Idem., *Finding Time for the Old Stone Age. A history of Palaeolithic archaeology and Quaternary geology in Britain, 1860–1960* (Oxford: Oxford University Press, 2007); Royal Society of London, 'Obituary notices of fellows deceased between 30th Nov. 1864 and 30th Nov. 1865', (1865): xiv–xx;

Leonard G. Wilson, 'Brixham Cave and Sir Charles Lyell's "The Antiquity of Man": the roots of Hugh Falconer's attack on Lyell', *Archives of Natural History* 23 (1996): 79–97.

3   Many of Falconer's papers and letters are kept at the Museum (see also https://falconermuseum.co.uk/learning-and-resources/hugh-falconer-banners/).

4   See Ruth Barton, *The X Club: Power and authority in Victorian science* (Chicago: University of Chicago Press, 2018); Adrian Desmond, *Huxley* (London: Penguin, 1998); Adrian Desmond and James Moore, *Darwin* (London: Penguin, 1992).

5   See, for example, Roy Porter, 'Gentlemen and geology: the emergence of a scientific career 1660–1920', *The Historical Journal* 21.4 (1978): 809–36.

6   There are several excellent discussions of the role of the East India Company in the development of the science of natural history in mid-Victorian Britain. See, for example, David J. Arnold, *The Tropics and the Traveling Gaze: India, landscape, and science, 1800–1856* (Seattle: University of Washington Press, 2006); Joyce Brown, 'A memoir of Colonel Sir Proby Cautley, F.R.S., 1802–1871, engineer and palaeontologist', *Notes and Records of the Royal Society of London* 34 (1980): 185–225; Pratik Chakrabarti, and Joydeep Sen, '"The world rests on the back of a tortoise": science and mythology in Indian history', *Modern Asian Studies* 50.3 (2016): 804–40; Vinita Damodaran, Anna Winterbottom and Alan Lester, eds., *East India Company and the Natural World* (London: Palgrave Macmillan, 2015); Donal P. McCracken, *Gardens of Empire: Botanical institutions of the Victorian British Empire* (London: Leicester University Press, 1977); Jessica Ratcliff, 'The East India Company, the Company's museum, and the political economy of natural history in the early nineteenth century', *Isis* 107 (2016): 495–517.

7   Anon., 'Wallich, Nathaniel (1786–1854)' in *The Plant Collectors Collection*. Accessed 4 February 2022 https://plants.jstor.org/stable/10.5555/al.ap.person.bm000009055.

8   Edward P. F. Rose, 'Geologists and the army in nineteenth century Britain: a scientific and educational symbiosis?', *Proceedings of the Geologist's Association* 107 (1996): 129–41 presents an interesting discussion of this practice in action.

9   See, for example, Hugh Falconer, 'Abstract of a discourse by Dr Falconer, on the fossil fauna of the Sewalik Hills', *Journal of the Royal Asiatic Society* 8 (1846): 107–11; Om Prakash Kejariwal, *The Asiatic Society of Bengal and the Discovery of India's Past, 1784–1838* (Oxford: Oxford University Press, 1988).

10 Brown, 'A memoir of Colonel Sir Proby Cautley'; B. B. Woodward, revised by Mark Harrison, 'Royle, John Forbes (1798–1858)', in *Oxford Dictionary of National Biography*. https://doi.org/10.1093/ref:odnb/24239.

11 The Siwalik fauna is of the first importance in the history of palaeontology, and represented an extraordinary resource that has been more effectively understood in recent times. See, for example, Stephen J. Gould, *The Structure of Evolutionary Theory* (Cambridge: Harvard University Press, 2002); Idem., *Punctuated Equilibrium* (Harvard University Press, 2007); Kenneth A. R. Kennedy, and Russell L. Ciochon, 'A canine tooth from the Siwaliks: first recorded discovery of a fossil ape?', *Journal of Human Evolution* 14 (1999): 231–53.

12 See Claudine Cohen and Jean-Jacques Hublin, *Boucher De Perthes. Les Origines Romantiques De La Préhistoire* (Paris: Belin, 1989); William Boyd Dawkins, *Cave Hunting* (London: Macmillan, 1874); John Evans, 'On the occurrence of flint implements in undisturbed beds of gravel, sand, and clay' *Archaeologia* 38 (1860): 280–307; Donald K. Grayson, *The Establishment of Human Antiquity* (New York: Academic Press, 1983); John Lubbock, *Pre-Historic Times* (London: John Murray, 1865); Charles Lyell, *Geological Evidence of the Antiquity of Man,* second edition), (London: John Murray, 1863); Anne O'Connor 'Brixham Cave and the antiquity of man: reassessing the archaeological and historical significance of a British cave site.' *Lithics* 21 (2000): 20–8; Idem., 'Hugh Falconer, Joseph Prestwich and the Gower caves'; Idem., *Finding Time for the Old Stone Age*; William Pengelly, 'Report on Windmill Hill Cavern, at Brixham, Devonshire. Drawn up by Mr. Pengelly, in 1862, for the Cavern Committee, at the request of the chairman, Dr. Falconer. Forwarded to the committee, at their request, December 4, 1865', *Report and Transactions of the Devonshire Association for the Advancement of Science* 6 (1873): 46–60; Paul Pettit and Mark J. White, 'Cave men: stone tools, Victorian science, and the "primitive mind" of deep time', *Notes and Records of the Royal Society of London* 65 (2011): 25–42; Joseph Prestwich, 'On the occurrence of flint implements, associated with the remains of animals of extinct species in beds of a late geological period, in France at Amiens and Abbeville, and in England at Hoxne', *Philosophical Transactions of the Royal Society of London* 150 (1860): 277–318; Idem., 'Report of the exploration of Brixham Cave', *Philosophical Transactions of the Royal Society* 163 (1873): 471–572; Nathalie Richard, *Inventer La Préhistoire:*

Les Débuts De L'archéologie Préhistorique En France (Paris: Vuibert, 2008); A. Bowdoin Van Riper, *Men among the Mammoths: Victorian science and the discovery of human prehistory* (Chicago: University of Chicago Press, 1993); Wilson, 'Brixham Cave and Sir Charles Lyell's "The Antiquity of Man"'.
13 Royal Society, 'Obituary Notices'; Murchison, *Palaeontological Memoirs*.
14 David J. Meltzer, 'The seventy-year itch: controversies over human antiquity and their resolution', *Journal of Anthropological Research* 61 (2005): 433–68; Martin J. S. Rudwick, *Georges Cuvier, Fossil Bones, and Geological Catastrophes* (Chicago: University of Chicago Press, 1997); Idem., *Bursting the Limits of Time. The reconstruction of geohistory in the age of revolution* (Chicago: University of Chicago Press, 2005); James Sackett, 'Human antiquity and the old stone age: the nineteenth century background to paleoanthropology', *Evolutionary Anthropology* 37 (2000): 36–49; Efrem Sera-Shriar, *The Making of British Anthropology, 1813–1871* (Pittsburgh: University of Pittsburgh Press, 2016); Idem., ed., *Historicizing Humans: Deep Time, Evolution, and Race in Nineteenth-Century British Sciences. Science and culture in the nineteenth century* (Pittsburgh: University of Pittsburgh Press, 2018); George C. Stocking Jr., *Victorian Anthropology* (New York: Free Press, 1987).
15 The best discussion of this is found in Boylan, 'The controversy of the Moulin-Quignon jaw'.
16 Grace Milne was a keen correspondent and developed into an accomplished illustrator and writer working with Falconer. Her letters (and a memoir of her life written by her sister Louisa Milne) provide an intimate portrait of her life with Falconer and Prestwich and her developing role as a popular communicator of geology. See Grace Anne Prestwich, *Essays Descriptive and Biographical*, especially pp. 1–70; Kristine Larsen, *The Women Who Popularized Geology in the 19th Century*. (Cham: Springer, 2017); J. D. Mather and I. Campbell, 'Grace Anne Milne (Lady Prestwich): more than an amanuensis?', in *The Role of Women in the History of Geology*, eds. Cynthia V. Burek and Bettie Higgs (London: Geological Society of London, 2007), 251–64; Marilyn Ogilvie, Joy Harvey and Margaret Rossiter, eds., *The Biographical Dictionary of Women in Science: Pioneering lives from ancient times to the mid-20th century* (London: Routledge, 2000).
17 See footnote 12.
18 The best discussion of this complex and sometimes murky business can be found in Dawson, '"The Great O. versus the Jermyn St. pet"; Dawson, *Show Me the Bone*; Dawson and Lightman, eds., *Victorian Scientific Naturalism*.
19 Hugh Falconer, 'Letter', *Athenaeum* 1848 (1863): 459–60. For Falconer's debates with Darwin, see Gould, *The Structure of Evolutionary Theory*. For his debates with Lyell, see Bynum, 'Charles Lyell's "Antiquity of Man and its critics"'. Barton, *The X Club*, discusses the operations of the X Club.
20 Desmond, *The European Discovery of the Indian Flora*; McCracken, *Gardens of Empire*.
21 See W. Harry G. Armytage, *The Rise of the Technocrats: A social history* (London: Routledge, 1965, 2007).
22 Royal Society, 'Obituary notices'.

Bibliography

Anon., 'Wallich, Nathaniel (1786-1854)' in *The Plant Collectors Collection*. Accessed 3 February 2022 https://plants.jstor.org/stable/10.5555/al.ap.person.bm000009055.
Armytage, W. Harry G., *The Rise of the Technocrats: A social history* (London: Routledge, 1965, 2007).
Arnold, David J., *The Tropics and the Traveling Gaze: India, landscape, and science, 1800–1856* (Seattle: University of Washington Press, 2006).
Barton, Ruth, *The X Club: Power and authority in Victorian science* (Chicago: University of Chicago Press, 2018).
Boylan, Patrick J., *The Falconer Papers, Forres* (Leicester: Leicestershire Museums, Art Galleries and Records Service, 1977).
Boylan, Patrick J., 'The controversy of the Moulin-Quignon jaw: the role of Hugh Falconer', in *Images of the Earth: Essays in the history of the environmental sciences*, eds. Ludmilla J. Jordanova and Roy S. Porter (Chalfont St. Giles: British Society for the History of Science, 1979).

Brown, Joyce, 'A memoir of Colonel Sir Proby Cautley, F.R.S., 1802–1871, engineer and palaeontologist', *Notes and Records of the Royal Society of London* 34.2 (1980): 185–225.

Bynum, William F., 'Charles Lyell's "Antiquity of Man and Its Critics"', *Journal of the History of Biology* 7 (1984): 153–87.

Chakrabarti, Pratik and Joydeep Sen, '"The world rests on the back of a tortoise": science and mythology in Indian history', *Modern Asian Studies* 50 (2016): 804–40.

Cohen, Claudine and Jean-Jacques Hublin, *Boucher De Perthes. Les Origines Romantiques De La Préhistoire* (Paris: Belin, 1989).

Damodaran, Vinita, Anna Winterbottom and Alan Lester, eds., *East India Company and the Natural World* (London: Palgrave Macmillan, 2015).

Dawkins, William Boyd, *Cave Hunting* (London: Macmillan, 1874).

Dawson, Gowan, '"The great O. versus the Jermyn St. pet": Huxley, Falconer, and Owen on paleontological method', in *Victorian Scientific Naturalism*, eds. Gowan Dawson and Bernard Lightman (Chicago: University of Chicago Press, 2014), 27–52.

Dawson, Gowan, *Show Me the Bone. Reconstructing prehistoric monsters in nineteenth-century Britain and America* (Chicago: University of Chicago Press, 2016).

Dawson, Gowan and Bernard Lightman, eds., *Victorian Scientific Naturalism* (Chicago: University of Chicago Press, 2014).

Desmond, Adrian, *Huxley* (London: Penguin, 1998).

Desmond, Adrian and James Moore, *Darwin* (London: Penguin, 1992).

Desmond, Ray, *The European Discovery of the Indian Flora* (Oxford: Oxford University Press, 1992).

Evans, John, 'On the occurrence of flint implements in undisturbed beds of gravel, sand, and clay', *Archaeologia* 38 (1860): 280–307.

Falconer, Hugh, 'Abstract of a discourse by Dr Falconer, on the fossil fauna of the Sewalik Hills', *Journal of the Royal Asiatic Society* 8 (1846): 107–11.

Falconer, Hugh, 'On Prof. Huxley's attempted refutation of Cuvier's Laws of correlation, in the reconstruction of extinct vertebrate forms', *Annals and Magazine of Natural History* n.s. 17 (1856): 476–93.

Falconer, Hugh, 'On the ossiferous caves of the Peninsula of Gower, in Glamorganshire, South Wales', *Quarterly Journal of the Geological Society of London* 16 (1860): 487–91.

Falconer, Hugh, 'On the ossiferous Grotta Di Maccagnone, near Palermo', *Quarterly Journal of the Geological Society of London* 16 (1860a): 99–106.

Falconer, Hugh, 'Letter', *Athenaeum*, no. 1848 (1863): 459–60.

Falconer, Hugh, with G. Busk and W.B. Carpenter, 'An account of the proceedings of the late conference held in France to inquire into the circumstances attending the asserted discovery of a human jaw in the gravel at Moulin-Quignon, near Abbeville; including the procès verbaux of the sittings of the conference, with notes thereon', *Natural History Review* n.s. 3 (1863): 423–62.

Falconer, Hugh and G. Busk, 'On the fossil contents of the Genitsa Cave, Gibraltar', *Quarterly Journal of the Geological Society of London* 21 (1865): 364–70.

Falconer, Hugh and Proby T. Cautley, *Fauna Antiqua Sivalensis, Being the Fossil Zoology of the Sewalik Hills, in the North of India, Part I, Proboscidea* (London: J. Frances etc., 1849).

Gould, Stephen J., *The Structure of Evolutionary Theory* (Cambridge, MA: Harvard University Press, 2002).

Gould, Stephen J., *Punctuated Equilibrium* (Cambridge, MA: Harvard University Press, 2007).

Grayson, Donald K., *The Establishment of Human Antiquity* (New York: Academic Press, 1983).

Gruber, Jacob, 'Brixham Cave and the antiquity of man', in *Context and Meaning in Cultural Anthropology*, ed. Melford E. Spiro (New York: Free Press, 1965), 373–402.

Kejariwal, Om Prakash, *The Asiatic Society of Bengal and the Discovery of India's Past, 1784–1838* (Oxford: Oxford University Press, 1988).

Kennedy, Kenneth A. R. and Russell L. Ciochon, 'A canine tooth from the Siwaliks: first recorded discovery of a fossil ape?', *Journal of Human Evolution* 14 (1999): 231–53.

Larsen, Kirstine, *The Women Who Popularized Geology in the 19th Century* (Cham: Springer, 2017).

Lubbock, John, *Pre-Historic Times* (London: John Murray, 1865).

Lyell, Charles, *Geological Evidence of the Antiquity of Man*, second edition (London: John Murray, 1863).

Mather, J. D. and I. Campbell, 'Grace Anne Milne (Lady Prestwich): more than an amanuensis?', in *The Role of Women in the History of Geology*, eds. Cynthia V. Burek and Bettie Higgs (London: Geological Society of London, 2007), 251–64.

McCracken, Donal P., *Gardens of Empire: Botanical institutions of the Victorian British Empire* (London: Leicester University Press, 1977).

Meltzer, David J., 'The seventy-year itch: controversies over human antiquity and their resolution', *Journal of Anthropological Research* 61 (2005): 433–68.

Moore, D. T., 'Falconer, Hugh (1808–1865), palaeontologist and naturalist.' In *Dictionary of National Biography*. https://doi.org/10.1093/ref:odnb/9110.

Murchison, Charles, *Palaeontological Memoirs and Notes of the Late Hugh Falconer, Edited, with a Biographical Sketch* (London: R. Hardwicke, 1868).

O'Connor, Anne, 'Brixham Cave and the antiquity of man: reassessing the archaeological and historical significance of a British cave site', *Lithics* 21 (2000): 20–8.

O'Connor, Anne, 'Hugh Falconer, Joseph Prestwich and the Gower caves', *Studies in Speleology* 14 (2006): 75–79.

O'Connor, Anne, *Finding Time for the Old Stone Age. A history of Palaeolithic archaeology and Quaternary geology in Britain, 1860–1960* (Oxford: Oxford University Press, 2007).

Ogilvie, Marilyn, Joy Harvey and Margaret Rossiter, eds., *The Biographical Dictionary of Women in Science: Pioneering lives from ancient times to the mid-20th century* (London: Routledge, 2000).

Pengelly, William, 'Report on Windmill Hill Cavern, at Brixham, Devonshire. Drawn up by Mr. Pengelly, in 1862, for the Cavern Committee, at the request of the chairman, Dr. Falconer. Forwarded to the committee, at their request, December 4, 1865', *Report and Transactions of the Devonshire Association for the Advancement of Science* 6 (1873): 46–60.

Pettit, Paul and Mark J. White, 'Cave men: stone tools, Victorian science, and the 'primitive mind' of deep time', *Notes and Records of the Royal Society of London* 65 (2011): 25–42.

Porter, Roy, 'Gentlemen and geology: the emergence of a scientific career 1660–1920', *The Historical Journal* 21.4 (1978): 809–36.

Prestwich, Grace Anne, *Essays Descriptive and Biographical* (Edinburgh–London: William Blackwood, 1901).

Prestwich, Joseph, 'On the occurrence of flint implements, associated with the remains of animals of extinct species in beds of a late geological period, in France at Amiens and Abbeville, and in England at Hoxne', *Philosophical Transactions of the Royal Society of London* 150 (1860): 277–318.

Prestwich, Joseph,, 'Report of the exploration of Brixham Cave', *Philosophical Transactions of the Royal Society* 163 (1873): 471–572.

Ratcliff, Jessica, 'The East India Company, the Company's museum, and the political economy of natural history in the early nineteenth century', *Isis* 107 (2016): 495–517.

Richard, Nathalie, *Inventer La Préhistoire: Les Débuts De L'archéologie Préhistorique En France* (Paris: Vuibert, 2008).

Rose, Edward P. F., 'Geologists and the army in nineteenth century Britain: a scientific and educational symbiosis?', *Proceedings of the Geologist's Association* 107.2 (1996): 129–41.

Royal Society of London, 'Obituary notices of fellows deceased between 30th Nov. 1864 and 30th Nov. 1865' (1865): xiv–xx.

Rudwick, Martin J. S., *Georges Cuvier, Fossil Bones, and Geological Catastrophes* (Chicago: University of Chicago Press, 1997).

Rudwick, Martin J. S.,, *Bursting the Limits of Time. The reconstruction of geohistory in the Age of Revolution* (Chicago: University of Chicago Press, 2005).

Sackett, James, 'Human antiquity and the old stone age: the nineteenth century background to paleoanthropology', *Evolutionary Anthropology* 37 (2000): 36–49.

Sera-Shriar, Efrem, *The Making of British Anthropology, 1813–1871* (Pittsburgh: University of Pittsburgh Press, 2016).

Sera-Shriar, Efrem, ed., *Historicizing Humans: Deep time, evolution, and race in nineteenth-century British sciences. science and culture in the nineteenth century* (Pittsburgh: University of Pittsburgh Press, 2018).

Stocking, George C. Jr., *Victorian Anthropology* (New York: Free Press, 1987).

Van Riper, A. Bowdoin, *Men among the Mammoths: Victorian science and the discovery of human prehistory* (Chicago: University of Chicago Press, 1993).

Wilson, Leonard G., 'Brixham Cave and Sir Charles Lyell's "The Antiquity of Man": the roots of Hugh Falconer's attack on Lyell', *Archives of Natural History* 23 (1996): 79–97.

Woodward, B. B., revised by Mark Harrison, 'Royle, John Forbes'. In *Dictionary of National Biography*. https://doi.org/10.1093/ref:odnb/24239.

11
Personal and professional connections in early nineteenth-century Egyptology: The letters of Conrad Leemans to Thomas Pettigrew

Gabriel Moshenska

Introduction

In his study of personal archives as sources for archaeological biographies, Kaeser observes that 'the biographer should take into consideration not only letters that can be labelled as properly scientific, but also (as far as possible) purely private exchanges, which can be very useful as well'.[1] In practice few lives, relationships or sources are so neatly compartmentalised, and most of the archived correspondence of value for archaeological life-writing is somewhere on the continuum between these two poles of 'scientific' and 'private'. With the growth of interest in networks as units of analysis in the history of archaeology these categories are further blurred as scholars map evolving webs of professional, financial, familial, sexual, adversarial and amicable relationships.[2] The connections between two individuals are the smallest unit or building block of such networks: a close examination of a single such link can provide a starting point for network-building, just as archived correspondence that provides context and detail to the relationship can also point to further associations and points of contact.

This chapter focuses on the social and intellectual relationship between the Dutch Egyptologist Conrad Leemans and the British surgeon and antiquarian Thomas Pettigrew. It draws on a variety of sources, but is primarily based on a set of 14 letters sent by Leemans to Pettigrew dating from 1836, when Leemans first visited London, through to 1843, around the time that Pettigrew's active involvement in the study of ancient Egypt began to decline. The letters provide insights into the early years of Leemans' career as he began to establish himself as one of the nineteenth century's foremost scholars of ancient Egyptian texts. They show the value of personal introductions for scholars travelling to foreign countries, as well as forms of intellectual tribute and collaboration, and the economies and geographies of scholarly publication. The letters shed light on Leemans' heartfelt Anglophilia and his hopes of finding employment in a museum or collection in Britain but also reveal something about Pettigrew's career in Egyptology. As British scholarship on ancient Egypt developed beyond antiquarianism, Pettigrew became increasingly marginalised, before ultimately shifting his attention to British antiquities.

Leemans, in contrast, has long been recognised as a pioneer in the study of ancient Egypt, and a short volume containing a biography and selected letters was published by a descendent, W. F. Leemans, in 1973. The majority of the letters in this volume were those received by Leemans, and the volume included an appeal for information:

> Je ne connais que très peu des lettres, que C. Leemans a sans doute écrit en grand nombre à ses collègues. Si quelqu'un pouvait en retrouver, il me rendrait un grand service en me les signalant.[3]

My much-belated response to this appeal draws on letters held in Pettigrew's archived correspondence at the British Library and at the Beinecke Rare Book and Manuscript Library at Yale. Returning to Kaeser's point of the scientific and the private in personal correspondence, one of the most interesting and charming aspects of Leemans' letters to Pettigrew is precisely the mixture of personal and professional information that they impart, often shifting swiftly from the one to the other, and revealing something of the internal workings of the international networks of archaeological, Egyptological and related scholarship of the period, complicated by family ties, friendships and loyalties.

Correspondence and networks in the history of archaeology

The archaeological and philological advances in the study of ancient Egypt during the first half of the nineteenth century laid the foundations for the modern discipline of Egyptology.[4] This period saw the emergence of a professional strand within the intellectual community, with a small but growing number of scholars of ancient Egypt employed in museums across Europe. From a historical perspective, the function and composition of this community of individuals and institutions can be traced as a network of intersecting professional and personal connections. To understand the movement of ancient Egyptian texts, artefacts, ideas and the scholars themselves, it is necessary to trace this network of personal and intellectual connections, taking into account the influencing factors of nationality, religion, socio-economic class, professional status and scholarly reputation. The value of network analyses in propelling a more nuanced and theoretically informed history of archaeology has been demonstrated in recent work by Thornton, who argues that:

> In order to examine a social network in any comprehensive sense sponsors, patrons, friends, spouses, teachers, families, clubmates should all be considered; this information builds up a more complex picture and contributes to reconstructing and interpreting the historical context. In this way, the history of archaeology moves beyond the still popular narrative of great excavators, sites and objects, towards a more nuanced understanding of archaeology within social, cultural, political and economic arenas.[5]

The move towards microhistorical studies of this kind, focusing on connections between individuals over fairly narrow timespans, allows a fine-grained analysis of these contexts at a human scale of space and time in which primary sources such as correspondence are vital. Kaeser described microhistorical archive-based research in the history of archaeology: 'At a very small scale and from fine traces in the archive material scrutinised intensively, it endeavours to reconstruct the complex web of past actions, relations and social networks.'[6] Díaz-Andreu has written on the particular value of archived letters in this work:

> Today these letters are an important documentary source for the history of archaeology. They are far more than anecdotal evidence … They contain proof of the process of events as they were experienced and felt by the individuals living through them. In the study of correspondence between scholars, letters help us to understand the tempo of a social relationship.[7]

The aims of this study are to examine the values of interpersonal relationships as a unit of analysis in life-writing in the history of archaeology, and to highlight the utility of archived correspondence in unravelling the minutiae of these relationships.

Conrad Leemans, 1809–1893

Conrad Leemans was born in Zaltbommel in the Netherlands in 1809. He studied theology at university before coming under the influence of a family friend Caspar Reuvens, the world's first professor of archaeology, at Leiden University. Reuvens employed Leemans on several of his excavations on Roman sites in the Netherlands, where he became a skilled fieldworker. In 1829 Leemans and Reuvens travelled to Paris, where they studied Egyptology and spent time at the Louvre.[8]

Leemans continued to work with Reuvens at the National Museum of Antiquities in Leiden until the Belgian Revolution in 1830, when he volunteered for military service. He was wounded in an ambush in August 1831 and returned to the Netherlands to recuperate and work on his doctoral thesis in Egyptology. After Reuvens' death in 1835, Leemans was appointed conservator of the National Museum of Antiquities and later became its director. In his career of more than 50 years at the museum he published huge and ground-breaking catalogues of the collections, including the first ever comprehensive publication of a corpus of ancient Egyptian texts.[9] In 1836 Leemans visited England and spent several months studying the collections at the British Museum, as well as some private collections. During his visit he became acquainted with most of the key figures in the then-small community of British Egyptologists, including Thomas Pettigrew.

Thomas Pettigrew, 1791–1865

Thomas Pettigrew was born in London in 1791, which made him some 18 years older than Leemans. The son of a workhouse surgeon who had served for many years in the Royal Navy, he was apprenticed to a surgeon friend of his father who ran a private medical school. Through his involvement in the Royal Humane Society and the Medical Society of London, he became honorary surgeon to the Duke and Duchess of Kent, a role which included vaccinating the future Queen Victoria. He later became surgeon and librarian to the Duke of Sussex.[10]

Pettigrew had a long-standing interest in history and archaeology and accumulated a substantial collection of antiquities. During the 1830s and 1840s he became famous for unrolling Egyptian mummies for invited or paying audiences in museums, operating theatres, conference halls and private homes.[11] He published extensively on Egyptological, antiquarian and archaeological subjects, as well as studies in the history of medicine, and was a co-founder and long-time Vice President of the British Archaeological Association until his death in 1865. He is chiefly remembered today for his work on Egyptian mummies, as well as for his sensational and scandalous biography of Admiral Nelson: an exercise in life-writing based largely on a collection of Nelson's private letters that Pettigrew purchased at auction.[12]

Leemans in London

Leemans seems to have come into contact with Pettigrew during his visit to London in early 1836. The purpose of this visit was to continue his Egyptological training, building on his time in Paris in 1829. Leemans' time in London was spent studying at the British Museum and visiting private collections of Egyptian antiquities, including those of John Lee and Sir John Soane. His painstaking copies of the inscriptions in these collections are still preserved in the museum at Leiden. During this trip, as his biographer notes:

> Il y rencontra tout les anglais de temps intéressés par l'ancienne Égypte, Edward Hawkins, Wilkinson, Lee, Pettigrew, et l'égyptologue débutant Samuel Birch; il fut invité a l'Athenaeum Club … Jeune homme, ayant, par son éducation, l'habitude de monde, il eut ses entrées dans les familles anglaises et il s'adapta facilement aux costumes et à la mode anglaise, qui, à cette époque, servit d'exemple en Europe continentale … Il entretiendra des relations épistolaires pendant plusieurs années avec les familles qu'il avait rencontrées, avec sir Henry Ellis (directeur de Musée Britannique), avec les Gray (John Edward Gray, conservateur de la collection zoologique de Musée Britannique), les Pettigrew, John Lee, Lord Prudhoe, C.J. London et d'autres.[13]

Leemans first wrote to Pettigrew in March 1836, soon after his arrival in London, at which point he was staying in rooms on Hunter Street, Bloomsbury, close to the British Museum, where most of his work was carried out.[14] He wrote to request permission to view Pettigrew's collection of Egyptian antiquities, during a forced break in his work on

Egyptian inscriptions due to the Easter closure of the British Museum. Pettigrew's reply has not survived, but in May Leemans wrote again, sending a draft copy of his notes and a description of a sarcophagus in Pettigrew's collection.[15] These letters indicate that Pettigrew was a significant enough collector of Egyptian antiquities to pique Leemans' interest and that Leemans had in due course visited Pettigrew's home to study his collection and meet his family.[16]

During his visit to London Leemans became ill, as evidenced by his letter to Pettigrew giving an account of his fever, shivering, perspiration, and the state of his 'lower regions'.[17] Pettigrew enjoyed a good reputation as a society surgeon, and many of his friends, colleagues and correspondents seem to have called upon his professional skills at various points. For example, the Egyptologist John Gardner Wilkinson wrote to Pettigrew from the Mediterranean for advice on the treatment of an extremely unpleasant venereal disease, the symptoms of which he described in detail.[18]

Leemans is said to have returned from London to Holland as something of a 'dandy', wearing the most fashionable London outfits, much to the amusement of his friends [19]. His Anglophilia is evident in his wish, repeated several times in his correspondence, for a job in a British museum, and in his lament to Pettigrew that 'really I don't know how to remain alive this year, without breathing Albion's air, together with my dear friends there'.

International correspondence

In December 1836, after his return to Holland, Leemans wrote to Pettigrew, whom he still addressed as 'my dear Sir', touching upon various medical, archaeological and personal topics.[20] Like Pettigrew, Leemans father was a medical professional, and Leemans wrote to thank Pettigrew for sending copies of his various pamphlets and offprints on subjects such as cholera and 'hydrophobia', or rabies. Pettigrew's pamphlet on cholera was published in 1831 as the second cholera pandemic raged across Europe, but before it reached Britain the year after, causing thousands of deaths.[21] Leemans also referred in passing to Pettigrew's feud with the Charing Cross Hospital, which was at the time in the process of firing him for corruption, after he extracted a payment of £500 for appointing a friend to a lucrative post.[22] Leemans' comments:'I am very glad to hear that the hospital affair turned into the shame of your base opposers' seem to suggest that Pettigrew had prevailed in this dispute, but this was not the case.[23] Much of this letter and several that follow are made up of gossip about the National Museum of Antiquities, enquiries about relatives and mutual friends, and discussions of Leemans' and Pettigrew's research.

These shared interests were by no means restricted to Egyptology. Leemans published a paper on British archaeology shortly after his visit, and his correspondence with Pettigrew shows that both men were studying Chinese and Indian antiquities.[24] From 1837 Pettigrew began to compile his four-volume collection of biographical studies of famous figures in the history of medicine, the *Medical Portrait Gallery*, as a distraction after the death of his eldest son in India.[25] Each entry in the collection included a portrait and, where possible, an autograph of the figure in question, and Pettigrew enlisted Leemans in his search for a portrait and autograph of the Dutch physician Herman Boerhaave.[26] Leemans in turn used Pettigrew to advertise and distribute his books to British antiquarians, and the two discussed and exchanged copies of their publications for several years.[27]

This exchange of sources, references and texts is a familiar aspect of international academic correspondence and networks through to the present, and was by no means one-sided. In 1837 Richard William Howard Vyse blasted and broke his way into the Great Pyramid of Giza and uncovered a number of new inscriptions, including the first evidence that Khufu was the builder of the pyramid.[28] Vyse's discoveries were not published in full for some time, and Leemans – then close to completing his first published collection of Egyptian inscriptions – wrote to Pettigrew twice, in 1837 and 1838, asking for a draft copy of the pyramid texts that had been deposited at the Royal Society of Literature.[29]

Leemans also requested a copy of the Sanskrit inscription on an Indian bronze statue in Pettigrew's collection, and sent sheets of the appropriate paper along with detailed instructions on making pressings, to be carried out by Pettigrew's son William.[30] Here again we see an international scholarly network in operation: the pressing was not for Leemans but formed part of a collection of Indian inscriptions he was collecting on behalf of his friend Eugène-Vincent-Stanislas Jacquet (1811–38), who intended to publish a *Corpus Inscriptionum Indicoreum*.[31] Jacquet was a brilliant and precocious linguist and a member of the Asiatic Society of Paris: within six months of Leemans' letter Jacquet had dropped dead of exhaustion, pencil in hand, surrounded by a collection of artefacts.[32] The exchange of pressings highlights the significance of correspondence networks and 'invisible colleges' in the movement of material objects as well as information during this period.[33]

In the mid-1830s Leemans' situation at the National Museum of Antiquities was still insecure, and the museum itself was woefully underfunded.[34] It is perhaps unsurprising that a few months after his return to Holland he was still feeling nostalgic for the British Museum and his friends in London, writing wistfully about the possibilities of employment ('My constant wishes are to get a situation in England … I wish Sir John Soane would make me the director of his collection'), but also confessing that 'a place at the Br. Museum would hardly agree to my aversion of being bound to do my duty, by laws and instructions'.[35] Leemans' description of his work in Leiden wavered between contentment at the freedom he enjoyed and dissatisfaction at the lack of money, books and resources: the Dutch economy was still recovering from the expensive wars of the early 1800s, with lasting impacts on what had been a world-leading scientific and intellectual community.[36]

Networks of people and things

In the early nineteenth century a number of major collections of Egyptian antiquities were brought to Britain and sold, some at auction, and most divided into multiple sales: many European museums can trace large proportions of their Egyptian collections, or even their origins, to these sales. Some had originated as private collections, while others like Henry Salt's were accumulated for the purpose of export and sale. These sales served as important nexuses for the international Egyptological community, often being preceded by lavish exhibitions of the antiquities, and with published sales catalogues that formed significant elements of the meagre scholarly literature.[37] The second sale of Giovanni d'Athanasi's collection was scheduled for March 1837,[38] and Leemans wrote to Pettigrew in December 1836 rather wistfully:

> Perhaps, if my occupations allow me in the spring an absence of ten or 12 days, I would try to cast an eye at the Athanasi's collection, the catalogue of which you had the kindness to procure me, but, as I doubt very much, if I shall be able to fulfill this plan, perhaps I am to trouble you afterwards for some information about some lots, before the collection is to be sold.[39]

Leemans' plan came to fruition, and the following March found him in London, assessing the choice artefacts including a high-status sarcophagus, and making arrangements to have breakfast with Pettigrew before the auction commenced.⁴⁰ He also made some purchases on behalf of the museum, as noted in the catalogue of Egyptian antiquities he published in 1840:

> Quelques achats partiels, à l'occasion des ventes des collections SALT en 1825 et D'ATHANASI en 1837 à Londres, ont contribué à augmenter les trésors des antiquités Égyptiennes et à assurer au Musée des Pays-Bas une place distinguée parmi ceux du premier rang.⁴¹

In the same catalogue introduction, he cites Pettigrew's *History of Egyptian Mummies* as the authoritative text on Egyptian mummification. In these transactions we can glimpse the operation of one fragment of an international scholarly network: in Pettigrew's acquiring the sales catalogue and sending it to Leemans in Leiden; in Leemans' travelling to London for the sale; and in his return to Leiden with antiquities transported from Egypt to Britain by a Greek dealer.⁴² The value of nineteenth-century correspondence networks as sources in the history of collections is well attested.⁴³

Letters of introduction

Beyond the exchange of data and materials, Leemans' letters reveal a great deal about the activities of international scholarly networks through recommendations and introductions. Leemans clearly appreciated the warm reception he received from the Pettigrew family, and felt secure enough in the ensuing friendship to offer introductions to the Pettigrews to friends and colleagues travelling to London. Presumably these would have been part of a set of introductions to various relevant figures in London's social and intellectual circles, but Leemans' letters also suggest that he recognised the value of Pettigrew's networks beyond their immediate shared areas of interest. Leemans' letters include introductions to five people: a scientist, a linguist, an Egyptologist, an artist and a physician, and it is worth considering these in a little more detail.

The first introduction comes in November 1837, naming one 'Dr F Crausz', a family friend of Leemans who was travelling to the Cape via London.⁴⁴ Leemans states that Crausz is keen to gather information on zoology, mineralogy and other areas of natural history and asks Pettigrew to provide introductions to suitable scholars and societies, as well as hospitality to a young man alone in a foreign city. It is most likely that

'F Crausz' is Christian Ferdinand Friedrich von Krauss (1812–1890), a German scientist and collector. Krauss studied zoology and mineralogy and was awarded his PhD at Heidelberg in 1836. In 1838 he sailed from Britain to the Cape Province in South Africa. Many of the items he collected during his travels were sold to the British Museum, and he subsequently worked at the Staatliches Museum für Naturkunde in his hometown of Stuttgart. He subsequently served as director of the museum from 1856.[45]

Leemans' next introduction was given to his friend Dr Benjamin Frederik Matthes (1818–1908), who was enjoying a 'scientific stay in London' and had brought with him a copy of one of Leemans' Egyptological publications to give to Pettigrew.[46] Leemans introduced Matthes to Pettigrew's daughter Eliza in particular, stating that 'Eliza will remember his sister and brothers; we used to meet with them at Kroonesteyn … I may perhaps hope that her protection will be granted to my friend'.[47] At the time, Matthes, then just 20 or 21 years old, was embarking on a long and successful career as a missionary, linguist and Bible translator: much of his work took place in Indonesia.[48] A later traveller in the region recalled having met Matthes many years earlier, and that '[h]e wrote a grammar and a dictionary of both the Booginese and the Macassar tongues [and] translated the Bible into these languages', but noted that '[h]is success as a converter to the Christian faith has not been lasting'.[49] Translations of religious texts may have been an interest that Matthes and Pettigrew shared: through his work as librarian to the Duke of Sussex, Pettigrew had catalogued and studied a vast collection of religious texts including hundreds of different translations of the Bible.[50]

The only Egyptologist that Leemans introduced to the Pettigrews was the young German scholar Karl Lepsius (1810–1884). Leemans' note is brief: he introduced Lepsius as 'one of the first hieroglyphical scholars now existing' and that he had given him a letter to pass on to Eliza Pettigrew.[51] It is likely that by 1838 Pettigrew would have been aware of Lepsius, whose work during this period was focused on refining Champollion's work on Egyptian grammar.[52] Lepsius had studied archaeology and philology at Leipzig, Göttingen and Berlin, and spent time in Paris where he became interested in Egyptology. He subsequently travelled around Europe for several years to study Egyptian collections in Italy; Holland, where he presumably met Leemans; and Britain, where he arrived with an introduction to Pettigrew. In later years Lepsius worked at Berlin University and the Egyptian Museum of Berlin: he is widely acknowledged as one of the foremost Egyptologists of the nineteenth century and an important figure in the development of the discipline.[53]

The fourth introduction in this collection was given to the lithographer and engraver James Erxleben.[54] Unlike Krauss, Matthes and Lepsius,

Erxleben was looking for paid work in London and Leemans' introduction to Pettigrew is professional rather than personal in tone, although he notes that Erxleben 'has been introduced here in Leyden in the best family circles'.[55] Leemans introduced Erxleben to Pettigrew as an anatomical illustrator, perhaps knowing that Pettigrew had employed several skilled artists including George Cruikshank in illustrating his own anatomical and archaeological publications. I have found few records of Erxleben's life: born in Germany, he was based in Leiden around 1830–1839 and is best known for his zoological and anatomical lithographs, as well as his later work with the palaeontologist Richard Owen.[56] This professional success fulfilled Leemans' promise to Pettigrew that 'I feel convinced, that after having made some [portraits] in London, he shall get plenty of occupation.'[57]

In his final introduction, Leemans asked Pettigrew's support for a medical student named Fleck, then studying at Leiden but planning to study surgery in London subsequently.[58] This is most likely Francis Le Sueur Fleck of the Cape Province, who would have been around 20 years old at the time of writing in 1841. Leemans introduced Fleck as a model student and a family friend, and asks for Pettigrew's professional support as a prominent surgeon: he also asks that the Pettigrew family make Fleck welcome in their home.[59] Fleck's obituary indicates that after his return to South Africa he served as a medic with the military in the Seventh Xhosa War of 1846–1847, a particularly unpleasant conflict during which his 'constitution not naturally strong received a shock by which it was ever after affected'.[60] Fleck subsequently suffered from poor health and died in Cape Town in 1851 at the age of 30.

In considering these letters of introduction, it is worth bearing in mind the generational difference between Leemans, born in 1809, and Pettigrew, born in 1791. At the time of writing, Krauss, Lepsius, Fleck and Matthes were all young men in their twenties, within a few years of Leemans' own age and the contemporaries of Pettigrew's older children (of whom more below). This suggests that correspondence of this kind can illuminate the intergenerational as well as the international dimensions of intellectual and personal networks in the history of archaeology, and themes such as power, patronage and influence.

The Pettigrew and Leemans families

Leemans' letters shed some light on Pettigrew's immediate family: the letters often include greetings to Pettigrew's wife Elizabeth and their children Eliza, William, Augustus, Samuel, Emily and Julia. Leemans writes of the Pettigrew children with familiarity and affection, referring to Emily and Julia as 'the little Chinese apples', presumably from the Dutch word for orange, 'sinaasappel', which derives from 'Sina', the antiquated European term for China.[61] It seems that, on his 1836 visit, Leemans found the Pettigrew family to be warm and welcoming to a young foreigner: this atmosphere of domestic harmony and openness is recalled in the memoirs of Pettigrew's son Samuel.[62] Leemans added a PS to one of his letters with warm regards to Mrs Pettigrew, noting 'the marks of friendship & interest, she favoured me with'.[63]

Part of the reason for Leemans' nostalgia for Britain might be found in the repeated references in his letters to Pettigrew's oldest daughter Eliza, who at the time of his first visit in 1836 was 24 years old, unmarried and living at home.[64] The letters indicate that, a few months after Leemans returned to Holland in 1836, Eliza went to visit him there. A letter of December 1836 sends her greetings from Leemans' younger brother and enclosed letters to Eliza from his mother and sister, and from the widow of Caspar Reuvens.[65] In a letter of 1838, by which time he had begun to address Pettigrew as 'my dear friend!' he wrote that 'I owe a long letter to Eliza.'[66] Later that year in his letter of introduction for Lepsius, Leemans mentioned that 'I have given to Dr Lepsius a letter for Elise, which will give you further particulars, but as I feared that perhaps she might not yet be returned from the country, I take the liberty to send a recommendation to you personally.'[67] This suggests that Leemans' correspondence with Eliza was at least as frequent as his letters to her father.

Pettigrew's children generally married well, and Leemans appears to have been reasonably independently wealthy.[68] However, on a visit to his hometown in 1840, Leemans met Maria Cornelia de Virieu, who came from a moderately aristocratic family, and the pair were married later that year. His wife suffered from extreme sea-sickness, which not only prevented a planned trip to Egypt but meant that Leemans' visits to Britain ended as well.[69] The friendship with Eliza seems to have been maintained, and when in 1841 he wrote to report the birth of his first child he noted that he owed Eliza a letter, and that she had informed him of the death of her sister-in-law, for which he sent his condolences.[70] In 1843 Eliza, then 31, married a family friend, Captain (later Admiral) Sir William Henry Dillon, at 63 more than twice her age and some 12 years older than her father.[71]

The end of the correspondence

After 1843 the archived correspondence comes to an end, at roughly the same time as Pettigrew's active involvement in Egyptology. In 1834 his

History of Egyptian Mummies had been a modest sensation, and in 1836 his mummy unrolling at the Royal Institute had been attended by all the prominent figures in British Egyptology as well as leading scientists. But the field of Egyptology was developing fast, driven in part by the growing number of translations of ancient Egyptian texts.[72] I suspect, but cannot be certain, that Pettigrew could read hieroglyphic texts but that his knowledge of the languages of ancient Egypt was relatively slight. In 1842 he began to publish the *Encyclopaedia Aegyptiaca*, aiming to produce a comprehensive overview of the field. The first volume, covering only the short section AAH–ABO, was the only one produced, as the work failed to attract sufficient subscribers.[73]

Nonetheless, when in 1843 Samuel Birch sought references for his post at the British Museum, he approached Leemans as a distinguished colleague, saying that 'I shall be glad of your testimony to my slight writs to join with these of the English Egyptian antiquaries Mrs. Osburn and Pettigrew'.[74] Despite this deference, Birch, Leemans and Lepsius were part of the new generation of Egyptologists grounded in philology, whereas Pettigrew, who had by this point begun holding public mummy unrollings to make money, was part of the old.[75]

Whether the friendship faded once Leemans' visits to Britain ended or for some other reason is difficult to say, not least as the Pettigrew papers are incomplete. In John Lee's letters to Leemans he reports in 1847 that '[y]our friends Mr Gray, Mr Pettigrew and Mr Burgon are well'.[76] In 1864 Lee informed Leemans, 'Your old friend Mr Pettigrew is cheerful but an invalid, he resides near London and with his daughters and he publishes the transactions of the British Archaeological Association'.[77] A year later Pettigrew died, and was buried with his wife in Brompton Cemetery.

Conclusion

Leemans' letters to Pettigrew trace fragments of the geography of Egyptological knowledge, and of the interpersonal relationships that provided the foundations and scaffolding for these scholarly networks. Written at a time when postal correspondence was growing swifter, cheaper and more reliable, they provide a fascinating insight into a relationship, both personal and intellectual, that encompassed family and friends across several countries.[78] The warmth of the household towards a young foreign visitor seems to have kindled Leemans' lasting affection for the Pettigrews and perhaps for Britain in general.

One of the aims of this chapter was to evaluate a set of correspondence between two individuals to consider what insights it could offer into wider intellectual, historical, spatial, personal and social contexts. The relative wealth of material outlined above, in particular the insights into international networks demonstrated in the letters of introduction, support the idea that interpersonal correspondence has considerable value in tracing both intellectual and personal lives and networks in the history of archaeology. Given the scale, it might be excessive to speak of an 'invisible college' in early nineteenth-century European Egyptology, but these different forms of connections are nonetheless of interest. The letters from Leemans to Pettigrew trace the movement of scholars, texts, data and expertise across national, institutional, generational and linguistic boundaries, while providing levels of personal detail that allow us to weave these threads of connection into more lifelike portraits of the individuals involved. Amongst Pettigrew's surviving correspondence, Leemans' letters are distinctively lively, for example skipping quickly from a very moving, detailed account of his son's birth to thoughts on his forthcoming publications, and then to a comment on Pettigrew's complicated relationship with the Duke of Sussex, and finally to a testimony for a friend.[79] The letters show snapshots of the brief points of intersection in the lives of two notable Egyptologists set against the social, intellectual and familial worlds of early nineteenth-century Europe.

Notes

1. Marc-Antoine Kaeser, 'Biography, science studies and the historiography of archaeological research: managing personal archives', *Complutum* 24 (2013): 103.
2. Amara Thornton, 'Social networks in the history of archaeology: placing archaeology in its context', in *Historiographical Approaches to Past Archaeological Research*, eds Gisela Eberhardt and Fabian Link (Berlin: Edition Topoi, 2015), 69–94.
3. W. F. Leemans, *L'Egyptologue Conrade Leemans et sa Correspondance: Contribution à L'Histoire d'une Science* (Leiden: E.J. Brill, 1973), 25.
4. David Gange, *Dialogues with the Dead: Egyptology in British culture and religion, 1822–1922* (Oxford: Oxford University Press, 2013); David J. Wortham, *The Genesis of British Egyptology 1549–1906* (Norman: University of Oklahoma Press, 1971).
5. Thornton, 'Social networks', 71.
6. Marc-Antoine Kaeser, 'Biography as microhistory: the relevance of private archives for writing the history of archaeology', in *Archives, Ancestors, Practices: Archaeology in the light of its history*, eds Nathan Schlanger and Jarl Nordbladh (Oxford: Berghahn, 2008), 11.
7. Margarita Díaz-Andreu, *Archaeological Encounters: Building networks of Spanish and British archaeologists in the 20th century* (Newcastle: Cambridge Scholars Publishing, 2012), 6.
8. Ruurd B. Halbertsma, *Scholars, Travellers and Trade: The pioneer years of the National Museum of Antiquities in Leiden, 1818–1840* (Abingdon: Routledge, 2003), 143.
9. Halbertsma, *'Scholars, Travellers and Trade'*, 143.
10. Warren R. Dawson, *Memoir of Thomas Joseph Pettigrew F.R.C.S., F.R.S., F.S.A. (1791-1865)* (New York: Medical Life Press, 1931).

11 Gabriel Moshenska, 'Unrolling Egyptian Mummies in Nineteenth-Century Britain', *British Journal for the History of Science* 47, 3 (2014): 451–77; Thomas J. Pettigrew, *A History of Egyptian Mummies, and an Account of the Worship and Embalming of the Sacred Animals by the Egyptians, with Remarks on the Funeral Ceremonies of Different Nations, and Observations on the Mummies of the Canary Islands, of the Ancient Peruvians, Burman Priests &c.* (London: Longman, Rees, Orme, Brown, Green, and Longman, Paternoster Row: 1834).
12 Thomas J. Pettigrew, *Memoirs of the Life of Vice-Admiral Lord Viscount Nelson, K.B., Duke of Bronté, etc. etc. etc.* (London: T. & W. Boone, 29 New Bond Street, 1849). For an overview of Pettigrew's work on ancient Egypt, see Gabriel Moshenska, 'Thomas 'Mummy' Pettigrew and the Study of Egypt in Early Nineteenth-Century Britain', in *Histories of Egyptology: Interdisciplinary Measures*, ed. William Carruthers (Abingdon: Routledge, 2015), 201–14.
13 Leemans, '*L'Egyptologue*', 4–5.
14 Beinecke Rare Book and Manuscript Library Osb. Mss. 113/7/332, Letter from Conrad Leemans to Thomas Pettigrew (March 22, 1836).
15 Beinecke Rare Book and Manuscript Library Osb. Mss. 113/7/332, Letter from Conrad Leemans to Thomas Pettigrew (May 19, 1836).
16 Dawson, 'Memoir'; Moshenska, 'Thomas 'Mummy' Pettigrew'.
17 Beinecke Rare Book and Manuscript Library Osb. Mss. 113/7/332, Letter from Conrad Leemans to Thomas Pettigrew (June 18, 1836).
18 Gabriel Moshenska, 'Diagnosing Sir John Gardner Wilkinson: A footnote to the history of Egyptology', *Antiquity* 85 (2011). http://www.antiquity.ac.uk/projgall/moshenska328/.
19 Halbertsma 2003; Leemans 1973, 5.
20 British Library Add. Mss. 56230/14, Letter from Conrad Leemans to Thomas Pettigrew (December 19, 1836).
21 Thomas J. Pettigrew, *Observations on Cholera; Comprising a Description of the Epidemic Cholera of India, the Mode of Treatment, and the Means of Prevention* (London: S. Highley, 1831).
22 Rubeigh J. Minney, *The Two Pillars of Charing Cross: The story of a famous hospital* (London: Cassell, 1967).
23 Leemans to Pettigrew, December 19, 1836. In fact, a committee at the Charing Cross Hospital found that Pettigrew, then Chief Surgeon of the hospital, 'had acted unjustifiably and in a manner unbecoming a Governor and an officer of this Institution'. They condemned him for his moral impropriety and dismissed him instantly from the service' (Minney 1967, 66).
24 Leemans to Pettigrew, December 19, 1836; British Library Add. Mss. 56230/16, Letter from Conrad Leemans to Thomas Pettigrew (January 28, 1838); Conrad Leemans, 'Observations on three Roman Sepulchral Inscriptions found at Watermore, near Cirencester, in Gloucestershire, in 1835 and 1836', *Archaeologia*, 27 (1838): 211–28.
25 Thomas J. Pettigrew, *Medical Portrait Gallery: Biographical Memoirs of the Most Celebrated Physicians, Surgeons etc. etc. who have Contributed to the Advancement of Medical Science* (London: Whittaker and Co., 1840).
26 Beinecke Rare Book and Manuscript Library Osb. Mss. 113/7/332, Letter from Conrad Leemans to Thomas Pettigrew (January, 1839).
27 Beinecke Rare Book and Manuscript Library Osb. Mss. 113/7/332, Letter from Conrad Leemans to Thomas Pettigrew (September 18, 1838); British Library Add. Mss. 56230/20, Letter from Conrad Leemans to Thomas Pettigrew (March 25, 1840).
28 Wortham, 'Genesis'.
29 Beinecke Rare Book and Manuscript Library Osb. Mss. 113/7/332, Letter from Conrad Leemans to Thomas Pettigrew (November 17, 1837); British Library Add. Mss. 56230/16, Letter from Conrad Leemans to Thomas Pettigrew (January 28, 1838).
30 Leemans to Pettigrew, January 28, 1838.
31 Leemans to Pettigrew, January 28, 1838.
32 Jérôme Petit, 'Eugene Jacquet and his Pioneering Study of Indian Numerical Notations', *Ganita Bharati: Bulletin of the Indian Society for History of Mathematics* 31, 1–2 (2009): 23–33.
33 Brian Ogilvie, 'Correspondence networks', in *A Companion to the History of Science*, ed. Bernard Lightman (Chichester: Wiley Blackwell, 2011), 358–71.
34 Halbertsma, '*Scholars*'.
35 Leemans to Pettigrew, December 19, 1836.
36 David Knight, *The Making of Modern Science* (Cambridge: Polity, 2009).
37 Meira Gold, 'British Egyptology (1822–1882)', in *UCLA Encyclopedia of Egyptology*, eds. Rune Nyord and Willeke Wendrich (Los Angeles: UCLA, 2022); Warren R. Dawson,

'Pettigrew's demonstrations upon mummies: a chapter in the history of Egyptology', *Journal of Egyptian Archaeology*, 20 (1934): 170–82.
38 Rachel Mairs and Maya Muratov, *Archaeologists, Tourists, Interpreters: Exploring Egypt and the Near East in the late 19th–early 20th centuries* (London: Bloomsbury, 2015).
39 Leemans to Pettigrew, December 19, 1836.
40 Beinecke Rare Book and Manuscript Library Osb. Mss. 113/7/332, Letter from Conrad Leemans to Thomas Pettigrew (March 12, 1837).
41 Conrad Leemans, *Description raisonnée des monumens égyptiens du Musée d'Antiquités des Pays-Bas à Leide* (Leiden: H.W. Hazenberg, 1840), viii.
42 Ogilvie, 'Correspondence networks', 362.
43 Agnès Garcia-Ventura and Jordi Vidal, 'International networks and the shaping of nineteenth-century Spanish collections: a glance at the correspondence of Juan Facundo Riaño', *Journal of the History of Collections*, 32, 3 (2020): 481–90.
44 Leemans to Pettigrew, November 17, 1837.
45 Bo Beolens, Michael Watkins and Michael Grayson, *The Eponym Dictionary of Reptiles* (Baltimore: Johns Hopkins University Press, 2011), 146.
46 Conrad Leemans, *Lettre à M. François Salvolini: Sur les monumens égyptiens, portant des légendes royales, dans les musées d'antiquités de Leide, de Londres, et dans quelques collections particulières en Angleterre, avec des observations concernant l'histoire, la chronologie et la langue hiéroglyphique des Égyptiens, et une appendice sur les mesures de ce peuple* (Leiden: H.W. Hazenberg, 1838).
47 British Library Add. Mss. 56230/18, Letter from Conrad Leemans to Thomas Pettigrew (May 10, 1838).
48 Herman van den Brink, *Dr. Benjamin Frederik Matthes: Zijn leven en arbeid in dienst van het Nederlandsch Bijbelgenootschap* (Amsterdam: Nederlandsch Bijbelgenootschap, 1943).
49 Adriaan J. Barnouw, *A Trip Through the Dutch East Indies* (Gouda: Doch and Knuttel, 1920), 59.
50 Gabriel Moshenska, 'The Duke of Sussex's Library and the First Debates on the Authorship of De Doctrina Christiana', *Milton Quarterly* 47, 1 (2013): 1–12; Gabriel Moshenska, "The Finest Theological Library in the World': the Rise and Fall of the Bibliotheca Sussexiana', in *Book collecting in Ireland and Britain, 1650–1850*, ed., Elizabeth Boran (Dublin: Four Courts Press, 2018), 168-87.
51 Beinecke Rare Book and Manuscript Library Osb. Mss. 113/7/332, Letter from Conrad Leemans to Thomas Pettigrew (September 18, 1838).
52 Morris L. Bierbrier, *Who Was Who in Egyptology*, fourth revised edition (London: Egypt Exploration Society, 2012), 324–6.
53 *Ibid*.
54 Beinecke Rare Book and Manuscript Library Osb. Mss. 113/7/332, Letter from Conrad Leemans to Thomas Pettigrew (February 26, 1839).
55 Leemans to Pettigrew, February 26, 1839.
56 Darryl Wheye and Donald Kennedy, *Humans, Nature, and Birds: Science art from cave walls to computer screens* (New Haven, CT: Yale University Press, 2008), 157.
57 Leemans to Pettigrew, February 26, 1839.
58 British Library Add. Mss. 56230/22, Letter from Conrad Leemans to Thomas Pettigrew (September 23, 1841).
59 Leemans to Pettigrew, September 23, 1841.
60 'Obituary of Francis Le Sueur Fleck Esq MD MRCSL', *South African Commercial Advertiser*, 22 October 22, 1851.
61 Leemans to Pettigrew, January 28, 1838.
62 Samuel T. Pettigrew, *Episodes in the Life of an Indian Chaplain* (London: Sampson Low, Marston, Searle, & Rivington: 1882).
63 Leemans to Pettigrew, January 28, 1838.
64 Dawson, 'Memoir'.
65 Leemans to Pettigrew, December 19, 1836.
66 British Library Add. Mss. 56230/18, Letter from Conrad Leemans to Thomas Pettigrew (May 10, 1838).
67 Leemans to Pettigrew, September 18, 1838.
68 Dawson, 'Memoir'.
69 Leemans, 'L'Egyptologue'.
70 British Library Add. Mss. 56230/22, Letter from Conrad Leemans to Thomas Pettigrew (September 23, 1841).

71 Dawson, 'Memoir'.
72 Gange, 'Dialogues'; Wortham, 'Genesis'.
73 Dawson, 'Memoir'; Thomas J. Pettigrew, *Encyclopædia Ægyptiaca; or, Dictionary of Egyptian Antiquities. General View of Ancient Egypt: Forming the Preliminary Discourse. AAH ABO* (London: Whittaker and Co., Ave Maria Lane, 1842).
74 Leemans, *'L'Egyptologue'*, 58.
75 Moshenska, 'Thomas "Mummy" Pettigrew'
76 Leemans, *'L'Egyptologue'*, 42.
77 Leemans, *'L'Egyptologue'*, 45.
78 Ogilvie, 'Correspondence Networks'.
79 Leemans to Pettigrew, September 23, 1841.

Bibliography

Anon. 'Obituary of Francis Le Sueur Fleck Esq MD MRCSL', *South African Commercial Advertiser*, October 22, 1851.
Barnouw, Adriaan J., *A Trip Through the Dutch East Indies* (Gouda: Doch and Knuttel, 1920).
Beolens, Bo, Michael Watkins and Michael Grayson, *The Eponym Dictionary of Reptiles* (Baltimore: Johns Hopkins University Press, 2011).
Bierbrier, Morris L., *Who Was Who in Egyptology*, fourth revised edition (London: Egypt Exploration Society, 2012).
van den Brink, Herman, *Dr. Benjamin Frederik Matthes: Zijn leven en arbeid in dienst van het Nederlandsch Bijbelgenootschap* (Amsterdam: Nederlandsch Bijbelgenootschap, 1943).
Dawson, Warren R., 'Pettigrew's demonstrations upon mummies: a chapter in the history of egyptology', *Journal of Egyptian Archaeology*, 20 (1934): 170–82.
Dawson, Warren R., *Memoir of Thomas Joseph Pettigrew F.R.C.S., F.R.S., F.S.A. (1791–1865)* (New York: Medical Life Press, 1931).
Díaz-Andreu, Margarita, *Archaeological Encounters: Building networks of Spanish and British archaeologists in the 20th Century* (Newcastle: Cambridge Scholars Publishing, 2012).
Gange, David, *Dialogues with the Dead: Egyptology in British culture and religion, 1822–1922* (Oxford: Oxford University Press, 2013).
Garcia-Ventura, Agnès and Jordi Vidal, 'International networks and the shaping of nineteenth-century Spanish collections: A glance at the correspondence of Juan Facundo Riaño', *Journal of the History of Collections*, 32, 3 (2020): 481–90.
Gold, Meira, 'British Egyptology (1822–1882)', in *UCLA Encyclopedia of Egyptology*, eds. Rune Nyord and Willeke Wendrich (Los Angeles: UCLA, 2022).
Halbertsma, Ruurd B., *Scholars, Travellers and Trade: The pioneer years of the National Museum of Antiquities in Leiden, 1818–1840* (Abingdon: Routledge, 2003).
Kaeser, Marc-Antoine, 'Biography, science studies and the historiography of archaeological research: managing personal archives', *Complutum* 24, 2 (2013): 101–8.
Kaeser, Marc-Antoine, 'Biography as microhistory: the relevance of private archives for writing the history of archaeology', in *Archives, Ancestors, Practices: Archaeology in the light of its history*, eds., Nathan Schlanger and Jarl Nordbladh (Oxford: Berghahn, 2008), 9–20.
Knight, David, *The Making of Modern Science* (Cambridge: Polity, 2009).
Leemans, Conrad, *Description raisonnée des monumens égyptiens du Musée d'Antiquités des Pays-Bas à Leide* (Leiden: H.W. Hazenberg, 1840).
Leemans, Conrad, 'Observations on three Roman sepulchral inscriptions found at Watermore, near Cirencester, in Gloucestershire, in 1835 and 1836', *Archaeologia* 27 (1838): 211–28.
Leemans, Conrad, *Lettre à M. François Salvolini: Sur les monumens égyptiens, portant des légendes royales, dans les musées d'antiquités de Leide, de Londres, et dans quelques collections particulières en Angleterre, avec des observations concernant l'histoire, la chronologie et la langue hiéroglyphique des Égyptiens, et une appendice sur les mesures de ce peuple* (Leiden: H.W. Hazenberg, 1838).
Leemans, W.F., *L'Egyptologue Conrade Leemans et sa Correspondance: Contribution à L'Histoire d'une Science* (Leiden: E.J. Brill, 1973).
Mairs, Rachel and Maya Muratov, *Archaeologists, Tourists, Interpreters: Exploring Egypt and the Near East in the late 19th–early 20th centuries* (London: Bloomsbury, 2015).

Minney, Rubeigh J., *The Two Pillars of Charing Cross: The story of a famous hospital* (London: Cassell, 1967).

Moshenska, Gabriel, '"The finest theological library in the world": the rise and fall of the Bibliotheca Sussexiana', in *Book Collecting in Ireland and Britain, 1650–1850*, ed., Elizabeth Boran (Dublin: Four Courts Press, 2018), 168–87.

Moshenska, Gabriel, 'Thomas "Mummy" Pettigrew and the study of Egypt in early nineteenth-century Britain', in *Histories of Egyptology: Interdisciplinary measures*, ed. William Carruthers (Abingdon: Routledge, 2015), 201–14.

Moshenska, Gabriel, 'Unrolling Egyptian mummies in nineteenth-century Britain', *British Journal for the History of Science* 47, 3 (2014): 451–77.

Moshenska, Gabriel, 'The Duke of Sussex's Library and the first debates on the authorship of *De Doctrina Christiana*', *Milton Quarterly* 47, 1 (2013): 1–12.

Moshenska, Gabriel, 'Diagnosing Sir John Gardner Wilkinson: A footnote to the history of Egyptology', *Antiquity Project Gallery* 85 (2011). https://www.antiquity.ac.uk/projgall/moshenska328/.

Ogilvie, Brian, 'Correspondence networks', in *A Companion to the History of Science*, ed. Bernard Lightman (Chichester: Wiley Blackwell, 2011), 358–71.

Petit, Jérôme, 'Eugene Jacquet and his pioneering study of indian numerical notations', *Ganita Bharati: Bulletin of the Indian Society for History of Mathematics* 31, 1–2 (2009): 23–33.

Pettigrew, Samuel T., *Episodes in the Life of an Indian Chaplain* (London: Sampson Low, Marston, Searle, & Rivington: 1882).

Pettigrew, Thomas J., *Memoirs of the Life of Vice-Admiral Lord Viscount Nelson, K.B., Duke of Bronté, etc. etc. etc.* (London: T. & W. Boone, 1849).

Pettigrew, Thomas J., *Encyclopædia Ægyptiaca; or, Dictionary of Egyptian Antiquities. General View of Ancient Egypt: Forming the Preliminary Discourse. AAH–ABO* (London: Whittaker and Co., 1842).

Pettigrew, Thomas J., *Medical Portrait Gallery: Biographical memoirs of the most celebrated physicians, surgeons etc. etc. who have contributed to the advancement of medical science* (London: Whittaker and Co., 1840).

Pettigrew, Thomas J., *A History of Egyptian Mummies, and an Account of the Worship and Embalming of the Sacred Animals by the Egyptians, with Remarks on the Funeral Ceremonies of Different Nations, and Observations on the Mummies of the Canary Islands, of the Ancient Peruvians, Burman Priests &c.* (London: Longman, Rees, Orme, Brown, Green, 1834).

Pettigrew, Thomas J., *Observations on Cholera: Comprising a description of the epidemic cholera of India, the mode of treatment, and the means of prevention* (London: S. Highley, 1831).

Thornton, Amara, 'Social networks in the history of archaeology: placing archaeology in its context', in *Historiographical Approaches to Past Archaeological Research*, eds. Gisela Eberhardt and Fabian Link (Berlin: Edition Topoi, 2015), 69–94.

Wheye, Darryl and Donald Kennedy, *Humans, Nature, and Birds: Science art from cave walls to computer screens* (New Haven, CT: Yale University Press, 2008).

Wortham, David J. *The Genesis of British Egyptology 1549–1906* (Norman: University of Oklahoma Press, 1971).

12
Life-writing Vere Gordon Childe from secret surveillance files

Katie Meheux

Scramble the letters of the word 'file' and the result is a 'life'.
(Fiona Capp 1993, 3)

Introduction

This study will examine the secret surveillance files kept by the Security Service (MI5) on Vere Gordon Childe (1892–1957), one of the most admired archaeologists of the twentieth century[1]. Childe's use of Marxist approaches in his work has been widely studied, but his associated political activities have received much less attention. Security Service files offer uniquely comprehensive insights for life-writing him politically. They reveal the full diversity of Childe's political activities – civil liberties and anti-fascist campaigner, pacifist and anti-nuclear advocate, internationalist and 'progressive' intellectual – and provide an overarching narrative or biography that charts his political life from Conscientious Objector to 'extreme Socialist', communist fellow traveller and, perhaps briefly, member of the Communist Party of Great Britain (hereafter CPGB). Early surveillance of Childe, carried out for a few intense months in 1917 during the First World War, was followed by flurries of interest in 1919 and 1922. From 1932, entries were added annually until 1955, when his file was closed. Childe died with an open security file kept on him by the Australian Security Intelligence Organization (hereafter ASIO), however, the balance of evidence suggests he was not an 'MI5 target', rather only of tangential interest.[2]

Childe's files allow us to reinterpret his political life-path, interactions, networks and allegiances. They also offer new perspectives on accepted narratives, challenging for example, long-held ideas that Childe died disillusioned with communism.[3] Most significantly, the files allow us to see Childe's life against the backdrop of the political turbulence of the twentieth century and within the context of the rich creativity of left-wing 'progressive' culture and science, Marxist and otherwise. This contextualised examination reframes Childe as a progressive intellectual, bound into left-wing culture by shared interests and long friendships, rather than merely an isolated 'Marxist' archaeologist.

Life-writing from secret surveillance files

Secret surveillance files released into the public domain, many from totalitarian regimes, have been increasingly used for history and life-writing.[4] They are not without their challenges: inaccuracies, inadequacies of data preservation and bias.[5] They need to be contextualised, compared with other security service files[6] and life-writing sources, and examined against security services' history and practice to gain a balanced understanding.

Surveillance files are eclectic collections of intelligence gathered by techniques ranging from stealing documents, to eavesdropping on conversations, informant allegations and intercepting wireless signals. Methods of acquisition are often unreliable, for example, partially overheard conversations.[7] Information is collected at random and little effort made to give shape and coherence to events. Narratives are marked by repetitions, inaccuracies and the slow accretion of details that attempt to characterise the subject and fit them into networks of 'subversion'. Sources are diverse: forms, press clippings, letters, photographs, reports and bureaucratic memos.[8]

For life-writing, security files act as biographies constructed from political and bureaucratic perspectives.[9] These biographies are hostile, lacking balance or sympathetic perspective. They are unauthorised: all information was obtained illegally.[10] They are akin to criminal records, but function not to identify crimes, rather to characterise subjects as dangerous social types.[11] Yet these same files contain information of enormous value. Security files were accrued during subjects' lifetimes by trained, experienced operatives who were external to their lives, offering valuable, alternative perspectives and helping us avoid the pitfalls of presentism, nostalgia and false memory.[12] They provide a wealth of corroborative detail and often include vital chronologies of movements, activities, associations and networks.[13]

Some studies see MI5 files as impersonal, neutral records.[14] However, we must be wary of the 'reality effect' created by detailed official reportage and bureaucracy. We must also be wary of claims of neutrality. MI5 was a civilian organisation with no executive powers and its personnel had no power to arrest or detain individuals, but they could still intimidate or misrepresent suspects, in the process changing surveillance records from passive knowledge stores to active, transformative agents.[15] Left-wing intellectuals and communists, including Childe, knew they were being spied upon and this awareness impacted upon their lives.[16] While based at Dingwall as a Royal Commissioner for Ancient Monuments in Scotland, Childe became convinced that his mail was being secretly opened and spent a day travelling to and from Kingussie to post a letter outside the Highland Security Zone. He was not paranoid; his mail *was* being opened.[17]

KV2/2148 and KV2/2149: Gordon Childe and the 'Red Menace'

In March 2006, the secret surveillance files kept on Childe by MI5 were released by the National Archives into the public domain.[18] This release was unexceptional; the files were merely included in the fourteenth batch of records of historical interest released since the Intelligence Services Act of 1994.[19] The majority of MI5 files released have been Personal (PF Series) Files (reference KV2): thousands of personal files of alleged foreign agents, dissidents, right and left-wing extremists, pacifists and anti-conscriptionists kept under surveillance as potential threats to national security.[20] This seemingly widespread surveillance should be kept in perspective. In 1991, the short-lived opening of former Soviet Committee for State Security (KGB) archives revealed 9.5 million files; many more had been destroyed.[21]

Childe's files were included in a release of KV2 files on 'Communists and suspected Communists', but no mention of him was made in the accompanying publicity.[22] This lack of interest emphasises that whilst Childe is the only British archaeologist known (so far) to possess a security file, he was merely one of thousands of individuals kept under surveillance for communist connections. The security services considered the 'Red Menace' to be the greatest threat to the stability of the British Empire.[23] Childe was a regular visitor to Central and Eastern Europe and much admired by colleagues there (Figure 12.1). These visits, networks and admiration made him suspect in the eyes of both MI5 and MI6.

Records held by MI5 on Childe were released in two files: KV2/2148 (1917–1952) and KV2/2149 (1952–1955).[24] The break

Figure 12.1 Vere Gordon Childe with a teddy bear given to him by students from Brno University, now in the Czech Republic. Date and photographer are unknown. UCL Institute of Archaeology Archives, oversized photos box.

between the KV2 files was associated with bureaucratic process: in 1952, MI5 was transferred from the War Office to the Home Office and record-keeping was transferred to a new administrative 'A' branch.[25] When compared to other contemporary KV2 files, little is exceptional about Childe's files, except the documents from the First World War, which rarely survive in KV2 files.[26]

MI5 files were internal documents formulated to assess security risks and provide advice for government agencies. They were the result of a system established during the 1930s: an observation section investigated suspects; their reports were sent to the Registry.[27] Registry staff opened a single file on an individual and all relevant papers, along with extracts from other files, were placed within it.[28] A 'look up', a request for an internal search of records, on Childe prepared in April–May 1941 offers us a rare summary of the complex investigative files then cross-referenced to Childe's personal file:[29]

- SF455/6 V9.294 and SF455/15 V5.163A referring to national security, enemy propaganda or communist activities
- OF 73/1 3X, identifying an organisation to which Childe belonged
- L12A, 8A, 15A, 18A, etc., 'list' files relating to investigations carried out on individuals or organisations. L197A/27 (mis-numbered as L107A/27) referred to Childe's friend, German archaeologist and refugee Gerhard Bersu
- SZ 5309/F 29.7.31 from Scotland Yard's police countersubversion files, probably Childe's 1920s Special Branch file.

Childe's KV2 files are primarily the product of MI5 investigations but also include documents from other organisations. The earliest surveillance of Childe was by the Home Office during the First World War.[30] Childe was subsequently investigated by police forces, notably Special Branch, the countersubversion unit of the London Metropolitan Police, the British Secret Intelligence Service, known as SIS or its military intelligence cover designation MI6, and Indian Political Intelligence (IPI), established to monitor revolutionary Indian nationalism.[31]

Childe's KV2 files contain many Special Branch documents. He also had separate Special Branch files, but these cannot be accessed as Special Branch files remain closed.[32] Special Branch defined subversion more broadly than MI5, keeping files on nationalists, atheists, trade unionists and pacifists.[33] This means that Special Branch records preserved in Childe's KV2 files are particularly useful in revealing his involvement with a broad range of 'left' organisations, notably the Association of Scientific Workers and the National Council for Civil Liberties (NCCL).

Individuals kept under surveillance in one country often ended up under surveillance in others, for the security services were linked together by networks of communication and shared intelligence. This was particularly true of Britain, where security networks also embraced countries of the Empire/Commonwealth and allied nations. A summary of Childe's political and academic life produced for MI6 in 1955 was shared with ASIO; the document still remains in Childe's ASIO file.[34] Childe also had a file with their predecessor, the Counter Espionage Bureau, established in Australia during the First World War. This file was kept between 1917 and 1919 and started on MI5 advice because of Childe's war-resistance; no trace of it survives.[35] Childe was an international traveller throughout his life and other, similar surveillance files may await discovery elsewhere.

Comparison with other KV2 files reveals that surveillance of Childe was irregular and inconsistent. His files do not include any photos or descriptions of him, which would have been needed for personal surveillance, such as following him. His phones were never tapped, nor his car number plates recorded.[36] Information was added to Childe's files every year sporadically between 1932 and 1955, but this often consisted of short references, for example an entry in April 1955, reporting on an article Childe had written for the 'Communist' journal *Past and Present*.[37] Childe's interest to MI5 was essentially tangential, resulting from his involvement with the political organisations that were their real focus, including the Marx Memorial Library, whose board Childe joined in 1938 (Figure 12.2), and the Society for Cultural Relations with the Soviet Union.[38] Surveillance of him appears to have been justified and self-perpetuated as much by historical information as his current activities.

Childe was a direct target for investigation on only three occasions, all during wartime: in 1917, 1940–1941 and 1950–1951.[39] The World Wars and the Korean War (1950–1953) caused MI5 and wider society in general to regard Childe and others with unorthodox political opinions with increased suspicion.[40] Childe was aware of this: when asked in 1943 by the CPGB to protest at the release of British fascists detained without trial under the controversial wartime Defence Regulation 18B, he refused:

> I am not prepared to protest against the release of any 18B detainee. This monstrous regulation is far more likely to be used under the present administration against you and me than against reactionaries.[41]

Figure 12.2 The Marx Memorial Library, 7a Clerkenwell Green, London. The library, founded in 1933, was kept under observation by MI5 because of its close association with the CPGB. Reproduced from Wikimedia Commons under the terms of CC BY-SA 2.0. Uploaded 6 December 2005 by user Justinc.

Childe's files as sources for life-writing, biography and history

Childe's files, as will be seen, allow us to reconstruct an over-arching, nuanced narrative for life-writing him politically. But it should be recognised that the files are, nonetheless, both imperfect and problematic: in preservation, contextualisation and bias, and as interpretation. There are significant gaps in the files. Childe's files have been released with many documents withheld, stamped 'retained in Department under section 3(4) of the Public Records Act'. Two entries are omitted because they are MI6 files: material from a 1950 operation 'STAND'; MI6 prohibits the release of any documents.[42] Omissions do not necessarily relate to Childe; one omitted document, for example, protected the identity of an undercover agent.[43]

Omissions dating to the 1920s are most significant. Entries in KV2/2148 jump from 9 to 24a, with the gap between numbered both 10 and 23a and labelled with the name and personal file number of Childe's friend Raymond Postgate, one of the founders of the CPGB.[44] This suggests that 13 documents relating to Childe were placed in Postgate's file. This file has never been released and may no longer exist: a frustrating hiatus in our understanding of Childe's early relationship with the CPGB and wider nascent communist and pacifist networks.[45] Sir Basil Thomson, then Head of Special Branch, commented that pacifists were 'busy tearing off their disguise and reappearing under their proper garb as revolutionaries'.[46]

Most information in Childe's file was gathered using Home Office Warrants (HOWs), which authorised the interception of mail.[47] A HOW was first taken out on Childe on 25 June 1917 and closed after his return to Australia on 25 October 1917. A second HOW was taken out by Scotland Yard on 28 September 1922 on Childe's address at 34 Cartwright Gardens.[48] This HOW was never cancelled. The context of intercepted letters is not always clear, as they were placed in Childe's file separate from main investigations. But they allow us to see 'light and shade' in his political opinions. One letter, for example, that he sent to the communist-dominated Second World Student Congress in Prague on 1 May 1950 points to an internationalist perspective:

> Students should everywhere combine for the advancement of knowledge, the pooling of human experience and the benefit of Mankind across the artificial boundaries and curtains that have been erected by politicians. I trust your congress in Praha will promote such co-operation on a truly international scale and wish all success to your deliberations.[49]

Another demonstrates that Childe's devotion to Soviet Russia was not unquestioning. To his friend John Lewis, CPGB member and editor of *Modern Quarterly* journal, Childe wrote in 1945: 'Russia was swell, though it left doubts on certain fronts.'[50]

An intercepted letter apparently inviting Childe to be Vice-President of the Australia-New Zealand Civil Liberties Society in 1952 shows the unreliability of uncorroborated information.[51] In 1954, the Society mounted a campaign to save from execution three men found guilty of the murder of Cecil Larsen, Resident Commissioner of the Pacific island of Niue. A letter from the honorary secretary to Childe, asking him to support their appeal, reveals that he was not in fact the Society's Vice-President, had no association with them and was unconvinced by the case.[52]

Because the papers in Childe's files have been siphoned off from investigative files, we often have only frustrating glimpses of his activities. In 1947, for example, taps on the phone of leading CPGB intellectual Maurice Cornforth revealed that Childe was interested in joining the Engels Society, an association of Marxist scientists.[53] In 1948, the Engels Society became involved in the Lysenko Controversy, the dismissal of Western genetics as 'unsound Neo-Darwinism' by Soviet scientist Lysenko that became a fiercely fought Cold War debate about scientific freedom.[54] Many communist scientists, notably geneticist J. B. S. Haldane, struggled to ally their commitment to scientific freedom with their allegiance to Soviet Communism.[55]This intriguing, isolated reference reveals Childe's involvement in the debate and raises possible reasons for his post-war disenchantment with intellectual Soviet Communism.

Recognition and balancing of bias are also vital. Childe attended a garden party on 17 July 1936 given in honour of the Russian ambassador Ivan Maisky by the Edinburgh branch of the Society for Cultural Relations with the USSR. Childe's role as the Society's President was taken as evidence that he was a 'communist' by Glasgow police.[56] This idea was perpetuated and recycled in his files to the extent that the Secretary of State for Scotland refused to appoint Childe as a Royal Commissioner of Ancient Monuments in Scotland because he was a 'communist', although this accusation was later refuted.[57] Newspaper reports suggest, however, that the party was a social and diplomatic event held in the garden of an Edinburgh clergyman, Rev. J. E. Hamilton. The entry thus reflects not the activities of revolutionary communists, rather the prejudices of the security services.[58]

Childe's Marxist writings have been used by archaeologists as primary evidence of his political beliefs and loyalties, but they are absent from his KV2 files.⁵⁹ This absence serves as a much-needed reminder not only that Childe's political life and literary output were often unrelated, but that the central weakness of the files for life-writing is the absence of Childe's own subjective political experience. Instead, we see him always through the gaze of others: policemen; security services operatives; colleagues in the CPGB; informants.

Reconstructing Childe's political biography: A life-writing narrative

The security services kept Childe under sporadic observation for nearly 40 years, most of his adult life, in the process inadvertently providing an overarching narrative or biography of his political life. This narrative allows us to order evidence from other sources for Childe's life and contextualise it within contemporary political and culture developments. It also identifies gaps in our knowledge and offers possibilities for future research. In the long term, this tentative 'biography' or framework also provides potential for comparing and contrasting the development of Childe's political, largely Marxist, thought and writings with his political activities.

1917: Conscientious Objector; war resister; international socialist; civil liberties campaigner

Childe's KV2 file begins with investigations by MI5 in summer 1917 following the official reporting to the Home Office of comments that he made to his friend and fellow student, Conscientious Objector Philip T. Davies, then imprisoned in Dorchester Prison. Officials decided that Childe had 'expressed himself in favour of German submarine success and of a Revolution here' and referred him to MI5, standard practice where espionage or subversion was suspected. MI5 took out a HOW on Childe and he was followed by Oxford City police; Assistant Superintendent Nawes reported 'visits to theatre, pictures'. Entries describe Childe as 'probably the ugliest man in the world' and 'thoroughly perverted', demonstrating the prejudice and hostility of serving military officers towards Childe. Such language was commonly used to describe war-resisters, who were considered 'unmanly', cowardly, shirking and homosexual, echoing the unfounded accusations of Childe's infatuation with Davies found in the files.⁶⁰

Despite this surveillance, no concrete evidence of wrongdoing emerged. Childe was permitted to return to Australia, although MI5 informed their Australian counterparts that Childe needed to be kept under observation. Major Frank Hall, in charge of MI5's section covering the dominions, colonies and Ireland, ensured Childe had to take the longest and most dangerous sea route back to Australia, demonstrating the untrammelled secret power of MI5 during war-time.[61]

We must be careful not to take the 'reality effect' produced by the reports at face value, rather contextualise them within both the wider social approbation displayed towards war-resisters and the war-time fears and prejudices of MI5, then a military organisation.[62] Childe was a committed international socialist, pacifist and war-resister, involved with several pioneering civil liberties organisations: the No Conscription Fellowship, the Union of Democratic Control, the National Council against Conscription and the pacifist Independent Labour Party. He kept questionable company at Oxford University (Figure 12.3): several of his friends from the Guild Socialist Movement were Conscientious Objectors; three had been imprisoned for their beliefs.[63]

As an Australian, Childe could not be conscripted, and as his radical friends fell afoul of the British war machine, he increasingly acted for them. A letter from Alan Kaye, a friend of Childe and a leader of the Guild Socialists, to Labour MP Thomas Edmund Harvey, a supporter of Conscientious Objectors, suggests that Childe was not acting upon an infatuation, rather visiting Davies on behalf of his wider political friendship group, with Davies' agreement, to keep him informed of political developments and show support.[64] Childe's comments about submarine warfare emphasise this. They were not his own opinions, rather the common call of anti-war protestors in 1917 who wanted a negotiated peace, notably the Union of Democratic Control.[65] It is also interesting to note that Childe's closest friend and roommate at Oxford, future CPGB leader Rajani Palme Dutt, was expelled the same month that Childe visited Davies for spreading 'international socialist propaganda', including pledging support to the Bolshevik revolutionary cause.[66]

However, we must also recognise that the fears of MI5 were not unwarranted. Childe showed signs of being a Revolutionary. In June 1917, a conference was convened in Leeds to honour the Russian Revolution. Nearly 20,000 people attended amid calls for immediate negotiated peace, universal suffrage and independence for India and Egypt. Short-lived 'soviets' or workers councils were established.[67] Childe, as President of the Oxford Union of Democratic Control, was a

Figure 12.3 Childe at Oxford, wearing graduation robes and probably dating to 1916/17. Photographer unknown. UCL Institute of Archaeology Archives. Childe Notes and Miscellaneous. Box 23.12.

delegate to the conference.[68] He was also willing to lie and subvert authority; he misrepresented himself to the prison authorities, referring to 'my friend the Pro-Provost of Queens'.[69] MI5, as they saw it, had reason to be suspicious.

1919–1922: Transnational socialism and revolution

Fragmentary entries in Childe's file dated between May and August 1919,[70] while he was still in Australia, relate primarily to Australian and British security concerns about his contributions to the British pacifist newspaper *Labour Leader*, the official newspaper of the Independent Labour Party, banned from export in 1917.[71] *Labour Leader* supported the Bolshevik regime, promoted international socialism and criticised the government.

Special Branch were also concerned about letters Childe was receiving from 'RTD', who was linked with an Egyptian medical student, Mohammed Amin El-Biblawi, a suspected Egyptian revolutionary. The Egyptian insurgency of March 1919 challenged the stability of the British Empire and was actively encouraged by students introducing socialist ideas from Europe.[72] 'RTD' appears to have been Childe's friend, Rajani Palme Dutt, who was deeply involved in anti-imperialist agitation.[73] Childe's activism in Australia at this time is well attested, but his KV2 files reveal fascinating new details not only of his anti-colonialism and radicalism, but also of the covert transnational networks that supported and sustained it. Childe was not alone in this transnational activism: his fellow Australian, radical internationalist Hessel Duncan Hall, is also mentioned.

In September 1922, less than a year after his return to Britain, a HOW was taken out on Childe as 'an extreme socialist' closely connected to communists.[74] Childe's contribution to the radical, communist-funded *Labour Monthly* seems to have been to blame; Special Branch took the warrant out at the end of September 1922, the same month his article was released.[75] Whilst this seems an overreaction, there was a widespread contemporary belief that a 'Bolshevik' revolution was imminent.[76]

MI5 also took careful note of Childe's continuing friendship with Oxford graduate Raymond Postgate, now a left-wing journalist, emphasising the importance of radical friendships and networks in both Childe's political life and his writings, an importance obscured by traditional interpretations of Childe as a political 'loner'. Frustratingly, files for this period are inaccessible and further details are missing, emphasising the important clues the KV2 files provide. However, we know that Childe did not become a communist, nor did he join the Society for Cultural Relations with the Soviet Union when it was founded in 1925.[77] Instead, he focused on his archaeological career, maintaining his political activities through left-wing organisations that occupied the Marxist middle ground, including the Labour Research Department Summer School and the Plebs League.[78]

Only when Childe was established as Abercromby Professor do hints of his political activities re-emerge. In 1928, he was making plans to visit Russia.[79] There are strong hints he retained his radical left-wing politics; Childe's friend, archaeologist Alexander Keiller, teased him that he would find even another old friend, Socialist MP George Lansbury, 'unpleasantly and unsatisfactorily pink'.[80] However, he still had little interest in the CPGB, telling his friend, Mary Alice Evatt in 1931 that the Communist Party was 'quite hopeless here'.[81]

The 1930s: the Society for Cultural Relations with the Soviet Union, Aid Spain, the India League, the Communist Party, the Association of Scientific Workers and the peace movement

Childe's KV2 files are rich with details of his activities during the 1930s, painting an unrivalled picture of his involvement with radical organisations. The range of organisations, anti-imperialist, anti-fascist and communist, and Childe's own writings and statements, suggest that he was an active member of the Popular Front against Fascism.[82] Childe's political activities during this period have largely escaped notice from scholars, but one of his students recalled that 'he was a Marxist, President of the Anglo-Soviet Society and a militant atheist, and these views obtruded into his lectures'.[83]

Most reports in Childe's files from this period come from the Chief Constables of Edinburgh and Glasgow police forces, reflecting his tenure as Abercromby Professor of Archaeology at the University of Edinburgh. Reports from the Chief Constable of Glasgow are particularly interesting, for Glasgow was the centre of Scottish activity in support of the Republicans in the Spanish Civil War (1936–1939).[84] Childe was a patron of the Spanish Relief Committee and a critic of the Foreign Enlistment Act, designed to prevent volunteers travelling to Spain to fight.[85] He may also have had a secret role, with the Chief Constable of Glasgow alerting MI5 to a report by communist 'David Mackenzie' that their 'undercover man' known as the 'Professor', was most likely Childe.[86] Childe was in Spain (Palma de Mallorca) in April 1936, on the eve of war and was friends with Pedro Bosch-Gimpera, archaeologist and Republican Minister.[87] Keiller also intriguingly asked Childe's help for the son of his dentist, who had travelled to Spain to join the International Brigades.[88]

Plainclothes detectives attended meetings of the Glasgow and Edinburgh branches of the Society for Cultural Relations with the Soviet Union; Childe was president and founder, in 1932, of the Edinburgh branch. The security services were suspicious of the Society, which was both a genuine institution for studying Russian culture and an international communist 'front' organisation.[89] Hints of these complexities are revealed in a report on a meeting of 11 February 1932 at Calders Restaurant in Glasgow, with a string band and dancing, a lecture, Russian literature for sale and advertisements for Russian classes.[90]

Childe had visited India and was openly opposed to British colonial rule, but it was only in November 1938, when Childe became chairman of a new branch of the India League in Edinburgh, that an Indian Political Intelligence 'cross-reference' occurs in his MI5 file.[91] Indian Political Intelligence was concerned, as they believed the India League, a left-wing organisation dedicated to Indian independence, was communist controlled.[92] Its leading figure, Vengalil Krishna Krishnan Menon, was part of the same libertarian, anti-fascist and anti-imperialist circles as Childe. In November 1938 he gave the inaugural speech for Childe's Edinburgh branch, stating that Indian independence was part of an international struggle for peace and democracy.[93]

Childe also played a significant role in the new cultural institutions of the CPGB. He was on the board of the Marx Memorial Library and the editorial board of the *Modern Quarterly* journal.[94] Launched in 1937, the *Modern Quarterly* was described as 'a progressive journal' in which there was an 'attempt to discuss scientific and historical problems from a point of view that is Marxist, although some of our editorial board are not actually Marxists'.[95] Childe, as an internationally acclaimed archaeologist and Marxist intellectual, was an important cultural asset for the CPGB. In 1943, an intercepted phone call advised: 'he is an important fellow and one we have to keep on good terms with'.[96]

Childe changed his attitude to Marxism and the CPGB with far greater regularity than is generally portrayed.[97] In 1937, he claimed that he would prefer a chair in Pittsburgh to Russia.[98] This intriguing comment suggests that, like his fellow socialist scientists Lancelot Hogben, J. G. Crowther and Julian Huxley, Childe may have been briefly enticed away from communism by the success of Roosevelt's New Deal public programme; Pittsburgh was a stronghold of the New Deal.[99] In 1938, he was reluctant to become involved in the Marx Memorial Library, concerned it would 'tie a label' around his neck that he was 'anxious to avoid'.[100] At times, he was hostile about Soviet intellectuals, criticising their 'lapsed scholasticism' and 'pseudo-Marxism'.[101]

The Popular Front provided an exciting range of political identities to explore during the 1930s. A range of left-wing affiliations of no interest to the security services are visible in newspapers, for example, Childe supported writer Naomi Mitchison in her unsuccessful bid as Socialist candidate for the University of Edinburgh Parliamentary seat.[102] Also missing from Childe's KV2 files, because it was now 'respectable', are traces of Childe's strong commitment to pacifism during the interwar period.[103] These 'respectable' political activities warn us of the dangers of relying solely on the KV2 files to examine Childe's political life.

The interwar period was probably the most dynamic and creative period of Childe's political life. He was involved in multiple organisations:

the Left Book Club, the India League, the Edinburgh Branch of Scientific Workers, the Spanish Relief Committee, the Society for Cultural Relations with the USSR and the peace movement. He may also have undertaken undercover work and travels. However, there are remarkably few traces of these activities in Childe's contemporary archaeological work and Childe has been viewed as an isolated radical figure in Scotland.[104] This interpretation should be revised: he was a leader of progressive left-wing culture in Scotland and a major intellectual contributor to the Popular Front against Fascism.

World War II: A communist 'Fifth Column', the German Archaeological Institute, Gerhard Bersu, anonymous denunciation and growing closer to the 'Party'

The outbreak of the Second World War turned Childe's left-wing political activism into a liability. On 3 May 1940, as 'spy fever' gripped Britain, an anonymous letter was handed into the Edinburgh military permit office, denouncing Childe and his friend Cathcart Roland (Roly) Wason (Figure 12.4):

> The following persons should be examined as their views on Anti-Scottish and Anti-British propaganda and as to their reputed work in Britain organising crimson Soviet enterprises and other subversive and vicious affairs.[105]

Both men had worked together for the League of Prehistorians, an archaeological society set up by Childe's students in the early 1930s, and it is possible that Childe and Wason were denounced by a member of the society, perhaps by one of their own students.[106] One former student accused Childe of 'attempting to use the League for the propagation of his communist views'.[107] Childe's friendship with German archaeologist Gerhard Bersu also became problematic following Bersu's tribunal as an 'enemy alien' in 1940, as did Childe's membership of the *Deutsches Archäologisches Institut* (German Archaeological Institute).[108]

Scottish Command drew the conclusion that 'Professor Childe was said to have had very socialist views and although he is opposed to the present government, he has never been suspected of being disloyal to this country.'[109] However, he was kept under sporadic surveillance for the rest of the war, perhaps because he displayed an increasingly strong commitment to communism, even defending the Russian invasion of Finland as 'a necessary

Figure 12.4 Archaeologists and activists. Gordon Childe (centre) and Roly Wason (right) with Finnish archaeologist Carl Axel Nordman (left in hat), on a field trip during Nordman's visit to Scotland in 1932. Finnish Heritage Agency. Kind permission to reproduce. Open Access at http://bit.ly/43rz94X

defensive move' and praised the Soviet Union for building 'a new world order'.[110] As the war progressed, so did his involvement with communism (Figure 12.5). In 1945, he visited Russia and criticised the British government's decision to withhold the travel permits of eight physicists.[111] In 1946, he was a member of the British Soviet Unity Council calling for 'practical day-to-day co-operation' to promote the alliance between the two countries.[112] At a Society for Cultural Relations with the Soviet Union meeting in March 1946, Childe claimed that the 'real purpose of America in retaining the secret of the atomic bomb was to enable American industry which was in the hands of a few powerful trusts to keep this new force for exploitation in industry and for personal profit'.[113] His allegiances seemed clear, but in the deteriorating political climate, increasingly problematic.

Post War, Cold War: CPGB Member? Or fellow traveller? International communism, conflict and suspicion

In 1947, MI5 came to believe that Childe was a card-holding member of the CPGB. Any membership was nonetheless short-lived; he is reported

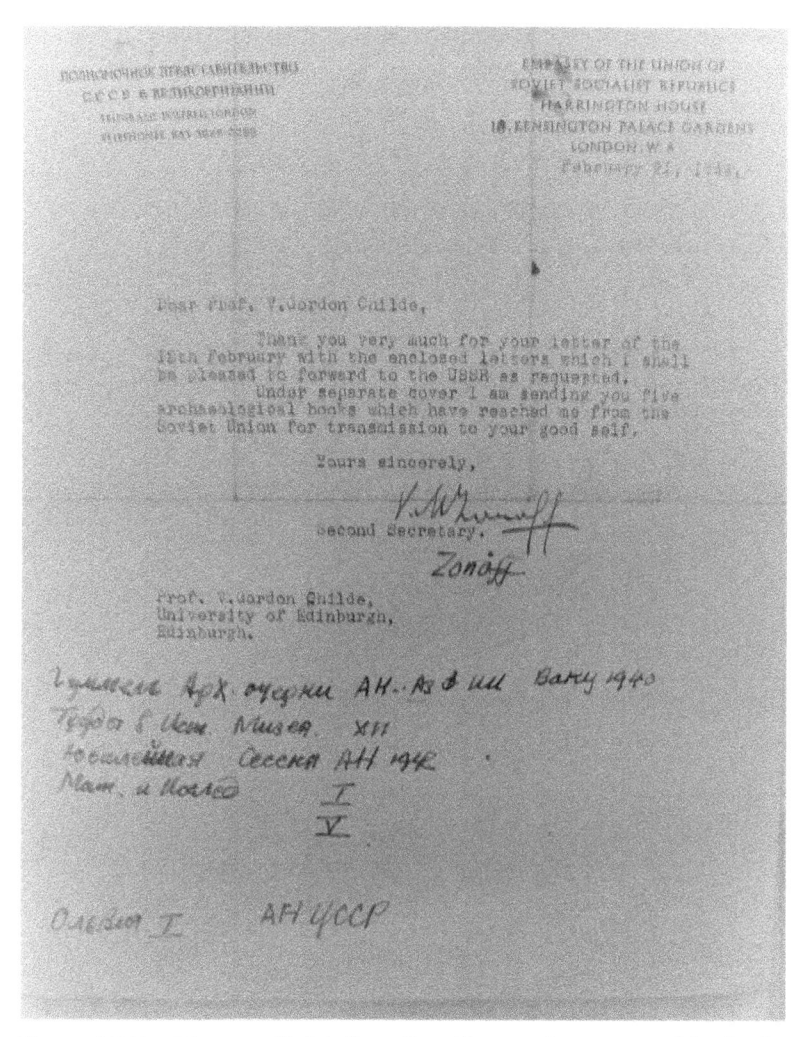

Figure 12.5 A letter to Childe from Zonoff, second secretary of the Soviet Embassy in London, 21 February 1944. Evidence of his growing engagement, both intellectual and political, with Marxism and the Soviet Union. UCL Institute of Archaeology Archives, Childe Correspondence 1/14.

as being only 'close with the Party' in the winter of 1948, but by 1949, no longer a member.[114] MI5's conclusions are supported by evidence from the CPGB. In October 1948, Childe was asked to attend a Party culture conference amongst the 'well known non-party people' and in 1949, he was described as 'very close to us'.[115] This close agreement is not surprising. In 1949, MI5 gained covert access to Party membership records.[116] The absence of a membership form in Childe's KV2 files indicates that at the height of the Cold War, when his actions, affiliations and travels were most scrutinised, Childe was not a CPGB member. Indeed, in 1948, Childe wrote to American anthropologist Lesley White stating explicitly that he was 'not a member of the party'.[117]

Childe was, however, heavily involved in Party cultural groups during 1947: the Historians Group, the Engels Society and the Social Philosophy Group.[118] As an eminent Marxist intellectual, he did not have to join the CPGB to take part in these groups, as he shared close connections with CPGB intellectuals.[119] His membership of the Historians Group may have been incorrectly interpreted by MI5 as evidence of wider Party membership.

Childe was an active participant in many of the 'front' organisations of the early Cold War and contributed to both the *Anglo-Soviet Journal* and the journal of the Historians Group, *Past & Present*. Three secret 'sources' inside the Society for Friendship with Bulgaria, the Hampstead Peace Council and the MacDonald Discussion Group reveal this active and wide-ranging participation.[120] The MacDonald Discussion Group, a private left-wing discussion group of professionals from theatre, film and architecture, was monitored by MI5 between 1951 and 1954 because of fears of communist penetration of the entertainment industry.[121] MI5 feared the cultural influence of communist intellectuals generally, including Childe's friend J. D. Bernal and Childe himself:

> It is understood from source that Childe has been extremely active in archaeology in the past two or three years in trying to impose the sort of regimentation on archaeologists which Bernal attempted through the Royal Society to impose of scientists generally.[122]

This assessment reveals the extent to which MI5 were paranoid and distrusting of left-wing intellectuals during the early Cold War; it misrepresents reputable, well-documented attempts by the Association of Scientific Workers and the new British Sociological Association, of which Childe was a founding member, to ensure adequate post-war government funding and recognition of the social sciences.[123]

In 1951, William Fagg, Secretary of the Royal Anthropological Institute contacted MI5, reporting that without permission or discussion, Childe had used the membership list of the Institute to circulate 'a very innocent and persuasive letter' concerning the anti-nuclear (and pro-Soviet) Stockholm Peace Appeal, asking people to sign up to it; Childe could still be unscrupulous in pursuit of political ends.[124] Instead of confronting him, Fagg wrote a letter signed 'Anthropologist' to the

Daily Telegraph and *Manchester Guardian* newspapers denouncing Childe and the British Peace Council and advising everyone receiving a similar letter to post it back unsigned, thus contributing '2 ½ d to the strengthening of British defence' through the price of the stamp.[125] Childe had encountered a colleague as willing to fight the Cold War as himself – only from the other side.

Post-war, Childe must have been on the Special Branch list of individuals whose luggage was to be searched at British airports; there are reports from both Northolt and London airports, reflecting suspicions of communist fellow travellers and fears of Soviet espionage.[126] MI6 became more involved in tracking Childe when Foreign Office officials became concerned about his participation in official visits to countries behind the Iron Curtain, for example a visit by Childe to Czechoslovakia in August 1949 as a member of the 'Communist-penetrated Association of Scientific Workers'.[127] In 1955, he was reported as 'very progressive', a 'peace propagandist' and a 'willing instrument of the Communist Party'.[128]

The security services could not see that Childe's connections with communist countries were not merely political, they were also vital for his archaeological research, reflective of a lifetime's travels and friendships and a vital intellectual bridge between Communist East and Transatlantic West.[129] However, their fears were not unjustified: a BBC monitoring report on the Soviet radio service on 30 September 1953 contained an interview with Childe entitled 'Soviet Central Asia No Russification' in which he spoke approvingly of the contentious policy of 'Russification' of the ethnic minorities of Central Asia.[130]

Closing the files: observing Childe's later political life

Childe's KV2 files came to an end in 1955, probably due to a need to redirect precious MI5 resources.[131] Gathercole has claimed that Childe had become disillusioned with communism towards the end of his life,[132] but there is no sign of this in the final entries in Childe's KV2 files and it is noticeable how active he was in the British–China Friendship Association.[133] Childe may have become disillusioned by Soviet Russia, but like many left-wing intellectuals, he embraced China.[134] He remained deeply involved in communist front organisations, travelling with international delegations behind the Iron Curtain and forging independent relationships with the Warsaw Pact countries. But Childe's later political life was largely that of an intellectual and less of an activist, as he perhaps grew wary of the increasingly hostile atmosphere.[135]

Security services maintained their watch on Childe until his death. A file kept on him by ASIO during the last months of his life in 1957 recognised that Childe had committed suicide; they were concerned that 'his actions in taking his own life could have been influenced by factors of counterespionage significance', although they never made their knowledge public and his suicide remained an open secret.[136] Investigation may have been prompted by local gossip; Childe's friend, archaeologist James Stewart, claimed that he had been murdered by 'a certain political party'.[137] In 1958, a scandalised Glyn Daniel, visiting Finland, wrote to R. E. M. Wheeler that 'Brasyov', presumably Russian archaeologist Aleksandr Bryusov, had been spreading:

> the wicked rumour that Childe left England because the British government would not let him work in peace, forced him to resign prematurely and that he committed suicide in Australia because the Australian government was persecuting him.[138]

Bryusov was better informed about Childe's death than his British friends, perhaps attesting to interest in Childe by the Soviet security services.

For much of the final years of Childe's life, he was identified in his KV2 files as a 'communist sympathiser'. The definitive conclusion was delivered in 1955 by Millicent Bagot, MI5's communist 'expert':

> There is no documentary evidence that at the moment Childe is a card-holding member of the Communist Party but there is no doubt that in the recent past, he has been a willing instrument of the Party. He kept in close touch with the Communist Party for a number of years and as can be seen from the foregoing is an active member of several 'front' organisations. His public utterances have generally been in accord with the prescribed Party line.[139]

'Communist' identities were multiple and mutable: fervent, life-long membership of individuals and families; the reading of communist literature; support for communist Parliamentary candidates; even spies.[140] Childe had become, if not as early as the 1930s, by the end of his life, a communist fellow traveller, one of a group of left-leaning intellectuals, fascinated by the Soviet Union and disillusioned with their own democracies.[141] Fellow travellers have been portrayed as Moscow's dupes, but they were conscious promoters of Soviet and communist goals.[142] Some intellectuals, for example Bernal and Haldane, pursued their beliefs from within the CPGB.[143] Others, like Childe, pursued them from outside, as his good friend, Max Mallowan, recognised: 'the Party was too clever ever to admit him formally. Outside it he was an invaluable ally; from within he would have been a menace'.[144]

Conclusion

The KV2 security services files kept on Vere Gordon Childe, although not unproblematic, provide an unparalleled source for life-writing him politically. They provide not only vital, often unique details, but also an overarching life-path or narrative which allows us to track his changing beliefs, associations and networks. Research into Childe's politics has long focused on his Marxist thought, but the files reveal the broader base of Childe's activism. He was a life-long pacifist and war-resister, vehemently opposed to atomic warfare. He was both a pioneering and a sustained civil liberties activist. These political attachments are scarcely visible in his archaeological work, warning us of the dangers of relying on his writings to understand his politics. Only by drawing together his lived political experience, his public statements and his writings can we gain a full understanding of Childe the political activist and thinker.

Childe was radicalised by the moral shock of conscription and desired to become a 'revolutionary' and 'rebel'. This early radicalism did not fade with academic fame and success. In Scotland, for example, he was at once an influential professor and a successful and sought-after radical leader. However, the extent of this radicalism seems to have been concealed from archaeological colleagues (who perhaps also preferred not to see it), misdirected and performed to the extent that many doubted it. His friend, Robert Stevenson, said of him:

> It was always difficult with Childe to know what was deep and what was superficial. I suspect that will always be one of the problems in writing about Childe, it was the case in knowing him.[145]

Behind the aimiable, forgetful exterior – half performance, half real – was a more ruthless and mercurial man managing two complex and intertwining lives, the archaeological and the political.

Childe's activism was a life-long commitment, but not one he undertook alone. In archaeological circles, his radicalism may have made him an outsider, but more widely, he contributed to some of the most brilliant left-wing thought of the twentieth century. In the post-Cold War world, although such allegiances are once again problematic, we should acknowledge the scientific and cultural contributions made by leading communists and communist fellow travellers. They were not naïve dupes, rather brilliant, committed intellectuals, selective and ruthless in their responses to the vision offered to them by Soviet and later International Communism. Childe's political life was of ultimately of his own choosing: mutable, rich, inspiring and always idiosyncratic.

Notes

1. The National Archives (TNA). KV2/2148: *Vere Gordon Childe*. 1917–1952; KV2/2149: *Vere Gordon Childe*. 1952–1955.
2. Tim Cornwell, 'Skara Brae archaeologist was MI5 target', *Sunday Times* (London), 17 December 2017: 13.
3. Leo S. Klejn, *Soviet Archaeology: Trends, schools and history* (Oxford: Oxford University Press, 2012); Peter Gathercole, 'Childe, Empiricism and Marxism', Unpublished Paper Presented at the Annual Meeting of the American Anthropological Association, 1974, typescript.
4. For example, John Callaghan and Mark Phythian, 'State surveillance and communist lives: Rose Cohen and the early British Communist milieu', *Journal of Intelligence History* 12 (2013): 134–55; Michael D. Lever, 'A person of interest: Gordon Childe and MI5', *Buried History* 51 (2015): 19–30; Tim Champion, 'Childe and Oxford', *Journal of European Archaeology* 12 (2009): 11–33.
5. Jonathan Haslam, 'Archival Review. Collecting and assembling pieces of the jigsaw: coping with Cold War archives', *Cold War History* 4 (2004): 140–50; Bennett, Gill, 'Declassification and release policies of the UK's Intelligence Agencies', *Intelligence and National Security* 17 (2002): 21–32.
6. KV2 files are personal files held in the National Archives that relate to specific individuals who were investigated for reasons related to national security.
7. Rodney Brunt, 'Information management of British military intelligence: the work of the documentalists, 1909–1945', *Library Trends* 62 (2013): 364.
8. Margaret Henderson and Alexandra Winter, 'Memoirs of our nervous illness: the Queensland Police Special Branch files of Carole Ferrier as political auto/biography', *Life Writing* 6.3 (2009): 360.
9. Alison Lewis, Valentina Glajar and Corina L. Petrescu, 'Introduction', in *Secret Police Files from the Eastern Bloc: Between Surveillance and Life Writing*, eds. Alison Lewis, Valentina Glajar and Corina L. Petrescu (Woodbury, Suffolk: Boydell and Brewer, 2016), 9–10; Vatulescu, 'Arresting biographies', 244.
10. Alison Lewis, 'Reading and writing the Stasi File: on the uses and abuses of the file as (auto) biography', *German Life and Letters* 56 (2003): 377, 385; Henderson and Winter, 'Memoirs', 350.
11. *Ibid*, 355, 387; Fiona Capp, *Writers Defiled: Security surveillance of Australian authors and intellectuals 1920–1960* (Victoria, Australia: McPhee Gribble, 1993), 4.
12. Haslam, 'Archival Review', 150; James K. Lyon, 'The FBI as literary historian: the file of Bertolt Brecht', *The Brecht Yearbook* 11 (1982): 230.
13. Lyon, The FBI, 222; Lewis, Glajar and Petrescu, 'Introduction', 10–11.
14. Alastair Black and Rodney Brunt, 'Information management in MI5 before the age of the computer', *Intelligence & National Security* 16 (2001): 158–65; Brunt, 'Information management of British military intelligence'; Thurlow, 'Historiography and source materials'.
15. Chris Northcott, 'The role, organization and methods of MI6', *International Journal of Intelligence and Counterintelligence* 20 (2007): 453–79.
16. Smith, James, *British Writers and MI5 Surveillance 1930–1960* (Cambridge: Cambridge University Press, 2013): 7.
17. Graham, 'In Piam Veterum Memoriam', 224; TNA. KV2/2148, 31a-49a: Childe.

18 National Archives 2006. Security Service MI5. History: 1 March 2006 Releases. Accessed 3 February 2022 https://webarchive.nationalarchives.gov.uk/20090511151559/ http://www.mi5.gov.uk/output/1-march-2006-releases.html.
19 Kevin Quinlan, *The Secret War between the Wars. MI5 in the 1920s and 1930s* (Woodbridge: The Boydell Press, 2014); Gill Bennett, 'Declassification and release policies of the UK's intelligence agencies'.
20 Richard C. Thurlow, 'The historiography and source materials in the study of international security in modern Britain (1885–1956)', *History Compass* 6 (2008): 147–71; Charmain Brinson and Richard Dove, *A Matter of Intelligence. MI5 and the surveillance of anti-Nazi refugees 1933–1950* (Manchester: Manchester University Press, 2014).
21 Cristina Vatulescu, 'Arresting biographies: the secret police file in the Soviet Union and Romania', *Comparative Literature* 56 (2004): 243–61.
22 (KV2/2148-2198) National Archives 2006. Security Service MI5.
23 Christopher Andrew, *The Defence of the Realm: The authorized history of MI5* (London: Penguin, 2010). Many of Childe's friends possessed KV2 files, including Communist leader Rajani Palme Dutt (KV2/1807-1809), writer Jack Lindsay (KV2/3252-3259), economist Maurice Dobb (KV2/1758-1759), scientist James Gerald Crowther (KV2/3341-3344) and historian Christopher Hill (KV2/3941-3946).
24 These files were formerly designated as PF32/V1 and PF.P.P.32 and kept in MI5's central registry.
25 Northcott, 'MI5', 457.
26 Richard C. Thurlow, 'The charm offensive: the 'coming Out' of MI5', *Intelligence and National Security* 15 (2000): 186.
27 Smith, *British Writers*, 11; Brunt, 'Information management', 364.
28 Black and Brunt, 'Information management', 160.
29 TNA. KV2/2148, 33a: Childe.
30 TNA. KV2/2148, 190711. This file does not survive and was probably destroyed in 1921–1922 during a purge by the Ministry of Health of all files kept on former war resisters.
31 Richard J. Popplewell, *Intelligence and Imperial Defence: British intelligence and the defence of the Indian empire 1904–1924* (Oxford: Routledge, 1995); Nigel West, *MI6: British secret intelligence service operations 1909–1945* (London: Panther, 1983).
32 TNA. KV2/2148, 36a: Childe: a probable early file SZ 5309/F 29.7.31 and R.F.402/48/221; Wilson and Adams, Special Branch, xvi–xix.
33 Andrew, *Defence of the Realm*, 129.
34 TNA, KV2/2148, 122a; Australian National Archives. A6126/279, 18. Vere Gordon Childe. Australian Security Intelligence Organization file. https://recordsearch.naa.gov.au/SearchNRetrieve/Interface/ViewImage.aspx?B=1073025. A second file, dating to 1951 and associated with Childe's protests about the treatment of Communists in Australia is also available to view https://recordsearch.naa.gov.au/SearchNRetrieve/Interface/ViewImage.aspx?B=278246.
35 Champion, 'Childe and Oxford'; Sally Green, *Prehistorian: A Biography of V. Gordon Childe* (Bradford-on-Avon: Moonraker, 1981), 22–24; TNA. KV2/2148, 190711. Childe.
36 Andrew, *Defence of the Realm*, 336. The installation of eavesdropping devices, usually requiring burglary and approval of the Home Office, was saved for major targets, in particular CPGB leaders. For example Betty Reid, wife of Childe's friend John Lewis, who had six personal files (KV2/2042-2047) dated between 1936 and 1955.
37 TNA. KV2/2149, 106z: Childe.
38 Thurlow, 'Historiography and Source Materials', 149.
39 TNA. KV2/2148, 190711, 36b, 32x, 32y, 74a: Childe.
40 Scott Lyall, "The Man is a Menace': MacDiarmid and Military Intelligence', *Scottish Studies Review* 8.1 (2007): 13; Karyn Burnham, *The Courage of Cowards. The untold story of First World War conscientious objectors* (London: Pen & Sword Military, 2014); Tom Buchanan, 'Loyal believers and disloyal sceptics: propaganda and dissent in Britain during the Korean War, 1950–1953', *History* 101 (2016): 736–55.
41 TNA. KV2/2148, 45a: Childe; Jennifer Grant, 'The role of MI5 in the internment of British Fascists during the Second World War'. *Intelligence and National Security* 24 (2009): 499–528.
42 TNA. KV2/2148, 67a, 68a. Thurlow, 'Historiography and Source Materials', 147; Quinlan, *Secret War*, 5, 188; Bennett, 'Declassification and Release Policies', 27.

43 E.g. TNA. KV2/2149, 94a, 97a, 98a, 99a and 100a.
44 Kevin Morgan, *Bolshevism and the British Left. Part One: Labour legends and Russian gold* (London: Lawrence & Wishart, 2006), 36-7.
45 The filing of these documents relates to changes in MI5 Registry record-keeping between the wars. See Black and Brunt, 'Information Management', 162–3.
46 Quinlan, *Secret War*, 70.
47 *Ibid*, 3; Andrew, *Defence of the Realm*, 11.
48 TNA. KV2/2148, 224788: Childe.
49 Eugene G. Schwartz, and Robert L. West, 'The World Student Congress and International Education of American Students', *Higher Education* 7.14 (1951): 157–62; TNA. KV2/2148, 66A: Childe.
50 TNA. KV2/2148, 50a: Childe.
51 TNA. KV2/2148, 77a: *Ibid*.
52 University of London Archives. Institute of Commonwealth Studies ICS157/1/4. Letter from R. Marmach to Vere Gordon Childe (3 February 1954); University of London Archives. Institute of Commonwealth Studies ICS157/1/4. Letter from Vere Gordon Childe to R. Marmach (4 February 1954).
53 TNA. KV2/2148, 53a: Childe; TNA (KV2/2335, 241a): Maurice Campbell Cornforth and Kitty Karoline Cornforth. 1944–1950. Also known as the Communist Party Science Group.
54 William DeJong-Lambert and Nikolai Krementsov, 'On labels and issues: The Lysenko controversy and the Cold War', *Journal of the History of Biology* 45 (2012): 373–88.
55 Andrew Brown, *J. D. Bernal: The Sage of Science* (Oxford: Oxford University Press, 2005), 304–12.
56 TNA. KV2/2148, 27a, 31a: Childe.
57 George F. Geddes, 'The Royal Commission on the Ancient and Historical Monuments of Scotland, Angus Graham and Gordon Childe (1935–1946)', *Proceedings of the Society of Antiquaries of Scotland* 146 (2016): 290–1.
58 'Russia's Aim. To Safeguard World Peace. M. Maisky in Edinburgh', *The Scotsman* (Edinburgh), 22 June 1936: 10.
59 E.g. Peter Gathercole, 'Patterns in prehistory: an examination of the later thinking of V. Gordon Childe', *World Archaeology* 3.2 (1971): 225–32; Peter Gathercole, 'Childe's early Marxism', in *Critical Traditions in Contemporary Marxism*, eds. Valerie Pinsky and Alison Wylie (Cambridge: Cambridge University Press, 1989), 80–7.
60 Champion, 'Childe and Oxford'; Katie Meheux, 'Eight conscientious objectors at the University of Oxford, 1914–1918', *Oxoniensia* 82 (2017): 165–200; David Englander, 'Military intelligence and the defence of the realm: the surveillance of soldiers and civilians during the First World War', *Bulletin of the Society for the Study of Labour History* 52 (1987): 24–30.
61 TNA. KV2/2148, 190711: *Ibid*; Englander, 'Military intelligence and the defence of the realm'.
62 Lois S. Bibbings, 'State reaction to conscientious objection', in *Frontiers of Criminality*, ed. Ian Loveland (London: Sweet & Maxwell, 1995), 25.
63 Meheux, 'Eight conscientious objectors'.
64 Society of Friends Archives. T. Edmund Harvey Archives, MSS 835/c/3. Letter from Alan Kaye to Thomas Edmund Harvey (15 June 1917).
65 Marvin Schwartz, *The Union of Democratic Control in British politics during the First World War* (Oxford: Clarendon Press, 1971), 152.
66 TNA. KV2-1807_1: Rajani Palme Dutt.
67 Stephen White, 'Soviets in Britain: the Leeds Convention of 1917', *International Review of Social History* 19 (1974): 165–93.
68 William J. Peace, 'The Enigmatic Career of Gordon Childe: A Peculiar and Individual Manifestation of the Human Spirit', PhD dissertation. Columbia University, 1992, 56–7.
69 Meheux, 'Eight Conscientious Objectors'; TNA. KV2/2148, 190711: Childe.
70 TNA. KV2/2148, 5–8: *Ibid*.
71 TNA. KV2/1918: Archibald Fenner Brockway. 1916–1921; Cain, Origins of Political Surveillance, 195–197.
72 Tareq Y. Ismael and Rifa'at El-Sa'id, *The Communist Movement in Egypt, 1920–1988* (Syracuse: Syracuse University Press, 1990), 3.
73 Shompa Lahiri, *Indians in Britain. Anglo-Indian Encounters: race and identity, 1880–1930* (London, Portland: Frank Cass, 2000), 128.
74 TNA. KV2/2148, 9–10: Childe; Green, Prehistorian, 49.

75 Vere Gordon Childe, 'When Labour ruled – in Australia, by an ex-ruler', *Labour Monthly* 3 (1922): 171–80; TNA. KV2/2148, 9: Childe.
76 TNA. KV2/2148, 5: *Ibid*.
77 Green, Prehistorian, 41; Childe's name is not on the original intercepted membership list for the society; ROSTA (Russian Telegraph Service)/TASS. TNA. KV2/1109. The ROSTA office in London, and the TASS office. May–June 1925.
78 Green, Prehistorian, 41.
79 Alexander Keiller Museum, Avebury. Keiller Archives. Letter from Alexander Keiller to Vere Gordon Childe (11 December 1928).
80 Oliver Hill-Andrews, 'Interpreting Science. JG Crowther and the Making of Interwar British Culture', PhD dissertation. University of Sussex, 2015, 12; Alexander Keiller Museum, Avebury. Keiller Archives. Letter from Alexander Keiller to Gordon Childe (20 September 1928).
81 Flinders University, Australia. Special Collections. Mary Alice Evatt Papers. Letter from Vere Gordon Childe to Mary Alice Evatt (23 June 1931).
82 Katie Meheux, 'A work from an "unknown member of the proletariat": digitising and re-examining Vere Gordon Childe's 'Dawn of European Civilization'', *Archaeology International* 20 (2017): 91–105; John Fyrth, *Britain, Fascism and the Popular Front* (London: Lawrence and Wishart, 1985).
83 George Robert Gayre, *Gayre of Gayre & Nigg. An Autobiography* (Edinburgh: Edinburgh Impressions, 1987), 19.
84 Daniel Gray, *Homage to Caledonia: Scotland and the Spanish Civil War* (Glasgow: Luath Press, 2009).
85 'Varsity Notes. Spanish Relief Committee', *Edinburgh Evening News* (Edinburgh), 6 February 1939: 5; Vere Gordon Childe, 'Points of View. The Foreign Enlistment Act', *The Scotsman* (Edinburgh), 13 January 1937: 3.
86 TNA. KV2/2148, 29A, 52A: Childe.
87 Jordi Vidal, 'Bosch Gimpera y Gordon Childe: Una Controversia Ideológica', *Revista D'Arqueologia de Ponent*, 24 (2014): 75–80. Accessed 3 February 2022 https://www.raco.cat/index.php/RAP/article/view/288707/376958.
88 Alexander Keiller Museum, Avebury. Keiller Archives. Letter from Vere Gordon Childe to Alexander Keiller (8 May 1937).
89 Phillips, Secret Twenties, 224–6; Emily Lygo, 'Promoting Soviet Culture in Britain: the history of the Society for Cultural Relations between the Peoples of the British Commonwealth and the USSR, 1924–1945', *The Modern Language Review* 108.2 (2013): 571–96.
90 TNA. KV2/2148, 24z: *Ibid*.
91 TNA. KV2/2148, 30a: *Ibid*.
92 British Library. India Office Records and Private Papers. IOR: L/PJ/12/451. The India League, 1938.
93 TNA. KV2/2509: Krishna Vengalil Krishna Menon. 1929–1941.
94 TNA. KV2/2148, 29b: Childe.
95 UCL Special Collections. Haldane Archive 5/5/1/14. Letter from J.B.S. Haldane to N. Vavilov (4 May 1939). https://digital-collections.ucl.ac.uk/R/VKH262VXTK9R98H8Q4H931FE196 K2FS7L6TTFJ55VUMI143FF7-02781?func=results-jump-full&set_entry=000001&set_number=755688&base=GEN01.
96 TNA. KV2/2148, 41a: Childe.
97 e.g. Gathercole, 'Childe's Early Marxism'; Gathercole, 'Childe, Empiricism and Marxism'.
98 Alexander Keiller Museum, Avebury. Keiller Archives. Letter from Vere Gordon Childe to Alexander Keiller (8 May 1937).
99 Oliver Hill-Andrews, 'A New and Hopeful Type of Social Organisation: Julian Huxley, J. G. Crowther and Lancelot Hogben on Roosevelt's New Deal' *British Journal of the History of Science* 52 (2019): 645–71.
100 People's History Museum, Manchester. Labour History Archive and Study Centre. CP/IND/Dutt. Letter from Vere Gordon Childe to Rajani Palme Dutt (14 October 1938).
101 'Distorting Prehistory. Forcing Facts to Fit Dogma', *The Scotsman* (Edinburgh), 23 August 1938: 13.
102 'By-Election Candidate', The Scotsman (Edinburgh), 5 June 1935: 18.
103 Martin Ceadel, *Pacifism in Britain, 1914–1945: The defining of a faith* (Oxford: Clarendon Press, 1980), 235; Vere Gordon Childe, 'War and Culture', in Eleventh Hour Questions, ed. Wallace Browning Tavener (Edinburgh: The Moray Press, 1937), 133–44.

104 Graham, 'In Piam Veterum Memoriam', 224; Ralston, 'Scottish Archaeology'.
105 TNA. KV2/2148, 32a: Childe. Wason had been lecturer in Classical Archaeology at the University of Edinburgh, but by 1938 had abandoned his academic career to become organiser of the Argyll Labour Party and a lens grinder in Glasgow. Graham Wason, 'Obituary: Roly Wason', *The Independent* (London), 24 January 1998. Accessed 3 February 2022 https://www.independent.co.uk/news/obituaries/obituary-roly-wason-1140579.html.
106 *Ibid*; Ralston, 'Scottish Archaeology'.
107 Gayre, Gayre & Nigg, 20, 44.
108 TNA. KV2/2148, 32z, 36a: *Ibid*.
109 TNA. KV2/2148, 32a: *Ibid*.
110 Vere Gordon Childe, 'Points of View. British Offer to Russia. Invasion of Finland', *The Scotsman* (Edinburgh), 19 November 1940: 7.
111 Green, Prehistorian, 101; Vere Gordon Childe, 'Soviet suspicions. The Russian standpoint', *The Scotsman* (Edinburgh), 26 February 1946: 4.
112 'British-Soviet Unity. Bathgate Bailie's Resolution', *Supplement to the West Lothian Courier* (Dundee), 1 February 1946.
113 TNA. KV2/2148, 52a: Childe.
114 TNA. KV2/2148, 55a; 60a; 65a; 70a: *Ibid*.
115 TNA. KV2/2148, 57a: *Ibid*; KV2/2148, 6a: *Ibid*.
116 Andrew, *Defence of the Realm*, 400–401.
117 William J. Peace, 'Vere Gordon Childe and American Anthropology', *Journal of Anthropological Research* 44 (1988): 419.
118 TNA. KV2/2148, 55a: Childe; KV2/2148, 53a: *Ibid*; TNA. KV2/2335, 189a, 193a: Cornforth.
119 In December 1952, for example, he invited Christopher Freeman, Robert Browning and Andrew Rothstein to lunch at the Institute of Archaeology; TNA. KV2/2149, 84a: Childe.
120 TNA KV2/2149, 113Z, 113b: Childe; KV2/2149, 85A: *Ibid*; KV2/2149, 85A: *Ibid*.
121 James Smith, 'The MacDonald Discussion Group: A communist conspiracy in Britain's Cold War film and theatre industry—or MI5's honey-pot?' *Historical Journal of Film, Radio and Television*, 35.3 (2015): 454–72.
122 TNA. (KV2/2148, 69a). *Ibid*.
123 Anon. 'Science in social affairs'. *Nature* 161 (1948): 68.
124 TNA. KV2/2149, 74a: *Ibid*. The Stockholm Appeal was launched by the World Peace Council on 19 March 1950 to promote nuclear disarmament. It was sponsored by the British Peace Council, of which Childe was a member, and was regarded as Soviet propaganda by the British government. Weston Ullrich, 'Preventing 'Peace': The British Government and the Second World Peace Congress', *Cold War History* 11 (2011): 344.
125 TNA. KV2/2149, 74a: *Ibid;* Anthropologist, 'Stockholm Appeal', *The Manchester Guardian* (Manchester), 1 September 1950: 6.
126 TNA. KV2/2149, 64a, 79a, 91a: *Ibid*.
127 TNA. KV2/2147, 65a: *Ibid*.
128 TNA. KV2/2149, 121A, 122a: Childe.
129 Klejn, *Soviet Archaeology*, 161–171; Jacek Lech and Franciszek Stepniowski, *V. Gordon Childe and Archaeology in the 20th Century* (Warsaw: Polish Academy of Sciences. The Pre-and Protohistorical Sciences Committee Works, volume III, 1999); Attila Laszlo, 'The young Gordon Childe and Transylvanian archaeology: the archaeological correspondence between Childe and Ferenc Laszlo', *European Journal of Archaeology* 12 (2009): 35–46.
130 TNA. KV2/2149, 93a: Childe.
131 Andrew, *Defence of the Realm*, 399–512.
132 Gathercole, 'Childe, Empiricism and Marxism', 5.
133 TNA. KV2/2149, 81a, 81z, 82a: *Ibid*.
134 Tom Buchanan, *East Wind: China and the British Left, 1925–1976* (Oxford: Oxford University Press, 2012), 144–78.
135 Gathercole, 'Childe, Empiricism and Marxism', 5.
136 Australian National Archives. A6126/279, 17-18. Vere Gordon Childe. Australian Security Intelligence Organization file; Glyn Daniel, 'Editorial', *Antiquity* 54.210 (1980): 1.
137 Judy Powell, *Love's Obsession. The lives and archaeology of Jim and Eve Stewart* (Kent Town, Australia: Wakefield Press, 2013), 174.
138 UCL Special Collections. UCL Wheeler Archive, WHEELER/B/4. Letter from Glyn Daniel to R. E. M. Wheeler (21 May 1958).

139 Andrew, *Defence of the Realm*, 330; TNA. KV2/2149, 122a: Childe.
140 David Aaronovitch, *Party Animals: My family and other communists* (London: Jonathan Cape, 2016); Morgan et al., Communists and British Society, 13; John Costello, *Mask of Treachery* (London: Collins, 1988), 224.
141 Ludmila Stern, *Western Intellectuals and the Soviet Union, 1920–1940. From Red Square to the Left Bank* (London: Routledge, 2007); David Cautes, *The Fellow Travellers* (London: Weidenfeld and Nicolson Ltd, 1973).
142 For example, Stephen Koch, *Double Lives: Stalin, Willi Munzenberg and the seduction of the intellectuals* (London: Harper Collins, 1996); Smith, British Writers, 154.
143 Cautes, *Fellow Travellers*, 219.
144 Max Mallowan, *Mallowan's Memoirs* (London: Collins, 1977), 234.
145 Peace, 'Enigmatic Career', 204–5.

Bibliography

Aaronovitch, David, *Party Animals: My family and other communists* (London: Jonathan Cape, 2016).
Andrew, Christopher, *The Defence of the Realm: The authorized history of MI5* (London: Penguin, 2010).
Anthropologist, 1950. 'Stockholm Appeal'. *The Manchester Guardian* 1 September 1950: 6.
Bennett, Gill, 'Declassification and release policies of the UK's intelligence agencies', *Intelligence and National Security* 17 (2002): 21–32.
Bibbings, Lois S., 'State reaction to conscientious objection', in *Frontiers of Criminality*, ed. Ian Loveland (London: Sweet & Maxwell, 1995), 57–81.
Black, Alastair and Rodney Brunt, 'Information management in MI5 before the age of the computer', *Intelligence & National Security* 16 (2001): 158–65.
Brinson, Charmain and Richard Dove, *A Matter of Intelligence. MI5 and the surveillance of anti-Nazi Refugees 1933–1950* (Manchester: Manchester University Press, 2014).
'British-Soviet Unity. Bathgate Bailie's Resolution', *Supplement to the West Lothian Courier* (Dundee), 1 February 1946.
Brown, Andrew, *J. D. Bernal. The sage of science* (Oxford: Oxford University Press, 2005).
Brunt, Rodney, 'Information management of British military intelligence: The work of the documentalists, 1909–1945', *Library Trends* 62 (2013): 360–77.
Buchanan, Tom, *East Wind: China and the British Left, 1925–1976* (Oxford: Oxford University Press, 2012).
Buchanan, Tom, 'Loyal believers and disloyal sceptics: Propaganda and dissent in Britain during the Korean War, 1950–1953', *History* 101 (2016): 736–55.
Burnham, Karyn, *The Courage of Cowards. The untold story of First World War conscientious objectors* (London: Pen & Sword Military, 2014).
'By-Election Candidate', *The Scotsman* (Edinburgh), 5 June 1935: 18.
Cain, Frank, *The Origins of Political Surveillance in Australia* (London, Sydney, Melbourne: Angus & Robertson Publishers, 1983).
Callaghan, John and Mark Phythian, 'State surveillance and communist lives: Rose Cohen and the early British Communist milieu', *Journal of Intelligence History* 12. (2013): 134–55.
Capp, Fiona, *Writers Defiled: Security surveillance of Australian authors and intellectuals 1920–1960* (Victoria, Australia: McPhee Gribble, 1993).
Cautes, David, *The Fellow Travellers* (London: Weidenfeld and Nicolson Ltd, 1973).
Ceadel, Martin, *Pacifism in Britain, 1914–1945: The defining of a faith* (Oxford: Clarendon Press, 1980).
Champion, Tim, 'Childe and Oxford', *Journal of European Archaeology* 12. (2009): 11–33.
Childe, Vere Gordon, 'When Labour ruled – in Australia, by an ex-ruler', *Labour Monthly* 3 (1922): 171–80.
Childe, Vere Gordon, 'Points of view. The Foreign Enlistment Act', *The Scotsman* (Edinburgh) 13 January 1937: 13.
Childe, Vere Gordon, 'War and culture', in *Eleventh Hour Questions*, ed. Wallace Browning Tavener (Edinburgh: The Moray Press, 1937): 133–44.

Childe, Vere Gordon, 'Points of view. British offer to Russia. Invasion of Finland', *The Scotsman* (Edinburgh), 19 November 1940: 7.
Childe, Vere Gordon, 'Soviet suspicions. The Russian standpoint', *The Scotsman* (Edinburgh), 26 February 1946: 4.
Cornwell, Tim, 'Skara Brae archaeologist was MI5 Target', *Sunday Times* (London), 17 December 2017: 13.
Costello, John, *Mask of Treachery* (London: Collins, 1988).
Daniel, Glyn, 'Editorial', *Antiquity* 54 (1980): 1–3.
DeJong-Lambert, William and Nikolai Krementsov, 'On labels and issues: The Lysenko controversy and the Cold War', *Journal of the History of Biology* 45 (2012): 373–88.
'Distorting prehistory. Forcing facts to fit dogma', *The Scotsman* (Edinburgh), 23 August 1938: 13.
Englander, David, 'Military intelligence and the defence of the realm: the surveillance of soldiers and civilians during the First World War', *Bulletin of the Society for the Study of Labour History* 52 (1987): 24–30.
Fyrth, John, *Britain, Fascism and the Popular Front* (London: Lawrence and Wishart, 1985).
Gathercole, Peter, 'Patterns in prehistory: an examination of the later thinking of V. Gordon Childe', *World Archaeology* 3 (1971): 225–32.
Gathercole, Peter, 'Childe, Empiricism and Marxism', Unpublished Paper Presented at the Annual Meeting of the American Anthropological Association, 1974, typescript.
Gathercole, Peter, 'Childe's early Marxism', in *Critical Traditions in Contemporary Marxism*, eds., Valerie Pinsky and Alison Wylie (Cambridge: Cambridge University Press, 1989), 80–7.
Gayre, George Robert, *Gayre of Gayre & Nigg. An Autobiography* (Edinburgh: Edinburgh Impressions, 1987).
Geddes, George, F., 'The Royal Commission on the Ancient and Historical Monuments of Scotland, Angus Graham and Gordon Childe (1935–1946)', *Proceedings of the Society of Antiquaries of Scotland* 146 (2016): 275–306.
Graham, Angus, 'In Piam Veterum Memoriam', in *The Scottish Antiquarian Tradition. Essays to Mark the Bicentenary of the Society of Antiquaries of Scotland and its Museum, 1780–1980*, ed. A. S. Bell (Edinburgh: John Donald Publishers Ltd, 1981), 212–26.
Grant, Jennifer, 'The role of MI5 in the internment of British Fascists during the Second World War', *Intelligence and National Security* 24 (2009): 499–528.
Gray, Daniel, *Homage to Caledonia: Scotland and the Spanish Civil War* (Glasgow: Luath Press, 2009).
Green, Sally, *Prehistorian: A biography of V. Gordon Childe* (Bradford-on-Avon: Moonraker, 1981).
Haslam, Jonathan, 'Archival review. Collecting and assembling pieces of the jigsaw: coping with Cold War archives', *Cold War History* 4.3 (2004): 140–52.
Henderson, Margaret and Alexandra Winter, 'Memoirs of our nervous illness: the Queensland Police Special Branch files of Carole Ferrier as political auto/biography', *Life Writing* 6 (2009): 349–67.
Hill-Andrews, Oliver 'Interpreting Science. JG Crowther and the Making of Interwar British Culture', PhD dissertation. University of Sussex, 2015.
Hill-Andrews, Oliver, 'A new and hopeful type of social organisation: Julian Huxley, J. G. Crowther and Lancelot Hogben on Roosevelt's New Deal', *British Journal of the History of Science* 52 (2019): 645–71.
Ismael, Tareq Y. and Rifa'at El-Sa'id, *The Communist Movement in Egypt, 1920–1988* (Syracuse: Syracuse University Press, 1990).
Klejn, Leo S., *Soviet Archaeology: Trends, schools and history* (Oxford: Oxford University Press, 2012).
Koch, Stephen, *Double Lives: Stalin, Willi Munzenberg and the seduction of the intellectuals* (London: Harper Collins, 1996).
Lahiri, Shompa, *Indians in Britain. Anglo-Indian Encounters: race and identity, 1880–1930* (London, Portland: Frank Cass, 2000).
Laszlo, Attila, 'The young Gordon Childe and Transylvanian archaeology: the archaeological correspondence between Childe and Ferenc Laszlo', *European Journal of Archaeology* 12 (2009): 35–46.
Lech, Jacek and Franciszek Stepniowski, *V. Gordon Childe and Archaeology in the 20th Century* (Warsaw: Polish Academy of Sciences. The Pre-and Protohistorical Sciences Committee Works, volume III, 1999).
Lever, Michael D., 'A person of interest: Gordon Childe and MI5', *Buried History* 51 (2015): 19–30.

Lewis, Alison, 'Reading and writing the Stasi file: on the uses and abuses of the file as (auto) biography', *German Life and Letters* 56 (2003): 377–97.

Lewis, Alison, Valentina Glajar and Corina L. Petrescu, 'Introduction', in *Secret Police Files from the Eastern Bloc. Between surveillance and life writing*, eds. Alison Lewis, Valentina Glajar and Corina L. Petrescu (Woodbury, Suffolk: Boydell and Brewer, 2016), 1–24.

Lyall, Scott, '"The man is a menace": MacDiarmid and military intelligence', *Scottish Studies Review* 8.1 (2007): 37–52.

Lygo, Emily, 'Promoting Soviet culture in Britain: the history of the Society for Cultural Relations between the Peoples of the British Commonwealth and the USSR, 1924–1945', *The Modern Language Review* 108 (2013): 571–96.

Lyon, James K., 'The FBI as literary historian: the file of Bertolt Brecht', *The Brecht Yearbook* 11 (1982): 213–31.

Mallowan, Max, *Mallowan's Memoirs* (London: Collins, 1977).

Meheux, Katie, 'Eight conscientious objectors at the University of Oxford, 1914–1918', *Oxoniensia* 82 (2017): 165–200.

Meheux, Katie, 'A work from an "unknown member of the proletariat": digitising and re-examining Vere Gordon Childe's "Dawn of European Civilization"', *Archaeology International* 20 (2017): 91–105.

Morgan, Kevin, *Bolshevism and the British Left. Part One: Labour legends and Russian gold* (London: Lawrence & Wishart, 2006)

Morgan, Kevin, Gidon Cohen and Andrew Flinn, *Communists and British Society 1920–1991* (London, Sydney and Chicago: Rivers Oram Press, 2007).

National Archives 2006. *Security Service MI5. History: 1 March 2006 Releases*. Accessed 3 February 2022 https://webarchive.nationalarchives.gov.uk/20090511151559/ http://www.mi5.gov.uk/output/1-march-2006-releases.html.

Northcott, Chris, 'The role, organization and methods of M16', *International Journal of Intelligence and Counterintelligence* 20 (2007): 453–79.

Peace, William J., 'Vere Gordon Childe and American anthropology', *Journal of Anthropological Research* 44 (1988): 417–33.

Peace, William J. 'The Enigmatic Career of Gordon Childe: A Peculiar and Individual Manifestation of the Human Spirit', PhD dissertation. Columbia University, 1992.

Phillips, Timothy, *The Secret Twenties: British intelligence, the Russians and the Jazz Age* (London: Granta Books, 2017).

Popplewell, Richard J., *Intelligence and Imperial Defence: British Intelligence and the defence of the Indian empire 1904–1924* (Oxford: Routledge, 1995).

Powell, Judy, *Love's Obsession. The lives and archaeology of Jim and Eve Stewart* (Kent Town, Australia: Wakefield Press, 2013).

Quinlan, Kevin, *The secret war between the Wars. MI5 in the 1920s and 1930s* (Woodbridge: The Boydell Press, 2014).

Ralston, Ian, 'Gordon Childe and Scottish Archaeology: the Edinburgh years 1927–1946', *European Journal of Archaeology* 12 (2009): 47–90.

'Russia's aim; to safeguard world peace. M. Maisky in Edinburgh', *The Scotsman* (Edinburgh), 22 June 1936: 10.

Schwartz, Marvin, *The Union of Democratic Control in British politics during the First World War* (Oxford: Clarendon Press, 1971).

Schwartz, Eugene G. and Robert L. West, 'The World Student Congress and international education of American Students', *Higher Education* 7.14 (1951): 157–62.

Smith, James, *British Writers and MI5 Surveillance 1930–1960* (Cambridge: Cambridge University Press, 2013).

Smith, James, 'The MacDonald Discussion Group: A communist conspiracy in Britain's Cold War film and theatre industry—or MI5's honey-pot?', *Historical Journal of Film, Radio and Television*, 35 (2015): 454–72.

Stern, Ludmila, *Western Intellectuals and the Soviet Union, 1920–1940. From Red Square to the Left Bank* (London: Routledge, 2007).

Thurlow, Richard C., 'The charm offensive: the "coming out" of MI5', *Intelligence and National Security* 15 (2000): 183–90.

Thurlow, Richard C., 'The historiography and source materials in the study of international security in modern Britain (1885–1956)', *History Compass* 6 (2008): 147–71.

Ullrich, Weston, 'Preventing "peace": The British Government and the Second World Peace Congress', *Cold War History* 11 (2011): 341–62.

'Varsity Notes. Spanish Relief Committee', *Edinburgh Evening News* (Edinburgh), 6 February, 1939: 5.

Vatulescu, Cristina, 'Arresting biographies: the secret police file in the Soviet Union and Romania', *Comparative Literature* 56 (2004): 243–61.

Vidal, Jordi, 'Bosch Gimpera y Gordon Childe: Una Controversia Ideológica', *Revista D'Arqueologia de Ponent,* 24 (2014): 75–80. Accessed 3 February 2022. https://www.raco.cat/index.php/RAP/article/view/288707/376958.

Wason, Graham, 'Obituary: Roly Wason', *The Independent* (London), 24 January 1998. Accessed 3 February 2022. https://www.independent.co.uk/news/obituaries/obituary-roly-wason-1140579.html.

West, Nigel, *MI6. British Secret Intelligence Service Operations 1909–1945* (London: Panther, 1983).

White, Stephen, 'Soviets in Britain: the Leeds Convention of 1917', *International Review of Social History* 19 (1974): 165–93.

Wilson, Ray and Ian Adams, *Special Branch. A history: 1883–2006* (London: Biteback publishing, 2015).

Part III
Reflections on practice

13
Alternative narratives in the history of archaeology: Exploring diaries as a form of reflexivity

Oscar Moro Abadía

Introduction

The history of science that emerged in the first half of the nineteenth century was initially conceived as the story of scientists who had contributed to scientific progress. For instance, in his influential *History of the Inductive Sciences*, William Whewell explained that:

> in tracing the progress of the various provinces of knowledge [...] it will be important for us to see that, at all such epochs [...] some man or men come before us, who have possessed, in an eminent degree, a clearness of the ideas which belong to the subject in question, and who have applied such ideas in a vigorous and distinct manner to ascertained facts and exact observations.[1]

Hagiographical biographies remained popular during the late nineteenth century and the beginnings of the twentieth century. However, starting in the 1960s, a number of historians and sociologists of science, including Thomas Kuhn, George Canguilhem and others, called the hagiographical focus on the lives of great scientists into question.[2] As a result of these critiques, few respectable historians of science focused on scientific biographies in the 1980s and the 1990s and even fewer adopted the laudatory tone typical of the beginning of the century.[3] Instead, historians and sociologists of science focused on 'more and more detailed, and more contextually sensitive, accounts of scientific episodes',[4] including discoveries and scientific controversies.

However, in the past 20 years, we have witnessed an increasing interest in biographical approaches.[5] In particular, historians of science have reflected on the place of biography in the historiography of science.[6] Similarly, biographical approaches have become popular among historians of archaeology.[7] In this field, scholars have explored new sources for archaeological biography, including oral sources, correspondence and, especially, diaries and personal archives.[8] In a theoretical context marked by a growing emphasis on subjectivity and reflexivity, a number of archaeologists have suggested that diaries provide important information for understanding the archaeological process.[9] I suggest in this chapter that diaries can also contribute to enriching the field of the history of archaeology by encouraging reflexivity in historical research. In fact, diaries constitute privileged documents for understanding both the process of writing archaeological histories and the final results. I illustrate this point with an example from my own work on the history of archaeology. In 2014, I spent two months at the École des Hautes Études en Sciences Sociales (Paris) co-writing a paper on the relationships between André Leroi-Gourhan and structuralism (later published in the *Cambridge Archaeological Journal* in 2015). During that time, I kept a diary in which I recorded relevant information to help conceptualise my writing process. This diary is not only helpful to identity the different strategies, ideas and problems that I followed during the writing of the paper, but also those which I ultimately included in the final paper.

In this chapter, I present an edited version of the diary that I kept in those months. The original document was a chaotic amalgamation of entries written in English, French and Spanish. I have therefore edited the entries and have introduced a considerable number of clarifications. Similarly, I have removed a number of non-academic references that likely would have held little meaning or interest for readers. Still, as much as possible, I have aimed to remain close to the original document. I have also edited the text to avoid duplication with the published paper. That said, the publication of a scholarly diary inevitably poses the question of redundancy, that is, the fact that 'diary writers are repeating, often perfectly, the language of other media'.[10] My case is not different. Although my diary captures some original perspectives, there is some repetition with some published sources, especially our 2015 paper in the *Cambridge Archaeological Journal*. That said, I tend to agree with Allison Mickel who suggest that 'the fact that so much information from the more conventional modes of recording is repeated in the diary entries should not be seen as evidence for the diaries' nonutility but instead as a rational practice that conforms to and contributes to archaeological epistemology'.[11] This is related to the fact that redundancy does not eliminate the different character of these two media. Quite the opposite, repetition 'embodies the criteria and culture of successful knowledge production'[12] and, therefore, highlights what can be said in one context and what needs to be omitted in the other. In my case, while in the academic publication I focused on Leroi-Gourhan, in the diary I mainly reflect on the position of Annette Laming-Emperaire in French academia. This also features some important considerations about gender in the history of archaeology.

1 May 2014

We arrived in Paris yesterday after a 20-hour trip. The trip with our two and a half year old daughter went fairly smoothly and the apartment that we rented on rue Beaunier was bigger than expected. Because of the holiday, everything is closed today so I will meet Dominique Richard from the *Fondation Maison des Sciences de l'Homme* tomorrow. Ms. Richard is responsible for the *Pôle Scientifique* of the *Programme Directeurs d'Études Associés*. In February, they had invited me to spend six weeks in Paris to develop a number of projects on the history of archaeology. In particular, I wanted to finish work on Leroi-Gourhan that I have begun two years prior.

The story of this chapter goes back to September 2006 when I defended my PhD dissertation at the Universidad de Cantabria in Santander, Spain. Alain Schnapp was the president of the jury and, after the (successful) defence, we went out for dinner at a local restaurant. Once seated, we spoke about prehistoric art and, at some point, I made a comment about Leroi-Gourhan's structuralism. Schnapp turned toward me and, with an expression of surprise on his face, told me that Leroi-Gourhan was not a structuralist. Given the respect I hold for Schnapp, I gently responded that, in the field of prehistoric art, Leroi-Gourhan was unanimously considered as the father of structuralism. He smiled in a somewhat ironic way and said that this was the *American* view of French prehistory.[13] The conversation ended then but I have thought about his remark for years. Time passed and Jo McDonald and Peter Veth invited me to write a paper on the hermeneutics of rock art for a companion that they were editing.[14] On that occasion, I read several of Leroi-Gourhan's books and, almost immediately, the question of structuralism became relevant again. Eduardo Palacio-Pérez, a historian of archaeology at the Universidad de Cantabria and I thus began a project on the relationships between Leroi-Gourhan and structuralism. To begin, I contacted a number of Leroi-Gourhan's former students, including Denis Vialou, Brigitte Delluc, Gilles Delluc and Françoise Audouze. Significantly, not one of them defined Leroi-Gourhan as 'structuralist'. For instance, Françoise Audouze commented that 'Leroi-Gourhan reacted in a strong way when someone told him that he was '"structuralist"' for he conceived his own research in diachronical terms, from an evolutive or evolutionist perspective'.[15] At the same time, other scholars supported the opposite view. In an interview, George Sauvet categorically stated that Leroi-Gourhan was *the* person who introduced structuralism in the analysis of prehistoric art. In sum, these conversations evidenced that the relationship between Leroi-Gourhan and structuralism was problematic.

In this setting, Eduardo and I spent two years looking for signs of structuralism in Leroi-Gouhan's work. We read his published works and I have spent time in the Leroi-Gourhan archives at the Maison de l'Archéologie et de l'Ethnologie (MAE) at Université Paris X-Nanterre. Our position, however, remains ambiguous. On the one hand, Leroi-Gourhan never declared himself as a 'structuralist' and we are persuaded that the main trends that oriented his work are not related to this theoretical framework.[16] On the other hand, it is hard to deny that, starting in 1958, a number of parallels can be established between Leroi-Gourhan's analysis of Paleolithic art and Lévi-Strauss's structural approach. The more we work on his works the more we are trapped in this paradox.

6 May 2014

I have started working at the library of the Fondation Maison des Sciences de l'Homme on the avenue de France. The library's location is not as central as it was before it moved from the boulevard Raspail, but the space is bright and I am grateful for its proximity to the Bibliothèque Nationale de France. I met Dominique Richard last Friday and she extended several kindnesses. My library card should be ready by the end of the week and she granted me access to the canteen in the building's basement.

Yesterday, I met Denis Vialou at the Institut de Paléontologie Humaine and our conversation made me think about certain reactions that our paper could engender. Vialou works as professor at the Musée National d'Histoire Naturelle and he was one of the most successful of Leroi-Gourhan's students. He did not believe that Leroi-Gourhan was a structuralist, but he insisted that he revolutionised the study of prehistoric art in the 1960s. This is a widespread notion among rock art specialists, especially in France, where it is generally accepted that Leroi-Gourhan's approach represented a widespread break from the work of his predecessors, especially Henri Breuil. In my reading, however, Leroi-Gourhan's and Breuil's approaches are related in a number of fundamental ways. This idea first came to mind when I read Stephen Jay Gould's *Up against a wall*,[17] a short essay in which he argued that, in addition to a number of differences concerning the meanings of prehistoric art, Breuil and Leroi-Gourhan shared a progressivist view according to which Paleolithic paintings evolved from simple and rudimentary images to complex and realistic representations. This progressivist view of prehistoric art is one of the many continuities that can be established between Breuil and Leroi-Gourhan.[18] For instance, they shared a Christian-informed view of prehistoric art and a teleological conception of art and culture that was likely related to their faith. While I do not deny the existence of important differences between Leroi-Gourhan and Breuil, I do not see a radical rupture between them. This being said, I understand that the idea of a discontinuity between both authors goes against the dominant interpretation of the history of prehistoric art and, more importantly, calls into question a symbolic landmark for an entire generation of French scholars who have built their work on Leroi-Gourhan's 'revolution'. In this setting, I hope we find the right course to navigate these troubled waters.

12 May 2014

Our daughter has been happy with her babysitter and my work on Leroi-Gourhan is going well. Yesterday I sent a draft of the paper to Eduardo and I am waiting for his comments. I work most days at the Fondation Maison des Sciences de l'Homme and occasionally at the library at the Musée National d'Histoire Naturelle in the Jardin de Plantes. It is not far to walk to from our apartment and the space is beautiful.

Tomorrow I will meet with Philippe Soulier at the MAE. Soulier has been working for several years on a biography of Leroi-Gourhan and has a profound knowledge of his work. I first met him in 2012 when I started researching this paper. At that time, I visited Leroi-Gourhan's archive at the MAE and Soulier kindly helped me navigate hundreds of boxes of documents. Most importantly, he suggested a paper – a short article published in an encyclopedia of anthropology edited by Jean Poirier in 1968[19] – that is particularly important to understand the ambiguous relationship between Leroi-Gourhan and structuralism. The paper is relevant not only because it constitutes one of the rare occasions in which Leroi-Gourhan explicitly discussed structuralism, but because it is indicative of his equivocal position toward this theoretical movement. This short paragraph illustrates this point:

> [For structuralists authors] the specific facts taking place in the life of ethnic groups correspond [...] to a non-random arrangement which have to be reconstructed every time anew [...] This is the inverse procedure of the one used by biologists, who reconstruct the living animal on the basis of its skeleton. The two procedures are, however, very similar; in both cases one begins with a previously known organisational scheme, which is then put in parallel with the organisational scheme to be discovered. Both the inversion of the methods and their profound analogies are striking when we compare *Mythologies* and the *Préhistoire de l'Art Occidental*.[20]

I have read this paragraph several times and I am still not sure I fully understand it. Still, it is clear that Leroi-Gourhan establishes two comparisons: One between structuralism and biology and another between his approach and that of Lévi-Strauss. In so doing, he also establishes an explicit analogy between (1) Lévi-Strauss and structuralism, and (2) his own method and the one used by biologists. More importantly, Leroi-Gourhan suggests that Lévi-Strauss and he himself used 'inversed methods' (it is important to note that he did not write 'opposed methods') connected by 'profound analogies'. In other words, this paragraph can be read at the same time as the evidence of Leroi-Gourhan's rejection of structuralism and his affiliation to this movement. And this is not the only case. In an interview with Claude-Henri Rocquet in 1982, Leroi-Gourhan declared that he and Lévi-Strauss 'were poles apart, but poles that have finished by approaching each other'.[21] In short, the question about the relationship between Leroi-Gourhan and structuralism is a difficult one because Leroi-Gourhan held a very ambiguous position *vis-à-vis* Lévi-Strauss. This is why it is so difficult to achieve any kind of definitive conclusion on this issue.

15 May 2014

The meeting with Philippe Soulier went well. We spoke about many things but, especially, about Leroi-Gourhan's Catholicism. I think that this question is particularly relevant to understand his interpretation of art and culture. One of the most recurrent traits of Leroi-Gourhan's work is the idea that natural and cultural processes are directed towards an end or shaped by a purpose. This understanding is especially obvious in his conception of the evolution of technology and prehistoric art. In this sense, Leroi-Gourhan is not far from a teleological view of progress that, in France, can be traced back to Lamarck. Leroi-Gourhan's teleological view is rooted in his religious beliefs. In fact, historical evidence shows he was a pious Catholic who often engaged with Catholic intellectuals in Lyon and Paris. However, Leroi-Gourhan rarely expressed his religious views openly. As far as I know, there is only one paper in which he elaborated on the influence of Catholic theology upon his work.[22] I asked Philippe about this question but, for whatever reason, Soulier was somewhat reluctant to talk about this topic. Given his generosity toward me, I do not push him on this point.

We also talked about a 156-page manuscript entitled '*Leroi-Gourhan: Historien de l'art et de la religion préhistorique*' that he had shared with me a couple of years ago. It is a detailed compilation of Leroi-Gourhan's work on prehistoric art. Moreover, there is a section about the reception of Leroi-Gourhan's work among French art historians. While there are very few references to structuralism, the document provides invaluable resources to explore the influence of art history upon Leroi-Gourhan's work.

19 May 2014

This morning, I reread Meg Conkey's *The Structural Analysis of Paleolithic Art*.[23] In many ways, this paper, first published in 1989, established the reputation of Leroi-Gourhan as a 'structuralist' author among American archaeologists. The article is a remarkable analysis of Leroi-Gourhan's work and is a classic on the topic. I am concerned about how Meg will react to our paper. She and I have been friends since I spent several months at Berkeley in 2001. Her work has always been a source of inspiration for me. My main concern is that our paper *can be read* as a critical response to her article, even if this is not our intention. We do not call into question her work, but we criticise the vulgate that, without trying to understand Leroi-Gourhan in his context, automatically catalogues him as 'structuralist'. We argue that Leroi-Gourhan's work reflected different influences and, therefore, multiple interpretations are possible.

22 May 2014

Today I discovered something interesting. I was reading Lévi-Strauss *Race and History*, an essay on race and racism that he wrote for UNESCO, when I found the following passage:

> According to one of the commonest explanations derived from the theory of cultural evolution, the rock paintings left behind by the middle palaeolithic societies were used for purposes of magic ritual in connexion with hunting. The line of reasoning is as follows: primitive peoples of the present day practise hunting rites, which often seem to us to serve no practical purpose; the many pre-historic paintings on rock walls deep in caves appear to us to serve no practical purpose; the artists who executed them were hunters; they were therefore used in hunting rites [...] While we are on the subject of cave paintings, we must point out that, except for the cave paintings found in South Africa (which some hold to be the work of native peoples in recent times), 'primitive' art is as far removed from Magdalenian and Aurignacian art as from contemporary European art, for it is marked by a very high degree of stylization, sometimes leading to complete distortion, while prehistoric art displays a striking realism. We might be tempted to regard this characteristic as the origin of European art; but even that would be untrue, since, in the same area, palaeolithic art was succeeded by other forms of a different character; the identity of geographical position does not alter the fact that different peoples have followed one another on the same stretch of earth, knowing nothing or caring nothing for the work of their predecessors, and each bringing in conflicting beliefs, techniques and styles of their own.[24]

This paragraph is relevant to our research for a number of reasons. First, as far as I know, it constitutes one of the rare occasions in which Lévi-Strauss commented on prehistoric art. Second, Lévi-Strauss calls into question Breuil's hunting-magic theory, the dominant paradigm in prehistoric art research until the 1960s. Third, Lévi-Strauss explicitly criticises the use of ethnographic analogies in archaeology. In this context, it is important to note that Lévi-Strauss published this essay in 1952 (which means he probably wrote it in 1951), when Breuil was at his peak and dominated prehistoric art research. I wonder: did Leroi-Gourhan read Lévi-Strauss's *Race and History*? Leroi-Gourhan only called into question Breuil's paradigm in 1958, six years after the publication of

Lévi-Strauss's *Race and History*. This means that, if he had read the booklet, it had a very late influence upon his published work.

28 May 2018

Today I reread the three papers by Leroi-Gourhan published in 1958. I'm excited because I think I might have found an important clue to explain Leroi-Gourhan's shift toward structuralism. Several scholars agree that these papers constitute a 'trilogy' that established a new paradigm in the history of prehistoric art research. Before 1958, Leroi-Gourhan had published several pieces on Chinese, Japanese and Lapp decorative art, but he had done very little work on prehistoric art. His primary publications on this topic were *The Reindeer Civilization* (published in 1936) in which he developed a comparison between Inuit and prehistoric art; a preface for a book by Fernand Windels about Lascaux[25] (1948), and a couple of papers on prehistoric art and aesthetics.[26] By the 1950s, Leroi-Gourhan visited several caves in France and Spain and had begun to establish a reputation as a prehistoric art specialist. For instance, André Malraux and Georges Salles asked him to write the first volume of *A Universal History of Art* in 1956.[27] Still, prior to 1958, Leroi-Gourhan was clearly under Breuil's influence. In 1957, he published a paper in which he explicitly subscribed to Breuil's theories. He wrote:

> The thousands of prehistoric images that we now know (female statuettes, engravings of figurative animals, the disposition of the images in the cave) leave no doubt about the magic-religious feelings of efficacy that engendered these images. This interpretation of prehistoric art harmonises in such a clear way with our detailed knowledge of modern primitive people (or, more generally, with what we know about modern humans) that it cannot divert from reality.[28]

However, *only one year later*, everything changed. In 1958, Leroi-Gourhan published three papers in *Bulletin de la Société Préhistorique Française* in which he developed a new approach to prehistoric art. These articles are conference proceedings from November 1957, February 1958 and May 1958. The first paper is about the function of symbols in Paleolithic cave art;[29] the second is on the meaning of Paleolithic signs[30] and the third examines the structure of Paleolithic cave paintings.[31] The change of tone is evident from the very beginning. The first article, for instance, starts with an explicit critique of the use of ethnographic analogies in archaeology. Leroi-Gourhan wrote:

> In this first paper, I will undertake neither a critique concerning the real meaning of the symbols nor a critique of the dangers associated with ethnographic comparisons [...] Rather, it seems better to explore the possibilities that examination of the whole of the decorated caves offers, discarding ethnographic comparisons and focusing on examination of [prehistoric] documents themselves.

Moreover, some of the most celebrated of Leroi-Gourhan's statements about prehistoric art were first enunciated in these papers: the notion that decorated caves were 'organised sanctuaries', the idea that images were not randomly placed on the walls of the caves, the conception that figurative and non-figurative representations constituted symbolic systems. Everything is there. So what might have happened in 1957 to change Leroi-Gourhan's views on prehistoric art? I thought about this question when I read, at the beginning of the first paper, the following paragraph:

> The questions that I posed of prehistoric documents were very different to those that we ordinarily ask [...] I wondered whether the decorated caves were organised sanctuaries [...] As I undertook this work, I discovered Ms Laming-Emperaire's views on an intentional nature of the association of certain animals in the main compositions of Lascaux and other caves. I then felt the need to examine the highest possible number of caves to establish the exact position of images, as well as some statistics about their location.[32]

Reading these lines, I felt I come across a significant statement. My impression is that it was Laming-Emperaire who influenced Leroi-Gourhan's shift towards a structuralist-like approach. Now to see if I can confirm this impression in the next couple of weeks.

30 May 2018

The story of Laming-Emperaire and Leroi-Gourhan is well known. Annette Laming-Emperaire completed a bachelor degree in philosophy. In 1946, she was appointed by the Conseil National de la Recherche Scientifique (CNRS) where she became interested in cave paintings. In 1947, she began a PhD on cave art under the supervision of Étienne Souriau, professor of aesthetics. They worked together for almost 10 years, a period during which she published a number of works on archaeological methods. In 1956, Laming-Emperaire asked Leroi-Gourhan to supervise her doctoral thesis. A year later, she successfully defended her PhD dissertation. This chronology is relevant for a number of reasons. First, Laming-Emperaire's thesis was almost completed when Leroi-Gourhan became her supervisor in 1956 (she defended her dissertation on 18 June 1957). Second, taking into account the abovementioned chronology, it is highly likely that Leroi-Gourhan read Laming-Emperaire's thesis at the end of 1956 or the beginning of 1957. Put differently, this was around the same time as he developed a new paradigm for the study of prehistoric art. Third, based on these premises, it is likely that Laming-Emperaire influenced Leroi-Gourhan, and not the other way around. Indeed, Leroi-Gourhan recognised Laming-Emperaire's influence upon his work several times, evoking two main narratives to explain it. The first narrative, suggested in the 1958 paper, established that Laming-Emperaire's work changed his views on prehistoric art. The second narrative was a version of what Merton called 'multiple discoveries', or the idea that different scientists working independently from one another made similar discoveries. According to this idea, Leroi-Gourhan and Laming-Emperaire had simultaneously 'discovered' the organisation of Paleolithic caves. As Leroi-Gourhan suggested in *Préhistoire de l'Art Occidental*, 'It was at that moment that I realised, together with Laming-Emperaire, that we had independently followed two very similar paths. We decided then to continue our research separately in order to not influence each other until she finished *Signification de l'art parietal.*'[33]

Whether this was a case of multiple discoveries or not, there is no doubt that Laming-Emperaire influenced Leroi-Gourhan's work. So why does she have a secondary position in the history of Paleolithic art research? And, on a different note, did Laming-Emperaire read Lévi-Strauss? Was she influenced by structuralism?

2 June 2014

A few weeks ago, I met with Arnaud Hurel at the Institut de Paléontologie Humaine. Hurel has published several books on the history of French archaeology and he knows Breuil's work well. In our conversation in a restaurant near the Institut, Hurel mentioned a couple of letters in which Breuil made some references to Leroi-Gourhan and Laming-Emperaire located in the archives of the Musée National d'Histoire Naturelle. This was a great tip. For this reason, in the last two weeks, I spent several hours working there. Admittedly, the work conditions are not easy. Breuil's handwriting is difficult to read. I can take notes but pictures are prohibited.

I found a letter (that Arnaud had mentioned in a different email to me) in which Breuil is very critical of Laming-Emperaire. It is a letter addressed to Jean Bouyssonie on 6 May 1958.[34] While some words are illegible, the document illustrates Breuil's views on Laming-Emperaire:

> This young woman, protected by Leroi-Gourhan, then co-director of Musée de l'Homme, became interested in Paleo art [...] She helped me, as typist (nothing else) with the edition of *400 siècles d'art parietal* and she edited some booklets on a number of decorated caves [...] she claimed [...] to have found the golden key to open all the doors for the interpretation of caves [...] And, what is worse, she exerted upon Leroi-Gourhan an indescribable but incontestable influence [...] Last summer, she submitted a 700-page doctoral thesis (that she has prepared without my advice) entitled 'Signification de l'art rupestre paléolitique' at Sorbonne that I am currently reading and for which she received the highest qualification [...] I have not finished reading the thesis yet (I am at page 250) but, until now, there is nothing original [...] When I think about Leroi-Gourhan's conferences [...] they interpret systematically everything as sexual themes, even if there are bison and horses! And even if the signs = everything sexual, including the *tectiformes* and the *claviformes*! The method consisting in deducing the customs of prehistoric times and the magical function of art from ethnographical examples 'is without value' (of course the analogic argument can assure nothing...ethnography can only provide us with suggestions to understand the inaccessible past!) [...] And they ask me to help her to prepare her integration at the Scientific Research...but, is this scientific research??

I think this letter is relevant to our thinking for two reasons. In the first place, Breuil clearly suggests that Leroi-Gourhan was influenced by Laming-Emperaire's work, which could explain Leroi-Gourhan's turn in 1958. Second, the letter captures Breuil's animosity towards Laming-Emperaire. In fact, while he somewhat justified Leroi-Gourhan's position (it is important to keep in mind that Leroi-Gourhan had not yet published his three papers in the *Bulletin de la Société Préhistorique Française*), he is very critical of Laming-Emperaire. He not only called into question her methodology, but he is very critical of her sexual interpretation (an interpretation that, one year later, he would call a 'sexomaniac perspective' in a footnote that he introduced to the new edition of *Les hommes de la Pierre Ancienne*[35]). The gendered-sexist nature of the Breuil's comments are very obvious. Significantly, in a moment in which she could have received support from the 'Pope of Prehistory' (as they called him), she only received a harsh critique. Breuil's reputation ascended as Laming-Emperaire was ostracised in the field of prehistoric art.

Thinking in these terms, I decide to rewrite the second part of the paper. While I'm satisfied with our analysis of the relationship between Lévi-Strauss and Leroi-Gourhan, we need to incorporate a section on Laming-Emperaire's influence upon Leroi-Gourhan. Moreover, if Laming-Emperaire was the person who introduced a number of structuralist-like ideas in the analysis of prehistoric art, we also need to assess Lévi-Strauss's influence upon her thinking.

5 June 2014

I am reading Laming-Emperaire's books and papers on cave art and have now a better idea about her thinking. Like Leroi-Gourhan, Laming-Emperaire's early works in the field were in accordance with Breuil's art-as-magic theories. For instance, in 1951, she published a small booklet entitled *Prehistoric Art* in which she wrote:

> Hunter-gatherers have always performed magic rituals to guarantee big-game hunting; even today Aboriginal people from Australia paint animals and signs on the walls of the caves they invoke in their rituals [...] Likely, rituals were held in grandiose rooms or in the narrow corridors of the Paleolithic caves [...] The magic origins hypothesis of prehistoric paintings and engravings illuminates a number of facts that, otherwise, would be incomprehensible.[36]

Laming-Emperaire's positions on prehistoric art changed significantly over the 10 years in which she wrote her dissertation. In this work, entitled *La signification de l'art rupestre paléolithique*, she proposed replacing a methodology based on ethnographic comparisons with a detailed examination of prehistoric paintings and engravings. Moreover, she argued that the association between horse and bison was the main theme of prehistoric caves. From this organisation, she deduced that cave paintings reproduced a metaphysical conception of the world opposing female and male representations. Significantly, in the introduction to her thesis she mentioned an article by Lévi-Strauss entitled *History and Ethnology* published in 1949. While I can't be certain that Laming-Emperaire read *Race and History* (1952), this reference indicates that she was familiar with Lévi-Strauss's work. In fact, she cites him in a number of papers that she published in the late 1960s. In 1969 she published an article in the French journal *Annales: Economies, Sociétés, Civilizations* that is particularly relevant concerning this question.[37] In this paper, she suggested that there were three main paradigms to interpret prehistoric paintings. The first one was 'the ethnographic method' and could only serve for an initial approach to prehistoric images. She suggested that, even if there were some modern small-scale societies in existence with a social organisation similar to Paleolithic groups, the art of these groups could not be used for interpreting Paleolithic art.

The second paradigm, that Laming-Emperaire illustrated in her doctoral dissertation of 1957, consisted in examining Paleolithic paintings for their own sake. The third paradigm referred to Lévi-Strauss's works of structural anthropology that 'had opened a new, unexpected, way to address some of the interpretive problems of Paleolithic cave art'.[38] According to Laming-Emperaire, Lévi-Strauss had effectively demonstrated that all societies were organised in exchange systems defined by two main principles: symmetry and reciprocity. Since these principles were present in the organisation of Paleolithic paintings, Laming-Emperaire argued that Lévi-Strauss's rules of exchange could also explain the organisation of prehistoric images in caves like Lascaux.

It is clear to me now that if structuralism penetrated the analysis of prehistoric art, it was through Laming-Emperaire's work. I am going to rewrite the second part of the paper and send it to Eduardo.

13 June 2014

I have now rewritten the second part of the paper to suggest that Laming-Emperaire significantly influenced Leroi-Gourhan's work. In the course of the last two months, I have shifted from my initial focus on Leroi-Gourhan to my current interest in Laming-Emperaire. She did not receive the recognition that she deserved in her lifetime, but I hope that we can demonstrate her significant role in the history of archaeology. At the same time, I have to keep in mind that the paper is about Leroi-Gourhan and structuralism and, therefore, any discussions on Laming-Emperaire's work need to be related to the main topic.

Yesterday, Eduardo and I discussed potential journals to submit the article. He suggested *Cambridge Archaeological Journal* but I am not sure, as I submitted two papers to them in the past and they were both rejected. Another option was *Current Anthropology*, but I wonder whether our angle works for its focus. The *Journal of World Prehistory* was also an option, even if they typically publish empirically oriented research, much like the *Journal of Archaeological Method and Theory*. One of the challenges of working in the area of the history of archaeology is that there are few reputable journals in which papers can be published. We can also try the *Journal for the History of the Human Sciences*, even if I published a paper there a couple of years ago.

26 June 2014

We are leaving Paris on Tuesday. Alain Schnapp has invited us for dinner next Saturday and I will meet Claude Blanckaert for lunch on Monday. I wrote a message to Dominique Richard yesterday to see if it is possible to meet on Monday morning before we leave to thank her for these two months in Paris. We finish the paper. We have finally decided to submit it to *Cambridge Archaeological Journal*. We leave to spend a week in Santander to return to Canada by mid-July.

Post-scriptum: 25 July 2019

This diary is related to two of my main areas of academic interest. First, over the last few years, I have become interested in the roles of biography and life-writing for the history of science. More specifically, I have been fascinated by the field diaries that archaeologists have kept since the end of the nineteenth century. These documents provide precious insights into the making of archaeological knowledge and they offer a view of archaeological research that is more 'alive' than scientific publications. Second, since I read Bourdieu's *Sketch for a Self-Analysis*[39] I have been increasingly interested in the question of reflexivity in the history of science.[40] As David Bloor pointed out, 'there is no reason why a sociologist or any other scientist should be ashamed to see his theories and methods as emanating from society, that is, as the product of collective influences and resources and as peculiar to the culture and its present circumstances'.[41] The question is whether this actually relates to the reflexivity of historians themselves. I think the answer is positive but historians need to look at their own work critically. Following Bloor's position, I would like to conclude with some critical reflections on my own work and approach. In particular, I will try to make some explicit and reflexive comments on my own relationship with Leroi-Gourhan.

I first read from Leroi-Gourhan's corpus when I was a student of archaeology in the early 1990s. Coming from Cantabria (a northern Spanish region particularly rich in caves and shelters), I became interested in prehistoric art. At that time, Leroi-Gourhan's theories still dominated the field of prehistoric art. At the same time, archaeologists began to call into question his legacy. In this context, I developed two interrelated feelings regarding his work. On the one hand, I felt overwhelmed by the fact that his views were constantly evoked in prehistoric art research, as if his theories were able to explain everything. On the other hand, I began to develop a critical approach to his work that (I can see it now) in part mirrored the hostility towards him that began to emerge in academia in the years immediately after the discovery and dating of Grotte Chauvet. In this setting, it is unsurprising that I developed some critical views on Leroi-Gourhan in my first papers. For instance, in 2006, I published an article in which I questioned Leroi-Gourhan as a revolutionary of prehistoric art research. Instead, I suggested that, in many ways, he continued Breuil's work.[42] In 2007 and 2008, I published two papers that referred to Leroi-Gourhan's idea that Paleolithic paintings had evolved from simple to complex representations.[43] In short, I argued that this idea transferred a long-established assumption in art history to the analysis of Paleolithic art.[44] I then became interested in the relationships between Leroi-Gourhan and structuralism. Eduardo Palacio-Pérez and I argued that Leroi-Gourhan's views on prehistoric art were shaped by a number of ideas that, broadly speaking, had their origins in the anthropology and art history of the beginnings of the twentieth century. Finally, I began to interrogate myself regarding the respective legacies of Leroi-Gourhan and Laming-Emperaire in the history of rock art research. In short, as this briefly overview demonstrates, Leroi-Gourhan has been a constant presence in my nearly 20-year scholarly career. Significantly, I realise now, I have always developed a critical approach towards his work that probably has its origins in my formative years in which Leroi-Gourhan's work was so often referenced. Accepting this, my hope is that I have not been unduly biased in my writing regarding his importance to the discipline. I have always admitted that his work had a huge impact in rock art research. The proof of this impact is the fact that books like *Préhistoire de l'art Occidental* and *Le geste et la parole* were still so often referred to in Spain in the early 1990s. This being said, pretending that his theories were without flaws is not doing justice to him. Instead, treating his work in a respectful but a critical way may be the first step to understand the importance of his legacy.

However, my goal here is not to decentre Leroi-Gourhan's privileged position in the history of archaeology. The point of this chapter is to illustrate how, besides the redundancy between diaries and published papers (see, for instance, some parallels between this chapter and our 2015 article in *Cambridge Archaeological Journal)*, the former can offer a more intimate (and less socially conditioned) perspective on different historical events and, more importantly, they can open new avenues of research for historians of archaeology. In this case, the key point of my diary relates to the historical criticism and diminishment of Laming-Emperaire and the need to re-evaluate her figure in the history of rock art research.

Notes

1 William Whewell, *History of the Inductive Sciences: From the earliest to the present times* (London: John Parker, 1837), 9.
2 See, for instance, Thomas S. Kuhn, *The Structure of Scientific Revolutions* (Chicago: Chicago University Press, 1962); George Canguilhem, 'L'objet de l'histoire des science', in *Études d'Histoire et de Philosophie des Science*, ed. George Canguilhem (Paris: Vrin, 1983), 9–23; Pierre Bourdieu, 'L'illusion biographique', *Actes de la recherche en Sciences Sociales* 62/63 (1986): 69–72.
3 Biography was so discredited during the 1970s that Thomas Hankins wrote a paper in defence of biographical approaches. Thomas L. Hankins, 'In defense of biography: the use of biography in the history of science', *History of Science* 17 (1979): 1–16.
4 Steven Shapin and Simon Schaffer, '*Up for Air: Leviathan and the Air-Pump* a generation on', in *Leviathan and Air-Pump. Hobbes, Boyle, and the experimental life,* second edition. eds. Steven Shapin and Simon Schaffer (Princeton: Princeton University Press, 2011), xi–l.
5 Michael Shortland and Richard Yeo, *Telling Lives in Science. Essays on scientific biography* (Cambridge: Cambridge University Press, 1996); Lorraine Daston and H. Otto Sibum, 'Introduction: *Scientific Personae* and their histories', *Science in Context* 16 (2003): 1–8; Thomas Söderqvist, ed., *The History and Poetics of Scientific Biography* (Aldershot: Ashgate, 2007).
6 Theodore M. Porter, 'Is the life of the scientist a scientific unit?' *Isis* 97 (2006): 314–21; Mary Jo Nye, 'Scientific biography: history of science by another means?' *Isis* 97 (2006): 322–29; Mott T. Greene, 'Writing scientific biography', *Journal of the History of Biology* 40 (2007): 727–59.
7 Douglas R. Givens, 'The role of biography in writing the history of archaeology', in *Rediscovering Our Past: Essays on the history of American archaeology*, ed. Jonathan E. Reyman (Aldershot: Avebury, 1992), 51–66.; Tim Murray, 'Epilogue: the art of archaeological biography', in *Encyclopedia of Archaeology. The Great Archaeologists*, ed., Tim Murray (Santa Barbara: ABC–CLIO, 1999), 869–83; Marc-Antoine Kaeser, 'La science vécue. Les potentialités de la biographie en histoire des sciences', *Revue d'Histoire des Sciences Humaines* 8 (2003): 139–60.
8 Pamela J. Smith, Jane Callander, Paul G. Bahn and Genevi Pinçlon, 'Dorothy Garrod in words and pictures'. *Antiquity* 71 (1997): 265–70; Nathan Schlanger and Jarl Nordbladh, eds., *Archives, Ancestors, Practices. Archaeology in the light of its history* (Oxford–New York: Berghahn, 2008); Marc-Antoine Kaeser, 'Biography as microhistory. The relevance of private archives for writing the history of archaeology', in *Archives, Ancestors, Practices. Archaeology in the light of its history*, eds., Nathan Schlanger and Jarl Nordbladh (Oxford–New York: Berghahn, 2008),

9–20; Margarita Díaz-Andreu, Megan Price and Chris Gosden, 'Christopher Hawkes: his archive and networks in British and European archaeology', *The Antiquaries Journal* 89 (2009): 405–26.
9 Allison Mickel, 'Reason for redundancy in reflexivity: the role of diaries in archaeological epistemology', *Journal of Field Archaeology* 40 (2015): 300–9.
10 Mickel 2015: 'Reason for redundancy in reflexivity', 307.
11 Mickel 2015: 'Reason for redundancy in reflexivity', 307.
12 Mickel 2015: 'Reason for redundancy in reflexivity', 308.
13 Some years later, in an interview with Michael Shanks and Christopher Witmore, Alain Schnapp expressed himself in a similar way. Talking about Bruce G. Trigger's *A History of Archaeological Thought*, Schnapp commented: 'I said that it was a good book, but I argued that you cannot say that Leroi-Gourhan was a structuralist, as Trigger did. He did not understand the context in a French tradition of the work of Leroi-Gourhan.', in William L. Rathje, Michael Shanks and Christopher Witmore, *Archeology in the Making. Conversations through a discipline* (London and New York: Routledge, 2013), 205–6.
14 Oscar Moro Abadía and Manuel R. González Morales, 'Understanding Pleistocene art: an hermeneutics of meaning', in *A Companion to Rock Art*, eds. Jo McDonald and Peter Veth (Chichester: Wiley-Blackwell, 2012), 263–75.
15 "*Lors de nos discussions avec lui durant les fouilles à Pincevent, Leroi-Gourhan réagissait assez fort quand on lui disait qu'il était structuraliste parce qu'il concevait ses recherches dans la diachronie, dans une perspective évolutive ou évolutionniste*", Personal communication, May 14, 2013.
16 For a more detailed explanation, see Oscar Moro Abadía and Eduardo Palacio-Pérez, 'Rethinking the structural analysis of Paleolithic art: new perspectives on Leroi-Gourhan's structuralism', *Cambridge Archaeological Journal* 25 (2015): 657–72.
17 Stephen J. Gould, *Leonardo's Mountain of Clams and the Diet of Worms. Essays on natural history* (London: Harvard University Press, 2011), 161–78.
18 For a more detailed account, see Oscar Moro Abadía, 'La priori du progrès chez Breuil et Leroi-Gourhan: Une continuité masquée', *Les nouvelles de l'archéologie* 106 (2006): 29–33.
19 André Leroi-Gourhan, 'L'expérience ethnologique', in *Ethnologie générale. Encyclopédie de la Pléiade*, ed. Jean Poirier (Paris: Gallimard, 1968), 1815–25.
20 Leroi-Gourhan, 'L'expérience ethnologique', 1819.
21 André Leroi-Gourhan, *Les racines du monde. Entretiens avec Claude-Henri Rocquet* (Paris: Pierre Belfond, 1982), 114.
22 André Leroi-Gourhan, 'L'origine des hommes', in *Qu'est-ce que l'homme? Semaine des Intellectuels Catholiques*, (Paris: Pierre Horay, 1955), 50–61.
23 Margaret W. Conkey, 'The structural analysis of Paleolithic art', in *Archaeological Thought in America*, ed. Clifford C. Lamberg-Karlovsky (Cambridge: Cambridge University Press, 1989), 135–54.
24 Claude Lévi-Strauss, *Race and History* (Paris: UNESCO, 1952), 17–18.
25 Fernand Windels, *Lascaux. Chapelle Sixtine de la Préhistoire* (Montignac: Centre d'Études Préhistoriques, 1948).
26 André Leroi-Gourhan, 'Les cultures actuelles. Esthétique. La vie esthétique' in *Encyclopédie Clartés. L'homme. Races et mœurs, Vol. 4 (bis). Fascicule 4860*, ed. André Leroi-Gourhan (Paris: Clartés, 1957), 9–10.
27 Philippe Soulier, personal communication.
28 Leroi-Gourhan, 'Les cultures actuelles. Esthétique', 9–10.
29 André Leroi-Gourhan, 'La fonction des signes dans les sanctuaires paléolithique', *Bulletin de la société préhistorique de France* 55 (1958): 307–21.
30 André Leroi-Gourhan, 'Le symbolisme des grand signes dans l'art pariétal paléolithique', *Bulletin de la société préhistorique de France* 55 (1958): 384–98.
31 André Leroi-Gourhan, 'Répartition et groupement des animaux dans l'art pariétal paléolithique', *Bulletin de la société préhistorique de France* 55 (1958): 515–28.
32 Leroi-Gourhan, 'La fonction des signes dans les sanctuaires paléolithique', 307–8.
33 André Leroi-Gourhan, *Préhistoire de l'art occidental*, second edition. (Paris: Mazenod, 1971), 7.
34 The letter is located in *Fonds Jean Bouyssonie*, Box n°. 4.
35 Henri Breuil and Raymond Lantier. *Les hommes de la pierre ancienne. Paléolithique et Mésolithique* second edition. (Paris: Payot, 1959), 237.
36 Annette Laming-Emperaire, *L'art préhistorique. Peintures, gravures et sculptures rupestres* (Paris: Les éditions Braun, 1951), 8.

37 Annette Laming-Emperaire, 'Pour une nouvelle approche des sociétés préhistorique', *Annales. Économies, Sociétés, Civilisations* 5 (1969): 1261–9.
38 Laming-Emperaire, 'Pour une nouvelle approche des sociétés préhistorique', 1263.
39 Pierre Bourdieu, *Sketch for a Self-Analysis* (Chicago: The University of Chicago Press, 2008).
40 Michael Lynch, 'Against reflexivity as an academic virtue and source of privileged knowledge', *Theory, Culture and Society* 17 (2000): 28–54; Pierre Bourdieu, *Science of Science and Reflexivity* (Chicago: The University of Chicago Press, 2004); Yves Gingras, 'Sociological reflexivity in action', *Social Studies of Science* 40 (2010): 619–31.
41 David Bloor, *Knowledge and Social Imagery,* second edition (Chicago: The University of Chicago Press, 1991), 44.
42 Moro Abadía, 'L'a priori du progrès chez Breuil et Leroi-Gourhan: Une continuité masquée', 29–33.
43 Oscar Moro Abadía and Manuel R. González Morales, 'Thinking about style in the "post-stylistic era": Reconstructing the stylistic context of Chauvet', *Oxford Journal of Archaeology* 26 (2007): 109–25; Oscar Moro Abadía and Manuel R. González Morales, 'Palaeolithic art studies at the beginning of the 21st century: A loss of innocence', *Journal of Anthropological Research* 64 (2008): 529–52.
44 Oscar Moro Abadía, Manuel R. González Morales and Eduardo Palacio-Pérez, 'Naturalism and the interpretation of cave art', *World Art* 2 (2012): 219–40 ; Oscar Moro Abadía, 'Rock art stories: Standard narratives and their alternatives', *Rock Art Research* 30 (2013): 1–33.

Bibliography

Bloor, David, *Knowledge and Social Imagery*, second edition (Chicago: The University of Chicago Press, 1991).
Bourdieu, Pierre 'L'illusion biographique', *Actes de la recherche en Sciences Sociales* 62/63 (1986): 69–72.
Bourdieu, Pierre, *Science of Science and Reflexivity* (Chicago: The University of Chicago Press, 2004).
Bourdieu, Pierre, *Sketch for a Self-Analysis* (Chicago: The University of Chicago Press, 2008).
Breuil, Henri and Raymond Lantier, *Les hommes de la pierre ancienne. Paléolithique et Mésolithique,* second edition (Paris: Payot, 1959).
Canguilhem, George, 'L'objet de l'histoire des science', in *Études d'Histoire et de Philosophie des Science*, ed. George Canguilhem (Paris: Vrin, 1983), 9–23.
Conkey, Margaret W., 'The structural analysis of Paleolithic art', in *Archaeological Thought in America*, ed., Clifford C. Lamberg-Karlovsky (Cambridge: Cambridge University Press, 1989), 135–54.
Daston, Lorraine and H. Otto Sibum, 'Introduction: *Scientific Personae* and their histories', *Science in Context* 16 (2003): 1–8.
Díaz-Andreu, Margarita, Megan Price and Chris Gosden, 'Christopher Hawkes: his archive and networks in British and European archaeology', *The Antiquaries Journal* 89 (2009): 405–26.
Gingras, Yves, 'Sociological reflexivity in action', *Social Studies of Science* 40 (2010): 619–31.
Givens, Douglas R., 'The role of biography in writing the history of archaeology', in *Rediscovering Our Past: Essays on the history of American archaeology*, ed. Jonathan E. Reyman (Aldershot: Avebury, 1992), 51–66.
Gould, Stephen J., *Leonardo's Mountain of Clams and the Diet of Worms. Essays on natural history* (London: Harvard University Press, 2011).
Greene, Mott T., 'Writing scientific biography', *Journal of the History of Biology* 40 (2007): 727–59.
Hankins, Thomas L., 'In defense of biography: The use of biography in the history of science', *History of Science* 17 (1979): 1–16.
Kaeser, Marc-Antoine, 'La science vécue. Les potentialités de la biographie en histoire des sciences', *Revue d'Histoire des Sciences Humaines* 8 (2003): 139–60.
Kaeser, Marc-Antoine, 'Biography as microhistory. The relevance of private archives for writing the history of archaeology', in *Archives, Ancestors, Practices: Archaeology in the light of*

its history, eds., Nathan Schlanger and Jarl Nordbladh (Oxford–New York: Berghahn, 2008), 9–20.
Kuhn, Thomas S., *The Structure of Scientific Revolutions* (Chicago: Chicago University Press, 1962).
Laming-Emperaire, Annette, *L'art préhistorique. Peintures, gravures et sculptures rupestres* (Paris: Les éditions Braun, 1951).
Laming-Emperaire, Annette, 'Pour une nouvelle approche des sociétés préhistorique'. *Annales. Économies, Sociétés, Civilisations* 5 (1969): 1261–9.
Leroi-Gourhan, André, 'L'origine des hommes', in *Qu'est-ce que l'homme? Semaine des Intellectuels Catholiques* (Paris: Pierre Horay, 1955), 50–61.
Leroi-Gourhan, André, 'Les cultures actuelles. Esthétique. La vie esthétique', in *Encyclopédie Clartés. L'homme. Races et mœurs, Vol. 4 (bis). Fascicule 4860*, ed. André Leroi- Gourhan (Paris: Clartés, 1957), 9–10.
Leroi-Gourhan, André, 'La fonction des signes dans les sanctuaires paléolithique', *Bulletin de la société préhistorique de France* 55 (1958): 307–21.
Leroi-Gourhan, André, 'Le symbolisme des grand signes dans l'art pariétal paléolithique', *Bulletin de la société préhistorique de France* 55 (1958): 384–98.
Leroi-Gourhan, André, 'Répartition et groupement des animaux dans l'art pariétal paléolithique', *Bulletin de la société préhistorique de France* 55 (1958): 515–28.
Leroi-Gourhan, André, 'L'expérience ethnologique', in *Ethnologie générale. Encyclopédie de la Pléiade*, ed. Jean Poirier (Paris: Gallimard, 1968), 1815–25.
Leroi-Gourhan, André, *Préhistoire de l'art occidental,* second edition. (Paris: Mazenod, 1971).
Leroi-Gourhan, André, *Les racines du monde. Entretiens avec Claude-Henri Rocquet* (Paris: Pierre Belfond, 1982).
Lévi-Strauss, Claude, *Race and History* (Paris: UNESCO, 1952).
Lynch, Michael, 'Against reflexivity as an academic virtue and source of privileged knowledge', *Theory, Culture and Society* 17 (2000): 28–54.
Mickel, Allison, 'Reason for redundancy in reflexivity: the role of diaries in archaeological epistemology', *Journal of Field Archaeology* 40 (2015): 300–9.
Moro Abadía, Oscar, 'L'a priori du progrès chez Breuil et Leroi-Gourhan: Une continuité masquée', *Les nouvelles de l'archéologie* 106 (2006): 29–33.
Moro Abadía, Oscar, 'Rock art stories: Standard narratives and their alternatives', *Rock Art Research* 30 (2013): 1–33.
Moro Abadía, Oscar and Manuel R. González Morales, 'Thinking about style in the "post-stylistic era": Reconstructing the stylistic context of Chauvet', *Oxford Journal of Archaeology* 26 (2007): 109–25.
Moro Abadía, Oscar and Manuel R. González Morales, 'Palaeolithic art studies at the beginning of the 21st century: A loss of innocence', *Journal of Anthropological Research* 64 (2008): 529–52.
Moro Abadía, Oscar and Manuel R. González Morales, 'Understanding Pleistocene art: an hermeneutics of meaning', in *A Companion to Rock Art*, eds. Jo McDonald and Peter Veth (Chichester: Wiley-Blackwell, 2012), 263–75.
Moro Abadía, Oscar and Eduardo Palacio-Pérez, 'Rethinking the structural analysis of Paleolithic art: new perspectives on Leroi-Gourhan's structuralism', *Cambridge Archaeological Journal* 25 (2015): 657–72.
Moro Abadía, Oscar, Manuel R. González Morales and Eduardo Palacio-Pérez, 'Naturalism and the interpretation of cave art', *World Art* 2 (2012): 219–40.
Murray, Tim, 'Epilogue: The Art of archaeological biography', in *Encyclopedia of Archaeology. The Great Archaeologists*, ed. Tim Murray (Santa Barbara: ABC–CLIO, 1999), 869–83.
Nye, Mary Jo, 'Scientific biography: history of science by another means?', *Isis* 97 (2006): 322–29.
Porter, Theodore M., 'Is the life of the scientist a scientific unit?', *Isis* 97 (2006): 314–21.
Rathje, William L., Michael Shanks and Christopher Witmore, *Archeology in the Making. Conversations through a discipline* (London–New York: Routledge, 2013).
Schlanger, Nathan and Jarl Nordbladh, eds., *Archives, Ancestors, Practices. Archaeology in the light of its history* (Oxford–New York: Berghahn, 2008).
Shapin, Steven and Simon Schaffer, '*Up for Air: Leviathan and the Air-Pump* a generation on', in *Leviathan and Air-Pump. Hobbes, Boyle, and the experimental life,* second edition, eds., Steven Shapin and Simon Schaffer (Princeton: Princeton University Press, 2011), xi–l.

Shortland, Michael and Richard Yeo, *Telling Lives in Science: Essays on scientific biography* (Cambridge: Cambridge University Press, 1996).
Smith, Pamela J., Jane Callander, Paul G. Bahn and Genevi Pinçlon, 'Dorothy Garrod in words and pictures', *Antiquity* 71 (1997): 265–70.
Söderqvist, Thomas, ed., *The History and Poetics of Scientific Biography* (Aldershot: Ashgate, 2007).
Whewell, William, *History of the Inductive Sciences: From the earliest to the present times* (London: John Parker, 1837).
Windels, Fernand, *Lascaux. Chapelle Sixtine de la Préhistoire* (Montignac: Centre d'Études Préhistoriques, 1948).

14
Archaeologists, curators, collectors and donors: Reflecting on the past through archaeological lives

David W. J. Gill

One of my earliest memories of encountering the history of archaeology was through the purchase (at Foyle's in London) of Glyn Daniel's *The Origins and Growth of Archaeology*.[1] This introduced me to some of the perceived great figures in the development of archaeology as a discipline: in particular, the antiquarian William Stukeley and his work on British prehistory, and Jean-François Champollion and the decipherment of Egyptian hieroglyphs through the study of the Rosetta Stone. These accounts brought new insights to me as I visited the rich archaeological landscapes of Wiltshire or viewed the global finds in the British Museum.

One of the themes of my academic research has been the development and history of classical archaeology. It has ranged from the eighteenth century with the formation of collections during the Grand Tour of Italy right through to the present day. The theme falls within the parameters of my wider research into the history of collecting, and specifically on cultural property issues. The passing of objects from collector to collector, or sometimes the alleged transfer between them, has complemented the research on specific individuals.[2]

The study of past material culture is accessed through museum collections, excavation reports and other bodies of material. It is important to recall that these presentations and interpretations are shaped by the diverse communities of academic writers, private collectors and museum curators. The personal choices of what to collect and display has influenced the way that bodies of archaeological material are received, considered and understood by the public.

Identifying donors to the Fitzwilliam Museum

Early in my career I was appointed Museum Assistant in Research at the Fitzwilliam Museum in Cambridge with curatorial responsibilities for the Greek and Roman collection. This developed my interest in the donors and former owners of the objects. My responsibilities included the digitisation of the departmental records using MODES (Museum Object Data Entry System) that had been developed by the Museum Documentation Association (MDA) (now the Collections Trust), an organisation based in Cambridge. The cataloguing of the definitive accession registers and object slip books (that record subsequent publications and additional information) meant that, stage by stage, an index could be created of the figures and institutions associated with the collection.[3] The information recorded on the data system allowed an analysis of previous publications, former owners, find spots and places where the objects had been displayed. For example, at least 11 pieces acquired in 1865, 1896 and 1924 had once formed part of the collection formed by Sir Alfred Biliotti who had excavated in the cemeteries of Rhodes in the 1860s on behalf of the British Museum;[4] finds from this fieldwork had been central to my own doctoral research.[5] This approach to an object's history that is defined by its previous owners, as well as the sales and galleries through which it passed, allowed a new approach to cataloguing acquisitions from the collection,[6] and provided the methodological basis for studying the way that cultural property was acquired by collectors and museums.[7]

At the heart of the Fitzwilliam Museum's sculpture collection were the pieces that had been donated to the University of Cambridge in 1850 by Dr John Disney of The Hyde near Ingatestone in Essex (Figure 14.1). The sculptures had been displayed as 'The Disney Marbles' for many years, and some had (and continue to have) 'Disney' painted on them. The collection itself had derived in part from the pieces acquired by Thomas Hollis and Thomas Brand-Hollis on their eighteenth-century Grand Tour of Italy. This collection, along with Brand-Hollis's home of The Hyde, had been bequeathed to Disney's father, the Reverend John Disney. Further pieces of sculpture, including some Etruscan items, had been added to the collection by Dr Disney during his visits to Italy after the Napoleonic Wars. However, these items contained several modern creations that had been purchased as ancient. Some of the Disney sculptures formed part of a Cambridge Festival exhibition, 'Antiquities of the Grand Tour', and the accompanying catalogue included a discussion of the display of the classical casts in the main grand entrance to the

Figure 14.1 The funerary monument of the Disney family in the churchyard of St Mary the Virgin, Fryerning in Essex. It contains the remains of Dr John Disney, founder of the chair of archaeology at Cambridge. © David Gill

museum.[8] Other Disney items in the museum's collection that arrived later than the original gift included a statue of Apollo that had been restored by John Flaxman, and a Paestan figure-decorated krater that was retained by the family, dispersed at auction and subsequently presented to the museum.[9]

This research on Disney coincided with the museum's preparation of a definitive catalogue of classical gems and finger-rings that were held by the Fitzwilliam.[10] These gems were largely spread between the Department of Antiquities and the Department of Coins and Medals. One of the tasks was to prepare an index of previous collections and owners, in particular identifying material from antiquarian collections and cabinets, such as the Marlborough Collection. These lists were then checked against some of the early printed catalogues that were located in the Founder's Library of the Museum.

Museum curators are sensitive to the display of modern creations or forgeries alongside ancient works of art.[11] A key piece in the Fitzwilliam

Museum was the supposedly Minoan stone goddess that had been acquired in 1926 and formed a central part of the newly created Prehistoric Gallery and then, from the 1960s, part of the prehistoric displays in the Greek and Roman Gallery.[12] The purchase of the statue was on the recommendation of Sir Arthur Evans, and it had been acquired through Charles Seltman of Queens' College, Cambridge. It had been said to have been found near Knossos, a piece of information that helped to lend authenticity to the piece. The unpacking of the story revealed the academic rivalries in Cambridge during the 1920s, as well as Evans's strong hostility towards Alan Wace, the former Director of the British School at Athens, who had been invited to write the monograph that was published by Cambridge University Press.[13] It was the later discovery of further statues, the so-called sisters, among Seltman's belongings in Cambridge that suggested that the Fitzwilliam statue was part of an elaborate scheme to pass off recent creations as ancient art. Indeed, Sir Leonard Woolley recalled in his autobiography the identification of a sophisticated forger's workshop, along with the forger's deathbed confession, on Crete at this very time.[14] His memoir – *As I Seem to Remember* – even prompted the detail that one of the workshop pieces had been acquired by Cambridge.

Archaeological lives and the Bronze Age Aegean

The story of the Fitzwilliam goddess had provided some of the background to the personalities who had been presenting the history of the Aegean Bronze Age from the nineteenth and early part of the twentieth centuries. This sculpture was displayed alongside a range of Bronze Age finds from the British excavations at Phylakopi on Melos, and Palaikastro in eastern Crete, as well as marble (and shell) Cycladic figures collected during travels in the southern Aegean. At the heart of Daniel's history of archaeology was the role of Heinrich Schliemann, and the dream of visiting 'at my leisure the scene of those events which had always had such an intense interest for me, and the country of the heroes whose adventures had delighted and comforted my childhood'.[15] Schliemann's account of how he received a Christmas gift in 1829 of Georg Ludwig Jerrer's *Universal History* was unpacked by David Traill.[16] In particular, Traill showed that the thought of excavating at Troy had not occurred to him until 1868.[17] The research by Traill revealed how the received picture of Schliemann was not always accurate and that at times Schliemann deliberately misled his readership.[18] Schliemann had overshadowed the pioneering work of Frank Calvert who was responsible for identifying the likely site of Troy but again largely overlooked in histories of archaeology.[19]

These critical encounters with Schliemann and Calvert prepared me for a series of engagements with archaeological lives. From the early 1990s I had been invited to contribute to a series of collaborative writing projects led by Paul Bahn.[20] One of these commissions was the writing of sections on classical archaeology for the *Cambridge History of Archaeology*.[21] The work was arranged chronologically and allowed the reader to grasp the global changes in archaeology (e.g. 'Antiquarians and Explorers, 1760–1820', and 'Archaeology Comes of Age, 1920–1960'). This integrated study included the contribution of the work of the French School at Delphi, the German School at Olympia and the American School in the Athenian Agora. The complete work was much later revised and reworked into area chapters.[22]

Egyptologists and South Wales

At this same point of time I had been asked to take on the honorary curatorship of the Egyptian collection formed by Sir Henry Wellcome,[23] the pharmaceutical millionaire, that had been placed on loan at Swansea University. The award of major grants allowed the collection to be moved from its cramped quarters as a departmental museum (in a converted seminar room) to a purpose-built Egypt Centre on the university campus as part of the Taliesin Arts Centre.[24] The preparations for the display of the collection included the researching of the personalities behind Wellcome's collection, such as the Reverend William MacGregor whose major collection had been dispersed at auction in 1922.[25] Additional research showed the Welsh connections of Sir Gardner Wilkinson, who can be considered as a founder of Egyptology in the United Kingdom:[26] he was buried at Llandovery under an elaborate funerary monument that incorporated a pyramid (Figure 14.2). One of the inscriptions on the monument records that he 'devoted nearly sixty years of his life to the elucidation of classical and other antiquities, and Egyptian history, archaeology, and topography more especially as regards their bearing on Biblical research. The large number of his published works bear but a small proportion to the results of these studies which were always freely placed at the disposal of scholars of all countries.' The Swansea Museum (a separate institution) also had a Ptolemaic coffin that had formed part of the collection of Francis Wallace Grenfell, First Baron Grenfell, the sirdar of the Egyptian army (1885–1892). A Middle Kingdom

Figure 14.2 The Egyptianising grave of Sir Gardner Wilkinson in the churchyard of St Dingat's at Llandingad near Llandovery in Carmarthenshire, Wales. © David Gill.

head of Amenemhat III, found at Aswan and belonging to Grenfell, had formed part of the Fitzwilliam's Egyptological collection and had been celebrated in the Middle Kingdom exhibition 'Pharaohs and Mortals', curated by Janine Bourriau.[27] These Swansea connections with the creation of modern Egyptology were explored in a festival exhibition, 'The Face of Egypt', at the Glynn Vivian Art Gallery in Swansea, supported by the generous loans of Wilkinson's artefacts, including his portrait, from the National Trust's property at Calke Abbey in Derbyshire.[28]

The Oxford Dictionary of National Biography

During the late 1990s research began on the revision of the *Oxford Dictionary of National Biography* (*ODNB*) with parts of Bahn's team being invited to revise or write new entries on British archaeologists. I was invited initially to revise or write anew several entries for figures associated with classical sites. This project required the identification of obituaries in both newspapers and academic journals, the listing of key publications, the noting of images and portraits, and the consultation of archive material. It became clear that newspaper obituaries often contained statements and details that clearly had not been checked and the 'facts' needed careful exploration and testing, often through Oxbridge college archives. These inaccuracies can perhaps be explained in part by the need for newspaper obituaries to be written or revised at speed so that they could appear relatively soon after the death had been announced. This is not a complete response because some newspapers now have obituaries prepared well in advance of the subject's death. More accurate and extended obituaries tended to be found in journals as the *Proceedings of the British Academy*.[29] The revision of previous memoirs sometimes brought attention to aspects of the subject's life that had been omitted. Thus, J. D. Beazley's associations with the poet James Elroy Flecker were overlooked in the original.[30] It was Flecker who dedicated one of his poems, 'Invitation', to Beazley encouraging him to 'abandon archaeology'. The relationship between Richard M. Dawkins and Baron Corvo (Frederick William Rolfe) was mentioned but left unexplored.[31]

One of the themes among the biographies was a series of memoirs on the early directors of the British School at Athens: four had studied at Cambridge – Ernest A. Gardner, Robert Carr Bosanquet, Richard M. Dawkins and Alan J.B. Wace, and two at Oxford – David G. Hogarth and Humfry G. G. Payne. Their substantial contribution to the work and life of the School could be assessed through the Annual Reports that were published in the *Annual of the British School at Athens,* as well as through excavation reports and other academic publications.

Gardner was the first Cambridge student to be admitted to the British School at Athens.[32] He had recently worked with Flinders Petrie on the Greek trading establishment of Naukratis in the Nile Delta that was described by the Greek historian Herodotus.[33] Gardner was appointed the second director of the School and was instrumental in developing the work of the Cyprus Exploration Fund; a share of the finds, including pottery from Marion and classical sculptures from Salamis, was acquired by the Fitzwilliam as part of the division resulting from the sponsorship of the project. Gardner subsequently prepared the catalogue of the Greek pottery at the Fitzwilliam.[34]

David Hogarth was the first Oxford student to be admitted to the School (arriving just after Gardner).[35] He was the fourth director of the School and was subsequently involved in excavations as part of the Cretan Exploration Fund.[36] He worked on the Dictaean Cave but failed to locate the Bronze Age palace at Kato Zakro in the east of the island. Hogarth was succeeded by Bosanquet who had served as his Assistant Director.[37] Bosanquet excavated at Palaikastro in eastern Crete, and then, when the School's emphasis moved back to the mainland, to the excavation of the sanctuary of Artemis Orthia at Sparta. It was thanks to Bosanquet that the Fitzwilliam had made a series of acquisitions from various islands in the Cyclades: Amorgos, Naxos and Pholegandros. His memoir was enhanced through the publication of a series of letters published by his widow, Ellen.[38] Bosanquet was succeeded by Dawkins who had also excavated at Palaikastro.[39] Dawkins took over the work at Sparta for the rest of his time as director, as the focus of the School's work switched from Crete to the Peloponnese.

Dawkins was succeeded by Wace, who had travelled extensively in Central Greece and Macedonia.[40] The routes travelled were mapped not only by the reports in the *Annual of the British School at Athens* but also by the presentation of sherds and stone objects to the Fitzwilliam (though they are now for the most part in the collection of the Museum of Classical Archaeology in Cambridge). Wace's time in Athens coincided with the outbreak of the First World War and ensuing restrictions on archaeological fieldwork. However, in 1920 Wace initiated the British work at Mycenae in collaboration with Carl Blegen of the American School.[41] Wace faced the hostility of Evans who was promoting the primacy of Crete over the mainland, and Wace's appointment as Director was not renewed. The School, under its new director, Arthur M. Woodward, turned its attentions back to Sparta, the site of its work before the war. My final memoir for a director of the School was on Humfry Payne who worked on Crete, as well as the important archaic site of Perachora on the Gulf of Corinth.[42] He died tragically from blood-poisoning and was buried at Mycenae; I can remember visiting his grave (inscribed with 'Mourn not for Adonais'), erected by his widow Dilys Powell,[43] on a day off during fieldwork in the Argolid (Figure 14.3).

The *ODNB* concentrated on the better-known names who held roles such as the director of institutes abroad. However, there were some gaps in the coverage, such as Woodward, the director between Wace and Payne. In addition, few of the Assistant Directors had been included in the memoirs as their subsequent work had not been deemed to be significant: George C. Richards and Henry J. W. Tillyard, for example, did not appear. A parallel biographical project, the *Dictionary of British Classicists* (*DBC*), was in preparation under the editorship of Robert Todd, and this allowed a wider range of individuals to be discussed.[44] Some 37 students at the British School were included (the work of 14 different contributors), among them were entries for Richards and Woodward.[45]

Women excavating in the Aegean and Egypt

During the interwar years, Winifred Lamb had been the honorary keeper of Greek antiquities at the Fitzwilliam. She had excavated with Wace at Mycenae, and then with Woodward at Sparta, before developing her own digs at Thermi and Antissa on Lesbos, Kato Phana on Chios, and Kusura in western Turkey. Lamb had also been the curator who had supported the acquisition of the Fitzwilliam goddess, a forgery presented as a Minoan sculpture. A study of the history of the Classical Tripos at Cambridge provided an opportunity to review the contribution that Lamb had made to the development of the classical collections at the Fitzwilliam particularly during the 1920s and 1930s.[46] It became clear that Lamb, or her relations, were purchasing items to fill the perceived gaps in the collection. The two main themes for Lamb were Greek and Roman bronzes, and then (largely Athenian) figure-decorated pottery; both categories featured in her study of bronzes and the two fascicules of the Fitzwilliam's pottery collection that appeared in the *Corpus Vasorum Antiquorum*.[47] Getzel Cohen at the University of Cincinnati was working on a volume of pioneering women archaeologists and invited me to contribute an essay on Lamb.[48] Helen Waterhouse, the author of the centenary history of the School,[49] provided me with access to a typescript of Lamb's letters home to her mother during her time at the British School.

Figure 14.3 The grave of Humfry Payne in the cemetery at Mycenae. A paperback copy of *The Traveller's Journey is Done*, the biography by his widow, Dilys Powell, had been placed by the gravestone by a passing group of mourners who had written messages inside the cover (2004). © David Gill.

Lamb's extended diary of her travels in north-west Greece in search of a prehistoric site to excavate provided insights into her fieldwork strategy.[50] Lamb featured in *ODNB* in the conscious move to include more women archaeologists.[51] Apart from Lamb, Cohen's volume on pioneering women included a study of Theresa Goell who excavated the mountain burial site of Nemrud Dağ in eastern Turkey.[52]

Subsequent to this study for the Cohen volume, a member of Lamb's family made the discovery in the family home of a cache of previously unseen diaries, unpublished reports and lectures. This provided the opportunity for a detailed study that followed her parallel careers as honorary keeper at the Fitzwilliam, and active field archaeologist in the Aegean and Anatolia.[53] A subsequent study explored her role in naval intelligence during the First World War when she worked alongside Beazley.[54] This highlighted the way that the techniques to identify anonymous German code-senders were used to identify the hands of anonymous Athenian pot-painters. Together Lamb and Beazley presented an Attic black-figured amphora to the Ashmolean that they had purchased during one of their forays to the sales during their work at the Admiralty.

The research on the formation of Sir Henry Wellcome's Egyptological collection brought an interest in some of the personalities in the history of Egyptology. The research on Lamb had raised the contribution of women to classical archaeology. For British Egyptology, the focus has been on Amelia Edwards, whose name is celebrated in the UCL Chair of Egyptology.[55] Yet the contribution of her contemporary, Mary Brodrick, is usually overlooked.[56] It was Brodrick's work on translating Egyptological works that made the subject more accessible to a British public. The memoir was a reminder of how history has allowed some key figures to slip from view. One unexpected insight into the presentation of Egyptology was through the essay 'Leaving Home' (1906) and the poem 'Swedes' (1915) by Edward Thomas that explored the excavation of the tomb of Yuya and Tjuyu in the Valley of the Kings in February 1905.[57] Thomas's reference to 'long-dead Amen-hotep' may allude to the tomb of Amenhotep II discovered in 1898 and described by Mary Brodrick. The comparison between the Egyptian tomb and a swede clamp in rural Hampshire may have been suggested by the protective covers that were being put in place in the British Museum in 1915 to protect the collections from Zeppelin bombing-raids.[58]

Lamb's active contribution to fieldwork during the interwar years was in a marked contrast to the earlier phase of the School.[59] The role of women at the British School before the First World War was reviewed.[60] This was in part to identify how the contribution of women such as Lamb differed from her predecessors who had been largely excluded from fieldwork. An exception was Dorothy Lamb. Although no relation of Winifred Lamb, Dorothy, like Winifred, was also a student at Newnham College. Dorothy Lamb had excavated at Phylakopi on Melos.[61] Her presence at the excavation probably explains the criticism of women on digs that was made by John P. Droop in his Cambridge University Press handbook to archaeological excavations that was ridiculed by Winifred Lamb and other women in the immediate post-war years.[62]

The School architect for the interwar years was Piet de Jong who worked at Mycenae and Sparta. During the excavations, he made a series of caricatures of those involved with the excavations including Wace and Lamb.[63] Jong is also well known for his architectural drawings for the American School during their work on the Athenian agora.[64]

Students at the British School at Athens

The research on the students admitted to the British School at Athens in the years prior to the First World War provided information for other studies. One was an overview of the life of Frank W. Hasluck, librarian at the British School, and his wife Margaret M. Hardie.[65] In particular, the research looked beyond the confines of Greece to British archaeological work in the Ottoman Empire especially in Anatolia. Such survey work can be traced back to the earliest years of the School and served as a legacy from the Asia Minor Exploration Fund. The work of British archaeologists, often based at the British School at Athens, in the Ottoman Empire included the travels, almost certainly for intelligence gathering, of Harry Pirie-Gordon,[66] who prepared the map that T. E. Lawrence later used for his 'archaeological' work in Syria. Pirie-Gordon's work during Allenby's Palestine Campaign during the First World War became the basis for a tourist guide to the area.[67] The work of former British School students in intelligence roles during the First World War, especially as part of the Macedonian Expeditionary Force, also allowed them to identify archaeological remains that were revealed during military trench digging.[68] These finds were displayed in a museum created in the White Tower at Thessalonike. Among the notorious exploits of School students were the raids on the Anatolian mainland by John Myres, known as 'Blackbeard of the Aegean'.[69] It was on Samos that Myres was confronted by the Greek wife of William R. Paton whose estates had been damaged.[70] Paton was a friend of Oscar Wilde and stood by him after his release from Reading Gaol.

The information gathered for both *ODNB* and *DBC* had provided information on many of the students at the British School from its foundation in 1886 up to the First World War. This gave the idea of preparing a history of the institution as seen through the personalities. It developed the earlier history that had been written for the centenary of the School in 1986.[71] A similar history had been prepared for the American School of Classical Studies at Athens.[72] The new study included a summary of each of the British students alongside their publications, education and careers.[73] Such an approach allowed the emphasis on students from Oxford and Cambridge to be identified, and through the identification of particular colleges, the influence of particular academics who directed their students to develop their interests in Greece. At the same time, in the early 2010s, the Fitzwilliam was reinstalling the Greek and Roman galleries and reassessing the formation of its collection, and this provided an opportunity to write a study of the School's Cambridge students who had donated objects to the museum in this same period.[74] The travels of the Cambridge students had brought about the presentation of finds to the Fitzwilliam, such as the collection of Minoan seals acquired from John H. Marshall who had collected them during his journeys through Crete while taking part in the Palaikastro excavations.[75] Other students with an interest in the Cyclades and other parts of mainland Greece presented a range of finds, often sherd material, that formed part of the prehistoric collection in the Fitzwilliam; Dawkins' loan of Cycladic material was withdrawn from the Fitzwilliam after the First World War when he moved to Oxford.[76]

The British School at Rome

At the start of my career, I had been a Roman Scholar at the British School at Rome. The School was greatly influenced by its early director, Thomas Ashby, who contributed so much to the understanding of the topography of the area around the city.[77] The *ODNB* provided an opportunity to review his life against new biographical studies.[78] One of the early directors of the British School at Rome was Henry Stuart-Jones, who is best known for his work on Liddell and Scott's Greek–English Lexicon rather than as an archaeologist.[79] However, his research on the Rome-based sculpture collections was linked to the work of Alan Wace, reflecting how scholars from the two schools had worked together in the years preceding the First World War.[80] One of the students who was admitted to the British School at Rome but then moved to Athens was (Sir) John Beazley.[81] Beazley's work on the Athenian figure-decorated pottery found in Italy laid the foundations of his later extensive lists of Athenian pot-painters.[82]

Cambridge lives

My earlier knowledge of Dr John Disney allowed me to return to his generous donation of his sculptural collection to the University of Cambridge as well as to the foundation of the Chair of Archaeology that bore his name.[83] Material from The Hyde's archive in Essex was complemented by walking part of Disney's estates in Dorset that had been purchased by Thomas Hollis. Research in Dr Williams' Library in London confirmed the link between the Reverend John Disney and Thomas Brand-Hollis of The Hyde; Brand-Hollis was a benefactor of the Essex Street Chapel in London where the Reverend Disney had been appointed one of the ministers when he left the Church of England. This research permitted a more detailed biographical study of Disney (and his family) to be made.[84] It had to take in the move of his uncle and cousin (and future wife) to Paris and their flight to Italy during the French Revolution, where, incidentally, they made some acquisitions of Greek figure-decorated pottery. Disney's legacy included the foundation of the Essex Archaeological Society and the formation of the Chelmsford Museum.

I completed two further Cambridge memoirs. A. B. Cook, the great authority on Zeus, and the first holder of the Laurence Chair of Classical Archaeology in Cambridge.[85] Part of Cook's Cambridge circle included the Cambridge philosopher Francis Cornford, author of *Microcosmographia academica* that presented advice to the young career academic.[86] Cornford was married to the poet Frances Darwin, daughter of Francis Darwin, and granddaughter of Charles Darwin; one of the documents in the Cornford archive in Cambridge is 'The Tale of the Three Francis'. Cornford was part of the Cambridge circle that included Jane Harrison who was such an influence on women at Newnham.[87] Cornford's son, the poet John Rupert Cornford, was named in honour of the Cornford's close friend the poet Rupert Brooke; John was killed during the Spanish Civil War.[88] Incidentally, I was able to access the memoir of John's life in the Miner's Library in Swansea where it had been preserved among the anti-Fascist pamphlets and documents relating to the Spanish Civil War.

Contemporary lives

While most of my biographical studies have been on individuals who died some decades earlier, three memoirs were of recently deceased individuals. This brings with it the challenge of writing sensitively about the deceased and being discreet about some of the details; however, information about some of the other figures was derived from children and grandchildren.

The Cambridge educated Lord William Taylour had worked with Wace on the post-Second World War excavations at Mycenae, and then at the American excavations at Nestor's Palace at Pylos in the Peloponnese.[89] He bequeathed a sculpture of Cybele to the Fitzwilliam while I was working there.

A memoir for William Francis Grimes, former director of the Institute of Archaeology in London, had (surprisingly) not been commissioned for the original series of *ODNB*, and I was asked to prepare an entry.[90] Though Grimes is well known for his excavation of the London Mithraeum, with his second wife Audrey Williams, his archaeological fieldwork included prehistoric sites in Wales and as well as the excavation of the ship burial at Sutton Hoo in Suffolk when he was working for the Ordnance Survey.[91] He brought with him the experience of excavating prehistoric ships during his time in Wales. Grimes' third wife was able to share some of her memories and to show me some of the drawings made during excavations during the construction of airfields during the Second World War.

The third person had been my personal tutor, mentor and doctoral examiner, Brian Shefton.[92] His parents had fled from Germany in the early 1930s, and Shefton's father had been given a generous welcome in Oxford. My research was able to shed light on his war service, as well as his subsequent career including time as a student at the British School at Athens. More recently I contributed to a volume that explored some of the objects that he acquired for the Greek Museum that now forms part of the Great North Museum in Newcastle upon Tyne.[93] My own essay was on an Attic black-glossed stamped bolsal – a type of stemless cup – that had once formed part of the collection at Nostell Priory in Yorkshire.

As we entered the year of the Pandemic, I was asked to turn my hand to writing an obituary for my former Fitzwilliam colleague, Paul Woudhuysen, formerly Keeper of Printed Books and Manuscripts.[94] While he was well known as a librarian and collector of material published during the Nazi occupation of Holland, Woudhuysen had also excavated in Israel, as well as in Cambridge, prior to the development of Castle Hill.

Conclusion

This series of publications on archaeological lives has made me focus on the legacy of these individuals to their subject. But it is often in unexpected ways that it is possible to make connections and detect influences.

For example, a study of official guidebooks for heritage sites in Wales that is based around the authors, has a section on C. A. Ralegh Radford, who served as a director of the British School at Rome during the 1930s. Ralegh Radford had, as a School student, travelled with Winifred Lamb in Aetolia to look for possible prehistoric sites to excavate. Bosanquet, it should be remembered, excavated not only in the Aegean but also at the Roman fort of Housesteads on Hadrian's Wall, as well as at a series of Roman sites in Wales, under the auspices of the Committee for Excavation and Research in Wales and the Marches, when he became professor at Liverpool.[95] Other School students such as John H. Hopkinson and Leonard Cheesman were active in exploring Roman sites in Britain including Corbridge.[96] Conversely, the artist Alan Sorrell, who is well known for his archaeological reconstructions for sites in Britain, undertook some drawing work for the American School in the Agora.[97]

An unexpected outcome was the use of the material from my research on the British School at Athens as a contribution to Kamila Shamsie's *A God in Every Stone*.[98] The plot starts with a fictional archaeologist, Vivian Rose Spencer, excavating at Labraunda in Anatolia on the eve of the First World War, and this drew on my study of students in Anatolia. In contrast, the life of Grimes and his important contribution to the excavation of the ship burial at Sutton Hoo was overlooked in John Preston's *The Dig* (2007) and then misunderstood in the subsequent film (2021). Such fictional dramatisations can influence the public perception of archaeology and archaeologists.

Do such memoirs serve a purpose? Future generations of students need to know and be aware of those that they are following. This was made clear in Eric Cline's *Three Stones Make a Wall* and these histories form the basis for the foundations of archaeological theory.[99] Other histories have emphasised the place of classical scholarship in North America or in Germany, or activities in a particular region such as the Ottoman Empire.[100] The major contribution of foreign institutes in Rome and Athens to archaeological research is now being recognised.[101] Museum histories present a blend of a narrative that draws on significant acquisitions (and their former owners) and the curatorial staff who interpret and present the objects.[102] The names of archaeologists, collectors and museum curators are also important for the study of museum-based objects especially to perform due diligence checks on potential acquisitions. Above all, these lives remind us of the interdependence of scholarship and the networks that are formed often at the start of archaeological careers. Most of all, these biographical studies are a reminder of our own mortality and force us to ask ourselves about our own legacy to the subject.

Acknowledgements

I am grateful to Christopher Stray for his comments and observations over several decades, and Amara Thornton has reminded me of the importance of archaeological networks within the writing of institutional histories. Natalia Vogeikoff of the American School of Classical Studies at Athens made some helpful suggestions for this chapter.

Notes

1. Glyn Daniel, *The Origins and Growth of Archaeology* (London: Penguin, 1967).
2. David W. J. Gill, 'Thinking about collecting histories: a response to Marlowe', *International Journal of Cultural Property* 23 (2016): 237–44.
3. David W. J. Gill, *Donors and Former Owners of Greek and Roman Antiquities in the Fitzwilliam Museum, Cambridge* (Cambridge: Fitzwilliam Museum, 1992).
4. David W. J. Gill, 'Biliotti, Alfred (1833–1915; Kt 1896)', in *The Dictionary of British Classicists*, ed. R. B. Todd (Bristol: Thoemmes Continuum Gill, 2004), vol. 1:80–1.
5. David W. J. Gill, *Attic Black-glazed Pottery in the Fifth Century BC: Workshops and Export*. Unpublished D.Phil. dissertation, Oxford University, 1986.
6. David W. J. Gill, 'Recent acquisitions by the Fitzwilliam Museum, Cambridge, 1971–1989', *Journal of Hellenic Studies* 110 (1990): 290–4.
7. David W. J. Gill and Christopher Chippindale, 'Material and intellectual consequences of esteem for Cycladic Figures.' *American Journal of Archaeology* 97 (1993): 601–59; Christopher Chippindale and David W. J. Gill, 'Material consequences of contemporary classical collecting', *American Journal of Archaeology* 104 (2000): 463–511; see Elizabeth Marlowe, 'What we talk about when we talk about provenance: a response to Chippindale and Gill', *International Journal of Cultural Property* 23 (2016): 217–36. For a case study using the Ashmolean Museum: Christopher Chippindale, David W. J. Gill, Emily Salter, and Christian Hamilton, 'Collecting the Classical world: first steps in a quantitative history', *International Journal of Cultural Property* 10 (2001): 1–31.
8. David W. J. Gill, *Antiquities of the Grand Tour of Italy* (Cambridge: Fitzwilliam Museum, 1990); David W. J. Gill, 'Antiquities from the Grand Tour: The Disney Collection at the Fitzwilliam Museum', *Cambridge* 26 (1990): 34–7.
9. David W. J. Gill, '"Ancient fictile Vases" from the Disney Collection', *Journal of the History of Collections* 2 (1990): 227–31.
10. Martin Henig, *Classical Gems: Ancient and modern intaglios and cameos in the Fitzwilliam Museum, Cambridge* (Cambridge: Cambridge University Press, 1994).
11. J. Spier, 'Blinded with science: the abuse of science in the detection of false antiquities', *Burlington Magazine* 132 (1990): 623–31; Oscar W. Muscarella, *The Lie Became Great: The forgery of ancient Near Eastern cultures*. Studies in the Art and Archaeology of Antiquity 1 (Groningen: Styx, 2000); T. Hardwick, '"The Sophisticated Answer": A recent display of forgeries held at the Victoria and Albert Museum', *Burlington Magazine* 152 (2010): 406–08. For the impact of forgeries: Christos Tsirogiannis, David W. J. Gill, and Christopher Chippindale, 'The forger's tale: an insider's account of corrupting the corpus of Cycladic figures', *International Journal of Cultural Property*, 29 (2022): 369–385.
12. Kevin Butcher and David W. J. Gill, 'The director, the dealer, the goddess and her champions: the acquisition of the Fitzwilliam goddess,' *American Journal of Archaeology* 97 (1993): 383–401; see also Kenneth D. S. Lapatin, *Mysteries of the Snake Goddess: Art, desire, and the forging of history* (Boston and New York: Houghton Mifflin, 2002).
13. Alan J. B. Wace, *A Cretan Statuette in the Fitzwilliam Museum: A Study in Minoan costume* (Cambridge: Cambridge University Press, 1927).
14. Leonard Woolley, *As I Seem to Remember* (London: Allen and Unwin, 1962): 21–3.
15. Quoted in Daniel, *The Origins and Growth of Archaeology*, 150.

16 David A. Traill, *Excavating Schliemann: Collected Papers on Schliemann*, Illinois Classical Studies, suppl. vol. 4 (Atlanta: Scholars Press, 1993): 29–40.
17 See also David W. J. Gill, 'Review of Traill, *Excavating Schliemann*', in *Bryn Mawr Classical Review* 5 (1994): 57–64.
18 David A. Traill, *Schliemann of Troy: Treasure and deceit* (London: John Murray, 1995).
19 Susan Heuck Allen, *Finding the Walls of Troy: Frank Calvert and Heinrich Schliemann at Hisarlik* (Berkeley–Los Angeles: University of California Press, 1999); see also David W. J. Gill, 'Review of Allen, *Finding the Walls of Troy*', *Antiquity* 73 (1999): 968–9.
20 For example, Paul G. Bahn (ed.), *The Collins Dictionary of Archaeology* (Glasgow: Collins, 1992); see also Paul G. Bahn (ed.), *The Penguin Archaeology Guide* (Harmondsworth: Penguin, 2001).
21 Paul G. Bahn (ed.), *The Cambridge Illustrated History of Archaeology* (Cambridge: Cambridge University Press, 1996).
22 Paul G. Bahn (ed.), *The History of Archaeology: An introduction* (London: Routledge, 2014); see also David W. J. Gill, 'The Classical world: antiquarian pursuits', in *The History of Archaeology: An introduction*, ed. Paul G. Bahn (London: Routledge 2014): 57–72.
23 Robert Rhodes James, *Henry Wellcome* (London: Hodder and Stoughton, 1994).
24 David W. J. Gill, 'From Wellcome Museum to Egypt Centre: Displaying Egyptology in Swansea', *Göttinger Miszellen* 205 (2005): 47–54.
25 David Brown, 'MacGregor, William (1848–1937)', in *Oxford Dictionary of National Biography*. https://doi.org/10.1093/ref:odnb/73478.
26 Jason Thompson, *Sir Gardner Wilkinson and His Circle* (Austin: University of Texas Press, 1992).
27 Janine Bourriau, *Pharaohs and Mortals: Egyptian art in the Middle Kingdom* (Cambridge: Cambridge University Press, 1988): 44–5, n. 31.
28 Alison Lloyd and David W. J. Gill, *The Face of Egypt. Swansea Festival Exhibition 1996: 5 October 1996–5 January 1997. Glynn Vivian Art Gallery* (Swansea: City and County of Swansea, 1996).
29 For example, A. H. Sayce, 'David George Hogarth, 1862–1927', *Proceedings of the British Academy* 13 (1927): 379–83; A. H. Smith, 'Thomas Ashby (1874–1931)' *Proceedings of the British Academy* 17 (1931): 515–41.
30 But see A. L. Rowse, 'A buried love: Flecker and Beazley', *The Spectator* (21–28 December 1985): 58–60.
31 See M. J. Benkovitz, *Frederick Rolfe: Baron Corvo* (London: Hamish Hamilton, 1977).
32 J. M. C. Toynbee and H. D. A. Major, revised by David Gill, 'Gardner, Ernest Arthur (1862–1939)', in *Oxford Dictionary of National Biography*. https://doi.org/10.1093/ref:odnb/33327.
33 W. M. Flinders Petrie and Ernest A. Gardner, *Naukratis*, Third Memoir of the Egypt Exploration Fund (London: Trübner, 1886).
34 Ernest A. Gardner, *A Catalogue of the Greek Vases in the Fitzwilliam Museum, Cambridge* (Cambridge: Cambridge University Press, 1897).
35 David W. J. Gill, 'Hogarth, David George (1862–1927)', in *Oxford Dictionary of National Biography*. https://doi.org/10.1093/ref:odnb/33924.
36 Davina Huxley, ed., *Cretan Quests: British explorers, excavators and historians* (London: British School at Athens, 2000).
37 Ellen S. Bosanquet, revised by David W. J. Gill, 'Bosanquet, Robert Carr (1871–1935)', in *Oxford Dictionary of National Biography*. https://doi.org/10.1093/ref:odnb/31976.
38 Ellen S. Bosanquet, ed., *Robert Carr Bosanquet: Letters and Light Verse* (Gloucester: John Bellows Ltd., 1938).
39 W. R. Halliday, revised by David W. J. Gill, 'Dawkins, Richard MacGillivray (1871–1955)', in *Oxford Dictionary of National Biography*. https://doi.org/10.1093/ref:odnb/32749.
40 David W. J. Gill, 'Wace, Alan John Bayard (1879–1957)', in *Oxford Dictionary of National Biography*. https://doi.org/10.1093/ref:odnb/74552.
41 Carol Zerner, *Alan John Bayard Wace and Carl William Blegen: A friendship in the realms of bronze* (Athens: American School of Classical Studies at Athens, 1989).
42 David W. J. Gill, 'Payne, Humfry Gilbert Garth (1902–1936)', in *Oxford Dictionary of National Biography*. https://doi.org/10.1093/ref:odnb/35422.
43 Dilys Powell, *The Traveller's Journey is Done* (London: Hodder and Stoughton, 1943).
44 Robert B. Todd, ed., *The Dictionary of British Classicists* (Bristol: Thoemmes Continuum, 2004).

45 David W. J. Gill, 'Richards, George Chatterton (1867–1951)', in *The Dictionary of British Classicists*, vol. 3, ed. R. B. Todd (Bristol: Thoemmes Continuum, 2004), 814–5; David W. J. Gill, 'Woodward, Arthur Maurice (1883–1973)', in *The Dictionary of British Classicists*, vol. 3, ed. R. B. Todd (Bristol: Thoemmes Continuum, 2004), 1075–6.
46 David W. J. Gill, 'Winifred Lamb and the Fitzwilliam Museum', in *Classics in 19th and 20th Century Cambridge: Curriculum, culture and community*, ed. Christopher A. Stray, Cambridge Philological Society suppl. vol. 24 (Cambridge: Cambridge Philological Society, 1999): 135–56.
47 Winifred Lamb, *Greek and Roman Bronzes* (London: Methuen, 1929); Winifred Lamb, *Cambridge, Fitzwilliam Museum, fascicule 1*, Corpus Vasorum Antiquorum, (Oxford: Clarendon Press, 1930); Winifred Lamb, *Cambridge, Fitzwilliam Museum, fascicule 2*, Corpus Vasorum Antiquorum, (Oxford: Clarendon Press, 1936).
48 David W. J. Gill, 'Winifred Lamb (1894–1963)', in *Breaking Ground: Pioneering women archaeologists*, eds. Getzel Cohen and Martha S. Joukowsky (Ann Arbor: University of Michigan Press, 2004): 425–81.
49 Helen Waterhouse, *The British School at Athens: The first hundred years*, British School at Athens suppl. vol., (London: Thames & Hudson, 1986).
50 David W. J. Gill, 'Winifred Lamb: Searching for prehistory in Greece', in *Travellers to Greece*, ed. Christopher A. Stray (London: Classical Association, 2006): 33–53.
51 David W. J. Gill, 'Lamb, Winifred (1894–1963)', in *Oxford Dictionary of National Biography*. https://doi.org/10.1093/ref:odnb/67872.
52 D. H. Sanders and David W. J. Gill, 'Theresa B. Goell (1901–1985)', in *Breaking Ground: Pioneering women archaeologists*, eds. Getzel Cohen and Martha S. Joukowsky (Ann Arbor: University of Michigan Press, 2004): 482–524.
53 David W. J. Gill, *Winifred Lamb: Aegean Prehistorian and Museum Curator*, Archaeological Lives (Oxford: Archaeopress, 2018). The project was supported by a grant from the British Academy.
54 David W. J. Gill, 'Cryptography and vasology: J.D. Beazley and Winifred Lamb in Room 40', in *Wonders Lost and Found: Papers in honour of Michael Vickers*, ed. by N. Sekunda (Gdansk: The Institute of Archaeology, Gdańsk University, 2020): 194–8.
55 J. Rees, *Amelia Edwards: Traveller, novelist & Egyptologist* (London: The Rubicon Press, 1998).
56 David W. J. Gill, 'Brodrick, Mary (1858–1933)', in *Oxford Dictionary of National Biography*. https://doi.org/10.1093/ref:odnb/48602.
57 David W. J. Gill and Caroline Gill, '"Leaving Town" and "Swedes": Edward Thomas and Amenhotep', *Notes and Queries* 50.3 (2003): 325–7.
58 The concerns for the collection were raised by Charles Ricketts and Charles Shannon whose collection, including classical antiquities, was bequeathed to the Fitzwilliam; see Cecil Lewis, ed., *Self-portrait Taken from the Letters and Journals of Charles Ricketts, R.A.* (London: Peter Davies, 1939).
59 David W. J. Gill, 'Winifred Lamb: Her first year as a student at the British School at Athens', in *Archaeology and Women: Ancient and modern issues*, eds. Sue Hamilton, Ruth D. Whitehouse, and Karen I. Wright (Walnut Creek: Left Coast Press, 2007): 55–75.
60 David W. J. Gill, '"The Passion of Hazard": Women at the British School at Athens before the First World War', *Annual of the British School at Athens* 97 (2002): 491–510.
61 David W. J. Gill, 'Dorothy Lamb (1887–1967): A pioneering Mediterranean field-archaeologist', Brown University, 2004. https://www.brown.edu/Research/Breaking_Ground/bios/Lamb_Dorothy.pdf.
62 John Percival Droop, *Archaeological Excavation*, The Cambridge Archaeological and Ethnological Series, (Cambridge: Cambridge University Press, 1915).
63 Rachel Hood, *Faces of Archaeology in Greece: Caricatures by Piet de Jong* (Oxford: Leopard's Head Press, 1998).
64 John K. Papadopoulos, ed., *The Art of Antiquity: Piet de Jong and the Athenian Agora* (Princeton: American School of Classical Studies at Athens, 2007); see David W. J. Gill, 'Review of John K. Papadopoulos, ed., *The Art of Antiquity: Piet de Jong and the Athenian Agora* (Princeton: American School of Classical Studies at Athens, 2007)', *Bryn Mawr Classical Review* 2008.
65 David W. J. Gill, 'The British School at Athens and archaeological research in the Late Ottoman Empire', in *Archaeology, Anthropology and Heritage in the Balkans and Anatolia: The Life and Times of F. W. Hasluck, 1878–1920*, vol. 1, ed. David Shankland (Istanbul: The Isis Press, 2004), 223–55; David W. J. Gill, 'A preliminary bibliography of the works of F. W. Hasluck and of M. M. Hardie (Mrs F. W. Hasluck)', in *Archaeology, Anthropology and Heritage in the Balkans and*

Anatolia: The life and times of F. W. Hasluck, 1878–1920, vol. 2, ed. David Shankland (Istanbul: The Isis Press, 2004), 485–90.

66 David W. J. Gill, 'Harry Pirie-Gordon: Historical research, journalism and intelligence gathering in the Eastern Mediterranean (1908–18)', *Intelligence and National Security* 21 (2006): 1045–59.

67 David W. J. Gill, 'Harry Pirie-Gordon and the Palestine guide books', *Public Archaeology* 11 (2013): 169–78.

68 David W. J. Gill, 'Excavating under gunfire: archaeologists in the Aegean during the First World War', *Public Archaeology* 10 (2011): 187–99; see also Andrew Shapland and E. Stefani, eds., *Archaeology Behind the Battle Lines: The Macedonian Campaign (1915–19) and its Legacy*, British School at Athens: Modern Greek and Byzantine Studies (London: Routledge, 2017).

69 J. N. L. Myres, *Commander J.L. Myres, R.N.V.R.: The Blackbeard of the Aegean*, J. L. Myres Memorial Lecture, vol. 10 (London: Leopard's Head Press, 1980).

70 David W. J. Gill, 'Paton, William Roger (1857–1921)', In *Oxford Dictionary of National Biography*. https://doi.org/10.1093/ref:odnb/53496.

71 Waterhouse, *The British School at Athens*.

72 Louis E. Lord, *A History of the American School of Classical Studies at Athens 1882–1942: An intercollegiate project* (Cambridge: American School of Classical Studies at Athens, 1947); Lucy Shoe Meritt, *History of the American School of Classical Studies at Athens 1939–1980* (Princeton: American School of Classical Studies at Athens, 1984).

73 David W. J. Gill, *Sifting the Soil of Greece: The early years of the British School at Athens (1886–1919)*, Bulletin of the Institute of Classical Studies suppl. vol. 111 (London: Institute of Classical Studies, 2011).

74 David W. J. Gill, 'From the Cam to the Cephissus: the Fitzwilliam Museum and students of the British School at Athens', *Journal of the History of Collections* 24 (2012): 337–46.

75 David W. J. Gill, 'Collecting for Cambridge: John Hubert Marshall on Crete', *Annual of the British School at Athens* 95 (2000): 517–26; see also V. E. G. Kenna, *Die englischen Museen II*, Corpus der minoischen und mykenischen Siegel, Band VII (Berlin: Mann, 1967).

76 Gill, *Winifred Lamb: Aegean prehistorian and museum curator*, 92–93. For Dawkins' collection now in Oxford: Susan Sherratt, *Catalogue of Cycladic Antiquities in the Ashmolean Museum: The captive spirit* (Oxford: Oxford University Press, 2000).

77 I. A. Richmond, revised by David W. J. Gill, 'Ashby, Thomas (1874–1931)', in *Oxford Dictionary of National Biography*. https://doi.org/10.1093/ref:odnb/30468; see also Andrew Wallace-Hadrill, *The British School at Rome: One hundred years* (London: The British School at Rome, 2001).

78 Richard Hodges, *Visions of Rome: Thomas Ashby, archaeologist* (London: The British School at Rome, 2000).

79 H. E. D. Blakiston, revised by David W. J. Gill, 'Jones, Sir Henry Stuart (1867–1939)', in *Oxford Dictionary of National Biography*. https://doi.org/10.1093/ref:odnb/34232.

80 Alan J. B. Wace, 'Fragments of Roman historical reliefs in the Vatican and Lateran Museums', *Papers of the British School at Rome* 3 (1906): 273–94; Henry Stuart-Jones, ed., *A Catalogue of the Ancient Sculptures Preserved in the Municipal Collections of Rome 1: The sculptures of the Museo Capitolino* (Oxford: Clarendon Press, 1912).

81 Martin Robertson, revised by David W. J. Gill, 'Beazley, Sir John Davidson (1885–1970)', in *Oxford Dictionary of National Biography*. https://doi.org/10.1093/ref:odnb/30664.

82 Beazley's approach is celebrated in J. Michael Padgett, ed., *The Berlin Painter and His World: Athenian vase-painting in the early Fifth Century B.C.* (New Haven: Princeton University Art Museum, 2017).

83 David W. J. Gill, 'Disney, John (1779–1857)', in *Oxford Dictionary of National Biography*. https://doi.org/10.1093/ref:odnb/7686.

84 David W. J. Gill, *The World of Disney: From antiquarianism to archaeology*, Archaeological Lives (Oxford: Archaeopress, 2020); see also David W. J. Gill, 'The Collection of John Disney, Antiquarian and University Benefactor', With Fresh Eyes: Conference Proceedings Portsmouth 2013 and Colchester 2014, ed. A. Khreisheh, *The Museum Archaeologist* 36 (2017): 68–79.

85 A.D. Nock, revised by David W. J. Gill, 'Cook, Arthur Bernard (1868–1952)', in *Oxford Dictionary of National Biography*. https://doi.org/10.1093/ref:odnb/32538.

86 Reginald Hackforth, revised by David W. J. Gill, 'Cornford, Francis Macdonald (1874–1943)', in *Oxford Dictionary of National Biography*. https://doi.org/10.1093/ref:odnb/32571; see also Gordon Johnson, *University Politics: F. M. Cornford's Cambridge and his advice to the young academic politician* (Cambridge: Cambridge University Press, 1994).

87 Mary Beard, *The Invention of Jane Harrison*, Revealing Antiquity, vol. 14 (Cambridge: Harvard University Press, 2000).
88 P. A. Sloan, *John Cornford: A memoir* (London: Jonathan Cape, 1938).
89 David W. J. Gill, 'Taylour, Lord William Desmond (1904–1989)', in *Oxford Dictionary of National Biography*. https://doi.org/10.1093/ref:odnb/67874
90 David W. J. Gill, 'Grimes, William Francis (1905–1988)', in *Oxford Dictionary of National Biography*. https://doi.org/10.1093/ref:odnb/67870
91 J. Shepherd, *The Temple of Mithras, London: Excavations by W.F. Grimes and A. Williams at the Walbrook*, Archaeological Report, vol. 12 (London: English Heritage, 1998); David W. J. Gill, 'William F. Grimes: The making of a prehistorian', *Bulletin of the History of Archaeology* 10 (2000): 1–8.
92 David W. J. Gill, 'Shefton, Brian Benjamin (1919–2012)', in *Oxford Dictionary of National Biography*. https://doi.org/10.1093/ref:odnb/104851; David W. J. Gill, 'Brian Shefton: Classical archaeologist', in *Ark of Civilization: Refugee scholars and Oxford University, 1930–1945*, eds. S. Crawford, K. Ulmschneider, and J. Elsner (Oxford: Oxford University Press, 2017), 151–60.
93 David W. J. Gill, 'The Nostell Priory Bolsal', in *On the Fascination of Objects: Greek and Etruscan art in the Shefton Collection*, eds. John Boardman, Andrew Parkin, and Sally Waite (Oxford: Oxbow, 2015), 95–106; see also Brian B. Shefton, 'The Greek Museum, The University of Newcastle upon Tyne', *Archaeological Reports* 16 (1969/70): 52–62.
94 David W. J. Gill, 'Paul Woudhuijsen (Woudhuysen) (1935–2020)', *The Book Collector* 69 (2020): 543–5.
95 Gill, *Sifting the Soil of Greece*, 238.
96 Gill, *Sifting the Soil of Greece*, 237–38. For Corbridge: M. C. Bishop, *Corstopitum: An Edwardian excavation. photographs from the 1906–14 excavations of the Roman site at Corbridge, Northumberland* (London: English Heritage, 1994).
97 Julia Sorrell and Mark Sorrell, *Alan Sorrell: The man who created Roman Britain* (Oxford: Oxbow, 2018.)
98 Kamila Shamsie, *A God in Every Stone* (London: Bloomsbury, 2014).
99 Eric H. Cline, *Three Stones Make a Wall: The story of archaeology* (Princeton: Princeton University Press, 2017); see also David W. J. Gill, 'Review of Eric H. Cline, *Three Stones Make a Wall: The story of archaeology* (Princeton: Princeton University Press, 2017)', *Bryn Mawr Classical Review* (2017). For the theoretical basis: Bruce G. Trigger, *A History of Archaeological Thought* (Cambridge: Cambridge University Press, 1989).
100 S. L. Dyson, *Ancient Marbles to American Shores: Classical archaeology in the United States* (Philadelphia: University of Pennsylvania Press, 1998); S. L. Dyson, *In Pursuit of Ancient Pasts: A history of Classical archaeology in the nineteenth and twentieth centuries* (New Haven–London: Yale University Press, 2006); Suzanne L. Marchand, *Down from Olympus: Archaeology and philhellenism in Germany, 1750–1970* (Princeton: Princeton University Press, 1996); Debbie Challis, *From the Harpy Tomb to the Wonders of Ephesus: British archaeologists in the Ottoman Empire 1840–1880* (London: Duckworth, 2008).
101 Frederick Whitling, *Western Ways: Foreign schools in Rome and Athens* (Berlin: De Gruyter, 2019).
102 David M. Wilson, *The British Museum: A history* (London: The British Museum Press, 2002); S. Panayotova, *I Turned It Into a Palace: Sydney Cockerell and the Fitzwilliam Museum* (Cambridge: The Fitzwilliam Museum, 2008); Lucilla Burn, *The Fitzwilliam Museum: A history* (Cambridge: The Fitzwilliam Museum/PWP, 2016).

Bibliography

Allen, Susan Heuck, *Finding the Walls of Troy: Frank Calvert and Heinrich Schliemann at Hisarlik* (Berkeley-Los Angeles: University of California Press, 1999).
Bahn, Paul G., ed., *The Collins Dictionary of Archaeology* (Glasgow: Collins, 1992).
Bahn, Paul G., ed., *The Cambridge Illustrated History of Archaeology* (Cambridge: Cambridge University Press, 1996).
Bahn, Paul G., ed., *The Penguin Archaeology Guide* (Harmondsworth: Penguin, 2001).
Bahn, Paul G., ed., *The History of Archaeology: An introduction* (London: Routledge, 2014).

Beard, Mary, *The Invention of Jane Harrison*, Revealing Antiquity, vol. 14. (Cambridge: Harvard University Press, 2000).
Benkovitz, M. J., *Frederick Rolfe: Baron Corvo* (London: Hamish Hamilton, 1977).
Bishop, M. C., *Corstopitum: An Edwardian excavation: photographs from the 1906–14 excavations of the Roman site at Corbridge, Northumberland* (London: English Heritage, 1994).
Blakiston, H. E. D., revised by David W. J. Gill, 'Jones, Sir Henry Stuart (1867–1939)', in *Oxford Dictionary of National Biography*. https://doi.org/10.1093/ref:odnb/34232.
Bosanquet, Ellen S., ed., *Robert Carr Bosanquet: Letters and light verse* (Gloucester: John Bellows Ltd., 1938).
Bosanquet, Ellen S., revised by David W. J. Gill, 'Bosanquet, Robert Carr (1871–1935)', in *Oxford Dictionary of National Biography*. https://doi.org/10.1093/ref:odnb/31976.
Bourriau, Janine, *Pharaohs and Mortals: Egyptian art in the Middle Kingdom* (Cambridge: Cambridge University Press, 1988).
Brown, David, 'MacGregor, William (1848–1937)', in *Oxford Dictionary of National Biography*. https://doi.org/10.1093/ref:odnb/73478.
Burn, Lucilla, *The Fitzwilliam Museum: A history* (Cambridge: The Fitzwilliam Museum/ PWP, 2016).
Butcher, Kevin and David W. J. Gill, 'The director, the dealer, the goddess and her champions: the acquisition of the Fitzwilliam Goddess', *American Journal of Archaeology* 97 (1993): 383–401.
Challis, Debbie, *From the Harpy Tomb to the Wonders of Ephesus: British archaeologists in the Ottoman Empire 1840–1880* (London: Duckworth, 2008).
Chippindale, Christopher and David W. J. Gill, 'Material consequences of contemporary classical collecting', *American Journal of Archaeology* 104 (2000): 463–511.
Chippindale, Christopher, David W. J. Gill, Emily Salter, and Christian Hamilton, 'Collecting the Classical world: first steps in a quantitative history', *International Journal of Cultural Property* 10 (2001): 1–31.
Cline, Eric H., *Three Stones Make a Wall: The story of archaeology* (Princeton: Princeton University Press, 2017).
Daniel, Glyn, *The Origins and Growth of Archaeology* (London: Penguin, 1967).
Droop, John Percival, *Archaeological Excavation*, The Cambridge Archaeological and Ethnological Series. (Cambridge: Cambridge University Press, 1915).
Dyson, S. L., *Ancient Marbles to American Shores: Classical archaeology in the United States* (Philadelphia: University of Pennsylvania Press, 1998).
Dyson, S. L., *In Pursuit of Ancient Pasts: A history of Classical archaeology in the nineteenth and twentieth centuries* (New Haven–London: Yale University Press, 2006).
Gardner, Ernest A., *A Catalogue of the Greek Vases in the Fitzwilliam Museum, Cambridge* (Cambridge: Cambridge University Press, 1897).
Gill, David W. J., Attic Black-glazed Pottery in the Fifth Century BC: Workshops and Export. Unpublished D.Phil. dissertation, Oxford University, 1986.
Gill, David W. J., '"Ancient fictile vases" from the Disney Collection', *Journal of the History of Collections* 2 (1990): 227–31.
Gill, David W. J., 'Antiquities from the Grand Tour: the Disney Collection at the Fitzwilliam Museum', *Cambridge* 26 (1990): 34–7.
Gill, David W. J., *Antiquities of the Grand Tour of Italy* (Cambridge: Fitzwilliam Museum, 1990).
Gill, David W. J., 'Recent acquisitions by the Fitzwilliam Museum, Cambridge, 1971–1989', *Journal of Hellenic Studies* 110 (1990): 290–4.
Gill, David W. J., *Donors and Former Owners of Greek and Roman Antiquities in the Fitzwilliam Museum, Cambridge* (Cambridge: Fitzwilliam Museum, 1992).
Gill, David W. J., 'Review of D. A. Traill, *Excavating Schliemann: Collected Papers on Schliemann*, Illinois Classical Studies suppl. 4 (Atlanta: Scholars Press, 1993)', *Bryn Mawr Classical Review* 5 (1994): 57–64.
Gill, David W. J., 'Review of Susan Heuck Allen, *Finding the Walls of Troy: Frank Calvert and Heinrich Schliemann at Hisarlik* (Berkeley-Los Angeles: University of California Press, 1999)', *Antiquity* 73 (1999): 968–9.
Gill, David W. J., 'Winifred Lamb and the Fitzwilliam Museum', in *Classics in 19th and 20th Century Cambridge: Curriculum, culture and community*, ed. Christopher A. Stray, Cambridge Philological Society, suppl. vol. 24 (Cambridge: Cambridge Philological Society, 1999): 135–56.

Gill, David W. J., 'Collecting for Cambridge: John Hubert Marshall on Crete', *Annual of the British School at Athens* 95 (2000): 517–26.

Gill, David W. J., 'William F. Grimes: The making of a prehistorian', *Bulletin of the History of Archaeology* 10 (2000): 1–8.

Gill, David W. J., '"The Passion of Hazard": Women at the British School at Athens before the First World War', *Annual of the British School at Athens* 97 (2002): 491–510.

Gill, David W. J., 'Biliotti, Alfred (1833–1915; Kt 1896)', in *The Dictionary of British Classicists*, vol. 1, ed. R. B. Todd, (Bristol: Thoemmes Continuum, 2004), 80–1.

Gill, David W. J., 'The British School at Athens and archaeological research in the Late Ottoman Empire', in *Archaeology, Anthropology and Heritage in the Balkans and Anatolia: the life and times of F. W. Hasluck, 1878–1920*, vol. 1, ed. David Shankland (Istanbul: The Isis Press, 2004), 223–55.

Gill, David W. J., 'Brodrick, Mary (1858–1933)', in *Oxford Dictionary of National Biography*. https://doi.org/10.1093/ref:odnb/48602.

Gill, David W. J., 'Disney, John (1779–1857)', in *Oxford Dictionary of National Biography*. https://doi.org/10.1093/ref:odnb/7686.

Gill, David W. J., 'Dorothy Lamb (1887–1967): A pioneering Mediterranean field-archaeologist'. Brown University, 2004. Accessed 5 February 2022 https://www.brown.edu/Research/Breaking_Ground/bios/Lamb_Dorothy.pdf

Gill, David W. J., 'Grimes, William Francis (1905–1988)', in *Oxford Dictionary of National Biography*. https://doi.org/10.1093/ref:odnb/67870.

Gill, David W. J., 'Hogarth, David George (1862–1927)', in *Oxford Dictionary of National Biography*. https://doi.org/10.1093/ref:odnb/33924.

Gill, David W. J., 'Lamb, Winifred (1894–1963)', in *Oxford Dictionary of National Biography*. https://doi.org/10.1093/ref:odnb/67872.

Gill, David W. J., 'Paton, William Roger (1857–1921)', in *Oxford Dictionary of National Biography*. https://doi.org/10.1093/ref:odnb/53496.

Gill, David W. J., 'Payne, Humfry Gilbert Garth (1902–1936)', in *Oxford Dictionary of National Biography*. https://doi.org/10.1093/ref:odnb/35422.

Gill, David W. J., 'A preliminary bibliography of the works of F. W. Hasluck and of M. M. Hardie (Mrs F. W. Hasluck)', in *Archaeology, Anthropology and Heritage in the Balkans and Anatolia: the life and times of F.W. Hasluck, 1878–1920*, vol. 2, ed. David Shankland (Istanbul: The Isis Press, 2004), 485–90.

Gill, David W. J., 'Richards, George Chatterton (1867–1951)', in *The Dictionary of British Classicists*, vol. 3, ed. Robert B. Todd (Bristol: Thoemmes Continuum, 2004), 814–5.

Gill, David W. J., 'Taylour, Lord William Desmond (1904–1989)', in *Oxford Dictionary of National Biography*. https://doi.org/10.1093/ref:odnb/67874.

Gill, David W. J., 'Wace, Alan John Bayard (1879–1957)', in *Oxford Dictionary of National Biography*. https://doi.org/10.1093/ref:odnb/74552.

Gill, David W. J., 'Winifred Lamb (1894–1963)', in *Breaking Ground: Pioneering women archaeologists*, eds. Getzel Cohen and Martha S. Joukowsky (Ann Arbor: University of Michigan Press, 2004), 425–81.

Gill, David W. J., 'Woodward, Arthur Maurice (1883–1973)', in *The Dictionary of British Classicists*, vol. 3, ed. Robert B. Todd (Bristol: Thoemmes Continuum, 2004), 1075–6.

Gill, David W. J., 'From Wellcome Museum to Egypt Centre: Displaying Egyptology in Swansea', *Göttinger Miszellen* 205 (2005): 47–54.

Gill, David W. J., 'Harry Pirie-Gordon: Historical research, journalism and intelligence gathering in the Eastern Mediterranean (1908–18)', *Intelligence and National Security* 21 (2006): 1045–59.

Gill, David W. J., 'Winifred Lamb: searching for prehistory in Greece', in *Travellers to Greece*, ed. Christopher A. Stray (London: Classical Association, 2006), 33–53.

Gill, David W. J., 'Winifred Lamb: her first year as a student at the British School at Athens', in *Archaeology and Women: Ancient and Modern Issues*, eds. Sue Hamilton, Ruth D. Whitehouse, and Karen I. Wright (Walnut Creek: Left Coast Press, 2007), 55–75.

Gill, David W. J., 'Review of John K. Papadopoulos, ed., *The Art of Antiquity: Piet de Jong and the Athenian Agora* (Princeton: American School of Classical Studies at Athens, 2007)', *Bryn Mawr Classical Review* (2008). https://bmcr.brynmawr.edu/2008/2008.04.22/.

Gill, David W. J., 'Excavating under gunfire: Archaeologists in the Aegean during the First World War', *Public Archaeology* 10 (2011): 187–99.

Gill, David W. J., *Sifting the Soil of Greece: The early years of the British School at Athens (1886–1919)*, Bulletin of the Institute of Classical Studies, suppl. vol. 111 (London: Institute of Classical Studies, 2011).

Gill, David W. J., 'From the Cam to the Cephissus: the Fitzwilliam Museum and students of the British School at Athens', *Journal of the History of Collections* 24 (2012): 337–46.

Gill, David W. J., 'Harry Pirie-Gordon and the Palestine guide books', *Public Archaeology* 11 (2013): 169–78.

Gill, David W. J., 'The Classical World: antiquarian pursuits', in *The History of Archaeology: An introduction*, ed. Paul G. Bahn (London: Routledge, 2014), 57–72.

Gill, David W. J., 'The Nostell Priory Bolsal', in *On the Fascination of Objects: Greek and Etruscan art in the Shefton Collection*, eds. John Boardman, Andrew Parkin, and Sally Waite (Oxford: Oxbow, 2015), 95–106.

Gill, David W. J., 'Shefton, Brian Benjamin (1919–2012)', in *Oxford Dictionary of National Biography*. https://doi.org/10.1093/ref:odnb/104851.

Gill, David W. J., 'Thinking about collecting histories: a response to Marlowe', *International Journal of Cultural Property* 23 (2016): 237–44.

Gill, David W. J., 'Brian Shefton: Classical archaeologist', in *Ark of Civilization: Refugee scholars and Oxford University, 1930–1945*, eds. S. Crawford, K. Ulmschneider, and J. Elsner (Oxford: Oxford University Press, 2017), 151–60.

Gill, David W. J., 'The collection of John Disney, antiquarian and university benefactor', With Fresh Eyes: Conference Proceedings Portsmouth 2013 and Colchester 2014, ed. A. Khreisheh, *The Museum Archaeologist* 36 (2017): 68–79.

Gill, David W. J., 'Review of Eric H. Cline, *Three Stones Make a Wall: The story of archaeology* (Princeton-Oxford: Princeton University Press, 2017)', *Bryn Mawr Classical Review* (2017). https://bmcr.brynmawr.edu/2008/2008.04.22/.

Gill, David W. J., *Winifred Lamb: Aegean prehistorian and museum curator*, Archaeological Lives (Oxford: Archaeopress, 2018).

Gill, David W. J., 'Cryptography and vasology: J. D. Beazley and Winifred Lamb in room 40', in *Wonders Lost and Found: Papers in honour of Michael Vickers*, ed. N. Sekunda (Gdansk: The Institute of Archaeology, Gdańsk University, 2020), 194–8.

Gill, David W. J., 'Paul Woudhuijsen (Woudhuysen) (1935–2020)', *The Book Collector* 69 (2020): 543–5.

Gill, David W. J., *The World of Disney: From antiquarianism to archaeology*, Archaeological Lives (Oxford: Archaeopress, 2020).

Gill, David W. J. and Christopher Chippindale, 'Material and intellectual consequences of esteem for Cycladic figures', *American Journal of Archaeology* 97 (1993): 601–59.

Gill, David W. J. and Caroline Gill, '"Leaving Town" and "Swedes": Edward Thomas and Amen-hotep', *Notes and Queries* 50.3 (2003): 325–7.

Hackforth, Reginald, revised by David W. J. Gill, 'Cornford, Francis Macdonald (1874–1943)', in *Oxford Dictionary of National Biography*. https://doi.org/10.1093/ref:odnb/32571.

Halliday, W. R., revised by David W. J. Gill, 'Dawkins, Richard MacGillivray (1871–1955)', in *Oxford Dictionary of National Biography*. https://doi.org/10.1093/ref:odnb/32749

Hardwick, T., '"The Sophisticated Answer": a recent display of forgeries held at the Victoria and Albert Museum', *Burlington Magazine* 152 (2010): 406–8.

Henig, Martin, *Classical Gems: Ancient and modern intaglios and cameos in the Fitzwilliam Museum, Cambridge* (Cambridge: Cambridge University Press, 1994).

Hodges, Richard, *Visions of Rome: Thomas Ashby, archaeologist* (London: The British School at Rome, 2000).

Hood, Rachel, *Faces of Archaeology in Greece: Caricatures by Piet de Jong* (Oxford: Leopard's Head Press, 1998).

Huxley, Davina, ed., *Cretan Quests: British explorers, excavators and historians* (London: British School at Athens, 2000).

James, Richard Rhodes, *Henry Wellcome* (London: Hodder and Stoughton, 1994).

Johnson, Gordon, *University Politics: F.M. Cornford's Cambridge and his advice to the young academic politician* (Cambridge: Cambridge University Press, 1994).

Kenna, V. E. G., *Die englischen Museen II*, Corpus der minoischen und mykenischen Siegel, Band VII (Berlin: Mann, 1967).

Lamb, Winifred, *Greek and Roman Bronzes* (London: Methuen, 1929).

Lamb, Winifred, *Cambridge, Fitzwilliam Museum, Fascicule 1*. Corpus Vasorum Antiquorum. (Oxford: Clarendon Press, 1930).
Lamb, Winifred, *Cambridge, Fitzwilliam Museum, Fascicule 2*. Corpus Vasorum Antiquorum. (Oxford: Clarendon Press, 1936).
Lapatin, Kenneth D. S., *Mysteries of the Snake Goddess: Art, desire, and the forging of history* (Boston-New York: Houghton Mifflin, 2002).
Lewis, Cecil, ed., *Self-portrait Taken From The Letters and Journals of Charles Ricketts, R.A.* (London: Peter Davies, 1939).
Lloyd, Alison, and David W. J. Gill, *The Face of Egypt. Swansea Festival Exhibition 1996: 5 October 1996–5 January 1997. Glynn Vivian Art Gallery*. (Swansea: City and County of Swansea, 1996).
Lord, Louis E., *A History of the American School of Classical Studies at Athens 1882–1942: An intercollegiate project* (Cambridge: American School of Classical Studies at Athens, 1947).
Marchand, Suzanne L., *Down From Olympus: Archaeology and philhellenism in Germany, 1750–1970* (Princeton: Princeton University Press, 1996).
Marlowe, Elizabeth, 'What we talk about when we talk about provenance: a response to Chippindale and Gill', *International Journal of Cultural Property* 23 (2016): 217–36.
Meritt, Lucy Shoe, *History of the American School of Classical Studies at Athens 1939–1980* (Princeton: American School of Classical Studies at Athens, 1984).
Muscarella, Oscar W., *The Lie Became Great: The forgery of ancient Near Eastern cultures*, Studies in the Art and Archaeology of Antiquity 1 (Groningen: Styx, 2000).
Myres, J. N. L., *Commander J. L. Myres, R.N.V.R.: the Blackbeard of the Aegean*, J. L. Myres Memorial Lecture, vol. 10 (London: Leopard's Head Press, 1980).
Nock, A. D., revised by David W. J. Gill, 'Cook, Arthur Bernard (1868–1952)', in *Oxford Dictionary of National Biography*. https://doi.org/10.1093/ref:odnb/32538.
Padgett, J. Michael, ed., *The Berlin Painter and His World: Athenian vase-painting in the early fifth century B.C.* (New Haven: Princeton University Art Museum, 2017).
Panayotova, S., *I Turned It Into a Palace: Sydney Cockerell and the Fitzwilliam Museum* (Cambridge: The Fitzwilliam Museum, 2008).
Papadopoulos, John K., ed., *The Art of Antiquity: Piet de Jong and the Athenian Agora* (Princeton: American School of Classical Studies at Athens, 2007).
Petrie, W. M. Flinders, and Ernest A. Gardner, *Naukratis*, Third Memoir of the Egypt Exploration Fund (London: Trübner, 1886).
Powell, Dilys, *The Traveller's Journey is Done* (London: Hodder and Stoughton, 1943).
Rees, J., *Amelia Edwards: Traveller, novelist & Egyptologist* (London: The Rubicon Press, 1998).
Richmond, Ian A., revised by David W. J. Gill, 'Ashby, Thomas (1874–1931)', in *Oxford Dictionary of National Biography*. https://doi.org/10.1093/ref:odnb/30468.
Robertson, Martin, revised by David W. J. Gill, 'Beazley, Sir John Davidson (1885–1970)', in *Oxford Dictionary of National Biography*. https://doi.org/10.1093/ref:odnb/30664.
Rowse, A. L., 'A buried love: Flecker and Beazley', *The Spectator*, 21–28 December 1985: 58–60.
Sanders, Donald H. and David W. J. Gill, 'Theresa B. Goell (1901–1985)', in *Breaking Ground: Pioneering women archaeologists*, eds. Getzel Cohen and Martha S. Joukowsky (Ann Arbor: University of Michigan Press, 2004), 482–524.
Sayce, A. H., 'David George Hogarth, 1862–1927', *Proceedings of the British Academy* 13 (1927): 379–83.
Shamsie, Kamila, *A God in Every Stone* (London: Bloomsbury, 2014).
Shapland, Andrew, and E. Stefani, eds., *Archaeology Behind the Battle Lines: The Macedonian Campaign (1915–19) and its legacy*, British School at Athens: Modern Greek and Byzantine Studies (London: Routledge, 2017).
Shefton, Brian B., 'The Greek Museum, The University of Newcastle upon Tyne', *Archaeological Reports* 16 (1969/70): 52–62.
Shepherd, John, *The Temple of Mithras, London: Excavations by W.F. Grimes and A. Williams at the Walbrook*, Archaeological Report, vol. 12 (London: English Heritage, 1998).
Sherratt, Susan, *Catalogue of Cycladic Antiquities in the Ashmolean Museum: The captive spirit* (Oxford: Oxford University Press, 2000).
Sloan, P. A., ed., *John Cornford: A Memoir* (London: Jonathan Cape, 1938).
Smith, A. H., 'Thomas Ashby (1874–1931)', *Proceedings of the British Academy* 17 (1931): 515–41.
Sorrell, Julia, and Mark Sorrell, *Alan Sorrell: The man who created Roman Britain* (Oxford: Oxbow, 2018).

Spier, J., 'Blinded with science: the abuse of science in the detection of false antiquities', *Burlington Magazine* 132 (1990): 623–31.

Stuart-Jones, Henry, ed., *A Catalogue of the Ancient Sculptures Preserved in the Municipal Collections of Rome 1: The sculptures of the Museo Capitolino* (Oxford: Clarendon Press, 1912).

Thompson, Jason, *Sir Gardner Wilkinson and His Circle* (Austin: University of Texas Press, 1992).

Todd, Robert B., ed., *The Dictionary of British Classicists* (Bristol: Thoemmes Continuum, 2004).

Toynbee, J. M. C. and H. D. A. Major, revised by David Gill, 'Gardner, Ernest Arthur (1862–1939)', in *Oxford Dictionary of National Biography*. https://doi.org/10.1093/ref:odnb/33327.

Traill, David A., *Excavating Schliemann: Collected papers on Schliemann*, Illinois Classical Studies, suppl. vol. 4 (Atlanta: Scholars Press, 1993).

Traill, David A., *Schliemann of Troy: Treasure and Deceit* (London: John Murray, 1995).

Trigger, Bruce G., *A History of Archaeological Thought* (Cambridge: Cambridge University Press, 1989).

Tsirogiannis, Christos, David W. J. Gill, and Christopher Chippindale, 'The forger's tale: An insider's account of corrupting the corpus of Cycladic figures', *International Journal of Cultural Property* 29 (2022): 369–385.

Wace, Alan J. B., 'Fragments of Roman historical reliefs in the Vatican and Lateran museums', *Papers of the British School at Rome* 3 (1906): 273–94.

Wace, Alan J. B., *A Cretan Statuette in the Fitzwilliam Museum: A study in Minoan costume* (Cambridge: Cambridge University Press, 1927).

Wallace-Hadrill, Andrew, *The British School at Rome: One hundred years* (London: The British School at Rome, 2001).

Waterhouse, Helen, *The British School at Athens: The first hundred years*, British School at Athens suppl. vol. (London: Thames & Hudson, 1986).

Whitling, Frederick, *Western Ways: Foreign schools in Rome and Athens* (Berlin: De Gruyter, 2019).

Wilson, David M., *The British Museum: A history* (London: The British Museum Press, 2002).

Woolley, Leonard, *As I Seem to Remember* (London: Allen and Unwin, 1962).

Zerner, Carol, *Alan John Bayard Wace and Carl William Blegen: A friendship in the realms of bronze* (Athens: American School of Classical Studies at Athens, 1989).

15
The ghosts of Ann Mary Severn Newton: Grief, an imagined life and (auto)biography

Debbie Challis

Two drawings of colossal sculptures by artist Ann Mary Severn Newton hang near to a bust of her husband Charles Thomas Newton at the entrance to the Department of Greek and Roman Antiquities at the British Museum (Figure 15.1). Mary Severn Newton's (1832–1866) art is little known today and her archaeological drawings are barely footnotes in such biographies of her that there are. Even Charles Thomas Newton (1812–1894) gets little recognition outside the fields of classics and archaeology. Yet, in his time, he was recognised as a discoverer of the Mausoleum of Halicarnassos in Bodrum Turkey, a 'Wonder of the World' and popularly known as 'Mausoleum Newton'. When Keeper of the Department of Greek and Roman Antiquities, Newton helped transform antiquarianism into archaeology and put in place a more professional curatorial practice, albeit one that reflected the unethical acquisition practices of his time, at the British Museum.

By 1858, when Mary (I am using her first name to differentiate her from her husband or father) entered the field of archaeology, she was 26 years old and an accomplished artist who had financially supported her family for six years. A student of portrait artist George Richmond and an artist encouraged by John Ruskin, Mary had a critical reputation for finely rendered portraits in pencils and watercolours. Her life changed when Charles Newton commissioned her to draw the newly discovered sculptures from the Mausoleum of Halicarnassos. It was a new direction for Mary, personally as well as professionally since it led to her marriage to Newton in 1861. Although it was not easy for female artists in the

Figure 15.1 The two large drawings by Mary Severn Newton of the colossal sculpture of Artemisia and Mausolos are reproduced as plates in Charles Newton Travels and Discoveries. Vol. II (1865); (a), Plate 8, (b) Plate 10.

FEMALE FIGURE.

FOUND UNDER PYRAMID STEPS.

MAUSOLEUM.

Figure 15.1 (Continued)

nineteenth century to combine the commitments of married life with professional development, her work illustrated significant changes in medium and direction from 1859 to the time of her early death in 1866. Mary arguably had opportunities to travel and paint after marriage that she otherwise may not have had.

Mary is not unknown, but where there is information about her there are often errors. For example, in the Tate catalogue of female artists in its collection, it states that she died of measles when 'she was abroad' in Rhodes, when she was in fact in Gower Street.[1] Although this seems petty, the errors echo the way in which information can be lifted from one inaccurate or biased biographical source and repeated. In this chapter, I position Mary as a predecessor to the female artists prominent in later archaeological digs, most notably those of William Matthew Flinders Petrie in the early twentieth century, such as Anne Pirie Quibell.[2] In doing so, I place her in context as a working woman, an artist, within the patriarchal structures of mid-Victorian Britain and whose family depended upon the commission of her art. Drawing on the 'patterns of friendship' defined by the social and cultural networks of her family and friends, I try to recreate the intellectual world in which Mary moved. By situating her within these social networks as well as the legal framework within which she lived and worked, I am consciously writing a feminist historical account of Mary and drawing attention to an overlooked female artist.

Writing a life: Methodology

In writing this account, I also recognise my own role as a biographer constructing a life within personal and ideological frameworks.[3] I utilise the methodology of the sociologist historian Liz Stanley, whose term 'auto/biography' describes my approach here. Stanley describes 'auto/biography' as:

> [...] a term which refuses any easy distinction between biography and autobiography, instead recognising their symbiosis; and it also collects into it social science and other apparently 'objective' ways of producing and using life histories of different kinds.[4]

This approach means I am not chasing every fact about Mary and presenting it objectively. It is outside the scope of this volume. Rather, I am concentrating on her career as a professional artist who moved into archaeological work, which came about due to her relationship with

Charles Newton, first as employee and then as wife, although a wife in nineteenth-century Britain was in effect an employee, or more accurately property, of her husband.

The most extensive account of Mary is in the biographies of her father Joseph Severn and brother Walter Severn that are written by Sheila, Countess of Birkenhead, particularly her second book *Illustrious Friends* (1965). Sheila Birkenhead was married to the great grandson of Joseph Severn; her mother-in-law was Margaret Furneaux, Mary's niece and the daughter of sister Eleanor's daughter (Figure 15.2). Birkenhead drew extensively on Margaret's extensive private collection of letters and diaries, that have, for the most part, so far remained unpublished. Birkenhead comments in her second biography that her favourite of the Severn family is in fact Mary, Joseph's 'gifted daughter'.[5] Despite this, she overshadows Mary's life by that of her less talented father and brother due to their close friendship with John Keats and John Ruskin, respectively. Birkenhead draws extensively from her grandmother (in law) Eleanor Severn's diary and letters, but how accurately reported they are it is difficult to say. A more recent academic biographer of Joseph Severn, Grant Scott describes both Joseph Severn's nineteenth-century biographer William Sharp and Birkenhead's use of extracts of letters that are now in the London Metropolitan Archives as 'often transcribed inaccurately'.[6] In any case, Mary's section within *Illustrious Friends* reads as a romance with her faith

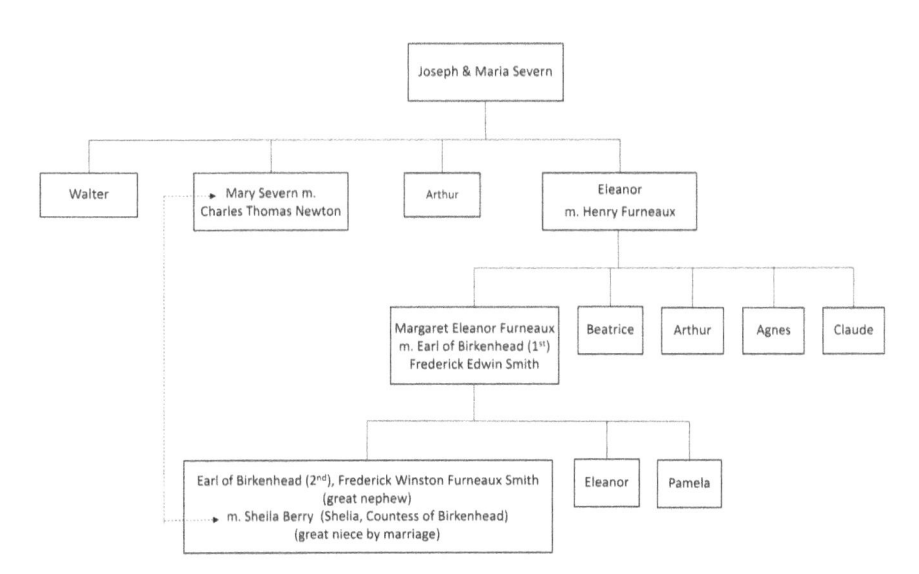

Figure 15.2 The Mary Newton family tree. Source: Author.

in God stressed, her attraction to the sardonic Newton tense and her desire for children speculated upon.

I have attempted several times to research this barely known female artist's life and then gave up for personal reasons. This chapter recognises the personal feelings that made me relinquish the research and uses that recognition for greater critical reflection in reading and constructing a woman's life. My feeling that my life was beginning to reflect Mary's, then realising that it was the other way around, made me stop my work on her. When I began researching and writing her life again, I was plunged into such grief that her husband's account of his own sorrow at her untimely death eerily echoed mine. Here I touch on how life-writing can be fraught with ambiguity and imagined meanings, even spectres, belonging to the researcher/writer rather than the subject of the writing. A researcher has a relationship with their subject. Recognition of this relationship can generate greater critical reflection and a richer study of the subject, their history and the role of historical and personal memory.

Working artist

A letter from Joseph Severn in 1842 described Mary's talent at the age of 10, writing: 'Mary has drawn some portraits of Mr Macpherson, which I really had thought were by some of the artists coming here.'[7] Mary's father Joseph Severn (1793–1879) was an artist who had practised in Rome for 20 years by the time the Severn family moved to London in 1842. He is best known for being the poet John Keats' faithful friend, as well as promoting Keats and his work after his death. The Severns were an artistic family; Mary's older brother Walter and younger brother Arthur also became artists. George Richmond (1809–1896), an old friend of Severn's from Rome, tutored Mary. Richmond was a specialist at work, principally portraiture, in pencils, watercolours and crayons, with which Mary mainly worked.[8] Deborah Cherry has pointed out that daughters in artist-families during the nineteenth century benefited not just from tuition, but:

> Most importantly they were encouraged to develop a professional attitude in contradistinction to the amateur practice which signified dependent domesticity. Artist-families provided material and psychic spaces for middle-class girls to grow into professional artists.[9]

The domestic space in which women developed depended hugely upon their family sphere and outlook in Victorian Britain, not just within artistic families.[10] The professional attitude that Mary was encouraged to take was important as by the late 1840s her father's work had become unfashionable and he had financial difficulties. The family became increasingly reliant on Mary's commissions and her brother Walter's salary.

Mary worked professionally (i.e. for an income) from around 1850. She exhibited a painting, *The Twins,* at the Royal Academy for the first time in 1852 and studied with the artist Ary Scheffer in Paris a year later.[11] An obituary of Scheffer notes his ability to break free from the classical school of art that was prominent in the early 1800s, along with fellow artists Gericault and Delacroix.[12] Beside portraiture, Scheffer painted genre and religious or poetic work. The freedom of Paris for female artists in the late nineteenth century has been well documented. At this time British women travelled to Paris to study in the studios of male artists who were 'more sympathetic' to giving access to the male aetelier's system, including life drawing, than the drawing schools and academies in Britain.[13] In the 1850s, a generation earlier, Mary may not have had access to life drawing but did have access to a much higher level of training than was available to women at this time. This training later enabled her to have an aptitude and skill for drawing ancient sculpture.

In her early career, Mary specialised in portraiture in crayon, chalk and watercolours; both the medium and the genre were considered appropriate for a female artist.[14] From 1853 she travelled from one great house to another in England and Ireland, making portraits, particularly of children. This may explain why so little of her work is in public collections and is possibly still in private hands.[15] Cherry has outlined how a system of 'matronage' worked in commissioning these portraits: the female head of a, usually aristocratic, household commissioned portraits of family members based on recommendations from other women.[16] Mary's mother Eliza (née Montgomerie) was well connected with 'Society', even if she was illegitimate and her marriage to Severn was not approved of by her guardian. From 1852, Mary's commissions kept the family financially afloat and her father from debtors' prison. In the summer of that year, Joseph Severn went into hiding to escape arrest for debt and the family moved. As soon as Mary turned 21, the lodgings for her parents and younger siblings were put into her name so creditors could not claim Severn's debts through the family home and belongings.[17]

Mary's work consisted of mixing business with pleasure as she visited clients or accompanied them on holidays, usually accompanied by one of the twins (her younger sister or brother) as a chaperone. Eleanor was, for example, with her when she was staying with Rev. Wharton Marriott, a housemaster at Eton, to make sketches of the schoolboys in

1857. During this visit, Mary made a portrait of the Duchess of Kent, Queen Victoria's mother, which the Queen recorded as being 'very good' in her journal.[18] In an example of matronage, Victoria then commissioned Mary to make portraits of her children, including the Prince of Wales, as well as copies of old masters for Prince Albert. Mary made a watercolour of Princess Beatrice (Figure 15.3), then a year old, and a sketch of Princesses Helena and Louise, for which she received 30 guineas.[19] These are still in the Royal Collection at Windsor. The royal portraits were also engraved and sold as lithographs by Richard Lane, thus bringing in more revenue.

The Severn family – Mary's brother Walter was important in establishing younger generation connections – had a large circle of friends and acquaintances including poet and barrister Arthur Munby, museum curator William Vaux and art critic John Ruskin. Although Ruskin had first met Joseph Severn in Rome, he took an interest in Mary's work and sometimes accompanied her sketching in the National Gallery. A wry caricature by Mary of herself and Ruskin drawing in September 1860 – *A Contrast in Styles* – corresponds to Walter Munby's notes from his discussion with her in November 1860:

> We were soon full in talk – about Ruskin – whom Miss S. had of late been discoursing with, and he has been copying a picture too by her side at the National Gallery. It was a head, and he couldn't do it at all, and gave it up [...].[20]

Mary had made her own friends and connections through her work and constant travel for commissions. One of the most significant was her stay with various members of the extended Anglo-Irish Palliser family in Ireland. Not only did Mary get a number of commissions from this family, she met like-minded female artists, such as Mary Palliser, who later accompanied her at the British Museum and became engaged to artist (and later Director of the National Gallery in London) Frederic Burton.[21] She also met and was influenced by the artist and illustrator Louisa Bereford, Marchioness of Waterford.[22]

Despite her success, Birkenhead implied that by 1858 Mary longed for a change, writing that she was enthusiastic when offered an opportunity to draw newly excavated sculpture at the British Museum:

> She had felt she was getting a little stale in her work lately. Since finishing her portraits of the older Princesses, she had exhibited several pictures at the Academy and had plenty of commissions, but

Figure 15.3 Princess Beatrice of Battenberg by Richard James Lane, after Ann Mary Newton (née Severn), lithograph, 1858. Courtesy National Portrait Gallery.

somehow she felt dissatisfied and restless. It would be something quite new, and she would learn a great deal about Greek art.[23]

How much of this is paraphrased from Mary's own diary is difficult to say, but significantly she accepted the commission brought to her by an old family friend and an assistant curator at the British Museum, William Vaux.

Charles Thomas Newton, art and archaeology

In 1840, after leaving Christchurch College at the University of Oxford, Charles Thomas Newton had been appointed as an assistant to Edward Hawkins, Keeper of the Department of Antiquities at the British Museum. Other assistants were Samuel Birch and William Vaux. All educated at Oxford, these young men were ambitious to reform the stagnant British Museum and antiquarianism that they saw as corrupting archaeology. Henry Wentworth Acland, another friend of Newton's from Oxford, was also in London studying surgery but with an interest in art and archaeology. John Ruskin, a fellow student at Christchurch, frequently visited the museum in the 1840s to see Newton whose 'passion for classical archaeology, so little in accord with Ruskin, gave them plenty to argue about'.[24] Despite their disagreements, while recovering from a serious illness at his parents' house in Herefordshire in 1843, Newton asked Ruskin for instruction on drawing.[25] Ruskin told Newton that he would learn more about art through drawing than the many hours he had spent at the museum gazing at antiquities.[26] The discussion between the two about drawing techniques and accurate illustration reveal how seriously Newton took making copies of sculpture, as both an art form and for archaeological accuracy.

Newton's emphasis on accuracy is further illustrated when Henry Acland, now the Lee's Reader in Anatomy at Oxford, invited him to lecture at the Oxford Art Society in 1849 and the Oxford meeting of the Archaeological Institute a year later. In a letter to Acland on yet another lecture in 1851, he refers to his request for money to buy casts to illustrate the lecture to the Archaeological Institute and commented that the amount he received was not enough to get his point across. Newton concluded that he could not deliver the lecture without adequate illustrations as he does not have 'the technical knowledge of anatomy it would require'.[27] Newton had previously worked with the artist George Scharf junior on illustrations of sculpture. (Scharf had been the official artist for Charles Fellows on the 1843 British Museum expedition to remove antiquities from Lycia in Turkey). Newton told Acland that he would send and pay for Scharf to go to Oxford as he was 'used to lecturing and preparing drawings on large scale for the lecture room'.[28] Newton's unwillingness to lecture without accurate visual aids underlay his emphasis on the importance of illustration for archaeological understanding.

Newton left the British Museum to become Vice Consul on Lesvos in 1852, excavating small sites on islands around Lesvos and Rhodes, before leading a major expedition that discovered and excavated the Mausoleum of Halicarnassos at Bodrum. Newton was one of the first excavators to use photography systematically. Newton had many friends within the contemporary British art scene such as G. F. Watts and in 1850 was painted by Watts in his fresco *The Hemicycle of Law Givers* at Lincoln's Inn Court. Even from a distance, the tall bearded figure of Newton is distinctive as Edward I, who put in place the basic statute law of England. Newton was also a juror at the 1851 Great Exhibition on 'Class XXX Sculpture, Models and Plastic Art', along with the sculptor John Gibson and designer A. W. Pugin. Although on the outer circles of the contemporary art world, he recorded his frustration with being 'overrun' by painters – George Frederic Watts, Valentine Cameron Prinsep and John Roddam Spencer Stanhope – when excavating in Halicarnassus, Turkey. Newton had in fact invited the artists on the expedition but found them of little use, bar his old friend G. F. Watts. Photography for Newton was the more exact and scientific form of recording excavations and objects than drawing and could be used to position archaeology as an area of scientific study.

Newton was pedantic as to the detail and quality of the illustrations in his first publication – *A History of Discoveries* (1863) – as evidenced by letters to Anthony Panizzi (also Antonio, the Principal Librarian of the British Museum) in 1859 – and decided to publish with the more exclusive Day & Son rather than the more popular John Murray.[29] Newton paid the same attention to illustrations for the lectures he was giving to archaeological societies in Oxford and Cambridge in the autumn of that year. However, reproducing photographs was expensive and getting the detail large enough to be seen by an audience in a lecture hall impossible in 1858 when Newton returned to Britain to give a series of lectures on his excavations. He wanted the sculptures reproduced by an artist with an eye for detail. George Scharf had been appointed Director of the new National Portrait Gallery in 1856 and so was not available for commission. His former museum colleague William Vaux suggested Mary as an artist who had a reputation for accuracy and had made copies of old masters for Prince Albert as Queen Victoria's Christmas present in 1857.

Work and marriage

It is unlikely that Mary had met Newton previously, despite having many mutual friends, as he left for the Ottoman Empire when she began her professional career as an artist visiting grand families. Newton was probably influenced to follow his former colleague Vaux's advice by his friend Ruskin's approval of Mary's work. Drawing from the antique was a principle taught at the art colleges that admitted women from the 1870s on, but it was an unusual activity for a professional female artist in 1858. Newton commissioned Mary to draw the newly unpacked sculpture from Halicarnassus at the British Museum. She was sometimes accompanied by fellow artist and friend from Ireland Mary Palliser and occasionally by Ruskin.[30] These drawings were used for Newton's lectures and publications and he inspected them all thoroughly, which Mary captured in some wry sketches poking fun at his exactness and her supposed artistic ineptitude.

From his letters it is clear that Newton was an imperious man with a caustic sense of humour but how Birkenhead describes him in *Illustrious Friends* is problematic. He is depicted as a sardonic romantic hero in the manner of Mr Rochester in *Jane Eyre*. For example:

> The door opened and he came in. He was tall and held himself well. He was forty years old and his body was spare and strong. With his stern face and unconscious air of distinction the whole impression given was one of austerity, until you noticed the rather grim lines of humour around the mouth and piercing eyes.[31]

The fanciful romantic description of their courtship in this biography overshadows both the significant work that Mary carried out for Newton and undermines the dilemma that his proposal of marriage gave her. Before he returned to the diplomatic service, Newton proposed marriage to Mary, but – according to Birkenhead's reading of her journal – she felt she could not accept as she was the principal breadwinner for her family.[32]

Marriage would mean no economic independence for Mary as her earnings would go to her husband and any lease in her name would also become her husband's. Her family were reliant on Mary's income and the lease for their house had been in her name since the day she turned 21. Mary would have been well aware of this, particularly as the rights of married women (or lack of them) was being much debated in the 1850s and 1860s, including by those she knew such as Ruskin and Walter Munby.[33] It is within this context that Ruskin delivers his lecture 'Of Queen's Gardens' on the role of the wife within marriage in 1865; now seen as conservative but at the time considered radical since it argued for the moral influence of women to be recognised and cultivated. The first Married Women's Property Act, allowing women some ownership of property and right to their own income, was not passed until 1870. In addition to the economic and legal issues surrounding marriage for a working woman, there was also the issue of creative independence. Marriage would bring a 'dramatic change in life-style' for Mary, especially as she relied for commissions on visits to families (which would no longer be possible) and lived at home where her mother ran the household, rather than conforming to the domestic duties presumed of a wife.[34]

After spending 1860 as Consul in Rome, that is the official representative of the British government in the then Papal state, Newton was appointed in a new post as the Keeper of the Department of Greek and Roman Antiquities. Through various contacts and connections, including Ruskin and Richmond, Mary's father Joseph Severn was appointed Consul in Newton's place by the Foreign Office, despite being much older than the required age for a diplomatic appointment. This meant that Severn could support himself and his family. Mary married Newton on 27 April 1861 and was now outside the artist family nucleus. Deborah Cherry has painted a damning picture of Newton's marriage with Mary, which she says was 'accompanied by censure of her professional practice, criticism of her work and that of her teacher [George Richmond]'. Cherry contends that Severn gave up her professional practice in watercolours and took up oil painting, as well as mainly producing drawings for her husband's lectures and publications 'which were valued less for their artistic merit than for their correctness'.[35] This criticism appears to be entirely based on Birkenhead's description, rather than looking at Mary's work after her marriage, and is problematic. There is no doubt that women were expected to rearrange their lives and careers (if they had one) after marriage as well as change their 'sense of self', while husbands were not. However, if Mary was looking for a change in direction, rather than the constant movement in the ambiguous role of guest and employee as well as the responsibility for providing for her family, she got one.

Mary did illustrate her husband's editions of archaeological works, though much of this seems to have been based on material she had made for his lectures in 1858 (Figure 15.4). After her marriage Mary changed both the medium she used and her genre. She stepped away from the accepted feminine practice of portraiture and into genre painting and archaeological illustration. She continued to work in watercolours but also created more work in oils. One of the few pieces of her work in a public collection is a self-portrait which was exhibited at the Royal Academy in 1863 and is now in the collection of the National Portrait Gallery, having been bequeathed there by Newton on his death in 1895 (Figure 15.5). Mary depicts herself in artistic dress holding a leather folio of drawings looking straight at the observer. When it was exhibited at the

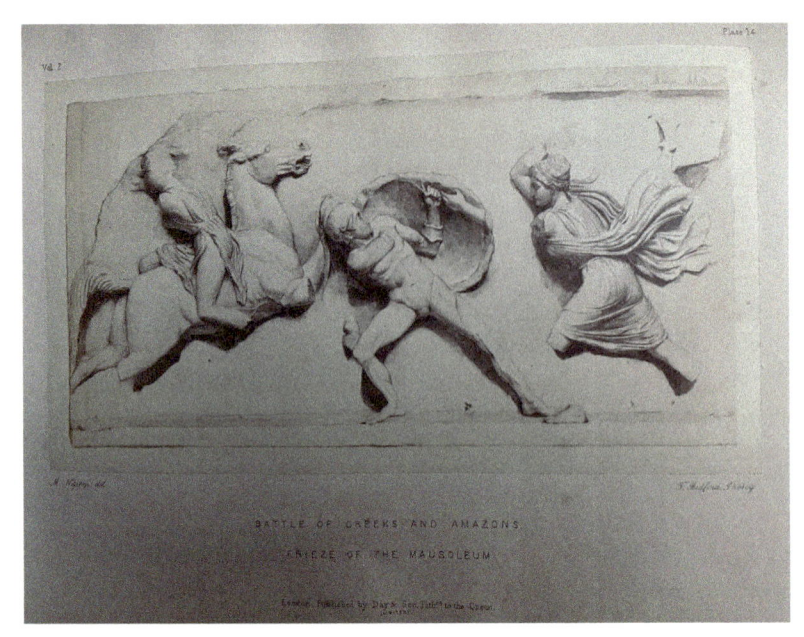

Figure 15.4 Mary Severn Newton, Amazons and Greeks - Frieze of the Mausoleum of Halicarnassos, Travels and Discoveries. Vol. II (1865), Plate 14.

Figure 15.5 Mary Severn Newton, Self-portrait (1863). Courtesy National Portrait Gallery.

Royal Academy in 1863, it attracted a positive response from *The Times*, which described it 'as something more than a graceful portrait of herself':

> Mrs Newton's head is one of the best pieces of colour among the portraiture of the year, and is excellently drawn besides. The same lady's *Elaine* (337), though hung too high for fair judgement, seems to have both beauty of face and grace of form.[36]

The review listed Mary among several female artists who 'should write R.A. after her name' – women could not then be members of the Royal Academy. *Elaine* was an Arthurian subject based on Tennyson's *Idylls of the King* and as such was evidence of new work in a historical genre, possibly pre-Raphaelite influenced.

Travel and archaeology

Mary accompanied Newton on his travels, including two trips to Rome in which time she visited her father and copied sculpture and painting while Newton was acquiring antiquities for the British Museum. Soon after Joseph Severn took up his position in Rome, his wife Eliza Severn died in France on her way to join him. Mary organised her mother's burial and gravestone in France with little help from her hapless father. Shortly after, Joseph Severn became embroiled in a complicated personal and political scandal in which Newton had to get involved and for which Mary admonished her father.[37] After dealing with her father's continual financial and then diplomatic (in all senses of the word) problems, marriage to the exacting Newton would certainly have been different for Mary.

In 1863 Newton and Mary went on a three-month tour of Asia Minor and Greece in order to assist him with writing *Travels and Discoveries in the Levant* (1865). Mary's companion for drawing, while her husband inspected new excavations on their trip, was a young Gertrude Jekyll, whose father was a friend of the couple. Jekyll had recently attended the South Kensington School of Art, later exhibiting paintings at the Royal Academy and the Society of Female Artists. She is better known today for her garden design and collaboration with the architect Edwin Lutyens. A few years after this travel, Jekyll met and became good friends with Barbara Bodichon, an early campaigner for women's rights and suffrage. This connection no doubt influenced her design of the Godalming branch banner of the National Union of Women's Suffrage Societies.[38] With friends like Jekyll, it is likely that Mary would have been interested in, or at least informed about, the growing political movements to reform the position of women in society.

Jekyll kept a journal, which was illustrated by lively watercolour sketches and pencil drawings by herself and Mary of their trip.[39] She records that on 13 October 1863 they travelled to Trieste via Paris, Munich and Vienna where they explored museums copying art and met Newton's curatorial colleagues. Mary and Jekyll drew throughout the journey, even on the boat where the Captain got a group of Cretan men to sit for them. They sailed to Izmir (then known as Smyrna) via the Cycladic Islands and on reaching Turkey travelled by train to meet John Turtle Wood, the engineer who had just began excavating at Ephesus. The party then spent most of November in Rhodes where Newton helped Alfred Biliotti with his excavations at Kameiros, while Mary and Gertrude visited 'native families' and the women's part of Turkish houses.[40] Both Biliotti and the Pasha of Rhodes took an interest in their drawing and sent them Turkish men as sitters.

On 23 November they moved to Istanbul where, aside from visiting scholarly contacts in the city, Newton looked at manuscripts in the Library of Seraglio and Mary was put to work drawing a bas-relief of an Amazon in the Istanbul museum, which Newton thought belonged to the Mausoleum (Figure 15.6).[41] They also drew from the sights around Istanbul, such as St Sophia and Scutari, and visited the daughters of an Ottoman official and a black slave woman in a Turkish house. In the 'Orient' their gender meant they acquired access to the harem (or women's quarters), one of the 'defining symbols of the Orient for Europeans'.[42] By mid-December they were in Athens where they were shown round the Acropolis and recent excavations at the Theatre of Dionysos by the historian George Finlay, who was about to publish his cutting-edge *History of Greece*, a history from the Roman conquest to the present day of 1864.

Newton's *Travels and Discoveries* owes much to the reproduction of the photographs made of Mary's drawings of ancient sculpture and gives a glimpse of the high-quality illustrations she made for Newton's lectures. Newton used a combination of etchings, by Mary's brothers Walter and Arthur, of photographs taken by Dominic Ellis Colnaghi with original drawings by Mary to illustrate the book. The lengthy excursion across Greece and Turkey gave Mary new subjects and experiences to paint and it is likely, had she lived, that she would have accompanied her husband on more of his journeys. The loan watercolour in the Tate Collection by her is a 'View of Naples' from her visit there with Newton. Jekyll spent much time with the Newtons after their return to London, copying paintings at the National Gallery and elsewhere with Mary. Mary's sense

Figure 15.6 Mary Severn Newton, Fragment of Frieze of the Mausoleum Bas-relief Amazon in the Museum of the Seraglio, Travels and Discoveries. Vol. II (1865), Plate I.

of humour is captured in caricatures of her life with Newton: a few are reprinted in Birkenhead and more are described by Betty Massingham in her biography of Gertrude Jekyll. An example Massingham provides from an exhibition of Mary's work (alongside Max Beerbohm's caricatures) in 1922 reads 'C.T.N. and M.N. become so wise. He has taught her to read Greek' (Frame III, 14.).[43] Mary is poking fun at herself and her new knowledge will, of course, be useful to Newton, but being taught to read Greek by her husband suggests he respected her intelligence. Even women with access to more education and books than most were not encouraged to learn Greek; something Elizabeth Barrett Browning satirises in *Aurora Leigh* (1857) when Aurora's cousin (and suitor) Romney finds her book with 'lady's Greek' written in it, which he compares to 'witchcraft' (Book 2, 75–80).

Descriptions of the paintings that were unfinished at the time of her death two years later, and posthumously exhibited at the Dudley Gallery in 1866, give a glimpse of her new direction and the influence of travel upon her work. Arthur Munby, a friend of the Severn family, describes going to the Newtons' house shortly after Mary's death and looking at her last drawings: 'sketches taken in the East – of Syrian women, of Scutari burial grounds – lovely all of them'.[44] *The Times* reviewed the Dudley Gallery exhibition and commented on the 'eastern drawings of the late and lamented Mrs Charles Newton', describing the depiction of 'Levantine Lady' and the 'Jewess of Smyrna' as 'leaving nothing unsupplied but what helps the imagination to the desired impressions of beauty and sorrow.'[45] Mary arguably took her career in a new direction, not just assisting her husband with his work, and made archaeological illustration – for publication and lectures – a professional art practice that other female artists would continue.

Speculating on fertility

Sally Festing's biography of Gertrude Jekyll, like Deborah Cherry in *Painting Women*, uncritically quotes from Birkenhead's *Illustrious Friends*, repeating the concern around the 'stress' of Mary's marriage. Festing writes, closely following Birkenhead, that 'obsessed by the suspicion that she might never be able to bear a child, she [Mary] was sublimating her fears in work'.[46] Compare Birkenhead, who was apparently drawing on Mary's letters to her sister: 'She worked all the harder to keep the miserable thought away that perhaps she might never have a child.' It is true that as a married woman Mary would have been unusual, since childless marriages comprised only 8.6% of all marriages in 1874.[47]

It is likely given her friends and their conversations, such as one recorded about Darwin by Arthur Munby in 1859, that she would have been aware of the idea that women performing cognitive work affected menstruation and the ability to conceive. This idea became popular in the mid-nineteenth century and by 1873, Herbert Spencer was using a mixture of Darwinism, economics and racial ideology to warn of the danger that highly cultured 'Anglo-Saxon' women with 'high-class brains' were evolving beyond motherhood.[48] Not only does this argument outline the supposed danger affecting the 'race', with all the racial and sexist prejudices implied, it also underlines how motherhood and women were perceived.

I stopped working on Mary around ten years ago, as I began to imagine her as haunted by the faces of the children she had drawn, particularly the winsome portrait of Princess Beatrice that I had examined at the Royal Archives in Windsor. I had enough self-awareness to recognise that my own involuntary childlessness – I was about to start fertility treatment that would eventually lead to IVF – made me obsess about Mary's imagined imaginary children. Mary may have had difficulties, even miscarriages, but in my head I projected my 'shame' around being 'barren' on her own situation.[49] It has been recognised that 'exposure to the rhetorical imperatives of published life-writing can influence the form and content of personal narratives'.[50] The reverse can happen too. I realised that I could not write or present on Mary until I had dealt with my own issues around not being biologically able to have a baby. This aspect of Mary's life has overshadowed her position as a working female artist following a new direction in her work at a time when to do that posed considerable difficulties. Looking back, I also realise how much involuntary childlessness, or infertility (whether real or imagined in Mary's case) is still the subject of myths and moralising whether in the nineteenth century or more recently.

An Attic headstone

Mary Severn Newton died at her home on Gower Street on 2 January 1866 of measles, which she had caught from a little boy whose portrait she had been painting. Measles could then be deadly. Newton was held partially responsible for Mary's early death by the Severn family as she was apparently exhausted with both her work and keeping his household. Birkenhead describes Newton as driving Mary 'as he drove himself, but she was more delicately made'.[51] She also stresses how laid down Mary was by her inability to have a child. Newton's behaviour was verified by Arthur Munby, who had been attracted to Mary and was a close friend of her brother, who described Newton as 'spoiling' Mary with hard work.[52] Of course, the Severns and Munby may not have approved of Newton teaching Mary Greek or encouraging intellectual pursuits. Her father Joseph Severn wrote that 'Mary was my favourite and gifted daughter and almost from her infancy had been my artistic companion and ever since my greatest pride.'[53] Mary had provided her family with a home both before and, to some extent, by her marriage. Newton himself was devastated and went to Bournemouth, writing to his friend Acland that he needed a 'change' since his eyes filled Mary's usual chair 'with her form'.[54]

Whatever the truth of Mary's marriage, her early death shattered a promising career as well as a lively young woman. Queen Victoria recorded her shock in her diary and sent a letter of condolence. Mary was buried in Kensal Green Cemetery with a grave that was modelled on, and is rumoured to contain, an ancient Athenian headstone.[55] Newton was later buried in the same plot in 1895. The gravestone now lies in several pieces on the ground, or it did when I last visited it in 2015 (Figure 15.7). The deep sorrow Newton felt is apparent in a letter on the death of Henry Acland's wife in 1878; his words to his friend are a moving testimony of grief:

> I have read with very great sorrow the announcement that terrible stroke which fell upon me twelve years ago has fallen on you too. Too, too well I know what is before you, the vain strivings to take [solace] in a fathomless sea of grief, the breaking up of long deep watered associations; the bleak and dreary experiences which are within the heart till it struggles into a sort of maimed and blighted life like a tree transplanted into an ungenial climate.[56]

A precursor of this account of Mary's life was given for me at a seminar at UCL by my friend and colleague Dr Amara Thornton in January 2015 as I was too ill with my own grief to deliver it. Having psychologically accepted that I was physically infertile and adopting a little boy, I was unexpectedly pregnant when I accepted the invitation to give a lecture on Mary Severn Newton's contribution to the visual history of archaeology in nineteenth-century Britain. I had expected to give the lecture heavily pregnant, but my baby was born early, at 32 weeks, and died eight days later. Bizarrely, perhaps, I still chose to write the lecture and give it to someone I trusted to present it. When I wrote out that quote from Charles Newton, I felt every word of it.

Figure 15.7 Photograph of the gravestone for Mary Severn Newton and Charles Newton in Kensal Green Cemetery. Taken in 2015 by Debbie Challis.

Looking back and revisiting Mary's life from a very different emotional place, I have tried to think about her life through an alternative intellectual and historical lens. For example, giving birth to a daughter in 2016, a year after writing that lecture, I recognised that to me, my daughter at around 10 months looked like Mary's drawing of Princess Beatrice. I have had to reflect on my own experiences in order to think about this artist in a different way.[57] My own struggles with my biology, namely my inability to conceive and then the neonatal death of my baby, and the multiple identities involved in motherhood (both being a woman without and then with children), has made me question the simple narrative construction of Mary's childlessness and marital misery. I positioned Mary and her work within a wider network of relationships and historical context, approaching her biography from the critical position as a feminist historian and biographer.

Mary Severn Newton was an artist, not an archaeologist in either a nineteenth-century or a contemporary sense. However, her work is still hung on both sides of the bust of her husband in a corner of the British Museum and contributed to the nineteenth-century visual culture that was influenced by new archaeological interpretations of the ancient world. She was a precursor of the female artists who worked as, or alongside, archaeologists from the late nineteenth century and early twentieth century. Her work moved in a new direction after she met Charles Newton, with sketches made from her travels to Italy and the Ottoman Empire as well as the exhibition of more imaginative works in oils. Her early death leaves questions about where her work might have led. The circles Mary moved in and the friends she had also point to an interest in greater freedoms for women. Newton himself was later involved in the Lectures for Women on Greek at Kings' College London in the 1880s and supported the early careers of budding classical archaeologists Jane Harrison and Eugenie Sellars.[58] It is possible that Mary and the memory of her influenced Newton, who had a more progressive attitude than many of his peers. It is time to bring Mary out from the shadows of her husband, her brother and father. Mary Severn Newton was a working female artist with an original creative vision, who contributed to archaeology and the art world in mid-nineteenth-century Britain.

Notes

1   Alicia Foster, *Tate Women Artists* (London: Tate Publishing, 2004), 52.
2   Amara Thornton, *Archaeologists in Print: Publishing for the People* (London: UCL Press, 2018), 6. See also Thornton's 'Chapter Three: The women who did', 48–74.

3   Liz Stanley, *The Auto/biographical I: The Theory and Practice of Feminist Auto/biography* (Manchester: Manchester University Press, 1992), 10.
4   Stanley, *The Auto/biographical I*, 127.
5   Sheila Birkenhead, *Illustrious Friends: The Story of Joseph Severn and his son Arthur* (London: Hamish Hamilton, 1965), xiii.
6   Grant F. Scott, ed., *Joseph Severn: Letters and memoirs* (Aldershot: Ashgate, 2005), xxi.
7   Joseph Severn, 'Letter to Elizabeth Severn, 10–12 January 1842', in Scott, *Joseph Severn*, 402, n.100.
8   Birkenhead, *Illustrious Friends*, 114–5; Derek Hudson, *Munby: A man of two worlds: The life and diaries of Arthur J. Munby 1828–1910* (London: Abacus, 1974), 33.
9   Deborah Cherry, *Painting Women: Victorian women artists* (London: Routledge, 1993), 21.
10 Philippa Levine, *Feminist Lives in Victorian England: Private roles and public commitment* (Oxford: Basil Blackwell, 1990) 9.
11 Scott, *Joseph Severn*, 'Letter to Elizabeth Severn (No. 126), 22 October 1853', 454.
12 'Facts and thoughts about Ary Scheffer', *The Crayon*, 6.11 (1859): 340.
13 Frances Borzello, *A World of Our Own: Women as artists* (London: Thames and Hudson, 2000) 131.
14 Cherry, *Painting Women*, 21.
15 Rowena Fowler, 'Newton [née Severn], (Ann) Mary (1832–1866)', *Oxford Dictionary of National Biography*. https://doi.org/10.1093/ref:odnb/20048.
16 Cherry, *Painting Women*, 103.
17 Birkenhead, *Illustrious Friends*, 117–8.
18 Queen Victoria's Journal, vol. 44 (5 November 1857): 86: http://www.queenvictoriasjournals.org/search/displayItem.do?FormatType=fulltextimgsrc&QueryType=articles&ResultsID=3251858359925&filterSequence=0&PageNumber=1&ItemNumber=1&ItemID=qvj09062&volumeType=PSBEA. Accessed 10 July 2021.
19 Delia Millar, *The Victorian Watercolours and Drawings in the Collection of her Majesty the Queen*, Vol. 2 (London: Philip Wilson, 1995), 797–8.
20 Hudson, *Munby*, 84.
21 Birkenhead, *Illustrious Friends*, 116.
22 Patricia Butler, 'A Victorian watercolourist', *Irish Arts Review Yearbook* 10 (1994): 157–62.
23 Birkenhead, *Illustrious Friends*, 125.
24 Tim Hilton, *John Ruskin: The early years 1819–1859* (London: Yale University Press, 1991), 76.
25 Balliol Manuscripts 414, Balliol College, Oxford, Ruskin MSS. John Ruskin, to Charles Newton. January 1843, f. 2.
26 Balliol Manuscripts 414, Balliol College Oxford, Ruskin to Newton, January 1843, f. 2.
27 Bodleian Library, Oxford. MSS. Acland 64, Letters to H. W. Acland 1847–66, Newton to Acland, 29 January 1851, f. 97.
28 Bodleian Library, Oxford. MSS. Acland 64, Letters to H. W. Acland 1878–79, Newton to Acland, 29 January 1851, f. 99.
29 British Library, London. Add. MSS Panizzi 36720, Newton, Charles: Letter to A. Panizzi, 21 August 1859, f. 108.
30 Birkenhead, *Illustrious Friends*, 128.
31 Birkenhead, *Illustrious Friends*, 126.
32 Birkenhead, *Illustrious Friends*, 130.
33 Levine, *Feminist Lives*, 114–5.
34 Pat Jalland, *Women, Marriage and Politics 1860–1914* (Oxford: Oxford University Press, 1988), 101.
35 Cherry, *Painting Women*, 39.
36 'Exhibition of the Royal Academy', *The Times*, 9 April 1863 (25467), 12, Col. E.
37 Some of this is told in Severn, ed., *Scott* (2005), 494–6.
38 Sally Festing, *Gertrude Jekyll* (London: Penguin, 1991), 81; Elizabeth Crawford, *Art and Suffrage: A biographical dictionary of suffrage artists* (London: Francis Boutle Publishers, 2018), 133.
39 Gertrude Jekyll's journal is reprinted in Francis Jekyll, *Gertrude Jekyll. A memoir* (London: Jonathan Cape, 1934), 39.
40 Jekyll, *Gertrude Jekyll*, 48.
41 Jekyll, *Gertrude Jekyll*, 65.
42 Nicholas Tromans, 'Harem and home', in *The Lure of the East: British Orientalist painting* ed. Nicholas Tromans (London: Tate Publishing, 2008), 128.

43 Betty Massingham, *Miss Jekyll: Portrait of a great gardener* (London: Country Life, 1966), 33.
44 Hudson, *Munby*, 216.
45 *The Times*, 9 April 1866 (25467), 12 Col. E.
46 Festing, *Gertrude Jekyll,* 34; Birkenhead, *Illustrious Friends*, 157.
47 Levine, *Feminist Lives*, 146.
48 Robin E. Jensen, *Infertility: Tracing the history of a transformative term* (Pennsylvania: Pennysylvania State University Press, 2016), 48.
49 Rochelle Ratner, 'Introduction', in *Bearing Life: Women's writing on childlessness* (New York: The Feminist Press, 2001), 137.
50 Antonia Harbus, 'Exposure to life-writing as an impact on autobiographical memory', *Memory Studies* 4 (2011): 209.
51 Birkenhead, *Illustrious Lives*, 157.
52 Hudson, *Munby*, 124.
53 Keats' House Collection, London Metropolitan Archives, K/MS/02/076, Severn Family Manuscripts 1821–1879, Letter from Joseph Severn to Maria Severn, 8 February 1866, f. 63.
54 Bodleian Library Oxford, MS. Acland, Letters to H. W. Acland 1847–66, Charles Newton, 11 January 1866, f. 104–5.
55 This rumour was told to the author by the chair of the Friends of Kensal Green Cemetery in 2008.
56 Bodleian Library Oxford, MS. Acland 84, Letters to H. W. Acland 1878–79, Charles Newton, 29 October 1878, ff. 52–53.
57 Stanley, *The Auto/biographical I.*, 243.
58 Annabel Robinson, *The Life and Work of Jane Ellen Harrison* (Oxford: Oxford University Press, 2002), 55; Stephen L. Dyson, *Eugenie Sellars Strong: Portrait of an archaeologist* (London: Duckworth, 2004), 35.

Bibliography

Birkenhead, Sheila, *Illustrious Friends: The Story of Joseph Severn and his Son Arthur* (London: Hamish Hamilton, 1965).
Borzello, Frances, *A World of Our Own: Women as artists* (London: Thames and Hudson, 2000).
Butler, Patricia, 'A Victorian watercolourist', *Irish Arts Review Yearbook*, 10 (1994): 157–62.
Challis, Debbie, '"The duty of truth": The friendship and influence between John Ruskin and Charles Newton', *The Ruskin Review and Bulletin*, 5.1 (2009): 5–15.
Challis, Debbie, *From the Harpy Tomb to the Wonders of Ephesus: British archaeologists in the Ottoman Empire 1840–1880* (London: Duckworth, 2008).
Cherry, Deborah, *Painting Women: Victorian women artists* (London: Routledge, 1993).
Crawford, Elizabeth, *Art and Suffrage: a biographical dictionary of suffrage artists,* (London: Francis Boutle Publishers, 2018).
Dyson, Stephen L., *Eugenie Sellars Strong: Portrait of an archaeologist* (London: Duckworth, 2004).
'Exhibition of the Royal Academy', *The Times*, 9 April 1863, 12, Col. E.
'Exhibition at the Dudley Gallery', *The Times*, 9 April 1866.
'Facts and thoughts about Ary Scheffer', *The Crayon*, 6.11 (1859): 340–5.
Festing, Sally, *Gertrude Jekyll* (London: Penguin, 1991).
Foster, Alicia, *Tate Women Artists* (London: Tate Publishing, 2004).
Fowler, Rowena, 'Newton [née Severn], (Ann) Mary (1832–1866)', *Oxford Dictionary of National Biography*. https://doi.org/10.1093/ref:odnb/20048.
Gould, V. F., *G. F. Watts. The Last Great Victorian* (London: Yale University Press, 2004).
Harbus, Antonia, 'Exposure to life-writing as an impact on autobiographical memory', *Memory Studies*, 4 (2011): 206–20.
Hilton, Tim, *John Ruskin. The Early Years 1819–1859* (London: Yale University Press, 1991).
Hudson, Derek, *Munby: A man of two worlds: The life and diaries of Arthur J. Munby 1828–1910* (London: Abacus, 1974).
Jalland, Pat, *Women, Marriage and Politics 1860–1914* (Oxford: Oxford University Press, 1988).
Jekyll, Francis, *Gertrude Jekyll. A Memoir* (London: Jonathan Cape, 1934)
Jensen, Robin E., *Infertility: Tracing the history of a transformative term* (Pennsylvania: Pennsylvania State University Press, 2016).

Levine, Philippa, *Feminist Lives in Victorian England: Private roles and public commitment* (Oxford: Basil Blackwell, 1990).
Massingham, Betty, *Miss Jekyll. Portrait of a great gardener* (London: Country Life, 1966).
Millar, Delia, *The Victorian Watercolours and Drawings in the Collection of Her Majesty the Queen*, vol. 2 (London: Philip Wilson, 1995).
Newton, Charles, *A History of Discoveries at Halicarnassus, Cnidus and Branchidae* (London: Day & Son, 1863).
Newton, Charles, *Travels and Discoveries in the Levant* (London: Day & Son, 1865).
Queen Victoria's Journal, vol. 44 (5 November 1857). Accessed 10 July 2021. www.queenvictoriasjournals.org.
Ratner, Rochelle, 'Introduction', in *Bearing Life: Women's writing on childlessness* (New York: The Feminist Press, 2001).
Robinson, Annabel, *The Life and Work of Jane Ellen Harrison* (Oxford: Oxford University Press, 2002).
Scott, Grant F., ed., *Joseph Severn: Letters and memoirs* (Aldershot: Ashgate, 2005).
Scott, Grant F., 'Writing Keats's last days: Severn, Sharp, and romantic biography', *Studies in Romanticism*, 42.1 (2003): 3–26.
Stanley, Liz, *The Auto/biographical I: The theory and practice of feminist auto/biography* (Manchester: Manchester University Press, 1992).
Thornton, Amara, *Archaeologists in Print: Publishing for the people* (London: UCL Press, 2018).
Tromans, Nicholas, 'Harem and home', in *The Lure of the East: British Orientalist painting*, ed., Nicholas Tromans (London: Tate Publishing, 2008), 128–37.

Index

Page numbers in italics are figures; with 't' are tables.

Acland, Henry Wentworth 388, 398
Agassiz, Louis 30, *32*, *38*, 39
Allberry, Charles 201, 202
Alma-Tadema, Sir Lawrence 187, 194–5, *194*
American School of Classical Studies at Athens 365
Ancient Times (Breasted) 99, 102–3
Anthes, Rudolf 56–7, *57–9*, 62
Anver (horse) 129, 130, 132, 133–5, 136–7, 143
anxiety 4–5
archaeobiography 11
archaeological dimension, dig writing 155, *157*, 158–63, *159*, *162*
archival research 34–9, *35*, *38*, 111–12, 282
Archives of European Archaeology (AREA) 8
AREA (Archives of European Archaeology) 25, 26
Ashby, Thomas 365
Athanasi, Giovanni d' 288–9
Audouze, Françoise 334
autobiography 4, 5, 7, 382
    and EILs 120–2, 141

Babelon, Ernest 242
Bahn, Paul 357
Baines, John 46–7
Ball, Terry 172
Bardo Museum (Tunis) 237, 240, 244, 245, 247, 250, 254
Battershill, Ann 171
Bayet, Charles 250, 252
BBC 165
Beatrice, Princess of Battenberg 386, *387*, 397
Beazley, Sir John (J. D.) 359, 365
Bernal, J. D. 316, 318
Bersu, Gerhard 303, 313
Bielefield School 46
Biliotti, Sir Alfred 354
biographical encyclopaedias 6
biographic illusion 33–4
biography 2, 154–5, 184, 215–17
    and archival research 34–9, *35*, *38*
    definition 382
    and history 74–5
    and narrative 76–7
    and science studies 25–33, *31–2*, 39–40, *40*
        archival research 34–9, *35*, *38*
        previous scholarship 33–4

Birch, Samuel 285, 293, 388
Birkenhead, Sheila, Countess of Birkenhead 383, 386–7, 391, 397–8
    Illustrious Friends 383–4, 390, 396
Bissing, Baron Friedrich Wilhelm von 50–1, 54–5, 56, 57, 77
Bloor, David 345–6
Bordy (engineer) 245
Bosanquet, Robert Carr 359–60, 368
botany *see* Falconer, Hugh
Boucher de Perthes 269, 270
Bourdieu, Pierre 33–4, 345
Brand-Hollis, Thomas 354, 366
Breasted, James Henry 9, 92, 93–8
    early fund-raising in Egyptology 93–8, *93–4*, *97*
    fund-raising in Near Eastern research 98–102, *101*
    Oriental Institute 110–11
    and multidisciplinary studies 104–7, *106*
    plan for 102–4
Breuil, Henri 334, 338–9, 341–2, 346
    and Laming-Emperaire 342–3
British School at Athens 79, 356, 359–60, 363–4
    students 364–5
British School at Rome 222, 365, 368
Brodrick, Mary 363
Bronze Age Aegean 356–7
Browning, Elizabeth Barrett 396
Brown, Judith M. 74
Bryusov, Aleksandr 318
Budge, Wallis 185

Cagnat, René 240, 242, 244, 245, 246, 251
Calvert, Frank 357
Cambon, Paul 240
Cambridge University 366
    Egyptology 184–5
        Thompson archive 185–6
        Herbert Thompson donations 202–4
    see also Fitzwilliam Museum
Capp, Fiona 299
Carnegie, Andrew 95
Carr, Lydia, *Tessa Verney Wheeler* 10–11
Carruthers, William 48
Carswell, John 169
Carton, Louis 244–5, 247, 248, 249–52

INDEX   405

Cautley, Sir Proby 266, 268
Champollion, François 290, 353
Charles-Picard, Gilbert 234, 254
Charmes, Xavier 240, 243
Cheesman, G. L. 219
Cheesman, G. L. (Leonard) 219, 368
Cherry, Deborah 384, 385, 391
Childe, Vere Gordon 9, 299–300, *302*, 307, *314*
　death of 318
　surveillance files 301–4, *304*, 319–20
　　1917 9, 307–9, *309*
　　1919-1922 309–10
　　1930s 311–13
　　World War II 313–14, *315*
　　post World War II 314–17
　　later political life 317–19
　　as sources 305–7
Cockerell, Douglas 197–8
Cohen, Getzel 361, 363
Collective Biography of Archaeology in the Pacific project 16
collective memory 122, 124
Collingwood, R. G. (Robin) 215, 220, 222–3, 224
colonialism, and France 234, 237–8, 253
Communist Party of Great Britain (CPGB) 299, 304, *304*, 305–7, 308, 310, 312, 314–16, *315*, 318
Conkey, Meg, *The Structural Analysis of Paleolithic Art* 337
Cook, A. B. 366
Corbett, Dennis 169
Cornford, Francis 366
Cornford, John Rupert 366
Corvo, Baron (Frederick William Rolfe) 359
Crausz, Dr F. 289–90
critical approaches 4
Crum, Walter Ewing Crum 184, 189–91, 192, 198, 201–2, 203

Daniel, Glyn 318, 356
　The Origins and Growth of Archaeology 353
Darwin, Charles 266, 270–1, 274, 366, 397
　on Falconer's death 272, 273
Davies, Philip T. 307
Dawkins, Richard M. 359–60, 365
Dawson, Warren, *Who Was Who in Egyptology* 6
Delattre, Alfred-Louis 233–5, 253–5
　author's approach to 235–6
　in Carthage 237–41, 249–50
　　and the organisation of research 240–1
　　conflict with Gauckler 238–9, 241, 242–5, 250–1
　　and Gauckler's removal 250–3
　　importance to archaeology of Carthage 236–7
　　death 253–4
　　threat to museum 245–7, 250
Desor, Édouard 9, 26, *31*, *38*, 39, 75, 184
diaries 5, 34, 36–7
　author's as reflexivity 331–3, 347
　excerpts 333–45
　Édouard Desor's 38, *38*
　see also dig writing
Díaz-Andreu, Margarita 283

Dictionary of British Classicists (*DBC*) 361, 364
dig writing 153–5
　dimensions and sources 154–7, *157*
　and the history of archaeology 172–4, *173*
　Tell es-Sultan 157–8
　　archaeological dimension 158–63, *159*, *162*
　　emotional dimension 170–2
　　social dimension 163–70, *165*, *168*
dimensions
　and dig writing 155–6, *157*
　see also archaeological dimension; emotional dimension; social dimension
Disney, John 354–5, *355*, 368
Dorrell, Peter 166
Dreyfus Affair 248–9
Dutt, Rajani Palme 308, 310
Dvořák, Max 77–8, 83

Edwards, Amelia 186, 204, 363
　A Thousand Miles up the Nile 1
ego documents 120
Egypt Exploration Fund (EEF)
　and Herbert Thompson 189, 193, 205
　and T. E. Peet 123, 124–5, 126–8, 129, 133
Egypt Exploration Society (EES) (formerly EEF) 119, 137–8, 139, *140*, 141
Egyptian Labour Corps (ELC) 125
Egyptological inaugural lectures (EILs) 119, 120–2, 141
Egyptology
　English/British 186, 363
　German 62–4
　　and biography 46–8
　　primary sources 56–62, *57–60*
　　scholarship and politics 45–6, 48–51
　　Steindorff list 51–6, *51–3*
　and South Wales 357–9, *358*
　see also Breasted, James Henry; Leemans, Conrad; Peet, Thomas Eric; Thompson, Sir Herbert
Ellingson, Mary Ross 81
emotional dimension, dig writing 155, *157*, 170–2
Endesfelder, Erika 50
Erman, Adolf 133, 138, 190
Erxleben, James 290–1
Evans, Sir Arthur 356, 360
Evans, Sir John 266, 269

Fagg, William 316–17
Fahmy, Khaled 125, 136
Falconer, Hugh 265–6, 274–5
　early life and work at British East India Company 267–9, *267*
　return to Europe 269–71
　death 271–4
Farge, Arlette 36
Festing, Sally 396
fiction 368
Fitzwilliam Museum (Cambridge) 365
　Egyptian artefacts 185, 359
　and Herbert Thompson 193, *194*
　recording donors to 354–6
　and Winifred Lamb 361, 363

406　LIFE-WRITING IN THE HISTORY OF ARCHAEOLOGY

Flecker, James Elroy 359
Fleck, Francis Le Sueur 291
Fowler, George Herbert 198, 201
France
  and colonialism 234, 237–8, 253
  education and the École Normale 240–1, 253
  separation of church and state 248–50, 252, 253, 254
Franken, Henk 161, *162*, 168, 171
Freeman, Philip 215, 221
Frere, Sheppard 213, 215, 220, 225
Fry, Roger 5
Fulbrook, Mary 120, 137

Gange, David 48–9
Gardiner, Sir Alan 122, 123, 133, 137, 138–9, 143
  and Herbert Thompson 192, 203
Gardner, Ernest 129, 359, 360
Gardner Wilkinson, Sir John 286, 357, *358*, 359
Garstang, John 123, 123t
Gates, Frederick T. 96–7, 98, 102
Gathercole, Peter 317
Gauckler, Paul 233–5, 253–5
  career successes 248
  in Carthage 238, 241
  conflict with Delattre 238–9, 241, 242–5, 250–2
  and Delattre's museum 245–7, 250
  as director of the Tunisian Antiquities Service 245
  importance to archaeology of Carthage 237
  letter attacking Catholics 249
  removal 250–3
Germany *see* Egyptology, German
Ginzburg, Carlo 62, 75, 83
Givens, Douglas R. 7, 154, 183, 215, 216, 255
Glanville, Stephen 192, 195, 204–5
Goodwin, Charles 184
Gordon, Lyndall 216
Govoni, Paola 216
graphic novel biographies 15–16
Grapow, Hermann 50, 54, 57, 63
Grenfell, Francis Wallace, First Baron Grenfell 357, 359
Griffith, Francis Llewellyn 122, 197, 204
  and Herbert Thompson 184, 186, 189, 190–1
Grimes, William Francis 367, 368
Gsell, Stéphane 241, 248
Günther-Mayer, Alžbeta 82
Güterbock, Bruno 60
Güterbock, Hans Gustav 30, 57, 60–1, *60*, 62–3
Gutron, Clémentine 234, 254

Haldane, J. B. S. 306, 318
Hale, George Ellery 99–100, 102
Halicarnassos (Bodrum, Turkey) 379, *380–1*, 389, 390, *392*
Hankins, Thomas L. 28, 347n3
Harding, Gerald Lankester 167
Harper, William Rainey 93, 94
Haverfield, Francis 215, 217–23

Hawkes, Jacquetta, *Mortimer Wheeler* 10
Hogarth, David G. 359–60
Hollis, Thomas 354, 366
homosexuality 66n36, 234, 241–2, 307
Hooker, Sir Joseph 266, 270–1, 272–4
Hurel, Arnaud 341–2
Huxley, Thomas 188, 198, 270
Hyvärinen, Matti 76

internalism 3

Jacquet, Eugène-Vincent-Stanislas 287
Jansová, Libuše 81
Jekyll, Gertrude 393–4, 394
Jericho *see* Tell es-Sultan
Journal of Egyptology (JEA) 124–5, 133, 139

Kaeser, Marc-Antoine 3, 9–10, 74, 184, 235, 283
  L'univers du préhistorien 75
Kamal, Ahmed 124
Keats, John 383
Kees, Hermann 49–50, 54, 56
Keiller, Alexander 310
Kenyon, Frederic 195, 199
Kenyon, Kathleen 157, 158, *159*, 160, 163, *168*, 171, *173*
  on financing the dig 168
  and health and safety 162–3
  and the local labourers 169
  rush mats 161
  on the unrest in Jordan 167–8
Klejn, Leo 7, 9
Koch, Friedrich 97
Krauss, Christian Ferdinand Friedrich von 290, 291

La Blanchère, René du Coudray de 238, 240, 241, 242, 245
Lacau, Pierre 124
Lamb, Dorothy 364
Lamb, Winifred 361, 363–4, 368
Laming-Emperaire, Annette 333, 340–4
Lavigerie, Charles, Cardinal 236, 237, 238, 239, 242
Lawrence, T. E. 364
Lee, John 285
Leemans, Conrad 281–2, 284, 293–4
  correspondence with Pettigrew 286–8, 292–3
  family 291–2
  letters of introduction 289–91
  in London 285–6
Lepore, Jill 75, 121, 142
Lepsius, Karl/Richard 97, 290, 291, 292, 293
Leroi-Gourhan, André 333–6, 337, 339–40, 346–7
  and Catholicism 336–7
  and Laming-Emperaire 333, 340–4
  and Lévi-Strauss 338–9
Levi, Giovanni 29
Lévi-Strauss, Claude 334, 336
  History and Ethnology 344
  Race and History 338
Liard, Louis 248, 250

life-writing
  archaeological 6–7
  defined 1–5
  new directions 15–16
  recent developments in 8–11
Loder, Kate 187
Lonsdale, William 267–8
Lubbock, Sir John 266, 269
Lyell, Sir Charles 266, 271
Lysenko Controversy 306

Macaulay, Rose 218, 226
Mallowan, Max 10, 319
Manichaeism, and Herbert Thompson 201
marriage 390–1
Married Women's Property Act 390
Marshall, Dorothy 172
Marshall, John 219, 365
Marx Memorial Library (London) 304, *304*, 312
Massingham, Betty 396
Matthes, Benjamin Frederik 290, 291
Maupertuis, Pierre-Louis Moreau de 75–6
media, and the excavation at Tell es-Sultan 164–5
Merlin, Alfred 249, 251, 253
Mickel, Allison 332–3
microhistory 9, 283
  and biography 30–3, *31–2*, 75–6, 84–5
  and Thomas Eric Peet 121, 137, 142
Millet, René 244, 245–6, 248
Milne, Grace (later Lady Prestwich) 266, 270
Milne, Joseph Grafton 128, 192
Monceaux, Paul 241, 245
Mond, Sir Robert 126
Morelli method 121–2
Munby, Arthur 386, 396, 397, 398
Munby, Walter 386, 390
Murray, Tim, *Encyclopaedia of Archaeology* 6–7
Myres, John 364

narrative, and biography 76–7
Nasaw, David, *American Historical Review* 74
Naville, Édouard 123, 124
Neugebauer, Otto 138
Newberry, Percy 122, 123, 127–8, 129, 130, 133, 134, 136, 137–8
Newton, Ann Mary Severn 379, *380–1*, 382
  author, methodology 382–4, *383*
  author and 398, 500
  and Charles Thomas Newton 388–9
  fertility 396–7
  marriage 389–93
  death 396, 397–400, *399*
  travel and archaeology 393–6, *395*
  as a working artist 384–7, *387*, 389–93, *392*
Newton, Charles Thomas 379, 383, *383*, 388–9
  marriage to Mary Severn Newton 389–93, 397–8
  Travels and Discoveries 380–1, *392*, 393, 394, *395*
Nordman, Carl Axel *314*

obituaries 4, 33–4, 359
  and Delattre 236
  and the *Oxford Dictionary of National Biography* 359
  'The Oriental Institute' (University of Chicago) 60, 92, 100, 104, 107, 110
  and the Rockefellers 108–9, *109*
Oxford Dictionary of National Biography (*ODNB*) 359–60, 364, 365

Palacio-Pérez, Eduardo 333–4, 335, 346
Palliser, Mary 386, 390
Paton, William R. 364
Patricia (daughter of Peet) 126, *127*, 129–30, *130–1*, 131–5, *135*, 136–7, 142
Payne, Humfry G. 359–60, 360, *362*
Peet, Thomas Eric (T. Eric Peet) 119, 119–20, 141–3
  biographical information 122–5, 123t
  correspondence 126–37, *127*, *130–1*, *135*
  and Oxford 140–1
  return to Britain 137–9, *140*
Perrot, Georges 241, 252
Petrie, William Mathew Flinders 47, 186, 382
  and Herbert Thompson 188–90, 199, 203
Pettigrew, Eliza 290, 291–2
Pettigrew, Thomas 281–2, 284–5
  family 291–2
  and Leemans 285–6, 286–8, 292–3
Peuckert, Sylvia 61
philanthropy 91–2, 110–11
  see also Breasted
Picard, Charles 78, 79
Pichon, Stephen 249, 250, 251, 252
Pinchon, 249
Pirie-Gordon, Harry 364
Poidebard, Antoine 39, *40*
Polanyi, Michael 76
politics, and German Egyptology 48–51
Poni, Carlo 75, 83
Postgate, Raymond 305, 310
Powell, Dilys 361, *362*
Power, Bill 161, *162*
presentism 154
Prestwich, Sir Joseph 266, 269
  see also Milne, Grace
pseudo-collective biographies 34

Quibell, J. E. 191, 192

Ralegh Radford, C. A. 368
Randall-MacIver, David 122
Raue, Dietrich 55
'reality effect' 36–7, 300, 308
Rebenich, Stefan 63
Reinach, Salomon 240, 241, 242, 243, 250
Reisch, 77–8
Renier, Léon 237, 242
representativeness 28–9
Reuvens, Caspar 190, 284, 292
Revel, Jacques 30
Richard, Dominique 333, 334, 345
Richmond, George 379, 384, 391
Robinson, David 81
Rockefeller, Abby Aldrich 102
Rockefeller, John D. 92, 94, 98

Rockefeller, John D., Jr. 92, 96, 98, 102–3, 104
  and the Oriental Institute 108–9, *109*
Rolfe, Frederick William *see* Corvo, Baron
Roman archaeology *see* Taylor, Margerie
  Venables
Roosevelt, Theodore 102
Royal Academy of Arts, and Mary Severn
  Newton 391, 393
Royle, John Forbes 268
Rublack, Ulinka 120, 137
Ruskin, John 379, 383, 386, 388, 389, 390,
  391

Sadoux, Eugène 247, 251
Said, Edward W. 64n4
Salač, Antonín 73, 76, 77–80, 85
Saladin, Henri 248, 251
Sauvet, George 334
Scharf, George 388, 389
Scheffer, Ary 385
Schliemann, Heinrich 356–7
Schnapp, Alain 333, 345
Schneider, Thomas 48, 49–50, 55
Schwab, Friedrich, La Tène collection *35*
science studies, and biography 27–33, *31–2*
Seltman, Charles 356
Sethe, Kurt 54, 195
Severn, Arthur *383*, 384, 394
Severn, Joseph 383, *383*, 384, 385, 386,
  391
Severn, Walter 383, *383*, 384, 385, 386, 394
Shamsie, Kamila, *A God in Every Stone* 368
Shapin, Steven 28
Shefton, Brian 367
Sheila, Countess of Birkenhead *see* Birkenhead,
  Sheila, Countess of Birkenhead
Smith, John Merlin Powis 102
social dimension, dig writing 155, *157*,
  163–70, *165*, *168*
social self 137
sociology, and biography 28–9
Soden, Wolfram von 60–1
Söderqvist, Thomas 4
Sorrell, Alan 368
Soulier, Philippe 335, 336–7
Spiegelberg, Wilhelm 191–2, 195
Spurgeon, David 164
Stanley, Liz 382
Steindorff, Georg 51–6, *51–3*, 61, 62
Stevenson, Alice 141
Stevenson, Robert 319
Stocking, George 4–5
Stray, Christopher 224
structuralism, and Leroi-Gourhan 333–6, 337,
  339–40, 343–4, 346
Stuart-Jones, Henry 365
surveillance files 300–1

Taylor, Margerie Venables 213, *214*
  biographical details 217–20
  contribution to Roman archaeology
    224–6
  during World War II 223–4
  Haverfield bequest 219–23
  sources 217
Taylour, Lord William 367

Tell es-Sultan 157–8
  dig writing
    archaeological dimension 158–63, *159*,
      162
    emotional dimension 170–2
    social dimension 163–70, *165*, *168*
Telling, Kathryn 124, 125, 142
Terrall, Mary 75–6
Thackray, Arnold 28
Thomas, Edward 363
Thompson, Jason 47–8
Thompson, Sir Herbert 183–4
  archive 185–6, 204–7
  biographical information 187–8, 190, 191,
    205
    move to Bath 201–2
    move to the country 198–201
    personal interests 193–5, *194*
  Cambridge University
    before Thompson 184–5
    donations to 202–4
  early career 188
  and Egyptology 189–90, 205–7
  notes and correspondence 195–8, *196–7*
  publications 190–1, 192–3, *193*
    A Family Archive from Siut 199–200,
      200, 206
  visit to Egypt 191–2
Thornton, Amara 283, 398
The Times, on Mary Severn Newton *392*, 393,
  396
Too and Tee (owls) 130, *130–1*, 132,
  134, 143
Toutain, Jules 241, 244, 245
Traill, David 356
Trigger, Bruce, *A History of Archaeological
  Thought* 110
Trümpener, Hans-Josef 46–7
Tunisia, archaeology in 240–1

Vaux, Père Roland de 167, *168*
Vaux, William 386, 387, 388, 389
Verney Wheeler, Tessa 10–11
Vialou, Denis 334–5
Victoria, Queen 386, 389, 398
Villefosse, Antoine Héron de 240, 242, 245,
  246, 248, 249, 251–2
Voss, Susanne 55
Vyse, Richard William Howard 287

Wace, Alan J. B. 356, 359–60, 365, 367
Wade, Alexander 132
Wallace, Colin 6
Wallich, Nathaniel 267–8
Waquet, Françoise 121
Wason, Cathcart Roland (Roly) 313, *314*
Watts, George Frederic 389
Weickert, Carl 56
Wellcome, Sir Henry 357, 363
Western, Cecil 161
Weyde, Gisela 73–4, 77–80, 83–5
  in Bratislava 80–2
  in Halle 82–3
Wheeler, Margaret 164, 169
Wheeler, Sir R. E. M. (Mortimer)
  10, 318

Whewell, William, *History of the Inductive Sciences* 331
White Fathers 234, 236, 237, 239, 243, 249, 250–3
White, Hayden 76
White Tower Museum (Thessalonike/Salonika) 129, 130–2, 141, 364
Whitworth, Mike 129
Wilson, John A. 51, 124
Wolters, Paul 77, 79

women
 in archaeology 10, 78–81, 83, 214–15, 361–4
 artists 379, 382, 384–5, 390
 and fertility 397
 Married Women's Property Act 390
Woodward, Arthur M. 360–1
Woolf, Virginia, *A Sketch of the Past* 5
Woudhuysen, Paul 367

Milton Keynes UK
Ingram Content Group UK Ltd.
UKHW051513070224
437437UK00026B/323